DAYSOUTUK

2007-2008

GW00599305

sponsored by

www.daysoutuk.com

DaysOutUK Credits

Days Out UK
PO Box 427
Northampton
NN1 3YN

Telephone:
01604 622445
Fax:
01604 633866 or 629900
Email:
info@daysoutuk.com

Web:
www.daysoutuk.com

ISBN 0-9543899-4-8
A catalogue record for this book is
available from the British Library.

© **Days Out UK 2007**

Part of Johnston Press Plc.

Printed and bound by
Cromwell Press, Wiltshire

**Database Manager /
Edited by**
Julia J. Smith

Front Cover Design
David Thomas

Graphic Design / Maps
Sara Tyler-Reese

Administration Manager
Kathy Eele

Sales & Administration
Berni Frost
Trudy Wakelin

Days Out UK discount vouchers

Attractions offering a discount will have their voucher offer highlighted within their listing. Towards the rear of this guide you will find over 350 discount vouchers offering you savings in excess of £2,000.

These vouchers appear in alphabetical order for ease of use. Simply cut-out the voucher you wish to use and exchange at the ticket booth of your selected attraction. Please ensure you read the full terms and conditions prior to making your journey.

Days Out UK Online Discount Club

...for everyone who wants a great deal on a great day out!

For online access to even more visitor attraction information, discount vouchers, and membership benefits, why not join the **Days Out UK Club?** Membership costs just £14.95 for 12 months and provides you with:

- Web access to the entire range of Days Out UK discount vouchers and visitor attraction data (updated daily).

- Specially discounted hotel accommodation from our 2007-2008 sponsor, Superbreak Mini Holidays Ltd.

- Theatre, music and sport booking service and offers from our entertainment ticketing partner, Ticketmaster.

- The opportunity to win some fabulous competition prizes.

- You can also book a table at some exclusive restaurants at specially negotiated prices, courtesy of Top Table.

For more information, or to subscribe please visit our website, **www.daysoutuk.com**

DaysOutUK Contents

DaysOutUK Contents

DaysOutUK Key to Facility Symbols

All weather attraction	Haunted / resident ghost/s
Allow 1-2 hours for visit	Historic Scotland
Allow all day for visit	Licensed for alcohol
Allow half a day for visit	Licensed for weddings
Baby changing facilities	National Trust
Beach / coastal area	National Trust for Scotland
Cadw Welsh Preservation	No dogs (except guide dogs)
Café / Restaurant on site	Offering a discount voucher
Celebration catering	Offers corporate facilities
Credit cards accepted	Parking is charged
Disabled access (full)	Parking nearby
Education packs available	Parking on site
English Heritage	Photography is allowed
Family friendly	Picnic areas
Gift Shop and/or shop/s	Pushchair access
Good weather attraction	Recommended for adults
Guided tours available	Refreshments available

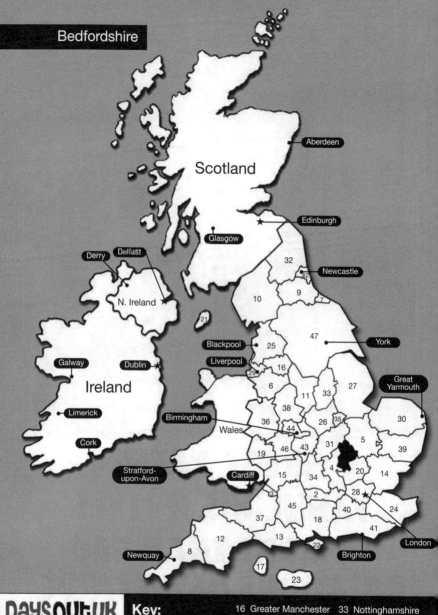

Bedfordshire

Scotland

Aberdeen

Edinburgh

Glasgow

Derry
Belfast
N. Ireland

Galway
Dublin

Ireland

Limerick

Cork

Newcastle

32
42

10
9
7

47
York

Blackpool
25
Liverpool
16
29
6
11
33
27
21
38
Birmingham
36
44
26
35
Great
Yarmouth
30
Wales
19
46
43
31
5
39
Stratford-
upon-Avon
Cardiff
15
34
4
20
14
13
2
28
London
45
40
24
37
18
41
12
13
22
Brighton
Newquay
8
17
23

Key:

1 Bedfordshire
2 Berkshire
3 Bristol
4 Buckinghamshire
5 Cambridgeshire
6 Cheshire
7 Cleveland
8 Cornwall
9 County Durham
10 Cumbria
11 Derbyshire
12 Devon
13 Dorset
14 Essex
15 Gloucestershire

16 Greater Manchester
17 Guernsey
18 Hampshire
19 Herefordshire
20 Hertfordshire
21 Isle Of Man
22 Isle Of Wight
23 Jersey
24 Kent
25 Lancashire
26 Leicestershire
27 Lincolnshire
28 London
29 Merseyside
30 Norfolk
31 Northamptonshire
32 Northumberland

33 Nottinghamshire
34 Oxfordshire
35 Rutland
36 Shropshire
37 Somerset
38 Staffordshire
39 Suffolk
40 Surrey
41 Sussex
42 Tyne & Wear
43 Warwickshire
44 West Midlands
45 Wiltshire
46 Worcestershire
47 Yorkshire

Animal Attractions

Bird of Prey and Conservation Centre

Old Warden Park Biggleswade Bedfordshire
SG18 9EA
Tel: 01767 627527 Fax: 01767 627752
www.birdsofpreycentre.co.uk

[Plenty of on-site parking available]

Open all year, the UK's largest Bird of Prey Centre with a collection of 300 birds. Three flying displays daily. Each show lasts approximately 40 minutes with a "hands on" opportunity with the birds after each display. There are guided tours aboard "Little Red", also Nature Trail tours. There is an adventure playground for your little ones to go wild on, or have a picnic beside the lake. Don't forget the Reptile & Exotic Shows twice daily. The place to visit in 2007.

Spring-Summer 10.00-17.00, Autumn-Winter 10.00-16.00. Three flying displays daily: 11.30 - Owls of the World, 13.30 - Birds of the World, 15.00 - Out of Africa

A£8.00 C£5.00 OAPs£7.00, Family Ticket £25.00. Group rate: £6.00

Discount Offer: One Child Free

Mead Open Farm

Stanbridge Road Billington Leighton Buzzard
Bedfordshire LU7 9HL
Tel: 01525 852954 Fax: 01525 852964
www.meadopenfarm.co.uk

[Off A4146 or A5, follow brown tourist signs. Plenty of on-site parking available]

Mead Open Farm offers heaps more play and stacks more smiles. With a jam-packed programme of 'hands-on' events, get really close. Cuddle rabbits, bottle feed lambs, milk cows or meet our new baby animals! Plus in Shaggy's PlayWorld, you can enjoy over 10,000 sq feet of indoor play. Brave giant drop slides, scramble zig zag net climbers and zoom down firemans poles. For toddlers there's a designated soft play zone. Combined with go-karts, outdoor log play adventure and during the summer months, tractor and trailer rides, there's so much to do. So much in fact, you will have deserved your break in the tea room or Shaggy's PlayWorld café. Check out the website for children's parties.

All year daily 10.30-18.30. Closed 25 Dec-1 Jan inclusive

Please check website for up to date prices

Thurleigh Farm Centre

Cross End Thurleigh Bedford Bedfordshire
MK44 2EE
Tel: 01234 771597
Animal feeding and petting, play area with swings, pedal carts, tractors, trampoline system, assault course, and aerial runway.

Woburn Safari Park

Woburn Park Woburn Bedfordshire MK17 9QN
Tel: 01525 290407
Set in 350 of the 3,000 acres of parkland surrounding Woburn Abbey. Safari Drive, Wild World Leisure area, Sea Lion Cove, miniature railway, adventure playgrounds and boats.

Woodside Animal Farm and Leisure Park

Woodside Road Slip End Luton Bedfordshire LU1 4DG
Tel: 01582 841044 Fax: 01582 840626
www.woodsidefarm.co.uk

[From N exit M1 J10, follow dual carriageway to roundabout, take turning for Harpenden (A1081) & follow brown tourist signs for Wildfowl Park. From S exit M1 J9, turning N onto A5 in direction of Dunstable, turn R onto B4540 Luton Rd & follow brown tourist signs for Wildfowl Park. Public transport, Rail to Luton main station, then bus service 30, 32, 46 or 231. Plenty of on-site parking available]

Woodside Animal Farm is an exciting and fun filled day out for all the family. With so many farm and zoo animals and birds to see and feed, everyone is encouraged to get "touchy-feely" with many of them in the daily "animal encounter" and handling sessions. The farm also allows visitors to feed a lot of the animals by selling special pots of feed for them. Included in the price are animal encounter sessions, tractor rides, reptile encounter session, rabbit cuddling, cow milking and egg collecting sessions. As well as bouncy castles and trampolines, visit our traditional country fun fair, rides include helter skelter, teacups and saucers ride, carousel, coconut shy, basketball throw and hook a duck. There are also outdoor play areas and the brand new large heated indoor play area. Farmer Woods 18 hole crazy golf course, a huge sandpit, electric tractors and "hook-a-duck", plus special event days throughout the year, please see the website for further details. Large coffee shop, farm shop and pet store. Please note that some activities are seasonal and/or dry weather activities.
All year Mon-Sat 08.00-18.00, Sun 10.00-18.00. In the winter the Playbarn and shop will remain open until 18.00, the farm park will close at dusk. Please contact farm office for details of Christmas

& New Year opening times
A£6.95 C&OAPs£5.95 C(1 yr old)£2.95 C(under1)£Free. Disabled visitors £2.95, accompanying carers £3.95. Group rates (for 20+) available on request

Art Galleries

Cecil Higgins Art Gallery

Castle Lane Bedford Bedfordshire MK40 3RP
Tel: 01234 211222 Fax: 01234 327149
www.cecilhigginsartgallery.org

[J13 M1 to centre of Bedford. Located in grounds leading to river embankment. Short walk from Midland Rd Train Station]

Cecil Higgins Art Gallery is situated in an attractive setting beside the beautiful Castle Gardens. Recreated Victorian house including many items from the Handley-Read collection and a fascinating William Burges bedroom. A modern gallery displays an internationally renowned collection of watercolours, prints and drawings, ceramics, glass and lace. Small coffee bar. There is a charge for guided tours and viewing of reserve collections. Disabled access. Visitors wishing to see particular works are advised to telephone beforehand.
Jan-17 June 2007 Tue-Sat 11.00-17.00, Sun & Bank Hol Mon 14.00-17.00. Closed Mons & Good Fri. (The Gallery will close from 18 June 2007 for refurbishment and re-open in 2009)
Admission Free

Birds, Butterflies & Bees

Bedford Butterfly Park

Renhold Road Wilden Bedford Bedfordshire
MK44 2PX
Tel: 01234 772770 Fax: 01234 772773
www.bedford-butterflies.co.uk

*[J13 off M1, follow A421 for Bedford, take
bypass towards Cambridge follow signs for
Wilden. Plenty of on-site parking available]*

For a really enjoyable outing in any weather,
come and visit us at Bedford Butterfly Park.
We're sure you'll have a great time. We have
wild flower meadows outside, and tropical butterflies in our hot house. There are animals, a
playground, a tea room for your lunch and a gift
shop for souvenirs. You'll also find a nature trail,
a room full of creepy crawlies and on weekends
and school holidays there is extra fun for the
kids in our activity barn.
*11 Feb-31 Oct daily 10.00-17.00, 1 Nov-18 Dec
Thur-Fri 10.00-16.00*
A£4.75 C(under3)£Free C£3.90, Family Ticket
(A2+C2) £16.00

Discount Offer: One Child Free

Country Parks & Estates

Dunstable Downs

Dunstable Downs Countryside Centre
Whipsnade Road Kensworth Dunstable

Bedfordshire LU6 2TA
Tel: 01582 608489
Commands outstanding views over the Vale of
Aylesbury and surrounding countryside.

Forest Centre and Millennium Country Park

Station Road Marston Moretaine Bedford
Bedfordshire MK43 0PR
Tel: 01234 767037 Fax: 01234 762606
www.marstonvale.org

[Plenty of on-site parking available]

Stretching over 250 hectares, the park has a
mosaic of habitats from wetlands to woodlands
- lakes and lagoons. It is now home to a wealth
of wildlife - in particular wild birds. Discover
some of the new inhabitants who can be
viewed from paths, boardwalks and bird hides.
Trails are surfaced, flat and safe. The Forest
Centre is family friendly and provides the perfect
facilities for a day out. A fully licensed lakeside
café and bar, kids' adventure play area, bike
hire, interactive exhibition, an art gallery and gift
shop, full of beautiful, unusual and fun things for
everyone.
*All year daily, Summer 10.00-18.00, Winter
10.00-16.00*
Admission Free. Wetland Reserve: A£2.75
C&Concessions £2.25

Discount Offer: Free One-Day Family Wetland Pass

Priory Country Park

Bedford Bedfordshire
Tel: 01234 211182
The park covers over 300 acres including two
large lakes, flower grassland and wooded areas.

Festivals & Shows

Bedfordshire Steam and Country Fayre

Old Warden Park nr Biggleswade Bedfordshire
SG18 9EP
Tel: 01462 851711 Fax: 01462 851711
www.bseps.org.uk

*[2mi W on A1 Biggleswade. Plenty of free on-site
parking available]*

Admission includes entrance to The
Shuttleworth Collection. See steam, tractor and
heavy horse working demonstrations, steam
ploughing, miniature steam, fairground organs,
aerobatic display, working crafts, trade and
market stalls, motor show, clay pigeon shooting, archery, off-road driving, working dog
demonstrations, vintage vehicles, old time fairground and Morris dancing. Plus licensed bar
and refreshments.
15-16 September 2007 (09.00-18.00)
Sat & Sun A£10.00 C(5-16)£5.00 OAPs£7.00,
Family Ticket(A2+C2) £25.00. Includes free
admission to The Shuttleworth Collection, the
Bird of Prey Centre & Swiss Garden

Folk & Local History Museums

Bedford Museum

Castle Lane Bedford Bedfordshire MK40 3XD
Tel: 01234 353323 Fax: 01234 273401
www.bedfordmuseum.org

*[Close to two town-centre car parks & a short
walk from Allhallows Bus Station & Midland Rd
Railway Station. Limited on-site parking available]*

Embark on a fascinating journey through the
human and natural history of North
Bedfordshire, pausing briefly to glimpse at wonders from more distant lands. Go back in time
to visit the delightful rural room sets and the Old
School Museum, where Blackbeard's sword,
'Old Billy' the record breaking longest-lived
horse and numerous other treasures and
curiosities can be found. Housed in the former
Higgins and Sons Brewery, Bedford Museum is
situated within the picturesque gardens of
Bedford Castle, beside the Great Ouse
embankment. The charming courtyard and well
laid out galleries provide an excellent setting for
the rich and varied nature of the collections.
Family activities on selected days. There is a
charge for guided tours which must be booked
in advance. Facilities available for people with
disabilities. Museum shop and coffee shop.
Rooms available for hire.
*All year Tue-Sat 11.00-17.00, Sun & Bank Hol
Mon 14.00-17.00. Closed Mons, Good Fri,
Christmas and New Year*
Admission Free

Forests & Woods

Whipsnade Tree Cathedral

Dunstable Bedfordshire
Tel: 01582 872406
Covers a tranquil 3.82ha (9.5 acres) and contains many tree specimens uniquely planted in the plan of a medieval cathedral.

Historical

Moggerhanger Park

Park Road Moggerhanger Bedford Bedfordshire MK44 3RW
Tel: 01767 641007 Fax: 01767 641515
www.moggerhangerpark.com

[A1, A603 1.5mi or M1(A421), J13, A603. Rail: Bedford or Sandy. Plenty of on-site parking available]

The Grade 1 listed Georgian Country House has recently been restored in keeping with the original design of its architect, Sir John Soane and is set in 33 acres of parkland originally landscaped by Humphry Repton. Restaurant and tea rooms open throughout the year. Do visit the first restaurant to be awarded a Bedfordshire 'Food Mark'! Guided tours daily throughout the summer. Functions and conference facilities available. Moggerhanger House has 3 executive conference suites making it an ideal venue for conferences, promotions and corporate entertainment.

Restaurant & Tea Rooms: All year daily 11.00-16.00 & Fri-Sat evenings. Guided Tours of Historic Rooms. 16 June-7 Sept daily 12.00 & 14.30. Pre-booked group tours are also available

Guided Tours of Historic Rooms: A£6.00 Concessions£5.00 C(under16)£Free. Group rates available on request.

Discount Offer: Two for the Price of One

Military & Defence Museums

Shuttleworth Collection

Old Warden Aerodrome Biggleswade Bedfordshire SG18 9EP
Tel: 01767 627927 Fax: 01767 627949
www.shuttleworth.org

[2mi W of A1 Biggleswade. Plenty of on-site parking available]

A traditional grass aerodrome, with a world-famous collection of aircraft from a 1909 Bleriot to a 1942 Spitfire, plus veteran and vintage motor vehicles and a coachroom of nineteenth-century horse-drawn vehicles all displayed indoors. The aircraft and the vehicles are kept in working order. Please allow a minimum of two hours for your visit.

All year daily, 1 Apr-31 Oct 10.00-17.00, 1 Nov-31 Mar 10.00-16.00. Closed Christmas and New Year week
A£10.00 Accompanied C(0-16)£Free OAPs£9.00. Group rate (20+): £6.50, School Parties £3.50. Prices on flying days A£20.00

Railways

Leighton Buzzard Railway

Page's Park Station Billington Road
Leighton Buzzard Bedfordshire LU7 4TN
Tel: 01525 373888 (24hours)
Fax: 01525 377814
www.buzzrail.co.uk

[On A4146 Hemel Hempstead Rd, near J with A505 Dunstable / Aylesbury Rd. Rail: Leighton Buzzard station 2m. Bus: Arriva service 31 (Luton Airport) links Leighton Buzzard Station, canal & town centre with Stanbridge Rd, which is a short walk from Page's Park station along Billington Rd. Plenty of on-site parking available]

The Leighton Buzzard Railway lets you experience public transport as it was in the early part of the twentieth century, and discover the line's unique history, dating back over 85 years. The 70-minute return journey takes you through the edge of the town and out into the countryside, and features level crossings, sharp curves and steep gradients. Most trains are hauled by an historic steam engine from one of Britain's largest collections of narrow-gauge locomotives. *Sundays: 11 Mar-28 Oct, 11 Nov, Mondays: 9 Apr, 7 & 28 May, 27 Aug, Tuesdays: 31 July-21 Aug, Wednesdays: 4 & 11 Apr, 30 May-22 Aug, 24 Oct, Friday 6 Apr, Saturdays: 7 Apr, 5 & 26 May, 4-25 Aug, 8 Sept, 6 Oct. Dec: Christmas specials. Check website for latest information, including train times*
A£6.00 C(0-2)£Free C£(2-15)£3.00 OAPs£5.00
Day Rover £11.00, Family Ticket £14.00-£17.00

Discount Offer: One Child Free

Wildlife & Safari Parks

ZSL Whipsnade Zoo

Whipsnade Dunstable Bedfordshire LU6 2LF
Tel: 01582 872171 Fax: 01582 872649
www.zsl.org

[Plenty of on-site parking available]

Escape with your family on a big animal adventure for a day out full of excitement and fun at ZSL Whipsnade Zoo! Set in the beautiful Chiltern Hills, ZSL Whipsnade Zoo is home to over 2,500 rare and exotic animals. Don't miss the chance to go 'In with the Lemurs' in our new walk-through experience - Opening 30th March 2007! Be amazed by our spectacular free-flying bird displays and sea lion demonstrations or take a trip on the Jumbo Express to experience our elephants and rhinos close-up! See the highlights of the park, including our 'Lions of the Serengeti' in their African Village enclosure, our new baby Greater One-horned Rhino and our latest baby elephant. Don't forget to visit the Discovery Centre, which is home to a fascinating array of tropical species. Book online at zsl.org to save 10% for a day out that will captivate you and your family.
All year daily from 10.00. Closed Dec 25
Please see website for details

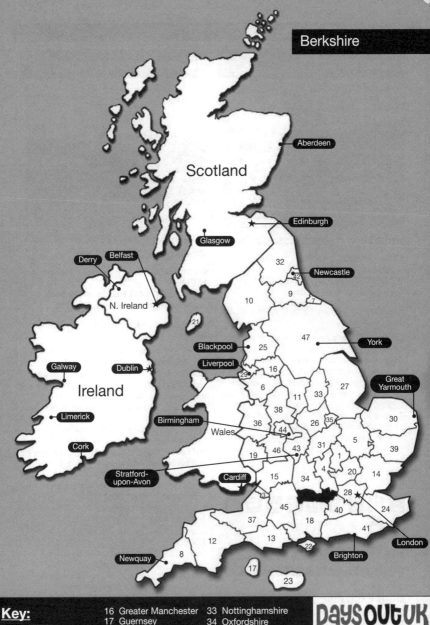

Berkshire

Aberdeen

Scotland

Edinburgh

Glasgow

Newcastle

Derry   Belfast

N. Ireland

32
42
9
7
10

21

Blackpool   25   47   York

Galway   Dublin

Liverpool   16

Ireland   29

6   Great
Yarmouth

Limerick   11   33   27   30

38

Birmingham   36   44   26   35   39

Cork   Wales   46   43   31   5

19   1

Stratford-
upon-Avon   Cardiff   15   34   4   20   14

45   28   24

London

37   40   41

12   18   Brighton

Newquay   13   22

8   17   23

Key:

1	Bedfordshire	16	Greater Manchester
2	Berkshire	17	Guernsey
3	Bristol	18	Hampshire
4	Buckinghamshire	19	Herefordshire
5	Cambridgeshire	20	Hertfordshire
6	Cheshire	21	Isle Of Man
7	Cleveland	22	Isle Of Wight
8	Cornwall	23	Jersey
9	County Durham	24	Kent
10	Cumbria	25	Lancashire
11	Derbyshire	26	Leicestershire
12	Devon	27	Lincolnshire
13	Dorset	28	London
14	Essex	29	Merseyside
15	Gloucestershire	30	Norfolk
		31	Northamptonshire
		32	Northumberland

33	Nottinghamshire
34	Oxfordshire
35	Rutland
36	Shropshire
37	Somerset
38	Staffordshire
39	Suffolk
40	Surrey
41	Sussex
42	Tyne & Wear
43	Warwickshire
44	West Midlands
45	Wiltshire
46	Worcestershire
47	Yorkshire

Animal Attractions

Lambourn Trainers Association

Windsor House Crowle Road Lambourn
Hungerford Berkshire RG17 8NR
Tel: 01488 71347 Fax: 01488 72664
www.lambourntraining.org

[M4 J14. Rail: Newbury. Plenty of on-site parking available]

Lambourn Trainers Association will escort visitors around their stables, giving a fascinating insight into the racing world not seen by the public before. Lambourn - Valley of the Racehorse, is highly respected for its enviable record for success, including the winners of the Cheltenham Gold Cup in 2000 and last two years of 2000 Guineas and Champion Stakes. Lambourn Trainers Open Day on 6th April 2007.
All year Mon-Sat 10.00-12.00 by appointment.
Open Day: 6 Apr 08.30-17.00. Closed Bank Hols & Sun
Tours £7.00+vat C£Free

Arts, Crafts & Textiles

Corn Exchange

Market Place Newbury Berkshire RG14 5BD
Tel: 01635 582666
This west Berkshire entertainment venue hosts drama, comedy, music, dance, exhibitions, films, along with their resident orchestra.

Country Parks & Estates

Wellington Country Park

Odiham Road Riseley Reading Berkshire
RG7 1SP
Tel: 0118 932 6444 Fax: 0118 932 6445
www.wellington-country-park.co.uk

[Signposted off A33. Plenty of on-site parking available]

Wellington Country Park, Riseley, near Reading, has 350 acres of wonderful parkland within the Duke of Wellington's estate, providing an ideal venue for a family outing. Explore the nature trails round the lakes. Play in the adventure playground, and explore our fantastic new play areas. Younger children will enjoy the lovely sandpit, animal farm and miniature railway. Finish off with a family tournament on the crazy golf course! Acres of space for your own picnics and barbecues, with areas provided. Camping and caravanning site in the park. An ideal touring site for Winchester, Salisbury, Legoland, Windsor and Oxford. Dogs welcomed. Special events throughout the year. Please call for further information.
Feb-Nov daily 10.00-17.30
A£6.00 C(under3)£Free C(3-15)£5.00
OAPs£5.00, Family Ticket (A2+C2) £19.50.
Group rates (for 20+) available on request.
Season tickets: £45.00 for first family member, £30.00 for subsequent family member

Discount Offer: One Child Free

Historical

Basildon Park

Lower Basildon Reading Berkshire RG8 9NR
Tel: 0118 984 3040 Fax: 0118 984 7370
www.nationaltrust.org.uk/basildonpark

[J12 M4 between Pangbourne & Streatley. Rail: Pangbourne. Plenty of on-site parking available]

Basildon Park is a beautiful and unusual Palladian mansion that starred in the 2005 feature film adaptation of Jane Austen's 'Pride and Prejudice.' This unique property is set in 400 acres of parkland and there are wonderful gardens for visitors of all ages to explore. We have a fantastic shop, a child-friendly restaurant (serving home-cooked food) and an exhibition about the filming of the Hollywood movie. The house was nearly demolished in the early twentieth century, but it was saved by Lord and Lady Iliffe who then gave the house and land to the National Trust in 1978. Since then the property has welcomed visitors to share some of Basildon Park's magic. The house itself has fine interiors, including original delicate plasterwork, an unusual octagonal room, a decorative shell room and an elegant staircase.
21 Mar-28 Oct (Wed-Sun inclusive). Also open Bank Hols
A£6.00 C£3.00, Family Ticket £15.00

Cliveden

Taplow Maidenhead Berkshire SL6 0JA
Tel: 01628 605069
Spectacular estate overlooking the Thames.

Highclere Castle

Highclere Newbury Berkshire RG20 9RN
Tel: 01635 253210
This splendid early Victorian mansion stands in beautiful parkland.

Windsor Castle

Windsor Berkshire SL4 1NJ
Tel: 020 7766 7304
Official Residences of Her Majesty The Queen.

Roman Era

Museum of Reading

The Town Hall Blagrave Street Reading Berkshire RG1 1QH
Tel: 0118 939 9800 Fax: 0118 939 9881
www.readingmuseum.org
[Rail: Reading Station]
Housed within The Town Hall in the centre of Reading, the family friendly Museum of Reading features 12 interactive galleries with plenty to see and do. From Romans to Rodin, biscuit tins to beetles there is something for everyone to explore. Drop in and join one of the hands-on friendly activity sessions, or to catch one of the changing art exhibitions. Experience the fascinating Roman Silchester gallery and the world's only full-size copy of the Bayeux Tapestry, and discover Reading's Royal Abbey. Admission is free and there's a great gift shop and buggy friendly café. Call for details of special events or see website.
All year Tue-Sun & Bank Hol
Admission Free

Science - Earth & Planetary

Look Out Discovery Centre

Nine Mile Ride Bracknell Berkshire RG12 7QW
Tel: 01344 354400 Fax: 01344 354422
www.bracknell-forest.gov.uk/be

[J10 M4, J3 M3 off A322 on B3430. Rail: Bracknell. Plenty of on-site parking available]

The Look Out Discovery Centre in Bracknell is a great day whatever the weather. The main attraction is an exciting hands on, interactive science and nature exhibition that offers over 70 bright and fun filled exhibits within five themed zones; Light and Colour, Sound and Communication, Forces and Movement, Woodland and Water and Body and Perception. Come and launch the hot air balloon, freeze your shadow on the wall or climb through a giant mole hole. In the surrounding 2,600 acres of Crown Estate woodland, visitors can enjoy nature walks, cycle trails, a picnic area and a child's play area. With child and adult mountain bike hire (or bring your own), coffee shop, gift shop and Tourist Information Centre. This offers an action packed day for the whole family at very reasonable prices. Birthday parties catered for.

All year daily 10.00-17.00. Closed Christmas
A£5.45 Concessions£3.60, Family Ticket £14.55

Discount Offer: One Child Free

Spectator Sports

Ascot Racecourse

High Street Ascot Berkshire SL5 7JX
Tel: 0870 727 1234 Fax: 0870 460 1238
www.ascot.co.uk

[Rail: Reading, London Waterloo. Plenty of on-site parking available]

The highlight of our year is Royal Ascot which takes place from Tuesday 19th to Saturday 23rd June inclusive. The quality of racing at the Royal Meeting is simply outstanding with over £3.5 million in prize money on offer and a total of seventeen pattern races (the UK's top rated races) over the five-day meeting. Outside Royal Ascot we have 21 other racedays that offer something for everyone with each of our 26 racedays offering its own unique atmosphere and entertainment programme. Highlights include six Family Days, a Beer Tasting Festival in association with the Campaign for Real Ale, an Easter Egg Hunt, a Wine Tasting Day, a Day for the Third Age with the shopping village, a Stallion Parade, a Firework Display as well as some of the best racing action in the UK. For further information or to book tickets go to web-site or call.

June-Dec
From A£10.00 C(0-16)£Free. Restaurant packages start from £70.50.

Sport & Recreation

Coral Reef Water World

Nine Mile Ride Bracknell Berkshire RG12 7JQ
Tel: 01344 862525 Fax: 01344 869146
www.bracknell-forest.gov.uk/be
*[From J3 M3, follow A322 to Bracknell for 3.7mi,
from J10 M4 follow A329 to Bracknell, then follow
A322 to Bagshot for 4.1mi. On-site parking]*
Fun at Coral Reef - so let the water excitement
start here. Coral Reef Bracknell's Water World is
a tropical paradise providing fun for all the family. There are three giant water slides and other
water features including the wild water rapids,
erupting volcano, firing cannons, squirting
snakes and bubbling spas. After all this fun,
why not visit our air-conditioned restaurant on
the first floor with views over the pool. Sauna
World is available to over 18s only so you can
relax in the tranquil surroundings of a saunarium
(a mix of dry and wet heat), two saunas and our
two tier steam room. There is a cool pool and
footspa to invigorate the whole body. Light
refreshments are also available in Sauna World.
Coral Reef is open all year round. Please note
that at all times there is a maximum of two children under 8 years to one adult (over 18).
*All year Mon 10.30-21.00, Tue-Fri 10.30-21.45,
Sat & Sun 09.00-17.45. Please note Wed & Fri
19.00-21.45 over 21s only. Early Bird sessions
Mon-Fri 06.30-9.30 excluding Bank Hol. Term
Time Only: Mon-Fri 10.30-15.30 are special
Parent & Toddler Sessions*
Off peak times: Mon-Fri 10.30-15.30 (term
time): A&C£3.60 C(0-4)£Free, Peak times: Mon-Fri 15.30 21.00/21.45 & Sat & Sun 09.00-17.45
A£6.35 C£4.40 C(0-4)£Free. Disabled, over 50s
and party rates available. Please telephone
venue for price change after Apr 2007

Queen Mother Reservoir

Horton Road Colnbrook Berkshire
Tel: 01753 683872
At 216 hectares, this is one of the largest
waters in southern England.

Stately Homes

Frogmore House

Windsor Berkshire SL1 1SL
Tel: 020 7321 2233
Set amid the extensive Home Park of Windsor
Castle, Frogmore House is surrounded by fine
and picturesque gardens.

Theme & Adventure Parks

Go Ape! High Wire Forest Adventure

The Look Out Nine Mile Ride Swinley Forest
Bracknell Berkshire RG12 7QW
Tel: 0870 420 7876
www.goape.co.uk

*[M3 J3 or M4 J10, off A322 on B3430. Plenty of
on-site parking available]*

Take to the trees and experience an exhilarating
course of rope bridges, 'Tarzan Swings' and
zip-slides up to 40 feet above the ground! Share
approximately three hours of memorable fun
and adventure, which you'll be talking about for
days. Book online and watch people Go Ape! at
www.goape.co.uk. Minimum height 1.4m.
Maximum weight 130 kg (20.5 stone). Under-18s must be accompanied by a participating
adult. One adult can supervise either two chil-

dren (where one or both of them in under 16 years old) or up to five 16-17 year olds. Pre-booking is essential to avoid disappointment. Book online or by telephone (there is a £1.00 booking fee on all telephone bookings).
10-25 Feb, 23 Mar-2 Nov daily, Nov Sat-Sun. Closed Dec-Jan
Gorillas (18yrs+) £25.00, Baboons (10-17yrs) £20.00

Discount Offer: Two for the Price of One

LEGOLAND Windsor

Winkfield Road Windsor Berkshire SL4 4AY
www.legoland.co.uk
[On B3022 Windsor-Ascot road, well signposted from M4 & M3. Plenty of on-site parking available]

Vikings are invading LEGOLAND Windsor! In summer 2007, LEGOLAND will unveil the amazing, humungous and hilarious 'Vikings' River Splash' ride. Take a wild, wet voyage through a Viking world built from thousands of LEGO® bricks but try to avoid a complete soaking! All in all, LEGOLAND has over 50 rides, live shows and attractions set in 150 acres of parkland. Log onto www.LEGOLAND.co.uk and check out their fantastic special events programme held throughout the season. At LEGOLAND Windsor, there's too much fun to squeeze into one day, so why not stay with one of their local hotel partners? A 2-day Pass plus hotel accommodation for one night including breakfast starts at just £154 for a family of four.* To make a booking, please visit www.LEGOLANDHolidays.com or call 0845 373

2643. *Price based on 2 adults and 2 children (under 16) sharing a family room. Please note that Days Out UK discount vouchers cannot be used for holiday bookings.
17 Mar-28 Oct. Opening times vary, for more information please visit our website

Discount Offer: Save up to £25.00!

Wildlife & Safari Parks

Beale Park

Lower Basildon Reading Berkshire RG8 9NH
Tel: 0870 777 7160 Fax: 0870 777 7120
www.bealepark.co.uk
[Signposted from J12 M4, follow brown tourist signs. Plenty of on-site parking available]

This glorious Thameside Wildlife and Leisure Park has something for everyone. Unique collection of rare and endangered birds, pets corner, deer park, paddling pools, adventure playground, gardens, trails, narrow gauge railway, picnic areas, shop, restaurant, fishing, little tikes village and jubilee gardens by Pantiles Nurseries and much more.
Mar-end Oct daily 10.00-18.00 (or dusk)
High Season: A£8.00 C£5.50 OAPs£6.50. Low Season: A£6.00 C£4.00 OAPs£4.50

Discount Offer: One Child Free

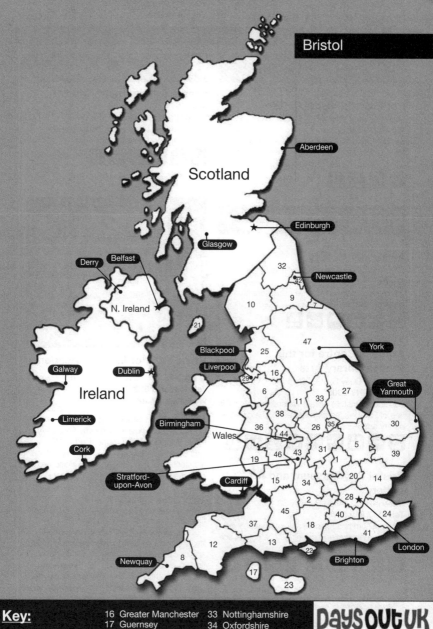

Bristol

Scotland

Aberdeen

Edinburgh

Glasgow

Derry | Belfast

N. Ireland

Newcastle

32

42

9

7

10

21

Galway | Dublin

Ireland

Limerick

Cork

Blackpool

Liverpool

25

29

16

6

11

33

27

York

Great Yarmouth

38

Birmingham

Wales

36

44

26

35

30

46

43

31

5

39

Stratford-upon-Avon

19

Cardiff

15

34

4

1

20

14

London

45

2

28

24

37

18

40

41

Newquay

8

12

13

22

Brighton

17

23

Key:

DAYSOUTUK
The place to look for places to go

Animal Attractions

HorseWorld Vistor Centre
Staunton Lane Bristol BS14 0QJ
Tel: 01275 540173
Set in stone farm buildings on the southern edge of Bristol, HorseWorld's Visitor Centre offers a great day out for everyone.

Art Galleries

Alexander Gallery
122 Whiteladies Road Clifton Bristol BS8 2RP
Tel: 0117 973 4692
We are exclusive world wide publishers of signed limited editions by Beryl Cook.

Arnolfini Centre for the Contemporary Arts
16 Narrow Quay Bristol BS1 4QA
Tel: 0117 917 2300
Located in Bristol's vibrant waterside, Arnolfini is one of Europe's leading centres for the contemporary arts.

Bristol City Museum and Art Gallery
Queens Road Clifton Bristol BS8 1RL
Tel: 0117 922 3571
The museum has regional and international collections representing ancient history, natural sciences, and fine and applied arts.

Country Parks & Estates

Ashton Court Estate and Gardens
Ashton Court Long Ashton Bristol BS41 9JN
Tel: 0117 963 9174
A sixteenth-century house and deer park with a nineteenth-century garden.

Exhibition & Visitor Centres

Create Environment Centre
Smeaton Road Bristol BS1 6XN
Tel: 0117 925 0505
Art gallery, recycling exhibition, cafe and demonstration Ecohome.

Royal West of England Academy
Queens Road Clifton Bristol BS8 1PX
Tel: 0117 973 5129
www.rwa.org.uk

The magnificent Grade II listed building of the Royal West of England Academy Art Gallery (RWA) is open all year round. Built in 1844 it was Bristol's first art gallery and boasts stunning architecture of this period. The exhibition programme includes a variety of shows, which appeal to all tastes from digital and new media to painting, drawing, printmaking and sculpture. The increasingly popular Autumn Exhibition is the largest open art show in the region. It includes all types of work, such as portraits, still life, abstracts and landscapes most of which are for sale. The RWA has its own collection of fine art, which it displays in free exhibitions throughout the year. The New Gallery has free entry and hosts 12 exhibitions a year with works for sale, often by artists from the south west region. For an up to date preview of what's on visit the RWA website.
All year daily Mon-Sat 10.00-17.30, Sun 14.00-17.00. Closed Easter Sun & 25 Dec-3 Jan
A£3.00 Concessions £2.00 C£Free

Watershed

1 Canons Road Harbourside Bristol BS1 5TX
Tel: 0117 927 5100
Watershed opened as Britain's first media centre in June 1982. Cinema, digital media, events and cafe/bar.

Festivals & Shows

Discovery Channel International Balloon Fiesta 2007

Ashton Court Long Ashton Bristol BS41 9JN
Tel: 0117 953 5884
The 2007 fiesta promises to be as fun-filled and exciting as those before it! We have the famous mass balloon ascents at 6am and 6pm every day, and the amazing night glows on Thursday and Saturday at 9.30pm.
9-12 August 2007, Thur-Sun

Maritime

SS Great Britain

Great Western Dock Gas Ferry Road Bristol BS1 6TY
Tel: 0117 926 0680
Step back in time on board Brunel's SS Great Britain – the world's first great ocean liner. Explore the beautifully recreated First Class Dining Saloon, steerage quarters and new Engine Room. Audio tours of passengers' lives and authentic smells help bring the nineteenth century experience alive.

Multicultural Museums

British Empire and Commonwealth Museum

Station Approach Temple Meads Bristol BS1 6QH
Tel: 0117 925 4980
Using authentic objects, rare film, photographs, sound recordings and costumes, visitors journey through British and world history.

Performing Arts

Bristol Old Vic

King Street Bristol BS1 4ED
Tel: 0117 987 7877
One of the UK's best known and most successful theatre companies, producing a wide range of modern classics, Shakespeare, new plays, children's shows, musicals, and attracting exceptional actors.

Places of Worship

Bristol Cathedral

College Green Bristol BS1 5TJ
Tel: 0117 926 4879
Founded as an abbey in 1140, it became a cathedral in 1542 and developed architecturally throughout the ages.

Science - Earth & Planetary

Explore-At-Bristol

Anchor Road Harbourside Bristol BS1 5DB
Tel: 0845 345 1235 Fax: 0117 915 7200
www.at-bristol.org.uk

[M5 J18 follow A4 (Portway) to The Centre. M4 J19, M32 to city centre where signposted. Entrance located on Canons Way, off Anchor Rd. Rail: GWR, Wales & West or Virgin trains to Bristol Temple Meads - 20min walk, 10min bus (8, 508, 9, 509), or 5min taxi. Bus: all buses stop at The Centre which is 5min walk away. Plenty of on-site

parking available 06.30-00.30]

Explore-At-Bristol... an amazing world of hands-on discovery. With action-packed exhibits, live shows and a planetarium, Explore really is one of the UK's most exciting interactive science centres. Put your mind and body to the test, get into a spin on a human gyroscope, have a game of virtual volleyball and experience the wonky side of life in the leaning lounge. Explore involves people of all ages in an incredible journey through the workings of the world around us. Plus there is always something new to discover with Explore's programme of special exhibitions - from animation to flight, illusions and sport! The chrome-plated, futuristic sphere in Millennium Square is the Planetarium, where you can sit back and take a trip to the stars beneath an immersive domed screen in our new seasonal star show.

Term time Mon-Fri 10.00-17.00, Sat-Sun & School Hols 10.00-18.00

Explore: A£9.00 C(under3)£Free C(3-15)&Concessions£6.50, Family Ticket (A2+C2) or (A1+C3) £26.00

Social History Museums

Blaise Castle House Museum
Henbury Road Henbury Bristol BS10 7QS
Tel: 0117 903 9818
The 'castle' is an eighteenth-century mansion built for a Quaker banker, and is now Bristol's Museum of Social History.

Sport & Recreation

Bristol Climbing Centre
St Werburgh's Church Mina Road St Weburgh's Bristol BS2 9YH
Tel: 0117 941 3489
A beginner? An expert? Whatever standard you are this climbing centre will have the facilities and provide the challenge you are looking for.

Zoos

Bristol Zoo Gardens
Clifton Bristol BS8 3HA
Tel: 0117 974 7399 Fax: 0117 973 6814
www.bristolzoo.org.uk
[Follow brown tourist signs from J17 M5 or J18 or city centre. Rail: from Bristol Temple Meads take No. 8 or 9 bus to zoo gates. Limited on site-parking available]

Bristol Zoo has more than 400 species and supports wildlife conservation and education. It takes part in local, national and international breeding programmes. Visit the lemur garden in the new 'Monkey Jungle' and see red ruffed and ring-tailed lemurs in a naturalistic, barrier-free environment. Other neighbours are lion-tailed macaques, black howlers and De Brazza's monkeys. The western lowland gorillas and their new baby have their own island. There's the award-winning 'Seal and Penguin Coast' with above and below water viewing. 'Bug World' houses the zoo's invertebrate collection. 'Twilight World' exchanges night and day so that nocturnal animals including fruit bats, sand cats, sloths and aye-ayes can be observed during the day. There are over 70 species in the 'Aquarium'. There's also a 'Reptile House' with snakes, iguana, and dwarf crocodiles. Walk through the 'Wallace Aviary' with its enchanting birds or visit 'Zona Brazil' to see South American animals including golden lion tamarins, tapirs and capybaras.
All year daily: Summer 09.00-17.30, Winter 09.00-17.00. Closed 25 Dec
Please see website for prices

Discount Offer: One Child Free

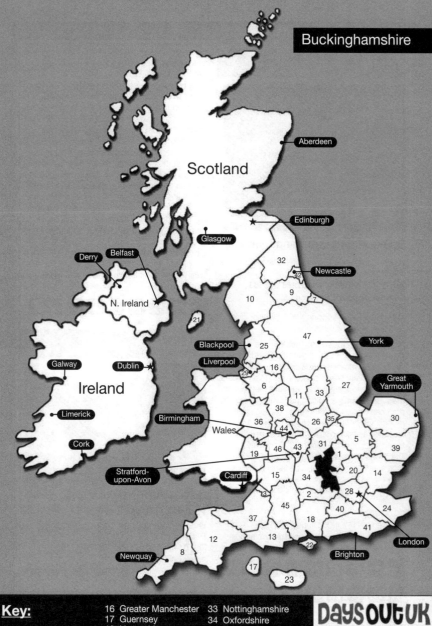

Buckinghamshire

Aberdeen

Scotland

Edinburgh

Glasgow

Derry Belfast

N. Ireland

Newcastle

32

42

10

9

7

21

47 York

Blackpool

25

Liverpool

16

29

Galway Dublin

Ireland

Limerick

Cork

6

11 33

27

Great Yarmouth

38

36 26 35 30

Birmingham

44

5 39

Wales

19 46 43 31 1

Stratford-upon-Avon

15 34 20 14

Cardiff

2 28

45 40 London

37 18 24

12 13 22 41

Newquay

8 Brighton

17

23

DAYS OUT UK
The place to look for places to go

Animal Attractions

Bucks Goat Centre and Mini Zoo

Layby Farm Stoke Mandeville Buckinghamshire HP22 5XJ
Tel: 01296 612983 Fax: 01296 613663
www.bucksgoatcentre.co.uk

[3mi outside Aylesbury, on A4010. Plenty of free on-site parking available]

A children's miniature zoo that features a wide range of animals from all over the world, including llamas, wallabies, birds, reptiles, pigs, donkeys and every breed of domestic goat native to the UK. Visitors are invited to hand-feed our animals, and there's a petting farm where small children can make friends with our guinea pigs and rabbits. Other facilities include a toyshop, a picnic lawn, a children's play area (featuring a giant trampoline) and the Naughty Nanny Café. Tractor rides are available throughout the summer (weather permitting). Children's parties are catered for, please telephone for more information. All attractions have easy disabled access.
All year daily: Summer 10.00-17.00, Winter 10.00-16.00
A£5.00 C(2-16)£4.00 C(under2)£Free OAPs£4.50. Group rates available on request

Odds Farm Park Rare Breeds Centre

Wooburn Common High Wycombe Buckinghamshire HP10 0LX
Tel: 01628 520188
www.oddsfarm.co.uk
[M40 J2 or J3 or M4 J7 then follow brown signs]
This award winning 40-acre open farm is a 'must-visit' children's attraction. With hundreds of furry friends, there are plenty of rabbits to pet, new babies to meet, ponies to pat and greedy sheep to feed. Plus the daily activities give you even more 'hands-on' animal fun. Updated frequently, the jam-packed programme includes sheep racing, rabbit world, bottle feed lambs, the goat show and piggies tea time. Daily shows include a sheep show, cow milking, sheep sheering and a goat show. The fun continues in the new PlayBarn. Loose yourself in the giant bale climb, zoom down the new astra slide and board new ride-on-toys. Add for the under 2's, plenty of soft play too. Parents can sit back and relax from the new heated gallery. Combined with log play areas, crazy golf, go karts, ball games and tractor & trailer rides (weather permitting), there's so much to do at Odds Farm Park!
All year daily from 10.00. Closed 25-26 Dec & 1 Jan. Please see website for admission prices

Caverns & Caves

Hellfire Caves

West Wycombe Caves Ltd.High Wycombe Buckinghamshire HP14 3AJ
Tel: 01494 533739 Fax: 01494 471617
www.hellfirecaves.co.uk
[On A40. Rail: High Wycombe. On-site parking]
Go underground for a unique adventure… Sir Francis Dashwood excavated the caves at West Wycombe in the 1750s. They are steeped in history, much of it centred on the notorious 'Hell-fire Club.' The history is told in an audio-visual presentation as you wind your way half a mile underground, through passages, down to the banqueting hall and finally, to the Inner Temple by the River Styx - some 300 feet beneath the church at the top of the hill. See the caves come alive with numerous statues dressed in period costume. Finish your day out by visiting our tearoom and gift shop (with its

award-winning murals).
*All year, Weekends & School Hols 11.00-17.00.
Apr-Oct daily 11.00-17.00.*
A£5.00 C(3-16)£4.00, Family Ticket £15.00

Discount Offer: Two for the Price of One

Exhibition & Visitor Centres

thecentre:mk
24 Silbury Arcade Milton Keynes
Buckinghamshire MK9 3ES
Tel: 0870 890 2530 Fax: 01908 604306
www.thecentremk.com
[J13 / J14 (M1), or follow signs for 'Central Shopping' from A5]
thecentre:mk is a regional shopping centre situated in the heart of Milton Keynes. With over 230 stores, cafés and restaurants (all under one roof), it is anchored by John Lewis, House of Fraser, Marks & Spencer and Next. As the premier shopping destination in the region between London and Birmingham, Cambridge and Oxford, it includes a varied programme of free events throughout the year, including bridal shows, fashion events, motor shows and the award-winning Christmas display. All this is easily accessible because it's all on one level. thecentre:mk has unrivalled customer service and provides excellent facilities for families, the disabled and children in a safe, clean, all-weather environment.
All year daily: Mon-Wed 9.30-18.00, Thu-Fri 9.30-20.00, Sat 9.00-18.00, Sun 11.00-17.00. Extended shopping hours at Christmas

Folk & Local History Museums

Bucks County Museum and the Roald Dahl Children's Gallery
Church Street Aylesbury HP20 2QP
Tel: 01296 331441
Innovative touchable displays about Buckinghamshire, family exhibitions, and regular events and activities.

Cowper and Newton Museum
Orchard Side Market Place Olney
Buckinghamshire MK46 4AJ
Tel: 01234 711516 Fax: 0870 1640 662
www.cowperandnewtonmuseum.org.uk
[N of Newport Pagnell (via A509)]
John Newton was a former slaver turned evangelical preacher who also wrote world-famous hymns, including 'Amazing Grace'. He was a close friend of the poet who lived in the present buildings of the Cowper and Newton Museum. William Cowper, a leading poet of this time, was a major influence on Jane Austen and Wordsworth. The museum also has a nationally renowned lace collection, dinosaur bones, a costume gallery and trade rooms housing a collection of Olney's social history from the early eighteenth century. Another bonus is the extensive gardens which are home to eighteenth-century (or earlier) plants. The museum is of early Georgian origins.
1 Mar-23 Dec Tue-Sat 10.30-16.30. Also open Bank Hol Mons & Shrove Tue. Closed Good Fri
Museum & Gardens: A£3.00 C(under12)£Free Concessions£2.00. Group rates (for 12+) available on request. Gardens Only: £1.00

Discount Offer: Two for the Price of One

Gardens & Horticulture

Stowe Landscape Gardens

Buckingham Buckinghamshire MK18 5EH
Tel: 01280 822850 / 01280 818825
Fax: 01280 822437
www.nationaltrust.org.uk/stowegardens
[3mi NW of Buckingham via Stowe Ave, off A422 Buckingham - Banbury rd. Plenty of on-site parking available]
Be inspired by the extraordinary, living, breathing work of art that is Stowe Landscape Gardens. With its ornamental lakes, glorious open spaces, wooded valleys and adorned with over 40 monuments and temples, this magnificent landscape is one of the supreme creations of the Georgian era. Given to the National Trust in 1989, the gardens, Stowe House (opened to the public by Stowe Preservation Trust) and the surrounding 750 acres of parkland have been undergoing an ambitious programme of restoration to recapture their former unparalleled magnificence. Described as a 'work to wonder at' Stowe Landscape Gardens explores ideas about love, liberty, virtue and politics, inspiring writers, artists and visitors for over three centuries. Today, the splendour and magic of Stowe can be enjoyed by all. Whether you want to enjoy the peace and tranquillity of beautiful surroundings, an unspoilt setting for a family picnic or an invigorating walk in the parkland, Stowe is the perfect place for a day out. A full programme of fun and educational events for children and adults is available.
1 Mar-30 Oct Wed-Sun 10.30-17.30, 4 Nov-25 Feb Sat-Sun 10.30-16.00. Closed 27 May
Gardens: A£6.00 C£3.00, Family Ticket £15.00. Group rate (15+): 15% discount

Heritage & Industrial

Milton Keynes Museum

Stacey Hill Farm McConnell Drive Wolverton Milton Keynes Buckinghamshire MK12 5EL
Tel: 01908 316222
Explore 200 years of local and national history.

Chiltern Open Air Museum

Newland Park Gorelands Lane Chalfont St. Giles Buckinghamshire HP8 4AB
Tel: 01494 871117 Fax: 01494 872774
www.coam.org.uk
[From J17 M25, follow signs to Maple Cross & then brown tourist signs. Also signposted from A413 at Chalfont St Giles & Chalfont St. Peter. Plenty of on-site parking available]

Chiltern Open Air Museum is an independent charity that's open to the public every day from 31st March to October 26th (2007 season). Now the biggest tourist attraction in southern Buckinghamshire, the museum was established 31 years ago in Chalfont St Giles with the aim of preserving some of the historic buildings that are unique examples of the heritage of the Chilterns. Visitors can explore more than 30 historic buildings (that span 2000 years of history) all rescued from demolition and re-erected on the museum's beautiful 45-acre woodland and parkland site. Lots to see and do for all the family, please visit www.coam.org.uk for details.
31 Mar-26 Oct daily 10.00-17.00
A£7.50 Concessions£6.50 C(5-16)£4.50 C(under5)£Free, Family Ticket (A2+C2) £21.50

Stowe House

Buckingham Buckinghamshire MK18 5EH
Tel: 01280 818166 / 818229
Fax: 01280 818186
www.shpt.org
[4mi N of Buckingham town. On-site parking]
As the most important temple set in the landscape gardens (now owned by the National
Trust), Stowe House is recognised as one of the
most influential neo-classical palaces in Europe.
The house and its contents were sold off sepa-
rately in 1922, when the last member of the
Temple-Grenville family could no longer maintain
it. It has been owned by Stowe School (a major
public school) since 1923, and in 1997, it was
passed into the care of Stowe House
Preservation Trust, which was established to
restore and preserve the house, and to open it
up to the public. Phase 2 of a six-phase
restoration plan was completed in 2005, restoring the magnificent marble saloon and south
front portico. An interpretation centre chronolog-
ically explains the rise of the family and the evolution of the house. Stowe House is licensed for
civil weddings and is also available for private
and corporate functions.
*12-15 &17-18 Feb (14.00 tours only), 3-4, 11,
17-18, 24-25 Mar (14.00 tours only), 4-13, 15,
18-22 12.00-17.00 (tour 14.00) & 28-29 Apr
(tour 14.00 only), 2-4 May (14.00 tours only), 6-7
May 12.00-17.00 (tour 14.00), 9-13 & 19-20
May (14.00 tours only), 27 May-1 June 12.00-
17.00 (tour 14.00), 9-10, 16-17 & 23-24 June
(14.00 tours only), 18-19, 22, 25-27 & 29 July
12.00-17.00 (14.00 tour), 1-3, 5, 8-10, 12, 15-
16, 22-23 & BH 27 Aug 12.00-17.00 (tour
14.00), 12-16 19-23 & 26-30 Sept (14.00 tours
only), 3-7, 10-14 Oct (14.00 tour only) & 22-25
Oct 14.00-17.00 (14.00 tour), 17-18 Nov (14.00
tours only), 15-16 Dec (14.00 tours only). For further information please call or visit our website.
Group visits all year by arrangement*
Admission & Tour A£4.00 C£2.50 C(under
5)£Free. HHA Members £Free, Reduction for
NT members

Waddesdon Manor

Aylesbury Buckinghamshire HP18 0JH
Tel: 01296 653211 / 653226
Fax: 01296 653212
www.waddesdon.org.uk
*[At W end of Waddesdon Village, 6mi NW of
Aylesbury on Bicester Rd A41. Bus: Red Rover 1,
15, 16 from Aylesbury. Plenty of on-site parking]*
Waddesdon Manor was built (1874-89) for
Baron Ferdinand de Rothschild to display his
vast collection of eighteenth-century art trea-
sures, which include French Royal furniture,
Savonnerie carpets and Sèvres porcelain as well
as important portraits by Gainsborough and
Reynolds. It has one of the finest Victorian gar-
dens in Britain, a fully stocked Rococo-style
aviary, wine cellars, shops and licensed restau-
rants. Many events are organised throughout
the year. For more information please call the
Booking Office.
*Gardens, Aviary, Children's Woodland Playground,
Restaurant & Shops: 6 Jan-18 Mar Sat-Sun, 21
Mar-23 Dec Wed-Sun, 27-31 Dec 10.00-17.00
open Bank Hols. House & Wine Cellars: 21 Mar-
28 Oct & 14 Nov-23 Dec Wed-Fri 12.00-16.00
Sat-Sun 11.00-16.00 Open Bank Hols. Bachelors'
Wing 21 Mar-28 Oct Wed-Fri 12.00-16.00*
Gardens, Aviary, Children's Woodland
Playground, Shops & Restaurants: 6 Jan-18
Mar A£5.50 C(5-16)£2.75 Family Ticket£13.75
21 Mar-31 Dec Wed-Fri A£5.50 C£2.75 Family
Ticket£13.75 Sat-Sun & Bank Hols A£7.00
C£3.50 Family Ticket£17.50. House & Gardens,
Wine Cellars, Aviary, Children's Woodland
Playground, Shops & Restaurants: 21 Mar-28
Oct Wed-Fri A£13.20 C£9.35 Sat-Sun & Bank
Hols A£15.00 C£11.00, 14 Nov-23 Dec Wed-Fri
A10.00 C£5.00 Sat-Sun A£12.00 C£6.00.
Bachelors' Wing 21 Mar-28 Oct: A£3.30
C£3.30. NT Members £Free. Timed tickets to
House can be bought up to 24hrs in advance,
£3.00 per transaction, please call 01296
653226 Mon-Fri 10.00-16.00. Children wel-
come under parental supervision in House,
babies must be carried in front sling

Military & Defence Museums

Bletchley Park Museum

The Mansion Bletchley Park, Wilton Avenue
Bletchley Milton Keynes MK3 6EB
Tel: 01908 640404
Bletchley Park was home to the World War II
codebreakers that cracked the Nazi Enigma
code. It is now open as a heritage site,

Model Towns & Villages

Bekonscot Model Village and Railway

Warwick Road Beaconsfield Buckinghamshire
HP9 2PL
Tel: 01494 672919 Fax: 01494 675284
www.bekonscot.com

*[2.7mi from J2 M40, signposted, 4mi from J16
M25. Plenty of on-site parking available]*

Good things do come in small packages! BE A
GIANT in this miniature wonderland where
nobody grows up. Established in 1929
Bekonscot Model Village captures a delightful
and timeless image of a lost age, depicting rural
England in the 1930s. An unforgettable day out
for everyone and all profits are donated to charity! There are six charming little villages in a 1.5
acre miniature landscape of farms, fields, castles, churches, woods and lakes. Walking
around you'll tower over the tiny population
enjoying the fun of the fair, the zoo or lazily
watching a cricket match. Interesting buildings
including castles, a Tudor house, thatched cottages, and a replica of Enid Blyton's 'Green
Hedges'. There are also moving models, such
as a coal mine, nodding donkey and the fun fair.
Bekonscot boasts the ultimate train set, and its
historic Gauge 1 line has been famous since
1929 for being one of the largest, most exciting

and complex in Great Britain. The busy railway
race between the villages, over bridges and
under your feet. There is a full-size signal box in
control of ten scale miles of track, seven stations and often more than eight trains. There is
also a sit-on railway running at weekends and
school holidays. Bekonscot has a refreshment
kiosk, souvenir shop, playground, picnic areas
and free parking. Our log cabin is a fun place to
hold a children's birthday party.

10 Feb-28 Oct daily 10.00-17.00
A£6.50 C£4.00 Concessions£4.50. Special
rates for school groups £3.40

Discount Offer: One Child Free

Nature & Conservation Parks

Tiggywinkle's Wildlife Visitor Centre

Aston Road Haddenham Aylesbury
Buckinghamshire HP17 8AF
Tel: 01844 292292
A two storey building allows the visiting public
to understand the work of the hospital, and follow the past, present and future medical
advances in wildlife rehabilitation.

Sport & Recreation

XScape: Milton Keynes

602 Marlborough Gate Milton Keynes
Buckinghamshire MK9 3XS

Tel: 0871 200 3220

Features 'real' snow slopes, bowling, a cinema,
gym plus bars and restaurants and shops

Stately Homes

Hughenden Manor Estate

Hughenden Manor High Wycombe
Buckinghamshire HP14 4LA
Tel: 01494 755573 Fax: 01494 474284
www.nationaltrust.org.uk
[1.5mi N of High Wycombe. Rail: High Wycombe. Plenty of on-site parking available]
A hidden gem nestled amongst the Chiltern Hills, Hughenden Manor was the home of Benjamin Disraeli, the most charismatic of Queen Victoria's prime ministers. Discover more about the private world of a famous Victorian, enjoy lunch in the Stables Restaurant, spend half an hour browsing in the National Trust shop and take a refreshing walk in the beautiful surrounding woodlands.

Mar-Oct Wed-Sun 11.00-17.00 (plus some days in December - please call for details)
A£6.40 C£3.20

Transport Museums

Buckinghamshire Railway Centre
Quinton Road Station Quainton Aylesbury

Buckinghamshire HP22 4BY

Tel: 01296 655450 Fax: 01296 655720
www.bucksrailcentre.org

[6mi N of Aylesbury, 15mi from Milton Keynes, 10mi from Bicester, 20mi from Oxford & Watford & 25mi from Luton. Off A41 Aylesbury / Bicester rd signposted from A41 at Waddesdon & A413 at Whitchurch. Plenty of free on-site parking]

Buckinghamshire Railway Centre is a working steam museum where you can step back in time to the golden age of railways. The centre has one of the largest private railway collections in the country with many steam locomotives from express passenger types to the humble shunting engine. The museum's interesting items of rolling stock on display include a coach from the Royal Train of 1901 and another used by Winston Churchill and General Eisenhower for wartime planning meetings. On steaming open days visitors can take a steam hauled train ride in vintage carriages and on our extensive miniature railway system whilst on certain days you can also ride in open wagons. The centre's new visitor centre is housed in the 1851 former Oxford Rewley Road Station moved from the centre of Oxford. In its new location it provides the perfect setting for displays of historic locomotives, carriages and smaller items. Also included are refreshment rooms and a gift shop. The centre is fully disabled accessible.

Mar-Oct Wed-Sun & Bank Hol Mons 10.30-17.30 (16.30 weekdays) for viewing. Train rides available on Sun & Bank Hol Mons plus Wed in School Hols

Special Events: A£8.00 C(5-15)£5.00 OAPs£6.50, FamilyTicket (A2+C4) £23.00. Steaming Days: A£7.00 C(5-15)£4.50 OAPs£6.00 Family Ticket (A2+C4) £21.00. Static Viewing: A£5.00 C(5-15)£2.50 OAPs£4.00 Family Ticket (A2+C4)£14.00. 'Day Out With Thomas': Please apply for details

Discount Offer: Two for the Price of One

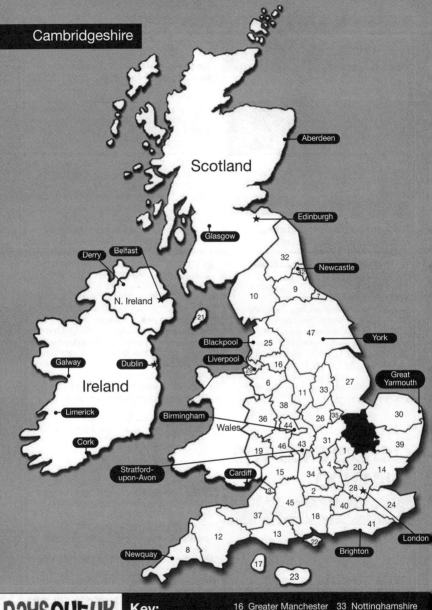

Cambridgeshire

Aberdeen

Scotland

Edinburgh

Glasgow

Derry • Belfast

Newcastle

N. Ireland

32

42

9

7

10

21

Blackpool

25

47

York

Liverpool

16

29

27

Great Yarmouth

Galway • Dublin

6

33

Ireland

11

30

Limerick

38

26

35

39

Birmingham

36

44

Wales

19

46

43

31

1

20

14

Stratford-upon-Avon

Cardiff

15

4

28

London

Cork

3

34

2

40

24

45

18

41

Newquay

37

13

22

Brighton

12

8

17

23

DAYS OUT UK

The place to look for places to go

Agriculture / Working Farms

Sacrewell Farm and Country Centre

Thornhaugh Peterborough Cambridgeshire
PE8 6HJ
Tel: 01780 782254
www.sacrewell.org.uk

[Situated just E of A1/A47 intersection, clearly signposted on approaching intersection from either direction on both A1 & A47. Plenty of on-site parking available]

Hidden deep in the heart of the countryside nestles an award winning farm and eighteenth-century watermill. Friendly farm animals, Shire Horse Centre, indoor and outdoor play areas, tractor rides, range of listed buildings, working watermill, gardens, farm bygones, and farm trails. Miller's Country Café serves delicious home-cooked food with views over the beautiful countryside. Browse through the Three Little Ducks quality farm & gift shop for local produce and interesting gifts. Special events held throughout the year. Birthday parties, conferences, meeting and many other events catered for. Camping and caravan facilities, with electric hook-ups, toilets and showers. Dogs allowed.
All year daily, Mar-Sept 09.30-17.00, Oct-Dec 10.00-16.00. Closed 24 Dec-1 Jan
A£5.50 C£4.00 OAPs£4.50, Family Ticket £16.00. Prices may vary for special events. Group rates (for 10+) available on request, pre-booking is essential

Discount Offer: One Child Free

Animal Attractions

Wimpole Home Farm

Arrington Royston Cambridgeshire SG8 0BW
Tel: 01223 206000
Home to many rare breeds of sheep, cattle, pigs, poultry, horses and goats. One of the Rare Breed Survival Trust's Approved Conservation Centres.

Wood Green Animal Shelters (HQ)

King's Bush Farm London Road
Godmanchester Cambridgeshire PE29 2NH
Tel: 08701 904090
Based in 52 acres of Cambridgeshire farmland, this is Europe's most progressive shelter for unwanted animals. Coffee shop and play areas.

Archaeology

Flag Fen: Britain's Bronze Age Centre

The Droveway Northey Road Peterborough
Cambridgeshire PE6 7QJ
Tel: 01733 313414 Fax: 01733 349957
www.flagfen.com

[A1 onto A1139, signed Fengate & Flag Fen. Plenty of free on-site parking available]

What will you discover? Flag Fen is one of the finest Bronze Age archaeological sites in Europe, with the oldest wheel in England and an ancient wooden track-way stretching across the Fens. With over 29 acres of parkland and historic reconstructions, you can discover how people lived 4000 years ago. Take a walk on the wild side around the mere and the fields, marvel at the ancient tools, jewellery and wood-work. Special events run monthly throughout the summer (highlights include pond-dipping, artefact-handling, enactments and experimental archaeology). Learn a new skill at a weekend workshop from willow sculpture to Celtic cos-tume, flint-knapping to basketry. Hands-on activities for all the family are run on selected days during the school holidays.

Mar-Oct: Tue-Sun & Bank Hols 10.00-16.00. Closed Nov-Feb

A£5.00 C£3.75 OAPs£4.50, Family Ticket (A2+C3) £13.75. Group rates (12+) available on request

Arts, Crafts & Textiles

Fitzwilliam Museum

Trumpington Street Cambridge Cambridgeshire CB2 1RB
Tel: 01223 332900
The Fitzwilliam Museum houses one of the finest art collections in the UK including antiqui-ties, manuscripts, sculpture, furniture and pot-tery.

Stained Glass Museum

The South Triforum Ely Cathedral Ely Cambridgeshire CB7 4DL
Tel: 01353 660347
An exhibition of over one hundred original stained glass panels rescued from redundant churches, illustrating the history of this ancient craft from medieval to modern times.

Birds, Butterflies & Bees

Raptor Foundation

The Heath St Ives Road Woodhurst
Cambridgeshire PE28 3BT
Tel: 01487 741140 Fax: 01487 841140
www.raptorfoundation.org.uk

[From A14 exit at St. Ives follow ring road, follow signs to Industrial Estate, R turn onto B1040 to Somersham follow brown tourist sign. From A1 exit at Huntingdon, follow signs to St. Ives, then B1040 to Somersham, follow brown tourist signs. Plenty of on-site parking available]

Come visit a unique and exciting place for children and adults alike and meet and learn about owls, hawks, falcons, buzzards, eagles and vultures. Located in 30 acres, home to over 210 raptors and more than 44 species, many of whom are threatened or endangered. We hold special events including: Twilight Flying - guest receives a meal. Over half term we will have children's activity days, where they can make an owl design for a t-shirt or make an owl out of feathers. Refreshments are available from our 'Silent Wings' restaurant/tearoom. Gifts are also available from 'Mad About Owls' and 'Raptor Krafts'. We have a large children's play area and educational room. Ask about out 'Lullabye of Birdland'. Stay with us at the 'Falcon's Nest', a 3-star Visit Britain B&B featured in BBC2s 'B&B the Best'. Fall asleep with soft hooting of owls. Wake up to the song of the Lark. Cast your 'eagle eye' over beautiful, historic Cambridgeshire.

All year daily 10.00-17.00. Flying displays at 12.00, 14.00 & 16.00

A£4.00 C(5-14)£2.50 C(2-4)£1.00 OAPs£3.00, Family Ticket £11.00. Private groups welcome. Registered Charity No. 1042085. All proceeds contribute to the care and rehabilitation of injured birds of prey

Discount Offer: Two for the Price of One

Country Parks & Estates

Milton Country Park

Cambridge Rd Milton Cambridgeshire CB4 6AZ
Tel: 01223 420060
A haven of peace and quiet not far from the city of Cambridge. A network of paths over 2 miles in length that run throughout the area.

Festivals & Shows

Cambridge Summer Music Festival

8 Horn Lane Linton Cambridge CB3 0AQ
Tel: 01223 894161 Fax: 01223 892945
www.cambridgesummermusic.com

[From London take A10 or M11. Most events (with a few exceptions) take place in Cambridge]

The Cambridge Summer Music Festival is held in over 25 historic venues in the City and features over 50 classical music events, including college chapels (such as the famous King's College Chapel), museums and concert halls. There'll be orchestras, choirs and chamber music (both serious and entertaining) by national and international performers. Highlights include the King's College Chapel Choir, The Academy of Ancient Music, the Endellion String Quartet (with Sam West), Musicians of the Globe, Acoustic Triangle, Katzenjammer, Haydn Youth Orchestra, Opera East, trumpeter Alison Balsom, and the Aurora Orchestra with Ben Grosvenor. 'Music for Kids' is a programme of workshops and concerts that will be great fun for all ages. As well as the festival there is a Spring Concerts series that runs in May, and Christmas Shopper Concerts that run in December. Details for all events can be found on our website. If you'd like a brochure, please write to us with your name and address.

12 July - 4 August 2007 (please see website or brochure for details of individual events)
£2.00-£35.00 depending on event (some events are free)

Folk & Local History Museums

Peterborough Museum and Art Gallery
Priestgate Peterborough PE1 1LF
Tel: 01733 343329
Displays showing the history of Peterborough, including marine dinosaurs, local archaeology and natural history.

Ramsey Rural Museum
Wood Lane Ramsey Cambridgeshire PE26 2XE
Tel: 01487 815715/814030
www.ramseyruralmuseum.co.uk

[In Ramsey which can be accessed via A141 from Huntingdon then B1040. Plenty of on-site parking available]

The Museum is housed in seventeenth-century farm buildings set in open countryside with ample space for parking and full disabled access. The collections include: agricultural tools and machinery, an old village store, chemist's shop, cobbler's shop, Victorian kitchen, bedroom, living room, Victorian school-room and blacksmith's forge. RAF and World War II related displays. Extensive local and family history archive. Census returns, photographs, maps etc. Many annual events such as mammoth book sale and Country Fair.

Apr-Oct Sun & Bank Hol Mon 14.00-17.00, Thur 10.00-17.00
A£4.00 C£2.00 OAPs£3.00 C(under5)£Free

Discount Offer: Two for the Price of One

Forests & Woods

Brampton Wood
Brampton Huntingdon Cambridgeshire
Tel: 01954 713500
Brampton Wood is at least 1,000 years old and an area of fine ancient woodland now owned and managed by The Wildlife Trust. At 324 acres, it is one of the largest and most important woodlands in East Anglia.

Heritage & Industrial

Prickwillow Drainage Engine Museum
Main Street Prickwillow Ely Cambridgeshire CB7 4UN
Tel: 01353 688360
Engines and artifacts associated with land drainage of the Fens. Large photographic and information display area.

Historical

Anglesey Abbey, Gardens and Lode Mill

Quy Road Lode Cambridge CB5 9EJ
Tel: 01223 810080
House dating from 1600 on site of Augustinian Priory. Now houses the Fairhaven collection of furnishings and paintings.

Elton Hall

Peterborough Cambridgeshire PE8 6SH
Tel: 01832 280468 Fax: 01832 280584
www.eltonhall.com

[On A605 5mi W of Peterborough. Plenty of on-site parking available]

This romantic house has been in the Proby family for over 350 years. The house, with its mixture of medieval, gothic and classical styles, reflects the family's passion for collecting, and this is shown in the remarkable contents. The Victorian and Edwardian gardens have been energetically restored in recent years which make Elton highly visitable. The parterre, sunken garden, rose garden, and the new millennium orangery gardens are the high spots. Best in June and July. Member of the Historic Houses Association.
27-28 May (last Sun & Mon), June Wed only, July-Aug Wed-Thur & Sun, also open 27 Aug (Bank Hol Mon) 14.00-17.00
Hall & Gardens: A£7.50 Accompanied C(under16)£Free Concessions£6.50. Gardens Only: A£5.00 Concessions£4.50

Oliver Cromwell's House

29 St. Mary's Street Ely Cambridgeshire CB7 4HF
Tel: 01353 662062 Fax: 01353 668518
www.eastcambs.gov.uk/tourism

[In heart of city, short walk from major car-parks. Signposted]

Oliver Cromwell was born on April 25th 1599. Since his death as Lord Protector in 1658 his fascinating life, ambitions, motives and actions have been the subject of much investigation and debate. Cromwell's family moved to Ely in 1936 and remained for some ten years. Today his home can be visited and we invite you to experience what domestic life would have been like in the seventeenth century in a variety of re-created period rooms as well as exhibitions detailing the Civil War and Cromwell's connection with fen life including a video on the draining of the fens. See Mrs Cromwell's kitchen, and meet Oliver Cromwell in his study, before visiting the haunted bedroom - if you dare! Guided tours and group visits by arrangement. The house also doubles as the Tourist Information Centre and has a delightful gift shop full of gift ideas as well as souvenirs relating to Cromwell and the area. Check out our website for events at the house or call for further information.
Apr-Oct daily 10.00-17.30, Nov-Mar Mon-Fri 11.00-16.00, Sat 10.00-17.00, Sun 11.00-16.00
A£3.95 C£2.70 Concessions£3.45, Family Ticket £11.00

Discount Offer: One Child Free

Ramsey Abbey Gatehouse

Abbey School Ramsey Huntingdon
Cambridgeshire PE17 1DH
Tel: 01480 301494
Site of one of the oldest English monasteries (as
early as the seventh century). A carved fifteenth-
century gatehouse with ornate oriel window.

Military & Defence Museums

Imperial War Museum, Duxford

Imperial War Museum Duxford Cambridge
Cambridgeshire CB2 4QR
Tel: 01223 835000
Nearly 200 aircraft on display including Spitfires,
Concorde and a Harrier Jet.

Natural History Museums

Dragonfly Project (formerly The National Dragonfly BioMuseum)

Wicken Fen (National Trust) Lode Lane Wicken
Ely Cambridgeshire CB7 5XP
Tel: 01733 204286
Information and exhibitions with lots of fascinating facts about dragonflies. Guided dragonfly
'safaris' with experts on hand. A study of dragonflies in art and a superbly stocked gift shop.

Nature & Conservation Parks

Wicken Fen (NT) Nature Reserve

Lode Lane Wicken Ely CB7 5XP
Tel: 01353 720274
The oldest nature reserve in the country, the
National Trust's 538 hectare wetland reserve is
rich in plant and insect life. A wide variety of
habitats for birds of scrub, marsh, reeds and
water. 9 Bird Hides offer views across a variety
of habitats. Dogs on leads only; not in Fen
Cottage.

Places of Worship

Duxford Chapel

Whittlesford Cambridgeshire
Tel: 01223 443000
*[adjacent to Whittlesford station off A505. Rail:
Whittlesford]*
A medieval chapel, once part of the Hospital of
St John. Dogs permitted on leads only.

Ely Cathedral

Chapter House The College Ely Cambridgeshire
CB7 4DL
Tel: 01353 667735 Fax: 01353 665658
Ely Cathedral towers over the Fens for miles
around. Dominating the skyline, it is one of
England's largest (and most beautiful) cathe-
drals. Known locally as the 'Ship of the Fens'
it's famous for its octagonal tower, which (when
lit) can be seen for tens of miles. Join a guided
tour, climb the octagonal tower and the west
tower for fine views of the Fens. Visit the
Stained Glass Museum (housed within the
cathedral), tour the college buildings and see
Prior Crauden's Chapel, which remains a symbol of the cathedral's monastic past.
All year daily
Mon-Sat: A£5.20 C(under12)£Free OAPs£4.50.
Group rates available on request. Admission
free to all on Sundays

Isleham Priory Church

Isleham Mildenhall Cambridgeshire
Tel: 01223 582700

[in Isleham 16m NE of Cambridge on B1104. Rail: Newmarket 8.5m, Ely 9m]

Rare example of an early Norman church. It has survived little alteration despite being later converted to a barn.

King's College Chapel

King's College Cambridge Cambridgeshire CB2 1ST
Tel: 01223 331212

King's College Chapel is the chapel to King's College of the University of Cambridge, and is one of the finest examples of late English Gothic or Perpendicular style. Members of the public are welcome to visit the chapel and the grounds of King's College.

Peterborough Cathedral

Minster Precincts Peterborough Cambridgeshire PE1 1XS
Tel: 01733 355300 Fax: 01733 355316
www.peterborough-cathedral.org.uk

[A1 on J with A605 / A47, follow City Centre signs]

Peterborough Cathedral "an undiscovered gem". With one of the most dramatic West Fronts in the country, it's three arches an extraordinary creation of medieval architecture, it would be easy for the interior to be an anticlimax, but it is not. The dramatic Romanesque building is little altered since its completion 800 years ago and it has recently undergone extensive cleaning and restoration following the serious fire of November 2001. Highlights include the unique painted nave ceiling, elaborate fan vaulting in the 'new' building, Saxon carvings from an earlier church, elaborately carved Victorian choir stalls and the burial place of two queens. An excellent exhibition tells the cathedral's story. Freshly prepared meals and snacks are available at Beckets restaurant opposite the West Front and the cathedral shop is next door. Disabled access to most areas. A range of tours can be booked in advance: please contact the Cathedral Office for details.

All year Mon-Fri 09.00-18.30 Sat 09.00-17.00, Sun 12.00-17.00. Some access restricted during services

Donations are politely requested; A£3.50 Concessions£2.50 suggested

Science - Earth & Planetary

Whipple Museum of the History of Science

Free School Lane Cambridge Cambridgeshire CB2 3RH
Tel: 01223 330906

A collection of scientific instruments and models dating from the Middle Ages to the present day.

Victorian Era

Cambridge Museum of Technology

The Old Pumping Station Cheddars Lane Cambridge Cambridgeshire CB5 8LD
Tel: 01223 368650

A preserved Victorian Pumping Station and working museum. The Cambridge Museum of Technology is based in the Old Steam Pumping Station which retains the original engines, pumps and boilers.

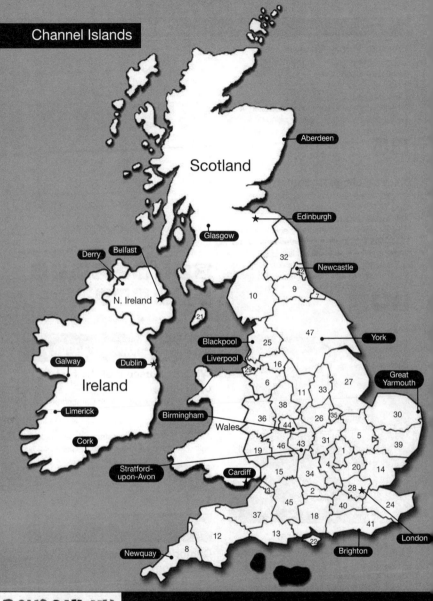

Channel Islands

Scotland

Aberdeen

Edinburgh

Glasgow

Derry Belfast

Newcastle

N. Ireland

32

42

10 9 7

Blackpool

21

47 York

25

Galway Dublin

16

Liverpool

Ireland

29

27

Great
Yarmouth

6 11 33

Limerick

38

26 35 30

Birmingham

36 44

Cork

Wales

5 39

19 46 43 31

1 20 14

Stratford-
upon-Avon

4

Cardiff

15 34

28 London

2 24

45

40 41

Brighton

37 18

12 13 22

Newquay

8

Days Out UK

The place to look for places to go

Archaeology

La Hougue Bie Museum
Princes Tower Road St. Saviour Jersey
Channel Islands JE2 7UD
Tel: 01534 853823
La Hougue Bie Museum is dominated by a
Neolithic burial mound.

Arts, Crafts & Textiles

Guernsey Tapestry
St James College Street St Peter Port Guernsey
Channel Islands GY1 1XF
Tel: 01481 727106
The Bailiwick of Guernsey Millennium Tapestry
illustrates 1000 years of local history.

Harbour Gallery and Studios
Le Boulevard St Aubin Jersey Channel Islands
JE3 8AB
Tel: 01534 743044
The Harbour Gallery is Jersey's largest exhibit-
ing and selling gallery.

Costume & Jewellery Museums

Jersey Goldsmiths: A Treasure Park
Lion Park St Lawrence Jersey Channel Islands
JE3 1GX
Tel: 01534 482098
See local goldsmiths create jewellery, or create
your own at the Quick Silver school of jewellery.
Gold-panning and a 'Diamondology' depart-
ment. Lake and gardens. Children's play areas.

The Guernsey Diamond Museum
Ray & Scott Jewellers Ltd The Bridge
St Sampsons Guernsey Channel Islands
GY2 4QN
Tel: 01481 244610
An insight into the sparkling world of diamonds.

Exhibition & Visitor Centres

Eric Young Orchid Foundation
La Rue du Moulin du Ponterrin Trinity Jersey
Channel Islands JE3 5HH
Tel: 01534 861963
One of the finest collections of orchids in the
world.
All year Wed-Sat

Jersey's Living Legend Village
La Rue du Petit Aleval St. Peter Jersey
Channel Islands JE3 7ET
Tel: 01534 485496
Enter the unforgettable Jersey Experience and
let us introduce you to some famous islanders.

Factory Outlets & Tours

Bouchet Agateware Pottery
Haut du Marais Forge Rue des Marettes St
Ouen Jersey Channel Islands JE3 2HW
Tel: 01534 482345
Tony Bouchet is the only person in the world
today who can make agateware pottery.

Catherine Best Jewellery
The Mill Steam Mill Lane St Martin Guernsey
Channel Islands GY4 6XE
The Windmill Les Chenolles St Peter Jersey
Channel Islands JE3 7DN
Tel: 01534 485777 (Jersey)
Tel: 01481 237771 (Guernsey)
Award-winning jewellery business that offers
classic jewellery with a modern feel. There are
also restaurants and children's play areas.

Jersey Pearl
Five Mile Road St Ouen Jersey JE3 2FN
Tel: 01534 862137
The largest collection of quality pearl jewellery in
the Channel Islands. In the workshop, crafts
people create individual pieces.

Jersey Pottery
Gorey Village Main Road Gorey Jersey
Channel Islands JE3 9EP
Tel: 01534 850850
See all the stages of production, from throwing
to hand decoration. Showroom, museum, a
'do-it-yourself' painting studio and a restaurant.

Folk & Local History Museums

German Occupation Museum
Les Houards Forest Guernsey Channel Islands
GY8 0BG
Tel: 01481 238205
The Channel Islands' largest collection of
authentic Occupation items.
Tue-Sun

Guernsey Museum and Art Gallery
Candie Gardens St Peter Port Guernsey
Channel Islands GY1 1UG
Tel: 01481 726518
Set in attractive Victorian gardens, overlooking
St. Peter Port, the main exhibition in the muse-
um tells the Story of Guernsey.
Feb-Dec daily

Jersey Museum
Weighbridge St. Helier Jersey Channel Islands
JE2 3NF
Tel: 01534 633300
The Jersey Museum, winner of the Museum of
the Year Award 1993, is a specially designed
purpose-built venue.

Food & Drink

La Mare Vineyards & Distillery
St Mary Jersey Channel Islands
Tel: 01534 481178
Experience everything from wine to chocolate.
Plenty for children too.

Gardens & Horticulture

Jersey Lavender Farm
La Rue du Pont Marquet St. Brelade Jersey
Channel Islands JE3 8DS
Tel: 01534 742933
Visitors can see the complete process of laven-
der production from cultivation through to har-
vesting and distillation to the bottling.

Reg's Garden
Route des Genots St Brelade Jersey
Channel Islands JE3 8DB
Tel: 01534 743756
A garden filled with thousands of flowering
shrubs and bushes, a large waterfall and an
aviary. Unusual 180ft-long pond full of koi carp.
Newly created Fairy Garden.

Historical

Little Chapel
Les Vauxbelets College Complex
Les Vauxbelets St. Andrew Guernsey
Channel Islands GY6 8XY
[Boullan Rd. Bus: 4, 5 & 5A]
Possibly the smallest chapel in the world, deco-
rated with seashells, pebbles and colourful
pieces of broken china.

Maison d'exil de Victor Hugo
Hauteville House 38 Hauteville Street
St Peter Port Guernsey Channel Islands
GY1 1DG
Tel: 01481 721911
Built around 1800 the house was bought by
Victor Hugo, the great French writer, in 1856.
Apr-Sept Mon-Sat. Closed Bank Hol

Sausmarez Manor
St. Martin Guernsey Channel Islands GY4 6SG
Tel: 01481 235571
The Manor has been owned by the same family
for seven and a half centuries.

Maritime

Fort Grey and Shipwreck Museum

Rocquaine Bay St Pierre du Bois Guernsey
Channel Islands GY7 9BY
Tel: 01481 265036
Built in one of the most picturesque areas of the
Island to defend against French invasion.
Easter-Sept daily

Maritime Museum

New North Quay St. Helier Jersey
Channel Islands JE2 3ND
Tel: 01534 811043
Through specially-designed exhibits, visitors can
explore the maritime forces which have shaped
the experience of life in Jersey.

Military & Defence Museums

Jersey War Tunnels

Les Charrieres Malorey St Lawrence Jersey
Channel Islands JE3 1FU
Tel: 01534 863442
Captive Island, the award-winning exhibition of
the German occupation of Jersey 1940-1945, is
housed in this underground hospital tunnel.

La Valette Underground Military Museum

La Valette St Peter Port Guernsey
Channel Islands GY1 1AX
Tel: 01481 722300
Covers all aspects of Guernsey's history in a
well-lit, air-conditioned German tunnel complex.

Places of Worship

St Matthew's Church (The Glass Church)

La Grande Route de St Aubin St Lawrence
Jersey Channel Islands JE3 1LN
Tel: 01534 720934
Known as 'the Glass Church' because of the
unique art deco interior decorations made by
Rene Lalique.

Science - Earth & Planetary

Treasures of the Earth

La Route De L'etacq St. Ouen Jersey
Channel Islands JE3 2FD
Tel: 01534 484811
An exhibition of a beautiful and bizarre collection
of gems, rocks, fossils and minerals.

Sealife Centres & Aquariums

Guernsey Aquarium

La Vallette St Peter Port Guernsey
Channel Islands GY1 1AX
Tel: 01481 723301
There are currently 47 separate displays.

Theme & Adventure Parks

aMaizin

La Hougue Farm La Grande Route de St Pierre
St Peter Jersey JE3 7AX
Tel: 01534 482116
An all-inclusive attraction that includes: crazy
golf, go-kart tracks, barnyard, maze, tractor
rides, craft centre and much more.

Zoos

Jersey Zoological Park - Durrell Wildlife Conservation Trust

La Profonde Rue Trinity Jersey JE3 5BP
Tel: 01534 860000
Green open spaces, free-living animals and an
exciting programme of visitor activities.

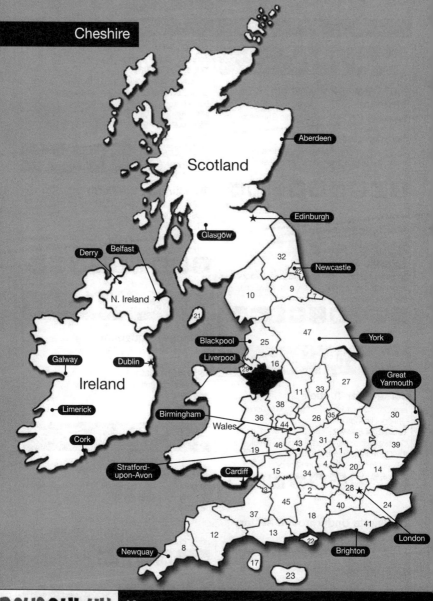

Cheshire

Aberdeen

Scotland

Edinburgh

Glasgow

Newcastle

Derry Belfast

N. Ireland

32

10 9 7

Galway Dublin

Ireland

Limerick

Cork

21

Blackpool 25

47 York

Liverpool 16

29 11 33 27

Great Yarmouth

38 30

Birmingham 36 44 26 35

Wales 5 39

19 46 43 31

Stratford-upon-Avon 4 20 14

Cardiff 15 34 2 28 24

45 40 London

37 18 41

12 13 Brighton

Newquay 8 22

17

23

Key:

1	Bedfordshire	16	Greater Manchester	33	Nottinghamshire
2	Berkshire	17	Guernsey	34	Oxfordshire
3	Bristol	18	Hampshire	35	Rutland
4	Buckinghamshire	19	Herefordshire	36	Shropshire
5	Cambridgeshire	20	Hertfordshire	37	Somerset
6	Cheshire	21	Isle Of Man	38	Staffordshire
7	Cleveland	22	Isle Of Wight	39	Suffolk
8	Cornwall	23	Jersey	40	Surrey
9	County Durham	24	Kent	41	Sussex
10	Cumbria	25	Lancashire	42	Tyne & Wear
11	Derbyshire	26	Leicestershire	43	Warwickshire
12	Devon	27	Lincolnshire	44	West Midlands
13	Dorset	28	London	45	Wiltshire
14	Essex	29	Merseyside	46	Worcestershire
15	Gloucestershire	30	Norfolk	47	Yorkshire
		31	Northamptonshire		
		32	Northumberland		

Animal Attractions

Stapeley Water Gardens and The Palms Tropical Oasis

London Road Stapeley Nantwich Cheshire CW5 7LH
Tel: 01270 623868 Fax: 01270 624919
www.stapeleywg.com

[J16 M6, 1mi S of Nantwich on A51 to Stone follow brown tourist signs. Plenty of on-site parking available]

There's something for everyone at Stapeley Water Gardens. The Palms Tropical Oasis is the perfect destination whatever the weather! With tamarin monkeys, toucans, piranhas, sharks and a crocodile, the Palms provide a unique experience of being in a tropical rainforest with all its fascinating and intriguing plants and animals. There's plenty of exciting areas to explore; from the humid setting of the Tropical House to the creepy Jungle Floor. There's also the Zoo Room and the Tunnel of Underwater Life to discover. The Palms also have a range of children's activities during school holidays and "Meet the Keeper" sessions every Saturday plus Mondays and Wednesdays throughout school holidays. Not only can you visit the Palms, there are fabulous selections of plants, gifts, pets, fish and water gardening at the Garden Centre, plus large Angling and Camping Centres.

Summer (Mid Mar-Mid Sept): Garden & Angling Centres: Mon-Sat 09.00-18.00, Wed open until 20.00. Bank Hol 10.00-18.00, Sun 10.00-16.00, Palms Tropical Oasis: daily 10.00-17.00, Winter: Garden & Angling Centres: Mon-Fri 09.00-17.00, Sat 09.00-18.00, (Angling Centre: Wed open till 20.00), Bank Hol 10.00-17.00, Sun 10.00-16.00. Palms Tropical Oasis: daily 10.00-17.00. Closed 25 Dec except for booked lunches. Garden & Angling Centres also closed Easter Sunday

The Palms Tropical Oasis: A£4.45 C£2.60 OAPs£3.95. Group rates (15+): A£3.95 C£2.35 OAPs£3.55

Discount Offer: One Child Free

Art Galleries

Stockport Art Gallery

War Memorial Building Greek Street Stockport Cheshire SK3 8AB
Tel: 0161 474 4453
Changing exhibitions of contemporary art, photography and craft.

Arts, Crafts & Textiles

Blakemere Craft Centre

Chester Road Sandiway Northwich Cheshire CW8 2EB
Tel: 01606 883261
Blakemeres' 30 craft shops offer individually handcrafted items.

Country Parks & Estates

Etherow Country Park

George Street Compstall Stockport Cheshire
Tel: 0161 427 6937
Etherow Country Park is a popular retreat from urban living.

Marbury Country Park

Comberbach Northwich Cheshire CW9 6AT
Tel: 01606 77741

Marbury Country Park is the parkland of Marbury Hall, which was demolished in 1968.

Tatton Park

Knutsford Cheshire WA16 6QN
Tel: 01625 534400 / 534435
50 acres of gardens, Tudor old hall, working
1930's farm and Neo-classical mansion. Shops
and adventure playground.

Festivals & Shows

RHS Flower Show at Tatton Park

Tatton Park Grounds Knutsford Cheshire
Tel: 0870 842 2229
www.rhs.org.uk/flowershows

[Plenty of on-site parking available]

In the heart of Cheshire, the RHS hosts the
spectacular annual RHS Flower Show at Tatton
Park. One of the finest flower shows in gardening calendar, the RHS Flower Show is set
against the beautiful parkland and historic houses of Tatton Park. Breathe in the fresh air (and
the fresh ideas for your garden) as top designers unveil their inspiring show gardens, the best
nurseries open for business and the numerous
caterers tempt your taste-buds. Seek out the
back-to-back gardens and unearth tips and
tricks to enhance your own. There'll be RHS
advisors who are happy to provide all the one-
to-one advice you'll need.
*19-22 July 2007 (Thur-Sat 10.00-18.30, Sun
10.00-17.00)*
£22.00 (£20.00 if booked in advance) C(5-
15)£5.00 C(under5)£Free

Food & Drink

Cheshire Ice Cream Farm

Drumlan Hall Farm Newton Lane Tattenhall
Chester Cheshire CH3 9NE
Tel: 01829 770446
A working dairy farm open to the public.
Animals include sheep, donkeys and rabbits.

Gardens & Horticulture

Cholmondeley Castle Garden

Cholmondeley Malpas Cheshire SY14 8AH
Tel: 01829 720383 Fax: 01829 720877
*[Off A49 Whitchurch / Tarporley road. Rail:
Crewe. Plenty of on-site parking available]*

Extensive ornamental gardens dominated by a
romantic Gothic Castle, built in 1801 of local
sandstone. Beautiful Temple water garden, rose
garden and many mixed borders. Ruin water
garden and memorial mosaic designed by
Maggy Howarth. Lakeside walk with picnic site,
children's play areas, rare breeds of farm animals, including Llamas, children's corner with
rabbits, chickens and free flying aviary birds.
Private chapel in the park. Gift shop and tea
room. Plants for sale. The castle is not open to
the public.

*1 Apr-30 Sept Wed-Thurs Sun & Bank Hols
11.30-17.00*
A£4.00 C£2.00 Group rates available on
request

Hare Hill

Over Alderley Macclesfield Cheshire SK10 4QB
Tel: 01625 584412 / 0870 609 5391
A woodland garden with azaleas, rhododendrons and a delightful walled garden at its heart.

Ness Botanic Gardens

Neston Road Ness Neston CH64 4AY
Tel: 0151 353 0123
Boasts plants from all over the world.

Norton Priory Museum and Gardens

Tudor Road Manor Park Runcorn Cheshire
WA7 1SX
Tel: 01928 569895 Fax: 01928 589743
www.nortonpriory.org
[Plenty of on-site parking available]

Visit the remains of a medieval priory - there's a museum to tell the story of the site, tranquil gardens, plant sales, the Refectory Café and much, much more.
Apr-Oct: Mon-Fri 12.00-17.00, Sat-Sun & Bank Hols 12.00-18.00 (Walled Garden 13.30-16.30). Nov-Mar: Daily 12.00-16.00. Closed Dec 24-26 & Jan 1
A£4.95 Concessions£3.50, Family Ticket (A2+C3) £12.75

Discount Offer: Two for the Price of One

Heritage & Industrial

Hat Works - The Museum of Hatting, Stockport

Wellington Mill Wellington Road
South Stockport Cheshire SK3 0EU
Tel: 0845 833 0975 Fax: 0161 480 8735
www.hatworks.org.uk
[Wellington Mill's landmark chimney is highly visible & is located on main throughfare, A6 Wellington Rd South. Opposite bus station, close to railway station. 2min walk from Merseyway Shopping Centre & town centre shops. Parking available in & around town centre. Nearest car parks are: Heaton Lane, Mersey Way & Grand Central]

The UK's first and only museum dedicated to the exciting world of hats and hat-making. Learn about Stockport's historic links with hatting and how the industry flourished employing over 4,500 people by the end of the nineteenth century. Take a step back in time to Hope Street with a glimpse into a Hatter's Cottage, marvel at the machines restored to full working order - giving a noisy and thrilling encounter with the town's industrial past. Interactive demonstrations reveal the art and mystery of hat making. The stunning display of hats from the early 1800s to modern day. There's so much to see and do, it is simply brimming over! Educational sessions: linked to Key Stages 1 & 2 with a dedicated Education Suite, details available upon request. The Level 2 internet café is open to all, visitor to the museum or not! Relax in stylish surroundings and choose from a range of coffees, pastries or light lunches.
All year daily Mon-Fri 10.00-17.00, Sat-Sun 13.00-17.00. Please call for Christmas & New Year opening times
Admission Free. Guided Tour: £2.00, Family Ticket £7.00

Macclesfield Silk Museums

Heritage Centre Roe Street Macclesfield
Cheshire SK11 6UT
Tel: 01625 612045
A visit to our three Silk Museums offers you the
chance to explore the history of a silk town.

Historical

Adlington Hall

Mill Lane Adlington Macclesfield Cheshire
SK10 4LF
Tel: 01625 829206
Home of the Leghs since 1315.

Boat Museum

South Pier Road Ellesmere Port South Wirral
Cheshire CH65 4FW
Tel: 0151 355 5017
Houses the world's largest floating collection of
canal craft within Ellesmere Port's historic dock.

Capesthorne Hall

Siddington Macclesfield Cheshire SK11 9JY

Tel: 01625 861221
Sculptures, paintings and a collection of
American Colonial furnishings.

Chester Castle: Agricola Tower and Castle Walls

Chester Cheshire
Tel: 0191 261 1585
Set in the angle of the city walls, this twelfth-
cetury tower contains a fine vaulted chapel.

Chester Roman Amphitheatre

Vicars Lane Chester Cheshire
Tel: 0191 261 1585
The largest Roman amphitheatre in Britain.

Staircase House

30-31 Market Place Stockport Cheshire
SK1 1ES
Tel: 0161 480 1460 Fax: 0161 474 0312
www.staircasehouse.org.uk

*[In centre of Stockport. 5min walk from bus &
train stations, follow signs to market place.
Parking within short walking distance, follow car
park signs to Merseyway]*

This award-winning new attraction invites you to
time travel through the history of Staircase
House from 1460 to WWII. With the help of a
state-of-the-art audio guide, the fascinating history of the house will unfold on a fun, accessible
and informative journey. The entire 18-room
town house is fully interactive. You are invited to
smell, touch and listen and to re-live its history
by pulling back the bedclothes on the four-
poster bed, peeling rush lights, and trying your
hand at seventeenth-century quill pen writing.
Perfect for a family day or simply to enjoy a
unique hands on historical experience. Staircase
House has an intriguing array of rooms linked
by narrow passages and the beautifully restored
Jacobean cage newell staircase - one of only
three surviving examples in Britain. Events
throughout the year. Visit on the last Saturday of
every month and meet characters from the past
in various rooms.
*Mon-Fri 12.00-17.00. Sat-Sun 10.00-17.00.
Group bookings welcome both inside & outside
normal opening hours by special arrangement*
A£3.95 Concessions(under16's & over
60's)£2.95, Leisure key: £2.00. Family Ticket
(A2+C3) £12.00

Tabley House

Knutsford Cheshire WA16 0HB
Tel: 01565 750151 Fax: 01565 653230
www.tableyhouse.co.uk

*[J19 M6 A556, 2mi W of Knutsford, entrance on
A5033. Plenty of on-site parking available]*

The only Palladian Mansion in the North West,
Tabley comprises an extraordinary collection of
family memorabilia. The First Lord de Tabley
was a distinguished patron of the arts and the
house comprises works by Reynolds, Fuseli,
Turner and Lawrence, to name a few. Furniture
by Bullock and Gillow. Knowledgeable and helpful stewards ensure an enjoyable afternoon out.
*Apr-end Oct Thur-Sun & Bank Hol 14.00-17.00.
Tea Room: 12.00-17.00*
A£4.00 C&Students(NUS/USI)£1.50

Military & Defence Museums

Hack Green Secret Nuclear Bunker

Nantwich Cheshire CW5 8AQ
Tel: 01270 629219
For over 50 years this vast underground complex remained a secret hidden on the outskirts
of a sleepy Cheshire town.

On the Water

Anderton Boat Lift

Lift Lane Anderton Northwich Cheshire
CW9 6FW
Tel: 01606 786777
The Anderton Boat Lift is one of the greatest
monuments to Britain's last canal age.

Places of Worship

Chester Cathedral

Abbey Square St Werburgh Street Chester
Cheshire CH1 2HU
Tel: 01244 324756 Fax: 01244 341110
www.chestercathedral.com

[In City Centre]

Founded as a Benedictine monastery in 1092 it
became a cathedral in 1541, this building is an
unusually well preserved example of a medieval
monastic complex, displaying all the main periods of Gothic architecture. Here you will find
amazing architecture, huge mosaics, stained
glass, medieval woodcarving and contemporary
works of art in the heart of the ancient City of
Chester. Admission includes a digital audio tour
of the Cathedral. There are daily services if visitors wish to join in.
All year daily 08.00-18.00
A£4.00 C£1.50 Concessions£3.00, Family
Ticket £10.00

Railways

Brookside Miniature Railway

Brookside Garden Centre Macclesfield Road
Poynton Cheshire SK12 1BY
Tel: 01625 872919
Steam and diesel engines draw up to 50 passengers at a time round the Garden Centre's landscaped maze of beautiful rockeries, flower beds and winding pathways.

Roman Era

Dewa Roman Experience

Pierpoint Lane Chester Cheshire CH1 1NL
Tel: 01244 343407
Stroll along reconstructed streets experiencing Roman Chester.

Science - Earth & Planetary

Catalyst: Science Discovery Centre

Mersey Road Widnes Cheshire WA8 0DF
Tel: 0151 420 1121 Fax: 0151 495 2030
www.catalyst.org.uk

[Rail: Runcorn then bus or taxi across bridge. By car J7 M62 0r J12 M56 follow brown & white tourism signs. Plenty of on-site parking available]

Experience an amazing journey of discovery in Catalyst's brand new Interactive Theatre and enter a colourful world of science and technology in our three interactive galleries. Visit our shop or café and travel 30 metres above the River Mersey in our external glass lift to marvel at the views from our glass-walled rooftop gallery. Science has never been so much fun!
All year Tue-Sun & Bank Hol Mon. Closed 24-26 Dec ,1st Jan & most Mons during school hols
A£4.95 C&Concession£3.95 C(under4)£Free Family Ticket£15.95

Discount Offer: One Child Free

Jodrell Bank Visitor Centre

Jodrell Bank Lower Withington Macclesfield Cheshire SK11 9DL
Tel: 01477 571339 Fax: 01477 571695
[Plenty of on-site parking available]
The Visitor Centre stands at the feet of one of the largest radio telescopes in the world, the Lovell telescope, a landmark in both Cheshire and in the world of astronomy.

All year daily 10.30-17.30 (subject to change). Closed 25 Dec, 6 July & 4 Oct
A&C£1.50

Discount Offer: Two for the Price of One

Sealife Centres & Aquariums

Blue Planet Aquarium

Longlooms Road Cheshire Oaks Ellesmere Port
Cheshire CH65 9LF
Tel: 0151 357 8804 Fax: 0151 356 7288
www.blueplanetaquarium.com

*[J10 M53, signposted. Easy to find from M6 &
M56. Plenty of on-site parking available]*

Blue Planet Aquarium is an experience you'll
never forget. A fascinating underwater world of
colours and close encounters. A voyage of discovery through rivers and reefs to where our
divers hand feed the sharks. Glide through the
most spectacular safari and be surrounded by a
carnival of Caribbean fish, including one of the
largest collections of sharks in Europe!!! Special
events held throughout the year, please call for
details.
*All year daily from 10.00. Please call to check
closing times as these may vary. Closed 25 Dec*
A£10.50 C(3-15)&Concessions£7.75
C(under3)£Free, Family Ticket (A2+C2) £35.50
Groovy Grandparent (OAPs2+C2) £30.50

Social History Museums

Grosvenor Museum

27 Grosvenor Street Chester Cheshire
CH1 2DD
Tel: 01244 402008

2,000 years of Chester's history: Yesterday's
fossils to today's countryside, life in the Fortress
of Deva, a Roman graveyard, sparkling silver
from Chester silversmiths and period rooms
bringing history to life.

Stockport Air Raid Shelters

61 Chestergate Stockport Cheshire SK1 1NE
Tel: 0161 474 1940 Fax: 0161 474 1942
www.stockport.gov.uk
[M60, J1, A6. Rail: Stockport, 10min]

First-hand experience of daily life in 1940s, war-
torn Britain. A labyrinth of tunnels under part of
the town centre provided shelter - and a way of
life - for Stockport and Manchester families
through the dark days of the Blitz. Take time to
wonder how everyone managed with those
bunks and benches; lights and sounds; toilet
arrangements and Red Cross facilities. Explore
authentic reconstructions in a core area of
sandstone tunnels. Sense the immense network
of structure; the thousands of people; their con-
cern and determination. Audio-experience the
sounds of 1940 - the historical context, the
songs and the reminiscences. Reflect on the
complexities of conflict in the 'Web of War' exhibition. Admire the contributions of Wardens,
WVS and other volunteers, experience the
atmosphere and respect the memories as you
stroll through the tunnels.

*All year daily 13.00-17.00. Open Bank Hols
except 25-26 Dec & 1 Jan times are subject to
change please call before visiting*
A£3.95 C&Concessions£2.95, Family Ticket
(A2+C2) £11.75

Stockport Story

29 Market Place Stockport Cheshire SK1 1ES
Tel: 0161 480 1460 Fax: 0161 474 0312
www.stockportstory.org.uk

[In centre of Stockport. 5min walk from bus & train stations, follow signs to market place. Parking within short walking distance, follow car park signs to Merseyway]

Stockport Story Museum is a brand new local history museum set in the heart of Stockport's historic market place. Visitors are invited to experience 10,000 years of history as they travel from prehistoric to present day Stockport. Explore the Origins gallery and see the fantastic finds from a local archaeological dig including original flint tools of the hunter-gatherers. Then travel through medieval Stockport in the Making of the Town gallery and find out about Stockport's once thriving textile industry. Journey on to the Work and Play gallery where you'll learn about Victorian Stockport and the industries of the town. Conclude your journey in the Changing Lives gallery where you can learn of the impact of the wars on Stockport, and how the town is shaping up today. There's also a temporary exhibition gallery with four exhibitions per year. The museum is family friendly with interactives and activities for all ages. Make a day of it by visiting Staircase House, which is right next door!

All year daily 10.00-17.00
Admission Free

Bramall Hall

Bramhall Park Bramhall Cheshire SK7 3NX
Tel: 0845 833 0974 Fax: 0161 486 6959
www.bramallhall.org.uk

[4mi S of Stockport off A5102, 10min from Stockport town centre. On-site parking available]

Magical Tudor House set in 70 acres of parkland. House contains sixteenth-century wall paintings, Elizabethan plaster ceilings, Victorian kitchens and Servants' quarters. Available for civil marriages and corporate entertaining. Wheelchair and pushchair access limited to ground floor only. Photography (but not flash) permitted. Guided tours by prior arrangement only.
1 Apr-end Sept Sun-Thur 13.00-17.00, Fri-Sat 13.00-16.00, Bank Hols only 11.00-17.00, 1 Oct-1 Jan Tue-Sun 13.00-16.00, 2 Jan-31 Mar Sat-Sun 13.00-16.00
A£3.95 C&OAPs£3.50. Group rates available on request

Discount Offer: Two for the Price of One

Dunham Massey Hall

Altrincham Cheshire WA14 4SJ
Tel: 0161 941 1025
Tour the house on your own and talk to the knowledgeable stewards, or join a guided tour,

Theme & Adventure Parks

Go Ape! High Wire Forest Adventure

Delamere Forest Park Linmere Visitor Centre
Northwich Cheshire CW8 2JD
Tel: 0870 420 7876
www.goape.co.uk

[10mi outside Chester, close to M56. Plenty of on-site parking available]

Take to the trees and experience an exhilarating course of rope bridges, 'Tarzan Swings' and zip-slides up to 40 feet above the ground! Share approximately three hours of memorable fun and adventure, which you'll be talking about for days. Book online and watch people Go Ape! at www.goape.co.uk. Minimum height 1.4m. Maximum weight 130 kg (20.5 stone). Under-18s must be accompanied by a participating adult. One adult can supervise either two children (where one or both of them in under 16 years old) or up to five 16-17 year olds. Pre-booking is essential to avoid disappointment. Book online or by telephone (there is a £1.00 booking fee on all telephone bookings).

10-25 Feb & 23 Mar-2 Nov daily, Nov Sat-Sun. Closed Dec-Jan
Gorillas (18yrs+) £25.00, Baboons (10-17yrs) £20.00

Discount Offer: Two for the Price of One

Gullivers World

Warrington Cheshire WA5 9YZ
Tel: 01925 444888/230088
From the juggling fun of Circus World, mosey on down to High Noon in Western World, walk with dinosaurs in the prehistoric Lost World, feel your knees tremble in Count's Castle and shiver your timbers in Smugglers Wharf. Be courageous and bold in Adventure World and splash around in Water World.

Tourist Information Centres

Chester Visitor Centre

Vicars Lane Chester Cheshire CH1 1QX
Tel: 01244 402111
The ideal starting point for exploring Chester. Guided walks including the Roman Soldiers Patrol. The centre also houses 'What's in a name' the fun way to trace the origins of family and first names.

Transport Museums

Mouldsworth Motor Museum

Smithy Lane Mouldsworth Chester Cheshire CH3 8AR
Tel: 01928 731781
Housed in a large Art Deco building close to Delamere Forest, a collection of over 60 motor cars, motorcycles and early bicycles.

Zoos

Chester Zoo

Upton-by-Chester Chester Cheshire CH2 1LH
Tel: 01244 380280
Chester Zoo has over 7,000 animals and is famous for its large enclosures and attractively landscaped gardens. Take the weight off your feet with our Zoofari overhead railway or a waterbus ride.

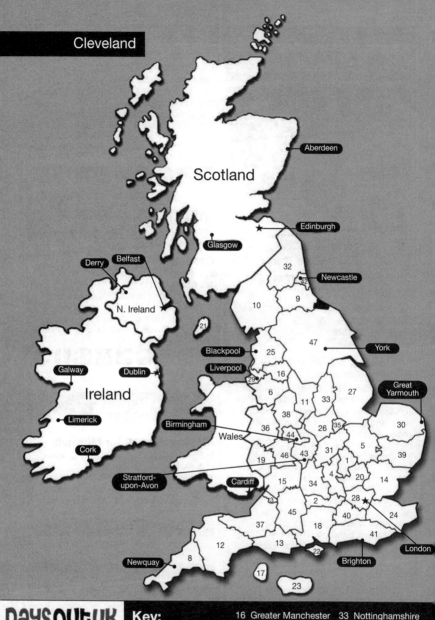

Cleveland

Scotland

Aberdeen

Edinburgh

Glasgow

Newcastle

Derry | Belfast

N. Ireland

32

42

9

10

21

Blackpool

25

Liverpool

16

47

York

6

29

Galway | Dublin

Ireland

Limerick

Cork

11 33

27

Great Yarmouth

38

36

26 35

30

Birmingham

44

Wales

19

46 43

31

5

39

Stratford-upon-Avon

Cardiff

15

34

4

1

20

14

13

2

28

London

45

40

24

37

18

41

13

22

Newquay

12

8

Brighton

17

23

DAYS OUT UK

The place to look for places to go

Art Galleries

Hartlepool Art Gallery
Church Square Hartlepool Cleveland TS24 7EQ
Tel: 01429 869706
Houses contemporary art exhibitions.

Arts, Crafts & Textiles

Cleveland Craft Centre
57 Gilkes Street Middlesbrough Cleveland
TS1 5EL
Tel: 01642 808090
Studio pottery and contemporary jewellery.

Birds, Butterflies & Bees

Butterfly World
Preston Park Yarm Road Stockton-On-Tees
Cleveland TS18 3RH
Tel: 01642 791414
An indoor tropical rainforest populated by exotic
free-flying butterflies and birds.

Festivals & Shows

Hartlepool Fireworks and Music Spectacular
Seaton Carew Seafront Hartlepool Cleveland
TS24 0JN
Tel: 01429 869706 (TIC)
www.destinationhartlepool.com
[South Shelter/Clock Tower. Park & Ride available]

One of the most popular firework displays in the
area. Children's funfair rides and stalls, entertainment and displays. Park and Ride shuttle
service available, see press for details or contact the Tourist Information Centre.
*3 November 2007 (Sat funfair from 16.00, enter-
tainment from 17.00, displays from 18.30)*
Admission Free

Stockton International Riverside Festival
Stockton-On-Tees Tees Valley TS18 3BB
Tel: 01642 527040 Fax: 01642 527037
www.sirf.co.uk
*[Various venues in Stockton. From A1(M) N take
A168 / A19 to Teeside leave A19 at A1046 to
Stockton. Trans-Penine Express from Manchester,
Leeds & York - alight at Thornaby, or East Coast
Main Line, change at Darlington. On-site parking]*
Stockton International Riverside Festival, the
UK's finest street arts festival, showcases the
best in street theatre, circus, dance and music.
For five days, artists from all over the world take
over the town with a series of stages and instal-
lations, from daredevil aerial and trapeze to
walkabout shows in the street. Meanwhile the
distinctive 'Fringe' offers a mix of cutting edge
and popular music and visual arts. Saturday's
Carnival and Parade brings a thousand costumed performers through the town in a riot of
colour and sound. This award winning, family
friendly Festival will finish with a bang as the
world's most famous firework company 'Groupe
F' provides the explosive Finale.
1-5 August 2007 (11.00-23.00)
Most events are free, others range from £3.00-
£10.00. Free festival programme available

Trafalgar Celebrations at Hartlepool's Maritime Experience

Maritime Avenue Hartlepool Cleveland
TS24 0XZ
Tel: 01429 860077 Fax: 01429 867332
www.hartlepoolsmaritimeexperience.com

[A19: A179 (N) or A689 (S). Plenty of on-site parking available]

Marking the 202nd anniversary of the British victory at the Battle of Trafalgar. Enjoy a visit to the North East's premier maritime attraction - a stunning recreation of an eighteenth-century Naval seaport complete with genuine historic ship. HMS Trincomalee is Europe's oldest warship afloat. Gun, cannon and sword-fighting displays and costumed guides adds to the experience.
20-21 October 2007
A£7.50 C£4.50 OAPs£5.75

Discount Offer: One Child Free

Folk & Local History Museums

Green Dragon Museum

Theatre Yard Calverts Lane Stockton-On-Tees
Cleveland TS18 1AT
Tel: 01642 606525
Local history museum showing the development of Stockton.

Heritage & Industrial

Cleveland Ironstone Mining Museum

Deepdale Skinningrove Saltburn-by-the-Sea
Cleveland TS13 4AP
Tel: 01287 642877
Experience the underground world of Cleveland's Ironstone Mining Past.

Historical

Ormesby Hall

Ladgate Lane Ormesby Middlesbrough
Cleveland TS7 9AS
Tel: 01642 324188
A mid eighteenth-century Palladian mansion, notable for its fine plasterwork and carved wood decoration.

Maritime

Hartlepool's Maritime Experience

Maritime Avenue Hartlepool Cleveland
TS24 0XZ
Tel: 01429 860077 Fax: 01429 867332
www.hartlepoolsmaritimeexperience.com

[From N A19 take A179 & follow signs for historic quay. From S A689 from A19 & follow signs for quay 1032. Plenty of on-site parking available]

The North East's premier maritime attraction. A voyage back in time to the sights and sounds of an eighteenth-century quayside. A full day of fun with loads of themed activities. Take a journey through an audio / visual tour of a frigate then board the real thing; the magnificent HMS Trincomalee, the oldest ship afloat in the UK where you can explore the decks accompanied by an audio guide. Skittle Square, the children's maritime adventure centre, outdoor wooden playship and a short film presentation 'Pressganged' are just a few of the attractions to enjoy. Costumed guides and regular sword fighting, cannon firing, musketry displays and pirate and marine re-enactors enhance the experience, please check the website to confirm details. Visit the free Museum of Hartlepool which tells the fascinating story of the town, including the monkey legend. Featuring a year long programme of exhibitions. Look around the restored paddle steam ship Wingfield Castle with coffee shop.

All year daily, summer 10.00-17.00, Winter Open daily please check website for times. Closed 25-26 Dec & 1 Jan
A£7.50 C£4.50 OAPs£5.75, Family Ticket £19.50

Discount Offer: One Child Free

Nature & Conservation Parks

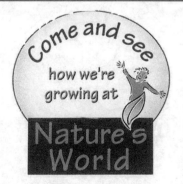

Come and see how we're growing at Nature's World

Nature's World
Ladgate Lane Acklam Middlesbrough Cleveland TS5 7YN
Tel: 01642 594895 Fax: 01642 591224

www.naturesworld.org.uk

[Signs from A19 onto A174. Plenty of on-site parking available]

The North of England's pioneering eco-experience! Featuring 'Futureworld' and tropical Hydroponicum. Also unique River Tees model, and over 20 acres of organic gardens and wildlife areas. Tearooms, shop and play areas.
1 Apr-30 Sept 10.00-17.00, 1 Oct-31 Mar 10.30-15.30
High Season: A£4.50 Concessions£4.00 C£2.50, Family Ticket £11.50, Low Season A£3.50 Concessions£3.00 C£1.50, Family Ticket £8.00

Discount Offer: £1.00 off per head (pre-booked groups of 20+)

Sport & Recreation

Stewart Park
Ladgate Lane Marton-in-Cleveland Middlesbrough Cleveland TS7 8AR
Tel: 01642 300202 / 515600
Captain Cooks Birthplace, Stewart Park offers a wide range of facilities including lakes, arboretum, walks and orienteering course.

Victorian Era

Preston Hall Museum and Park
Preston Park Yarm Road Stockton-On-Tees Cleveland TS18 3RH
Tel: 01642 781184
The museum illustrates Victorian social history, with reconstructions of period rooms and a street with working craftsman including blacksmith, farrier and toymaker.

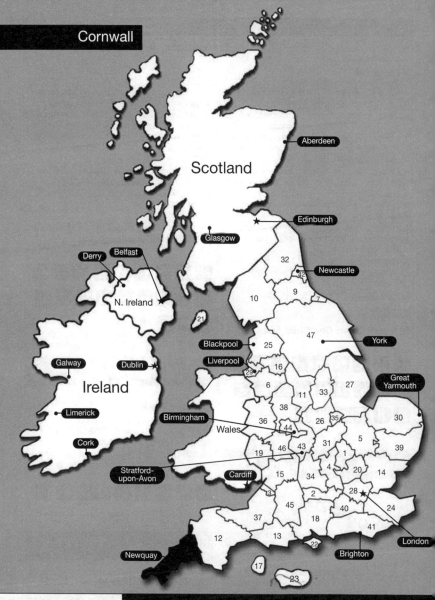

Cornwall

Scotland

Aberdeen

Glasgow

Edinburgh

Newcastle

Derry · Belfast

N. Ireland

Galway · Dublin

Ireland

Limerick

Cork

Blackpool

Liverpool

Birmingham

Wales

Cardiff

Stratford-
upon-Avon

York

Great
Yarmouth

London

Brighton

Newquay

The place to look for places to go

Key:

1	Bedfordshire	16	Greater Manchester
2	Berkshire	17	Guernsey
3	Bristol	18	Hampshire
4	Buckinghamshire	19	Herefordshire
5	Cambridgeshire	20	Hertfordshire
6	Cheshire	21	Isle Of Man
7	Cleveland	22	Isle Of Wight
8	Cornwall	23	Jersey
9	County Durham	24	Kent
10	Cumbria	25	Lancashire
11	Derbyshire	26	Leicestershire
12	Devon	27	Lincolnshire
13	Dorset	28	London
14	Essex	29	Merseyside
15	Gloucestershire	30	Norfolk
		31	Northamptonshire
		32	Northumberland

33	Nottinghamshire
34	Oxfordshire
35	Rutland
36	Shropshire
37	Somerset
38	Staffordshire
39	Suffolk
40	Surrey
41	Sussex
42	Tyne & Wear
43	Warwickshire
44	West Midlands
45	Wiltshire
46	Worcestershire
47	Yorkshire

Animal Attractions

Monkey Sanctuary

St. Martin Murrayton Looe Cornwall PL13 1NZ
Tel: 01503 262532 Fax: 01503 262532
www.monkeysanctuary.org

[Plenty of on-site parking available]

The Monkey Sanctuary near Looe had been home to a colony of Amazonian Woolly monkeys since 1964. Visitors can watch them in their extensive territory of interlinked enclosures, watch them scale trees, forage and socialize. Keepers are on hand daily to give talks and introduce you to the monkeys; their personality, likes and dislikes. The Monkey Sanctuary is also home to a small group of rescued capuchin monkeys brought to the Sanctuary from lives as isolation as pets. Visitors can learn about the problems of keeping intelligent and social monkeys in captivity, and learn about projects in South America working for monkeys in the wild. Visitors are also invited to get a closer look at a colony of lesser horseshoe bats who roost in our cellar courtesy of a CCTV link. There are beautiful gardens overlooking Looe bay for visitors to explore and follow the nature trail. Children can make Amazonian face masks in the activity room, and enjoy a bit of bouncing about of their own in the play area. The Monkey Sanctuary offers a gift shop, vegetarian café, ample parking and free picnic areas.
1 Apr-28 Sep Sun-Thur 11.00-16.30. Closed Fri-Sat
Please call for prices

National Seal Sanctuary

Gweek Helston Cornwall TR12 6UG
Tel: 01326 221874 Fax: 01326 221210
www.sealsanctuary.co.uk

[Follow signs to Helston then to Gweek. Plenty of on-site parking available]

This year the National Seal Sanctuary will be opening Sea Lion Lagoon. Here you can enjoy a close encounter with our Californian Sea Lions, getting up to all sorts of antics as they show off their amazing new surroundings. You can also meet their neighbours Caris and his new partner, the incredible Patagonian Sea Lions, who's meal times are their favourite part of the day. See animal welfare in action at the UK's busiest seal rescue centre. Our Animal Care Team work round the clock with sick and injured seal pups in the seal hospital. Meet our cheeky Asian short-clawed otters, Thai and Bamboo and learn more about otter conservation all over the world. Enjoy a close encounter of the marine kind at the Cornish Coast Experience, where visitors can meet some of the inhabitants from our local shores. Set on the beautiful Helford River estuary this has to be one of the most picturesque settings in the country. A wonderful day out for the whole family. Guided tours by prior arrangement. We welcome all well-behaved dogs.
All year daily from 10.00. Closed Christmas Day
Please call for admission prices

Discount Offer: One Child Free

Paradise Park and Jungle Barn

16 Trelissick Road Hayle Cornwall TR27 4HB
Tel: 01736 751020
www.paradisepark.org.uk
[A30 to Hayle/St. Ives roundabout, follow brown tourist signs to Helston Rd. On-site parking]

Chosen as 'Visitor Attraction of the Year' at the Cornwall Tourism Awards, you can be assured of a great day at Paradise Park. The exotic birds (especially parrots plus owls, touracos, pheasants and flamingos) and animals (otters, red pandas, red squirrels, alpacas) in tropical gardens were recently joined by a huge indoor play centre - making the park a perfect choice for families whatever the weather! The new Jungle Barn has giant drop slides, challenging soft play, a special toddlers area with ball fountain, and a café. But make sure you get out to enjoy the timetable of events - you can get up close at penguin and otter feeding, and at the brilliant summer free-flying displays with parrots, toucans, eagles, owls and falcons. The gardens really set the scene at the park; the terraced Gazebo Garden is planted with colourful sunloving plants, while Parrot Jungle is full of shade-loving bamboo and ferns. Home of the World Parrot Trust charity.
All year daily from 10.00. Closed 25 Dec
Please call for admission prices

Discount Offer: £1.00 off standard admission prices (for up to 5 people)

Porfell Animal Land

Herodsfoot Liskeard Cornwall PL14 4RE
Tel: 01503 220211
There are porcupines, wallabies, lemurs and many more TV favourites as.

Arts, Crafts & Textiles

Barbara Hepworth Museum and Sculpture Garden

Barnoon Hill St. Ives Cornwall TR26 1AD
Tel: 01736 796226
Sculptures can be seen in the late Dame Barbara Hepworth's house,

Tate St Ives

Porthmeor Beach St. Ives Cornwall TR26 1TG
Tel: 01736 796226
International Modern and Contemporary Art in the unique cultural context of St Ives.

Birds, Butterflies & Bees

Lost Gardens of Heligan

Pentewan St. Austell Cornwall PL26 6EN

Tel: 01726 845100 Fax: 01726 845101
www.heligan.com
[Signposted from A390 / B3273. Plenty of on-site parking available]
Heligan's 200-acre estate is home to a wealth of wildlife. A purpose-built hide enables you to watch the intimate lives of wildlife species including barn owls, badgers and bats, live on a series of screens and interactive displays. From the Hide's observation windows, nuthatches, goldfinches and woodpeckers are just some of the birds that can be observed. Heligan's outer estate landscape of woodlands, wetland and farmland is being managed as part of 'Heligan Wild'. This new initiative shows and interprets

this rich landscape using techniques and methods that encourage and provide habitats for wildlife. Guided walks and themed evenings run during the spring and summer months. Please see section under gardens and horticulture for more details on The Lost Garden's of Heligan.

All year daily, main season 10.00-18.00, winter season 10.00-17.00. Closed 24-25 Dec

A£8.50 C£5.00 OAPs£7.50, Family Ticket £23.50. Please note, pre-booking is essential for group visits

Porteath Bee Centre

St. Minver Wadebridge Cornwall PL27 6RA
Tel: 01208 863718
Porteath Bee Centre is a small bee keeping business with a shop, exhibition and café located on Cornwall's north coast.

Communication Museums

Porthcurno Telegraph Museum

Porthcurno Penzance Cornwall TR19 6JX
Tel: 01736 810966
[From Penzance take the Land's End rd (A30), turn L to St Buryan then follow signs to Porthcurno (& Wartime Telegraph Museum). Park in main valley car park]

This fascinating museum tells the story of the origins of today's Internet and the history of world communications, through the development of the telegraph network in Victorian times. The first telegraph station at Porthcurno opened in 1870, with the laying of an undersea cable to India, and by the start of the Second World War, it had become the largest and most important station in the world. Visitors get an insight into both the technological changes and the social changes, which took place during this time. The museum is housed in the underground tunnels, which were built during the war to protect the equipment from enemy damage. Visitors can see the secret escape stairs and enjoy lots of hands-on exhibits. There is something for all the family, with children's activities, additional exhibitions and demonstrations of the original equipment which help to bring it all to life.

Easter-Oct, daily 10.00-17.00 (Wed 19.30), Nov-Easter open Sun & Mon. Christmas & Winter half-term dates may vary- please ring for details

A£4.95 C£2.75 Concession£4.40 Family Ticket (2A+3C)£12.00 Student(NUS/USI)£3.50 (with dated photographic ID)

Discount Offer: 10% off Admission Prices

Festivals & Shows

Bude Jazz Festival

Bude Cornwall
Tel: 01228 356360
The twentieth Bude Jazz Festival will pack 166 jazz events into the eight days.

25 August-1 September 2007

Folk & Local History Museums

Royal Cornwall Museum

River Street Truro Cornwall TR1 2SJ
Tel: 01872 272205
Cornwall's oldest and most prestigious museum.

Smugglers at Jamaica Inn

Jamaica Inn Complex Bolventor Launceston
Cornwall PL15 7TS
Tel: 01566 86250 Fax: 01566 86177
www.jamaicainn.co.uk

[On A30 Launceston / Bodmin rd. Plenty of on-site parking available]

An attraction in three parts, designed to appeal to all the family. Employing the latest digital technology with traditional methods of interpretation. Visitors are first welcomed with a theatrical presentation of the Jamaica Inn story told in tableaux, light and sound, then on to see one of the finest collections of smuggling relics, dating from past to present. And finally, on to Dame Daphne Du Maurier's life and works including her Sheraton writing desk where she wrote so many of her famous novels.

Mid season daily 10.00-17.00, Summer daily 10.00-19.00, Part Winter 11.00-16.00

Museum Passport: A£3.50
C(under16)&OAPs£3.00, Family Ticket £8.95. Coach party rate: £2.50 per person

Food & Drink

Cornish Cyder Farm

Penhallow Truro Cornwall TR4 9LW
Tel: 01872 573356
Makes over forty varieties of delicious fruit products including farm scrumpy, sparkling cyder, country wines, jam, chutneys and spirits.

Gardens & Horticulture

Lost Gardens of Heligan

Pentewan St. Austell Cornwall PL26 6EN
Tel: 01726 845100 Fax: 01726 845101
www.heligan.com

[Signposted from A390 / B3273. On-site parking]

Heligan, seat of the Tremayne family for more than 400 years, is one of the most mysterious estates in England. At the end of the nineteenth century its thousand acres were at their zenith, but only a few years after the Great War of 1914-1918, bramble and ivy were already drawing a green veil over this 'Sleeping Beauty'. After decades of neglect with its restoration commenced by a small band of enthusiasts, Heligan was recently voted "The Nation's Favourite Garden" by Gardeners' World and now offers 200 acres open to the public. Set within beautiful Cornish countryside are: Victorian pleasure grounds, working buildings and historic glasshouses, productive gardens, a subtropical "Jungle" valley, lakes, wetlands, ancient broadleaved woodlands, and permanent pasture, where wildlife can be observed. Heligan is so much more than simply a garden restored; its own special atmosphere encourages exploration and contemplation, satisfying the broadest range of horticultural and wildlife interest. Please see section under Birds, Butterflies and Bees for more details on the Lost Garden's of Heligan.

All year daily Mar-Oct 10.00-18.00, Nov-Feb 10.00-17.00, Closed 24-25 Dec

A£8.50 C£5.00 OAPs£7.50, Family Ticket £23.50. Please note, prior booking is essential for group visits

Heritage & Industrial

Land's End Visitor Centre

Sennen Penzance Cornwall TR19 7AA
Tel: 0870 458 0044
Britain's most westerly point whose magic has drawn visitors for centuries.

Historical

King Arthur's Great Halls

Fore Street Tintagel Cornwall PL34 0DA
Tel: 01840 770526
Built in the 1930's, the building houses round tables, granite thrones and 72 stained glass windows. The shop stocks a whole array of specially commissioned Arthurian products.

Mount Edgcumbe House and Country Park

Cremyll Torpoint Cornwall PL10 1HZ
Tel: 01752 822236 Fax: 01752 822199
www.mountedgcumbe.gov.uk
[On Rame Peninsula via Torpoint Car Ferry from Plymouth. On foot: Ferry - Plymouth to Cremyll. Rail: Plymouth Liskeard. On-site parking available]

Tudor mansion, former home of the Earls of Mount Edgcumbe. Refurbished in eighteenth-century style. Family Treasures. Programme of special exhibitions and events. Features include shell seat in Earls 2 acre garden, historic buildings, formal gardens include Italian, French, English, American and New Zealand sections. One of 3 Grade I listed gardens in Cornwall. 865 acres of country park overlooking Plymouth Sound. Disabled and pushchair access limited, please call for details.

House & Earls Garden: 1 Apr-30 Sept Sun-Thur & Bank Hol Mons 11.00-16.30. Formal Gardens: All year daily 08.00-dusk
House & Gardens: A£4.50 C£2.25
Concessions£3.50, Family Ticket £10.00.
Season Ticket £7.50. Country Park: Admission Free

Discount Offer: Two for the Price of One

Prideaux Place

Padstow Cornwall PL28 8RP
Tel: 01841 532411 Fax: 01841 532945
www.prideauxplace.co.uk

[From A30 signposted Wadebridge/Padstow. Plenty of on-site parking available]

Situated above the picturesque port of Padstow is the Elizabethan mansion Prideaux Place. Completed in 1592 by Nicholas Prideaux and still lived in by the family who can trace their ancestry back to William the Conqueror. Surrounded by 40 acres of landscaped gardens and overlooking its ancient Deer Park this splendid house contains a wealth of family and royal portraits, an exquisite collection of porcelain, a growing Teddy Bear collection and a magnificent sixteenth-century plaster ceiling, the crowning glory of the Great Chamber with its stunning views across the Cornish countryside to distant Bodmin Moor. The gardens are undergoing extensive restoration, the family being helped by Tom Petherick who has been instrumental in the restoration of the gardens at Heligan. Visitors can enjoy woodland walks, a formal garden, a garden Temple and Roman antiquities. There is a fully licensed tearoom offering light lunches and renowned Cornish Cream Teas, on warm sunny days one can enjoy refreshments on the Terrace, a haven of peace away from the bustle of Padstow. *Easter Sun-12 Apr & 13 May-4 Oct Sun-Thur, House: 13.30-16.00, Grounds & Tearoom: 12.30-17.00. Group bookings open all year by appointment* A£7.00 C£2.00

St Catherine's Castle
Fowey Cornwall
Tel: 0117 975 0700
A small fort built by Henry VIII to defend Fowey Harbour.

St Michael's Mount
West End Marazion Cornwall TR17 0EF
Tel: 01736 710507 / 710265
Originally the site of a Benedictine priory and approached by a causeway at low tide, the dramatic castle dates from the twelfth century.

Tintagel Castle
Tintagel Cornwall PL34 0HE
Tel: 01840 770328
Legendary birthplace of King Arthur. A magical mystery audio visual tour through the ages, introduces visitors to the castle, its legends and history.

Maritime

Charlestown Shipwreck and Heritage Centre
Quay Road Charlestown St. Austell Cornwall PL25 3NJ
Tel: 01726 69897
The Shipwreck and Heritage Centre houses the largest display of shipwreck artefacts in the UK.

National Maritime Museum Cornwall
Discovery Quay Falmouth Cornwall TR11 3QY
Tel: 01326 313388 Fax: 01326 317878
www.nmmc.co.uk
[At SE end of Falmouth's harbour front, nr docks, car parking & railway station. Rail: Falmouth]

Located on the edge of Falmouth's stunning harbour, the National Maritime Museum Cornwall is a hands-on, twentyfirst-century, new generation of visitor attraction that will appeal to landlubbers and sailors alike. More than just a museum about boats, it's all about the sea, boats and Cornwall itself. Experience breathtaking views from the 29m tower, see the only natural underwater tidal zone in Europe and a stunning flying display of boats. Enjoy hands-on activities, an audio-visual immersive experience, talks, special exhibitions, and cruises. The National Maritime Museum Cornwall has something for everyone and is the perfect day out. The best way to get here is by boat! Use the 'Park & Float' and sail to the museum in a classic ferry (running May-September).
All year daily 10.00-17.00. Closed 25-26 Dec A£7.50 C(under5)£Free Concessions from £5.00, Family Ticket (A2+C3) £20.00

Discount Offer: Two for the Price of One

Nature & Conservation Parks

Eden Project
Bodelva Parr St Austell Cornwall PL26 2SG
Tel: 01726 811911
The Eden Project was established as one of the landmark Millennium projects in the UK. More than just a green theme park, Eden is about connecting plants, people and places.

Performing Arts

Minack Theatre and Exhibition Centre
Porthcurno Penzance Cornwall TR19 6JU
Tel: 01736 810694
Views from the theatre are spectacular, overlooking the Atlantic Ocean and across to the dramatic Logan Rock on Treen Cliff. In addition to live performances, there is a exhibition centre, cafe and gift shop for daytime visitors.

Places of Worship

Truro Cathedral
Truro Cornwall TR1 2AF
Tel: 01872 276782
The largest UK example of the Gothic Revival architectural style (fashionable during the nineteenth century).

Police, Prisons & Dungeons

Bodmin Jail
Berrycoombe Road Bodmin Cornwall
PL31 2NR
Tel: 01208 76292
Visit the dungeons below ground and find out just some of the crimes and punishments of our unfortunate ancestors.

Railways

Bodmin and Wenford Railway
Bodmin General Station Lostwithiel Road
Bodmin Cornwall PL31 1AQ
Tel: 0845 125 9678 Fax: 01208 77963
www.bodminandwenfordrailway.co.uk

[Free parking available at Bodmin General Station, situated on B3268 Lostwithiel rd nr Bodmin centre. From A30/A38 follow signs to Bodmin town centre then brown tourist signs to steam railway. Car parking NOT available at other stations. Rail: Mainline rail services operate to Bodmin Parkway. Through tickets to Bodmin & Wenford Railway are available tel: 08457 484950. Bus: Western Greyhound, 01637 871871]

The Bodmin and Wenford Railway offers a trip into nostalgia with steam trains operating from the historic town of Bodmin through scenic countryside along the preserved six-mile Great Western Railway branch line to Bodmin Parkway (for walks to Lanhydrock House) and Boscarne Junction (for the Camel Trail footpath). Steam locomotives include a newly-restored Great Western Railway prairie tank which returned to steam in 2003. The 75 year-old engine had been rescued from the scrapyard where it had been sent in 1960! The line is Cornwall's only standard-gauge steam railway - located about eight miles from the Eden Project. Bodmin General station (in Bodmin town centre) offers a refreshment room and souvenir shop. Evening specials offer a variety of music, brake van rides and murder mystery! Come and enjoy Sunday lunch in our First Class Dining Coaches, also available for private hire.

Opening times: June-Sept daily, also some days in Mar, Apr, May, Oct, Nov, Dec. Call for details
All Line Ticket (Return): A£10.00 C(under3)£Free C(3-16)£6.00, Family Ticket (A2+C4) £28.00.
Bodmin General & Boscarne Junction

Sealife Centres & Aquariums

Blue Reef Aquarium

Towan Promenade Newquay Cornwall TR7 1DU
Tel: 01637 878134 Fax: 01637 872578
www.bluereefaquarium.co.uk

[Follow brown tourist signs to car parks in town centre, Blue Reef is situated on Towan beach]

Take the ultimate undersea safari at the award winning Blue Reef Aquarium where there's a world of underwater adventure just waiting to be discovered. Over 30 living displays reveal the sheer variety of life in the deep; from native sharks and lobsters to seahorses and amazing jellyfish. At the aquarium's heart is a giant ocean tank where an underwater walkthrough tunnel offers incredibly close encounters with the stunning beauty of a tropical coral reef - home of hundreds of colourful fish. Blue Reef is a great place for visitors of all ages to discover more about the wonders of the deep. There's a full programme of entertaining, informative talks and feeding displays throughout the day. Learn more about native sea creatures including crabs, anemones and starfish at our popular Rockpool Encounters where our experts will be on hand to answer all your questions. New for 2007 - Seahorse Ranch. A spectacular experience whatever the weather.

All year daily from 10.00. Closed 25 Dec
A£7.50 C(3-16)£5.50
OAPs&Students(NUS/USI)£6.50. Discounted rates for groups and disabled visitors - please call for details

Discount Offer: One Child Free

Theme & Adventure Parks

Cornwall's Crealy Great Adventure Park

Tredinnick Newquay Cornwall PL27 7RA
Tel: 0870 1163333 Fax: 01395 233211
www.crealy.co.uk

[From A30: off A39 nr Wadebridge, fully signposted. Plenty of free on-site parking available]

Come to Cornwall's Crealy where family time is always Maximum Funtime - Guaranteed! Three NEW Showtimes: Heavy Horses on Parade, Cornwall's Falconry Displays and Swampy's Pirate Show - plus six unique areas of adventures, animals, enchantment, heritage, nature and wild water. The wildest rides, the UK's biggest outdoor play zones and 40,000 sq ft of indoor fun too. Find out more at on our website. Come to Cornwall's Crealy and have the most memorable, friendliest family day out - because the best days are Crealy days.

1 Apr-4 Nov daily 10.00-17.00 (Closed 5 Nov-14 Mar 08)
Low season: A&C£9.95, OAPs£6.50, C(under92cm)£Free, Family Ticket (4 people) £9.50 per person. High season: A&C£10.95 C(under92cm)£Free OAPs£7.50, Family Ticket (4 people) £10.50 per person

Discount Offer: One Free Ice-Cream

Flambards Experience

Helston Cornwall TR13 0QA
Tel: 01326 573404 Fax: 01326 573344
www.flambards.co.uk
[0.5mi S of Helston on A3083 towards Lizard]

The secret of Flambards' appeal is its huge variety; there is so much to do and see and so many places where all ages can enjoy themselves together inside and out. Inside, let your imagination lead you through the award winning Flambards Victorian Village, a compelling life-size re-creation of a lamp-lit village of bustling streets and alleyways with more than 50 shops, traders and homes. Or move forward to the

Second World War in Britain in the Blitz, an undercover, authentic life-size re-creation of a World War II blitzed street. Then, enjoy the fascinating exhibitions, step into Concorde, enjoy the Wildlife Experience or just let the children play in the Cool Zone undercover play area. And, outside, let rip on the best thrill rides in Cornwall, and children can play to their hearts' content in Ferdi Funland and the children's' ride area. With award winning gardens, top quality entertainment in the high season, a wide choice of picnic areas, catering and gift shops, every visitor can be confident of a superb full day out.
31 Mar-27 Oct daily 10.00/10.30-17.00/17.30 depending on season. Closed some Mon & Fri in low & shoulder season, please call for details
A(11-59)£12.95 C(under3)£Free C(3-10)£8.25
OAPs(60-79)£6.95 OAPs(80+)£Free, Family
Ticket (4 people)£41.00, (£10.25 per person)
with top ups: C(3-10)£7.00 each, A(11-59)
£12.00 each, OAPs(60-79) £6.00 each
Discount Offer: One Child Free

Hidden Valley Adventure Park

Tredidon St Thomas Launceston Cornwall
PL15 8SJ
Tel: 01566 86463
One of a kind adventure park, with exciting treasure hunts themed around an old shipwreck, gold mine and haunted cottage.

Miniatura Park

Halt Road Goonhavern Truro Cornwall TR4 9QE
Tel: 0870 458 4433
Relaxing fun for all the family with new and refurbished models, puzzles, sculptures, and grottos hidden throughout 12 acres of magical Cornish gardens.

Spirit of the Western American

Retallack Park Winnards Perch St. Columb
Cornwall TR9 6DE
Tel: 01637 881160
Wild west theme park, museums of cowboys, indians and American collections. Live action shows, a complete living history museum of the 1800s set in 100 acres.

Transport Museums

British Cycling Museum

The Old Station Camelford Cornwall PL32 9TZ
Tel: 01840 212811
Over 400 examples of cycles, old cycle repair workshop, over 1,000 cycling medals, fobs and badges from 1881.

Wax Works

Tunnels Through Time

St Michaels Road Newquay Cornwall TR7 1RA
Tel: 01637 873379
Cleverly brings to life the stories and legends of Cornwall.

Zoos

Newquay Zoo

Trenance Gardens Newquay Cornwall TR7 2LZ
Tel: 01637 873342 Fax: 01637 851318
www.newquayzoo.org.uk

[A30 Indian Queens, A392 to Newquay, turn R into Trevemper Rd, follow brown & white signs]

Visitor Attraction of the Year 2006 (Cornwall Tourism Awards). Award winning Newquay Zoo is set amongst exotic lakeside gardens with animals from all around the world ranging from the smallest monkey the Pygmy Marmoset to 'Ronnie' and 'Connie' the African Lions. Enjoy talks, animal encounters and feeding times throughout the day. See the very popular otter family playing in the stream in the Oriental Garden, Owston's Civets from Vietnam and stunning Hornbills from Asia. Look out for meerkats on sentry duty, penguins playing in their pool and the beautiful Red Pandas. Newquay Zoo is fun for all age groups with plenty of delights for children including the Tarzan trail, a children's play area, the village farm and the dragons maze. Face painting and a 'Wild Times' creative club are also available on most days during the summer. Events run throughout the year. The site is mainly level and is wheelchair friendly.

Apr-Sep daily 09.30-18.00, Oct-Mar daily 10.00-dusk. Closed 25 Dec
A£8.95 C(under3)£Free C(3-15)£6.00
OAPs&Students(NUS/USI)£6.45
Disabled/Carer£4.75, Family Ticket (A2+C2)
£25.00. Group rates available on request

Discount Offer: £1.00 off Per-Person (for up to 6 people)

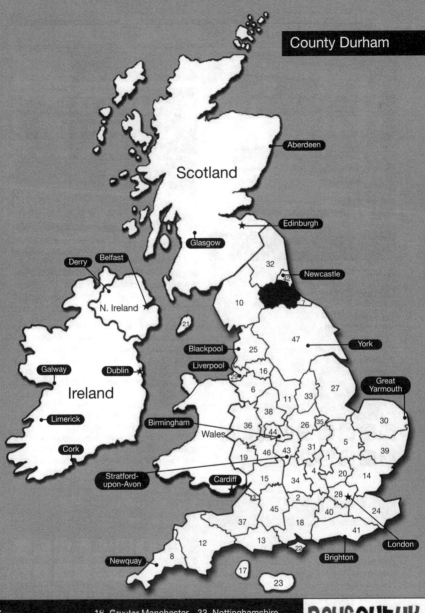

County Durham

Scotland

Aberdeen

Edinburgh

Glasgow

Derry | Belfast

Newcastle

32

42

N. Ireland

10

7

Galway | Dublin

21

Blackpool

25

York

47

Ireland

Liverpool

16

6

29

Great Yarmouth

Limerick

11

33

27

38

30

Cork

Birmingham

36

44

26

35

Wales

5

19

46

43

31

39

Stratford-upon-Avon

Cardiff

15

34

4

1

20

14

28

2

40

24

45

18

Brighton

London

37

41

Newquay

12

13

22

8

17

23

Key:

1 Bedfordshire	16 Greater Manchester	33 Nottinghamshire
2 Berkshire	17 Guernsey	34 Oxfordshire
3 Bristol	18 Hampshire	35 Rutland
4 Buckinghamshire	19 Herefordshire	36 Shropshire
5 Cambridgeshire	20 Hertfordshire	37 Somerset
6 Cheshire	21 Isle Of Man	38 Staffordshire
7 Cleveland	22 Isle Of Wight	39 Suffolk
8 Cornwall	23 Jersey	40 Surrey
9 County Durham	24 Kent	41 Sussex
10 Cumbria	25 Lancashire	42 Tyne & Wear
11 Derbyshire	26 Leicestershire	43 Warwickshire
12 Devon	27 Lincolnshire	44 West Midlands
13 Dorset	28 London	45 Wiltshire
14 Essex	29 Merseyside	46 Worcestershire
15 Gloucestershire	30 Norfolk	47 Yorkshire
	31 Northamptonshire	
	32 Northumberland	

Abbeys

Egglestone Abbey

Marwood Barnard Castle County Durham
DL12 8QN
Tel: 0191 261 1585
The remains of this Premonstratensian abbey
makes a picturesque sight on the right bank of
the River Tees. A large part of the church can
be seen, as can remnants of monastic buildings.

Animal Attractions

Hall Hill Farm

Lanchester County Durham DH7 0TA
Tel: 01388 731333
www.hallhillfarm.co.uk
[Plenty of on-site parking available]
Family farm set in attractive countryside with
opportunity to see and touch animals at close
quarters. Tractors and trailers, donkey rides,
feed the pet lambs, adventure play area, farm
tearoom and gift shop.
Apr-Sep 10.30-17.00
A£4.75 C£3.50

Archaeology

Old Fulling Mill, Museum of Archaeology

The Old Fulling Mill The Banks Durham County
Durham DH1 3EB
Tel: 0191 334 1823
The Museum houses a fascinating range of
archaeological material, mostly from North East
England, but also from Central Europe, Ancient
Greece and Rome.

Art Galleries

Bowes Museum (The)

Barnard Castle County Durham DL12 8NP
Tel: 01833 690606 Fax: 01833 637163
www.thebowesmuseum.org.uk
*[Historic Market Town of Barnard Castle. Plenty of
free on-site parking available]*

The first sight of The Bowes Museum never
ceases to amaze. Founded over 100 years ago
by wealthy businessman John Bowes and his
Parisian Wife Joséphine, the French-style
chateau was designed to house their acquisitions and to give 'ordinary' people a chance to
experience art for themselves. But the Museum
is more than a house of treasures: it curates its
own acclaimed exhibition programme, often
built around highlights from its own collections;
takes touring exhibitions from institutions,
stages fun-filled indoor and outdoor family
events, offers scholarly lectures and runs a significant education programme. The designated
collection includes some of the best examples
of European fine and decorative art in the UK,
with works by Goya, El Greco and Canaletto. It
also features fine ceramics, furniture, textiles
and a famous silver swan automaton. Situated
in beautiful grounds, the fabulous building is
also home to the acclaimed Café Bowes, and a
quality gift shop.
*All year daily 11.00-17.00. Closed 25-26 Dec &
1 Jan*
A£7.00 C(under16)£Free Concessions£6.00

**Discount Offer: Two for the Price of
One**

Darlington Arts Centre

Vane Terrace Darlington County Durham
DL1 5PW
Tel: 01325 483555
Darlington Arts Centre encompasses Myles Meehan Gallery, the Foyer exhibition space, the Window space and Glass Corridor Gallery. These exhibition spaces aim to provide opportunities for artists and groups to exhibit their work in new and exciting ways.

Country Parks & Estates

Hardwick Hall Country Park

Sedgefield Stockton-on-Tees County Durham
TS21 2EH
Tel: 0191 383 3594
A former landscape garden designed by James Paine in the eighteenth century. Contains the remains of several follies and the serpentine lake. A tree trail has been designed to introduce visitors to the huge variety of trees growing in the Country Park.

Folk & Local History Museums

Durham Heritage Centre

St Mary-le-Bow North Bailey Durham County Durham DH1 3ET
Tel: 0191 386 8719
The museum is in an historic church. Displays tell the story of Durham from the tenth century to the present day with models.

Weardale Museum of High House Chapel

Ireshopeburn County Durham
Tel: 01388 537417
Small folk museum in the Minister's House adjacent to eighteenth-century Methodist chapel where John Wesley preached.

Gardens & Horticulture

Eggleston Hall Gardens

Eggleston Barnard Castle County Durham
DL12 0AG
Tel: 01833 650115
Small informally laid out garden, with a stream, winding paths and lawns. Rare plants and shrubs.

Heritage & Industrial

Killhope The North of England Lead Mining Museum

Cowshill Weardale County Durham DL13 1AR
Tel: 01388 537505 Fax: 01388 537617
www.durham.gov.uk/killhope

[On A689 between Stanhope & Alston. Plenty of on-site parking available]

Work as a washerboy and find lead ore, experience the living conditions of Victorian lead miners, and walk the woodland trail. The Park Level Mine is an exciting trip deep underground. National Award Winning Museum.
Apr-31 Oct daily
A£4.50 C£1.50 Family Ticket (A2+C3)£11.50

Discount Offer: Two for the Price of One

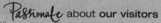

Passionate about our visitors
Winner of North East England Tourism Awards
Most Welcoming Experience 2005
Outstanding Customer Service Silver Award 2006

Award Winning

KILLHOPE

Open Daily
10.30 - 5.00pm
1st April - 31st
October 2007

The North of England Lead Mining Museum
Near Cowshill, Upper Weardale
Co. Durham DL13 1AR (A689)

For more information
✆01388 537505
www.durham.gov.uk/killhope

Making a difference where you live

Historical

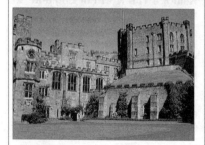

Durham Castle

Palace Green Durham County Durham
DH1 3RW
Tel: 0191 334 3800 Fax: 0191 334 3801
www.durhamcastle.com
*[Central Durham adjacent to Cathedral. Rail:
Durham 0.5m]*
Dating from 1072, Durham Castle, the former
residence of the Prince Bishops of Durham has
been the Foundation College of Durham
University since 1832. Along with the Cathedral
it forms part of Durham's World Heritage Site
dominating the skyline on all approaches to the
City. During University vacations the Castle acts
as a conference and holiday centre offering
accommodation. This includes the Bishop's
Suite, situated in an area of the Castle built in
the thirteenth century, with a sitting room hung
with seventeenth-century tapestries, overlooking
the River Wear. Each morning breakfast is
served in the Great Hall, one of the largest and
most impressive of its kind, with a 14 metre
high ceiling. Throughout the summer months
the Castle is a superb venue for wedding receptions, offering drinks in the courtyard and dinner
in the Great Hall. The Castle also offers regular
guided tours for both groups and individuals.
Please note that other events may result in the
cancellation of tours, please check availability.
*Guided Tours only: Apr-Sept daily 10.00-12.00 &
14.00-16.30, Oct-Mar Mon, Wed, Sat & Sun
14.00-16.00*
A£5.00 C&Concessions£3.50, Family Ticket
£12.00. Guide Book £2.50. Group rates (10-
40): A£4.50 C&Concessions£3.00

Superbreak Mini-Holidays - No 1 for UK short breaks

Raby Castle

Staindrop Darlington County Durham DL2 3AH
Tel: 01833 660202 Fax: 01833 660169
www.rabycastle.com
[On A688, 1mi N of Staindrop. Plenty of on-site parking available]

This dramatic mediaeval castle built by the mighty Nevills has been home to Lord Barnard's family since 1626. Set within a large deer park with walled gardens and a delightful rolling landscape, it is one of the most impressive castles in England. Discover the fine collections of furniture, impressive artworks and elaborate architecture. Highlights include the vast Baron's Hall, where it's rumoured that in 1569, 700 knights gathered to plot the doomed overthrow of Elizabeth I, a splendid Victorian octagonal drawing room that has emerged as one of the most striking interiors from the nineteenth century. And in contrast, a cavernous mediaeval kitchen that was used right up to 1954. There is an events programme that runs throughout the summer.
Easter (Sat-Mon), May-June & Sep (Sun-Wed & Bank Hol Sats), July-Aug (Sun-Fri): Castle 13.00-17.00, Park & Gardens 11.00-17.30. Closed Oct-Mar
A£9.00 C£4.00 Concessions£8.00, Family Ticket (A2+C3) £25.00

Nature & Conservation Parks

Low Barnes Nature Reserve

Witton-le-Wear Bishop Auckland County Durham DL14 OAG
Tel: 01388 488728
A 50 hectare wetland site with areas of mixed woodland and grassland. The Reserve is situated on an ex-gravel extraction site, which has been managed by Durham Wildlife Trust since operations ended in 1964.

Places of Worship

Durham Cathedral

The College Durham County Durham DH1 3EH
Tel: 0191 386 4266
The cathedral is a remarkable example of Norman architecture.

Railways

Locomotion: The National Railway Museum at Shildon

Shildon County Durham DL4 1PQ
Tel: 01388 777999
This attraction provides an enjoyable visit telling local, regional and international stories involving social and railway history.

Roman Era

Piercebridge Roman Bridge

Morbium Piercebridge County Durham
Tel: 0191 261 1585
[4m W of Darlington on B6275]
Visible Roman remains include the East Gate and defences, courtyard building and part of internal road. Also remains of the bridge which carried Dere Street over the Tees.

Social History Museums

Beamish: The North of England Open Air Museum

Beamish County Durham DH9 0RG
Tel: 0191 370 4000
A living, working experience of life as it was in the early 1800s and early 1900s.

Theme & Adventure Parks

Diggerland
Langley Park County Durham DH7 9TT
Tel: 08700 344437 Fax: 09012 010300
www.diggerland.com
[From A1(M) J62 head W, following signs to Consett, after 6mi turn L at roundabout signed to Langley Park, turn R into Riverside Industrial Estate. Rail: Durham (approx 5mi). Bus: 54 from station. Plenty of on-site parking available]

Diggerland is the best activity day out for all the family with all activities based around construction machinery. With over 15 rides and drives positioned in an adventure park situation. Experience the thrill of riding in Spindizzy and enjoy the view from the Sky Shuttle. Drive across rough terrain in the Super Track and enjoy a mystery ride in the Land Rover Safari. Test your co-ordination in the JCB Challenges and fasten your seat belt for the drive of your life in the Robots. A full day of fun can be had by all ages with everything onsite including refuelling at The Dig Inn and shopping at the Goodie store. Birthday parties are catered for, so if you fancy a party with a difference then contact us for details. Diggerland welcomes its 4th park in Yorkshire for 2007. Please see our website for more information.
Weekends & Bank Hols plus daily during half-term & school hols 10.00-17.00. Closed 25 Nov-Feb A&C£12.50 C(under3)£Free OAPs£6.25. Group rates (10+) 10% discount, (50+) 25%

Discount Offer: 10% off Admission Prices

Transport Museums

Darlington Railway Centre and Museum
North Road Station Station Road Darlington
County Durham DL3 6ST
Tel: 01325 460532 Fax: 01325 287746
www.drcm.org.uk

[1ml from Darlington town centre on A167. Plenty of on-site parking available]

Darlington Railway Centre & Museum, it's where trains were born and more than just a museum. Step back in time in one of the world's oldest railway stations and explore the birth of the railway age. See, touch, feel and smell railway heritage, marvel at the curiosities on show, from Victorian railway engines to yesterday's model trains. Enjoy family-friendly events, like 'A Day out with Thomas', 'Santa at the Station' and the 'Great Railway Easter Egg Hunt', to name just a few! There's always something to see and do, whatever the weather, with fun for everyone, from Grandma to the tiniest tot! Enjoy refreshments in the Station Café whilst the children use their creative skills in arts and crafts activities, puzzles, games and hands-on fun. Then stop on the way out at our gift shop to pick up a memento or send a postcard to a friend!
All year daily 10.00-17.00. Closed 25-26 Dec & 1 Jan
A£2.50, C&Concessions £1.50. Special prices apply for most events days

Discount Offer: Two for the Price of One

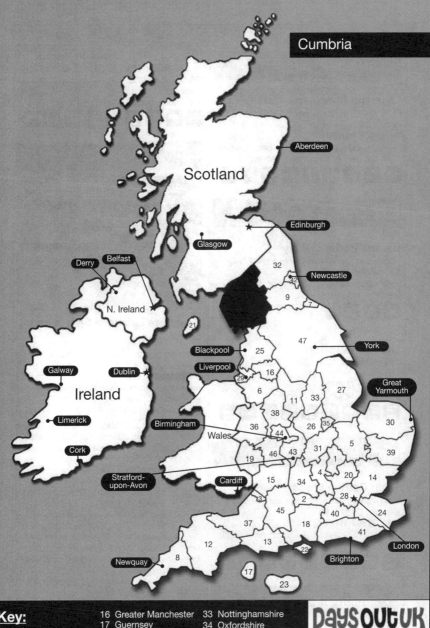

Cumbria

Scotland

Aberdeen

Edinburgh

Glasgow

Derry · Belfast

N. Ireland

Newcastle

32

42

9

7

21

Galway · Dublin

Ireland

Limerick

Cork

Blackpool

Liverpool

47

York

25

16

29

6

11

33

27

Great Yarmouth

Birmingham

38

Wales

36

44

26

35

30

19

46

43

31

5

39

Stratford-upon-Avon

Cardiff

15

34

4

1

20

14

13

2

28

London

45

40

24

37

18

41

12

13

22

Brighton

Newquay

8

17

23

Key:

1 Bedfordshire
2 Berkshire
3 Bristol
4 Buckinghamshire
5 Cambridgeshire
6 Cheshire
7 Cleveland
8 Cornwall
9 County Durham
10 Cumbria
11 Derbyshire
12 Devon
13 Dorset
14 Essex
15 Gloucestershire
16 Greater Manchester
17 Guernsey
18 Hampshire
19 Herefordshire
20 Hertfordshire
21 Isle Of Man
22 Isle Of Wight
23 Jersey
24 Kent
25 Lancashire
26 Leicestershire
27 Lincolnshire
28 London
29 Merseyside
30 Norfolk
31 Northamptonshire
32 Northumberland
33 Nottinghamshire
34 Oxfordshire
35 Rutland
36 Shropshire
37 Somerset
38 Staffordshire
39 Suffolk
40 Surrey
41 Sussex
42 Tyne & Wear
43 Warwickshire
44 West Midlands
45 Wiltshire
46 Worcestershire
47 Yorkshire

Animal Attractions

Lakeland Sheep and Wool Centre

Egremont Road Cockermouth Cumbria
CA13 0QX
Tel: 01900 822673
The Lakeland Sheep and Wool Centre is a purpose built centre, which houses sheep.

Arts, Crafts & Textiles

Beatrix Potter Gallery

Main Street Hawkshead Cumbria LA22 0NS
Tel: 015394 36355
An annually-changing exhibition of original
sketches and watercolours.

Birds, Butterflies & Bees

Eden Ostrich World

Langwathby Hall Farm Langwathby Penrith
Cumbria CA10 1LW
Tel: 01768 881771
The centre boasts rare breeds of animals and
plenty of ostriches.

Exhibition and Visitor Centres

Solway Coast Discovery Centre

Liddell Street Silloth-on-Solway Cumbria
CA7 4DD
Tel: 016973 33055
Discover how the ice age formed this area of
natural beauty.

Quaker Tapestry

Friends Meeting House Stramongate Kendal
Cumbria LA9 4BH
Tel: 01539 722975
A unique exhibition of 77 panels.

Rheged - The Village in the Hill

Redhills Penrith Cumbria CA11 0DQ
Tel: 01768 868000
Named after Cumbria's ancient Celtic Kingdom
and recently voted Cumbria's best attraction.

Festivals & Shows

Grasmere Lakeland Sports and Show

Grasmere Sportsfield Grasmere Ambleside
Cumbria LA22 9PZ
Tel: 015394 32127
www.grasmeresportsandshow.co.uk
*[M6 then A592. Rail: Windermere 8m. Plenty of
free on-site parking available]*

The world famous lakeland heritage and cultural
event. Celebrating 800 years of history. Features
Cumberland and Westmorland Wrestling inc. 11
stone World Championship. Also includes Inter
Family Fun Pull Tug-o-War, Fell Races, Mountain
Bike Races, The Scottish Terrier Racing Team,
Eagle and Vulture Show, The Adamson Military
Band, Elaine Hill Sheepdog Demonstrations,
Terrier Show, Trail Hound Puppy Show, Pet Dog
Show, Gundog Displays, Soaring Displays and
The Wordsworth Trust. Plus Made in Cumbria
Marquee, Crafts Marquee, Fairground, 150+
Trade Stands, Beer Tent and Catering. A great
family fun day out.
26 August 2007
A£7.50 C(5-14)£2.50

Discount Offer: Two for the Price of One

Folk & Local History Museums

Dock Museum
North Road Barrow-In-Furness Cumbria
LA14 2PW
Tel: 01229 876400
The museum presents the story of steel ship-building for which Barrow is famous and straddles a Victorian graving dock. Interactive displays, nautical adventure playground.

Keswick Museum and Art Gallery
Fitz Park Station Road Keswick Cumbria
CA12 4NF
Tel: 017687 73263
130 years of great customer service and 500 million years of Keswick History!

Tullie House Museum and Art Gallery
Castle Street Carlisle Cumbria CA3 8TP
Tel: 01228 534781
Enjoy a great day out with the family, discovering the tales of the "Border Reivers" (robbers or bandits), walking along a replica of Hadrian's Wall and sitting on a Roman saddle!

Forests & Woods

Grizedale Forest Park Visitor Centre
Grizedale Forest Park Grizedale Cumbria
LA22 0QJ
Tel: 01229 860010
The forest gives lovely views over the fells and lakes of South Lakeland.

Whinlatter Forest Park
Braithwaite Keswick Cumbria CA12 5TW
Tel: 017687 78469
Forests are fun and Whinlatter is on of Britain's best.

Heritage & Industrial

Cumberland Pencil Museum
Southey Works Great Bridge Keswick Cumbria
CA12 5NG
Tel: 017687 73626
Journey through the history of pencils and pencil making.

Florence Mine Heritage Centre
Egremont Cumbria CA22 2NR
Tel: 01946 820683
Florence Mine is the last working deep iron mine in Europe.

Printing Museum
102 Main Street Cockermouth Cumbria
CA13 9LX
Tel: 01900 824984
The Museum of Printing is based in a sixteenth-century building.

Rum Story
Jefferson's Wine and Spirit Merchants 27, Lowther Street Whitehaven Cumbria CA28 7DN
Tel: 01946 592933
Highlights an important facet of the town's history and explores the history of rum.

Sellafield Visitors Centre
Sellafield Seascale Cumbria CA20 1PG
Tel: 019467 27027
Designed to inform and entertain the whole family, the centre features 'hands-on' interactive scientific experiments.

Historical

Bow Bridge
Barrow-in-Furness Cumbria
Tel: 0191 261 1585
Late medieval stone bridge across Mill Beck, carrying a route to nearby Furness Abbey.

Brantwood

Coniston Cumbria LA21 8AD
Tel: 015394 41396 Fax: 015394 41263
www.brantwood.org.uk
[Off B5285. Plenty of on-site parking available]

Brantwood, the former home of eminent Victorian, John Ruskin, is the most beautifully situated house in the Lake District. This fascinating home is a treasure house of art and memorabilia and has extensive grounds and gardens with spectacular views over Coniston Water and the Coniston fells. The Gardens of Brantwood are like no other gardens in the world. Fashioned by John Ruskin and Joan Severn between 100 and 130 years ago, and restored and renovated today, they form a maze of strange and delightful features amidst more than 60 acres of ancient woodland and lakeshore. Explore Brantwood's estate and gardens, or experience contemporary art in the Severn Studio. Family fun with house and garden trails and activities for the children. Brantwood's bookshop, the Jumping Jenny Restaurant and Coach House Craft Gallery combine for a perfect day out!
Mar-Nov daily 11.00-17.30, Nov-Mar Wed-Sun 11.00-16.30
A£5.95 C£1.20, Family Ticket £11.95

Brougham Hall

Brougham Penrith Cumbria CA10 2DE
Tel: 01768 868184
Built in the thirteenth century, this historic home is now undergoing a program of restoration, and a range of craft workshops, a tea room and a gift shop have been established within the impressive outer walls.

Carlisle Castle

The Castle Carlisle Cumbria CA3 8UR
Tel: 01228 591922
A massive Norman keep contains an exhibition on the history of the castle.

Mirehouse Historic House and Gardens

Keswick Cumbria CA12 4QE
Tel: 017687 72287
www.mirehouse.com
[M6, J40 signs from A66 3mi N of Keswick on A591. Bus: regular bus service (X4, 555, 73, 73A), for details please call 0870 608 2 608. Limited on-site parking available]

Winner: Small Visitor Attraction of the Year 2006 (Cumbria for Excellence Awards). Simon Jenkins wrote in 'The Times', 'Mirehouse is more than the sum of its parts. It is the Lake District with its hand on its heart'. Strong ties of friendship bound it to Tennyson, Wordsworth and Southey and it remains a welcoming family home. Our visitors return for many reasons including: 'Excellent value', 'staff brilliant, especially with our children', 'could listen to the pianist all day', 'Magic! Natural playgrounds', the changing displays in the Poetry Walk, free children's nature notes regularly updated, an ancient wildflower meadow and a walled garden. The house is not open every day as it is a living family home and to conserve the delicate objects which are on display. The grounds are open every day, as is the tearoom, known for generous Cumbrian cooking. Many places for picnics.
Grounds: Apr-Oct daily 10.00-17.30. House: Apr-Oct Sun, Wed & Fri in Aug 14.00-17.00
House & Grounds: A£4.80 C£2.40, Family Ticket (A2+C4) £14.40. Grounds only: A£2.60 C£1.30

Muncaster Castle, Gardens and Owl Centre

Muncaster Castle Ravenglass Cumbria
CA18 1RQ
Tel: 01229 717614
Diverse attractions are offered at this castle.

Wordsworth Trust

Dove Cottage Grasmere Ambleside Cumbria
LA22 9SH
Tel: 015394 35544
This museum displays the Wordsworth Trust's unique collection of manuscripts, books and paintings.

Wordsworth House

Main Street Cockermouth Cumbria CA13 9RX
Tel: 01900 824805
The Georgian town house where William Wordsworth was born in 1770.

Laurel and Hardy Museum

4c Upper Brook Street Ulverston Cumbria
LA12 7BH
Tel: 01229 582292
The world famous museum devoted to Laurel and Hardy in Ulverston, the town where Stan was born on 16th June 1890.

Kendal Museum

Station Road Kendal Cumbria LA9 6BT
Tel: 01539 721374
With many examples of Lakeland flora and fauna, the museum charts developments from prehistoric times and into the twentieth century.

Lake District Visitor Centre at Brockhole

Windermere Cumbria LA23 1LJ
Tel: 01539 446601
Outstanding setting on the shores of Lake Windermere. 30 acres of award-winning gardens and grounds.

Ullswater 'Steamers'

The Pier House Glenridding Cumbria
CA18 1SW
Tel: 017684 82229
A cruise aboard an Ullswater 'Steamer' is undoubtedly the best way to enjoy 'England's most beautiful lake', opening up fantastic vistas of Helvellyn, the Pennines and the beautiful shoreline of the lake itself.

Windermere Lake Cruises

Bowness Promenade (also at Ambleside & Lakeside) Bowness-on Windermere Cumbria
LA23 3HQ
Tel: 015395 31188
Boats sail daily throughout the year between Ambleside, Bowness and Lakeside. Most vessels have onboard bars and coffee shops.

Carlisle Cathedral

7 The Abbey Castle Street Carlisle Cumbria
CA3 8TZ
Tel: 01228 548151
Founded in 1122 as a Norman Priory for Augustinian canons. The chancel roof is magnificent & the cathedral features an exquisite east window.

Roman Era

Ambleside Roman Fort

Ambleside Cumbria
Tel: 0191 261 1585
The remains of this first and second-century fort were built to guard the Roman road between Brougham and Ravenglass. Dogs permitted on leads only.

Birdoswald Roman Fort

Gilsland Carlisle Cumbria CA6 7DD
Tel: 01697 747602
This unique section of Hadrian's Wall has a most picturesque setting overlooking the Irthing Gorge.

Brocolitia (Carawburgh) Temple of Mithras

Hadrian's Wall Haydon Bridge Hexham Cumbria
[off B6318 which runs along this section of Hadrian's Wall]
Explore the ruins of this small, third-century temple (dedicated to the Roman god, Mithras) at Carrawburgh on Hadrians Wall.

Hare Hill

Lanercost Cumbria
[0.75m NE of Lanercost]
Part of Hadrian's Wall, a World Heritage Site. A short length of Wall standing nine feet high. Site managed by Cumbria County Council.

Ravenglass Roman Bath House

Ravenglass Cumbria
Tel: 0191 261 1585
[0.25mi E of Ravenglass, off minor road leading to A595]
The walls of the bath house are among the most complete Roman remains in Britain. Dogs permitted on leads only.

Roman Army Museum

Greenhead Carlisle Cumbria CA6 7JB
Tel: 01697 747485
Join the Roman Army after watching the recruitment film with audio visual effects.
Feb-Nov daily

Sealife Centres & Aquariums

Aquarium of the Lakes

Lakeside Newby Bridge Cumbria LA12 8AS
Tel: 015395 30153
Uncover the secret world of the lakes at Britain's unique freshwater aquarium.

Theme & Adventure Parks

Go Ape! High Wire Forest Adventure

Grizedale Forest Visitor Centre Grizedale Hawkshead Ambleside Cumbria LA22 OQJ
Tel: 0870 420 7876
www.goape.co.uk

[Nr Hawkshead on Satterthwaite Rd. Plenty of on-site parking available]

Take to the trees and experience an exhilarating course of rope bridges, 'Tarzan Swings' and zip-slides up to 40 feet above the ground! Share approximately three hours of memorable fun and adventure, which you'll be talking about for days. Book online and watch people Go Ape! at www.goape.co.uk. Minimum height 1.4m. Maximum weight 130 kg (20.5 stone). Under-18s must be accompanied by a participating

adult. One adult can supervise either two children (where one or both of them in under 16 years old) or up to five 16-17 year olds. Pre-booking is essential to avoid disappointment. Book online or by telephone (there is a £1.00 booking fee on all telephone bookings).
10-25 Feb & 23 Mar-2 Nov daily, Nov Sat-Sun. Closed Dec-Jan
Gorillas (18yrs+) £25.00, Baboons (10-17yrs) £20.00

Discount Offer: Two for the Price of One

World of Beatrix Potter
The Old Laundry Crag Brow Bowness-On-Windermere Windermere Cumbria LA23 3BX
Tel: 015394 88444
In an indoor recreation of the Lakeland countryside, complete with sights, sounds and smells.

Transport Museums

Cars of the Stars Motor Museum
Standish Street Keswick Cumbria CA12 5LS
Tel: 01768 773757
Film set displays and vehicles from Mad Max, Magnum, Batmobiles, Noddy, Postman Pat, The A Team, FAB1, James Bond, Chitty Chitty Bang Bang and Only Fools and Horses.
Feb-Dec

Wildlife & Safari Parks

Lakeland Wildlife Oasis
Hale Milnthorpe Cumbria LA7 7BW
Tel: 01539 563027
Educational, yet great fun, our exhibits range from chameleons to computers; from microscopes to meerkats and include creatures rarely seen in captivity, such as flying foxes and poison arrow frogs.

Trotters World of Animals
Coalbeck Farm Bassenthwaite Keswick Cumbria CA12 4RD
Tel: 017687 76239 Fax: 017687 76220
www.trottersworld.co.uk
[5mi NE of Cockermouth nr N end of Bassenthwaite lake. Plenty of on-site parking available]
Trotters World of Animals is home to hundreds of friendly animals including lemurs, wallabies and other exotic animals, along with reptiles and birds of prey and our family of gibbons will keep you amused for hours. Informative and amusing half hourly demonstrations will bring you closer to the animals. Indoor and outdoor play areas. This is one visit you can't afford to miss!
All year daily 10.00-17.30 or dusk. Closed 25 Dec & 1 Jan
A£6.50 C(3-14)£4.80 C(under3)Free

Discount Offer: One Child Free

Zoos

South Lakes Wild Animal Park
Crossgates Dalton-in-Furness Cumbria LA15 8JR
Tel: 01229 466086
The Lake District's only zoological park, recognised as one of Europe's leading conservation zoos.

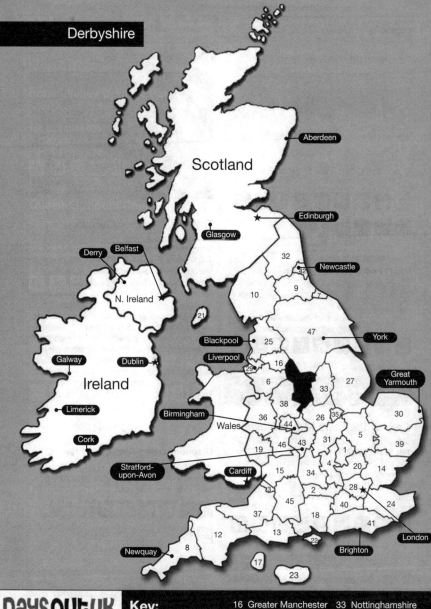

Derbyshire

Aberdeen

Scotland

Edinburgh

Newcastle

Derry   Belfast

N. Ireland

York

Galway   Dublin

Ireland

Blackpool

Liverpool

Limerick

Great
Yarmouth

Cork

Birmingham

Wales

Stratford-
upon-Avon

Cardiff

London

Newquay

Brighton

Key:

1 Bedfordshire
2 Berkshire
3 Bristol
4 Buckinghamshire
5 Cambridgeshire
6 Cheshire
7 Cleveland
8 Cornwall
9 County Durham
10 Cumbria
11 Derbyshire
12 Devon
13 Dorset
14 Essex
15 Gloucestershire

16 Greater Manchester
17 Guernsey
18 Hampshire
19 Herefordshire
20 Hertfordshire
21 Isle Of Man
22 Isle Of Wight
23 Jersey
24 Kent
25 Lancashire
26 Leicestershire
27 Lincolnshire
28 London
29 Merseyside
30 Norfolk
31 Northamptonshire
32 Northumberland

33 Nottinghamshire
34 Oxfordshire
35 Rutland
36 Shropshire
37 Somerset
38 Staffordshire
39 Suffolk
40 Surrey
41 Sussex
42 Tyne & Wear
43 Warwickshire
44 West Midlands
45 Wiltshire
46 Worcestershire
47 Yorkshire

Animal Attractions

Chestnut Centre, Otter, Owl and Wildlife Park

Castleton Road Chapel-en-le-Frith High Peak
Derbyshire SK23 0QS
Tel: 01298 814099
Here you will find one of Europe's largest collection of multi-specied otters, owls and other indigenous wildlife.

Art Galleries

Chesterfield Museum and Art Gallery

St Mary's Gate Chesterfield Derbyshire S41 7TD
Tel: 01246 345727
Chesterfield's rich historical heritage is explored in the town's museum and art gallery.

Derwent Gallery

Main Road Grindleford Hope Valley Derbyshire
S32 2JN
Tel: 01433 630458
The gallery displays fine art in a well-lit, open plan space with a mixture of original watercolours and oil paintings, sculpture and ceramics.

Arts, Crafts & Textiles

On A Wick and A Prayer

The Candle Workshop Tissington Derbyshire
DE6 1RA
Tel: 01335 390639
An exciting range of unique and original highly scented candles and unscented candles.

Caverns & Caves

Heights of Abraham: Cable Cars, Caverns and Hilltop Park

Matlock Bath Matlock Derbyshire DE4 3PD
Tel: 01629 582365
Unique hilltop park set at the top of a limestone gorge (reached by cable cars).

Peak Cavern

Peak Cavern Road Castleton Hope Valley
Derbyshire S33 8WS
Tel: 01433 620285
www.peakcavern.co.uk

[On A625, 15mi W of Sheffield, 25mi E of Manchester, in centre of Castleton village. Plenty of on-site parking available]

The Peak Cavern is the largest natural cavern in Derbyshire, and has the largest entrance to any cave in Britain. A village once existed inside the cave entrance, built and inhabited by rope makers, who carried out their craft in the cave for over 300 years. Today, ropemaking demonstrations are an integral part of every tour. Find out why it is called the devils arse!

All year, 1 Apr-31 Oct daily 10.00-17.00. Nov-Mar Sat & Sun 10.00-17.00 weekdays two tours per day (call for details. Open daily in school hols A£6.75 C(under5)£Free C(5-15)£4.75 Concessions£5.75, Family Ticket (A2+C2) £20.00 extra C£4.00. Joint ticket with Speedwell Cavern: A£11.50 C£8.00 Concessions£10.00, Family Ticket (A2+C2) £37.50 extra C£7.50. Group rates available on request

Discount Offer: Save up to £2.50

Poole's Cavern and Buxton Country Park

Green Lane Buxton Derbyshire SK17 9DH
Tel: 01298 26978 Fax: 01298 73563
www.poolescavern.co.uk

[Just off A515 Ashbourne rd or A53 Leek rd 15min walk from Buxton town centre. Plenty of on-site parking available]

Discover the secret world of caves Limestone rock, water and millions of years created this magnificent natural cavern. Our expert guides will escort you back in time through vast chambers and incredible stalactite formations on a one-hour tour, comfortable pathways with partial disabled access (contact us for details) and lighting throughout. Set in 100 acres of beautiful woodland. Trails lead towards to Solomon's temple, a panoramic viewpoint tower at the summit of Grin Low hill with spectacular peakland views. New for 2007, new visitor centre, shop, exhibition and restaurant open summer. Also GO APE high wire forest adventure aerial rope course. Fun for all the family. For bookings see www.goape.co.uk.

All year daily 09.30-17.30 contact us for seasonal variations. Tours leave every 20mins. Closed Christmas Day & New year
A£6.75 C£4.00 OAPs£5.50, Family Ticket £20.00. Group rates & joint Go Ape & Cavern visit discounts. Contact us for more details

Discount Offer: 20% off Adult Admissions

Speedwell Cavern

Castleton Hope Valley Derbyshire S33 8WA
Tel: 01433 620512 Fax: 01433 621888
www.speedwellcavern.co.uk

[Off A6187, 0.5mi W of Castleton Village. Plenty of on-site parking available]

Visited by boat, this cavern is a vast natural cave and an old lead mine worked in the early eighteenth century. Parties are taken by guides, who explain the full history and mysteries of this subterranean world 840 feet below the surface.

All year daily, 10.00-17.00
A£7.25 C£5.25 Concessions£6.25. Family Ticket (A2+2C) £25.00 extra C£5.25. Joint ticket with Peak Cavern: A£11.50 C£8.00 Concessions£10.00, Family Ticket (A2+C2) £37.50 extra C£7.50. Group rates available on request

Discount Offer: £1.50 off a Joint Adult Ticket OR £0.50 off a Joint Child Ticket OR £2.50 off a Joint Family Ticket

Treak Cliff Cavern

Buxton Road Castleton Hope Valley Derbyshire
S33 8WP
Tel: 01433 620571 Fax: 01433 620519
www.bluejohnstone.com

[Castleton is situated at centre of Peak National Park on A6187. 16mi from Sheffield & 29mi from Manchester within easy reach of M1 & M6. Plenty of on-site parking available]

Treak Cliff Cavern at Castleton has been a working Blue John mine since 1750 and open to the public as a visitor attraction since 1935. Visitors can see some of the finest stalactites and stalagmites in the Peak District whilst also experiencing the beauty of Blue John Stone. The largest areas of Blue John Stone ever revealed can be fully appreciated by the light of newly installed spotlights. The largest single piece ever discovered can still be seen in situ. This underground wonderland also contains thousands of stalactites and stalagmites plus all kinds of rocks, minerals and fossils. Multi coloured flowstone covers the walls of Aladdin's cave, whilst the most famous formation is The Stork, standing on one leg. The Cavern is enjoyed by visitors of all ages from all over the world. No wheelchair access - walking disabled only. Facilities for partially deaf visitors.
All year, Mar-Oct daily 10.00, last tour 16.20, Nov-Feb daily 10.00, last tour 15.20. Closed 24-26 Dec. Please call for further details of holiday opening times
A£6.80 C(5-15)£3.50 Concessions£5.80 OAPs&Students(NUS/USI)&YMA £5.80, Family Ticket(A2+C2) £18.50

Discount Offer: 10% off Adult Admissions

Denby Pottery Visitor Centre

Derby Road Denby Ripley Derbyshire DE5 8NX
Tel: 01773 740799 Fax: 01773 740749
www.denbyvisitorcentre.co.uk

[Next to Pottery on B6179, off A38, 2mi S of Ripley & 8mi N of Derby. Plenty of on-site parking available]

A warm welcome awaits you at Denby Visitor Centre. The centre has an attractive cobbled courtyard with shops, restaurant and play area. Activities include free cookery demonstrations, glass blowing studio and pottery tours. There are lots of bargains on offer in the seconds shop; other shops include gifts, paintings, garden centre, new Denby Home Store and Dartington Crystal. Factory tours are fully guided which gives a refreshing personal touch to the experience. Tours of the working factory and also a Craftroom Tour available. Here you find out about Denby stoneware past and present then have a go at painting a Denby plate with glaze and making a clay souvenir to take home. This tour is suitable for all ages and can accommodate wheelchairs. Please contact us for information on school holiday activities, special events and factory shop offers.
All year. Factory Tours: Mon-Thur 10.30 & 13.00 (excluding factory hols). Craftroom Tour daily 11.00-15.00. Centre open: Mon-Sat 9.30-17.00, Sun 10.00-17.00. Closed 25-26 Dec
Factory Tour: A£5.95 C&OAPs£4.95. Craftroom: A£4.50 C&OAPs£3.50

Discount Offer: Two for the Price of One.

Folk & Local History Museums

Eyam Museum

Hawkhill Road Eyam Hope Valley Derbyshire
S32 5QP
Tel: 01433 631371 Fax: 01433 631371
www.eyam.org.uk

[Off A623 signed R to Eyam on B6521, follow white & brown signs]

Bubonic Plague! Our main theme is the famous outbreak in Eyam in 1665-1666. You will see the world-wide spread of plague, leading to its arrival from London in 1665 in a fatally infected bundle of cloth. The awful symptoms are described, and some very strange ancient cures! Carefully researched stories of individual families are graphically told. You see the Rectors Mompesson and Stanley discussing the quarantining of the village, and the dreadful last days of Plague victim John Daniel. We go on to show how the village recovered. Silk, cotton, agriculture, shoes, lead and fluorspar mining, and quarrying played their part in Eyam's subsequent history. We end with a display of fine local minerals and fossils. A 30 seat lecture room is available for talks to pre booked parties. There is wheelchair access to the ground floor, and a stairlift is available.

27 Mar-4 Nov Tue-Sun & Bank Hol 10.00-16.30
A£1.75 C&OAPs£1.25, Family Ticket £5.00.
Group rates available on request

Old House Museum

Cunningham Place off North Church Street
Bakewell Derbyshire DE45 1DD
Tel: 01629 813642
www.oldhousemuseum.org.uk
[Off A6 Buxton-Matlock Rd at main square round-about. Disabled parking on-site only]

Situated behind Bakewell Church and a short walk from the main square, this Tudor house was built as a parsonage house during the reign of Henry VIII and is the oldest surviving domestic building in the lovely market town of Bakewell. In the late sixteenth century it was extended to become a gentlemen's residence and when Sir Richard Arkwright opened his third mill in Bakewell in the eighteenth century, he converted the Old House into tenements to house six families. Reminders of the past lives of the house are still visible, including stone-flagged floors, wattle and daub walls, and a massive Tudor fireplace. Nowadays, the Old House is a 11-room museum with an enjoyable collection featuring costumes, ceramics, toys, early cameras, a recreated Victorian kitchen, a Tudor parlour and even a rare Tudor toilet! All ages will enjoy experiencing the atmospheric Old House and discovering its fascinating collection.
1 Apr-31 Oct daily 11.00-16.00
A£3.00 C£1.00 C(under5)£Free

Discount Offer: One Child Free

Red House Stables Working Carriage Museum

Old Road Darley Dale Matlock DE4 2ER
Tel: 01629 733583
A unique collection of vehicles, started by

William Smith with his daughter carrying on the tradition.

Forests & Woods

Rosliston Forestry Centre

Burton Road Rosliston Swadlincote Derbyshire DE12 8JX
Tel: 01283 563483 Fax: 01283 563483
www.roslistonforestrycentre.co.uk

[On Rosliston to Burton rd, signposted off A444 at Castle Gresley. Bus: Arriva 22 from Swadlincote or Burton, Mon-Sat. Plenty of on-site parking available]

Woodland walks, indoor and outdoor play facilities, cycle hire, fishing, craft shop and restaurant - there's something for everyone at Rosliston Forestry Centre nestling at the heart of The National Forest. Education programmes, birds of prey demonstrations, archery, woodland laser game, laser clay shooting and inflatable laser game are also now available with prior booking. And why not turn your visit into a longer stay by booking into one of four on site luxury Forest Lodges designed to be accessible to all. For details of all the great things to see and to do at Rosliston Forestry Centre, including our year round events program, visit the website or contact the centre managers.
All year daily, 08.00-dusk
Admission Free. Some priced attractions and car park charges apply

Heritage & Industrial

Sir Richard Arkwright's Masson Mills

Working Textile Museum Derby Road Matlock Bath Derbyshire DE4 3PY
Tel: 01629 581001 Fax: 01629 581001
www.massonmills.co.uk

[On A6 0.5mi S of Matlock Bath. Rail: 1mi. Bus stop directly outside. On-site parking available]

Sir Richard Arkwright's Masson Mills were built in 1783 on the banks of the River Derwent at Matlock Bath, Derbyshire. These beautifully restored mills are recognised as the best surviving example of an eighteenth-century cotton mill and are the finest and best preserved example of one of the Arkwright's mills. They now house a shopping village and a fascinating Working Textile Museum illustrating Arkwright's Legacy, where you can experience the genuine atmosphere of Masson Mills and see authentic historic textile machinery spinning yarn and weaving cloth. Masson Mills form the Northern Gateway to the Derwent Valley Mills World Heritage Site. *Working Textile Museum: All year Mon-Fri 10.00-16.00 Sat 11.00-17.00 Sun 11.00-16.00. Closed Christmas Day & Easter Day*
A£2.50 C(5-16)£1.50 Concessions£2.00, Family Ticket £6.50. School Groups C£1.00. Group rate (30+): A£2.00

Discount Offer: Two for the Price of One

Strutt's North Mill

Derwent Valley Visitor Centre North Mill Bridgefoot Bolper Derbyshire DE56 1YD
Tel: 01773 880474 Fax: 01773 880474
www.belpernorthmill.org.uk
[Plenty of on-site parking available]

Strutt's North Mill and Visitor Centre is the gateway to the Derwent Valley Mills World Heritage Site. Built in 1804, William Strutt's technologically advanced 'fire-proof' mill shows by displays and original machinery the history and process of cotton spinning, the story of framework knitting, 'Brettles' renowned silk and cotton hosiery collection, Derbyshire's unique chevening and nailmaking. Leaders of the Industrial Revolution, the Strutt family changed Belper into a thriving industrial town. Our trained guides provide entertaining and informative tours, or we have self-guided audio handsets. Children can count the 'mill mice' and earn a certificate and a treat. The mill shop has books, gifts, drinks and snacks, and the adjacent renowned River Gardens has a playground, boating on the river and a bandstand.
All year Mar-Oct Wed-Sun & Bank Hol Mons 13.00-17.00, Nov-Feb Sat-Sun, 26 Dec & 1st Jan. Pre-booked groups at other times
A£3.00 C(7-16)£2.00 Concessions£2.50, Family Ticket £8.50

Discount Offer: One Child Free

Historical

Chatsworth
Bakewell Derbyshire DE45 1PP
Tel: 01246 582204 / 565300

Chatsworth has one of the richest collections of fine and decorative arts in private hands.

Nature & Conservation Parks

Linacre Reservoirs
Cutthorpe Chesterfield Derbyshire S42 7JW
Tel: 01246 567049 Fax: 01246 567049
Three small reservoirs in a wooded valley.

Upper Derwent Reservoirs
Fairholmes Visitor Centre Bamford Hope Valley
The Peak District Derbyshire S33 0AQ
Tel: 01433 650953
Refreshments and cycle hire at the Fairholme Visitor Centre.

On the Water

Carsington Water Reservoir
Carsington Ashbourne Derbyshire DE6 1ST
Tel: 01629 540696
Sailing club, Visitor Centre, and many opportunities for walking and cycling.

Places of Worship

Derby Cathedral
Derby Derbyshire DE1 3DT
Tel: 01332 341201
The smallest cathedral in England.

Sealife Centres & Aquariums

Matlock Bath Aquarium and Hologram Gallery
110 North Parade Matlock Bath Matlock Derbyshire DE4 3NS
Tel: 01629 583624
An aquarium housed in the original spa bathing pool and outbuildings.

Sporting History Museums

Donington Grand Prix Collection
Donington Park Castle Donington Derby Derbyshire DE74 2RP
Tel: 01332 811027 Fax: 01332 812829
www.doningtoncollection.com

[At Donington Park Grand Prix Circuit, just off A453, close to J23a/24 M1 & M42/A42. Plenty of on-site parking available]

The Donington Grand Prix Collection is the World's largest collection of Grand Prix racing cars, with a display of over 130 exhibits contained within five halls, depicting motor sport history from the early 1900s to the present day. Cars on display include those driven by 1938 Donington Grand Prix winner Tazio Nuvolari, Sir Henry Segrave, Sir Stirling Moss OBE, Jim Clark, Graham Hill, Damon Hill, Nigel Mansell, Eddie Irvine and many more. These include Nuvolari's personal 1934 2.9 litre Maserati 8CM, and the amazing 1936 Alfa Romeo Bimotore, which features twin engines, with a power output of 500 bhp and a top speed approaching 200mph. The World's largest collection of McLaren Formula One cars on public display also features, together with the world's most complete collection of Vanwalls, a line-up of Williams cars, and a fabulous display of BRMs.
All year daily 10.00-17.00. Closed certain days between Christmas & New Year
A£7.00 C(0-5)£Free C(6-16)£2.50 Concessions£5.00 Family Ticket (A2+C3) £14.00

Discount Offer: Two for the Price of One

Theme & Adventure Parks

Go Ape! High Wire Forest Adventure

Poole's Cavern Green Lane Buxton Derbyshire SK17 9DH
Tel: 0870 420 7876
www.goape.co.uk
[On Green Lane (0.5 mi from Buxton town centre). From A6 & A53 follow brown signs to B5059/A515 J & follow Green Lane for 0.5 mi. Plenty of on-site parking available]

Take to the trees and experience an exhilarating course of rope bridges, 'Tarzan Swings' and zip-slides up to 40 feet above the ground! Share approximately three hours of memorable fun and adventure, which you'll be talking about for days. Book online and watch people Go Ape! at www.goape.co.uk. Minimum height 1.4m. Maximum weight 130 kg (20.5 stone). Under-18s must be accompanied by a participating adult. One adult can supervise either two children (where one or both of them in under 16 years old) or up to five 16-17 year olds. Pre-booking is essential to avoid disappointment. Book online or by telephone (there is a £1.00 booking fee on all telephone bookings).
23 Mar-2 Nov (Nov weekends). Closed Dec-Jan
Gorillas (18yrs+) £25.00, Baboons (10-17yrs) £20.00

Discount Offer: Two for the Price of One

Gullivers Kingdom Theme Park
Temple Walk Matlock Bath Derbyshire DE4 3PG
Tel: 01925 444888

Cable cars, Royal Cave Tour, Wild West Street and Alpine Log Flume.

Transport Museums

Crich Tramway Village
Crich Matlock Derbyshire DE4 5DP
Tel: 01773 854321 Fax: 01773 854320
www.tramway.co.uk
[J28 M1, signs from A6 & A38, off B5035. Plenty of on-site parking available]
Crich Tramway Village, offers a family day out in the relaxing atmosphere of a bygone era. Explore the recreated period street with its genuine buildings and features, fascinating exhibitions and most importantly, its trams. Unlimited tram rides are free with your entry fee, giving you the opportunity to fully appreciate Crich Tramway Village and the surrounding countryside. Journey on one of the many beautifully restored vintage trams, as they rumble through the cobbled street past the Red Lion pub and restaurant, exhibition hall, workshops, viewing gallery, children's play and picnic area, before passing beneath the magnificent Bowes-Lyon Bridge. Next it's past the bandstand, through the woods, and then on to Glory Mine taking in spectacular views of the Derwent Valley. New Woodland Walk and Sculpture Trail.
10-25 Feb daily 10.30-16.00, Mar Sat-Sun 10.30-16.00, 31 Mar-28 Oct daily 10.00-17.30, Nov-16 Dec Sat-Sun 10.30-16.00
A£9.50 C(3-15)£5.00 OAPs£8.50, Family Ticket £26.00. Group rates (10+): A£8.50 C£4.50 OAPs£7.50

Discount Offer: One Child Free

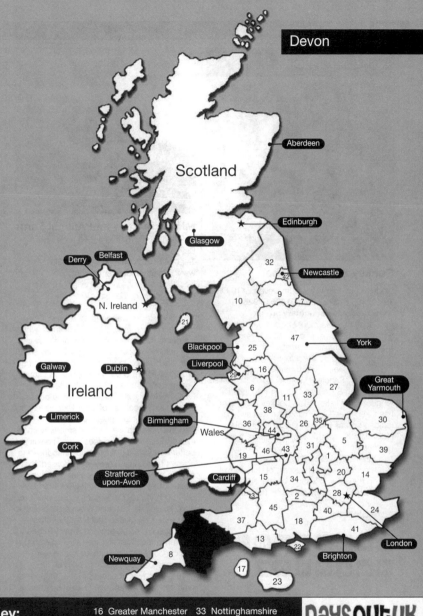

Devon

Aberdeen

Scotland

Edinburgh

32 Newcastle

Glasgow

9 7

Derry Belfast 10

N. Ireland

21 47 York

Blackpool 25

Galway Dublin Liverpool 16

Ireland 29 6

11 33 27 Great Yarmouth

Limerick 38

Birmingham 36 26 35 30

Cork Wales 44

Stratford- 19 46 43 31 1 5 39

upon-Avon Cardiff 15 34 4 20 14

13 2 28 London

45 40 24

Newquay 8 37 18 41

13 22 Brighton

17

23

Key:

1 Bedfordshire	16 Greater Manchester	33 Nottinghamshire
2 Berkshire	17 Guernsey	34 Oxfordshire
3 Bristol	18 Hampshire	35 Rutland
4 Buckinghamshire	19 Herefordshire	36 Shropshire
5 Cambridgeshire	20 Hertfordshire	37 Somerset
6 Cheshire	21 Isle Of Man	38 Staffordshire
7 Cleveland	22 Isle Of Wight	39 Suffolk
8 Cornwall	23 Jersey	40 Surrey
9 County Durham	24 Kent	41 Sussex
10 Cumbria	25 Lancashire	42 Tyne & Wear
11 Derbyshire	26 Leicestershire	43 Warwickshire
12 Devon	27 Lincolnshire	44 West Midlands
13 Dorset	28 London	45 Wiltshire
14 Essex	29 Merseyside	46 Worcestershire
15 Gloucestershire	30 Norfolk	47 Yorkshire
	31 Northamptonshire	
	32 Northumberland	

Animal Attractions

Donkey Sanctuary (The)

Slade House Farm Sidmouth Devon EX10 ONU
Tel: 01395 578222 Fax: 01395 579266
www.thedonkeysanctuary.org.uk
[At Slade House Farm, nr Salcombe Regis. Do not drive into Sidmouth or Salcombe Regis, but look for brown tourist information signs on A3052 between Sidford & turning for Branscombe. Plenty of on-site parking available]
The Donkey Sanctuary was founded in 1969 by Dr. Elisabeth Svendsen MBE. In the United Kingdom and Ireland, The Donkey Sanctuary has taken over 12,000 donkeys and also has major overseas projects in Egypt, Ethiopia, India, Italy, Kenya, Mexico, and Spain. It aims to prevent the suffering of donkeys worldwide through the provision of high quality, professional advice, training and support of donkey welfare. In the UK and Ireland, permanent sanctuary is provided to any donkey in need of refuge.
All year daily, 09.00-dusk
Admission Free

Hedgehog Hospital at Prickly Ball Farm

Denbury Road East Ogwell Newton Abbot Devon TQ12 6BZ
Tel: 01626 362319
Hedgehog hospital open to the public. A busy educational farm experience.

Miniature Pony and Animal Farm

Wormhill Farm North Bovey Newton Abbot Devon TQ13 8RG
Tel: 01647 432400 Fax: 01647 433662
www.miniatureponycentre.com
[B3212 just 2mi W of Moretonhampstead on Princetown Rd on Dartmoor. Plenty of on-site parking available]
"Our animals are waiting to meet you". See, meet and touch more than 150 animals, including our famous miniature ponies and donkeys that foal throughout the spring and early summer. Also waiting to meet you are Gulliver, our Shire horse, Chico and Harpo, our miniature horses, and Bubbles, Gabriel, Harry, George, Ollie, Freckles and Magpie, our riding ponies. You will also meet lots of other very friendly animals, including pigs, goats and lambs. In Pets Paddock you can meet lots of smaller animals, including rabbits, and guinea pigs. There is no better way for the children to be introduced to animals than here. There are supervised pony rides in our outdoor riding arena. With at least 9 different free activities every day, including a daily birds of prey display, the whole family can really join in. The activities change according to the season, so please check the Activities Timetable on the blackboard when you arrive, and remember, listen for the bell. Older children can choose between outdoor and indoor adventure play areas, or can burn off their excess energy on the trampolines. Younger children can choose between HorsePlay, our indoor soft play area, the Little Foals Play Park beside the picnic area, or test their driving skills in the mini tractor pen.
21 Mar-28 Oct daily 10.30-16.30 (July & Aug 10.00-17.00)
A£6.50 C£5.50 Concessions£5.00, Family Ticket (A2+C2) £22.00

Arts, Crafts & Textiles

Cardew Teapottery

Newton Road Bovey Tracey Devon TQ13 9DX
Tel: 01626 832172
The UK's largest ceramic playground attraction.

Birds, Butterflies & Bees

Buckfast Butterfly Farm and Dartmoor Otter Sanctuary

Buckfast Steam and Leisure Park Buckfastleigh
Devon TQ11 0DZ
Tel: 01364 642916
Tropical garden with free-flying butterflies and
moths from around the world. Otter sanctuary
with underwater viewing.

Quince Honey Farm

North Road South Molton Devon EX36 3AZ
Tel: 01769 572401
View honey bees without disturbing them in a
specially designed building with glass booths
and tunnels.

Caverns & Caves

Kent's Cavern Showcaves

The Caves Wellswood Torquay Devon TQ1 2JF
Tel: 01803 215136
Wander through an exhibition with sounds and
displays recreating scenes of the cave dwellers
and the first archaeological excavations.

Costume & Jewellery Museums

Totnes Costume Museum

Bogan House 43 High Street Totnes TQ9 5NP
Tel: 01803 862857
Exhibitions from the Collection, changed annual-
ly, on show in a Tudor Merchant House.

Country Parks & Estates

Escot Gardens, Maze and Fantasy Woodland

Escot Fairmile Nr Ottery St Mary Devon
EX11 1LU
Tel: 01404 822188 Fax: 01404 822903
www.escot-devon.co.uk
*[0.5mi off A30 Exeter to Honiton rd. From Exeter
exit at Pattesons Cross & follow signs. From
Honiton, exit at Iron Bridge & follow 'Fairmile'
signs. Plenty of on-site parking available]*
Originally laid out in the eighteenth century as
220 acres of Capability Brown parkland and
gardens, here you'll find an ark-full of animals
with woodland paths and trails and everywhere
beautiful flowers, shrubs and magnificent champion trees. A free visitor map will guide you to
the 4,000-Beech Hedge Maze, a real challenge
with its five hedge-leaping bridges and stunning
central look-out tower. Then on to the birds of
prey with their summertime displays, the otters
in their holt, the Pirates Playground, the pets
and the red squirrels, and the Aquatic Centre
housing one of the best collections of tropical
and pond fish in the West Country. At the
Coach House you'll find the Seahorse Trust, a
gift shop, and the restaurant serving delicious
home-cooked meals and cream teas using the
very best local produce. We even offer free
Escot letter-boxing, an unforgettable nature-
based treasure hunt. Escot is unique!
*All year daily 10.00-18.00 (10.00-17.00 Nov-
Easter). Closed 25-26 Dec*
A£5.95 C(0-2)£Free C(3-15)&OAPs£4.95,
Family Ticket (A2+C2) £18.50

Discount Offer: One Child Free

Northam Burrows Country Park

Northam Bideford Devon EX39 1LY
Tel: 01237 479708
A 254-hectare country park.

Exhibition & Visitor Centres

House of Marbles and Teign Valley Glass

The Old Pottery Pottery Road Bovey Tracey
Newton Abbot Devon TQ13 9DS
Tel: 01626 835358
Glass, games, marbles and Bovey Pottery.

Factory Outlets & Tours

Barbican Glassworks

Old Fishmarket The Barbican Plymouth PL1 2L5
Tel: 01752 224777
Tired of precinct shopping, try visiting the
Barbican with it's medieval maze of narrow
street layouts and Tudor dwellings. The
Barbican is adjacent to Sutton Harbour, the
original seaport of this historic area. Here you
can find the old Barbican Glassworks that now
houses the Dartington crystal showroom. Select
from a range of leading projects including, of
course our own world famous crystal and glassware. Shop for special offers on our products
and other well known brand names such as
Royal Brierley, Caithness, Waterford,
Wedgewood, Coalport and Edinburgh Woollen
Mill.
All year daily

Dartington Crystal

Linden Close Torrington Devon EX38 7AN
Tel: 01805 626242 Fax: 01805 626263
www.dartington.co.uk

*[At intersection of routes between Barnstaple,
Plymouth, Bideford, Exeter & South Molton, in
centre of Torrington. Follow brown tourist signs.
Rail: Exeter St. Davids change for Barnstaple,
taxis available from here. Plenty of on-site parking
available]*

Dartington Crystal is internationally famous for
it's beautiful, handmade glassware. Visitors to
the factory will be fascinated to watch the highly
skilled craftsmen blowing and shaping crystal,
perfecting an art form of 3,000 years in the
making. Discover the history of glass and the
unique Dartington story in the popular visitor
centre, or have fun and get hands-on in the
family activity area. You can also visit our glass,
gift and Edinburgh Woollen Mill shops for great
bargains at factory prices or simply relax in our
fully licensed restaurant.
*All year Visitor Centre, Factory Tour, Restaurant
and Shops: Mon-Fri 09.00-17.00, Sat 10.00-
17.00, Sun 10.00-16.00 (tours only available
Mon-Fri). Please call to confirm details of
Christmas, New Year & Bank Hol opening times.
Tour times, opening times & demonstrations may
be subject to change*
A£5.00 C(0-16)£Free OAPs£4.00

**Discount Offer: Two for the Price of
One**

Folk & Local History Museums

Allhallows Museum of Lace and Antiquities

High Street Honiton Devon EX14 1PG
Tel: 01404 44966
The museum has a wonderful display of Honiton lace, and there are lace demonstrations from June to August.

Sidmouth Museum

Hope Cottage Church Street Sidmouth Devon EX10 8LY
Tel: 01395 516139

Situated in the Hope Cottage by the Parish Church, the museum portrays the rich and varied history of this lovely regency town. Highlights of the collection include Regency prints, old photographs, Victoriana, costume, lace and artefacts of famous residents. A new land and man room depicts the geology and archaeology of the area. The world heritage coast is fully explained in these exhibits. Museum staff led guided tours of the town on Tuesdays and Thursday leaving the museum at 10.15 and Jurassic Coast on Wednesday at 10.15. Please call the museum for more information.
Apr-Oct, Mon 14.00-16.30, Tues-Sat 10.00-12.30 & 14.00-16.30
A&OAPs£1.50 C£Free

Food & Drink

Pack O' Cards Family Pub and Museum

High Street Combe Martin Ilfracombe Devon EX34 0ET
Tel: 01271 882 300
Built in the seventeenth century using the winnings of a card game, this Grade II Ancient Monument was constructed to resemble a deck of cards. Fine selection of real ales and excellent food.

Forests & Woods

Becky Falls Woodland Park

Manaton Bovey Tracey Devon TQ13 9UG
Tel: 01647 221259 Fax: 01647 221267
www.beckyfalls.com

[4mi W of Bovey Tracey off A382, signposted. Plenty of on-site parking available]

Voted Devon's Top Beauty Spot in 2006, Becky Falls Woodland Park is a unique mix of animals and adventure, world famous waterfalls, ancient woodland and stunning scenery. It's been attracting visitors and inspiring poets and writers for over 100 years as well as providing some of the most scenic and enjoyable walks in the Southwest. Providing loads of fun for all the family, the animals to meet and feed include Dartmoor ponies, miniature Shetland ponies, chipmunks and rescued birds of prey and owls. Children's letterboxing competition with small prize for every child. Full programme of children's entertainment during Easter, summer and October school holidays, including puppet shows, scary animal encounter shows, Victorian flea circus (for all ages) and storytelling (phone for details). Live musicians playing in the park on some Sundays throughout the season (phone for more information).
24 Mar-4 Nov 10.00-17.00
A£5.75-£6.75
C&OAPs&Students(NUS/USI)£4.75-£5.75, Family Ticket (A2+C2) £19.00-£23.00, extra C£3.50. Group rates available on request

Discount Offer: £2.00 off

RHS Garden Rosemoor

Great Torrington Devon EX38 8PH
Tel: 01805 624067
Come and see this enchanting garden set in the beautiful Torridge Valley.

Historical

Cadhay

Ottery St. Mary Devon EX11 1QT
Tel: 01404 812999
www.cadhay.org.uk
[1mi NW of Ottery St Mary. Plenty of on-site parking available]
The first reference to Cadhay is in the reign of Edward I as a sub-manor to the Manor of Ottery St. Mary. The main part of the present house was built circa 1550 by John Haydon. He retained the Great Hall of the earlier house, of which the fine timber roof dating between 1420-1470 can still be seen in the Roof Chamber. An Elizabethan long gallery was added early in the seventeenth century, thus forming a unique and lovely courtyard with statues of sovereigns on each wall described by Sir Simon Jenkins as "One of the treasures of Devon" in his book England's Thousand Best Homes. The house, surrounded by magnificent gardens with herbaceous borders and yew hedges, looks out over the original mediaeval fishponds, which may well have been used by the Warden and Canons of the Collegiate Church of St Mary of Ottery.
May-Sept Fri late Spring & Summer Bank Hols Sat-Mon 14.00-17.30
A£6.00 C£2.00. Group rates (for 20+) available on request

Castle Drogo

Drewsteignton Exeter Devon EX6 6PB
Tel: 01647 433306
This granite castle was built between 1910 and 1930 for the self-made millionaire Julius Drewe.

Chambercombe Manor

Ilfracombe Devon EX34 9RJ
Tel: 01271 862624
This is one of England's oldest houses (c1066), although there are sixteenth and seventeenth-century additions.

Clovelly Village

Bideford Devon EX39 5SY
Tel: 01237 431781
Unspoilt fishing village with steep cobbled streets. Donkeys and sledges are the only means of transport. Visitor centre and Kinsley Museum.

Compton Castle

Compton Marldon Paignton Devon TQ3 1TA
Tel: 01803 842382
This magical fortified manor house was built at three periods 1340, 1450 & 1520.

Dartmouth Castle

Castle Road Dartmouth Devon TQ6 0JN
Tel: 01803 833588
This brilliantly positioned defensive castle juts out into the narrow entrance of the Dart estuary.

Hound Tor (Deserted Medieval Village)

Dartmoor Devon
Tel: 0117 975 0700
[1.5m S of Manaton off Ashburton rd. Park in Hound Tor car park 0.5m walk]
Remains of three or four medieval farmsteads, first occupied in the Bronze Age.

Killerton House and Garden

Killerton House Broadclyst Exeter EX5 3LE
Tel: 01392 881345 Fax: 01392 883112
www.nationaltrust.org.uk
[Off B3181. From M5 northbound J30 via Pinhoe & Broadclyst. From M5 southbound J28 via Cullompton. Plenty of on-site parking available]

Built for the Acland family in 1778-79. Killerton House is furnished as a comfortable home. There is a substantial Victorian laundry and an interesting chapel, completed in 1841. 'Quilty Secrets' costume exhibition, taken from the extensive Killerton costume collection, is on display on the first floor throughout 2007. This explores the use of quilting for garments and accessories from the eighteenth to the twentieth century. The magnificent hillside garden was created in the 1770s by John Veitch, one of the greatest nurserymen and landscape designers of his day. Features include rhododendrons, magnolias, herbaceous borders and a collection of rare trees.
House: 14 Mar-4 Nov Wed-Mon, Aug daily, Oct Wed-Sun 11.00-17.00, 8-23 Dec daily 14.00-16.00. Garden: daily 10.30-19.00 or dusk if earlier. Please call for details
House & Garden: A£7.40 C£3.70, Family Ticket (A2+C3) £18.50 or Family Ticket(A1+C3) £11.10. Garden Only: A£5.60 C£2.80. Winter Garden Admission Charge (5 Nov-11 Mar 2008): A£3.50 C£1.75

Totnes Castle

Castle Street Totnes Devon TQ9 5NU
Tel: 01803 864406
A classic example of the Norman motte-and-bailey castle.

Morwellham Quay

Morwellham near Tavistock Devon PL19 8JL
Tel: 01822 832766 Fax: 01822 833808
www.morwellham-quay.co.uk
[4mi W of Tavistock. Plenty of on-site parking available]

In the heart of the spectacular Tamar Valley, amidst towering cliffs and gently rolling farmland, a lost world lives again. Costumed staff welcome visitors to the bustling 1860s port where history comes alive. All human life is here as you explore their cottages, gardens and workshops, or stroll along the riverside quays, which once housed vessels from all over the world. For many the highlight of a visit to Morwellham is the trip into the George and Charlotte mine. A small tramway follows the riverside before diving into the workings of a nineteenth-century copper mine. An experienced guide and son et lumiere presentations tell the fascinating story of the men who toiled deep underground to extract the valuable minerals that made the Tamar Valley rich. Young or old, there's something for everyone at Morwellham, peace and tranquillity, a beautiful landscape and intriguing glimpses of a bygone age.
All year daily 10.00-18.00. Closed 25-26 Dec & 1 Jan
A£8.90 C(5-16)£6.00 OAPs£7.80, Family Ticket (A2+C2) £19.50

Model Towns & Villages

Babbacombe Model Village

Hampton Avenue Babbacombe TQ1 3LA
Tel: 01803 315315
Set in four acres of beautifully maintained, miniature landscaped garden. The village contains 400+ models and a 1200ft model railway.

Natural History Museums

Royal Albert Memorial Museum

Queen Street Exeter Devon EX4 3RX
Tel: 01392 665858 Fax: 01392 421252
www.exeter.gov.uk/museums

[J30 M5 use city centre car parks or park & ride scheme]

Fun, family friendly and free. There's more in Exeter's museum than you might imagine, its 16 galleries of displays take visitors on a voyage of discovery from pre-history to the present day and from Exeter all around the world. There is likely to be something different to see every visit, from national touring shows to community displays as well as fine art from the city's collection and work by local artists and makers. The lively events programme includes talks, walks and classes for adults and a wide range of fun activities for children. Entry is free so come for an hour or stay all day. Displays drawn from the museum's own collections include glassware, West Country silver, clocks and watches, local history and archaeology. Exotic animals, birds and butterflies delight children in the Natural history section and the World Cultures galleries

display stunning items from all over the world.
All year Mon-Sat 10.00-17.00
Admission Free

Torquay Museum

529 Babbacombe Road Torquay Devon TQ1 1HG
Tel: 01803 293975 Fax: 01803 294186
www.torquaymuseum.org

[On B3199]

Take a journey through time in Devon's oldest museum. Fascinating artefacts from around the world, an interactive trail for children, the sights and sounds of country living in a reconstructed Devon farmhouse and the chance to detect the real life story behind a world famous writer in the Agatha Christie Gallery. A programme of temporary exhibitions and children's holiday activities means there's always plenty to see and do at Torquay Museum. Watch out for… the new interactive Explorers Gallery opening in 2007.
All year Mon-Sat 10.00-17.00, Mid July-Sep Sun 13.30-17.00
A£3.00 C&NUS/USI£1.50 Concessions£2.00, Family Ticket (A2+C3) £7.50. From July 2007 A£3.95 C£2.50, Concessions&NUS/USI£2.95, Family Ticket (A2+C3)£12.00. Group discounts available

Discount Offer: One Free "Explorers" Knapsack for Every Full-Paying Child

Nature & Conservation Parks

Dartmoor National Park
National Park Authority Headquarters Bovey Tracey Devon TQ13 9JQ
Tel: 01626 832093
The River Dart divides two high, boggy plateaux in the largest open space in southern England.

Exmoor National Park
Exmoor House Dulverton Exmoor Devon TA22 9HL
Tel: 01398 323665
A wide range of routes exists for exploring this magnificent landscape, from long distance walks to nature trails via cycle or horseback.

Gnome Reserve and Wildflower Garden
West Putford Bradworthy Devon EX22 7XE
Tel: 0870 845 9012
Over 1,000 gnomes and pixies in woodland garden with stream. Wild flower garden with 250 species of wild flowers. Studio making pottery pixies, hand-painted garden gnomes.

On the Water

Dart Pleasure Craft Ltd
5 Lower Street Dartmouth Devon TQ6 9AJ
Tel: 01803 834488
Five pleasure boats cruising on River Dart. Services operating between Paignton and Totnes.

Stuart Line Cruises
Exmouth Marina Exmouth Docks Exmouth Devon EX8 1DU
Tel: 01395 222144
Sail from Exmouth and enjoy relaxing River Exe cruises along the beautiful East Devon coastline. Sailing throughout the year.

Places of Worship

Exeter Cathedral
1 The Cloisters Exeter Devon EX1 1HS
Tel: 01392 285973
Exeter Cathedral, the 'jewel of the West', is one of England's most beautiful churches.

Railways

Paignton and Dartmouth Steam Railway
The Paignton and Dartmouth Steam Railway Queens Park Station Torbay Road Paignton Devon TQ4 6AF
Tel: 01803 555872 Fax: 01803 664313
www.paignton-steamrailway.co.uk
[Off M5 follow either A380 to Newton Abbot then follow signs for Paignton OR take A379 coastal rd to Paignton]
The holiday line with steam trains running for seven miles in Great Western tradition along the spectacular Torbay Coast to Kingswear, with ferry crossing to Dartmouth. Combined river excursions available 'The Round Robin' and 'Boat Train'. Special trains run for Dartmouth Regatta and the Red Arrows.
Apr, May & Oct. June-Sept daily
Train only Paignton-Kingswear: Return Fare: A£7.40 C(5-15)£5.10 OAPs£6.90, Family Ticket (A2+C2) £23.00. Train & Ferry to Dartmouth: A£9.00 C£6.00 OAPs£8.50, Family Ticket £28.00. Train, Ferry & 'Boat Train' Cruise: A£14.00 C£9.00 OAPs£13.00, Family Ticket £39.00. Train, Ferry, Cruise & Bus: Circular Trip: A£14.50 C£9.50 OAPs£13.50, Family Ticket £41.00

Pecorama

Underleys Beer Seaton Devon EX12 3NA
Tel: 01297 21542 Fax: 01297 20229
www.peco-uk.com

[Plenty of on-site parking available]

Pecorama, one of Devon's leading visitor attractions located high on the hillside above the fishing village of Beer, is the home of the famous PECO Model Railway Exhibition and the Beer Heights Light Railway. The exhibition hall displays wonderfully detailed railway layouts, with push-button controls enabling children to operate the trains whilst outdoors, a fleet of miniature steam locomotives pull passenger carrying trains for a mile long route through the grounds, over bridges, through steep-sided cuttings and a long, dark tunnel! Pecorama is also known for its Millennium Celebration Garden, a series of five stunning garden 'rooms' each linked by attractive walkways, whilst stunning stonework and special water features continually catch the eye. The individual garden names of Sun, Moon, Rainbow, Roof and Moat Garden reflect the nature and colour of the flowers, shrubs and trees to be found in each. Children can choose from a variety of activity areas whilst an extensive summer programme of entertainment runs each summer, with shows from mid July until the first Sunday in September. Whatever the weather, clowns, jesters and magicians provide daily (except Saturdays) entertainment under cover of our own "Big Top", the PECO Marquee.

2 Apr-27 Oct Mon-Fri 10.00-17.30, Sat 10.00-13.00, Sun 8 Apr & 27 May-2 Sept Inclusive 10.00-17.30
A£6.00 OAPs£5.50 C(4-14)£4.00 C(under4)&OAPs(80+)£Free

Seaton Tramway

Harbour Road Seaton Devon EX12 2NQ
Tel: 01297 20375 Fax: 01297 625626
www.tram.co.uk

[20mi SE of Taunton. Plenty of on-site parking available]

Seaton Tramway runs for three miles through East Devon's glorious Axe Valley. Views of the estuary and its wading birds are unrivalled from the popular open toppers, whilst enclosed saloons maintain comfort during bad weather. The Tramway originated from a miniature system in 1949, which evolved into Eastbourne Tramway (1954-1969). The move to Seaton occurred in 1970, after the company purchased the trackbed of the ex-BR branch. The terminus is in Harbour Road Car Park, Seaton, from where the trams take you through the Axe Valley to Colyton. You can break your journey at the station shop and restaurant, which offer a range of souvenirs, hot and cold food, and of course cream teas! The town centre is a short walk; sights include the twelfth-century church, with its unusual lantern tower. Special events include a Vintage Vehicle Rally, Bird Watching Trips, Santa Specials - and you can even learn to drive a tram!

10-25 Feb, 31 Mar-4 Nov, Weekends 3-25 Mar, 10 Nov-15 Dec
Return Journey A£7.95 OAPs£7.15 C£5.55
Single Journey A£4.75 OAPs£4.30 C£3.35

Discount Offer: One Child Free

National Marine Aquarium
Rope Walk Coxside Plymouth Devon PL4 0LF
Tel: 01752 600301
See jewel-bright tropical fish and other marine life.

Sport & Recreation

Doone Valley Holidays: Cloud Farm and the Doone Valley

Cloud Farm Oare Lynton Devon EX35 6NU
Tel: 01598 741234 Fax: 01598 741154
www.doonevalleyholidays.co.uk

[From A39 Porlock to Lynton take signposted rd to Doone Valley E of County Gate, turn R at Oare Church & Cloud Farm is 1mi along on L. Plenty of on-site parking available]

An unforgettable day out for all at Cloud Farm, with its lovely riverside location, stables, superb tearoom and gardens set one mile into the heart of Exmoor's idyllic Doone Valley. Walk in the tranquil countryside of Lorna Doone fame - the waterslide, village ruins, Badgworthy Water and wood are all on our doorstep. Ride with us through spectacular wooded valleys, hills and moorlands - friendly horses and ponies (and riding hats) for all ages and riding abilities; ring to book or just turn up! Turn the kids loose to paddle, fish, and explore the hills, rocks and woods. See the wildlife, from red deer, herons and kingfishers to rare flowers and ancient forests, and then... settle down in our gardens for refreshments, ice creams, snacks, lunches and cream

teas from our tearoom, shop and off-license. One visit is never enough...
All year daily, early to late
Please call for prices

Discount Offer: One Child Rides Half-Price

Theme & Adventure Parks

Big Sheep
Abbotsham Bideford Devon EX39 5AP
Tel: 01237 472366 Fax: 01237 477916
www.thebigsheep.co.uk
[A39. Plenty of on-site parking available]
The Big Sheep family entertainment park in Bideford, North Devon, is one of the West Country's top all weather attractions. A working family farm turned wacky tourist attraction, fun shows for adults and a massive Ewetopia indoor adventure zone for the children. Sheep racing and miniature sheepdog trials with dogs, ducks and children are among the highlights. Also features horse whispering shows, internet cafe, mountain boarding centre, quality restaurants and great shopping.
Daily, 31 Mar-31 Oct
A£8.50 C£7.50, Family Ticket (A2+C2) £30.00 or (A2+C3)£35.00 or (A2+C4)£40.00

Discount Offer: One Child Free

Devon's Crealy Great Adventure Park

Sidmouth Rd Clyst St Mary Exeter EX5 1DR
Tel: 01395 233200 Fax: 01395 233211
www.crealy.co.uk

[Crealy is Easy to Find - Hard to Leave! 4min from J30 M5, on Sidmouth Rd nr Exeter. Driving times: Birmingham 150min, Bournemouth 2h, Bristol 90min, London 3h, Plymouth 40min, Taunton 30min, Torbay 30min, Weymouth, 85min]

Devon's Crealy is the favourite family day out in the southwest - an unforgettable day packed with magical fun and adventures for all the family. New this year are the FUNambulist Challenge, King Henry's Golden Treasure Hunt, Water Wars - and dare to discover Dina's Lost World, opening for the 2007 summer holidays, where dinosaurs have never been so much fun! Special events throughout the year include the Easter M'Egga Hide 'n Seek, unique Summer Sunflower Maze, September Scarecrow Convention and Autumn PumpkinFest. The all weather play areas ensure maximum fun whatever the weather while you can relax and unwind on the Prairie Train tour around the Dragonfly Lake. With the most exciting rides and the friendliest animals, it's Family Maximum Funtime at Crealy. Crealy's Sir Walt's Restaurant and other cafes offer delicious west country food and drinks at great prices - so visit soon because the best days are Crealy days. Visit our website for all the inside information.

Open daily 1 Apr-4 Nov from 10.00, (also 5 Nov-14 Mar 08, Thurs-Sun & daily in School Hols) Closed 24-26 Dec & 1 Jan

Low season: A&C£9.95, OAPs£6.50, C(under92cm)£Free, Family Ticket (4 people) £9.50 per person. High season: A&C£10.95 C(under92cm)£Free OAPs£7.50, Family Ticket (4 people) £10.50 per person

Discount Offer: 1 Free Go-Kart Ride

Diggerland

Verbeer Manor Cullompton Devon EX15 2PE
Tel: 08700 344437 Fax: 09012 010300
www.diggerland.com

[Exit M5 J27. Head E on A38 towards Wellington for 0.5mi turn R at roundabout onto B3181. Diggerland is 3mi on L hand side. Rail: Tiverton Parkway (approx 4mi). Bus: 373 From Station to Willand. Plenty of on-site parking available]

Diggerland is the best activity day out for all the family with all activities based around construction machinery. With over 15 rides and drives positioned in an adventure park situation. Experience the thrill of riding in Spindizzy and enjoy the view from the Sky Shuttle. Drive across rough terrain in the Super Track and enjoy a mystery ride in the Land Rover Safari. Test your co-ordination in the JCB Challenges and fasten your seat belt for the drive of your life in the Robots. A full day of fun can be had by all ages with everything onsite including refuelling at The Dig Inn and shopping at the Goodie store. Birthday parties are catered for, so if you fancy a party with a difference then contact us for details. Diggerland welcomes its 4th park in Yorkshire for 2007. Please see our website for more information.

Weekends & Bank Hols plus daily during half-term & school hols 10.00-17.00. Closed 25 Nov-8 Feb

A&C£12.50 C(under3)£Free OAPs£6.25. Group rates: (10+) 10% discount, (50+) 25% discount

Discount Offer: 10% off Admission Prices

Milky Way Adventure Park

Clovelly Bideford Devon EX39 5RY
Tel: 01237 431255
The Clone Zone, Time Warp, The North Devon Bird of Prey and Sheepdog Centres, Pets Corner, railway and more.

Watermouth Castle

Berrynarbor Ilfracombe Devon EX34 9SL
Tel: 01271 867474
Overlooking the picturesque Watermouth Cove, Watermouth Castle Offers a unique and fun day out, with attractions and entertainment for all.

Woodlands Leisure Park

Blackawton Totnes Devon TQ9 7DQ
Tel: 01803 712598 Fax: 01803 712680
www.woodlandspark.com
[On A3122 8mi from Totnes. Plenty of on-site parking available]
Discover 60 acres of exhilarating action at this theme park, with a full day of variety for the whole family. Massive indoor venture zones, rides and 15 extensive playzones hidden in beautiful woodland. Ride 3 wild watercoasters and break the thrill barrier on 500m 'Toboggan Run.' Go slide crazy on the 'Arctic Gliders' or ride the 'Avalanche.' Explore the biggest indoor venture centre in the UK with high slides, net climbs and tumble towers, also three rides including heart stopping 50ft drop on the Trauma Tower. Five fun packed zones for under sevens plus dune buggies and 'Polar Pilots.' Enjoy the latest game on the planet as all the family blast 1000s of balls at one another in the

alien Master Blaster. Take time to relax in the superb Falconry centre with beautiful birds of prey displays then enjoy hundreds of animals and birds in Animal Funtime.

10 Mar-4 Nov daily 09.30-17.00. Nov-Mar Sat & Sun plus Devon School Hols
A&C£9.25, Family Ticket (A2+C2) £35.20

Discount Offer: Save up to £4.44!

Victorian Era

Bygones
Fore Street St. Marychurch Torquay Devon TQ1 4PR
Tel: 01803 326108
Life-size Victorian exhibition street.

Wildlife & Safari Parks

Combe Martin Wildlife and Dinosaur Park
Combe Martin Ilfracombe Devon EX34 0NG
Tel: 01271 882486 Fax: 01271 883869
www.dinosaur-park.com
[J27 M5. Go W on A361 towards Barnstaple. Turn R onto A399 following signs for Ilfracombe & Combe Martin. Plenty of on-site parking available]
The land that time forgot. A Sub Tropical Paradise with hundreds of birds and animals and the most realistic Dinosaurs on the planet. They move, they roar, they're alive! The UK's only full size animatronic Tyrannosaurus Rex

plus Dilophosaurus the Spitting Dinosaur - watch out you may get wet! Wander around 26 acres of beautiful botanical gardens with rare plants, cascading waterfalls and free flying exotic birds. Snow leopards, meerkats, apes and monkeys, sealions, timber wolves, tropical butterfly house and much more. Daily falconry displays, sealion shows, lemur encounters, and handling sessions. Spectacular lightshow, destination Mars, a truly out of this world experience! Earthquake Canyon, the most unique train ride in the UK. Experience a gigantic earthquake and survive! Enter the Tomb of the Pharaohs for a fascinating insight into Egypt - But watch out for the Mummy! Combe Martin has the UK's only Wolf Education and Research Centre. A great day out for all of the family. As seen on BBC television. Dogs not permitted.
17 Mar-4 Nov
A£12.00 C(under3)£Free C(3-15)£7.00 OAPs£8.00, Family Ticket (A2+C2) £34.00. Group rates available on request

Discount Offer: One Child Free

Exmoor Zoological Park
South Stowford Bratton Flemming Barnstaple Devon EX31 4SG
Tel: 01598 763352
Covering an area of 12 and a half acres with a waterfall, streams and a lake with penguins.

Zoos

Living Coasts
Beacon Quay Torquay Devon TQ1 2BG
Tel: 01803 202470
A range of fascinating coastal creatures from puffins to penguins and fur seals.

Paignton Zoo
Totnes Road Paignton Devon TQ4 7EU
Tel: 01803 697500
Meet some of the animal kingdom's most fantastic inhabitants.

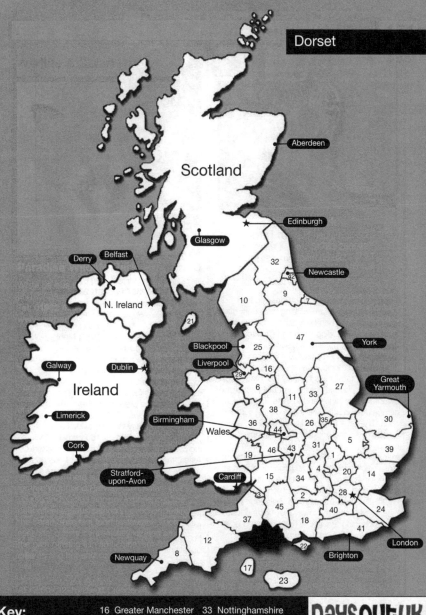

Dorset

Scotland

Aberdeen

Edinburgh

Glasgow

Newcastle

Derry
Belfast

N. Ireland

Blackpool

Liverpool

Galway
Dublin

Ireland

Limerick

Cork

Birmingham

Wales

Stratford-upon-Avon

Cardiff

Newquay

York

Great Yarmouth

London

Brighton

Key:

1 Bedfordshire	16 Greater Manchester
2 Berkshire	17 Guernsey
3 Bristol	18 Hampshire
4 Buckinghamshire	19 Herefordshire
5 Cambridgeshire	20 Hertfordshire
6 Cheshire	21 Isle Of Man
7 Cleveland	22 Isle Of Wight
8 Cornwall	23 Jersey
9 County Durham	24 Kent
10 Cumbria	25 Lancashire
11 Derbyshire	26 Leicestershire
12 Devon	27 Lincolnshire
13 Dorset	28 London
14 Essex	29 Merseyside
15 Gloucestershire	30 Norfolk
	31 Northamptonshire
	32 Northumberland

33 Nottinghamshire
34 Oxfordshire
35 Rutland
36 Shropshire
37 Somerset
38 Staffordshire
39 Suffolk
40 Surrey
41 Sussex
42 Tyne & Wear
43 Warwickshire
44 West Midlands
45 Wiltshire
46 Worcestershire
47 Yorkshire

DAYS OUT UK
The place to look for places to go

Animal Attractions

Farmer Palmer's Farm Park

Wareham Rd Organford Dorset BH16 6EU
Tel: 01202 622022 Fax: 01202 622182
www.farmerpalmers.co.uk
[4mi from Poole towards Bere Regis off A35]

Designed for families with children up to 8 years, this triple award winning farm park offers a timetable of fun and educational hands-on experiences including lamb and goat feeding, cow milking demonstration, as well as the opportunity to handle pigs, guinea pigs and groom ponies. Included in the 2,000 sq. m. of undercover facilities is the play barn with pedal tractors, pig bouncy castle and ball pits; straw mountain with slides and tunnels. The milking demonstration area and the two level soft play zone. The large outdoor sand playframe area, together with the go-karts, cow bouncy castle, bumpy tractor-trailer ride, maize maze (in summer) and woodland walk, makes for a busy day that's value for money. The large restaurant specialises in healthy traditional fare, catering for children and adults (try the homemade cakes!). Facilities include under 15mth baby soft play area, high chairs, microwave for heating food, 3 baby-changing areas, low hand washing units and wide ramps and doorways.
17 Feb-24 Mar daily 10.00-16.00, 25 Mar-27 Oct daily 10.00-17.30, 28 Oct-30 Dec Fri, Sat & Sun 10.00-16.00
Winter Admission (17 Feb-24 Mar incl) & (28 Oct-30 Dec incl) A&C£4.95 C(under2)£Free OAPs£4.75, Family Ticket (A2+C2) £19.00. Standard Admission (25 Mar-27 Oct) A&C£5.95 C(under2)£Free OAPs£5.75, Family Ticket (A2+C2) £22.00. Disabled person & carer £4.75 each in winter season & £5.75 in standard season. Group rates / season tickets on request.

Monkey World Ape Rescue Centre

Near Wareham Dorset BH20 6HH
Tel: 01929 462537 Fax: 01929 405414
www.monkeyworld.org
[Between Bere Regis & Wool off A35, signposted from Bere Regis. On-site parking available]
Since its establishment in 1987, Monkey World - Dorset's internationally-acclaimed ape rescue centre has helped change the lives of hundreds of primates from around the world. Combining fun with education on primate rescue and conservation, Monkey World works with foreign governments to prevent the illegal trade of primates from the wild. Set in 65 acres of beautiful woodland, Monkey World provides a stable, permanent home for over 160 primates including the largest group of chimpanzees outside Africa, the most important group of orangutans outside Borneo, woolly monkeys, gibbons and many more. Featured in the TV programme 'Monkey Business', the primates live naturally in large enclosures with the companionship of their own kind - a unique opportunity to see these fascinating creatures close up. Keepers hold half-hourly talks with a chance to ask questions. Monkey World also has the South's largest Great Ape Play Area for Kids, woodland walks, a pets corner, café, picnic areas and full facilities for the less-abled.
All year daily 10.00-17.00, July & Aug 10.00-18.00. Closed 25 Dec
A£10.00 C£7.00 Concessions£7.00, Family Ticket (A1+C2) £21.00 or (A2+C2) £30.00. Group rates available on request. School Parties C£5.50, Teacher £Free on (1:6) ratio

Archaeology

Dinosaurland
Coombe Street Lyme Regis Dorset DT7 3PY
Tel: 01297 443541
Jurassic Museum, free fossil clinic where visitors can bring in fossils for identification.

Terracotta Warriors Museum
Eastgate High Street East / Salisbury Street
Dorchester Dorset DT1 1JU
Tel: 01305 266040
The terracotta warriors created worldwide fascination when 6,000 of them were discovered in a pit in 1974.

Tutankhamun Exhibition
High West Street Dorchester Dorset DT1 1UW
Tel: 01305 269571
Experience the magnificence and wonder of the world's greatest discovery of ancient treasure.

Country Parks & Estates

Durlston Country Park
Lighthouse Road Swanage Dorset BH19 2JL
Tel: 01929 424443
Durlston is a 280-acre countryside paradise.

Kingston Lacy
Wimborne Minster Dorset BH21 4EA
Tel: 01202 883402 / 880413
The house contains the outstanding collection of paintings and other works.

Moors Valley Country Park Visitor Centre
Ashley Heath Horton Dorset
Tel: 01425 470721
Steam through the park in a traditional way, explore over 12 miles of tracks.

Exhibition & Visitor Centres

Brewers Quay and the Timewalk Journey
Brewers Quay Hope Square Weymouth Dorset DT4 8TR
Tel: 01305 777622 Fax: 01305 752338
[By road: Follow brown signs for Brewers Quay via Boot Hill & Rodwell Ave. By Foot: Follow the black and gold finger signs located in Weymouth town centre to the Old Harbour & Brewers Quay. Plenty of on-site parking available]

Brewers Quay is set within the historic Hope Square, alive with cafés, bars and bistros, with commanding views of the old Harbour. This imaginatively redeveloped Victorian Brewery houses a shopping village, award winning 'Timewalk' attraction, Museum, Courtyard restaurant and Excise House pub, offering a unique family experience all under one roof.
All year daily 10.00-17.30 (late nights Mon-Fri during School Summer Hols). Closed last 2 weeks of Jan

New Barn Field Centre
Bradford Peverell Dorchester Dorset DT2 9SD
Tel: 01305 268865
A fascinating and educational day out for all the family.

Festivals & Shows

Christchurch Food Festival

Christchurch Dorset
www.christchurchfoodfest.co.uk

The eighth Christchurch Food Festival promises to be the best yet, with a wide range of food-related events spread over eight days. Browse the International Food Market on the High Street with its 100+ stalls (12-13 May). Visit the Rangemaster Demonstration Kitchen in Saxon Square and see TV chefs demonstrate their skills (11-13 May). 'Kid's Kitchen' in Druitt Hall will host food tastings, a workshop, competitions and quizzes for 5 -11 year-olds (11-12 May). A full programme of meals and special events put on by local restaurants, pubs and cafés - please visit our website for further details.

11-18 May 2007

Cookery demonstrations are free of charge and prices vary for other events. VIP tickets (including ringside seats and lunch at a local restaurant) are available for some events

Tolpuddle Martyrs Festival

Main Road Tolpuddle Dorchester DT2 7EH
Tel: 01305 848237 Fax: 01305 848237
www.tolpuddlemartyrs.org.uk
[Tolpuddle Martyrs Museum & Grounds]

Every summer, the weekend of the third Sunday in July, the museum hosts the Tolpuddle Martyrs Festival. This FREE annual family festival combines celebration and tradition, offering both contemporary and traditional music. Join the famous 'Parade of Banners,' debates and discussions, or join thousands of others and listen to the guest speakers, bands and solo-artists on stage. On site there are stalls, a children's fun area, refreshments and beer tents. Festival Weekend camping is available by pre-booking only. The main Festival day is Sunday. Please visit our website for more information.
14-15 July 2007 (Sat pm-Sun 10.00-18.00)
Admission Free. £5.00 Parking

Folk & Local History Museums

Tolpuddle Martyrs Museum

Main Road Tolpuddle Dorchester DT2 7EH
Tel: 01305 848237 Fax: 01305 848237
www.tolpuddlemartyrs.org.uk

[Off A35. From Dorchester, Tolpuddle signposted at Troytown turn off. Continue along old A35 (C34), follow signpost. From Poole/Bournemouth take A31 then A35 to Dorchester then follow brown heritage signpost]

One dawn, in the bitter February of 1834, six Tolpuddle farm labourers were arrested after forming a trade union. A frightened Squire's trumped up charge triggered one of the most celebrated stories in the history of human rights. Packed with illustrative displays, this new state-of-the-art, interactive exhibition tells the Tolpuddle Martyrs story. Discover why the Judge and Squire were so vindictive - learn who

betrayed the Martyrs in the company of Death and the Skeleton - hear about their struggle for survival after transportation to Australia - share the relief of freedom and the pleasure of the homecoming. Call now for a FREE colour brochure, or email tolpuddle@tuc.org.uk.
All year, Summer: Tue-Sat 10.00-17.00, Sun 11.00-17.00. Winter: Thur-Sat 10.00-16.00, Sun 11.00-16.00. Open Bank Hols. Closed Mons & 22 Dec-4 Jan
Admission Free

Food & Drink

Palmers Old Brewery
West Bay Road Bridport Dorset DT6 4JA
Tel: 01308 427500
A traditional thatched working brewery. Palmers Brewery has been in operation since 1794.

Gardens & Horticulture

Abbotsbury Sub Tropical Gardens
Abbotsbury Weymouth Dorset DT3 4LA
Tel: 01305 871387
A magnificent 20-acre garden.

Bennetts Water Gardens
Putton Lane Chickerell Weymouth DT3 4AF
Tel: 01305 785150
Tranquil landscaped lakes with an outstanding display of water lilies.

Blue Pool
Furzebrook Road Wareham Dorset BH20 5AT
Tel: 01929 551408
The Blue Pool at Furzebrook was once a clay-pit, which accounts for a rare phenomenon that has attracted visitors from across the world.

Compton Acres Gardens
164 Canford Cliffs Road Poole BH13 7ES
Tel: 01202 700778 Fax: 01202 707537
www.comptonacres.co.uk

[On B3065. Plenty of on-site parking available]

Compton Acres - the South's finest privately owned gardens. Spectacular gardens, fine food and drink and a fantastic shopping experience. Compton Acres invites you to escape to a different world. In addition to ten acres of themed gardens, there are exciting shopping opportunities, restaurants, and a host of exhibitions and events happening throughout the year. You'll experience a day to remember, and there's something for everyone to enjoy - plus free parking.
All year daily. Summer: 09.00-18.00. Winter: 10.00-16.00. Closed 25 & 26 Dec. Last Admission: Summer 17.00, Winter 15.00
A£6.95 C£3.95 Concession£6.45, Family Ticket (A2+C3) £17.00

Discount Offer: Two for the Price of One

Cranborne Manor Private Gardens and Garden Centre
Wimborne St Cranborne Wimborne BH21 5PP
Tel: 01725 517248
Seventeenth-century gardens and a Jacobean garden and herb garden.

LULWORTH
CASTLE & PARK

The Knights of Lulworth
Summer Jousting Extravaganza*
Performed by Horses Impossible

LULWORTH

17th Century Castle. 18th Century Chapel.
Indoor Activity Room. Courtyard Shop.
Licensed Stable Cafe. Woodland Walk.
Animal Farm. Adventure Play Area.

Open Sunday to Friday. Follow the brown signs from the A352.
*For further information, event dates and times
0845 450 1054 or visit www.lulworth.com

Historical

Lulworth Castle and Park

East Lulworth Wareham Dorset BH20 5QS
Tel: 0845 4501054 Fax: 01929 400563
www.lulworth.com
[Off B3070. Fee on-site parking available]

A wonderful seventeenth-century Castle and
eighteenth-century Chapel set in extensive park-
land. Following a devastating fire in 1929, the
castle exterior has been restored to its former
glory whilst the bare walls of the interior and
many displays reveal past secrets and history.
Stunning views across the World Heritage
Jurassic Coast from the Castle Tower and
Castle lawn. Indoor children's activity room,
Courtyard Shop, licensed Stable Café.
Adventure playground and Animal Farm (open
Easter to September). Packed programme of
events throughout the year including the
Knights of Lulworth in Spectacular Summer
Jousting Shows, archery and concerts. See our
website for more details.
*All year Sun-Fri 1 Jan-23 Mar 10.30-16.00; 25
Mar-28 Sep 10.30-18.00; 30 Sep-31 Dec
10.30-16.00. Closed Sat (except Easter & some
special events), 24-25 Dec & 7-20 Jan*
Peak (22 Jul-27 Aug): A£9.00 C(4-15)£4.50
OAPs£7.50, Family Ticket (A2+C3)£26.50 or
(A1+C3)£17.50 (includes Jousting Shows). Off
Peak: A£7.00 C(4-15)£4.00 OAPs£6.00, Family
Ticket (A2+C3) £21.00 or (A1+C3) £14.00.
Season tickets also available; group rates avail-
able on request.

Discount Offer: One Child Free

Max Gate

Alington Avenue Dorchester Dorset DT1 2AA
Tel: 01305 262538
Poet and novelist Thomas Hardy designed and
lived in this house from 1885 until his death.

Nothe Fort

Barrack Road Weymouth Dorset DT4 8UF
Tel: 01305 766626
Fascinating coastal fortress dominates the
mouth of Weymouth Old Harbour and overlooks
the immense Portland Harbour.

Portland Castle

Castle Town Portland Dorset DT5 1AX
Tel: 01305 820539
One of the best preserved of Henry VIII's
coastal forts, built of white Portland stone.

Sherborne Castle

off New Road Sherborne Dorset DT9 5NR
Tel: 01935 813182 / 812072
Fax: 01935 816727
www.sherbornecastle.com

[From Bristol & W via Yeovil & A30; from Bournemouth & S via Blandford or Dorchester (A352); from Salisbury & E via A30. The Castle lies off New Rd about 0.75mi to E of centre of town. Plenty of on-site parking available]

Built by Sir Walter Raleigh in 1594 and stately home to the Digby family since 1617, the castle's state rooms reflect a glorious variety of decorative styles, with splendid collections of art, furniture and porcelain. The castle's cellars display Raleigh's original kitchen and a collection of finds from the castle grounds. No photography allowed inside the castle. Capability Brown created the lake in 1753 to give Sherborne the very latest in landscape gardening and today, 30-acres of beautiful lakeside gardens with sweeping lawns, borders and magnificent specimen trees extend around the 50-acre lake in a perfect lakeland setting. Come and explore this peaceful and natural landscape - bring a picnic, walk the dogs, watch the wildlife around the lake. There is disabled access in the gardens and ground floor of the castle. Make a day of Sherborne with its historic abbey and town close by. Enjoy morning coffees, light lunches and afternoon teas plus friendly gift shop.

1 Apr-31 Oct Tue-Thur & Sat-Sun 11.00-16.30, (Castle Interior opens later on Sat, 14.00). Open Bank Hol Mons

Castle & Gardens: A£8.50 C(0-15)£Free* OAPs£8.00. Gardens only: A£4.00 C£Free*. Group rates available for Castle & Gardens only. Private views also available. * a maximum of 4 children can be admitted per paying adult

Natural History Museums

Dinosaur Museum

Icen Way Dorchester Dorset DT1 1EW
Tel: 01305 269880 Fax: 01305 268885
www.thedinosaurmuseum.com
[Off main High East Street]

The only museum on mainland Britain solely devoted to dinosaurs, the award-winning Dinosaur Museum is a treat, especially for children. The museum combines life-sized reconstructions of dinosaurs with fossils and skeletons to create an exciting hands-on experience. Multimedia displays tell the story of the giant prehistoric animals and their enthralling world many millions of years ago. The Dinosaur Museum has twice been voted one of Britain's Top Ten Hands On Museums and is a former winner of the Dorset Family Attraction of the Year. It is frequently featured on national television including Blue Peter, The Tweenies and Tikkabilla. 'Fleshed-out' dinosaur reconstructions - including Tyrannosaurus rex, Stegosaurus and Triceratops - beg to be touched by little hands - and that's encouraged. New reconstructions include the 'sickle claw' Deinonychus and two troodons with feathers. The Dinosaur Museum is part of any Jurassic Coast experience. Its individual and exciting approach has made it extremely popular with visitors.

All year daily Apr-Oct 09.30-17.30, Nov-Mar 10.00-16.30. Closed 24-26 Dec

A£6.75 C(under4)£Free C£4.95 OAPs£5.75, Family Ticket (A2+C2) £21.00

On the Water

Bournemouth Seafront

Bournemouth Seafront Information Office
Undercliff Drive Bournemouth Dorset BH2 5AA
Tel: 01202 451781 Fax: 01202 451780
www.bournemouth.gov.uk/visitors/seafront

*[Seafront is brown sign-posted from A338 & A35
into Bournemouth. Beach office located on promenade to E of Bournemouth Pier. Plenty of on-site
parking available]*

Britain's best family seaside resort offering over
7 miles of soft, golden sand and spectacular
views of the Isle of Wight and the Purbecks.
Winner of 4 European Blue Flag Beach awards
for safe, clear water perfect for bathing in. RNLI
beach lifeguards and KidZone wristband
scheme provide a safe environment for families
to enjoy. Award winning restaurants, cafes and
ice-cream kiosks are located all along the promenade. Toilet facilities provided. Hire a beach
chalet for the day or week. Relax on a deck
chair or sunbed, take a Land Train trip along the
promenade between Alum Chine and
Boscombe Pier, featuring a pier café, children's
rides and arcade with all the latest games.
*Bournemouth Seafront Office: All year daily
09.00-17.00. Cliff Lifts Mar-Oct daily 09.00-
17.00. Land Train Mar-Oct daily 09.00-17.00.
Bournemouth Pier: All year daily 09.00-17.00*
Beach chalet hire from £7.50 a day. Land train
(one way) Family Ticket (A2+C3) £4.50

Places of Worship

St Catherine's Chapel

Abbotsbury Dorset
A small stone chapel set on a hilltop, with an
unusual roof and small turret used as a lighthouse.

Police, Prisons & Dungeons

Old Crown Courts and Cells

Dorchester Dorset
Tel: 01305 251010
Experience two hundred years of gruesome
crime and punishment in a setting little changed
over the years.

Railways

Swanage Railway

Station House Railway Station Approach
Swanage Dorset BH19 1HB
Tel: 01929 425800 Fax: 01929 426680
www.swanagerailway.co.uk

The Swanage Railway runs for six miles from
Swanage to Norden via the historic village of
Corfe Castle. Park and ride facilities available at
Norden.
*Apr-Oct & 22 Dec-1 Jan daily, Feb-Dec Sat &
Sun. Closed 25 Dec*
A£7.50 C(5-15)&OAPs£5.50, Family Ticket
(A2+C3) £21.00

Sealife Centres & Aquariums

Oceanarium

Pier Approach West Beach Bournemouth
Dorset BH2 5AA
Tel: 01202 311993 Fax: 01202 311990
www.oceanarium.co.uk

*[On seafront at Bournemouth, on West Beach
Promenade opposite Bournemouth Pier & close
to Bournemouth International Centre (BIC). From
A338 Wessex Way follow brown tourist signs for
Oceanarium, Pier & Beaches or BIC. Car parking
available at Bath Rd or BIC car parks]*

Explore the secrets of the ocean in an adventure that take you from the flesh-eating piranhas of the Amazon to the horn sharks of Key West and eerie depths of Abyss. Get even closer to reef sharks, turtles and stingrays in the underwater tunnel and, new for 2007, experience the world's first interactive dive cage! Immerse yourself in the dive cage experience to discover more about amazing sea creatures including great white sharks and manta rays, without getting wet! Relax in the contemporary Offshore Café or dine al fresco on the beachside terrace.

All year daily from 10.00. Closed 25 Dec

A£7.50 C(under3)£Free C(3-15)£5.00
Concessions£6.50

Weymouth Sea Life Park and Marine Sanctuary

Lodmoor Country Park Weymouth Dorset
DT4 7SX
Tel: 01305 788255 Fax: 01305 760165
www.sealifeeurope.com

[On A353]

New for 2007 - Come face to face with some of the world's most poisonous sea creatures in "VENOM". In this dangerous and fascinating new feature you will meet a variety of deadly characters including sea snakes, lionfish, porcupine puffer fish and moon jellyfish. Weymouth Sea Life Park and Marine Sanctuary have launched a unique Turtle Sanctuary that house several captive-bred sea turtles from the Cayman Islands. This amazing new facility will offer incredible views of these endearing, ancient animals and help raise awareness of the desperate plight of wild sea turtles, whose nest sites are being lost to tourist developments and whose numbers are in dramatic decline. With a unique mix of indoor and outdoor attractions our spacious seven-acre park provides a great day out whatever the weather. Highlights include an incredible otter sanctuary, a collection of comical Humbolt penguins, resident seals and the amazing Splash Lagoon, where adults can relax whilst our younger visitors can have a "splashing good time." Round off your day with a visit to our sister attraction Pirate Adventure Mini Golf for some swashbuckling action. Guided tours by prior arrangement.

All year daily from 10.00. Closed Christmas Day
Please call for prices

Discount Offer: One Child Free

Sport & Recreation

Tower Park Entertainment Centre

Yarrow Road Poole Dorset BH12 4NY
Tel: 01202 723671 Fax: 01202 722087
www.towerparkcentre.co.uk
[Follow signs for town centre, then brown & white signs for Tower Park, just off A3049. Plenty of on-site parking available]

Tower Park in Poole is the south coast's biggest leisure complex offering entertainment for all the family throughout the year. Tower Park has something for everyone whatever the weather. Tower Park includes; Splashdown - the area's only water flume attraction, tel. 01202 716123; Empire 10 screen cinema, tel. 0871 4714714; Bowlplex - with 24 computerised ten-pin bowling lanes, tel. 01202 715907; Gala Clubs - free membership, tel. 01202 739989; take on the latest Reeltime challenges in video game technology and fruit machines, tel. 01202 716604; Sticky Mickey - ice creams to snacks and candy, tel. 01202 745745; Exchange Bar & Grill - offers an extensive American style menu, tel. 01202 738308; Pizza Hut - provides the best pizzas and pastas, tel. 01202 718717; Burger King - restaurant and Drive Thru with varied menu and Kids Club meals, tel. 01202 736761; KFC - serves up the freshest chicken burgers and meal deals, tel. 01202 717173. New for 2006 Nandos 01202 718923, TGI Friday's 01202 746654 Flame Oriental 01202 718615, LA Fitness Gym and Pool 01202 714920 and Chiquitos Mexican Restaurant 01202 711680.
All year daily. Closed 25 Dec. Opening times of individual attractions do vary, please call for further information
Admission price vary according to season and attraction, please call for more information

Theme & Adventure Parks

Go Ape! High Wire Forest Adventure

Moors Valley Country Park Horton Road Ashley Heath Nr. Ringwood Dorset BH24 2ET
Tel: 0870 420 7876
www.goape.co.uk

[Follow brown tourist signs to Moors Valley Country Park from A31. Plenty of on-site parking available]

Take to the trees and experience an exhilarating course of rope bridges, 'Tarzan Swings' and zip-slides up to 40 feet above the ground! Share approximately three hours of memorable fun and adventure, which you'll be talking about for days. Book online and watch people Go Ape! at www.goape.co.uk. Minimum height 1.4m. Maximum weight 130 kg (20.5 stone). Under-18s must be accompanied by a participating adult. One adult can supervise either two children (where one or both of them in under 16 years old) or up to five 16-17 year olds. Pre-booking is essential to avoid disappointment. Book online or by telephone (there is a £1.00 booking fee on all telephone bookings).
10-25 Feb, 23 Mar-2 Nov daily, Nov Sat-Sun. Closed Dec-Jan
Gorillas (18yrs+) £25.00, Baboons (10-17yrs) £20.00

Discount Offer: Two for the Price of One

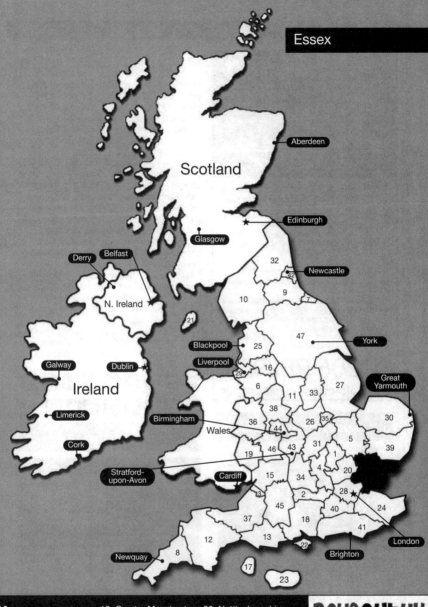

Essex

Scotland

Aberdeen

Edinburgh

Glasgow

Derry
Belfast

Newcastle

N. Ireland

32

42

9

7

10

Blackpool

21

47

York

25

Galway

Dublin

Liverpool

16

29

Ireland

6

11

33

27

Great
Yarmouth

Limerick

38

Cork

36

44

26

35

30

Birmingham

46

43

31

5

39

Wales

19

1

20

Stratford-
upon-Avon

Cardiff

15

4

34

28

London

Newquay

8

12

13

37

45

18

40

24

41

22

Brighton

17

23

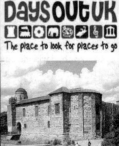
Key:

1	Bedfordshire
2	Berkshire
3	Bristol
4	Buckinghamshire
5	Cambridgeshire
6	Cheshire
7	Cleveland
8	Cornwall
9	County Durham
10	Cumbria
11	Derbyshire
12	Devon
13	Dorset
14	Essex
15	Gloucestershire
16	Greater Manchester
17	Guernsey
18	Hampshire
19	Herefordshire
20	Hertfordshire
21	Isle Of Man
22	Isle Of Wight
23	Jersey
24	Kent
25	Lancashire
26	Leicestershire
27	Lincolnshire
28	London
29	Merseyside
30	Norfolk
31	Northamptonshire
32	Northumberland
33	Nottinghamshire
34	Oxfordshire
35	Rutland
36	Shropshire
37	Somerset
38	Staffordshire
39	Suffolk
40	Surrey
41	Sussex
42	Tyne & Wear
43	Warwickshire
44	West Midlands
45	Wiltshire
46	Worcestershire
47	Yorkshire

See, Hear, Touch and Discover History in Colchester's Award-Winning Museums!

Colchester Castle Museum takes you through 2000 years of British history. Once the capital of Roman Britain, Colchester has experienced devastation by Boudica, invasion by the Normans and a siege during the English Civil War. Hands-on, interactive displays and special events bring this stunning building and collection to life.

Hollytrees Museum shows off 300 years of daily life with fun and humor in mind.

At the **Natural History Museum** a wild world awaits you! Journey through time, discover, see, hear and touch the creatures we share our lives with. At Tymperleys Clock Museum step back in time visiting this 15th Century timber-framed house.

01206 282939
www.colchestermuseums.org.uk

Agriculture/Working Farms

Barleylands Farm Centre and Craft Village

Barleylands Farm Barleylands Road Billericay
Essex CM11 2UD
Tel: 01268 290229 Fax: 01268 290222
www.barleylands.co.uk
[From M25, take J29, join A127 towards Southend then A176 & follow brown signs. From A12, take J16, join A176 & follow brown signs. Plenty of on-site parking available]

Visit Barleylands Farm… a unique family attraction! Come along to the Farm Centre and feed our friendly farm animals by hand. Animals include a donkey, sheep, cows, goats, pigs, ponies, rabbits, and an array of small furry friends. Bottle-feeding the young lambs takes place at 11am and 3pm seasonally. For added fun we also have giant trampolines, bouncy castles, miniature ride-on tractors, a huge indoor sandpit, and an adventure play area within the Farm Centre. Our miniature train now runs seven days a week (with a small additional charge) from March-October, with 'Derek the Diesel Engine' running Monday-Saturday and the steam engine running on Sundays. Visitors can bring along a picnic, or can visit one of several refreshment areas on site, including our new Farmyard Pantry. New in 2007: visitors will enjoy our new 'Dinocar' track and our 'Willow Walk,' plus we'll be unveiling our new Discovery Centre, with its massive collection of farming artefacts. Visitors to the farm can also explore our Craft Village, which houses probably the largest collection of working crafts in East Anglia.

All year daily Mar-Oct 10.00-17.00, Nov-Feb 10.00-16.00 (Craft Village closed on Mons)
Farm Centre: A&C£4.00, Family Ticket £12.00.
Craft Village: £Free

Animal Attractions

Redwings Ada Cole Rescue Stables

Broadlands Epping Road Broadley Common
Waltham Abbey Essex EN9 2DH
Tel: 0870 040 0033 Fax: 0870 458 1942
www.redwings.org.uk
[Off B181 in Broadley Common, nr Nazeing.

Plenty of on-site parking available]

In October 2005 Redwings Horse Sanctuary merged with the Ada Cole Memorial Stables, a charity with a long established reputation in the field of equine welfare and years of expertise in rehabilitating and re-homing horses and ponies. The Redwings Ada Cole Rescue Centre is home to more than 50 horses, ponies, donkeys and mules, many of which are being rehabilitated with a view to finding them caring foster homes. There is also a permanent herd, which includes five equines that are available for adoption. These include Boo the handsome Arab, Misfit the Shetland and Louie the donkey. The centre has pleasant paddock walks and guided tours plus a gift shop and information centre.
All year daily 10.00-17.00. Closed 25-26 Dec & 1 Jan
Admission Free
Discount Offer: One Free Poster

Tropical Wings

Wickford Rd South Woodham Essex CM3 5QZ
Tel: 01245 425394
Many different species of birds, insects and animals.

Archaeology

Colchester Castle Museum

Castle Park Colchester Essex CO1 1TJ
Tel: 01206 282939
www.colchestermuseums.org.uk

See, Hear, Touch and discover 2000 years of History in this award-winning Museum. Interactive displays and year round programme of events make learning fun, bringing history to

life. Colchester Castle Museum is the largest keep ever built by the Norman's. This beautiful castle is built on the Roman foundations of the Temple of Claudius over thousand years ago. The Roman vaults can still be visited today as part of a behind the scenes guided tour, available all year round. The museum is unique and extensive, boasting one of the finest collections of Roman archaeology in Europe. Please visit our website for events.
Mon-Sat 10.00-17.00, Sun 11.00-17.00.
Minicom 01206 507803
A£5.10 C(5-15)£3.30 C(under5)£Free Concessions£3.30 Saver Ticket(A2+C2)£13.50, tours of the Roman vaults and castle roof are available after admission to the Castle; A£2.00 C£1.00, prices valid until 31 December 2007

Arts, Crafts & Textiles

Blake House Craft Centre

Blake End Nr Braintree Essex CM77 6RA
Tel: 01376 344123
www.blakehousecraftcentre.co.uk

[Follow brown tourist signs from A120. Plenty of on-site parking available]

The carefully preserved farm buildings at Blake House Craft Centre are centered around a courtyard, which was previously the Blake House farmyard. Wander around the fine variety of art and craft shops in a friendly, relaxed atmosphere, where there really is something for everyone! From antique clothing to animal toys, from Steiff bears to stuffed olives and from electric guitars to elegant fabrics, you can treat yourself or find the perfect gift. Once you've looked around the shops, enjoy a bite to eat, challenge your friends to a round of crazy golf on our brand new mini-golf course and then test your wits against the maize maze challenge! Our licensed restaurant "Timbers" is housed in an eighteenth-century listed corn barn. For coffee, lunchtime snack, full restaurant meal, live band, or private venue, visit Timbers Restaurant. Open 7 days a week and Wednesdays - Saturday evenings! Please call 01376 552553 for bookings.

All year Tue-Sun 10.00-17.00. Individual shop times vary
Admission Free

Country Parks & Estates

Lee Valley Regional Park

Stubbins Hall Lane Crooked Mile Waltham Abbey Essex EN9 2EG
Tel: 01992 702200 Fax: 01992 899561
www.leevalleypark.org.uk
[Plenty of on-site parking available]
If you enjoy wildlife, sport, countryside, heritage, fantastic open spaces with great places to stay, then the Lee Valley Regional Park is for you. The Park is the regional destination for sport and leisure and stretches for 4,000 hectares between Ware in Hertfordshire, through Essex to the river Thames, and provides leisure activities to suit all ages, tastes and abilities. For more information about the park and what you can do - please phone or visit our website.

Discount Offer: One Child Free at the Lee Valley Park Farms

Weald Country Park

Weald Road South Weald Brentwood Essex CM14 5QS
Tel: 01277 261343
Features a visitor centre, gift shop, light refreshments, deer paddock, country walks, lakes, horse riding and cycling.

Folk & Local History Museums

Chelmsford Museum and Essex Regiment Museum

Oaklands Park Moulsham Street Chelmsford Essex CM2 9AQ
Tel: 01245 605700
Victorian villa houses, local and social history, Essex Regiment history; fine arts and natural history.

Epping Forest District Museum

39/41 Sun Street Waltham Abbey Essex EN9 1EL
Tel: 01992 716882
The museum is situated in two timber framed houses dating from c1520-c1760.

Museum of Harlow

Muskham Road Harlow Essex CM20 2LF
Tel: 01279 454959
Harlow is best known as a new town, but the museum tells its story from Prehistoric and Roman to modern times.

Prittlewell Priory Museum

Priory Park Southend-On-Sea Essex
Tel: 01702 434449
Originally a Cluniac monastery, now a museum of local history and natural history. Please telephone before visit to check opening times.

Saffron Walden Museum

Museum Street Saffron Walden CB10 1JL
Tel: 01799 510333
This friendly museum lies near the castle ruins in the centre of town.

Tymperleys Clock Museum

Trinity Street Colchester Essex CO1 1JN
Tel: 01206 282939

Tymperleys now houses part of the famous Bernard Mason Collection, one of the largest collections of clocks in Britain. All were made in Colchester between 1640 and 1840 and give a fascinating insight into this specialist trade.

Gardens & Horticulture

Gnome Magic

New Dawn Old Ipswich Road Dedham Colchester Essex CO7 6HU
Tel: 01206 231390

Set in 2 hectares (5 acres) and divided into two, Gnome Magic is an unusual treat. Enjoy the delightful garden which blends into an amazing wood where the growing number of 500 gnomes and their friends live.

Original Great Maze

Blake House Craft Centre Blake End Rayne Nr. Braintree Essex CM77 6RA
Tel: 01376 553146
www.greatmaze.info

[Follow tourist signs from A120. Plenty of on-site parking available]

Experience the latest challenge from the acclaimed 'maize maze' master David E. Partridge. The Original Great Maze returns for 2007, but this year it's bigger, better and harder! Sown from over half a million maize and sunflower seeds, the challenge is on! So come and get lost for a fun family day out of adventure or a competitive challenge for the experienced maze enthusiast. Many have turned their visit to the maze into an annual event, but don't worry if you are new to one of the greatest maze challenges in the world, there is a lost souls map available and a viewing platform to help you find your way out! When you have conquered the maze, why not take a look around the Blake House Craft Centre or enjoy a meal in our licensed restaurant, housed in an eighteenth-century listed corn barn. Fun for everyone, whatever the weather.

7 July-9 Sept daily 10.00-16.30
A£4.50 C£2.50 OAPs£3.50 Pushchairs & Wheelchairs Free

Discount Offer: One Child Free

ROYAL GUNPOWDER MILLS
Waltham Abbey

Open weekdays from May to September 2007. 11am - 5pm (last entry 3.30pm)

Five minutes from Junction 26 of the M25
Tel. 01992 707370
www.royalgunpowdermills.com

Exciting!
Science

An historic site since the days of the Gunpowder Plot, developments have made British gunpowder the envy of the world.

Beautiful!
Nature

The Royal Gunpowder Mills shares its secret history with you amongst 175 acres of stunning parkland.

Fascinating!
History

Exciting living history and re-enactment events most weekends including VE Day, Steam Fair and Military Vehicle Show.

from the formality of clipped hedges on the Hilltop to the naturalistic planting on Clover Hill. The wilder peripheries of the estate comprise sapling woodland, meadows, and a model garden for wildlife, which enhances biodiversity. A recent addition to the garden is four vegetable plots which we hope will inspire people to have a go at growing their own. The Thatched Barn Restaurant and Courtyard Tea Garden serves a wide selection of hot and cold food made on the premises, using locally sourced produce where possible. Round off your trip with a visit to our well-stocked plant and shop. We also offer a comprehensive range of events and educational programmes.

All year daily from 10.00. Closings times vary with the season. Closed 25 Dec
A£5.00 C(6-16)£1.50 C(0-5)£Free. Parties 10+ special rates available-booking essential. Carer for disabled visitor & blind visitors free

Discount Offer: Two for the Price of One

Heritage & Industrial

RHS Garden Hyde Hall

Buckhatch Lane Rettendon Chelmsford Essex CM3 8ET
Tel: 01245 400256 Fax: 01245 402100
www.rhs.org.uk
[A130 follow tourist signs. Plenty of on-site parking available]

Hyde Garden is an oasis of calm and serenity and a visit to the 360-acre estate is unforgettable in any season. The developed area of the garden, in excess of 24 acres, demonstrates an eclectic range of inspirational horticultural styles,

Royal Gunpowder Mills

Beaulieu Drive Waltham Abbey Essex EN9 1JY
Tel: 01992 707370 Fax: 01992 707372
[Follow A121 (M25 J26) towards Waltham Abbey. Royal Gunpower Mills is straight ahead at crossroads with McDonald's on L. Plenty of on-site parking available]

Set in 175 acres, the Royal Gunpowder Mills presents its 300-year history to the world. Listed structures and canals combine with extensive woodland, creating a hidden world with a thriving ecology. Take our self-guided nature walk with our map and information sheet, or (if you're feeling less energetic!) take the land train with our knowledgeable guide. For children, there's a special version of our nature walk with animals to spot and games to play that will introduce them to wildlife. Our interactive exhibition is a fun way to learn about history and our 1940s toyshop, general store, and kitchen will show them how children used to live. Our events programme includes the popular 'VE Weekend,' a mix of re-enactments, living history and the legendary Spitfire (performing an aerobic display on the final day). Other family-themed weekends include 'Home Front,' 'Victoriana' and 'Gunpowder, Treason and Plot.'

Sat-Sun & Bank Hols only 11.00-17.00. Other times by prior arrangement.
A£6.00 C(5-16)£3.50 Concessions£5.00, Family Ticket £19.00

Historical

Audley End House
Audley End Saffron Walden Essex CB11 4JF
Tel: 01799 522399
Enjoy over 30 lavishly decorated interiors and a wonderful collection of paintings.

Ha'penny Pier Vistor Centre
The Quay Harwich Essex CO12 3HH

Tel: 01255 503429
The pier ticket office is charming, typical example of late nineteenth-century architecture.

Hadleigh Castle
off Chapel Lane Hadleigh Essex SS7 2PP
Tel: 01223 582700
This thirteenth-century castle was first built by Hubert de Burgh.

Hedingham Castle
Bayley Street Castle Hedingham Halstead Essex CO9 3DJ
Tel: 01787 460261 Fax: 01787 461473
www.hedinghamcastle.co.uk

[On B1058 1mi off A1017 (between Colchester & Cambridge), close to Constable country. Easy reach of London & M11. Plenty of on-site parking available]

Hedingham Castle was built in 1140 by Aubrey de Vere II and was the home of the de Veres, Earls of Oxford for 550 years. The castle was besieged by King John in 1216, and attacked by the Dauphin of France in 1217. Hedingham has welcomed many royal visitors including King Henry VII, King Henry VIII and Queen Elizabeth I. The keep stands over 110 feet high with walls 12 feet thick. Most of the Norman architectural features remain around the keep - especially the chevron stone carvings and the splendid arch, which spans the entire width of the Banqueting Hall and is the widest Norman arch in Western Europe. There are beautiful woodland and lakeside walks and areas where visitors can enjoy a picnic. Unfortunately, disabled access is limited to the grounds. Dogs are allowed in the grounds if kept on leads. Member of the Historic Houses Association.

1 Apr-28 Oct Sun-Thurs 10.00-17.00. Closed Fri-Sat throughout
A£5.00 C£3.50 Concessions£4.50, Family Ticket £17.00

Discount Offer: One Child Free

For great hotel deals call Superbreak on 01904 679999 or visit www.superbreak.com

Educational and fun-packed days out

Open April - October; Sunday to Thursday

Feb - Snowdrop Sundays
& Photography competition

April - Medieval Siege Society

May - Lion Rampant

May - Jousting Tournament I

June - Jousting Tournament II

Aug - Jousting Tournament III

01787 460261
www.hedinghamcastle.co.uk

Hylands House

Hylands Park London Road Chelmsford Essex
CM2 8WQ
Tel: 01245 605500 Fax: 01245 605510
www.chelmsford.gov.uk/hylands

*[Nr Chelmsford, J28 M25 then J15 A12. Follow
signposts for Hylands. For House: Use entrance
on dual carriageway section of A414 (car park
next to house). For Park: use other entrances.
Plenty of on-site parking available]*

Hylands House is a beautiful grade II* listed
building, set in 574 acres of parkland. Visitors
can enjoy all of the spectacular rooms in the
house, ranging from the exquisitely gilded
Drawing Room, to the sumptuously ornate
Banqueting Room. The Repton Room on the
first floor provides stunning views over the landscaped parkland. The final stages of restoration
on the Stable Block (incorporating a gift shop,
restaurant, arts and crafts centre and visitor
centre) was completed and opened February
2007. Hylands House is also licensed for Civil
Ceremonies and can also be hired for Wedding
Receptions, Corporate Functions and Private
Hire. Hylands Estate is open throughout the
year and is a wonderful surrounding for a pleasant walk. Dogs and photography allowed in the
park.
*House: All Year Sun & Mon 11.00-18.00. (Oct-
Apr House closes at 18.00 on Mon). Available for
hire for weddings, corporate or private functions
Tue-Sat. Stables Centre: daily*
A£3.40 C(under16)£Free OAP's£2.40

**Discount Offer: Two for the Price of
One**

Ingatestone Hall

Hall Lane Ingatestone Essex CM4 9NR
Tel: 01277 353010
Tudor mansion in 11 acres of grounds.

Mistley Towers

Factory Lane Brantham Manningtree CO11 1NJ
Tel: 01206 393884
Famous lodges built in 1782 for the hall, and
two square, classic towers.

Moot Hall

High Street Maldon Essex CM9 5PN
Tel: 01621 857373
Built circa 1440 the old Courthouse and Council
Chambers are well preserved.

Mountfitchet Castle and Norman Village

Stansted Essex CM24 8SP
Tel: 01279 813237
Norman motte and bailey castle and village reconstructed as it was in Norman England.

Maritime

National Motorboat Museum

Wat Tyler Country Park Pitsea Hall Lane Pitsea Basildon Essex SS16 4UH
Tel: 01268 550077
Opened in 1986 the museum documents the history of motorboating concentrating mainly on sports and leisure.

Military & Defence Museums

Kelvedon Hatch Secret Nuclear Bunker

Brentwood Essex CM14 5TL
Tel: 01277 364883
Step inside the door of this rural bungalow nestling in the Essex countryside and discover the twilight world of the Government Cold War.

Natural History Museums

Central Museum and Planetarium

Victoria Avenue Southend-On-Sea Essex SS2 6EW
Tel: 01702 434449
A fine Edwardian building housing displays of archaeology, natural history and local history.

Natural History Museum

All Saints Church High Street Colchester Essex CO1 1DN
Tel: 01206 282941
Displays on the natural environment of north-east Essex from the Ice Age to today's town wildlife.

Nature & Conservation Parks

Two Tree Island

Nr Leigh Station Southend-On-Sea Essex
This lonely expanse of windswept grass and saltings is the site of a nature reserve. A wide variety of birds is seen, and particularly migrants.

On the Water

Clacton Pier

Clacton-on-Sea Essex CO15 1QX
Tel: 01255 421115
A major entertainment centre with rides, arcades, reptile house and undercover fairground, public house and beer garden with children's play area, shops, nightclub with cafés.

Southend Pier

Western Esplanade Southend-On-Sea Essex
SS1 1EE
Tel: 01702 215620 Fax: 01702 611889
www.southendpier.co.uk

*[A13 or A127 into Southend-On-Sea follow signs
to seafront]*

Following the tragic fire on 9 October 2005
Southend Pier walkway and railway is once
again fully open to the public. Visitors can travel
on the famous Pier train or walk down the mile-
long walkway and enjoy the stunning views.
Visitors can also see the lifeboats and browse
the RNLI gift shop. Despite the fire, Southend
Pier remains the longest pleasure pier in the
world.

*Pier open daily from 9.15 till dusk - please call the
Visitor Information Centre for specific
opening/closing times*
A£3.00 C&OAPs£1.50, Family Ticket £7.20.
Group rates available on request

Railways

East Anglian Railway Museum

Chappel and Wakes Station Station Road
Wakes Colne Colchester Essex CO6 2DS
Tel: 01206 242524
The museum has a wide collection of locomo-
tives and rolling stock, some of which are fully
restored and others are undergoing repair.

Sealife Centres & Aquariums

Sealife Adventure

Eastern Esplanade Southend-On-Sea Essex
SS1 2ER
Tel: 01702 442211 Fax: 01702 462444
www.sealifeadventure.co.uk
[On seafront 0.5mi E of pier]

Just along the seafront from Adventure Island,
the Sea Life Adventure themed aquarium is
bursting with a unique mixture of education and
fun that families will love. Journey through the
Sea Cavern, mosey on into the Seahorse
Rodeo, wander around the Ray Bay, walk under
the waves in Deepwater World, and examine
the Sea Nursery. On your journey you will enjoy
a wealth of marine marvels from starfish to
sharks, piranhas to stingrays, and every day
there is a full programme of demonstrations,
talks and presentations. Also, 'Adventure
Towers' children's activity centre and the Waves
Café.
*All year daily from 10.00 closing at either 17.00 or
19.00. Closed 25-26 Dec*
Please see our website for prices

**Discount Offer: Two for the Price of
One**

Sport & Recreation

Kursaal

Eastern Esplanade Southend-On-Sea Essex
SS1 2WW
Tel: 0871 550 1010
Something for everyone, from 30 lanes of Ten
Pin Bowling to an Amusement Arcade.

Theme & Adventure Parks

Adventure Island

Western Esplanade Southend-On-Sea SS1 1EE
Tel: 01702 443400 Fax: 01702 601044
www.adventureisland.co.uk

*[1h from central London, on both sides of
Southend Pier. M25 J29 then A127 or M25 J30
then A13]*

Adventure Island (on both sides of Southend's
world-famous pier) is the No.1 fun park in the
South-East of England. New for 2007: the most
thrilling roller coaster ride to come to
Southend... RAGE, with its 23-metre vertical lift
and its drop & loop, together with its 360-
degree 'barrel roll.' With over 40 rides and
attractions (including 3 more roller coasters and
22 junior rides) there's something for the whole
family to enjoy. Admission to Adventure Island is
FREE (you only pay if you play) and the best
way to play is with an all-day wristband.
*31 Mar-9 Sept daily from 11.00, Sept-Mar Sat-
Sun & school half-terms. Closing times vary
between 18.00 & 23.00. Closed 22-23 Dec*
Riders 1.2m & taller: All Day Wristbands (32
rides) £20.00. Riders 1.0-1.2m tall: Junior
Bands (22 rides) £15.00. Riders less than 1.m
tall: Mini Bands (14 rides) £10.00. Half-price

wristbands from 18.00 during July-Aug & weekends in June, Sep-Oct. Please see website for
off-peak times with even more savings.

**Discount Offer: 3 Wristbands for the
Price of 2**

Toy & Childhood Museums

Hollytrees Museum

High Street Colchester Essex CO1 1VG

Tel: 01206 282940
Colchester Hollytrees Museum is housed in a
beautiful Georgian town house.

House on the Hill Toy Museum

Grove Hill Stansted Essex CM24 8SP
Tel: 01279 813567
One of the largest toy museums in Europe,
housed on two floors.

Wildlife & Safari Parks

Mole Hall Wildlife Park

Mole Hall Widdington Saffron Walden Essex
CB11 3SS
Tel: 01799 540400
This wildlife park and butterfly pavilion offers a
relaxing day out.

Zoos

Colchester Zoo

Maldon Road Stanway Colchester Essex
CO3 0SL
Tel: 01206 331292
Colchester Zoo has over 200 species of ani-
mals.

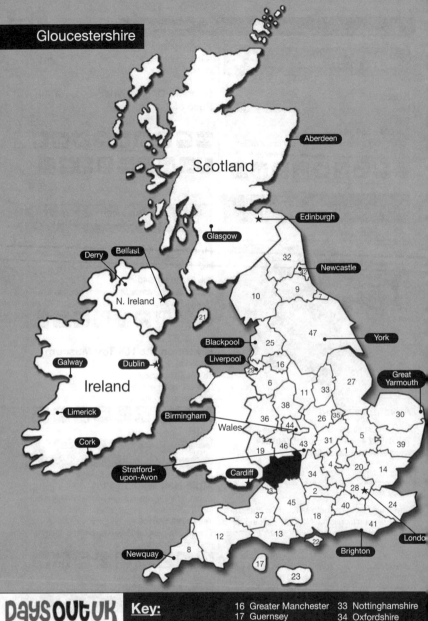

Gloucestershire

Aberdeen

Scotland

Edinburgh

Glasgow

Newcastle

Derry · Belfast

N. Ireland

32

42

9

10

7

21

York

47

Blackpool

25

Galway · Dublin

Liverpool

16

Ireland

29

6

Great
Yarmouth

11

33

27

Limerick

38

30

Cork

Birmingham

36

44

26

35

Wales

31

5

39

19

46

43

1

14

Stratford-
upon-Avon

13

34

4

20

Cardiff

28

London

24

45

2

40

41

37

18

Newquay

12

22

Brighton

8

13

17

23

Key:

1	Bedfordshire	16	Greater Manchester
2	Berkshire	17	Guernsey
3	Bristol	18	Hampshire
4	Buckinghamshire	19	Herefordshire
5	Cambridgeshire	20	Hertfordshire
6	Cheshire	21	Isle Of Man
7	Cleveland	22	Isle Of Wight
8	Cornwall	23	Jersey
9	County Durham	24	Kent
10	Cumbria	25	Lancashire
11	Derbyshire	26	Leicestershire
12	Devon	27	Lincolnshire
13	Dorset	28	London
14	Essex	29	Merseyside
15	Gloucestershire	30	Norfolk
		31	Northamptonshire
		32	Northumberland

33	Nottinghamshire
34	Oxfordshire
35	Rutland
36	Shropshire
37	Somerset
38	Staffordshire
39	Suffolk
40	Surrey
41	Sussex
42	Tyne & Wear
43	Warwickshire
44	West Midlands
45	Wiltshire
46	Worcestershire
47	Yorkshire

Animal Attractions

Cotswold Farm Park

Guiting Power Stow on the Wold Cheltenham Gloucestershire GL54 5UG
Tel: 01451 850307 Fax: 01451 850423
www.cotswoldfarmpark.co.uk

[J9 M5 off B4077 Tewkesbury/Stow rd. Plenty of free on-site parking available]

At Guiting Power, in the heart of the Cotswolds, lies the Cotswold Farm Park, Britain's first ever Rare Breeds farm to open to the public. Alongside its serious aims of conservation and education, the whole family will find themselves easily entertained whatever the weather. Very much a working farm, there is a comprehensive collection of rare breeds of British farm animals as well as lots of activities for the youngsters; rabbits and guinea pigs to stroke, lambs and calves to bottle feed, tractor and trailer rides, battery powered tractors and good safe rustic-themed play areas both indoors and outside. There is also a gift shop and Cotswold Kitchen. Audio tours are available for adults; nature trails, a woodland walk and plenty of space for a picnic. The Cotswold Farm Park also has its own 40-pitch camping and carvanning site, with electric hook-up, toilets and showers, so visitors never have to leave!

24 Mar-9 Sept daily, then Sat-Sun only to end Oct & Autumn Half Term (20-31 Oct incl) 10.30-17.00
A£5.75 C£4.75 OAPs£5.25, Family Ticket £19.00. Group rates available on request

Discount Offer: One Child Free

Art Galleries

Gloucester City Museum and Art Gallery

Brunswick Road Gloucester Gloucestershire GL1 1HP
Tel: 01452 396131 Fax: 01452 410898
www.gloucester.gov.uk/citymuseum

[Centre of Gloucester, 5min walk from Railway Station]

There is something for everyone with impressive collections. These include a wide range of Roman artefacts such as the Rufus Sita tombstone; the amazing Iron Age Birdlip Mirror; one of the earliest backgammon sets in the world; dinosaur fossils; wildlife from the City and the Gloucestershire countryside; and paintings by famous artists such as Turner and Gainsborough. The first floor has been completely re-displayed. The Time Gallery has a range of clocks from the 1680s to the twentieth century, with everything from sand glasses to sun dials. There are fine examples of eighteenth-century furniture and ceramics and one of the best collections of eighteenth-century glass in the country. Coins include a rare Viking ingot and a sensational seventeenth-century hoard. There are various interactive activities, including the opportunity to test bank notes and to use the Furniture Explorer to find some of the hidden secrets of the furniture. There is an exciting range of exhibitions throughout the year along with children's holiday activities and special events.

All year Tue-Sat 10.00-17.00
Admission Free

Nature in Art

Wallsworth Hall Twigworth Gloucester
Gloucestershire GL2 9PA
Tel: 01452 731422 Fax: 01452 730937
www.nature-in-art.org.uk
[On A38, 2mi N of Gloucester. Plenty of free on-site parking available]
Nature in Art is unique. It is the world's only museum and art gallery dedicated to all kinds of art inspired by nature. As well as organising a vibrant programme of temporary exhibitions, we regularly create new displays of our own exhibits. Our collection embraces two and three-dimensional work in all mediums and styles ranging from Picasso to Shepherd. Spanning 1500 years, it contains work by 600 artists from over 60 countries. So whether you prefer exotic oriental treasures or watercolour landscapes, the Flemish masters or contemporary glass, modern abstract interpretations or bronze sculpture - there will be something here for you.You are likely to make some discoveries too! You can also meet an artist as they demonstrate their skills - which could be painting, sculpting, woodcarving or many other art forms (February-November). Homemade snacks and cakes are served in the coffee shop overlooking the sculpture gardens. There are also indoor and outdoor activity areas for children and a gift shop with souvenirs and artists materials.
All year Tue-Sun & Bank Hol 10.00-17.00, Mon by arrangement. Closed 24-26 Dec
A£4.50 C&OAPs&Students(NUS/USI)£4.00 C(0-8)£Free, Family Ticket £13.00

Discount Offer: Two for the Price of One

Birdland

Rissington Road Bourton on the Water
Cheltenham Gloucestershire GL54 2BN
Tel: 01451 820480 Fax: 01451 822398
www.birdland.co.uk

Birdland is a natural setting of woodland, river and gardens, which is inhabited by over 500 birds; Flamingos, pelicans, penguins (the only group of King Penguins in England, Wales and Ireland), cranes, storks, cassowary and water-fowl can be seen on various aspects of the water habitat. Over 50 aviaries of parrots, falcons, pheasants, hornbills, touracos, pigeons, ibis and many more. Tropical and Desert Houses are home to the more delicate species. Take time out to wander, relax and learn in this tranquil environment and watch the activities of the birds on and around the River Windrush as it meanders through the Park on its journey to the Thames. Dogs are allowed, but must be kept on a lead at all times. Disabled access throughout and toilet facilities. The Penguin Café offers a range of food and beverages in comfortable surroundings; Play area, Picnic areas, Information Centre, Birds of Prey Encounters and much more. Also available Family Ticket, Season Ticket, Bird Adoptions and Educational sheets. See our website for more details e.g. 'Keeper for a Day' or 'Feed the Penguins'.
All year daily Apr-Oct 10.00-18.00, Nov-Mar 10.00-16.00. Closed 25 Dec
A£5.25 C(4-14)£3.00 OAPs£4.25, Family Ticket (A2+C2) £15.00

Discount Offer: One Child Free

Cotswold Falconry Centre

Batsford Park Moreton-in-Marsh
Gloucestershire GL56 9QB
Tel: 01386 701043

Housing 80-100 individual birds of prey at any
given time, the Cotswold Falconry Centre aims
to be one of the friendliest and most informative
raptor centres in the country. Daily flying displays. Browse one of the many breeding
aviaries, see owls, caracara vultures, eagles and
much more. Tearoom and gift shop.

National Birds of Prey Centre

Great Boulsdon Newent Gloucestershire
GL18 1JJ
Tel: 01531 820286 Fax: 01531 821389
[Plenty of on-site parking available]

Did you know we are the most significant, the
best and one of the largest collections of birds
of prey in the world? We have over 160 Birds of
Prey. Covering 50 species which includes 60
owls from the tiny little owl up to the largest
European eagle owl and there are many eagles
from the Bateleur eagle up to the American bald
eagle. All on view and all flying.

All year daily 10.30-17.30
A£8.50 C£5.50 OAPs£7.00, Family Ticket
£23.00

Clearwell Caves Ancient Iron Mines

Royal Forest of Dean Coleford Gloucestershire
GL16 8JR
Tel: 01594 832535 Fax: 01594 833362
www.clearwellcaves.com

*[1.5mi S of Coleford town centre on B4228 sign-
posted from Coleford town centre. Plenty of on-
site parking available]*

Selected as the 'Family Attraction for
Gloucestershire for 2003' by the Good Britain
Guide you will see why when you enjoy a journey of discovery to see how ochre and iron ore
have been 'won' here for over 5,000 years -
from the Neolithic period through to the present
day. The mines were famous for their ochre produced to make pigments for artist's and other
natural paints; red, yellow, brown and purple
ochre is still produced today and sold in the
mine shop. There are nine impressive caverns
to discover, with mining and geological displays
throughout. Visitors will also see the ochre
preparation area and blacksmith's workshop.
Excellent gift shop and tempting tearoom to visit
afterwards. Picnic area. Ample free parking. For
the more adventurous, 'Deep Level' visits can
be arranged for small groups.

*1 Mar-31 Oct daily 10.00-17.00. Christmas
Fantasy; 1-24 Dec 10.00-17.00*
A£4.50 C£2.80 Concessions£4.00, Family
Ticket £12.90

Discount Offer: One Child Free

Clearwell Caves

OPEN 10.00AM - 5.00PM
Clearwell, Near Coleford, Gloucestershire

The Royal Forest of Dean's Iron Mining Museum
A fascinating insight into an ancient iron mining tradition going back 4000 years

Tel: **01594 832535**
www.clearwellcaves.com

A GREAT UNDERGROUND EXPERIENCE FOR ALL THE FAMILY!

Festivals & Shows

Greenbelt Festival

Cheltenham Racecourse Cheltenham Gloucestershire
Tel: 020 7374 2760 (Tickets)
Fax: 020 7374 2731
www.greenbelt.org.uk
[M5 J10, A435 towards Bishops Cleeve & Evesham, within easy reach of M5 & A40/M40. Rail: Cheltenham Spa. Bus: Stagecoach 01242 522021]

Greenbelt is an all-age Arts Festival with its roots in the Christian faith and a welcome that's wide and inclusive. It's a place to learn, to experience, to be. It's like nothing else in the world, and that's what keeps thousands of people keep coming back year after year. Greenbelt features a great range of music on 5 stages showcasing brand new artists and bands. In addition, the Festival hosts a dynamic, incredibly rich and varied selection of talks, workshop and debates; exploring contemporary issues, faith, social justice, politics - and more. Greenbelt also has a visual and performing arts programme, exploring a variety of alternative worship styles, and runs a daily Children's Festival.
24-27 August 2007
A£90.00 Concessions£60.00 C(13-17)£50.00, C(4-12)£45.00 C(0-3)£Free, Family Ticket £235.00. Day Tickets available from May 2007 call 01242 227979 or see website.

Royal International Air Tattoo

RAF Fairford Gloucestershire GL7 4RB
Tel: 0870 758 1918 Fax: 01285 713268
www.airtattoo.com
[RIAT 2007 road signs will direct traffic to main designated entry routes, A417, A419. Rail: Swindon. Shuttle Buses from Swindon Bus Station. Plenty of on-site parking available]
An action-packed feast of entertainment for all the family is guaranteed this summer at one of the UK's biggest and most exciting days out. Visitors to the Royal International Air Tattoo Fairford in Gloucestershire on July 14-15 will be treated to a large slice of American Pie as the world's largest military airshow hosts Europe's biggest tribute to the US Air Force on it's 60th Anniversary. Expect to see fast jets, giant transporters, historic aircraft, the legendary Red Arrows plus a rare UK appearance by the awesome USAF Thunderbirds displays team! Only the Air Tattoo offers more than 300 aircraft from across the globe and a thrilling eight-hour flying display. On the ground, there's a breathtaking range of attractions including the critically acclaimed Tri@RIAT interactive showcase designed especially for youngsters, a robot arena, a funfair, classic car displays plus a fabulous free outdoor sunset concert.
14-15 July 2007
In advance: A£32.50 (advance tickets can be used for either day but not both). Tickets can be bought either online or by telephone. On the day: A£37.50. C(under16)£Free. Car parking: £Free

Folk & Local History Museums

Gloucester Folk Museum

99-103 Westgate Street Gloucester
Gloucestershire GL1 2PG
Tel: 01452 396868 / 396869
Fax: 01452 330495
www.gloucester.gov.uk/folkmuseum
*[10min walk from railway station. By rd from W
A40 & A48, from N A38 & M5, from E A40 &
B4073, from S A4173 & A38]*

Three floors of attractive Tudor and Jacobean II*
listed timber-framed buildings along with new
buildings housing the Dairy, Ironmonger's shop
and Wheelwright and Carpenter workshops.
Displays feature a wide range of local history,
domestic life, crafts, trades and industries from
1500 to the present. The making of brass pins
by hand was once carried out in the original
buildings and a Protestant martyr, Bishop John
Hooper, is said to have lodged here. There is
something for all the family, including a Toys and
Childhood gallery with hands-on toys and a
puppet theatre, the Siege of Gloucester of
1643, a Victorian Class Room, a Victorian
kitchen and laundry equipment. A wide range of
exhibitions, children's activities, events, demonstrations and role-play sessions are held
throughout the year. There is an atmospheric
cottage garden and courtyard for events, often
with live animals, and outside games.
All year Tue-Sat 10.00-17.00
Admission Free

Gardens & Horticulture

Batsford Arboretum and Wild Garden

Batsford Park Moreton-In-Marsh
Gloucestershire GL56 9QB
Tel: 01386 701441
One of the largest private collections of woody
plants in Great Britain.

Bourton House Garden

Bourton On The Hill Gloucestershire GL56 9AE
Tel: 01386 700754
Surrounding a delightful eighteenth-century
Cotswold manor house (not open) and six-
teenth-century tithe barn, this exciting 3-acre
garden positively fizzes with ideas.

Westonbirt - The National Arboretum

Tetbury Gloucestershire GL8 8QS
Tel: 01666 880220
A wonderful world of trees - beautiful all year.

Heritage & Industrial

Dean Heritage Centre

Camp Mill Soudley Cinderford Gloucestershire
GL14 2UB
Tel: 01594 822170 / 824024
Fax: 01594 823711
www.deanheritagemuseum.com
[On B4227. Plenty of on-site parking available]

The Dean Heritage Centre is set in beautiful
Soundley valley on 5 acres of natural woodland.
The centre is the only Heritage Centre for the
Forest of Dean and tells the story of this unique
area through 5 museum galleries, outdoor display, Forester's Cottage with livestock, re-constructed mine and charcoal burners hut and
area. The children will be entertained with the
adventure playground, Gloucester Old Spot
pigs, children's activities and gift shop.
Demonstrations and events are organised at the
centre throughout the year, with increased activities during the summer holidays. With an on
site café, changing art exhibition room and
nearby woodland walks there is plenty to see
and do for any visitor for any weather. Disabled
access and parking is available, no smoking or
dogs allowed on site (guide dogs only). Open
daily, free parking and group bookings welcome
with possible discount.
Summer: 10.00-17.00
A£4.90 C£2.50 Concessions£4.20, Family
Ticket(A2+C4) £14.00

Historical

Berkeley Castle

Berkeley Gloucestershire GL13 9BQ
Tel: 01453 810332 Fax: 01453 511915
www.berkeley-castle.com
*[On B4509 (1.5mi W of A38). Plenty of on-site
parking available]*

Simon Jenkins, in 'England's Thousand Best
Houses' describes Berkeley Castle as 'Britain's
rose red city half as old as time'. Visit this gem-
stone of England's ancient past for a unique
experience of architectural history - a living
home reflecting a thousand years of habitation.
In an amazing state of preservation and bursting
with stories of an eventful past, Berkeley Castle
is a treasure not to be missed. The Berkeley
family is one of England's best untold stories;
powerful players through turbulent centuries
who influenced the course of history while man-
aging to keep both their property and their lives
intact. Their influence can be seen throughout a
millennium and across the world, from the
founding of Berkeley Square in London to the
founding of the American colonies. Visit and you
will encounter the murder of a King, a struggle
with a Queen, a butcher's daughter who
became a Countess... and much, much more.
*1 Apr-30 Sept Tue-Sat & Bank Hol Mons 11.00-
16.00, Sun 14.00-17.00, Oct Sun 14.00-17.00
(Butterfly House closed in Oct). (Entry for Joust
Mediaeval Festival only on 21-22, 28-29 July)*
A£7.50 C(under5)£Free C(5-16)£4.50
OAPs£6.00, Family Ticket (A2+C2) £21.00.
Gardens only: A£4.00 C£2.00. Butterfly House:
A£2.00 C£1.00. Group rates (25+) A£7.00
C£3.50 OAPs£5.50 (must be pre-booked)

Discount Offer: One Child Free

Dyrham Park

Dyrham Nr Bath Gloucestershire SN14 8ER
Tel: 0117 937 2501 Fax: 0117 937 1353
www.nationaltrust.org.uk

*[8mi N of Bath on A46, 12mi E of Bristol & 2mi
from J18 of M24. On-site parking available]*

Dyrham Park is a beautiful Baroque country
house set in 110 hectares of parkland and gardens, designed by Talman for William Blathwayt,
Secretary at War during the reign of William III.
As a consequence of Blathwayt's royal connections and influential uncle, Thomas Povey, the
house was to become a showcase for his taste
in Dutch decorative arts. The collection includes
delftware, paintings and furniture, later additions
include furniture by Gillow and Linnell. Amongst
the restored Victorian domestic rooms are
kitchens, tenants' hall and delft-tiled dairy.
*16 Mar-28 Oct Fri-Tue, House: 12.00-16.45,
Restaurant & Shop: 11.00-17.00. Park: All year
daily 11.00-17.00 or dusk if earlier (Closed
Christmas day)*
House: A£9.60 C£4.80 Family Ticket £23.90.
Garden & Park: A£3.80 C£2.00, Family Ticket
£8.50. Park only available Wed & Thurs: A£2.50
C£1.20 Family Ticket £5.60. Discount for group
bookings

Frampton Manor

Frampton-on-Severn Gloucester
Gloucestershire GL2 7EP
Tel: 01452 740698
Medieval/Elizabethan timber framed Manor
House with walled garden. Admission by
appointment only.

Kelmscott Manor

Kelmscott Lechlade Gloucestershire GL7 3HJ
Tel: 01367 252486 Fax: 01367 253754
www.kelmscottmanor.co.uk

*[Situated approx 3mi from Lechlade & sign post-
ed from A417 & A4095]*

Kelmscott Manor, a Grade 1 listed Tudor farmhouse adjacent to the River Thames, was
William Morris' summer residence from 1871
until his death in 1896. Morris loved Kelmscott
Manor, which seemed to him to have 'grown up
out of the soil'. Its beautiful gardens with barns,
dovecote, a meadow and stream provided a
constant source of inspiration. The house,
which is perhaps the most evocative of all the
houses associated with Morris, contains an outstanding collection of the possessions and work
of Morris, his family and associates, including
furniture, textiles, pictures, carpets and ceramics.

*Public Open Days - House & Gardens: Weds,
Apr-Sept, 11.00-17.00 (Ticket office open from
10.30). The following Sat, 21 Apr, 19 May, 16
June, 7 & 21 July, 4 & 18 Aug & 15 Sept, 14.00-
17.00 (Ticket office open from 13.15) Group
bookings - House & Gardens: Thurs & Fri, must
be booked in advance. Garden only: June-Sept,
Thurs 14.00-17.00*

House & Garden: A£8.50 C(8-16)£4.25,
Students(in full-time education)£4.25 One carer
accompanying a disabled person: £Free.
Garden only: £2.00. Groups please phone for
tour prices

Sudeley Castle, Gardens and Exhibitions

Winchcombe Cheltenham Gloucestershire
GL54 5JD
Tel: 01242 602308 Fax: 01242 602959
www.sudeleycastle.co.uk
[On B4632. Plenty of on-site parking available]

Sudeley Castle sits against the backdrop of the beautiful Cotswold Hills and is steeped in history. With many royal connections, the Castle has played an important role in the turbulent and changing times of England's past. Sudeley is perhaps best known as the home of Queen Katherine Parr, who is entombed in St Mary's Church, situated in the grounds. The 14 acres of magnificent, award-winning gardens are a delight throughout the seasons and are managed on organic principles. The Pheasantry was established in 2004 and the collection includes 15 species of rare and endangered pheasants. Sudeley Castle Country Cottages are located midway between the castle and the historic town of Winchcombe, they're available all year round for short or long stays. Please visit the website for details of the groundbreaking contemporary art exhibition, historic exhibitions and our exciting new events programme!
Connoisseur tours of the Castle Apartments take place every Tuesday, Wednesday and Thursday. We have disabled access in the garden only.
31 Mar-28 Oct daily 10.30-17.00. Closed Nov-Mar
A£7.20 C£4.20 Concessions£6.20

Discount Offer: One Child Free

Woodchester Mansion

Nympsfield Stonehouse Gloucestershire
GL10 3TS
Tel: 01453 861541 Fax: 01453 861337
www.woodchestermansion.org.uk

[From M5 J13 follow directions for Stroud, at roundabout turn R onto B4066 for Selsey, Follow for 4mi, take L turn signposted Nympsfield. From M4 J18 take A46 signposted Stroud, at crossroads turn L until side road forks R to Nympsfield. At J (don't go into village) turn R onto B4066 & take next R. Gates to Mansion are then on your L]

Woodchester Mansion is an architectural masterpiece of the Victorian age that was abandoned by its builders before it could be completed. It's remained virtually untouched by time since the mid-1870s, and today it offers visitors a unique opportunity to explore a Gothic building in mid-assembly. The mansion is hidden in a secluded 400-acre landscape park of great beauty, sheltering an abundance of wildlife and rare-breed grazing stock. Enchanting woodland walks snake around its five man-made lakes. The mansion and its park are reputed to be haunted and regular events are held throughout the year for those who want to hunt our ghosts. Facilities for visitors include a tearoom (serving drinks, cakes and snacks) and a gift shop. Volunteers from the Woodchester Mansion Trust conduct guided tours of the house on a regular basis. The park (owned by the National Trust) is open to all.

Apr-Oct first Sat-Sun & every Sun. May, July & Aug Sat-Sun plus Bank Hols, 11.00-17.00
A£5.00 C(under14)£Free Concessions£4.00

Music & Theatre Museums

Keith Harding's World of Mechanical Music

Oak House High Street Northleach Cheltenham
Gloucestershire GL54 3ET
Tel: 01451 860181
A collection of antique clocks, musical boxes,
automats and mechanical musical instruments.

Nature & Conservation Parks

Cotswold Water Park and Keynes Country Park

Spratsgate Lane Shorncote Cirencester
Gloucestershire GL7 6DF
Tel: 01285 861459
Britain's largest Water Park.

Robinswood Hill Country Park & Rare Breeds Centre

Reservoir Road Gloucester Gloucestershire
GL4 6SX
Tel: 01452 303206
250 acres of Cotswold countryside with on-site
Rare Breeds Farm.

WWT Slimbridge Wetlands Centre

Slimbridge Gloucester Gloucestershire GL2 7BT
Tel: 01453 891900
One of the finest collections of water-birds in
the world.

Places of Worship

Gloucester Cathedral

Gloucester Gloucestershire GL1 2LR
Tel: 01452 528095
William the Conqueror ordered the construction
of the present building in 1089.

Railways

Dean Forest Railway

Norchard Station Forest Road Lydney
Gloucestershire GL15 4ET
Tel: 01594 843423 info line
www.deanforestrailway.co.uk

[B4234 N of Lydney. Plenty of on-site parking available]

"The Friendly Forest Line" Standard gauge steam (plus occasional diesel) passenger trains from Norchard to Lydney Junction and on the newly opened extension through the medieval forest to the delightful village of Parkend, for real ale pubs, forest walks and nature reserve. Also lake and children's park at Lydney. At Norchard there is a museum of railway relics, which includes the history of the Severn and Wye Railway from 1809. Special events include Days out with Thomas, Forties wartime re-enactment, Halloween Ghost trains, Santa specials, Sunday lunch dining car trains etc. Also steam and diesel locomotive driving courses.

Trains Run: Apr-May Sun, June-July Wed, Sat-Sun, Aug Tue-Thur & Sat-Sun, Sept Wed & Sat-Sun, Oct Sun. Also Bank Hols & selected dates in Oct & at Christmas
A£9.00 OAPs£8.00 C£5.00 C(under5)£Free, Family Ticket (A2+C2) £26.00. Pay once & ride all day! (Different prices apply for special events)

Gloucestershire Warwickshire Railway

The Railway Station Toddington Cheltenham Gloucestershire GL54 5DT
Tel: 01242 621405
www.gwsr.com

[J between B4632 / B4077 on Stow Rd (8mi from J9 M5). Plenty of on-site parking available]

The 'Friendly Line in the Cotswolds', offers a 20 mile round trip between Toddington and Cheltenham Racecourse. The views of The Cotswolds, Malverns and The Vale of Evesham are superb, since most of the line runs along embankments. The exciting 693 yard Greet Tunnel is one of the longest on a preserved railway and surely the darkest! Pop along and see the driver and fireman. Break your journey at picturesque Winchcombe Station with its tree lined picnic area or sample the delicious homemade cakes in the 'Flag & Whistle' tearooms at Toddington Station. Refreshments are also available from the buffet car on most trains. A well-stocked station shop sells a variety of 'railway' gifts. Special events are held throughout the year. Visiting locomotives. Wheelchairs can be catered for. Tickets give unlimited travel on the day of purchase. Special group rates available.

Mar-Dec Sat Sun & Bank Hol Mon & selected weekdays
Return tickets: A£10.00 C(0-4)£Free C(5-15)£6.00 OAPs£8.50, Family Ticket (A2+C3) £27.00. Group rates (for 20+) available on request

Cattle Country Adventure Park

Berkeley Heath Farm Berkeley Gloucestershire GL13 9EW
Tel: 01453 810510 Fax: 01453 811574
www.cattlecountry.co.uk
[Plenty of on-site parking available]

Why not have a fantastic, fun-filled day out at the Cattle Country Adventure Park? There's plenty to do both inside and out, with large adventure play areas (where adults are encouraged to join in with their children!). Equipment includes big slides, soft play, trampolines, and a huge jumping pillow. A miniature train will take you to Oakhill Station, where you can visit various small animals in the 'Animal Encounters' area. Follow our nature trail to the 'Willow Maze' and you'll pass a herd of American bison, red deer and other cattle on the way. Also, there'll be special tractor and trailer rides throughout the summer that'll bring you closer to the bison than ever before. There's also interesting giftshops, an excellent restaurant and a snack bar. We can accommodate private parties whenever the park is closed.

Feb Half-Term - Oct Half-Term

Discount Offer: 10% Discount on Admission & Gift Shop Purchases

Go Ape! High Wire Forest Adventure

Mallards Pike Lake Forest of Dean
Gloucestershire
Tel: 0870 420 7876
www.goape.co.uk
[From A48 at Blakeney, take Nibley-Parkend Rd, Mallards Pike is signposted. Plenty of on-site parking available]

Take to the trees and experience an exhilarating course of rope bridges, 'Tarzan Swings' and zip-slides up to 40 feet above the ground! Share approximately three hours of memorable fun and adventure, which you'll be talking about for days. Book online and watch people Go Ape! at www.goape.co.uk. Minimum height 1.4m. Maximum weight 130 kg (20.5 stone). Under-18s must be accompanied by a participating adult. One adult can supervise either two children (where one or both of them in under 16 years old) or up to five 16-17 year olds. Pre-booking is essential to avoid disappointment. Book online or by telephone (there is a £1.00 booking fee on all telephone bookings).
10-25 Feb & 23 Mar-2 Nov daily, Nov Sat-Sun. Closed Dec-Jan
Gorillas (18yrs+) £25.00, Baboons (10-17yrs) £20.00

Discount Offer: Two for the Price of One

Transport Museums

Bristol Aero Collection

Hangar A1 Kemble Airfield Kemble Cirencester
Gloucestershire GL7 6BA

Tel: 01285 771204
Aerospace and transport museum on an active airfield, with aircraft, vintage buses and a tram!
Apr-Oct, Sun & Mon

Cotswolds Motor Museum and Toy Collection

The Old Mill Sherbourne Street
Bourton-on-the-Water GL54 2BY
Tel: 01451 821255
Housed in a water mill, the museum has cars and motorcycles up to the 1950's.

National Waterways Museum

Llanthony Warehouse Gloucester Docks
Gloucester Gloucestershire GL1 2EH

Tel: 01452 318200
Situated in a Grade Two listed Victorian warehouse.

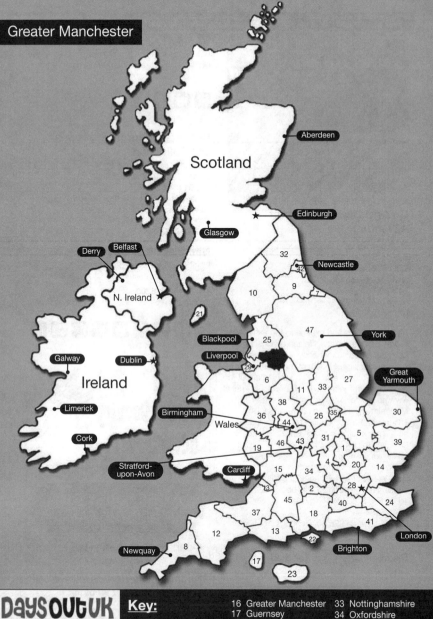

Greater Manchester

Aberdeen

Scotland

Edinburgh

Newcastle

Glasgow

32
42
9
7
10
47 — York
Derry
Belfast
N. Ireland

Blackpool
25
Liverpool
29
6
11 33 27
Great Yarmouth
Galway
Dublin
Ireland
38
30
26 35
Birmingham
36 44
5
39
Wales
46 43 31 1
19 4 20 14
Stratford-upon-Avon
Cardiff
15 34 28 — London
2 40 24
45
37 18 41
12 13 22 Brighton
Newquay 8
17
23

Limerick
Cork

Key:

1 Bedfordshire
2 Berkshire
3 Bristol
4 Buckinghamshire
5 Cambridgeshire
6 Cheshire
7 Cleveland
8 Cornwall
9 County Durham
10 Cumbria
11 Derbyshire
12 Devon
13 Dorset
14 Essex
15 Gloucestershire

16 Greater Manchester
17 Guernsey
18 Hampshire
19 Herefordshire
20 Hertfordshire
21 Isle Of Man
22 Isle Of Wight
23 Jersey
24 Kent
25 Lancashire
26 Leicestershire
27 Lincolnshire
28 London
29 Merseyside
30 Norfolk
31 Northamptonshire
32 Northumberland

33 Nottinghamshire
34 Oxfordshire
35 Rutland
36 Shropshire
37 Somerset
38 Staffordshire
39 Suffolk
40 Surrey
41 Sussex
42 Tyne & Wear
43 Warwickshire
44 West Midlands
45 Wiltshire
46 Worcestershire
47 Yorkshire

Manchester Airport Aviation Viewing Park

Wilmslow Old Road Manchester Airport
Tel: 0161 489 3000
The purpose-built viewing park has a visitor centre and a growing collection of aircraft exhibits.

Gallery Oldham

Greaves Street Oldham Cultural Quarter Oldham Greater Manchester OL1 1AL
Tel: 0161 770 4653 Fax: 0161 770 4669
www.galleryoldham.org.uk

[In Oldham town centre just off Union St, 10min walk from railway station. Rail: Oldham Mumps]

Gallery Oldham is an award winning landmark building, opened in 2002, which forms part of Oldham's new Cultural Quarter. Changing exhibitions at the gallery incorporate Oldham's extensive art, social and natural history collections alongside touring shows, newly commissioned art, international art and work produced with local communities. Regular events take place and include family activities, exhibition talks, live music and a comprehensive schools programme.
All year Mon-Sat 10.00-17.00
Admission Free

Manchester Art Gallery

Mosley Street Manchester Greater Manchester M2 3JL
Tel: 0161 235 8888 Fax: 0161 235 8899
www.manchestergalleries.org
[Corner of Mosley St & Princess St nr Manchester Town Hall]

Manchester Art Gallery houses the city's magnificent art collection and hosts a lively programme of exhibitions and events in stunning Victorian and contemporary surroundings. The gallery is located in the heart of the city centre, easily accessible by tram, bus, train, car and coach. Family favourites are available in the gallery's self-service, family style cafe. Choose chef's special hot pasta with sauces, pasta salad served with fresh bread or pick and mix your own Hungry Monkey Lunchbox! Hot food served daily from 12.00-14.00 plus sandwiches, salads and delicious cakes. Children's menu available. High chairs, baby bottle warmers and baby changing facilities available. The gallery shop stocks an impressive range of art books, prints, postcards and gifts inspired by the collection and a variety of children's products including the best selling, award winning book 'The Gallery Cat'. Families can enjoy a programme of events including hands-on activities in the Clore Interactive Gallery, family trail activity packs, story bags and the family audio tour, and can follow Tony Ross's humorous children's picture labels.

All year Tue-Sun 10.00-17.00. Closed Mon except Bank Hols, Good Fri, 24-26 & 31 Dec.
Admission Free

Salford Museum and Art Gallery

Peel Park The Crescent Salford
Greater Manchester M5 4WU
Tel: 0161 778 0800 Fax: 0161 745 9490
[A6 in front of Salford University to end of M602 signposted. Plenty of on-site parking available]

Discover the past at Salford Museum and Art Gallery! Visit Lark Hill Place - our fascinating reconstructed Victorian Street where you will find many shops and houses including a toy shop, chemist, grocer, blacksmith and a cottage. Our Spectacular Victorian Gallery compliments this with a display of Victorian sculpture and paintings. The lifetimes Gallery interprets different aspects of Salford's fascinating history whilst two temporary exhibition spaces present a varied programme of exhibitions. The Local History Library is also in the building and is a must for anyone researching the area or their Salfordian relatives. The venue is family friendly and has a full programme of activities for all ages.
All year Mon-Fri 10.00-16.45, Sat & Sun 13.00-17.00. Closed Good Fri & Easter Sat 2007 Christmas Opening 2007 to be confirmed.
Admission Free

Touchstones Rochdale

Esplanade Rochdale Greater Manchester
OL16 1AQ
Tel: 01706 864986
We are an arts and heritage centre, incorporating Rochdale Museum, Art Gallery (including a new community gallery).

Turnpike Gallery

Civic Square Leigh Greater Manchester
WN7 1EB
Tel: 01942 404469
Temporary exhibitions programme reflecting diverse range of arts practice and promotes young and contemporary artists.

Arts, Crafts and Textiles

Manchester Craft Centre

17 Oak Street Manchester Greater Manchester
M4 5JD
Tel: 0161 832 4274
Beautifully restored Victorian fish and poultry market with original glass roof, now housing 17 contemporary designers and crafts people making and retailing from their studios.

Urbis: The Museum of Urban Living

Cathedral Gardens Manchester M4 3BG
Tel: 0161 605 8200 / 605 8209
Our dynamic exhibition programme covers photography, design, architecture, music, contemporary art and much more.

Whitworth Art Gallery

Oxford Road Manchester M15 6ER
Tel: 0161 275 7450
Home to the largest collection of textiles and wallpapers outside London and an internationally famous collection of British watercolours.

Costume & Jewellery Museums

Gallery of Costume

Platt Hall Wilmslow Road Rusholme Manchester
Greater Manchester M14 5LL
Tel: 0161 224 5217
Housed in Platt Hall, an elegant eighteenth-century textile merchant's house.

Country Parks & Estates

Heaton Park

Prestwich Manchester Greater Manchester
M25 2SW
Tel: 0161 773 1085 Fax: 0161 798 0107
www.manchester.gov.uk/leisure
*[4mi from Manchester City Centre, close to J17
of M60. Plenty of on-site parking available]*

Heaton Park is one of the biggest public parks
in Europe, and offers a great day out for all ages
with most activities free of charge. The magnificent Heaton Hall is open throughout the summer months, with beautifully restored interiors
and collections of furniture, paintings, musical
instruments and an exhibition celebrating the
park's rich history. In the Animal Centre you can
watch alpacas, goats, sheep, pigs and cows.
There is a Transport Museum with working vintage trams and rowing boats can be hired at
the lake. The Horticultural Centre boasts beautiful demonstration gardens and plants for sale.
For the more energetic there are bowling
greens, horse riding, an 18 hole golf course and
a Pitch and Putt course. The park hosts a range
of exciting events throughout the year, including
outdoor theatre, concerts, themed family fun
days and a bonfire night, as well as sponsored
walks and runs. No dogs except guide dogs in
buildings.
*Park: All year daily 08.00-dusk. Hall: 8 Apr-1 Oct
Wed-Sun & Bank Hols 11.00-17.30*
Admission Free

Folk & Local History Museums

Bolton Museum and Art Gallery

Le Mans Crescent Bolton BL1 1SE
Tel: 01204 332211
Collections of archaeology, local and industrial
history, Egyptology, natural history, geology.

Ordsall Hall Museum

Ordsall Lane Ordsall Salford M5 3AN
Tel: 0161 872 0251 Fax: 0161 872 4951
*[The hall is situated 1mi from end of M602.
Disabled access in some areas. Plenty of on-site
parking available]*

Ordsall Hall Museum is a magnificent black and
white half-timbered manor house located in the
heart of Salford. It is fully furnished with seventeenth-century furniture and exhibits, and
stands in its own grounds. The Hall is rumoured
to be haunted - see if you can find the ghosts
that reside there! The Great Hall, kitchen and
Star Chamber take you back in time whilst galleries upstairs show a variety of temporary exhibitions of art, history and hands-on fun. Ordsall
Hall Museum has a full programme of family
friendly events - why not make a trip on the first
Sunday of the month and enjoy the family fun-
day!
*All year Sun-Fri. Mon-Fri: 10.00-16.00. Sun:
13.00-16.00. Closed 25-27 Dec. Closed Good
Fri, Easter Sat&Sun. Christmas opening 07 to be
confirmed*
Admission Free

Multicultural Museums

Manchester Jewish Museum
190 Cheetham Hill Road Manchester M8 8LW
Tel: 0161 834 9879
The museum is housed in a former Spanish and
Portuguese synagogue built in 1874.

Natural History Museums

Manchester Museum
The University of Manchester Oxford Road
Manchester Greater Manchester M13 9PL
Tel: 0161 275 2634
Draws on the 4 million objects in its collections.

Performing Arts

The Lowry
Pier 8 Salford Quays Manchester M50 3AZ
Tel: 0870 787 5780
West End shows to stand-up comedy.

Science - Earth & Planetary

Museum of Science and Industry in Manchester
Liverpool Road Castlefield Manchester M3 4FP
Tel: 0161 832 2244
See the wheels of industry turning in the Power
Hall and planes that made flying history.

Social History Museums

Imperial War Museum North
The Quays Trafford Wharf Road Trafford Park
Manchester Greater Manchester M17 1TZ
Tel: 0161 836 4000
Houses thousands of objects and engaging
exhibitions.

Sporting History Museums

Manchester United Museum and Tour Centre
Sir Matt Busby Way Old Trafford Manchester
Greater Manchester M16 0RA
Tel: 0870 442 1994 Fax: 0161 868 8861
www.manutd.com
[2mi from city centre off A56. Plenty of on-site parking available]
Re-live the Club triumphs, tragedies and trophies at the Manchester United Museum.
Follow the history of the Club from 1878 to the present day, including the Hall of Fame and dazzling Trophy Room. Delve behind the scenes at the Theatre of Dreams by taking the Stadium Tour. Sit in the heights of the North Stand for a bird's eye view of the pitch, stand in Sir Alex Ferguson's spot in the dug-out, sit in the Home changing room at your favourite player's peg and emerge from the players tunnel to the roar of the crowd. Not what you would expect from a museum and tour. Everything you would expect from Manchester United. For more information, or to book a tour, please telephone. Facilities provided for deaf and disabled customers, please give prior notice when booking a Stadium Tour.
All year daily 09.30-17.00. Match Day closing before kickoff, tours not available on match days. Closed 25 Dec
Tour & Museum: A£9.50 C(under5)£Free C&OAPs£6.50, Family Ticket £27.00. Museum only: A£6.00 C(under5)£Free C&OAPs£4.25, Family Ticket £17.50. All prices will rise by £0.50 after 1st June

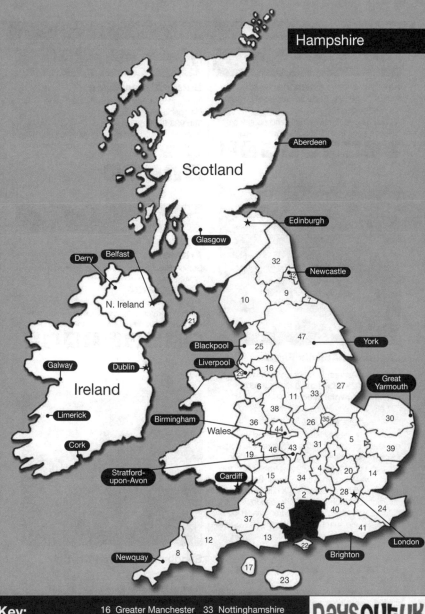

Hampshire

Aberdeen

Scotland

Edinburgh

Glasgow

Newcastle

Derry · Belfast

N. Ireland

32

42

9

7

10

21

47

York

Blackpool

25

Liverpool

16

29

Great Yarmouth

Galway · Dublin

Ireland

6

11

33

27

38

30

Limerick

Birmingham

36

44

26

35

5

39

Wales

46

43

31

1

Cork

19

20

14

Stratford-upon-Avon

Cardiff

15

34

4

28

London

13

2

40

24

45

37

13

41

12

22

Newquay

8

Brighton

17

23

Key:

1 Bedfordshire	16 Greater Manchester	33 Nottinghamshire
2 Berkshire	17 Guernsey	34 Oxfordshire
3 Bristol	18 Hampshire	35 Rutland
4 Buckinghamshire	19 Herefordshire	36 Shropshire
5 Cambridgeshire	20 Hertfordshire	37 Somerset
6 Cheshire	21 Isle Of Man	38 Staffordshire
7 Cleveland	22 Isle Of Wight	39 Suffolk
8 Cornwall	23 Jersey	40 Surrey
9 County Durham	24 Kent	41 Sussex
10 Cumbria	25 Lancashire	42 Tyne & Wear
11 Derbyshire	26 Leicestershire	43 Warwickshire
12 Devon	27 Lincolnshire	44 West Midlands
13 Dorset	28 London	45 Wiltshire
14 Essex	29 Merseyside	46 Worcestershire
15 Gloucestershire	30 Norfolk	47 Yorkshire
	31 Northamptonshire	
	32 Northumberland	

DAYS OUT UK
The place to look for places to go

Animal Attractions

Finkley Down Farm Park

Finkley Down Andover Hampshire SP11 6NF
Tel: 01264 352195
A wide range of farm animals and poultry can be seen here, including some rare breeds.

Longdown Activity Farm

Longdown Ashurst Southampton SO40 7EH
Tel: 023 8029 2837 Fax: 023 8029 3376
www.longdownfarm.co.uk
[Off A35 between Lyndhurst & Southampton. Plenty of on-site parking available]

Meet lots of friendly farm animals, and join in our range of daily activities - for example bottle-feeding goat kids or calves, small animal handling and goat feeding. Enjoy a tractor and trailer ride, weather permitting. Farmer Bryan can arrange a birthday party with a difference, for a minimum of 10 children. We have indoor and outdoor play areas where children can let off steam, in safe surroundings. We also have both outdoor and under-cover picnic areas.
17 Feb-28 Oct daily, Nov-Dec Sat-Sun 10.00-17.00, 17-22 Dec daily
A£6.50 C(3-14) £5.50, Family Ticket (A2+C2) £23.00. Season tickets & group discounts available, groups of 15+ are given a fully guided tour at no extra charge. Tours are tailored to suit the age range or particular interest of the group and must be pre-booked

Discount Offer: One Child Free

Archaeology

Butser Ancient Farm

Nexus House Gravel House Waterlooville Hampshire PO8 0QE
Tel: 023 9259 8838
A reconstructed British Iron Age (circa 300BC) farm. Features buildings, structures, animals and crops of the era.

Art Galleries

ArtSway

Station Road Sway Lymington Hampshire SO41 6BA
Tel: 01590 682260
ArtSway presents a high quality changing exhibition programme of contemporary visual art in a unique environment deep in the New Forest.

Sandham Memorial Chapel

Harts Lane Burghclere Hampshire RG20 9JT
Tel: 01635 278394 Fax: 01635 278394
www.nationaltrust.org.uk/sandham

[4mi S Newbury, 0.5mi E of A34. Rail: Newbury 4mi. Limited parking nearby]

This red brick chapel was built in the 1920s for the artist Stanley Spencer to fill with paintings of his experiences in the First World War. Inspired by Giotto's Arena Chapel in Padua, Spencer took five years to complete what is arguably his finest achievement. This extraordinary project illustrates the artist's experiences as a medical orderly and as a soldier in Macedonia. He celebrates the everyday routine of a soldier's life with an intensely personal religious faith, reaching its triumphant climax with the huge Resurrection of the Soldiers, which completely fills the east wall and dominates the entire chapel. The chapel is set amidst lawns and orchards with views across to Watership Down. Photography allowed in orchard. Note: There is no lighting in the chapel, it is best to view the paintings on a bright day. Wheelchair access via portable ramps. Dogs on leads in grounds.

3-18 Mar & 3-25 Nov Sat & Sun 11.00-16.00, 28 Mar-28 Oct Wed-Sun 11.00-17.00, 1-16 Dec Sat & Sun 11.00-15.00. Also open Bank Hol Mon. Other times by appointment only, & groups must book in advance

A£3.50 C£1.75 NT Members £Free

Southampton City Art Gallery

North Guild Civic Centre Commercial Road Southampton Hampshire SO14 7LP
Tel: 023 8063 2601
This is the largest gallery in the south of England, with the finest collection of contemporary art in the country outside London.

St Barbe Museum and Art Gallery

New Street Lymington Hampshire SO41 9BH
Tel: 01590 676969
St. Barbe Museum & Art Gallery tells the special story of the coastal strip between the New Forest and The Solent.

Arts, Crafts and Textiles

Whitchurch Silk Mill

28 Winchester Street Whitchurch Hampshire RG28 7AL
Tel: 01256 892065
Whitchurch Silk Mill was built on the River Test in Hampshire two hundred years ago.

Birds, Butterflies & Bees

Hawk Conservancy Trust

Sarson Lane Weyhill Andover SP11 8DY
Tel: 01264 773850 Fax: 01264 773772
www.hawkconservancy.org
[Signposted from A303. Plenty of on-site parking]

The Hawk Conservancy Trust, Andover, is a national award-winning family tourist attraction. Set in 22 acres of grounds (including woodland and a wildflower meadow), there is plenty to do for the whole family. There are three Bird-of-Prey flying displays every day (including the spectacular 2pm 'Valley of the Eagles' display), each featuring a different team of birds. Children can complete our 'Raptor Passport Trail' and nature trail, and enjoy the fun of ferret and runner duck racing. All visitors can hold a British Bird-of-Prey, and either walk or take a tractor ride around our beautiful wildflower meadow. Adults also have the opportunity to fly a Harris Hawk. Our facilities include: Gift Shop, Coffee Shop (serving light lunches and snacks throughout the day), BBQ (weekends and school holidays, when weather permits), Education Centre and Bird-of-Prey hospital. For more information please call or visit our website.

17 Feb-28 Oct daily 10.30-17.30. Nov-Feb Sat-Sun 10.30-17.30

A£9.00 C£5.75 OAPs£8.25 Students£8.00, Family Ticket (A2+C2) £28.50

Discount Offer: £1.00 off Child Admissions

Country Parks & Estates

Itchen Valley Country Park

Allington Lane West End Eastleigh
Southampton Hampshire SO30 3HQ
Tel: 023 8046 6091
A large area of unspoilt countryside beside the
River Itchen.

Queen Elizabeth Country Park

Gravel Hill Horndean Waterlooville Hampshire
PO8 0QE
Tel: 023 9259 5040
Hampshire's biggest country park. 1,400 acres
of open access woodland and downland.

Staunton Country Park

Middle Park Way Havant Hampshire PO9 5HB
Tel: 023 9245 3405
1000 acres of landscaped parkland and ancient
woodland.

Festivals & Shows

Winchester Hat Fair

Winchester Hampshire SO23 8RZ
Tel: 01962 849841
www.hatfair.co.uk
*[Various venues. Winchester is 70mi from London
& 9mi from Southampton. M3, J9/10 (Park &
Ride service at J) & follow signs to Winchester
City Centre. Rail: Winchester]*
Hat Fair is England's longest running free festival
of street theatre. More than 40 theatre companies from all over the world will perform in and
around the city, alongside workshops, large
scale theatre performances, pyrotechnic shows
and late night cabaret. Hat Fair is a FREE event;
it gets its name from the traditional voluntary
contribution of money in the hat to street performers. It draws an audience of around 50,000
people of all ages from all over Britain.
28 June-1 July 2007, 11.00-Late
Admission Free, donations welcome

Folk & Local History Museums

Breamore House and Countryside Museum

Breamore Fordingbridge Hampshire SP6 2DF
Tel: 01725 512468 Fax: 01725 512858
[On A338. Plenty of on-site parking available]

Breamore House is set in its own beautiful parkland amid surrounding farms and fields. The
grandeur and magnificence of the house has
changed little over the past 400 years. It is the
family home of the Hulses whose collections
include paintings, furniture, needlework and
porcelain. Life in a typical village like Breamore
can be relived in the Breamore Countryside
Museum which provides a fascinating insight
into the days when a village was self-sufficient.
Visitors can see full size replicas of a farm work-
er's cottage before the advent of electricity, a
blacksmith shop, a dairy, a wheelwright's shop,
a brewery, a saddler's shop and a cobbler's
shop. The village shop, school, cooperage, bak-
ers, laundry, village garage and clock maker
represent recent developments. The museum
also boasts one of the finest collections of
steam powered farm machinery. There is also a
children's adventure playground and the Great
British Maze.
*House: Easter weekend, Apr Tue & Sun, May-
Sept Tue-Thur, Sat-Sun & all Bank Hols, 14.00-
17.30. Countryside Museum: as House 13.00-
17.30*
A£7.00 C(5-16)£5.00 C(0-4)£Free
Concessions£6.00, Family Ticket (A2+C2)
£17.00

Discount Offer: Two for the Price of One

City Museum and Records Office

Museum Road Portsmouth Hampshire PO1 2LJ
Tel: 023 9282 7261 Fax: 023 9287 5276
www.portsmouthmuseums.co.uk
*[M27/M275 into Portsmouth, follow museum
symbol then City Museum on brown signposts.
Rail: Harbour Station, 10min walk. Bus: No. 6.
Limited on-site parking available]*

The museum is dedicated to local history and
fine and decorative art. 'The Story of
Portsmouth' displays room settings showing life
in Portsmouth from the seventeenth century to
the 1950s using modern audio-visual techniques. Experience the different life-styles of the
Victorian working poor in the 'Dockyard
Workers Cottage' and the affluent 'Victorian
Parlour'. A 1930s kitchen with everything
including the kitchen sink! A 1930s 'Art Deco'
dining room and a 1950s front room complete
with flying ducks on the wall and early television
showing "Listen With Mother". The 'Portsmouth
at Play' exhibition looks at all aspects of leisure
pursuits from the Victorian period to the 1970s.
"What the Butler Saw" machines on the pier, a
"Pennyfarthing" cycle and film archive's from the
1930s and 1960s. The museum has a temporary exhibition gallery with regular changing
exhibitions. New for 2007 - The World of
Sherlock Holmes, Sir Arthur Conan Doyle and
the creation of a hero exhibition. *All year Apr-
Sept daily 10.00-17.30, Oct-Mar daily 10.00-
17.00. Closed 24-26 Dec*
Admission Free

Havant Museum

East Street Havant Hampshire PO9 1BS
Tel: 023 9245 1155
The museum shares the former Town Hall build-
ing with a flourishing arts centre.

Westgate Museum

High Street Winchester Hampshire SO23 9AX
Tel: 01962 848269
This small museum of historical objects is
housed in the rooms over the medieval
Westgate of the city. No wheelchair access.

Forests & Woods

New Forest Museum and Visitor Centre

Main Car Park High Street Lyndhurst SO43 7NY

Tel: 023 8028 3444 Fax: 023 8028 4236
The Living Forest audio-visual show and exhibi-
tion displays, that include life-size models of
Forest characters and the famous New Forest
embroidery, bring to life the Forest's history, tra-
ditions, characters and wildlife.
Daily 10.00-17.00
A£3.00 Concessions£2.50 C(under8)£Free

Gardens & Horticulture

Bramdean House

Bramdean Alresford Hampshire SO24 0JU
Tel: 01962 771214
Famous mirror image herbaceous borders and
large collection of unusual plants.

Exbury Gardens and Steam Railway

The Estate Office Exbury Southampton Hampshire SO45 1AZ

Tel: 023 8089 1203 / 8089 9422
Fax: 023 8089 9940
www.exbury.co.uk

[3mi from Beaulieu off B3054, 20min from J2 M27. Plenty of on-site parking available]

Natural beauty is in abundance at Exbury Gardens, a 200 acre woodland garden on the east bank of the Beaulieu River. Created by Lionel de Rothschild in the 1920s, the Gardens are a stunning vision of his inspiration. The spring displays of rhododendrons, azaleas, camellias and magnolias are world famous. The daffodil meadow, rock garden, sundial garden, herbaceous borders, ponds and cascades ensure year round interest, and why not 'let our steam train take the strain' on a 1 1/4 mile journey over a bridge, through a tunnel across a pond in the Summer Lane Garden planted with bulbs, herbaceous perennials and grasses? Then travel along the top of the rock garden and across a viaduct into the American Garden. Fun for all the family and a day out at Exbury that the weather cannot spoil. Dogs allowed on short lead. Neighbouring 'Maize Maze' open Summer Holidays.

17 Mar-11 Nov daily 10.00-17.30 or dusk if earlier (includes Bank Hols)
High Season 17 Mar-10 June: A£7.50 C(under3)£Free C(3-15)£1.50 Concessions£7.00, Family Ticket (A2+C3) £17.50. Railway an additional £3.00 per person. Low Season: A£6.50 C(under3)£Free C(3-15)£1.50 Concessions£6.00 Family Ticket(A2+C3) £15.00. Railway an additional £3.00 per person. All paying visitors in High Season (17 Mar-10 June) will receive a free voucher to return to Exbury in Oct-Nov to see the autumn colours

Discount Offer: One Child Free

Heritage & Industrial

Beaulieu

John Montagu Building Beaulieu Brockenhurst Hampshire SO42 7ZN

Tel: 01590 612345 Fax: 01590 612624
www.beaulieu.co.uk

[Follow brown signs from J2 (M27). Plenty of on-site parking available]

Come to Beaulieu in the heart of the New Forest and discover the many delights that one of the South's leading tourist attractions has to offer. The National Motor Museum has over 250 vintage, veteran and classic cars, from the World Land-Speed Record Breakers and F1 racers to family cars of the 1970s. A ride on 'Wheels' will take you on a fascinating journey through 100 years of motoring history. Don't miss the James Bond Experience featuring the Lotus Submarine Car (recently voted the nation's favourite on-screen car). In Palace House (home of the Montagu family since 1538) tales from the butler, cook and housemaids give a fascinating insight into the workings of a Victorian household. The thirteenth-century abbey features an exhibition and film about the life of its Cistercian monk founders, while the Secret Army Exhibition tells the story of wartime Beaulieu and the training of secret agents.
1 Oct-25 May 10.00-17.00, 26 May-30 Sep 10.00-18.00. Closed 25 Dec
Please call or visit website for admission prices

Hollycombe Steam Collection

Midhurst Road Liphook Hampshire GU30 7LP
Tel: 01428 724900 Fax: 01428 723682
www.hollycombe.co.uk

[Off A3 (2mi SE). Follow brown tourist signs or local signs for Milland. Plenty of on-site parking available]

Britain's largest collection of working steam, Hollycombe is much more than an enthusiast's museum. Rather than just studying engines from the past, there is a complete, working Edwardian fairground and three different railways, all of which visitors can ride on. The emphasis is on enjoyment while recreating the golden age of steam, from a time when Britain was great. In addition, there are rides behind a steam traction engine, old film shows in the Bioscope, the forerunner of town cinemas, agricultural machinery and a whole lot more, all set in acres of historic woodland gardens. A new visitor centre brings the experience up to date while information signs and a brand new gallery around the site explain what is on show. While there are special events throughout the season, late May brings out the best in the gardens when the azaleas and rhododendrons are in flower.

1 Apr-6 Oct Sun & Bank Hols, 29 July-27 Aug daily 12.00-17.00, rides from 13.00

A£10.00 C£8.50 OAPs£9.00 Saver Ticket£35.00(A2+C3)

Discount Offer: One Child Free

Historical

Gilbert White's House and the Oates Museum

The Wakes High Street Selborne Alton Hampshire GU34 3JH
Tel: 01420 511275 Fax: 01420 511040
www.gilbertwhiteshouse.org.uk

[In Selborne town centre (on B3006). Free car park behind the Selborne Arms pub]

Gilbert White's House and the Oates Museum is set in a charming eighteenth-century house, once the home of the Rev. Gilbert White (1720-93), famous naturalist and author of 'The Natural History and Antiquities of Selborne'. Over 20 acres of garden and parkland, largely restored to its eighteenth-century form. Garden tours and introductory talks can be arranged for groups. The Oates Museum includes an exhibition about Lawrence Oates and his tragic death on Captain Scott's ill-fated expedition to the South Pole in 1911. Facilities include Tea Parlour serving delicious fare, much of it based on eighteenth-century recipes, such as Homity Pie and Toasted Wigs. Excellent shop stocking many unusual gifts.

All year Tue-Sun 11.00-17.00. Open daily June-Aug. Closed 23 Dec-1 Jan
A£6.50 C£Free Concessions£5.50. Group rates (10+): A£5.00 C£3.50

Discount Offer: Two for the Price of One

Southsea Castle

Clarence Esplanade Southsea Hampshire
PO5 3PA
Tel: 023 9282 7261 Fax: 023 9287 5276
www.portsmouthmuseums.co.uk
*[M27/M275 into Portsmouth, or A3(M), A27,
A2030 follow Seafront symbol then Southsea
Castle on brown signposts. Rail: Harbour Station.
Bus: No. 6 to Palmerston Rd (shopping area)
then 7min walk. Plenty of on-site parking avail-
able]*
This castle was built in 1544 as part of Henry
VIII's national coastal defences. In our amazing
Time Tunnel Experience, the ghost of the cas-
tle's first Master Gunner guides you through
dramatic scenes from the castle's eventful histo-
ry. Tudor, Civil War and Victorian history. Audio-
visual presentation and underground passages.
Apr-Sept daily 10.00-17.30 Oct 10.00-17.00
A£3.50 Concessions£2.50 OAPs£3.00, Family
Ticket (A2+C2) £9.50. Two free children under
13 free with full paying adult. Group rates available on request

**Discount Offer: 20% off Adult
Admissions**

The Vyne

Vyne Road Sherborne St. John Basingstoke
Hampshire RG24 9HL
Tel: 01256 883858
With over 500 years of history and 1000 acres
of beautiful gardens and parkland to explore,
The Vyne has something for everyone to enjoy.

Winchester College

College Street Winchester Hampshire
SO23 9HA
Tel: 01962 621209 Fax: 01962 621166
www.winchestercollege.org
*[From N J9 M3, from S J10 M3. Limited on-site
parking available]*

Founded in 1382, Winchester College is
believed to be the oldest continuously running
school in the country. Concentrating on the
medieval heart of the College, guided tours last
approximately 1 hour and include Chamber
Court (which takes its name from the Scholars'
and Fellows' chambers which surround it), the
Gothic Chapel (whose fourteenth-century vaulted roof is one of the earliest examples constructed from wood rather than stone), College
Hall (the original Scholars' dining room), the
School (a seventeenth-century red-brick schoolroom built in the style of Christopher Wren), and
the original Cloister, which contains a memorial
to Mallory the mountaineer.

*Guided Tours: All year daily except Christmas &
New Year. For individuals and small groups - walk
in tours Mon, Wed, Fri & Sat 10.45, 12.00,
14.15, 15.30; Tue & Thur 10.45, 12.00; Sun
14.15, 15.30. Group tours for parties of 10+
people can be arranged at times to suit but must
be booked in advance*

A£3.50 Concessions£3.00

Literature & Libraries

Charles Dickens' Birthplace

393 Old Commercial Road Portsmouth
Hampshire PO1 4QL
Tel: 023 9282 7261 Fax: 023 9287 5276
www.portsmouthmuseums.co.uk
*[From M275 turn L at 'The News' roundabout, fol-
low signpost for Charles Dickens Birthplace]*

Built in 1805, this is Dickens' birthplace and
early home. Restored and furnished to illustrate
middle-class taste of the early nineteenth centu-
ry, the museum displays items pertaining to
Dickens' work and the couch on which he died.
There are Dickens' readings at 15.00 on the first
Sunday of each month.
*Apr-Sept daily 10.00-17.30, Charles Dickens
Birthday 7 Feb 10.00-17.00*
A£3.50 Concessions£2.50 OAPs£3.00 Family
Ticket (A2+C2) £9.50. Two free children under
13 free with full paying adult. Group rates avail-
able on request

Discount Offer: 20% off Adult Admissions

Jane Austen's House

Chawton Alton Hampshire GU34 1SD
Tel: 01420 83262
The house is where Jane Austen lived and
wrote from 1809 to 1817.

Living History Museums

Milestones, Hampshire's Living History Museum

Leisure Park Churchill Way West Basingstoke
Hampshire RG21 6YR
Tel: 01256 477766 Fax: 01256 477784
www.milestones-museum.com
*[M3 J6, take ringway W & follow brown signs for
Leisure Park. Plenty of on-site parking available]*
Milestones brings Hampshire's recent past to
life all under one roof, inside one of the biggest
buildings in Basingstoke. Set within a recreated
town that encompasses houses, shops, facto-
ries and even a pub, a network of streets take
the visitor back in time, and on a journey
through the changing conditions and changing
technologies from the late Victorian era to
1940s Britain. Using the free audio guides, discover how a blacksmith turned car repairer, visit
a workshop with working machinery, learn how
different forms of transport were developed. See
how local industrialists responded to the changing technologies of the twentieth century and
world events in the nationally important collections of Thornycroft, Tasker and Wallis and
Steven's industrial vehicles all set in a realistic
context. Historical characters and for families,
hands-on activities, all add to the special
atmosphere of a visit to Milestones. Special
events and exhibitions throughout the year.
*All year Tue-Fri 10.00-17.00, Sat & Sun 11.00-
17.00, Bank Hol 10.00-17.00. Closed Mon, 25-
26 Dec & 1 Jan*
A£7.25 C(under5)£Free C(5-15)£4.25
Concessions£6.50, Family Ticket(A2+C2)
£21.00. Schools Visit C£3.60. Group rates:
(15+) A£5.00
Discount Offer: Two for the Price of One

Maritime

Portsmouth Historic Dockyard

Visitor Centre Victory Gate Portsmouth
Hampshire PO1 3LJ
Tel: 023 9283 9766 Fax: 023 9283 8228
www.historicdockyard.co.uk

*[5mi from M27 J12. M275 into Portsmouth & fol-
low 'Historic Waterfront' signs]*

Portsmouth Historic Dockyard is home to three
famous warships, Admiral Lord Nelson's HMS
Victory, the first iron hulled armoured battleship
HMS Warrior 1860 and King Henry VIII's
favourite warship the Mary Rose which sank in
1545. Attractions also include Action Stations,
which provides interactive displays and simula-
tors on the modern day Navy, the Royal Naval
Museum, Harbour Tours cruises and not to forget a range of retail and catering outlets. A
great day out for all the family at Portsmouth
Historic Dockyard. There will be a full calendar
of events happening throughout the year so be
sure to visit our website for more information.
*All year daily Apr-Oct 10.00-18.00, last ticket sold
16.30. Nov-Mar 10.00-17.30, last ticket sold
16.00. Closed 24-26 Dec*
An all-inclusive ticket gives one entry to each
attraction: A£16.00 Concessions£13.00, Family
Ticket (A2+C3) £46.00

**Discount Offer: 20% off One All-
Inclusive Ticket**

Royal Marines Museum

Eastney Esplanade Southsea Hampshire
PO4 9PX
Tel: 023 9281 9385 Fax: 023 9283 8420
www.royalmarinesmuseum.co.uk

*[M27, M3, A3M to Portsmouth Southsea front, at
Eastney follow brown tourist signs. Plenty of on-
site parking & dog 'park' available]*

At this award winning museum, in what was
one of the most stately Officers Messes in
England you can discover the exciting 340 year
story of the Royal Marines brought to life
through dramatic and interactive displays and
tour its world famous medal collection. Come
and find out for yourself how Hannah Snell
posed as a man and served as a marine in India
in 1740. Explore the Jungle warfare room but
watch out for the live snake and scorpion! Find
out how the elite troops of the Royal Marines
were closely involved in both World Wars, Battle
of Trafalgar, Falklands War - the list goes on.
Every year the Royal Marines play a key part in
resolving conflicts and keeping peace around
the world - here's your chance to see it all under
one roof. It's the closest you'll get to experiencing life as a Royal Marine without joining up!

*June-Aug daily 10.00-17.00, Sept-May daily
10.00-16.30. Closed 24-26 Dec*

A£5.25 C&Students(NUS/USI)£3.25
OAPs£4.25. Disabled£3.00. Group rates (10+):
10% discount (organiser & coach driver £Free)
Schools rates £Free plus 1 Teacher £Free for
each 8 children, Cadets £1.00 per head

**Discount Offer: Two for the Price of
One**

Royal Navy Submarine Museum

Haslar Jetty Road Gosport Hampshire
PO12 2AS
Tel: 023 9252 9217 Fax: 023 9251 1349
www.rnsubmus.co.uk
[Plenty of on-site parking available]

Dive into the past and the future and explore the challenges of the deep! Discover all about submarines and the men who sailed and fought in them. It's a story of remarkable bravery and exciting adventures, revealing how we grew to understand the science and dangers of the sea. Enjoy a guided tour of our World War 2 vintage submarine HMS Alliance, step onboard the fully restored Holland 1 (from 1901) and see inside X24, the only surviving World War 2 midget submarine. Command your own submarine and discover the power of the ocean and the secrets of the deep in our six interactive zones, or re-live life under the sea in our four History Galleries, which contain the personal belongings of submariners and a fascinating collection of photographs, artefacts and archive material. If you are feeling hungry, visit the Jolly Roger Café or take home a souvenir from our gift shop.

All year daily 10.00-17.30 (16.30 Nov-Mar). Closed 24-25 Dec
A£6.50 C&OAPs£5.00, Family Ticket (A2+C4) £15.00

Discount Offer: 25% off Admissions

D-Day Museum and Overlord Embroidery

Clarence Esplanade Southsea PO5 3NT
Tel: 023 9282 7261 Fax: 023 9287 5276
www.portsmouthmuseums.co.uk
[M27/M275 into Portsmouth, follow museum symbol then D-Day Museum on brown signposts. Rail: Harbour Station. Bus: No. 6 to Palmerston Rd (shopping area) then 7min walk]

Visit this year and see the Faces of History (Winston Churchill, Montgomery and Eisenhower) come alive in the magnificent 83 metre 'Overlord Embroidery' depicting scenes of 'Operation Overlord' - 6 June 1944. The Museum's unique and dramatic film show, which includes original, historic footage and archive film bringing this period of the Second World War alive to the visitor. Experience life on the 'Home Front' in an Anderson Shelter and the period front room of the ARP Warden. 'Listen While You Work' in the factory scene; keep vigil with the troops camped in the forest waiting their time to embark; eavesdrop on communications in 'The Map Room', Southwick House. Listen to the story behind the crashed Horda Glider; pass through the German pillbox to the 'Beach Landing' gallery with video / archive film of the landings and interactive touch screens. Tanks, jeep, Dingo Scout Car, anti-aircraft gun, military equipment, models, photographs, uniforms and veteran's memories, make this museum a necessity for military history enthusiasts.

All year daily Apr-Sept 10.00-17.30, Oct-Mar 10.00-17.00. Closed 24-26 Dec. Cafe facilities available May-Sept only
A£6.00 Concessions£4.20 OAPs£5.00, Family Ticket (A2+C2) £16.20. Group rates available

Discount Offer: 20% off Admissions

Explosion! The Museum of Naval Firepower

Priddy's Hard Heritage Way Gosport PO12 4LE
Tel: 023 9250 5600 Fax: 023 9250 5605
www.explosion.org.uk
[J11 M27, Follow A32 to Gosport & brown signs to Explosion! Rail: mainline route London to Portsmouth Harbour. Take ferry to Gosport (3min) then turn R & follow brown tourist signs (20min walk) or taxi to Forton Lake Bridge (3min). Plenty of on-site parking] Explosion! the Museum of Naval Firepower, is a hands on, interactive Museum set in the historic setting of a former gunpowder and munitions depot at Priddy's Hard, on the Gosport side of Portsmouth Harbour. Priddy's Hard was once a busy Naval Armament supply depot that provided the Royal Navy with its ammunition for over two hundred years. Telling the story of naval warfare from the days gunpowder to modern missiles, the two hour tour of the museum includes a stunning multi media film show set in the original eighteenth-century gunpowder vault, with the latest technology and interactive touch screens that bring the presentations to life. There's a fascinating social history too, including the story of how 2,500 women worked on the site during its peak in World War II. The Museum describes the role that Priddy's Hard played in naval operations worldwide for over 200 years, as well as its importance to the local Gosport community, which not only armed the Navy but also fed it.
All year Weekends only, 10.00-16.00
A£4.00 C(under5)£Free C(5-16)&Concessions£2.00 OAPs£3.00, Family Ticket£10.00

Discount Offer: Two for the Price of One

Royal Hampshire Regiment Museum and Memorial Garden

Serle's House Southgate Street Winchester Hampshire SO23 9EG
Tel: 01962 863658
www.royalhampshireregimentmuseum.co.uk

[Between St Thomas's Church & Hotel Du Vin]

This fine eighteenth-century early Georgian House contains an excellent collection of militaria showing the history of the Royal Hampshire Regiment 1702-1992. It includes weapons, medals, uniforms and many individual artefacts, the whole brought to life with pictures and photographs. The gardens in front of the house are maintained by the regiment as is the War Memorial and Garden of Remembrance. Photography is permitted on request. Families and children are welcome. An extensive archive exists from which information about the Regiment and its members can be provided - a telephone call in advance is advised.
All year Mon-Fri 10.00-16.00, Apr-Oct additional weekends & Bank Hol 12.00-16.00. Closed for 2 weeks during Christmas-New Year period
Admission Free

Mills - Water & Wind

Eling Tide Mill

Eling Hill Totton Southampton Hampshire SO40 9HF
Tel: 023 8086 9575
See natural tide power harnessed in the only surviving tide mill, still in regular production.

Nature & Conservation Parks

New Forest Otter, Owl and Wildlife Conservation Park

Deerleap Lane Longdown Marchwood
Southampton Hampshire SO40 4UH
Tel: 023 8029 2408 Fax: 023 8029 3367
www.ottersandowls.co.uk

[From M27 take exit 3 onto M271 signposted to Southampton Docks. At roundabout turn R onto A35 to Lyndhurst & Bournemouth. Follow brown tourist signs through two roundabouts then turn L into Deerleap Lane. We are just a mile down this rd. Plenty of on-site parking available]

An acknowledged Conservation Park set in 25 acres of ancient woodland within the New Forest National Park. Here you will find one of Europe's largest gathering of otters, owls and other indigenous wildlife all in their natural surroundings including pine martens, badgers, polecats, mink, foxes, Scottish wildcats, deer, lynx, wallabies and wild boar. Stroll through the animal house and watch otters swimming under water, ferrets chasing their tails and harvest mice building their homes on the top of corn stooks. Then take the Wildlife Walkabout past more otters to the Owlery and to all the other interesting animals. Throughout the day there are Keeper Sessions where you can learn more about them.

All year daily 10.00-17.30, weekends only in Jan
A£6.95 C£4.95, Family Ticket (A2+C2) £20.50.
Season Ticket: A£28.00 C£20.00, Family Ticket (A2+C2) £90.00

Discount Offer: One Child Free

Places of Worship

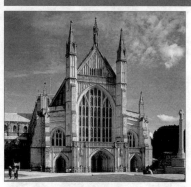

Winchester Cathedral

1 The Close Winchester Hampshire SO23 9LS
Tel: 01962 857200 Fax: 01962 857201
www.winchester-cathedral.org.uk

Explore more than 1000 year's of England's past. Walk in the footsteps of kings, saints, pilgrims, writers and artists in Europe's longest medieval cathedral. Uncover the secrets of how a diver saved the cathedral from collapse and learn why Jane Austen was buried in the nave. There's also a free children's trail available for families. The Cathedral Café (with its open-air terrace and spectacular views) has won awards for its architecture and food. The Cathedral Shop has a unique range of gifts and souvenirs, including CDs of the Cathedral Choir. A wide range of events take place throughout the year including exhibitions, markets, outside theatre, concerts and much more. Please visit our website for more information.

All year daily: Mon-Sat 08.30-18.00, Sun 08.30-17.30. Varies for services and special events
A£5.00 C(under16)£Free Concessions£4.00.
Group rate: £4.00 (please call 01962 857225)

Railways

Eastleigh Lakeside Railway

Lakeside Country Park Eastleigh Hampshire
Tel: 023 8061 2020
A miniature railway running to Monks Brook.

Royal Victoria Railway

Royal Victoria Country Park Netley Abbey
Southampton Hampshire SO31 5GA
Tel: 023 8045 6246
A scenic, one mile, ten and a quarter inch
gauge passenger miniature railway.

Watercress Line

The Railway Station Alresford Hampshire
SO24 9JG
Tel: 01962 733810 Fax: 01962 735448
www.watercressline.co.uk

*[Alresford & Alton stations are signposted off A31
Guildford to Winchester rd, follow brown tourist
signs. Leave J9 or J10 M3]*

Experience history in motion at the Mid-Hants
Railway 'Watercress Line'. Travel by steam or
heritage diesel train through 10 miles of beautiful Hampshire countryside between Alresford
and Alton. Many of our locomotives have been
fully restored by the engineering skills of volunteers. You can either join the line at the
Georgian town of Alresford (near Winchester) or
Alton, a bustling market town. On your journey
you can stop at Ropley and Medstead and Four
Marks stations and marvel at their preserved
history. We hold special events. We also run
pre-booked luxury dining trains, refreshments,
picnic areas, gift shops and children's play area.
*Jan-end Oct Sat-Sun & Bank Hols plus Tue-Thur
May-Sept*
Unlimited All-Day Travel: A£10.00 C(2-16)£5.00,
Family Ticket (A2+C2) £25.00

**Discount Offer: Two for the Price of
One**

Rockbourne Roman Villa

Rockbourne Fordingbridge Hampshire SP6 3PG
Tel: 01725 518541
Discovered in 1942, these remains of a 40-
room Roman Villa represent a fine display of
mosaics and hypocaust.

Natural History Museum and Butterfly House

Cumberland House Eastern Parade Portsmouth
Hampshire PO1 3JN
Tel: 023 9282 7261 Fax: 023 9287 5276
www.portsmouthmuseums.co.uk
*[M27/M275 into Portsmouth, follow Seafront sym-
bol then Southsea Castle on brown signposts. Or
A3(M), A27, A2030, follow Seafront then Castle
signposts. Rail: Harbour Station. Bus: No. 6 to
Festing Rd]*

The geology and natural history of the area are
explained, with a full-size reconstruction of a
dinosaur, a fresh water aquarium and British
and European free-flying butterflies. There are
seasonal displays of woodland, downland and
marshland ecology. New displays explore the
redisplayed area to discover more about
dinosaurs, butterflies and wildlife in our area.
Visit our new hands-on activities.
*Mar 10.00-17.00, Apr-Sept daily 10.00-17.30,
Oct-Mar 10.00-17.00. Closed 24-26 Dec*
Admission free. Children under 13 must be
accompanied by an adult

Sealife Centres & Aquariums

Blue Reef Aquarium

Clarence Esplanade Southsea Portsmouth
Hampshire PO5 3PB
Tel: 023 9287 5222 Fax: 023 9229 4443
www.bluereefaquarium.co.uk
[Situated on seafront rd midway between two piers. Signposted]

Take the ultimate undersea safari at the award winning Blue Reef Aquarium where there's a world of underwater adventure just waiting to be discovered. Over 40 living displays reveal the sheer variety of life in the deep; from native sharks, lobsters and adorable otters to seahorses, fascinating frogs and exotic fish. At the aquarium's heart is a giant ocean tank where an underwater walkthrough tunnel offers incredibly close encounters with the stunning beauty of a tropical coral reef - home of hundreds of colourful fish. Blue Reef is a great place for visitors of all ages to discover more about the wonders of the deep. There's a full programme of entertaining, informative talks and feeding displays throughout the day. Learn more about native sea creatures including crabs, anemones and starfish at our popular Rockpool Encounters where our experts will be on hand to answer all your questions. A spectacular experience whatever the weather.
All year daily from 10.00. Closed 25 Dec only
A£7.95 C(3-16)£5.50 Concessions£6.95

Discount Offer: One Child Free

Theme & Adventure Parks

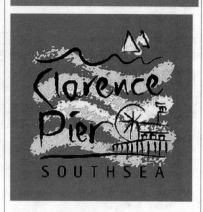

Clarence Pier

Clarence Esplanade Southsea PO5 3AA
Tel: 023 9282 1455 Fax: 023 9281 2552
www.clarencepier.co.uk

The original Clarence Pier was built in 1861, and was opened by the Prince and Princess of Wales who attended a concert given by the combined band of the Royal Marines Artillery and Royal Marines Light Infantry. Up until 1873 the Pier had a tramline from Portsmouth Town Railway Station (now Portsmouth & Southsea), which ran right onto the Pier, taking passengers and luggage to the Isle of Wight on steamers. In 1905 the Pier was extended to accommodate increased boat traffic. Further extensions were made in 1932 when a café, sun deck and concourse hall were added. Then on 1st June 1941 the Pier was bombed by the Luftwaffe during the heaviest air raid on Portsmouth of World War Two. It re-opened in its present form some twenty years later on 1st June 1961; the Pier with its funfair has been synonymous with Southsea, it boasted favourite concert parties and shows, and ever-changing rides and slot machines, video games etc., but many people's abiding memory of the Pier is the laughing sailor machine which stood outside. For a penny you could make him split his sides. The original machine has been preserved and is still owned by the present proprietors.
Mar-Sept daily 9.00-21.30. Closed 25 Dec
Pier: Admission Free, rides 1 token £0.50 with offers of buy 50 for the price of 40 or buy £20 worth & get another £5 worth free

Funland Amusement Park

1 Sea Front Hayling Island Hampshire
PO11 0AG
Tel: 023 9246 2820
A variety of attractions open subject to maintenance and weather conditions. Height Restrictions may apply.

Paultons Park

Ower Romsey Hampshire SO51 6AL
Tel: 023 8081 4455
Family leisure park with over 40 different attractions and rides. Dinosaurland, Kids Kingdom, Tiny Tots Town, Rabbit Ride and Magic Forest where nursery rhymes come to life. See the history of English gypsies in the Romany Experience.

Transport Museums

Sammy Miller Museum

Bashley Cross Road New Milton Hampshire
BH25 5SZ

Tel: 01425 620777

The museum complex is set in glorious countryside on the border of the New Forest. The complex has a number of attractions including a museum, spares shop, animal area, children's play area and tea rooms. This motor bike museum has machines dating back to 1900 with many machines that are the only surviving ones in the world.

Wildlife & Safari Parks

Hawthorn's Urban Wildlife Centre

The Common Southampton Hampshire
SO15 7NN
Tel: 023 8067 1921
Hawthorn's is a wildlife haven in the centre of the city with an information centre displaying live exhibits and hands-on activity room.

Zoos

Marwell Zoological Park

Colden Common Winchester Hampshire
SO21 1JH
Tel: 01962 777407 Fax: 01962 777511
www.marwell.org.uk
[J5 M27, J11 M3. Rail: Eastleigh/Winchester. Plenty of free on-site parking available]
Beautiful Marwell is six miles southeast of Winchester in Hampshire and makes a wonderful day out for all the family. There are over 200 species of rare animals including tigers in a magnificent enclosure. Don't miss the snow leopards, rhino and hippo! Marwell has one of Europe's largest collections of rare hoofed animals including zebra and antelope and is dedicated to the conservation of endangered species. There are many popular favourites such as giraffe, meerkats, kangaroos and gibbons. Enjoy the World of Lemurs, Into Africa, Tropical World, Penguin World, the Fossa Exhibit, Aridlands and the Bat House. Road and rail trains, gift shop and adventure playgrounds. Special activity days held throughout the year. Marwell offers a day full of fun and interest for all ages.

All year daily from 10.00. Closed 25 Dec
Please visit website for admission prices

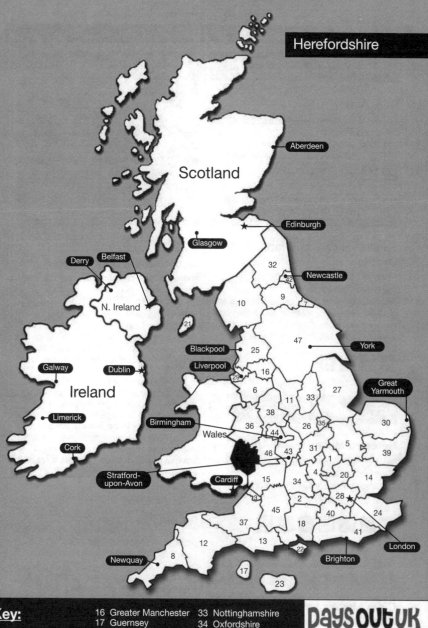

Herefordshire

Aberdeen

Scotland

Edinburgh

Glasgow

32

Newcastle

Derry · Belfast

N. Ireland

10   9   7

21

Galway   Dublin

Ireland   Blackpool   25   47   York

Liverpool   29   16   27   Great Yarmouth

Limerick   6   11   33   30

38   26   35

Cork   Birmingham   36   44   31   5   39

Wales   46   43   1

Stratford-upon-Avon   Cardiff   15   4   20   14

34   2   28   24

Newquay   45   40

37   18   41   London

12   13   22   Brighton

8   17   23

Abbeys

Dore Abbey

Ryefield Wormbridge Herefordshire HR2 9DB
Tel: 01981 570251
The abbey was founded by French monks in
1147. It is remarkable for its wealth of features.

Animal Attractions

Small Breeds Farm Park and Owl Centre

Kington Herefordshire HR5 3HF

Tel: 01544 231109
Discover lots of miniature, rare and unusual animals and birds. Enjoy interacting with the birds.
The Owl Centre has a superb variety of owls
which are beautifully displayed in the intimate
garden setting.

Arts, Crafts & Textiles

Hereford Museum and Art Gallery

Broad Street Hereford Herefordshire HR4 9AU
Tel: 01432 260692
The art gallery has regularly changing exhibitions
of fine art, photography, decorative arts and
crafts.

Food & Drink

Cider Museum and King Offa Distillery

21 Ryelands Street Hereford Herefordshire
HR4 0LW
Tel: 01432 354207
Housed in a former cider works, the museum
tells the fascinating story of cidermaking
through the ages.

Westons Cider Visitors Centre

The Bounds Much Marcle Ledbury
Herefordshire HR8 2NQ
Tel: 01531 660108 Fax: 01531 660619
www.westons-cider.co.uk

[Plenty of on-site parking available]

Nestling on a gentle hillside amongst apple and
perry pear orchards 'Westons Cider' with its
400 year old farmhouse is the centre piece to a
unique day out for all the family. Join a tour
around our cider mill and hear how cider is produced, from the planting of the orchards to the
moment it is poured into a glass. Sample our
ciders and perries free in our shop (adults only).
With our award winning Henry Weston
Courtyard Garden, Bottle Museum Tea Rooms,
Shire Horse Dray Rides, a Traditional and Rare
Breeds Farm Park, a children's playground, a
cider and gift shop and the award winning
Scrumpy House restaurant and bar, there is
something for everyone.

*All year Mon-Fri 9.00-16.30, Sat & Sun 10.00-
16.00, Cider Tours: daily 11.00 & 14.30, Farm
Park: Easter-end Sept Mon-Fri 9.00-16.30, Sat &
Sun 10.00-16.00. Christmas hol times may differ
please check our website for details*
Farm Park: A£2.50 C£1.50, Cider Tours:
A£4.00 C£2.50, Dray rides A£2.50 C£1.50
(phone for availability), Children's play area &
Henry Weston Courtyard Garden £Free

Discount Offer: One Child Free

WESTONS CIDER
— ESTD 1880 —
FREE ENTRY | VISITORS CENTRE

Monday-Friday 9.00-4.30, Saturday-Sunday 10.00-4.00. Park up, stay put and ENJOY...

★ FREE CHILDREN'S PLAY AREA

★ FREE THE HENRY WESTON COURTYARD GARDEN

★ TRADITIONAL & RARE BREEDS FARM PARK Including children's ride-on 'John Deere' pedal tractors. Open from Easter til the end of September. Admission prices: Adult: £2.50, Child £1.50.

★ THE BOTTLE MUSEUM TEA ROOMS Home-made sandwiches, cakes and cream teas.

★ SHIRE HORSE DRAY RIDES Subject to availability. Please call in advance to avoid disappointment.

★ GUIDED MILL TOURS Daily 11am & 2.30pm
Admission prices: Adult £4.00, Child £2.50

★ CIDER & PERRY SHOP, FREE TASTING

★ NEW CELLAR GIFT SHOP

★ FREE PARKING & PICNIC AREA

★ THE SCRUMPY HOUSE
Award-winning restaurant and bar.

Westons Cider
The Bounds, Much Marcle, Ledbury, Herefordshire HR8 2NQ

Telephone: 01531 660108 Website: www.westons-cider.co.uk

Gardens & Horticulture

Hampton Court Gardens
Hope-Under-Dinmore Leominster Herefordshire HR6 0PN
Tel: 01568 797777
Walled flower garden, herbaceous borders, canals, pavilions, follies, maze and secret tunnel, hermit's grotto and waterfalls.

Hergest Croft Gardens
Kington Herefordshire HR5 3EG
Tel: 01544 230160
There are spring and summer borders, unusual vegetables, and old-fashioned roses in the Kitchen Garden. There is also one of the finest collections of trees and shrubs in Britain spread over 50 acres.

Historical

Berrington Hall
Leominster Herefordshire HR6 0DW
Tel: 01568 615721
This seventeenth-century mansion is perfectly situated with stunning views to the Black Mountains and the Brecon Beacons.

Croft Castle
Croft Yarpole Leominster Herefordshire HR6 9PW
Tel: 01568 780246
Croft Castle illustrates the turbulent history of this part of England.

Kinnersley Castle

Kinnersley Herefordshire HR3 6QF
Tel: 01544 327507
Housing various fine oak panelled rooms and
the original 1588 plaster work ceiling of the
solar, it is set in grounds containing yew
hedges, a walled kitchen garden and a notable
ginko tree.

Places of Worship

Hereford Cathedral

5 College Cloisters Cathedral Close Hereford
Herefordshire HR1 2NG
Tel: 01432 374200
Hereford's beautiful Romanesque cathedral
dates from 676, and contains the famous
Mappa Mundi & Chained Library in the new
library building.

Stately Homes

Eastnor Castle

Eastnor Ledbury Herefordshire HR8 1RL
Tel: 01531 633160 Fax: 01531 631776
www.eastnorcastle.com
*[2mi E of Ledbury on A438 Tewkesbury Rd.
Alternatively, J2 M50 then A449/A438 to Eastnor.
Plenty of on-site parking available]*

Fairytale Georgian castle in magical surroundings, with Deer Park, Lake and Arboretum,
which contains the finest collection of Cedars in
Britain. Inside this family home you'll find richly
decorated Gothic interiors by Pugin, Fine Art,
Armour and much more. Adventure Playground
and Assault Course, Knight's Maze, Children's
Fun sheets, Tree trail, Lakeside and Woodland
Walks, tearoom serving light snacks and after-
noon tea and special events programme.
Disabled access, groups welcome. Member of
the Historic Houses Association.
*Easter weekend 5-9 Apr, every Sun & Bank Hol
Mon from 15 Apr-30 Sept. 16 July-31 Aug Sun-
Fri*
Castle & Grounds: A£7.50 C£4.50, Family
Ticket £19.50. Grounds: A£3.50 C£1.50. Group
rate (20+): £6.00. Guided Tours: £9.50

**Discount Offer: Two for the Price of
One**

Hellens Manor

Much Marcle Ledbury Herefordshire HR8 2LY
Tel: 01531 660504
www.hellensmanor.com
*[On Ledbury/Ross Rd (entrance opoposite
church). Plenty of on-site parking available]*
A Jacobean manor house that was named after
Walter de Helyon, who lived here in the fifteenth
century. Hellens has been continuously occupied ever since. See our collection of fine pictures and furniture. The manor is set in tranquil
gardens that feature a labyrinth, knot garden
and Elizabethan garden. A great day out for all
the family.
*Easter Sunday-31 Oct: Wed-Thu, Sun & Bank
Hol Mon 14.00-17.00. Guided tours on the hour
(other times by written appointment)*
A£5.00, Family Ticket £10.00

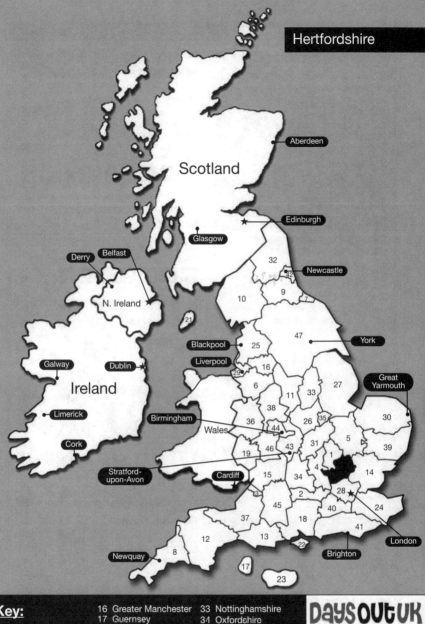

Hertfordshire

Aberdeen

Scotland

Edinburgh

Glasgow

Derry · Belfast

Newcastle

N. Ireland

32

42

Dublin

10

9

7

Galway

Belfast

21

Ireland

Blackpool

25

47

York

Liverpool

16

Limerick

29

6

27

Great Yarmouth

Cork

11

33

30

38

Birmingham

36

26

35

Wales

44

5

39

19

46

43

31

Stratford-upon-Avon

15

34

1

14

Cardiff

13

2

28

London

45

40

24

37

18

41

Brighton

Newquay

12

13

22

8

17

23

Animal Attractions

Willows Farm Village

Coursers Road London Colney St Albans
Hertfordshire AL2 1BB
Tel: 0870 129 9718 Fax: 0870 121 1665
www.willowsfarmvillage.com
[0.25mi from J22 M25, just off Coursers Rd.
Plenty of on-site parking available]

You'll find acres of fun for everyone at Willows
Farm Village. Discover our farmyard favourites,
special events and demonstrations plus enjoy
fun and adventure activities. Don't miss our Daft
Duck Trials, Bird-o-Batics Falconry Displays,
Tristian the Runaway Tractor, Sheepstakes
Sheep Racing, Farmyard Ferret Fun and Guinea
Pig Village. For fun there's the Bouncy
Haystacks trampolines, Tree House Adventure
and Country Fun Fair. Children can pan for gold,
peddle away in our mini tractors and enjoy the
children's shows. There's also a special area just
for the under 5s. A full day out for the whole
family with all events and activities included in
the entrance fee. Activities change throughout
the season please call or visit the website for
the latest information.

From 24 Mar 10.00-17.30
Please visit the website for admission prices

Discount Offer: One Child Free

Arts, Crafts & Textiles

Henry Moore Foundation

Dane Tree House Perry Green Much Hadham
Hertfordshire SG10 6EE
Tel: 01279 843333
Major works are displayed in the grounds and in
the studios where Moore worked.

Letchworth Museum and Art Gallery

Broadway Letchworth Garden City SG6 3PF
Tel: 01462 685647
Geology, art and archaeology galleries.

Caverns & Caves

Royston Cave

Melbourn Street Royston Hertfordshire
SG8 7DA
Tel: 01763 245484
[Nr crossroads Melbourn St & Kneesworth St]

Medieval manmade cave situated beneath the
town centre. Rediscovered in the seventeenth
century and excavated to reveal medieval carvings. Unique to Europe if not the world the cave
remains a mysterious and magical place.
Easter-Sept Sat-Sun 14.30-17.00 and Bank
Holiday Mondays
A£2.00 accompanied C£Free

Country Parks & Estates

Aldenham Country Park

Dagger Lane Elstree Borehamwood
Hertfordshire WD6 3AT
Tel: 020 8953 9602
The park consists of 175 acres of woodland
and parkland set around a large reservoir.

Fairlands Valley Park and Sailing Centre

Six Hills Way Stevenage Hertfordshire SG2 0BL
Tel: 01438 353 241
Fairlands Valley is a park of 120 acres within
which is a sailing centre offering watersports
courses. Paddling-pools and childrens play
area.

Knebworth House, Gardens, Adventure Playground and Park

Knebworth Hertfordshire SG3 6PY
Tel: 01438 812661 Fax: 01438 811908
www.knebworthhouse.com

*[Direct access from J7 A1(M) at Stevenage
South. Plenty of on-site parking available]*

Originally a Tudor manor house this magnificent
stately home with Victorian Gothic decoration is
set in 250 acres of parkland. Family tours of the
house run twice daily with hands on activities.
There is also a British Raj display on India. The
25 acres of formal gardens include the Jekyll
Herb Garden and re-instated Victorian Maze. A
self-guided Monsters and Mazes trail leads you
to discover more about the gardens including
the 72 life size models of dinosaurs in the
Wilderness Garden. Outdoor adventure playground and miniature railway. No dogs permitted in House or Gardens except guide dogs,
dogs permitted with leads in the Park.
*Daily 31 Mar-15 Apr, 26 May-3 June, 30 June-5
Sept. Sat, Sun & Bank Hols 24-25 Mar, 21 Apr-
20 May 9-24 June, 8-30 Sept. Park, Playground
& Gardens: 11.00-17.00. House & Exhibition:
12.00-17.00 Last Admission 16.15*
Including House: A£9.00 Concessions£8.50,
Family Ticket £31.00. Excluding House: A£7.00
Concessions£7.00, Family Ticket £24.00.
Group rates (for 20+) available on request

Discount Offer: Two for the Price of One

Stanborough Park

Stanborough Road Welwyn Garden City
Hertfordshire AL8 6DQ
Tel: 01707 327655
126 acres of parkland with two lakes, a sailing
centre, rowing boats, and a nature reserve.

Folk & Local History Museums

Barnet Museum

31 Wood Street Barnet Barnet Hertfordshire
EN5 4BE
Tel: 020 8440 8066
Archaeological and historical exhibits relating to
the area.

Hertford Museum

18 Bull Plain Hertford Hertfordshire SG14 1DT
Tel: 01992 582686
Fine collections from Hertford, Hertfordshire and
beyond.

Museum of St Albans

Hatfield Road St Albans Hertfordshire AL1 3RR
Tel: 01727 819340
The history of St Albans is traced from the
departure of the Romans up to the present day.

ROYSTON & DISTRICT MUSEUM

...TOGETHER WITH 'THE ROYSTON TAPESTRY'

Lower King Street, Royston, Hertfordshire SG8 5AL
T: 01763 242587 E: curator@roystonmuseum.org.uk
W: www.roystonmuseum.org.uk

Housed in the former congregational chapel schoolroom, the museum contains exhibits that trace the history and development of the town.

Please contact the curator for opening times

ROYSTON CAVE
Melbourn Street, Royston, Hertfordshire

Royston Cave is a medieval manmade structure hewn out of the chalk. Its exposed medieval carvings bring visitors from all over the world.

Open on Saturdays, Sundays & Bank Holiday Mondays, 14.30 to 16.30 (Apr - Sept)

Please call 01763 245484 for group visits

Royston and District Museum

Lower King Street Royston Hertfordshire SG8 5AL
Tel: 01763 242587
www.roystonmuseum.org.uk

[5min walk from Royston Railway Station]

Housed in the former congregational chapel school room, the museum contains exhibits which trace the history and development of the town. There is an excellent loan exhibition of twentieth-century ceramics. The Museum is home to the Royston Tapestry that traces the history of the town from earliest times. There are also temporary exhibitions by local artists and craftsman.
All year Wed-Thur & Sat from 10.00, Easter-end Sep Sun & Bank Hol Mon 14.00-16.45
Donations appreciated

Gardens & Horticulture

Gardens of The Rose

Chiswell Green Lane St Albans AL2 3NR
Tel: 01727 850461 Fax: 01727 850360
www.roses.co.uk
[2mi S of St Albans on B4630. Rail: St Albans City. Plenty of on-site parking available]

Over 30,000 roses on display including old garden roses and modern roses, complemented by a rich variety of companion plants.

Scott's Grotto

Scotts Road Ware Hertfordshire SG12 9JQ
Tel: 01920 464131
Recently restored by the Ware Society, it consists of underground passages and chambers decorated with flints, shells, minerals and stones.

Historical

Berkhamsted Castle

Castle Hill Berkhamsted Hertfordshire HP4 1HF
Tel: 01442 871737
Roads and a railway have cut into the castle site, but its huge banks and ditches remain impressive.

Garden at Hatfield House

Hatfield Hertfordshire AL9 5NQ
Tel: 01707 287010 Fax: 01707 287033
www.hatfield-house.co.uk
[7mi from J23 M25 & 2mi from J4 A1(M), oppo-site Hatfield railway station. Plenty of free on-site parking available]

Where Elizabethan history began. Celebrated Jacobean House and Tudor Old Palace steeped in Elizabethan and Victorian political history in a spectacular countryside setting. Built in 1607 and home of a Cecil family for 400 years. The Royal Palace of Hatfield (c1485) in the West Garden is where Elizabeth I spent her childhood and held her first council in 1558. Enjoy the scented garden; Knot garden, elegant parterres and borders. Picnic tables and children's play area in the extensive park. Dogs welcome in the park. Licensed restaurant and gift shop open daily. Unique venue for weddings, parties and corporate hospitality in the Old Palace and Riding School conference centre. The Hatfield Banquet with costumed players is held most Friday evenings throughout the year. Plenty of free parking. Entrance opposite Hatfield Station. Special events programme. Full information on the website.
Easter Sat 7 Apr-end Sept. House: Wed-Sun & Bank Hols 12.00-16.00. Guided tours: weekdays except Aug. Park & Garden: daily 11.00-17.30 throughout season. East Garden: Thurs only
House, Park & West Garden: A£9.00 C(5-15)£4.50 OAPs£8.50, Family Ticket (A2+C4) £25.00. Park & West Garden: A£5.00 C£4.00, Park only: A£2.50 C£1.50. East Garden: £3.50

Discount Offer: Two for the Price of One

Mill Green Museum and Mill

Mill Green Hatfield Hertfordshire AL9 5PD
Tel: 01707 271362 Fax: 01707 272511
www.welhat.gov.uk/museum

[Between Hatfield & Welwyn Garden City at J of A1000 & A414. Limited on-site parking available]

This fully restored, eighteenth-century, water-powered corn mill, adjacent to the museum, is in regular use grinding corn in the traditional way. Organic, wholemeal, stoneground flour is for sale in five different sizes. The local history museum for Welwyn Hatfield is based in the Mill House, formerly the home for generations of millers and their families. There are three galleries exhibiting aspects of the districts social history. Frequent changes in one gallery, coupled with the many events throughout the year, entertain and inform visitors whether you are 8 or 80! This is a great place to bring the family. The Jubilee Garden provides a lovely riverside setting, bring a picnic and spend the day at Mill Green. Cream teas are available in the garden on Sunday afternoons from Easter until the end of September. For a full programme of events please contact the museum.

All year Tue-Fri 10.00-17.00, Sat Sun & Bank Hol 14.00-17.00
Admission Free

Discount Offer: £0.50 off a Bag of Mill Green Flour

Music & Theatre Museums

St Albans Organ Theatre

320 Camp Road St Albans Hertfordshire
AL1 5PE
Tel: 01727 869693
www.stalbansorgantheatre.org.uk
*[2mi from St Albans city centre. Buses: S2 & C2
come from city centre and railway station.
Located next to Camp School. Plenty of on-site
parking available]*

A permanent playing exhibition of mechanical
musical instruments. Dance Organs by Decap,
Bursens, and Mortier; Mills Violano-Virtuoso self
playing violin and piano; reproducing pianos by
Steinway, Weber and Marshall & Wendell; musical
boxes. Wurlitzer and Rutt theatre pipe
organs. Regular monthly theatre organ concerts. Disabled access and toilet.
Every Sun 14.00-16.30. Other times by arrangement for groups. Closed 25 Dec
A£4.50 C£2.50 OAPs£3.50, Family Ticket
£10.00

Natural History Museums

Walter Rothschild Zoological Museum

Akeman Street Tring Hertfordshire HP23 6AP
Tel: 020 7942 6171
This museum was once the private collection of
Lionel Walter, 2nd Baron Rothschild, and is now
part of the Natural History Museum.

Places of Worship

St Albans Cathedral

Sumpter Yard Holywell Hill St Albans
Hertfordshire AL1 1BY
Tel: 01727 860780 Fax: 01727 850944
www.stalbanscathedral.org.uk

*[Centre of St. Albans, J3 A1(M), M1 from N J7,
from S J6, M25 from E J22, from W J21a]*

The setting for the shrine of Alban, Britain's first
Christian Martyr, a Norman Abbey Church built
with recycled Roman bricks from the nearby city
of Verulamium, a thriving parish church and
today a Cathedral. St. Albans offers you a journey through 1700 years of history. Highlights
include the great Norman Tower, a series of
twelfth and thirteenth-century wall-paintings
unequalled in England, the painted Presbytery
ceiling (1280), the Shrine of St. Alban (1308)
with a wooden watching loft (1400) and the
tomb of Humphrey Duke of Gloucester (1447).
Free guided tours every day, booked groups by
arrangement. Family Trails and children's activities often available during school holidays -
please contact for details. Bookstall, gift shop
and the 'Café at the Abbey'.
All year daily 08.00-17.45
Suggested Donation: £3.00

Roman Era

Verulamium Museum and Park

St. Michaels Street St Albans AL3 4SW
Tel: 01727 751810
Verulamium was one of the largest and most
important Roman towns in Britain.

Wildlife & Safari Parks

Paradise Wildlife Park

White Stubbs Lane Broxbourne Hertfordshire
EN10 7QA
Tel: 01992 470490 Fax: 01992 440525
www.pwpark.com/

[J25 (M25). Plenty of on-site parking available]

Paradise Wildlife Park is a fantastic place to discover wonderful exotic animals including tigers, lions, monkeys and zebras. What makes Paradise unique is the fact that you can get up close and personal, meeting and feeding many of the animals. The park has lots of new attractions including the amazing white lions and tigers, the penguins, the 'Tumble Jungle' and coffee shop. There are many other attractions including 3 themed adventure playgrounds, children's rides, indoor soft play area and tractor trailer rides. There is a small additional charge for the 'Woodland Railway,' 'On Safari' golf course and 'Gold Panning' experience. The park offers various catering options including the Safari Suite fast food restaurant. There are seasonal outlets conveniently located around the park offering fish and chips, hot dogs, ice-creams and hot and cold drinks.

All year daily 09.30-18.00
A£12.00 C(2-15)£9.00 C(under2)£Free

Discount Offer: One Child Free

Shepreth Wildlife Park

Willersmill Station Road Shepreth SG8 6PZ
Tel: 01763 262226 Fax: 01763 260582
www.sheprethwildlifepark.co.uk
[Just off A10 between Cambridge & Royston, next to train station. Plenty of on-site parking]

Established in 1979 the sanctuary has evolved from a quiet refuge for small and domestic animals into a remarkable safe haven for all creatures great and small! Now home to tigers, lynx, monkeys, otters and wolves to name a few, this popular attraction boasts a cat house overhead walkway allowing fantastic photographic opportunities of the tigers. It also offers a tropical pavilion where exotic birds and reptiles reside and where the new tortoise house and capybara houses can be found. The gift shop remains home to Waterworld and Bug City - an indoor fish and insect house that lays claim to being the inspiration behind the National Geographic Channel's series, 'Insects from Hell'. The most recent additions are our new toddlers soft play room, great fun for dry and wet days and an impressive new nocturnal house with a colony of flying fox fruit bats and more. When all the animals have been enjoyed and the fish and ponies fed, there remains one last place to take pleasure in, the Wild Sea Monkey! A pirate ship marooned in the children's play area.
All year daily 10.00-18.00 (10.00-dusk during Winter months). Closed 25 Dec
Park: A£7.95 C£5.95 OAPs£5.95. Bug City only: A£2.20 C£1.55 OAPs£1.85. Bug City (when combined with park) Combined Ticket: A£1.90 C£1.30 OAPs£1.50. Group rates (for 20+): 10% discount on the day, 20% if booked & paid for 3 weeks in advance.

Discount Offer: One Child Free

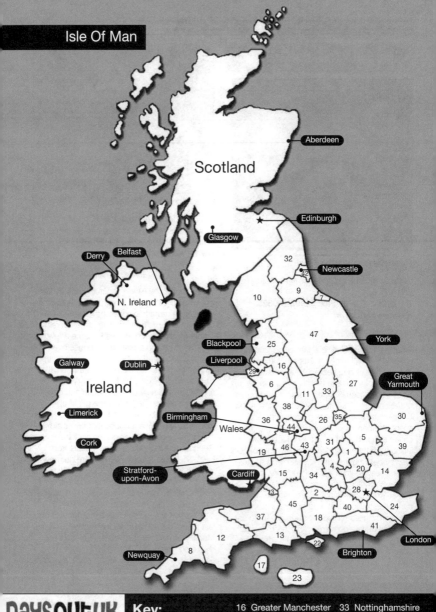

Isle Of Man

Scotland

Aberdeen

Edinburgh

Glasgow

Derry | Belfast

Newcastle

Derry

N. Ireland

32

42

9

7

10

Galway | Dublin

Ireland

Blackpool

Liverpool

25

47

York

Limerick

16

Great Yarmouth

Cork

29

6

11

33

27

30

38

Birmingham

36

26

35

Wales

44

5

39

Stratford-upon-Avon

19

46

43

31

1

20

14

Cardiff

15

34

4

28

London

2

40

24

45

41

37

18

Brighton

Newquay

12

13

22

8

17

23

Key:

1	Bedfordshire
2	Berkshire
3	Bristol
4	Buckinghamshire
5	Cambridgeshire
6	Cheshire
7	Cleveland
8	Cornwall
9	County Durham
10	Cumbria
11	Derbyshire
12	Devon
13	Dorset
14	Essex
15	Gloucestershire
16	Greater Manchester
17	Guernsey
18	Hampshire
19	Herefordshire
20	Hertfordshire
21	Isle Of Man
22	Isle Of Wight
23	Jersey
24	Kent
25	Lancashire
26	Leicestershire
27	Lincolnshire
28	London
29	Merseyside
30	Norfolk
31	Northamptonshire
32	Northumberland
33	Nottinghamshire
34	Oxfordshire
35	Rutland
36	Shropshire
37	Somerset
38	Staffordshire
39	Suffolk
40	Surrey
41	Sussex
42	Tyne & Wear
43	Warwickshire
44	West Midlands
45	Wiltshire
46	Worcestershire
47	Yorkshire

Animal Attractions

Home of Rest for Old Horses

Bulrhenny Richmond Hill Douglas Isle of Man IM4 1JH
Tel: 01624 674594/07624 463198 Fax: 01624 613278
[On A5 Airport Rd, half way up Richmond Hill approx 3mi S of Douglas. Home is on Bus route. Plenty of on-site parking available]

Not to be missed. Visit the wonderful Retirement Home for the Ex-Douglas Tram Horses and their friends, set in over 90 acres of glorious countryside. An Adoption Scheme supports the home and there are over 50 horses and donkeys to choose from. Come and browse around our newly refurbished gift shop where you can buy food to feed the horses, and then enjoy our home baking in our newly refurbished tea rooms. Afternoon teas and children's parties can be catered for by arrangement. Coaches are welcome by arrangement. The Home is a registered charity and supported entirely by voluntary contributions. Dogs must be kept on leads.
14 May-14 Sept Mon-Fri 10.00-16.00
Admission Free

Mann Cat Sanctuary

Ash Villa Main Road Santon Isle of Man IM4 1EE
Tel: 01624 824195
Many rescued cats and kittens (including Manx variety) in pleasant country setting. Also rabbits, a sheep, ducks and goats.
Sun only 14.00-17.00

Arts, Crafts & Textiles

Erin Arts Centre

Victoria Square Port Erin Isle of Man IM9 6LD
Tel: 01624 832662 Fax: 01624 836658
www.erinartscentre.com

The entertainment hub of the Isle of Man is Douglas but for visitors to the South the spotlight is on the Erin Arts Centre, Port Erin. It serves the fit and well, the young, the elderly, disadvantaged and disabled. This has been a centre of excellence for more than thirty years, hosting regular concerts, plays and exhibitions to cater for all tastes, and is hired by many local organizations including the Rushen Players. The Centre was founded in 1971 and since then has received international recognition as home to major cultural events, see section Festivals and Shows, and a great deal more, from instrumental and vocal competitions to visual arts and a film club. It is well worth a visit.
Exhibition Gallery: Tue-Fri 13.30-16.30

Tynwald Craft Centre

Tynwald Mills St. Johns Douglas Isle of Man IM4 3AD
Tel: 01624 801213
Country retail and leisure centre including 20+ shops, two cafes, art gallery, garden centre and conference centre.

Country Parks & Estates

Mooragh Park
Ramsey Isle of Man
Tel: 01624 810100
This large municipal park offers bowling, putting, tennis, a 12-acre boating lake, children's playground and BMX track.

Onchan Pleasure Park
Onchan Isle of Man
Tel: 01624 675564
Motor boats, go-karts, crazy golf, tennis, bowling, pitch and putt, children's playground and amusement arcade.

Exhibition & Visitor Centres

Ayres Visitor Centre
Conservation Centre Ballaghennie Bride Isle of Man
Tel: 01624 801985
Displays of local flora and fauna, books and gifts. Fascinating nature trail through coastal sand dunes.

Manx Wildlife Trust Scarlett Visitor Centre
Scarlett Point Castletown Isle of Man
Tel: 01624 801985
Scarlett Visitor Centre has information and displays on the area's geology and natural history.
May-Sep 14.00-17.00, closed Mon

Factory Outlets & Tours

Laxey Woollen Mills
Glen Road Laxey Isle of Man IM4 7AR
Tel: 01624 861395
Founded by John Ruskin in 1881. Still weaving cloths on traditional handlooms making Laxey Manx Tartan and Tweeds.

Festivals & Shows

Mananan International Festivals of Music and the Arts
Erin Arts Centre Victoria Square Port Erin Isle of Man IM9 6LD
Tel: 01624 832662 Fax: 01624 836658
www.erinartscentre.com/events/mananan_festival.html
[Signposted from Promenade]

The Celtic Sea God Mananan presides over this cornucopia of events in Port Erin in 2007. Its special blend of the very best of recitals, jazz, lectures, opera, theatre and cabaret promises a certain delight for those who venture to dip in. Includes Young Singer and Young Musician of Mann Competitions. The Erin Arts Centre also hosts the Lionel Tertis International Viola Competition and Workshop and The Barbirolli International Oboe Festival and Competition which are held triennial.
Summer Festival: June 21-July 1 2007. Opera Festival: 9-13 September 2007. Next Barbirolli event 2008 & next Tertis event August 2009
Prices vary according to event, please call for details or visit the website

Folk & Local History Museums

Castle Rushen
The Quay Castletown Isle Of Man IM9 1LD
Tel: 01624 648000
One of Britain's most complete medieval castles, Castle Rushen is a limestone fortress rising out of the heart of the old capital of the Island.

House of Manannan

Mill Road Peel Isle Of Man IM5 1TA
Tel: 01624 648000
This new £6 million centre is an unforgettable experience.

Forests & Woods

Silverdale Glen

Tel: 01624 823474
nr Ballasalla Isle of Man
Shop, amusements, radio-controlled boats, play park, a beautiful glen and a craft centre.

Historical

Peel Castle

Mill Road Peel Isle Of Man IM5 1TB
Tel: 01624 648000
One of the Island's principle historic centres, this fortress sits at the mouth of Peel Harbour.

Mining

Laxey Wheel and Mines Trail

Laxey Isle of Man
Tel: 01624 675522
The Great Laxey Wheel is the largest working water wheel in the world.

Performing Arts

Villa Marina and Gaiety Theatre Complex

Harris Promenade Douglas Isle of Man IM1 2HH
Tel: 01624 694555
Villa Marina, the Royal Hall, the Gaiety Theatre, 'Dragons' Castle' soft-play area and gardens.

Places of Worship

Rushen Abbey

Ballasalla Isle Of Man IM9 3DB
Tel: 01624 648000
The most substantial and important medieval religious site in the Isle of Man.

Railways

Isle of Man Steam Railway

Douglas Steam Railway Station Douglas Isle of Man
Tel: 01624 663366
A Victorian steam railway running through the Manx countryside from Douglas to Port Erin.
Easter-Oct

Science - Earth & Planetary

Camera Obscura

Douglas Head Douglas Isle of Man
Tel: 01624 686766
Offers visitors an incredible view of the Island.
Easter, then May-Sep. Sat 13.00-16.00, Sun 11.00-16.00 (weather permitting)

Sport & Recreation

National Sports Centre

Groves Road Douglas Isle Of Man IM2 1RB
Tel: 01624 688588
The Isle of Man's premier leisure facility.

Wildlife & Safari Parks

Curraghs Wildlife Park

Ballaugh Isle of Man IM7 5EA
Tel: 01624 897323
Exhibits a large variety of animals and birds in natural settings.

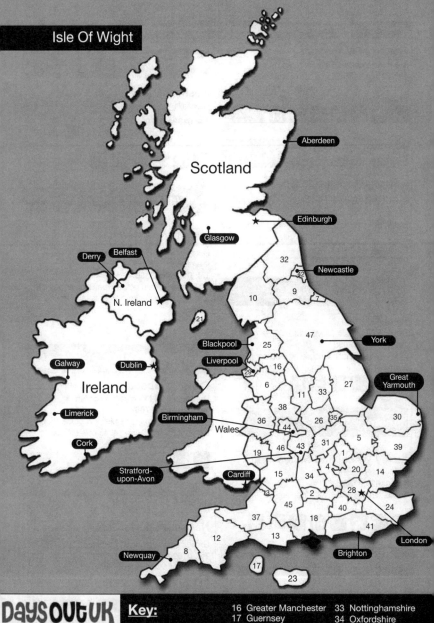

Isle Of Wight

Scotland

Aberdeen

Edinburgh

Glasgow

Newcastle

32

42

Derry
Belfast

N. Ireland

10

9

7

21

Blackpool

25

47

York

Galway
Dublin

Liverpool

16

Great
Yarmouth

Ireland

29

27

Limerick

6

33

30

Cork

11

38

39

Birmingham

36

44

26

35

5

Wales

19

46

43

31

1

20

14

Stratford-
upon-Avon

Cardiff

15

34

4

28

London

13

2

45

40

24

Newquay

37

18

41

8

12

13

Brighton

17

23

Key:

1	Bedfordshire	16	Greater Manchester
2	Berkshire	17	Guernsey
3	Bristol	18	Hampshire
4	Buckinghamshire	19	Herefordshire
5	Cambridgeshire	20	Hertfordshire
6	Cheshire	21	Isle Of Man
7	Cleveland	22	Isle Of Wight
8	Cornwall	23	Jersey
9	County Durham	24	Kent
10	Cumbria	25	Lancashire
11	Derbyshire	26	Leicestershire
12	Devon	27	Lincolnshire
13	Dorset	28	London
14	Essex	29	Merseyside
15	Gloucestershire	30	Norfolk
		31	Northamptonshire
		32	Northumberland

33	Nottinghamshire
34	Oxfordshire
35	Rutland
36	Shropshire
37	Somerset
38	Staffordshire
39	Suffolk
40	Surrey
41	Sussex
42	Tyne & Wear
43	Warwickshire
44	West Midlands
45	Wiltshire
46	Worcestershire
47	Yorkshire

Animal Attractions

Amazon World Zoo Park

Watery Lane Newchurch Sandown Isle of Wight
PO36 0LX
Tel: 01983 867122
Animals, birds, reptiles, fish and insects in recreated habitats.

Brickfields Horse Country

Newnham Road Binstead Ryde Isle of Wight
PO33 3TH
Tel: 01983 566801 / 615116
A unique family attraction with shire horses, miniature ponies, farm animals and donkeys.

Isle of Wight Zoo - Home of The Tiger and Big Cat Sanctuary and Lemurland

Yaverland's Seafront Sandown Isle of Wight
PO36 8QB
Tel: 01983 403883
Some of the planet's most endangered creatures.
Mar, Easter-Sept, Oct.

Arts, Crafts & Textile

Isle of Wight Studio Glass

Old Park St Lawrence Isle of Wight PO38 1XR
Tel: 01983 853526
Come and watch handmade decorative and functional studio glass being made.

Birds, Butterflies & Bees

Butterfly World and Fountain World

Staplers Road Wooton Isle of Wight PO33 4RW
Tel: 01983 883430
Exotic butterflies fly freely in the tropical indoor garden.

Factory Outlets & Tours

Isle of Wight Pearl

Chilton Chine Military Road Brighstone
Isle of Wight PO30 4DD
Tel: 01983 740352
Houses 35,000 items of jewellery. Specialist gold and silver shop.

Folk & Local History Museums

Museum of Island History

Guildhall High Street Newport Isle of Wight
PO30 1TY
Tel: 01983 823366
A new museum presenting the story of the Isle of Wight.

Gardens & Horticulture

Ventnor Botanic Garden

Undercliffe Drive Ventnor Isle of Wight
PO38 1UL
Tel: 01983 855397
New state-of-the-art visitor centre includes two exhibitions.

Historical

Appuldurcombe House / Isle of Wight Owl and Falconry Centre

Appuldurcombe Road Wroxall Ventnor
Isle of Wight PO38 3EW
Tel: 01983 852484
Set in the imaginatively restored servants' quarters of Appuldurcombe House.

Needles Old Battery

West Highdown Totland Bay Isle of Wight
PO39 0JH
Tel: 01983 754772
www.nationaltrust.org.uk/Isleofwight

*[At Needles Headland (B3322). Rail: Ferry
Yarmouth. Car park nearby at Alum Bay, free car
parking for NT members by kind permission of the
Needles Park, (disabled visitors should contact us
in advance for information)]*

Visit this spectacular cliff-top fort with views of
the Needles Rocks. Built in 1862, it has an
intriguing history that is brought to life in a child-
friendly comic book-style. Explore the underground tunnel with its unique birds-eye view of
the Needles. Enjoy our fascinating exhibitions
(that include memorabilia from World War II) and
our special 'Shipwreck' exhibition. Borrow a
Children's Discovery Pack and explore the site
as a soldier on watch during World War II. Relax
in our tearoom - housed in an old lookout tower
with dramatic views. A wide programme of special events throughout the season. New for
2007: Exhibition on the part played in Britain's
space programme (opening times vary).
*25 Mar-28 Oct 10.30-17.00. Closed Fri, except
Good Friday & during July-Aug. Closes in high
winds (please phone in advance to check)*
A&OAPs£4.20 C£2.10, Family Ticket £10.50,
NT Members: Free

Osborne House

East Cowes Isle of Wight PO32 6JY
Tel: 01983 200022
Visit the Swiss Cottage where the royal children
played.

Classic Boat Museum

Sea Close Wharf Newport Harbour Newport Isle
of Wight PO30 2EF
Tel: 01983 533493 Fax: 01983 533505
www.classicboatmuseum.org

*[Easy access by bus from Ryde, East & West
Cowes ferry terminals. Free parking at the door
via Seaclose Park]*

This Maritime Heritage Museum exhibits 60
small, attractive and unique water craft, both
power and sail. Each craft is displayed with
well-researched historic notes and with all
appropriate gear. An example is 'Flying Spray' a
beautiful 1912 Thames pleasure launch shown
with velvet upholstery and portable gramo-
phone! The topical displays are changed each
year and restoration of historic boats by volunteers is always on view. Research is undertaken
from the large archives and enquiries are welcome. The museum is open, daily in the summer and two days a week in winter, all being
undercover. Facilities are provided for all abilities
and there is a gift shop, and second-hand nautical books for sale. Tea and coffee are available. Group visits welcomed by prior arrangements. Parking is free via Seaclose Park with
level access everywhere. Buses from Ryde and
Newport stop 2 minutes away.

29 Mar-2 Nov daily
A£3.00 C(6-16)&Students(NUS/USI)£1.00
OAPs£2.00. Groups welcome by prior arrange-
ment

Natural History Museums

Dinosaur Isle

Culver Parade Sandown Isle of Wight
PO36 8QA
Tel: 01983 404344 Fax: 01983 407502
www.dinosaurisle.com
[Follow brown signs to Dinosaur Isle in Sandown area. Plenty of on-site parking available]

Dinosaur Isle is Britain's first purpose built dinosaur attraction just over the sea wall in Sandown where in a spectacularly shaped building reminiscent of a Pterosaur flying across the Cretaceous skies you can walk back through fossilised time to the period of the dinosaurs a 120 million years ago. Set in amongst a recreated landscape you will meet life sized models of the Isle of Wight's famous five dinosaurs - Neovenator, Eotyrannus, Iguanadon, Hypsilophodon and Polacanthus. Flying above you, amongst the haunting sounds of a long lost forest, are pterodactyls. You will see dinosaur skeletons as they are found by the fossil hunters and can watch our volunteers preparing the latest exciting finds. At Dinosaur Isle there are many hands on activities to try and you will be able to encounter the lost world of dinosaurs that once roamed freely across the Isle of Wight.
All year daily, Apr-Sept 10.00-18.00, Oct-Mar 10.00-16.00. Closed 24-26 Dec & 1 Jan. Please call to confirm opening times in Jan.
A£4.85 C£2.85, Family Ticket (A2+C2) £13.50

Discount Offer: One Child Free

Nature & Conservation Parks

Shanklin Chine

12 Pomona Road Shanklin Isle of Wight
PO37 6PF
Tel: 01983 866432 Fax: 01983 866145
www.shanklinchine.co.uk
[Signposted on A3055. Entrance from Shanklin Esplanade or Shanklin Old Village]

Part of our national heritage, this scenic gorge at Shanklin, Isle of Wight, is a magical world of unique beauty and a rich haven of rare plants, woodland, wildlife, including red squirrels and enchanting waterfalls. A path winds through the ravine with overhanging trees, ferns and other flora covering its steep sides. The exhibition 'The Island - Then and Now' is housed in the Heritage Centre and features 'Flora of the Island', also PLUTO (Pipe Line Under The Ocean) which carried petrol to the Allied troops in Normandy, and local history displays. The Memorial to 40 Royal Marine Commando, who trained here during the war in preparation for the Dieppe Raid of 1942, can be seen at the lower entrance. After dusk, during the main summer months, subtle illuminations create a different world. Gift shop and tea room. On the beach below, Fisherman's Cottage, built by William Colenutt in 1817, offers a choice of excellent food and real ale, which can be enjoyed on the sun terrace.
30 Mar-28 Oct daily, illuminated 25 May-9 Sept
A£3.75 C(5 14inol)£2.00 C(0 4)£Froo, OAPs£2.75, Disabled/Carer£1.50, Family Ticket (A2+C2) £9.50 or (A2+C3) £11.50. Group rate (10+): 10% discount (excluding schools).

Waltzing Waters

Aqua Theatre Westridge Centre Brading Road
Ryde Isle of Wight PO33 1QS

Tel: 01983 811333
The world's most elaborate water, light and
music production.

Isle of Wight Steam Railway

The Railway Station Havenstreet Village Ryde
Isle of Wight PO33 4DS
Tel: 01983 882204
A 10-mile 'round trip' through glorious Island
countryside.

Marine Aquarium

Fort Victoria Yarmouth Isle of Wight PO41 0RR
Tel: 01983 760283
Be amazed by the variety of bizarre creatures
found in our local waters.

Blackgang Chine Fantasy Park

Blackgang Ventnor Isle of Wight PO38 2HN
Tel: 01983 730330
Water gardens, maze and coastal gardens and
a water force high speed boat ride.
Mar-Oct

Needles Park

Alum Bay Isle of Wight PO39 0JD
Tel: 0870 458 0022 Fax: 01983 755260
www.theneedles.co.uk

*[Signposted on B3322. Plenty of on-site parking
available]*

Set in heritage coastline, offering a range of
attractions for all; the spectacular chairlift to the
beach provides marvellous views of the Island's
famous landmark and naturally coloured sandcliffs. On the beach there's the opportunity to
take a boat trip for a closer look at the dramatic
rocks and lighthouse and another chance to
view the unique sandcliffs. Back at the cliff top,
visit the sand shop and create your own unique
sand souvenir. At Alum Bay Glass you can
watch skilled glassblowers making beautiful
glassware and for those with a sweet tooth,
master sweetmakers demonstrate the art of traditional sweetmaking at the Isle of Wight Sweet
Manufactory. Junior Driver has proved popular
with children as they learn about road safety,
whilst driving an electric car and hopefully obey-
ing road signs and working traffic lights! The
Park has full catering and retail facilities including a licensed bar. New for 2007 Tea Cup ride
*1 April-end Oct 10.00-17.00, hours extended on
event days. Certain facilities open during winter
please call for details*
Admission free, all day parking £3.00 per car.
Plus a range of Pay-as-you-Go Attractions
Supersaver ticket provides great discounts.
Facilities subject to availability and certain
attractions have age/height restrictions

**Discount Offer: Three for the Price of
Two (Super-Saver ticket books)**

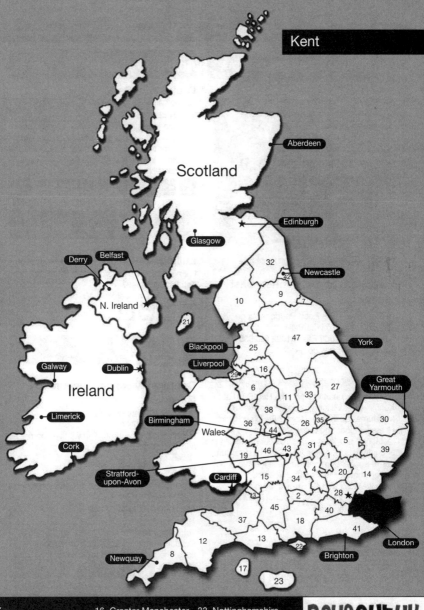

Kent

Scotland

Aberdeen

Edinburgh

Glasgow

Derry

Belfast

N. Ireland

Newcastle

32

42

9

7

10

21

47

York

Galway

Dublin

Blackpool

25

Ireland

Liverpool

16

29

6

27

Great Yarmouth

Limerick

11

33

30

38

Cork

Birmingham

36

44

26

35

5

Wales

19

46

43

31

1

39

Stratford-upon-Avon

Cardiff

15

4

20

14

34

2

28

London

45

40

37

18

41

12

13

Brighton

Newquay

8

22

17

23

Key:

1	Bedfordshire	16	Greater Manchester	33	Nottinghamshire
2	Berkshire	17	Guernsey	34	Oxfordshire
3	Bristol	18	Hampshire	35	Rutland
4	Buckinghamshire	19	Herefordshire	36	Shropshire
5	Cambridgeshire	20	Hertfordshire	37	Somerset
6	Cheshire	21	Isle Of Man	38	Staffordshire
7	Cleveland	22	Isle Of Wight	39	Suffolk
8	Cornwall	23	Jersey	40	Surrey
9	County Durham	24	Kent	41	Sussex
10	Cumbria	25	Lancashire	42	Tyne & Wear
11	Derbyshire	26	Leicestershire	43	Warwickshire
12	Devon	27	Lincolnshire	44	West Midlands
13	Dorset	28	London	45	Wiltshire
14	Essex	29	Merseyside	46	Worcestershire
15	Gloucestershire	30	Norfolk	47	Yorkshire
		31	Northamptonshire		
		32	Northumberland		

DAYS OUT UK
The place to look for places to go

Agriculture / Working Farms

Hop Farm at the Kentish Oast Village

Beltring Maidstone Road Paddock Wood Tonbridge Kent TN12 6PY
Tel: 01622 872068 Fax: 01622 872630
www.thehopfarm.co.uk

[On A228. M25 J5 on to A21 S & 15min from M20 J4. Plenty of on-site parking available]

Based in the heart of Kent, the Hop Farm at the Kentish Oast Village includes award winning Museums, Exhibitions, Animal Farm and Shire Horses, indoor and outdoor play areas and restaurant providing a great day out for all ages and interests. The Hop Farm also hosts a number of special events throughout the year, from Motor Shows, the 'War and Peace Show' the largest Military Vehicle Extravaganza in the world, to garden shows and craft shows. Picnic areas indoor and out.

All year daily 10.00-17.00
A£7.50 C£6.50, Family Ticket (A2+C2) £27.00
Prices vary on event days

Discount Offer: One Child Free

Animal Attractions

Druidstone Park

Honey Hill Blean Canterbury Kent CT2 9JR
Tel: 01227 765168
Druidstone is a garden park of peace and harmony; with an enchanted woodland walk which caters for the imagination where dwell the Sleeping Dragon, Old Man of the Oak and Magical White Deer.

Archaeology

Lullingstone Roman Villa

Lullingstone Lane Eynsford Kent DA4 0JA
Tel: 01322 863467
This villa was built around AD100.

Arts, Crafts & Textiles

Canterbury Royal Museum Art Gallery

High Street Canterbury Kent CT1 2RA
Tel: 01227 452747
Magnificent Victorian building with fine porcelain and art collections, notably by TS Cooper. Gallery for special exhibitions.

Metropole Galleries

The Leas Folkestone Kent CT20 2LS
Tel: 01303 244706
Outstanding artists are invited to create ambitious, thought-provoking exhibitions.

Tunbridge Wells Museum and Art Gallery

Civic Centre Mount Pleasant Royal Tunbridge Wells Kent TN1 1JN
Tel: 01892 554171
From Tunbridge-ware caskets, Victorian oil paintings, archaeology to historic fashions and dolls.

Birds, Butterflies & Bees

MacFarlane's World of Butterflies

Canterbury Road Swingfield Folkestone Kent
CT15 7HX
Tel: 01303 844244
www.macfarlanesgardens.co.uk
*[From A2 take A260 Folkestone exit. From M20
take A260 Hawkinge exit. Rail: Folkestone Central
Station. Bus: 16 & 16A to Canterbury service,
alight at Robert's Corner. Plenty of free on-site
parking available]*

Where can you see the world's largest moth or
discover a butterfly with the 'feathers' and
'eyes' of an owl? And where will you find a butterfly with wings so delicate you can see
through them? Surprisingly, in a quiet corner of
Kent, and it's the only place of its kind for miles
around. Watch the kids' eyes light up as they
stroll in a tropical 'rainforest' setting. Here you
will discover swallow tails, fritillaries, dainty heli-
conids and the giant Atlas moth as they flutter
freely among hibiscus, lantana and giant fruiting
banana plants, feeding on the nectar. We welcome school and adult groups, individuals and
families, and offer free guided tours with one of
our expert staff. After admiring the butterflies,
why not visit our gift shop or browse our
Nursery and Plant Centre or relax in the Red
Admiral Restaurant and sample mouth-watering
home cooking. Visit and open your eyes to the
wonderful world of butterflies!

31 Mar-30 Sept 10.00-17.00. Closed Easter Sun
A£3.00 C£2.00 Concessions£2.50, Family
Ticket (A2+C2) £8.50. Group rates available on
request

Discount Offer: One Child Free

Exhibition & Visitor Centres

Canterbury Tales
St. Margaret's Street Canterbury Kent CT1 2TG
Tel: 01227 479227
A fascinating audio-visual experience sited in
the heart of the city.

Festivals & Shows

Broadstairs Dickens Festival

Broadstairs Kent
Tel: 01843 861827/861118 event
*[M2 from London. Rail: London Victoria to
Broadstairs]*

Charles Dickens visited Broadstairs between
1837 and 1859. He named it 'Our English
Watering Place' and enjoyed its sun, sea and
air. For nine days every June you can mix with
crinolined ladies and their top hatted escorts.
See them promenade in Dickensian splendour
and even better, wear costume of the 1837-
1859 period and join in the fun. Many events,
both free and ticketed, including: Opening
Parade followed by; Opening Ceremony with
Entertainment, Victorian Cricket Match, Duels,
Melodramas, Festival Play, Victorian Bazaar,
Victorian Music Hall, Victorian Sea Bathing,
Talks, Victoriana Collectors' Fair, Morning Coffee
with the Dickensians, Musical Entertainment
and a Victorian Country Fayre.
16-24 June 2007
Many events are free. Ticketed events range
from £3.50-£17.00. Group Bookings of 10+ for
any ticketed event will get one free ticket

Canterbury Festival 2007

Festival Office Christ Church Gate The Precincts Canterbury Kent CT1 2EE
Tel: 01227 452853 Fax: 01227 781830
www.canterburyfestival.co.uk
[Held in venues across city & surrounding area]
The historic setting of Canterbury provides a unique location for the largest festival of arts and culture in the region. This year's festival offers something for everyone with over 200 events. Working with world-renowned musicians, international companies and local artists, the festival offers an exciting programme of classical concerts in the Cathedral, contemporary dance, theatre, opera, comedy, talks, walks and children's events in venues around the city and surrounding area. The popular and intimate festival club features an eclectic mix of jazz, folk, blues and world music.
13-27 October 2007
Prices vary, call 01227 378188 to book your tickets. Free brochure available from July, please call 01227 452853 to request

Caring Parent Show with Noddy

Kent Showground Detling Kent ME14 3JF
Tel: 0845 055 0719
www.caringparent.co.uk
[On A249 2mi M20 J7 & 5mi M2 J5. Rail: Maidstone East. Bus: from train station, Arriva 01622 69700. Channel Tunnel 35mi. Ashford International 20mi]
The Caring Parent Show offers new and expectant parents a one-stop shopping experience, family entertainment and the opportunity to learn about some of today's key maternity and family issues. Attracting over 100 exhibitors, you'll have the opportunity to sample or purchase items ranging from maternity wear, children's clothing, toys and books through to nursery furniture, the latest modes of baby transport, the newest baby monitors and safety equipment to hit the market place. A fun day out for all the family, so if you have little ones that need entertaining don't despair, new for 2007 is a dedicated entertainments zone for children. They'll have the opportunity to meet a children's favourite TV character Noddy, join in with one of the interactive play activities or sit back and watch the entertainers.
5-6 May 2007 10.00-17.00
In advance: A£4.00 C(0-16)£Free

Discount Offer: Two for the Price of One

Kent County Showground

Kent Event and Exhibition Centre Detling Maidstone Kent ME14 3JF
Tel: 01622 630975 Fax: 01622 630978
www.kentshowground.co.uk
[Off A249 Link Rd between M20 & M2. Plenty of on-site parking available]
County showground holding many special events. Kent Show - an enjoyable, entertaining, educational experience for all the family. See cattle, sheep, pigs, horses, show jumping, llamas, alpacas, ring displays, farming, food & wine, hundreds of trade stands, flower show and forestry area. Schools very welcome. It's a great day out! Also included are a tractor pulling display, kangaroo kid display, undercover craft and model displays, fair, beer tents, refreshments and free parking.
Kent County Show: 13-15 July 2007
Please call for further details

Folk & Local History Museums

Tenterden and District Museum

Station Road Tenterden Kent TN30 6HN
Tel: 01580 764310
www.tenterdentown.co.uk
[On A28 between Ashford & Hastings]

Opened in 1976, the Tenterden Museum is housed in an attractive weatherboard building originally built in 1850 as a stable and store. The collections are broad in type, ranging from agriculture and industry to textiles and archives, with very strong potential as a learning resource. The six rooms on two floors house all aspects of the town's social, commercial and agricultural history. Following the Charter Exhibition commemorating the incorporation of Tenterden into the Confederation of Cinque Ports in 1449, the museum now houses a diorama replicating medieval shipbuilding at Small Hythe. To compliment the exhibit, the entrance room houses the artefacts found by the 'Channel 4' TimeTeam when they excavated a site establishing that ships were built there for the medieval Royal fleet. Visitors are surprised how extensive and diverse the collection is with artefacts ranging from a 1500 BC flint axe head to the reproduction of a typical Victorian kitchen.
Easter-Oct Tue-Sun (& Bank Hols). Apr-June & Oct 13.30-16.30, July-Sep 11.00-16.30
A£1.00 C(under18)£0.25 C(under5)£Free OAPs£0.75. Group rates available on request

Discount Offer: Two for the Price of One

Food & Drink

Biddenden Vineyards and Cider Works

Little Whatmans Gribble Bridge Lane Biddenden Kent TN27 8DF
Tel: 01580 291726 Fax: 01580 291933
www.biddendenvineyards.com
[1.5mi outside Biddenden Village on A262, bear R at Woolpack Corner. Plenty of on-site parking available]

Biddenden Vineyards and Cider Works is Kent's oldest family owned vineyard and the Counties largest producer of ciders and apple juice. So why not visit us and enjoy a tranquil walk through 22 acres of vines. The grapes are grown on shallow sheltered slopes and the soil and climate is ideal for producing fresh fruity wines, which reflect the richness of the region. Biddenden Vineyards produce White, Red, Rosé and sparkling wines of the highest quality, which is reflected in the awards, received each year. Traditional strong still Ciders are also produced on site, including Monks Delight, a mulling cider and our Special Reserve, a cider oaked in whisky casks. Pure farm pressed apple juice with no added sugar is also an extremely popular product.

Mon-Sat 10.00-17.00. Sun & Bank Hols 11.00-17.00. Closed Sun in Jan-Feb. Closed 24 Dec-1 Jan. Guided Tours for 15+ adults only, subject to prior booking
Free Admission & Tastings

Discount Offer: One Free Cup of Tea or Coffee in the Café

Gardens & Horticulture

Broadview Gardens

Hadlow College Tonbridge Road Hadlow
Tonbridge Kent TN11 0AL
Tel: 01732 850551 Fax: 01732 853207
www.hadlow.ac.uk
[On A26. Plenty of on-site parking available]
Broadview Gardens is a unique garden originally
designed and maintained as a teaching
resource for students at Hadlow College, now
open to the public. The 8 acres of garden are
formed around a 100 metre long double mixed
border backed with clipped Yew hedges and
columnar Oak trees. From the border run two
grass avenues lined with clipped hedges. Each
year, from September to May, students build
new gardens on themes from domestic gardens, show gardens to public landscape styles
using an extensive variety of plants and materials in common and innovative ways. A selection
of the gardens currently able to be seen are The
Grasses Garden, The Medicinal Garden, The
Oriental Garden, The subtropical style Garden
(May to October), the Italian Garden and the
Dry Garden. There is also a natural style space
with lake, meadow and wooded areas, and an
ornamental planted lake with moist border. The
Gardens hold two National Collections; The
National Collection of Japanese Anemones,
flowering from August to October, and the
National Collection of Hellebores, flowering
February to March. Throughout the gardens
there is an extensive range of unusual plants
and collections, in addition to more familiar
plants used in unconventional ways. As part of
the learning experience of visiting the gardens
we aim to keep most of the plants labelled.
Broadview Gardens at Hadlow College are a
partner garden of the RHS Garden Wisley, and
are open twice a year for the National Garden
Scheme. The gardens have links with the
National Council for the Conservation of Plants
and Gardens (NCCPG) with the collections of
Hellebores and Japanese Anemones.
All year daily 10.00-16.00
£2.00

**Discount Offer: Two for the Price of
One**

Emmetts Garden

Ide Hill Sevenoaks Kent TN14 6AY
Tel: 01732 868381 / 750367
Fax: 01732 868193
www.nationaltrust.org.uk
*[4mi from M25, J5. 1.5mi S of A25 on
Sundridge-Ide Hill rd. 1.5mi N of Ide Hill off
B2042. Rail: Sevenoaks (4.5mi) or Penshurst
(5.5mi). Bus: JRS Traveline 404 from Sevenoaks,
alight Ide Hill (1.5mi). Plenty of on-site parking]*

Influenced by William Robinson, this charming
and informal garden - with the highest treetop in
Kent - was laid out in the late nineteenth century, with many exotic and rare trees and shrubs
from across the world. There are glorious shows
of daffodils and bluebells, azaleas, rhododendrons in spring and acers and cornus in
autumn. There is also a rose garden and rock
garden. Volunteer driven buggy can take visitors
and one folded wheelchair from car park to ticket hut. Garden, shop and tearoom largely
accessible and wheelchairs available. Note:
there is a sheer drop at the end of the shrub
garden. Occasional guided tours available.
*17 Mar-3 June Tue-Sun & Bank Hols, 6 June-1
July Wed-Sun, 4 July-28 Oct Wed, Sat-Sun,
11.00-17.00*
A£5.50 C£1.00, Family Ticket (A2+C3) £12.00
NT Members £Free. Group rates (15+): £4.30,
must be booked in advance

Groombridge Place Gardens and Enchanted Forest

Groombridge Place Groombridge
Tunbridge Wells Kent TN3 9QG
Tel: 01892 861444 Fax: 01892 863996
www.groombridge.co.uk

[Off A264 on B2110. Plenty of on-site parking available]

Experience magic and mystery, history and romance at these beautiful award winning gardens - such an unusual mix of traditional heritage gardens with the excitement, challenge and contemporary landscaping of the ancient forest - appealing to young and old alike. Set in 200 acres of wooded parkland, the magnificent walled gardens are set against the romantic backdrop of a seventeenth-century moated manor and include herbaceous borders, white rose garden, drunken topiary, secret garden and more. Wonderful colour through the seasons. In ancient woodland there's an 'Enchanted Forest' with quirky and mysterious gardens developed by innovative designer, Ivan Hicks, to excite and challenge the imagination. Children love the Dark Walk, Tree Fern Valley, the Groms Village, Romany Camp and the Giant Swings. Also Birds of Prey flying displays, canal boat cruises and a great programme of special events.
31 Mar-3 Nov daily 10.00-17.30
A£8.95 C(3-12)&OAPs£7.45, Family Ticket (A2+C2) £29.95. Season tickets & group rates available

Chartwell

Mapleton Road Westerham Kent TN16 1PS
Tel: 01732 868381/866368 Fax: 01732 868193
[2mi S of Westerham. Rail: Edenbridge, Oxted or Sevenoaks. Plenty of on-site parking available]

Home of Sir Winston Churchill. With pictures, maps, documents and personal mementoes. The gardens contain the lakes he dug, the water garden where he fed his fish and his garden studio. Chartwell has partial disabled access.
House: 17 Mar-1 July Wed-Sun, 3 July-2 Sept Tue-Sun, 5 Sept-28 Oct Wed-Sun 11.00-17.00
A£10.80 C£5.40 Pre-booked Groups£9.00, Family Ticket £27.00. NT Members free

Cobham Hall

Cobham Gravesend Kent DA12 3BL
Tel: 01474 823371 Fax: 01474 825904
www.cobhamhall.com
[Adjacent to A2 / M2 between Gravesend / Rochester. 8mi from J2 M25, 27mi from London.

Plenty of on-site parking available]

Cobham Hall is an outstandingly beautiful, red brick mansion in Elizabethan, Jacobean, Carolian and eighteenth-century styles. This former home of the Earls of Darnley is set in 150 acres of parkland and is now an Independent international boarding and day school. The Gothic Dairy and some of the classical garden buildings are being renovated. The grounds yield many delights for the lover of nature, especially in spring, when the gardens and woods are resplendent with daffodils, narcissi and a myriad of rare bulbs. The House is open to guided tours Wednesdays and Sundays with delicious cream teas available in the Gilt Hall.
Mar-Apr Wed, Sun & Easter Weekend 14.00-17.00, July-Aug Wed & Sun 14.00-17.00. Guided Tours: Weds & Sun 14.00-17.00
A£4.50 C&OAPs£3.50

Deal Castle
Victoria Road Deal Kent CT14 7BA
Tel: 01304 372762
Deal Castle was built by Henry VIII as an artillery fortress.

Dover Castle and Secret Wartime Tunnels
Dover Castle Dover Kent CT16 1HU
Tel: 01304 211067
Two exhibitions about the role Dover played when the country was threatened by invasion.

Down House
Luxted Road Downe Orpington Kent BR6 7JT
Tel: 01689 859119
Visit the family home of Charles Darwin.

Hever Castle and Gardens
Hever Castle Hever Edenbridge Kent TN8 7NG
Tel: 01732 865224
This romantic thirteenth-century moated Castle was the childhood home of Anne Boleyn.

Leeds Castle
Maidstone Kent ME17 1PL
Tel: 01622 765400 Fax: 01622 735616
www.leeds-castle.com

[6mi at J8 of M20/A20. Plenty of on-site parking available]

Leeds Castle was listed in the Domesday Book and was originally the site of a manor for the Saxon royal family. It has been a Norman stronghold, a royal residence for six of the medieval Queens of England, the palace of Henry VIII and a 1920s country retreat. The castle's last private owner, Lady Baillie, lovingly restored the castle to its former glory and also founded the Leeds Castle Foundation in 1974, which is a charitable trust. Today, visitors can journey through 1000 years of fascinating history as they explore the castle - a treasure house of furnishings, paintings, tapestries and antiques. Not to mention 500 acres of parkland, gardens and attractions, which include a maze, an underground grotto, falconry displays and an aviary, which is home to over 100 rare and endangered species of bird. A guaranteed great day out.

All year daily Apr-Sept 10.00-17.00 last admission, Oct-Mar 10.00-15.00 last admission. Closed 7 July, 3-4 Nov & 25 Dec
Castle & Grounds: A£14.00 C(under4)£Free C£8.50 Concessions£11.00. Group rates available for 15+ people

Lullingstone Castle

Lullingstone Park Eynsford Dartford Kent
DA4 0JA
Tel: 01322 862114
In house, Queen Anne State rooms, family por-
traits, armour. Church of Norman origin, herb
garden, flower borders.

Maidstone Museum and Bentlif Art Gallery

St. Faiths Street Maidstone Kent ME14 1LH
Tel: 01622 602838
www.museum.maidstone.gov.uk
[Close to Maidstone East Station in town centre]

An absolute must-see, this exceptionally fine
regional museum houses a number of intriguing
collections in an Elizabethan manor house.
Collections range from natural history to military
memorabilia and the costume gallery. Look out
for the life-size dinosaurs and the fossils under
your feet in the Earth Heritage Gallery, and don't
miss the real Egyptian Mummy! Interactive areas
and an exciting programme of temporary exhibitions, workshops and children's activities mean
that there is something to capture everybody's
imagination. Limited disabled access. Special
workshops for children during half term and
school holidays.
*All year Mon-Sat 10.00-17.15, Sun 11.00-16.00.
Closed 25-26 Dec & 1 Jan*
Admission Free

Penshurst Place and Gardens

Penshurst Tonbridge Kent TN11 8DG
Tel: 01892 870307 Fax: 01892 870866
www.penshurstplace.com

*[From M25, J5, follow A21 to Hastings, exit
Hildenborough then follow brown tourist signs.
From M26, J2a, follow A25 (Sevenoaks) then
A21 for Hastings then as above. Rail: Tonbridge.
Plenty of on-site parking available]*

Ancestral home of the Sidney family since 1552,
with a history going back six and a half centuries, Penshurst Place has been described as
'the grandest and most perfectly preserved
example of a fortified manor house in all
England'. At the heart of this medieval masterpiece is the Barons Hall, built in 1341, and the
adjoining Staterooms contain a wonderful collection of tapestries, furniture, portraits and
armour. The ten acres of gardens are as old as
the original house - the walls and terraces were
added in the Elizabethan era - which ensures a
continuous display from spring to autumn.
There is also a toy museum, venture playground, gift shop and garden tea room.
*3 Mar Sat-Sun, 24 Mar-28 Oct daily. House:
12.00-16.00. Grounds: 10.30-18.00 (last entry
16.00). Gift Shop: 10.30-18.00*
House & Grounds: A£7.50 C(5-16)£5.00
Concessions£7.00, Family Ticket (A2+C2)
£21.00. Gardens only: A£6.00 C£4.50
Concessions£5.50, Family Ticket £18.00.
Guided tours for groups: House A£7.50
C£4.50, Garden £8.50 C£5.00, House &
Garden £11.00

For great hotel deals call Superbreak on 01904 679999 or visit www.superbreak.com

Quex Museum, House and Gardens - The Powell Cotton Collection

Quex Park Birchington Kent CT7 0BH
Tel: 01843 842168 Fax: 01843 846661
www.quexmuseum.org

[In Birchington 0.5mi S of Birchington Square, SW of Margate, 13mi E of Canterbury. Signposted. Rail: Birchington. Plenty of on-site parking available]

Quex House is one of Kent's loveliest Regency Houses and has been home to five generations of the Powell-Cotton family. It sits at the heart of the fifteenth-century Quex Estate. Rooms in the House are open to the public on summer afternoons. Quex was the home of Major P.H.G. Powell-Cotton, the intrepid nineteenth-century explorer, collector and conservationist. His world-famous collections of African zoology are displayed in stunningly impressive dioramas and his ethnographic collections provide unique insights into the diversity of that continent. Further galleries contain fine examples of European and Chinese porcelain, Japanese, netsuke, an extensive series of weapons from all over the world and local archaeology. The gardens reward exploration: lawns, fountains, a woodland walk, Victorian walled garden, peacocks, dovecote and wildlife pond. The site has free parking, a shop (including plants for sale) a large licensed restaurant and good access for disabled visitors.

26 Mar-end Oct Sun-Thur 11.00-17.00, House from 14.00. Winter Sun 13.00-15.30 except Christmas & New Year

A£5.00 C(5-16)&OAPs£4.00, Family Ticket (A2+C3) £14.00. Group rates (for 20+) available on request

Maritime

Old Lighthouse

Dungeness Road Dungeness Romney Marsh Kent TN29 9NB
Tel: 01797 321300 Fax: 01303 258691
www.dungenesslighthouse.com

[From M20 J10 onto A2070 towards Brenzett & Lydd airport. After 12mi, turn L at roundabout & join A259. After 4mi turn R onto B2075 sign posted for Lydd. Immediately after bridge, take L hand fork. Turn L at roundabout onto Dungeness Rd. Continue for 4mi. Turn R into Dungeness & the Old Lighthouse is at end of rd]

Lighthouse constructed in 1901-1904 operated until 1960 redundant due to the construction of the nearby Power Station, which obscured the Main Beam. This imposing building is almost 46 metres high to the top of the weather vane 11 metres in diameter, constructed of engineering bricks with sandstone interior walls, over 3 million bricks were used to build the structure. Internally there are series of Mezzanine floors made of slate supported by the steel beams and massive rivets. Each floor is linked by concrete stairs, which hugs the walls, and has decorative iron banisters. Cambered casement viewing windows. On fine days it is possible to walk around the balcony. Climb the tower of 169 steps for panoramic views over the English Channel and the surrounding countryside. Binoculars well worth bringing. Dungeness Lighthouse offers unique and perfect views over the shingle ridges. No animals and no commercial photo shoots.

Easter Hols, May Sat-Sun & Bank Hols, 1-30 June Thurs-Sun, 1-24 July Tues-Sun, 25 July-end Aug daily, Sept Thurs-Sun, Oct Sat-Sun. 10.45-16.30. Closed Nov-Mar

A£3.00 C£2.00 OAPs£2.50, Family Ticket (A2+C4)£9.00 Student(NUD/NSI)£2.00

Ramsgate Maritime Museum

Clock House Pier Yard Royal Harbour
Ramsgate Kent CT11 8LS
Tel: 01843 570622
www.ekmt.fogonline.co.uk

[Follow A299 to Ramsgate. Follow signs to harbour]

The museum is housed in Ramsgate Harbour's historic Clock House, a Grade II* listed building. Its five galleries explore the maritime heritage of the Isle of Thanet and East Kent from ancient times up to the present day. Subjects covered include: the construction and history of the country's only Royal Harbour; the fishing and shipbuilding industries; maritime navigation and the search for longitude; the Royal Navy and Ramsgate's role in times of war; the lifeboat service, the Great Storm of 1703; and the dangers to shipping posed by the notorious Goodwin Sands. The museum also houses a fascinating marine archaeological collection composed of artefacts raised from vessels lost on the sands - including a unique Prince Rupert Patent Demi-Cannon, recovered complete with it's original wooden carriage from the wreck of the late Stuart warship Stirling Castle.

All year, Easter-Sept Tue-Sun 10.00-17.00, Closed Mon (except Bank Hol). Oct-Easter Thur-Sun 11.00-16.30. Closed Mon-Wed (except Bank Hol)
A£1.50 C£0.75 OAPs£0.75, Family Ticket £4.00

Discount Offer: Two for the Price of One

Explore the maritime heritage of Thanet and the East Kent coast.

Opening Times
Summer: Tue-Sun 10.00-17.00
Winter: Thu-Sun 11.00-16.30
(last admission: 30mins before closing)

The Clock House, Pier Yard, Ramsgate
Kent CT11 8LS

Tel: 01843 570622

www.ekmt.fogonline.co.uk

Military & Defence Museums

Canterbury Buffs Regimental Museum

Royal Museum and Art Gallery High Street
Canterbury CT1 2RA
Tel: 01227 452747
Display of uniforms, old arms, awards, campaign medals, regimental colours, pictures, trophies and souvenirs.

Princess of Wales's Royal Regiment and the Queen's Regiment Museum

Inner Bailey Dover Castle Dover Kent CT16 1HU
Tel: 01304 240121
Trace the fascinating story of The Princess of Wales's Royal Regiment from its beginnings in 1572 to present day.

Royal Engineers Museum

Prince Arthur Road Gillingham Kent ME4 4UG
Tel: 01634 822839

The prize-winning museum tells the story of Britain's soldier engineers - the Sappers. It is a treasure trove of the unexpected ranging from Wellington's battlemap of Waterloo to a Harrier Jump jet.

Music & Theatre Museums

Mills - Water & Wind

Crabble Corn Mill

Lower Road River Dover Kent CT17 0UY
Tel: 01304 823292
www.ccmt.org.uk

Crabble Corn Mill is run by volunteers from the local community. Since its restoration in 1989, it has won several awards including the Community Enterprise Award. The Mill is one of the finest working watermills in Europe and it is the only working watermill in Kent. This is a must-see visitor attraction and one of Dover's hidden gems.

Apr-Sep Tue-Sun, Feb-Apr & Oct-20 Dec Sun only 11.00-17.00
A£5.00 Concessions£3.50, Family Ticket £13.00

Finchcocks Living Museum of Music

Finchcocks Museum Riseden Goudhurst Kent TN17 1HH
Tel: 01580 211702 Fax: 01580 211007
www.finchcocks.co.uk

[M25, A21 then A262 from London. Plenty of on-site parking available]

This fine early Georgian house stands in a spacious park with a beautiful garden, and contains an outstanding collection of keyboard instruments from the seventeenth century onwards. They have been restored to playing condition, and there are musical tours on all open days and private visits. Visually handicapped visitors may touch the instruments as well as hear them. Special events include fairs (May & October) and Music Festival weekends in September. Both indoor and outdoor picnic areas.

Easter-Sept Sun & Bank Hol Mon 14.00-18.00, Aug Wed, Thur & Sun 14.00-18.00. Private groups by appointment Apr-Oct & Dec
A£8.00 C£4.00 daytime, A£9.00 evening

Discount Offer: Two for the Price of One

On the Water

Bewl Water
Bewlbridge Lane Lamberhurst Tunbridge Wells
Kent TN3 8JH
Tel: 01892 890661
Watersports, visitor centre and summer events.

Places of Worship

Canterbury Cathedral
Cathedral House The Precincts Canterbury Kent
CT1 2EH
Tel: 01227 762862
Mother Church of the Anglican Communion.

The Friars
Aylesford Priory Aylesford Kent ME20 7BX
Tel: 01622 717272
Dating back to the thirteenth century, the priory
has now been restored.

Railways

Kent and East Sussex Railway
Tenterden Town Station Tenterden Kent
TN30 6HE
Tel: 087 060 060 74 Fax: 01580 765654
www.kesr.org.uk
[On A28. Plenty of on-site parking available]
The Kent & East Sussex Railway owes much of
its charm to its origin as the world's first light
railway. Originally opened in 1900, the tightly
curved line with steep gradients is typical of
those rural railways that were developed on
shoestring budgets to bring the 'iron house' to
sparsely populated areas. Re-opened by dedicated volunteers as an attraction in 1974 following its demise in the 1950s, today it is one of
Britain's most loved, most original heritage railways, running steam and heritage diesel trains
for 10¼ miles from Tenterden in the Kentish
Weald through the Rother Valley brushing past
Northiam to Bodiam in East Sussex - where it
terminates a stone's throw from the magnificent
Bodiam Castle. An ever-evolving range of special events and offers provides temptation and
interest for all ages whether you're a regular visitor or one who has yet to discover the unique
charm of the Kent & East Sussex Railway.

*Please call the talking timetable on 01580
762943*
A£11.00 C£6.00 OAPs£10.00, Family Ticket
£29.00

Romney Hythe and Dymchurch Railway

New Romney Station Littlestone Road
New Romney Kent TN28 8PL
Tel: 01797 362353 Fax: 01797 363591
www.rhdr.org.uk
[M20, J11 signposted, Hythe station, other stations on A259. Plenty of on-site parking available]
The Romney, Hythe & Dymchurch Railway, is one of the world's unique railways running for nearly 14 miles across Kent's historic Romney Marsh, linking the Cinque Ports towns of Hythe and New Romney via the children's paradise of Dymchurch and St Mary's Bay, and on to the lighthouses at Dungeness, this is an ideal day out for all the family. Take a ride behind one of the superb fleet of one-third scale Steam and Diesel locomotives on rails just 15 inches (381mm) apart as they relive the days of the express locomotive. There are cafés at New Romney and Dungeness, gift shops at all major stations and a real gem is to be found at New Romney, above the Heywood Buffet is the Model Railway Exhibition, with a massive working model railway layout depicting scenes from mountains to the coast, there is also another working layout plus toys and models which bring back happy memories of yesteryear. The history of the line is featured in words and pictures telling the story of this, the worlds only mainline in miniature, which is still being kept alive by dedicated staff and volunteers. Opened in July 1927, The RH&DR was the brainchild of two former racing drivers, Captain J.E.P Howey and Count Louis Zborowski - who was perhaps better known as the driver of the original Chitty bang bang, (the second 'Chitty' was added for the film) unfortunately Count Louis was killed in a car racing accident before the RHDR was finished but Captain Howey with the help of world renowned model maker Henry Greenly kept the dream alive to build the biggest little railway in the world.
Regular services Easter-Sept daily also weekends in Mar & Oct, Feb-Oct half-terms daily

Fares depend on length of journey, C£half-price, discount for pre-booked parties of 20+. OAP concessions available

Spa Valley Railway

West Station Nevill Terrace Tunbridge Wells
Kent TN2 5QY
Tel: 01892 537715
www.spavalleyrailway.co.uk
[35mi from central London, 18mi from J5 M25 via A21 & A26]

Take a trip on the Spa Valley Railway through the beautiful Wealden Countryside. The heritage railway, primarily operating Steam hauled passenger trains, runs from the historic town of Royal Tunbridge Wells, via High Rocks, to the charming village of Groombridge. Tunbridge Wells West station is situated just off the A26, South of the town centre. The railway gift shop, buffet and engine shed are all situated here. The Pantiles historic shopping area, and the Chalybeate Spring are just a few minutes walk. High Rocks halt is situated adjacent to the historic High Rocks Inn. Investigate the spectacular sandstone rocks, enjoy the local footpaths or enjoy a meal or drink in the unique surroundings. Groombridge is currently the normal terminus for passenger trains. The station is in the heart of the attractive village, and just 10mins walk from the award winning Groombridge Place Gardens and Enchanted Forest.
Apr-Oct & Dec, please call for further details
Full line return, A£5.00 C&OAPs£4.00. Special fares for event weekends please call for futher details

Discount Offer: One Child Free

Theme & Adventure Parks

Diggerland

Medway Valley Leisure Park Roman Way Strood Kent ME2 2NU
Tel: 08700 344437 Fax: 09012 010300
www.diggerland.com
[M2 J2, A228 towards Rochester. At roundabout turn R, we are on R. Rail: Strood & Rochester. Bus: Arriva 151. Plenty of on-site parking available]

Diggerland is the best activity day out for all the family with all activities based around construction machinery. With over 15 rides and drives positioned in an adventure park situation. Experience the thrill of riding in Spindizzy and enjoy the view from the Sky Shuttle. Drive across rough terrain in the Super Track and enjoy a mystery ride in the Land Rover Safari. Test your co-ordination in the JCB Challenges and fasten your seat belt for the drive of your life in the Robots. A full day of fun can be had by all ages with everything onsite including refuelling at The Dig Inn and shopping at the Goodie store. Birthday parties are catered for, so if you fancy a party with a difference then contact us for details. Diggerland welcomes its 4th park in Yorkshire for 2007. Please see our website for more information.
Weekends & Bank Hols plus daily during half-term & school hols 10.00-17.00
A&C£12.50 C(under3)£Free OAPs£6.25. Group rates: (10+) 10% discount, (50+) 25% discount

Discount Offer: 10% off Admission Prices

Go Ape! High Wire Forest Adventure

Bedgebury Visitor Centre Bedgebury Road Goudhurst Kent TN17 2SJ
Tel: 0870 420 7876
www.goape.co.uk
[Bedgebury is signposted off A21 on B2079. Approx. 12mi SE of Tunbridge Wells & 16mi NW of Hastings. Plenty of on-site parking available]

Take to the trees and experience an exhilarating course of rope bridges, 'Tarzan Swings' and zip-slides up to 40 feet above the ground! Share approximately three hours of memorable fun and adventure, which you'll be talking about for days. Book online and watch people Go Ape! at www.goape.co.uk. Minimum height 1.4m. Maximum weight 130 kg (20.5 stone). Under-18s must be accompanied by a participating adult. One adult can supervise either two children (where one or both of them in under 16 years old) or up to five 16-17 year olds. Pre-booking is essential to avoid disappointment. Book online or by telephone (there is a £1.00 booking fee on all telephone bookings).

23 Mar-2 Nov (plus Nov weekends). Closed Dec-Jan
Gorillas (18yrs+) £25.00, Baboons (10-17yrs) £20.00

Discount Offer: Two for the Price of One

Wildlife & Safari Parks

Howletts Wild Animal Park

Bekesbourne Lane Bekesbourne Canterbury Kent CT4 5EL
Tel: 01227 721286 Fax: 01227 721853
www.totallywild.net
[Signposted off A2 (3mi S of Canterbury). Plenty of on-site parking available]
At Howletts Wild Animal Park, you can see world conservation in action n the heart of Kent. Set in 90 acres of beautiful ancient parkland, Howletts is now home to the world's largest family of gorillas in captivity and the UK's biggest herd of African elephants including two 'big babies' born last year. Rare and endangered species around every corner include black rhinos, Indian and Siberian tigers, clouded leopards, Brazilian tapirs, African hunting dogs, servals and bongos. You can walk alongside amazingly agile and inquisitive lemurs in their special open closure and enjoy one of the world's best vantage points for observing exceptionally rare Javan langurs. Don't miss this year's newest animal additions including rare Sumatran tigers and wild wolves from Iberia. Summer evening shuttle and walking safaris available - booking essential. Hot and cold dishes are available all day in the Pavilion Restaurant and Pizzeria. Please note that dogs (including guide dogs) are not allowed.
Daily, Summer 10.00-18.00, Winter 10.00-17.00. Closed 25 Dec
A£13.95 C(under4)£Free C(4-16)&OAPs£10.95

Discount Offer: Kid for a Quid

Port Lympne Wild Animal Park

Aldington Road Lympne Hythe, nr Ashford Kent CT21 4PD
Tel: 01303 264647 Fax: 01303 264944
www.totallywild.net
[J11 M20. Park is 5min away, signposted from J. Plenty of on-site parking available]

Port Lympne Wild Animal Park opens up an amazing world of exploration where many endangered and rare animals live in a sweeping, 600-acre estate of woodland, hills and grassland. One minute you could be on the plains of Africa - the next, in the heart of the jungle or rainforest. Magnificent views over Romney Marsh remind you that you are in one of the most picturesque corners of the Kent countryside. The 16-acre, beautifully landscaped gardens surrounding Port Lympne Mansion are an additional attraction. New for 2007; baby black rhino, African bull elephant 'Kruger', totally wild 'tree-jumping', overnight safaris from June (booking essential). There are also Barbary lions, lemurs, baboons, red pandas, 'flying monkeys', the world's largest family gorilla house, snow leopards, tigers, lynx, African hunting dogs and much more. For a small additional charge, you can enjoy a real safari in the 'African Experience' where giraffe, black rhino, zebra, wildebeest and antelope roam free. Please note that dogs (including guide dogs) are not allowed.
Summer 10.00-18.00. Winter 10.00-17.00. Closed 25 Dec
A£13.95 C(under4)£Free C(4-16)&OAPs£10.95

Discount Offer: Kid for a Quid

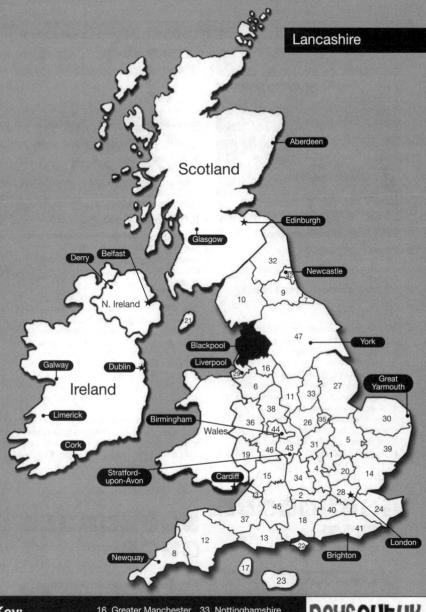

Lancashire

Scotland

Aberdeen

Edinburgh

Glasgow

Newcastle

Derry
Belfast

N. Ireland

York

Galway
Dublin

Blackpool

Liverpool

Ireland

Great
Yarmouth

Limerick

Birmingham

Wales

Cork

Stratford-
upon-Avon

Cardiff

London

Newquay

Brighton

32

42

9

10

7

47

21

16

6

11

33

27

38

36

44

26

35

30

19

46

43

31

5

39

15

34

1

4

20

14

28

2

24

45

40

41

37

18

13

12

22

8

17

23

Abbeys

Whalley Abbey

The Sands Whalley Clitheroe Lancashire
BB7 9SS
Tel: 01254 828400 Fax: 01254 825519
[J36 M6 Whalley A59 to village. Plenty of on-site parking available]

The ruins of a thirteenth-century Cistercian Abbey are set in the delightful gardens of the Blackburn Diocesan Retreat and Conference House, a sixteenth-century manor house with gardens reaching down to the River Calder. On site facilities include a picnic area within the kitchen garden, a coffee shop, gift shop and small exhibition area plotting the history of the Abbey. The conference house offers Bed and Breakfast accommodation, with a 4* Quality in Tourism rating, to compliment your visit.
All year daily 10.00-16.30. Limited opening over Christmas & New Year
A£2.00 C£0.50 OAPs£1.25 FamilyTicket £4.00

Agriculture / Working Farms

Bowland Wild Boar Park

Chipping Preston Lancashire PR3 2QS
Tel: 01995 61554
View wild boar, longhorn cows and deer in the scenic Ribble Valley Park. Meet the small animals and feed them if you wish.

Animal Attractions

ILPH Penny Farm

Preston New Road Peel Blackpool FY4 5JS
Tel: 01253 766983
www.ilph.org/pennyfarm
[On A583 a short distance from M55. Plenty of on-site parking available]

ILPH Penny Farm was opened to the public in June 2001 by HRH the Princess Royal. It is home to around 50 horses and ponies in over 100 acres and has many specialist facilities to allow us to rehabilitate horses and ponies giving them the chance of a new life through our loan scheme. Our volunteers undertake guided farm tours, relating the histories and progress of those equines on view in the yard and surrounding paddocks. Penny Farm has an informative visitor centre, which shows the work of the ILPH both at home and abroad. The coffee shop offers traditional, home made food fayre and occasionally plays host to children's' birthday parties 'with a difference'. Penny Farm is a great day out for all the family.
All year Weds, Sat-Sun & Bank Hols 11.00-16.00. Closed 25 Dec-1 Jan
Admission Free

Arts, Crafts & Textiles

Botany Bay

Canal Mill Botany Brow Chorley Lancashire
PR6 9AF
Tel: 01257 261220
Five floors of crafts, furniture, soft furnishings, collectables and memorabilia. There's also an indoor adventure play centre for children.

Birds, Butterflies & Bees

WWT Martin Mere

Fish Lane Burscough Ormskirk L40 0TA
Tel: 01704 895181 Fax: 01704 892343
www.wwt.org.uk
[Only 6mi from Ormskirk & 10mi from Southport. Situated off A59, signposted from M61, M58 & M6. Rail: Burscough (Southport - Manchester line) 1mi. Bus: 3 from Ormskirk (except Sun). Cyclists welcome. Plenty of on-site parking available]

Visit WWT Martin Mere at any time of year and you are guaranteed a great day out. Discover over a thousand ducks, swans, geese and flamingos in our 26 acre waterfowl gardens. Visit themed areas such as the South American Lake, the Oriental Pen and the African area, where you can see our African Crowned Cranes. As you wander around the waterfowl gardens feeding the waterfowl, bear in mind that your entrance fee has helped WWT to restore habitats and undertake captive breeding programmes for many of the rare birds that you have been feeding. After your walk around the waterfowl garden have lunch or a snack in the Pinkfoot Pantry and visit our gift shop for souvenirs.
All year daily Mar-Oct 09.30-17.30, Nov-Feb 09.30-17.00. Closed 25 Dec
A£7.95 C(4-16)£3.95 Concessions£5.95, Family Ticket (A2+C2) £18.95. (Prices include a voluntary donation of at least 10%, visitors can choose to pay standard admission price)

Factory Outlets & Tours

Oswaldtwistle Mills

Moscow Mill Collier Street Oswaldtwistle Accrington Lancashire BB5 3DE
Tel: 01254 871025 Fax: 01254 770790
www.o-mills.co.uk
[Just off J7 M65. Plenty of on-site parking]

A family attraction set within a working mill and its grounds. Oswaldtwistle Mills has something to amaze, charm and intrigue visitors of all ages. The former weaving mill has three licensed coffee shops, children's play area, sweet factory, wildfowl reserve and over 80 retailers selling clothing, giftware, homeware, furniture and more.
All year Mon-Sat 09.30-17.30 (Thur 20.00) Sun 10.00-17.00

Discount Offer: 10% Discount on Food & Drink Purchases in Café Nova

Festivals and Shows

Blackpool Illuminations

Promenade Blackpool Lancashire
Tel: 01253 478222
Using over one million bulbs, the Blackpool Illuminations are an awesome spectacle.
31 Aug-4 Nov 2007

British Lawnmower Museum

106-114 Shakespeare Street Southport
Lancashire PR8 5AJ
Tel: 01704 501336
Boasts a unique collection of restored garden
machinery and memorabilia.

Gawthorpe Hall

Padiham Burnley Lancashire BB12 8UA
**Tel: 01282 771004 Fax: 01282
770178/770353**
www.lancsmuseums.gov.uk

*[On E outskirts of Padiham, 0.75mi drive to house
on N of A671, M65, J8 towards Clitheroe, then
signposted from 2nd traffic light junction. Bus:
services from Burnley. Rail: Rose Grove (2mi)]*

Gawthorpe Hall was built between 1600 and
1605 for the Shuttleworth family on their estate
in East Lancashire. Possibly designed by Robert
Smythson, the man responsible for Hardwick
Hall, there are a number of similarities between
the two buildings and many of the original features can still be found at Gawthorpe. During
the mid nineteenth century, Sir Charles Barry
and Augustus Pugin were commissioned by Sir
James Kay-Shuttleworth to refurbish the house,
thereby creating the opulent interiors we see
today. In addition there are many notable paintings on loan from the National Portrait Gallery
and an unparalleled collection of needlework
assembled by Rachel Kay-Shuttleworth, the last
family member to live in the house. Today the
house is alive with exhibitions, events and family
activities.

*Hall: 1 Apr-28 Oct Tue-Thur & Sat-Sun (open
Good Fri & Bank Hol Mons) 13.00-17.00.
Garden: all year daily 10.00-18.00*
House: A£4.00 Concessions£3.00, C£Free.
Garden: Admission Free. Group rates available
on request

Lancaster Castle

Shire Hall Castle Parade Lancaster Lancashire
LA1 1YJ
Tel: 01524 64998 Fax: 01524 847914
www.lancastercastle.com
[Follow brown signs from A6 to the City Centre]

One of the country's hidden gems, Lancaster
Castle still serves as a prison and crown court,
but it is still possible to visit this intriguing place
by joining one of our celebrated guided tours.
From the imposing beauty of the Shire Hall to
the grim reality of the Old Cells and the Drop
Room, the castle reflects a thousand years of
history and tells the story of the many people
who have passes through its gates. Witches
and martyrs, kings and queens, heroes and vil-
lains: they all have their place here against a
unique setting. The castle is open daily for guided tours (except for Christmas/New Year period), but as well as that we offer regular musical
and theatrical events, talks and themed tours.
Please telephone or visit our website for more
information.
*All year daily 10.00-17.00, tours 10.30-16.00.
Closed Christmas & New Year*
A£5.00 C&OAPs£4.00, Family Ticket £14.00

Leighton Hall

Carnforth Lancashire LA5 9ST
Tel: 01524 734474 Fax: 01524 720357
www.leightonhall.co.uk

[J35 M6. Plenty of on-site parking available]

Award-winning Leighton Hall is the lived-in house of the famous furniture-making Gillow dynasty. Unravel the fascinating past of this ancient Lancashire family; wander through the spectacular grounds and witness breathtaking displays from trained birds of prey. Leighton also has a caterpillar maze, plant conservatory and charming tearooms. Children can run wild in the play area or explore a woodland trail; they're encouraged to get involved - there are no roped off areas! Leighton Hall is very much a 'lived in' house, brought to life by the enthusiasm of its guides. Leighton Hall can be found nestling in a bowl of parkland in the north of Lancashire, a few miles from the city of Lancaster. It's open to the public from May to September, pre-booked groups are welcome all year round and parking is free.

May-Sep Tue-Fri & Bank Hols 14.00-17.00. Aug only: Tue-Fri, Sun & Bank Hols 12.30-17.00. Groups of 25+ welcome all year round by prior arrangement. Birds-of-Prey fly at 15.30 (weather permitting)

Hall & Gardens: A£6.00 C£4.00 OAPs£5.00, Family Ticket (A2+C3) £18.00. Gardens Only: £2.00 (for all)

Discount Offer: Two for the Price of One

Rufford Old Hall

Liverpool Rd Rufford Lancashire L40 1SG
Tel: 01704 821254
One of the finest sixteenth-century buildings in Lancashire with a magnificent hall, built in 1530.

Landmarks

Blackpool Tower

Central Promenade Blackpool Lancashire FY1 4BJ
Tel: 01253 622242
Looming over Blackpool's Golden Mile, the Tower is one of the most famous seaside landmarks in England.

Model Towns & Villages

Blackpool Model Village

East Park Drive Stanley Park Blackpool Lancashire FY3 9RB
Tel: 01253 763827
Hundreds of models against a background of waterfalls, lakes and running streams.

Performing Arts

Doctor Who Museum

The Golden Mile Centre Central Promenade Blackpool Lancashire FY1 5AA
Tel: 01253 299982
The all-new Doctor Who Museum boasts the largest collection of programme exhibits ever.

Winter Gardens Blackpool

97 Church Street Blackpool FY1 1HL
Tel: 01253 625252
A large complex of theatres and conference facilities.

EAST LANCASHIRE RAILWAY

Bolton Street Station, Bury BL9 0EY

DISCOVER
The East Lancashire Railway
Relive the golden age of steam

Ride behind a vintage steam locomotive to view the scenic West Pennine Moors, break your journey at any station to visit Mill shops, Bury Market, cafes, restaurants, bars and many attractions nearby!
Special events: Day Out With Thomas, Teddy Bears Picnic, 1940s Weekend and more!!

Steam trains run every weekend and bank holidays throughout the year
+ Wednesday, Thursday and Friday (May to Sept)

Big discounts offered to coach parties!
Tel: 0161 764 7790

www.east-lancs-rly.co.uk
enquire@east-lancs-rly.co.uk

Heywood – BURY – Ramsbottom – Rawtenstall

Railways

East Lancashire Railway

Bolton Street Station Bolton Street Bury
Lancashire BL9 0EY
Tel: 0161 764 7790 Fax: 0161 763 4408
www.east-lancs-rly.co.uk
[M66 J2. Railway is signposted from all major rds. Plenty of on-site parking available]

A mainly steam hauled train service between

Bury to Ramsbottom, Rawtenstall and Heywood. This popular steam railway offers a day out for all the family with all the trimmings you expect on a railway (tunnels, level crossings etc). You can break your journey at any station to visit the shops at Dickensian Ramsbottom with its Farmers and Sunday markets. A riverside picnic area allows you to view the trains. Then, rejoin the train, and complete your journey with views of the Pennine Moors - an ideal day out for the family whatever the weather. Special events are held throughout the year and include a Day Out with Thomas, Teddy Bears Picnic, 1940s weekend and Santa Specials to name just a few. The Railway also runs Sunday Lunch and Diners trains and Drive a Steam Engine makes an ideal present.
Weekend service & Bank Hol also May-Sept Wed, Thur, Fri. Dec Santa specials. Closed 25 Dec
Full Line Return Ticket: A£11.00 C£7.40

Discount Offer: Two for the Price of One

Sealife Centres & Aquariums

SEA·LIFE
BLACKPOOL

Blackpool Sea Life Centre

Golden Mile Centre Promenade Blackpool
Lancashire FY1 5AA
Tel: 01253 621258 Fax: 01253 751647
www.sealifeeurope.com

[M55, signposted to venue]

Blackpool Sea Life is one of the most fascinating, exciting underwater adventures to visit. Experience close encounters with an amazing collection of marine and freshwater creatures, including sharks, rays, seahorses, Gary the Grouper and even piranhas. Relax in our seaview cafe whilst younger visitors can explore the soft play area, complete with slide and ball pit.

Feeding demonstrations throughout the day provide insight into the marvels of the marine world. Guided tours around our aquarium by prior arrangement. New for 2007! Step through our sunken galleon and discover pirates: The Legend of Blackbeard. Be surrounded by the beautiful Caribbean Reef and see the tropical sharks and shoaling fish that have made their home in the ghostly wreck. Stay around long enough and you're sure to hear the tale of how Blackbeard's ship came to rest from an old shipmate.

All year daily from 10.00. Closed Christmas day
Please call for price details

Discount Offer: One Child Free

Spectator Sports

Trax Motorsport Ltd

Wallend Road Ashton-On-Ribble Preston Lancashire PR2 2HW
Tel: 01772 731832

Trax is a 140-acre multi activity leisure site, it offers everything you need for the ultimate adrenaline thrill! Located in Preston on the Docklands we can provide a number of exciting activities to suit people of all ages. The activities range from Paintball, Karting, Junior Moto-x or Quad biking. If you own your own kart or motorbike (on or off road) we have a fantastic circuit available for you to use. If you want to have a great day out with the family or friends we are open every weekend and selected weekdays throughout the year.
For more information on any of these activities please call one of the following numbers: Karting 01772 769554; Paintball 07811 480 660; JM-X 01772 739334; MX Track 07710523430.

Sport & Recreation

Sandcastle Waterworld

South Promenade Blackpool FY4 1BB
Tel: 01253 343602
Enjoy the permanent heatwave at this swimming pool on Blackpool Promenade.

Theme & Adventure Parks

Camelot Theme Park

Park Hall Road Charnock Richard Chorley Lancashire PR7 5LP
Tel: 08702 204820 (24hr info)
Fax: 01257 452320
www.camelotthemepark.co.uk
[J27 N on M6, J28 S on M6, J8 M61. Plenty of on-site parking available]
Camelot Theme Park is a land of great knights and Amazing days where you can meet Merlin, King Arthur and his brave Knights of the Round Table and explore 5 magical lands filled with thrilling rides, spectacular shows and many more attractions. Thrill seekers will enjoy the mighty Whirlwind, and the scarey 'Knightmare' two terrifying roller coasters, designed to whip you into a frenzy, when you catch your breath dare to try the torturous Rack or brave the waters of Pendragon's Plunge. There's also a great selection of rides for our younger brave-hearts. Be amazed at the spectacular horsemanship of the Knights of the Round Table and cheer for your favourite Knight as they perform in a medieval Jousting Tournament or brush up on your magic skills by joining Camelot's grand weaver of spells for a master class in conjuring and magic at Merlin's School of Wizardry. It really is an amazing family day out!
31 Mar-28 Oct 10.00-17.00. Please call 24hr info line to check specific days
A&C£18.00 OAPs£12.00, Family Ticket (4 Guests) £60.00. Children under 1 metre in height £Free. Group rates (for 12+) available on request

Discount Offer: Two for the Price of One

Pleasure Beach, Blackpool

Blackpool Lancashire FY4 1EZ
Tel: 0870 444 5566 Fax: 01253 407609
www.blackpoolpleasurebeach.com

[M6 J32 then take M55, follow brown tourist signs. Plenty of on-site parking available]

With over 125 rides and attractions plus our spectacular shows, there's something for everyone at the Pleasure Beach. New for 2007: Infusion will take riders through a whirlwind water experience. Five incredible loops and rolls plus a double-line twist, all in one suspended looping coaster. Don't miss Bling: spin through the air at 100ft on our giant glittering gondolas. Don't miss the Pepsi Max Big One - Europe's tallest roller coaster (at 235ft) with over a mile of twists and turns at 87mph. Experience the thrills of one of the world's only twin-tracked coasters - The Grand National, plus much, much more. For more information, please telephone or visit our website.

10 Feb-25 Mar Sat-Sun, 30 Mar-4 Nov daily
Purchase wristbands or ride tickets, also available for Beaver Creek Children's Park. Wristbands give you unlimited riding all day long!

Discount Offer: Three Wristbands for the Price of Two Wristbands

British Commercial Vehicle Museum

King Street Leyland Preston Lancashire PR25 2LE
Tel: 01772 451011 Fax: 01772 451015
www.bcvm.co.uk

[5min from J28 M6. Plenty of on-site parking available]

Take a journey back in time and explore 100 years of British commercial vehicle history. The British Commercial Vehicle Museum at Leyland, Lancashire is the largest commercial vehicle museum in Europe. It houses the country's only national collection of historic vans, trucks and buses and illustrates the proud history of Britain's road transport industry through a collection of exhibits, including dramatic 'sound and light' sets, which bring the role of these vehicles alive. Throughout the season there are special events, exhibitions and rallies. Please contact the museum for up-to-date information or visit our website. School parties are very welcome. A lecture room is provided and a unique series of school curriculum materials featuring Britain's road transport heritage are provided free of charge to each visiting group. Private group visits individually catered for.

Apr-Sept Sun, Tue-Thur, Oct Sun only, open Bank Hol Mon 10.00-17.00
A£4.00 C(4-15)&OAPs£2.00, Family Ticket (A2+C3) £10.00

Victorian Era

Wigan Pier

Wallgate Wigan Lancashire WN3 4EU
Tel: 01942 323666
Provides an educational and fun packed day
out, transporting visitors back in time.

Wax Works

Louis Tussauds Waxworks

87/89 Central Promenade Blackpool FY1 5AA
Tel: 01253 625953 Fax: 01253 621611
www.louistussaudswaxworks.co.uk
[J1/2 M55, A583 to Promenade]

Join us at Louis Tussaud's Waxworks and you'll
feel like a star! See the all-new "CelebCity",
where you can mingle with the stars and get
closer to the A-list. Once you've walked the red
carpet, you'll be immersed in a world of celebrity, rubbing shoulders with Hollywood's A List
and the tabloid's favourites. Don't miss our all
new Coronation Street set where you can meet
the stars in the Rovers and gossip with Vera
and Jack outside on the UK's most famous
cobbles! You can even find out how the stars
became Waxworks legends, when you take a
fascinating look behind the scenes and find out
how the stars are modelled and how clothing,
accessories and scenery are created.
All year daily from 10.00 except Christmas Day
Please check prior to visit. Various Family
Tickets available

Zoos

Blackpool Zoo

East Park Drive Blackpool Lancashire FY3 8PP
Tel: 01253 830830 Fax: 01253 830800
www.blackpoolzoo.org.uk

[Close to M55. Plenty of on-site parking available]

Over 1500 animals live in our 32-acre zoo,
including big cats, elephants, gorillas, orang-
utans, sea lions and many more! The Dinosaur
Safari comprises 32 life-size dinosaurs on a fun
time trail. Realistic sounds, and an erupting volcano, complete this amazing experience. There
are two excellent catering facilities serving a full
range of meals and snacks. Three retail outlets
offer gifts from pocket-money prices to quality
collectables such as the Diane Fossey range of
gorillas. We also have a free exhibition area, a
state-of-the-art conference facility, and an outdoor theatre arena with sheltered seating for
events and shows. The entire site is fully accessible to wheelchair users. We also pride our-
selves on offering "talking tours" for the blind,
and signing for the deaf. No dogs allowed on
site. Our superb education team provide talks
and presentations for all ages and abilities and
can be contacted on 01253 830805.

Daily from 10.00. Closed Christmas Day
Prices: To be arranged - see website

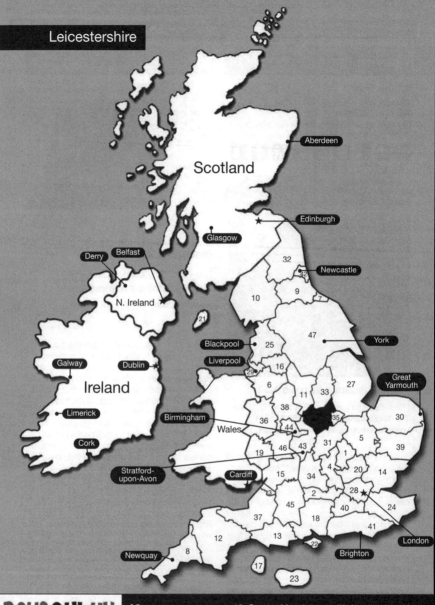

Leicestershire

Scotland

Aberdeen

Edinburgh

Glasgow

Newcastle

Derry   Belfast

N. Ireland

Blackpool

Liverpool

York

Galway   Dublin

Ireland

Great Yarmouth

Limerick

Birmingham

Wales

Cork

Stratford-upon-Avon

Cardiff

London

Newquay

Brighton

Key:

1	Bedfordshire
2	Berkshire
3	Bristol
4	Buckinghamshire
5	Cambridgeshire
6	Cheshire
7	Cleveland
8	Cornwall
9	County Durham
10	Cumbria
11	Derbyshire
12	Devon
13	Dorset
14	Essex
15	Gloucestershire
16	Greater Manchester
17	Guernsey
18	Hampshire
19	Herefordshire
20	Hertfordshire
21	Isle Of Man
22	Isle Of Wight
23	Jersey
24	Kent
25	Lancashire
26	Leicestershire
27	Lincolnshire
28	London
29	Merseyside
30	Norfolk
31	Northamptonshire
32	Northumberland
33	Nottinghamshire
34	Oxfordshire
35	Rutland
36	Shropshire
37	Somerset
38	Staffordshire
39	Suffolk
40	Surrey
41	Sussex
42	Tyne & Wear
43	Warwickshire
44	West Midlands
45	Wiltshire
46	Worcestershire
47	Yorkshire

Animal Attractions

Manor Farm Animal Centre and Donkey Sanctuary
Castle Hill East Leake Loughborough
Leicestershire LE12 6LU
Tel: 01509 852525
Set in 100 acres with over 200 tame animals, nature trails, pond dipping, straw maze, living willow sculpture, children's play area and fort adventure, donkey and quad rides.

Stonehurst Family Farm and Museum
Bond Lane Mountsorrel Loughborough
Leicestershire LE12 7AR
Tel: 01509 413216
It is the farm in the imagination of every child, where they can wander amongst and cuddle small sheep, pigs, rabbits, hens, horses, ponies and more.

Arts, Crafts & Textiles

Whitemoors Antiques and Crafts Centre
Main Street Shenton Market Bosworth
Leicestershire CV13 6BZ
Tel: 01455 212250 / 212981
Antiques, bric-a-brac, books, curios, extensive cultured Victorian gardens, delightful licensed tea room (seating 50+).

Birds, Butterflies & Bees

Tropical Birdland
Lindridge Lane Desford Leicestershire LE9 9GN
Tel: 01455 824603
Experience birds of the rainforest on your doorstep. Over 85 species, walk through aviaries, chick room, woodland walk and koi ponds.
Easter-Oct daily

Costume & Jewellery Museums

Wigston Framework Knitters Museum
42-44 Bushloe End Wigston Magna
Leicestershire LE18 2BA
Tel: 0116 288 3396
The house is a Master Hosier's house with a two storey Victorian frameshop in the garden.

Country Parks & Estates

Bradgate Country Park
Bradgate Road Newtown Linford Leicester
Leicestershire LE6 0HE
Tel: 0116 236 2713
This is Leicestershire's largest park, 850 acres, surrounding the ruins of the fifteenth-century Bradgate House, where Lady Jane Grey, Queen of England for nine days in 1553, lived for most of her life.

Foxton Locks Country Park
Gumley Road Foxton Market Harborough
Leicestershire LE16 7RA
Tel: 0116 267 1944
Landscaped car park and picnic site with woodland footpath to Grand Union Canal towpath, long flight of locks and remains of barge lift on inclined plane.

Market Bosworth Park Country Park
The Park Market Bosworth Leicestershire
Tel: 01455 290429
87 acres of rural park, including 11-acre arboretum. Children's Adventure Playground, and lake.

Watermead Country Park
off Wanlip Road Syston Leicester LE7 8PF
Tel: 0116 267 1944
230 acres of Country Park, with lakes, nature reserve, woodland walks, footpaths. Access to River Soar and canal.

Forests & Woods

Sence Valley Forest Park

Ravenstone Road Ibstock Leicestershire
Tel: 01889 586593 Fax: 01889 574217
www.forestry.gov.uk/nationalforest
[On A447 between Ibstock & Ravenstone. Plenty of on-site parking available]

The Forestry Commission's Sence Valley Forest Park is a wonderful example of how a disused opencast colliery can be transformed into a diverse wildlife haven. After being planted with over 98,000 trees this 150 acre site was opened to the public in September 1998 as part of The National Forest. The park contains woodland, lakes linking to the River Sence, grassland and a wildflower meadow. Thanks to the varied habitat 150 bird species have been recorded at the park. This along with the bird hide makes the site an excellent spot for bird-watchers. Opportunities for recreation at the park include fishing on one of the lakes, a bridleway, surfaced trails providing access for walkers, cyclists, and disabled visitors and a varied events programme.

All year daily during daylight hours. Car park open from 08.30-dusk. See notice in the car park for precise times. N.B. 2.2m height barrier at entrance. Arrangements for coaches & minibuses can be made. Please contact venue at least 48 hours before visit

Admission Free

Gardens & Horticulture

Kayes Garden Nursery

1700 Melton Road Rearsby Leicester LE7 4YR
Tel: 01664 424578
Situated in the lovely, rural Wreake Valley to the North-East of Leicester.

Heritage & Industrial

Moira Furnace Museum and Country Park

Furnace Lane Moira Leicestershire DE12 6AT
Tel: 01283 224667
Iron-making blast furnace housing an industrial history exhibition. Woodland, workshops and the restored Ashby Canal with narrowboats.

Snibston

Ashby Road Coalville Leicestershire LE67 3LN
Tel: 01530 278444 Fax: 01530 813301
www.snibston.com

[10min from J22 of M1. Plenty of on-site parking]

Visit Snibston and lift a Mini Cooper in our hands on gallery Extra Ordinary, which shows how technology has affected our every day life. Come and see the amazing selection of historic and contemporary costumes in the Fashion Gallery. Join real life miners on a tour of the colliery and experience what it was like to work underground. Take a ride on our diesel locomotive and get creative with our school holiday craft activities. Explore our nature reserve and hunt for local wildlife and let off some steam in our outdoor play area. Please see our website for further details. Some activities incur an additional charge.

All year Apr-Oct daily 10.00-17.00, Nov-Mar Mon-Fri 10.00-15.00, Sat, Sun & School hols 10.00-17.00

A£6.00 C£4.00 Family Ticket (A2+C2) £18.00 or (A2+C3) £20.00

Historical

Belgrave Hall
Church Road Belgrave Leicester LE4 5PE
Tel: 0116 266 6590
A delightful three-storey Queen Anne house dating from 1709.

Belvoir Castle
Grantham Leicestershire NG32 1PE
Tel: 01476 871000
Includes the museum of the Queen's Royal Lancers. The terraced gardens and sculptures.

Bosworth Battlefield Visitor Centre and Country Park
Ambion Hill Sutton Cheney Market Bosworth Leicestershire CV13 0AD
Tel: 01455 290429
Comprehensive interpretation of the battle by means of exhibitions, models and a film theatre.

Stanford Hall
Lutterworth Leicestershire LE17 6DH
Tel: 01788 860250
Beautiful 1690s house set in an attractive park besides Shakespeare's River Avon.

Railways

Battlefield Line Railway
Shackerstone Station Shackerstone Nuneaton Warwickshire CV13 6NW
Tel: 01827 880754
Runs from the grade-two listed Shackerstone Station.

Great Central Railway
Great Central Road Loughborough Leicestershire LE11 1RW
Tel: 01509 230726
Great Central Railway, Britain's only double track main line heritage railway.

Science - Earth & Planetary

National Space Centre
Exploration Drive Leicester LE4 5NS
Tel: 0116 261 0261 Fax: 0116 258 2100
www.spacecentre.co.uk
[Just off A6, 2mi N of Leicester City Centre, midway between Leicester's inner & outer ring rds. Brown signs direct all arterial routes around Leicester. Rail: Midland Mainline & Central Trains serve Leicester Station. Bus: First Leicester Yellow Line 54 stops at Abbey Lane, short walk from Centre. Bus can be picked up at London Rd station, Charles St, Belgrave Gate. Discover Leicester Tourbus also stops at Space Centre (summer only). Plenty of free on-site parking]
The award winning National Space Centre is the UK's largest attraction dedicated to space. From the minute you catch sight of the Space Centre's futuristic Rocket Tower, you'll be treated to hours of breathtaking discovery and interactive fun. Think you'll never see the whole universe close-up? Then take a seat in our high-tech full domed Space Theatre and prepare to be amazed. Human Space flight: Lunar Base 2025 is the new fantastic experience at the National Space Centre. Become an astronaut! Interactive exhibits test your mental and physical ability to survive in deep space. Blast off on a stunning 3D SIM journey to the ice moon Europa. The National Space Centre hosts many exciting weekend events. In 2007 these include 50 Years in Space Exhibition, an invasion by the UK Garrison for Star Wars Weekend and many more... see the website for full details.
All year Tue-Sun 10.00-17.00. During Leicestershire School Hols also Mon 10.00-17.00 A£11.00 C(4-16)&Concessions£9.00 Family Ticket (A2+C2) £34.00 or (A2+C3) £42.00. All children under the age of 14 must be accompanied by an adult. All tickets valid for 12 months for UK taxpayers

Breathtaking discovery & interactive fun

50 YEARS IN SPACE 2007

Six **Interactive** galleries
Lunar Base **astronaut experience**
The **SIM** • The **Space Theatre**
Rocket Tower • **Cargo Bay** shop
Boosters restaurant

Tel: **0870 607 7223**
National Space Centre • Leicester • LE4 5NS

www.spacecentre.co.uk

Theme & Adventure Parks

Twinlakes Park
Melton Spinney Road Melton Mowbray
Leicestershire LE14 4SB
Tel: 01664 567777 Fax: 01664 560070
www.twinlakespark.co.uk
[M1 J21A, A46, A607 into Melton Mowbray]
New Dynamic Duo due for 2007 and Creepy
Critters Reptile House now open. An exciting
variety of family rides and attractions is set in 60
acres of glorious countryside at Twinlakes Park,
Melton Mowbray where action packed play
zones entertain the whole family. Whatever the
weather expect a full day of play in massive
indoor venture centres complete with 5 rides.
Enjoy fascinating flying displays in the Falconry
Centre, friendly animals, ferret racing and cute
birds in Red Rooster Farm Centre. Live entertainers, workshops and events make school
holidays special. The soaring flying sensations
of the Icarus Sky Flyers and the speeding rocking Mercury Minicoaster are Twinlakes favourite
rides. Expect laughter and thrills on the
Spinning Spiders, Dune Buggies and Shark Bite
Rides. While the big thrill Trauma Tower is an
indoor scream machine. Bump, pedal and row
boats on lakes, pump iron on daring obstacles
of the Texan Assault Course, shoot down multi
slides, fly down zip slides and pedal like crazy
on Indy Karts. There's Big Zones for small kids
with interactive soft play centres, absorbing Wild
West City, Challenging attractions and a host of
activities to give maximum fun. Indoors the
massive Labyrinth has awesome challenges and
rides with four floors of super high slides, daring
tower climbs and multi swings. Enjoy bouncing
in Buccaneers Island and blasting balls at bud-
dies in the two Master Blaster areas. With
action, animals and acres of beauty there's all
weather fun at Twinlakes. Birthday catering.
All year daily from 10.00. Closed 24-27 Dec
24 Mar-1 Nov A&C£8.50 C(under92cm)£Free
OAPs£4.99, Family Ticket(A2+C2) £32.00.
Season Tickets £31.95, OAPs £19.00. After 1
Nov A&C£5.99 OAPs£3.75. Group discounts
available for 10 or more

Discount Offer: 15% Off Admission

Transport Museums

Foxton Canal Museum & Inclined Plane Trust
Middle Lock Gumley Road Foxton
Market Harborough Leicestershire LE16 7RA
Tel: 0161 279 2657
Victorian steam-powered boat lift, pub, shop,
museum, boat trips, boat hire, working boatyard
and interesting local walks. Interactive displays,
working models, play boat and much more.

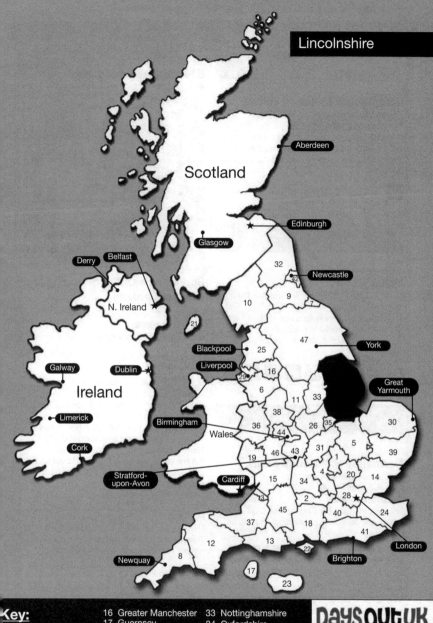

Lincolnshire

Aberdeen

Scotland

Edinburgh

Glasgow

32

Newcastle

42

Derry Belfast

9

Newcastle

10

7

N. Ireland

21

47

York

Blackpool

25

Liverpool

Galway Dublin

16

Great
Yarmouth

Ireland

6

11

33

30

Limerick

38

26

35

Birmingham

36

44

5

39

Wales

46

43

31

1

20

14

Cork

19

Stratford-
upon-Avon

Cardiff

15

34

4

London

13

2

28

24

Newquay

45

40

37

18

41

12

13

22

Brighton

8

17

23

Key:

1 Bedfordshire	16 Greater Manchester	33 Nottinghamshire
2 Berkshire	17 Guernsey	34 Oxfordshire
3 Bristol	18 Hampshire	35 Rutland
4 Buckinghamshire	19 Herefordshire	36 Shropshire
5 Cambridgeshire	20 Hertfordshire	37 Somerset
6 Cheshire	21 Isle Of Man	38 Staffordshire
7 Cleveland	22 Isle Of Wight	39 Suffolk
8 Cornwall	23 Jersey	40 Surrey
9 County Durham	24 Kent	41 Sussex
10 Cumbria	25 Lancashire	42 Tyne & Wear
11 Derbyshire	26 Leicestershire	43 Warwickshire
12 Devon	27 Lincolnshire	44 West Midlands
13 Dorset	28 London	45 Wiltshire
14 Essex	29 Merseyside	46 Worcestershire
15 Gloucestershire	30 Norfolk	47 Yorkshire
	31 Northamptonshire	
	32 Northumberland	

Archaeology

Gainsthorpe Medieval Village

Hibaldstow Lincolnshire
Tel: 0191 261 1585
Originally discovered and still best seen from the air, this hidden village comprises earthworks of peasant houses, gardens and streets. Dogs on leads only.

Art Galleries

Usher Gallery

Lindum Road Lincoln Lincolnshire LN2 1NN
Tel: 01522 527980
The Usher Gallery houses a collection of fine art, watches, porcelain, miniatures and has a changing display of contemporary art exhibitions.

Country Parks & Estates

Normanby Hall Country Park

Normanby Park Normanby Scunthorpe North Lincolnshire DN15 9HU
Tel: 01724 720588
Regency mansion, farming museum, gift shop, tea rooms, 350 acres of parkland, red and fallow deer.

Waters' Edge Country Park

Maltkiln Road Barton Upon Humber
North Lincolnshire
Tel: 01652 631500
Waters' Edge is situated on the waterfront at Barton upon Humber against the backdrop of the magnificent Humber Bridge.

Gardens & Horticulture

Springfields Outlet Shopping and Festival Gardens

Camelgate Spalding Lincolnshire PE12 6EU
Tel: 01775 760909
www.springfieldsshopping.com

[1mi E of Spalding signposted off A16. Plenty of on-site parking available]

Springfields Outlet Shopping and Festival Gardens in Spalding offers over 40 factory outlet shops, themed educational gardens, celebrity designed showcase gardens by Charlie Dimmock, Kim Wilde and Chris Beardshaw, striking water features and woodland walks. There is also a children's Play Barn and Adventure Golf along with places to eat and drink. The outlet shops sell well known brands all retailing at up to 75% off high street prices and brands include Marks & Spencer, Clarks, Reebok, Mexx and many more. Within the Festival Gardens are examples of Stephen Newby's wonderful blown steel sculptures. There is also the Festival Garden Centre, which houses the new Springfield's Restaurant.

All year Mon-Wed & Fri 10.00-18.00, Thur 10.00-20.00, Sat 09.00-18.00, Sun 11.00-17.00. Bank Hols 10.00-18.00

Admission free

Historical

Belton House

Grantham Lincolnshire NG32 2LS
Tel: 01476 566116 Fax: 01476 579071

[40min from Nottingham, Leicester & Lincoln, Belton House is on A607 Grantham / Lincoln rd easily reached & signposted from A1. Rail: Grantham. Plenty of on-site parking available]

Built 1685-88 for Sir John Brownlow. The rooms contain portraits, fine furniture, tapestries, oriental porcelain, family silver and Speaker Cust's silver. Formal gardens, an orangery and a magnificent landscaped park with a lakeside walk and the Bellmount tower. Adventure playground and miniature train rides. Braille, audio guides and Hearing Scheme. Family guide. Children's menu available in restaurant. Front baby slings on loan. Dogs on leads only in parkland.

House: 25 Mar-29 Oct Wed-Sun & Bank Hol Mon 12.30-17.00. Open Good Fri. Garden & Park 11.00-17.30, Shop & Restaurant 11.00-17.00. (Park may occasionally be closed for special events)
House & Garden: A£9.00 C(under5)£Free C(5-16)£5.50, Family Ticket (A2+C3) £24.00. Grounds only: A£7.00 C£4.50, Family Ticket £18.50. Reductions for pre-booked parties available

Gainsborough Old Hall

Parnell Street Gainsborough Lincolnshire DN21 2NB
Tel: 01427 612669 Fax: 01427 612779
www.lincolnshire.gov.uk/gainsboroughold-hall

[In Gainsborough town centre, 20mi W of Lincoln, 30mi E of Sheffield. Rail: Gainsborough Central 0.5mi, Gainsborough Lea Road 1mi]

A stunning medieval Manor House built in the 1460s containing a remarkable Great Hall and original kitchens which are one of the best surviving examples of medieval kitchens in the county. The Old Hall has welcomed royalty including Richard III and Henry VIII and his fifth wife Katherine Howard. The Mayflower Pilgrims and John Wesley were given religious freedom at the Old Hall during times of great religious conflict. There is an impressive collection of seventeenth and eighteenth-century furniture and interactive displays encouraging young and old to learn what life was like in this most impressive manor house. The tearooms at the Old Hall offer homemade cakes and flapjacks made on site with a selection of hot drinks and fresh locally made produce and is part of the 'Tastes of Lincolnshire' promotion. There is also an active events and exhibitions programme so please telephone for more information.
All year Mon-Sat 10.00-17.00, Easter-Oct Sun 13.00-16.30. Closed 24-26 Dec & 1 Jan
A£3.80 Concessions£2.60, Family Ticket £10.00. Please pre-book guided tours. Free audio tour also available

Discount Offer: One Child Free

GAINSBOROUGH
OLD HALL

Come and visit the finest Medieval manor house in the country!

Exciting programme of events throughout the year including -

Murder Mystery, Travels Through Time and a Victorian Christmas Craft Fair

For more information please contact the Hall on
01427 612669 or visit
www.lincolnshire.gov.uk/gainsboroughholdhall

ENGLISH HERITAGE   Lincolnshire

Lincoln Castle

Castle Hill Lincoln Lincolnshire LN1 3AA

Tel: 01522 511068
Nineteenth century connections and unique Victorian prison chapel.

Tattershall Castle

Tattershall Lincoln Lincolnshire LN4 4LR
Tel: 01526 342543
A vast fortified and moated red-brick tower, built in medieval times.

Woolsthorpe Manor

23 Newton Way Woolsthorpe-by-Colsterworth Grantham Lincolnshire NG33 5NR
Tel: 01476 860338
The birthplace and family home of Sir Isaac Newton.

Lincoln Cathedral

Minster Yard Lincoln Lincolnshire LN2 1PX
Tel: 01522 561600 Fax: 01522 561634
www.lincolncathedral.com

[Uphill Lincoln]

Lincoln Cathedral is one of the finest medieval buildings in Europe. It has been a major focus of worship for over 900 years and it is a centre of excellence for art, conservation, music and architecture. Find Katherine Swynford's tomb, St Hugh's Shrine and the famous Lincoln Imp. Take a guided tour or explore at your own pace; spend an afternoon browsing in the historic libraries; join us for worship or one of our events. Film buffs among you will be interested to search out the locations used for filming the "Da Vinci Code". Hollywood descended on the Cathedral in August 2005 and transformed the nave and chapter house into Westminster Abbey. A 'behind the scenes' exhibition and some of the set will be on display until September 2007.

All year daily summer; Mon-Sat 07.15-20.00, Sun 07.15-18.00, winter; Mon-Sat 07.15-18.00, Sun 07.15-17.00
A£4.00 C(under5)£Free C(5-16)£1.00 Concessions£3.00, Family Ticket £10.00. Annual visitor pass £15.00

Discount Offer: 10% discount on all gift shop purchases (when you spend £10.00 or more)

Theme & Adventure Parks

Butlins

Skegness Lincolnshire PE25 1NJ
Tel: 01754 762311 Fax: 01754 767833
www.butlins.com/dayvisitor

[Follow A52 heading towards Ingoldmells. 3mi from town centre. Plenty of on-site parking available]

For a great day out, come on holiday for the day! With 70 years experience entertaining holidaymakers, it's no wonder we know what makes the perfect holiday. So come and see how much you can pack in! With wet n wild Splash Waterworld, adventure forts, indoor soft play zones, traditional funfairs and fantastic entertainment under the Skyline Pavilion, there's more than enough to keep the whole family happy! Plus at Skegness you can try out our Yacht Club with gourmet dishes as well as the old classics, or adults can relax in the Health Spa and Hydrotherapy Pool.

1 May-4 Nov daily 10.00-18.00. Excludes 11-13 May, 5-7 Oct & 12-14 Oct
Afrom£7.50 Cfrom£6.00

Discount Offer: Two for the Price of One

Magical World of Fantasy Island

Sea Lane Ingoldmells Skegness Lincolnshire PE25 1RH
Tel: 01754 874668 Fax: 01754 874668
www.fantasyisland.co.uk

[Off A52. Plenty of on-site parking available]

Britain's first themed indoor family resort with traditional family fun to theme park thrills. Europe's largest 7 day open air market, over 30 rides to choose from, both inside and out including 2 of Europe's largest Coasters 1500 seater Show bar with acts showing from mid-day through till 2am, kiddies characters fun for all the family, Woodys Wine Bar for the younger generation with guest DJs nightly.

Mar-April weekends only. Easter daily. May-Oct daily. Market: Nov & Dec weekends only. (not theme park)
Admission free, rides charged tokens needed

Discount Offer: Spend £18.00 on Ride Tokens, get another £18.00 worth free

Pleasure Island Theme Park

Kings Road Cleethorpes Lincolnshire DN35 0PL
Tel: 01472 211511 Fax: 01472 211087
www.pleasure-island.co.uk

[M180 A180 to Cleethorpes or A46 A16 for scenic route. Rail: Cleethorpes bus runs from Railway to Park. Plenty of on-site parking available]

With oodles of great rides and attractions at Pleasure Island, where else can all the family have so much fun? There's 6 white knuckle rides including, new for summer 2007, the top spinning HydroMax. Youngsters are not forgotten in Tinkaboo Town with Kiddies' roundabouts and slides. One of the best things about Pleasure Island however, is the number of rides that can be enjoyed by all the family such as the themed water rides, the mini mine train and everyone's favourite, the dodgems, plus so much more. Don't forget that there are 6 fabulous family shows to see also, including the new show for summer 2007, Basil Brush.

1 Apr-3 Sept (the park will remain closed Mon & Tue during quiet times - call for further information), Sept-Oct weekends & 20-28 Oct daily A&C£14.50 C(0-3)£Free OAPs£8.50, Family Ticket £52.00 (admits any 4 people). Group rates available on request

Discount Offer: Two for the Price of One

Transport Museums

Trolleybus Museum at Sandtoft

Belton Road Sandtoft Doncaster
North Lincolnshire DN8 5SX
Tel: 01724 711391 Fax: 01724 711846
www.sandtoft.org.uk

[J2 M180 (A161) to Belton, R at roundabout & travel approx. 2.5m. Free bus from Doncaster]
The museum boasts the world's largest collection of historic trolleybuses (45), and they date from 1927 to 1985. Many of the exhibits are restored to working order and carry visitors around the museum, which has adopted a 1950s/1960s feel, with contemporary motorbuses, street scene and shop window displays, a prefab 'home' exhibition, cycle and lawnmower museum as well as an exhibition of trolleybus and transport artefacts. There is also adequate free parking, tours, gardens, play areas, picnic areas, AV shows, a souvenir shop, cafe and visiting attractions. Sandtoft Gathering is the museum's major annual event with many added attractions. There is disabled access to most areas, but wheelchair access to trolleybus rides is not always available. The operating company, Sandtoft Transport Centre Ltd is a Registered Charity (no. 514382), and is run by volunteer members. It was established to preserve the trolleybus as part of Britain's Transport Heritage.

Trolleydays: 7-9 Apr, 5-7 May (European Weekend), 26-28 May (Southern Weekend), 10 & 24 June, 8 July (Vintage Cycle Day), 28-29 July (Sandtoft Gathering 2007), 11-12 Aug (40s/50s Weekend), 25-27 Aug (East Midlands Weekend), 8-9 Sep (Model Weekend), 22-23 Sep (Six Wheel Weekend), 14 Oct (St. Leger Rally), 11 Nov (Twilight Running), 8-9 Dec (Santa Days). Gates Open: Trolleydays: 11.00-17.00; Sandtoft Gathering 29 July (Preview) 11.00-22.00, 30 July 10.00-18.00; Santa Days 11.00-16.00

Trolleydays & Pre-booked parties: A£5.00

Concessions£3.00 C(under5)£Free, Family Ticket (A2+C4) £15.00. Sandtoft Gathering: A£7.00

Concessions£4.00 C(under5)£Free. Please call for Santa Days prices

Discount Offer: One Adult admitted at the Concession Rate

Open daily, Mar-July 10.00-17.00, Aug 10.00-17.30, Sept-Oct 10.00-16.00, Closed 30 Oct-16 Mar
A£6.20 C£4.70 OAPs£5.70, Family Ticket(A2+C2)£19.00

Zoos

Skegness Natureland Seal Sanctuary

North Parade Skegness Lincolnshire PE25 1DB
Tel: 01754 764345
Natureland houses a specialised collection of animals.

Wildlife & Safari Parks

Butterfly and Wildlife Park

Long Sutton Spalding Lincolnshire PE12 9LE
Tel: 01406 363833 Fax: 01406 363182
www.butterflyandwildlifepark.co.uk
[A17. Plenty of on-site parking available]

The Butterfly and Wildlife Park voted Lincolnshire's Family Attraction of the Year 2003 by The Good Britain Guide has something to offer all age groups and is a very popular day out. One of the largest tropical houses in Great Britain has hundreds of colourful butterflies flying freely in a rainforest setting. There are also crocodiles, snakes, water dragons an ant room and an insectarium. Outdoors The Lincolnshire Birds of Prey Centre has eagles, owls, falcons, hawks and vultures and fly them at 12 noon and 3pm everyday (subject to the weather and one display at 2pm during September and October). You can see everything from wallabies to water buffalo in the rapidly expanding animal collection. Set in 20 acres is a large adventure playground with an activity castle, toddler's area, ride-on tractors, mini-golf and lovely gardens. The award winning tearooms and gift shop compliment this quality assured visitor attraction.

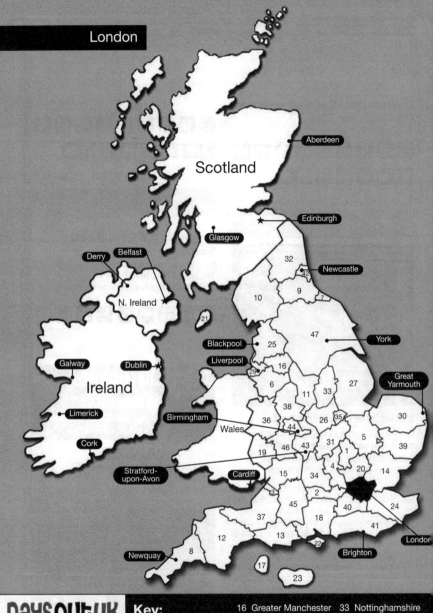

London

Aberdeen

Scotland

Edinburgh

Glasgow

Newcastle

Derry   Belfast

N. Ireland

32

42

9

7

10

21

47   York

Blackpool   25

Liverpool

16

Galway   Dublin

29

6

Ireland

11   33

27

Great
Yarmouth

38

30

Limerick

Birmingham

36

44

26   35

Wales

5

Cork

19   46   43

31   1

39

Stratford-
upon-Avon

Cardiff

15

34

20   14

13

2

24

45

40

London

37   18

41

Newquay

12   8

13

22

Brighton

17

23

Key:

1 Bedfordshire
2 Berkshire
3 Bristol
4 Buckinghamshire
5 Cambridgeshire
6 Cheshire
7 Cleveland
8 Cornwall
9 County Durham
10 Cumbria
11 Derbyshire
12 Devon
13 Dorset
14 Essex
15 Gloucestershire
16 Greater Manchester
17 Guernsey
18 Hampshire
19 Herefordshire
20 Hertfordshire
21 Isle Of Man
22 Isle Of Wight
23 Jersey
24 Kent
25 Lancashire
26 Leicestershire
27 Lincolnshire
28 London
29 Merseyside
30 Norfolk
31 Northamptonshire
32 Northumberland
33 Nottinghamshire
34 Oxfordshire
35 Rutland
36 Shropshire
37 Somerset
38 Staffordshire
39 Suffolk
40 Surrey
41 Sussex
42 Tyne & Wear
43 Warwickshire
44 West Midlands
45 Wiltshire
46 Worcestershire
47 Yorkshire

Abbeys

Westminster Abbey: Museum, St. Margarets Church, Chapter House and Pyx Chamber

Broad Sanctuary London SW1P 3PA
Tel: 020 7222 5152
[Tube: Westminster]
The present building is one of the most visited churches in the world.

Animal Attractions

London Aquarium

County Hall Westminster Bridge Road London SE1 7PB
Tel: 020 7967 8000 Fax: 020 7967 8029
www.londonaquarium.co.uk

[Tube: Waterloo or Westminster. Across Westminster Bridge from Houses of Parliament, next to London Eye]

At the London Aquarium, you will discover over 350 species of fish and animal life from the oceans, lakes, rivers and streams around the world. For the adventurous you can touch the rays in the touch pool. Throughout the year, the award winning London Aquarium runs themed weeks of activities, displays and presentations. Most of these are free and are available to adults and children.
All year daily 10.00-18.00
A£13.25 C(3-14)£9.75 Concessions£11.25, Family Ticket (A2+C2) £44.00

Discount Offer: One Child Free

Art Galleries

British Museum

Great Russell Street London WC1B 3DG
Tel: 020 7323 8000 Fax: 020 7323 8616
www.thebritishmuseum.ac.uk
[Tube: Holborn, Tottenham Court Rd, Russell Sq, Goodge St]
Founded in 1753, the British Museum's remarkable collections span over two million years of human history. Visitors enjoy a unique comparison of the treasures of world cultures under one roof, centred around the Great Court and the historic Reading Room. World-famous objects such as the Rosetta Stone, Parthenon Sculptures and Egyptian mummies are visited by up to 5 million visitors per year. In addition to the vast permanent collection, the museum's special exhibitions, displays and events are all designed to advance understanding of the collections and cultures they represent. Highlights of the exhibitions programme for 2007 include A New World: England's first view of America and First Emperor: China's Terracotta Army.
Galleries: All year daily Sat-Wed 10.00-17.30, Thur-Fri 10.00-20.30 Closed Good Fri, 24-26 Dec & 1 Jan. Certain Galleries are subject to different opening times. Full details are available from the Box Office/Information Desk or please check the web site

Admission Free

Cartoon Museum

35 Little Russell St Camden London WC1A 2HH
Tel: 020 7580 8155
[Tube: Tottenham Court Rd]
A recent addition to London's museum scene.

Dali Universe

County Hall Gallery Riverside Building London SE1 7PB
Tel: 0870 744 7485 Fax: 020 7620 3120
www.countyhallgallery.com

[Tube: Westminster & Waterloo]

London's most surreal experience lies in a labyrinth of atmospheric corridors and dreamlike effects in the heart of the thriving South Bank. Nestled between the Aquarium and the BA London Eye with a waterfront Thames vista across to the Palace of Westminster, Dalí Universe enjoys a unique location for a dramatic collection. Over 500 incredible pieces by genius and eccentric Salvador Dalí are on permanent exhibit within three themed areas - 'Dreams and Fantasy,' 'Sensuality and Femininity' and 'Religion and Mythology' - and the exhibition demonstrates Dalí's incredible creative versatility with extensive collections ranging from surreal furniture to rare graphics, etchings, jewellery and glass objects. The highlight is most certainly the extraordinary collection of surreal bronze sculpture. Boasting the largest exhibit of Dalí sculpture in the world, the Dalí Universe features classic and quirky pieces including 'Space Elephant,' 'Persistence of Memory,' 'Space Venus' and 'Woman Aflame.'
All year daily 10.00-18.30. Closed 25 Dec
Dali & Picasso: A£12.00 C(8-16)£8.00 C(4-7)£5.00 C(Under4)£Free Concessions£10.00, Family Ticket (A2+C2) £30.00. Group 10+ A£11.00 C(8-16)£7.00 C(4-7)£4.00 C(Under4)£Free Concessions£9.00. Audio guides £2.50

Discount Offer: Two for the Price of One

Dulwich Picture Gallery

Gallery Road Dulwich London SE21 7AD
Tel: 020 8693 5254 Fax: 020 8299 8700
www.dulwichpicturegallery.org.uk
[Just off A205 South Circular. Rail: Victoria / West Dulwich. Plenty of on-site parking available]
The oldest public picture gallery in England is also one of the most beautiful. Housed in a building designed by Sir John Soane in 1811, displaying a fine cross-section of Old Masters. The Gallery was recently reopened following a £9m refurbishment and extension. Development project includes facilities such as a lecture hall, practical art room and café. The Gallery puts on three critically acclaimed exhibitions each year.
All year Tue-Fri 10.00-17.00, Sat-Sun & Bank Hol 11.00-17.00. Closed Mon except Bank Hols. Guided tours Sat & Sun at 15.00. Closed Good Fri, 24-26 Dec & 1 Jan
A£4.00 C(0-16)&Disabled&UB40s£Free OAPs£3.00. Free to all on Fri

Discount Offer: Two for the Price of One

Foundling Museum

40 Brunswick Square London WC1N 1AZ
Tel: 020 7841 3600
[Tube: Russell Square]
Originally a hospital for abandoned children, the museum now tells their stories.

London International Gallery of Children's Art

O2 Centre 255 Finchley Road London
NW3 6LU
[Tube: Finchley Rd]
Tel: 020 7435 0903
A registered charity which celebrates the creativity of young people.

National Gallery

Trafalgar Square London WC2N 5DN
Tel: 020 7747 2885
[Tube: Leicester Square]
Huge range of European art, ranging from 1260 to 1900.

National Portrait Gallery

St Martins Place London WC2H 0HE
Tel: 020 7306 0055
[Tube: Charing Cross]
From Elizabeth I to Oscar Wilde, William Shakespeare to Florence Nightingale... With the largest collection of portraiture in the world.

Pump House Gallery

Battersea Park London SW11 4NJ
Tel: 020 7350 0523
[Tube: Sloane Square]
Built in 1861, the Pump House Gallery was originally a Victorian water tower supplying water to the lakes and cascades in Battersea Park. Following renovation, the building now houses a contemporary art gallery, gift shop and park information centre.

Royal Academy of Arts

Burlington House Piccadilly London W1J 0BD
Tel: 020 7300 8000
[Tube: Piccadilly Circus]
Famous for its exhibition programme, the Royal Academy is the oldest arts institution in Britain.

Serpentine Gallery

Kensington Gardens Kensington London
W2 3XA
Tel: 020 7298 1515 / 7402 6075
[Tube: Lancaster Gate]
A platform for contemporary artists, both British and international, with changing exhibitions.

Somerset House

Strand London WC2R 1LA
Tel: 020 7845 4600
[Tube: Temple or Embankment]
Gallery and former Tudor palace. Now a magnificent eighteenth-century art gallery.

Tate Britain

Millbank London SW1P 4RG
Tel: 020 7887 8888
www.tate.org.uk/britain
[Tube: Pimlico. Train: Vauxhall]

Tate Britain is the original Tate Gallery and holds the largest collection of British art in the world. Tate's collection of British art contains iconic masterpieces by artists including Hogarth, Gainsborough, Constable, Whistler, Sargent, Hepworth and Bacon. The gallery has a highly-acclaimed restaurant and the Tate Boat takes visitors between Tate Britain, Tate Modern and the London Eye. Pre-booking recommended for major exhibitions.
All year daily 10.00-17.50. Open until 22.00 first Fri of every month. Closed 24-26 Dec
Admission Free (charges for major exhibitions)

Tate Modern

Bankside London SE1 9TG
Tel: 020 7887 8888
www.tate.org.uk/modern

[Tube: Southwark/Blackfriars Train: London Bridge/Blackfriars]

Britain's national museum of modern and contemporary art from around the world is housed in the former Bankside Power Station on the banks of the Thames. The awe-inspiring Turbine Hall runs the length of the entire building and you can see amazing work by artists such as Cezanne, Bonnard, Matisse, Picasso, Braque, Giacometti, Rothko, Dali, Pollock and Warhol. Pre-booking is recommended for major exhibitions.

All year daily Sun-Thu 10.00-18.00, Fri & Sat 10.00-22.00. Closed 24-26 Dec

Admission Free (charges for major exhibitions)

TwoTen Gallery

The Wellcome Trust 210 Euston Road London NW1 2BE
Tel: 020 7611 8888
TwoTen Gallery presents temporary exhibitions on the interaction between contemporary medical science and art.

Wallace Collection

Hertford House Manchester Square London W1U 3BN
Tel: 020 7563 9500 Fax: 020 7224 2155
www.wallacecollection.org

[Tube: Bond St / Baker St. Off Oxford St, behind Selfridges]

The Wallace Collection is one of the finest collections of art ever assembled by one family and became a national museum in 1897. Today the eclectic, wondrous collection is shown in the family home, a tranquil oasis just minutes from the bustle of London's Oxford Street. Be amazed by the fantastic Old Master paintings by Titian, Canaletto, Rembrandt, Velázquez and Gainsborough amongst others. Be transported to eighteenth-century France, surrounded by the world's greatest selection of eighteenth-century paintings, furniture and Sèvres porcelain. Imagine Queen Marie-Antoinette and Madame de Pompadour sashaying down the staircase as you enjoy the splendour of the family's home. Relish the world-class armouries, perfect for both young boys and overgrown ones! Relax in the serenity of the glazed Courtyard, home to our restaurant The Wallace. Enjoy free exhibitions, family activities and public events throughout the year. Join our mailing list for up to date details.

Open daily 10.00-17.00. Closed 24-26 Dec
Admission Free

Arts, Crafts & Textiles

Design Museum

Butler's Wharf 28 Shad Thames London
SE1 2YD
Tel: 0870 909 9009
[Tube: Tower Hill]
The world's leading museum of modern design.
A changing programme of exhibitions covers
everything from engineering to fashion.

Museum of Brands, Packaging and Advertising

2 Colville Mews Lonsdale Road Notting Hill
London W11 2AR
[Tube: Notting Hill Gate]
Tel: 020 7908 0880
Unique museum charting British consumerism.
From Cornflakes to Ker-plunk.

Royal College of Art

Kensington Gore London SW7 2EU
Tel: 020 7590 4444
[Tube: Gloucester Road]
One of London's most prestigious art colleges.
The exhibition programme is a great way to
sample its work, past and present.

Sir John Soane's Museum

13 Lincoln's Inn Fields London WC2A 3BP
Tel: 020 7405 2107
[Tube: Holborn]
A higgledy-piggledy treasure trove of artefacts,
this extraordinary house is worth a rummage.

Victoria and Albert Museum

Cromwell Road South Kensington London
SW7 2RL
Tel: 020 7942 2000
[Tube: South Kensington]
Holds one of the world's largest and most
diverse collections of decorative arts.

William Morris Gallery

Lloyd Park Forest Road Walthamstow E17 4PP
Tel: 020 8527 3782
[Tube: Walthamstow Central]
The world's only museum devoted to William
Morris, the great Victorian artist and craftsman.

Birds, Butterflies & Bees

London Butterfly House

Syon Park Brentford Middlesex London
TW8 8JF
Tel: 020 8560 0378 Fax: 020 8560 7272
www.londonbutterflyhouse.com
[Tube: Gunnersbury]

The London Butterfly House invites you to
embark on a butterfly adventure. Enter our tropical garden and step into a world of endless
enjoyment for people of all ages, whatever the
weather. You will be surrounded by 1000s of
colourful butterflies from all around the world
and able to wonder among the exotic flowers
and shrubs in our tropical garden. You will be
able to search for butterfly eggs, caterpillars and
pupae hidden among the foliage and watch
butterflies emerge from their pupae in the specially designed emerging cages. Other attractions include a walk through aviary for tropical
soft-billed birds and an insect gallery with
amphibians and reptiles. The London Butterfly
House offers an experience to remember that
will captivate the whole family in a unique surrounding. In this our final year, we hope to welcome as many people as possible to enjoy the
experience we offer. Visit our website for further
information.

All year daily. Closed 25 & 26 Dec

WWT London Wetland Centre

Queen Elizabeth's Walk Barnes London
SW13 9WT
Tel: 020 8409 4400
[Tube: Rail: Barnes Bridge]
The Wetland Centre is a major new attraction for London that brings wildlife and wetlands into the heart of the city.

Caverns & Caves

Chislehurst Caves

Old Hill Chislehurst Kent BR7 5NB
Tel: 020 8467 3264 Fax: 020 8295 0407
www.chislehurstcaves.co.uk
[A222 between A20 & A21, at Chislehurst railway bridge, turn into Station Rd then R & R again into Caveside Cls. Bus: Bromley 269, 162. Rail: Charing Cross to Chislehurst, Caves are around corner from the station & entrance off Caveside Cls nr Bickley Arms Pub]

Miles of mystery and history beneath your feet! Grab a lantern and get ready for an amazing underground adventure. At Chislehurst Caves your whole family can travel back in time as you explore the labyrinth of dark mysterious passageways which have been hewn by hand from the chalk deep beneath Chislehurst.
Accompanied by an experienced guide on a 45 minute tour you will learn of the Druids, Romans and Saxons who used the caves, as well as the more recent history of this underground maze. In the 1950s and 60s, a series of concerts were held here and during World War Two they became the largest air raid shelter outside London. Included in the tours, which run on the hour, are visits to the Caves Church, the Druid Altar, the Haunted Pool and much more! The caves should hold the imagination of even the most easily-bored child and if nothing else, there are almost 20 miles of tunnels to wear them out!
All year Wed-Sun, tours run hourly 10.00-16.00. Open daily during local school hols except Christmas & New Year
45 Min Tour: A£5.00 C&OAPs£3.00

Discount Offer: One Child Free

Communication Museums

Discover: Making Stories Together

1 Bridge Terrace Stratford London E15 4BG
Tel: 020 8536 5555 Fax: 020 8522 1003
www.discover.org.uk

Come to Discover and experience a unique place for children (aged 0-8) and their families to make up stories and play together. We offer a fantastic space for children to explore and expand their imagination. They can dress up, record their own stories, play in the Story Garden on a big Space ship, cross a sparkley river and hunt for treasure in a secret cave. It is also possible to make a puppet, put on a puppet show or listen to stories. The possibilities to imagine are endless! Discover offers very reasonably priced Birthday Parties including Super Douper Hootah, Space and Jungle themed parties. All held in a great, colourful room with the help of one of expertly trained Discover Story Builders.
All year daily 10.00-17.00 except Mons during School Term
A&C£3.50, Family Ticket £11.00. Concessions available

Costume & Jewellery Museums

Fan Museum

12 Crooms Hill Greenwich London SE10 8ER
Tel: 020 8305 1441 Fax: 020 8293 1889
www.fan-museum.org

*[Rail: Greenwich opposite Greenwich Theatre.
DLR: Cutty Sark Maritime Greenwich]*

The Fan Museum is an award-winning museum
and has recently won the 'Visit London Gold
Award 2006' for 'Best Small Visitor Attraction'.
The world's only Fan Museum with its unsur-
passed collections of more than 4,000 fans and
fan leaves dating from the eleventh century is
housed in beautifully restored listed Georgian
houses. The fans are displayed in changing
exhibitions. Shop, workshop, study facilities.
Orangery and landscaped garden. Special tours
and private functions. Fan making classes.
Refreshments available by prior arrangement. A
programme of exhibitions are listed within the
special events section, you can contact the
museum for further details on the above number.

*All year Tue-Sat 11.00-17.00, Sun 12.00-17.00.
Afternoon tea available Tue & Sun from 15.00*
A£4.00 Concessions£3.00 C(under7)£Free,
Family Ticket £10.00

**Discount Offer: Two for the Price of
One**

Exhibition & Visitor Centres

Central Hall Westminster

Storey's Gate Westminster London SW1H 9NH
Tel: 020 7222 8010 Fax: 020 7222 6883
www.c-h-w.com

Opened in 1912, this unique historic Edwardian
building is situated in the heart of Westminster
London, just adjacent to Westminster Abbey.
Central Hall was designed by Lanchester &
Richards in Viennese Baroque style, and the
ceiling of the Great Hall is reportedly the second
largest of its type in the world. Many events of
national importance and eminent speakers have
been welcomed, perhaps the most famous
event being the Inaugural General Assembly of
the United Nations in 1946. Today Central Hall
offers a wide variety of event space, from a fine
wood panelled boardroom to the Great Hall,
which seats over 2,000 people theatre style.
The finest in cuisine is offered, together with the
latest in audio visual and technical support. One
of our events team will be dedicated to your
needs. Methodist Church only weddings are
available through the church.
All year daily 07.00-18.00 or as required

Earls Court Exhibition Centre

Warwick Road London SW5 9TA
[Tube: Earls Court]
Tel: 020 7385 1200
Earls Court hosts many shows and exhibitions
throughout the year, including the Ideal Home
Show and the Brit Awards.

Festivals & Shows

City of London Festival

12-14 Mason's Ave London EC2V 5BB
Tel: 020 7796 4949 Fax: 020 7796 4959
[Numerous venues & open spaces in city, all of which are within easy walking distance of London Underground, mainline stations & bus routes]

Set against the magnificent architecture of London's 'Square Mile' the Festival's recent theme of 'Trading Places', connecting London to other world centres, comes closer to home with a French theme in 2007. Taking place in some of the City's most beautiful and historic buildings the Festival celebrates music of all types, contemporary, classical, jazz and world, along with visual arts, film, architecture and an ever growing open-air programme. 2007 also marks the 200th Anniversary of the parliamentary Abolition of the Slave Trade and this rich subject will inspire a new opera. Please call the box office on 0845 120 7502.
25 June-12 July 2007
Free - £50.00

Notting Hill Carnival

Notting Hill London
[Tube: Westbourne Park]
Tel: 020 7730 3010
A massive procession of costume soca and steel bands. The area plays host to 45 licensed static sound systems, each playing their own soca, reggae, jazz, soul, hiphop, funk music plus hundreds of street stalls.

27 August 2007

Folk & Local History Museums

Bruce Castle Museum

Lordship Lane Tottenham Haringey London N17 8NU
[Rail: White Hart Lane]
Tel: 020 8808 8772
A Grade I listed, sixteenth-century manor house set in 20 acres of parkland. It now houses the Borough of Haringey's local history collections.

Church Farmhouse Museum

Greyhound Hill London NW4 4JR
Tel: 020 8359 3942 Fax: 020 8356 2885
www.churchfarmhousemuseum.co.uk

[J2 M1, off A41. Tube: Hendon Central. Plenty of on-site parking available]

Built c1660, with Victorian additions and alterations, this is the oldest surviving house in Hendon. Listed Grade II, it was the boyhood home of Mark Lemon, first Editor of Punch, in the early C19. The house, which is set in a small and public garden (now features a children's maze), has three C19 furnished rooms-dining room (decorated for a Victorian Christmas every December), kitchen and laundry room. The Museum presents a continuous programme of unique temporary exhibitions - one each year especially for children. Recent topics have included: Wedgwood pottery and glass, Punch and Judy, Hendon Aerodrome, fireworks, movable books and pop music in Barnet. Forthcoming exhibitions in 2007/8 will be on the history of Hampstead Garden Suburb; on Sherlock Holmes; and on old toys.
All year Mon-Thur 10.00-13.00 & 14.00-17.00, Sat 10.00-13.00 & 14.00-17.30, Sun 14.00-17.30. Closed on Fri & 25-26 Dec & 1 Jan
Admission Free

Livesey Museum for Children

682 Old Kent Road London SE15 1JF
[Rail: South Bermondsey]
Tel: 020 7639 5604
This Museum holds a lively programme of hands-on exhibitions for children up to 12 years, their schools, families and carers.

Museum of Richmond

Old Town Hall Whittaker Avenue Richmond
Surrey TW9 1TP
[Tube: Richmond]
Tel: 020 8332 1141
Deals with Richmond's rich and colourful history
in a lively and informative way.

Ragged School Museum

46-50 Copperfield Road London E3 4RR
Tel: 020 8980 6405
[Tube: Tube: Mile End]
Based in canalside warehouses that once
housed Barnardo's largest ragged school, this
museum focuses on the history of the East End.

Sherlock Holmes Museum

221b Baker Street London NW1 6XE
Tel: 020 7935 8866
[Tube: Baker St]
This famous address was opened as a museum
in 1990. The first floor rooms contain all the fea-
tures familiar to the Holmes enthusiast.

Food & Drink

Hard Rock Café

150 Old Park Lane London W1K 1QZ
Tel: 020 7514 1700
[Tube: Hyde Park Corner]
Still housing the first ever piece of memorabilia
donated to the Hard Rock Café (Eric Clapton's
Lead II Fender, originally donated to reserve a
space at the busy bar), the London café is as
charming today as it was 35 years ago.

Planet Hollywood

13 Coventry Street London W1D 7DH
Tel: 020 7287 1000
[Tube: Piccadilly Circus]
The world's only restaurant inspired by the
glamour of Hollywood was launched with the
backing of Hollywood stars Sylvester Stallone,
Bruce Willis and Arnold Schwarzenegger.

Gardens & Horticulture

Museum of Garden History

St-Mary-at-Lambeth Lambeth Palace Road
Lambeth London SE1 7LB
Tel: 020 7401 8865 Fax: 020 7401 8869
www.museumgardenhistory.org
*[On S side of River Thames, next to Lambeth
Palace, almost opposite Houses of Parliament at
SE end of Lambeth Bridge. Bus: 3/344/C10 to
Lambeth Rd & 507/77 to Lambeth Palace Rd
(507 weekdays only) Rail: Victoria / Waterloo,
then bus or short walk. Tube: Lambeth North
(Bakerloo), Westminster (District, Circle & Jubilee),
Vauxhall (Victoria), Waterloo (Bakerloo, Northern &
Jubilee)]*
The Museum of Garden History is in the former
Parish Church of St Mary at Lambeth, now a
listed building. It was the world's first Museum
dedicated to garden history. Tombs of the John
Tradescants, elder and younger, plant hunters
and the royal gardeners to Charles I and
Captain Bligh of the Bounty can be found in the
grounds, along with a reproduction seventeenth-century knot garden which provides a
peaceful haven, full of plants that can be traced
back to that period. Within the Museum there
are displays illustrating the history of the
Tradescants, local history and plant hunting,
and the development of garden design alongside a fine collection of historic garden tools and
curiosities. Seasonal exhibitions, lectures, concerts, fairs and art exhibitions are regularly held
throughout the year. Guided tours by appointment and photography allowed with permission.
Café and shop.
*All year daily 10.30-17.00. Closed over Christmas
& New Year, please call for details*
Voluntary donations requested, A£3.00
Concessions£2.50

Royal Botanic Gardens, Kew

Kew Richmond London TW9 3AB
Tel: 020 8332 5655
[Tube: Kew Gardens]
The world-famous visitor attraction houses more than 40,000 different kinds of plants.

Guided Tours

BBC Television Centre Tours

BBC Television Centre Wood Lane London W12 7RJ
Tel: 0870 60 30 304 (Booking)
Fax: 020 8576 7466
www.bbc.co.uk/tours

[Tube: White City (Central Line). Bus: 72, 95, 220 all stop opposite Television Centre. There is metered parking in nearby streets & a NCP car park off Rockley Rd, Shepherd's Bush.There is no coach parking at BBC Television Centre. For detailed pick up/drop off information, you can download pdf files from our website]

On a tour of London's BBC Television Centre, you will see behind the scenes of the most famous TV centre in the world. On the award winning tour, you may experience areas such as the News Centre, Weather Centre, dressing rooms and studios. Television Centre is a working building so we plan your exact itinerary around what is happening on the day, therefore no two tours are ever the same. Please note that visitors must be 9 years and over and tours must be pre-booked. Television Centre is a large complex and tours involve a lot of walking. We also offer a CBBC Tour for children aged 7-12 years old where you'll visit the Blue Peter garden, play in our interactive studio and have the opportunity to become 'Diddy Dick' and 'Diddy Dom'.
Tours run regularly throughout the week. Please call for further details
A£9.50 C(over7)&Students(NUS/USI)£7.00

Concessions£8.50, Family Ticket £27.00.
Group rate (15+): A£8.50
C&Students(NUS/USI)£6.00 Concessions£7.50
School Group (under16)£5.00, Teacher£7.00.
Staff Individual Rates (if taking up a public tour)
A£7.50 C£5.00. Please note, the maximum number on each tour is 22 people. Pre-booking essential, please state Television Centre when booking

The Original Tour - London Sightseeing

Jews Row Wandsworth London SW18 1TB
Tel: 020 8877 2120 Fax: 020 8877 1968
www.theoriginaltour.com
[Baker St Station Forecourt, Embankment Pier, Piccadilly Circus, Victoria, Trafalgar Square & Marble Arch]
Enjoy a capital day out in London aboard The Original Tour's traditional open-top buses. The world's first and largest sightseeing operator offers a flexible 'Hop-on Hop-off' service, with over 90 stops, delivering guests to the door of London's most famous sights and attractions. This entertaining and informative guide to London is presented by English-speaking Tour Hosts or a choice of seven digitally recorded language commentaries plus a children's channel. Children also receive a Kids' Club activity pack. The 24-hour tickets include a fantastic free Thames cruise.
Daily 08.30-17.00, with buses operating until 20.00 July-Aug
For further info please call or visit website

Discount Offer: Save Money - Book in advance through www.theoriginal-tour.com

Heritage & Industrial

Bank of England Museum

Threadneedle Street London EC2R 8AH
Tel: 020 7601 5545 Fax: 020 7601 5808
www.bankofengland.co.uk/museum
The Bank of England Museum tells the story of the Bank from its foundation in 1694 to its role in today's economy. Interactive programmes with graphics and video help to explain its many and varied roles. Popular exhibits include a unique collection of banknotes, a genuine gold bar which can be handled and free holiday events, please ring for details.
All year Mon-Fri 10.00-17.00. Closed Weekends, Public & Bank Hols
Admission Free

Historical

Apsley House

149 Piccadilly London W1J 7NT
Tel: 020 7499 5676
[Tube: Hyde Park Corner]
Was home to the great 'Iron' Duke of Wellington and contains his magnificent art collection.
All year Tue-Sun & Bank Hol Mon

Dennis Severs House

18 Folgate Street London E1 6BX
Tel: 020 7247 4013
[Tube/Rail: Liverpool St]
Lose youself in another time.
All year, 1st & 3rd Sun

Freud Museum

20 Maresfield Gardens Hampstead London NW3 5SX
Tel: 020 7435 2002 / 435 5167
[Tube: Finchley Rd]
A sensitive and wholly personal exhibition set in the Freud family home.
All year Wed-Sun

Geffrye Museum

136 Kingsland Road Shoreditch London E2 8EA
Tel: 020 7739 9893 Fax: 020 7729 5647
www.geffrye-museum.org.uk

[Tube: Liverpool St (then bus). Bus: 149, 242, 243, 67. Old St (then bus 243)]

One of London's most friendly and charming museums, the Geffrye presents the history of the English domestic interior from 1600 to the present day. A series of period rooms containing fine collections of furniture, paintings and decorative arts reflect the changing tastes and styles of the urban middle classes. The museum is set in delightful eighteenth-century almshouse buildings with attractive gardens, including a walled herb garden and series of period gardens.

All year daily Tue-Sat 10.00-17.00 & Sun 12.00-17.00. Closed 24-25 Dec, 1 Jan & Good Friday. Closed Mons except Bank Hols
Admission Free

Hermitage Rooms

South Building Somerset House Strand London
WC2R 1LA
Tel: 020 7845 4630
[Tube: Covent Garden]
The galleries provide a perfect backdrop for
rotating exhibitions offering a glimpse of some
of the magnificent treasures from the Hermitage
and other collections.

Houses Of Parliament

Westminster London SW1A 0AA
Tel: 0870 906 3773
www.parliament.uk

Once again this year, Parliament will be opening
its doors to allow visitors the opportunity to tour
this unique building. Visitors will be led by a
specially qualified Blue Badge Guide. The tour
through the Palace allows visitors to see the
Chamber of the House of Lords, Central Lobby,
The Chamber of the House of Commons and St
Stephen's Hall. Tours takes approximately 75
minutes, allowing you to plan your itinerary
around them. Tours are available in French,
German, Italian and Spanish at specific times.
Parliament remains a working building making
tours subject to changes and cancellations.

*Aug Mon-Tue & Fri-Sat 09.15-16.30, Wed-Thur
13.15-16.30, Sept-Oct Mon & Fri-Sat 09.15-
16.30, Tue-Wed & Thur 13.15-16.30*
A£12.00 C&Concessions£5.00 Others£8.00,
Family Ticket £30.00

Keats' House

Keats Grove Hampstead London NW3 2RR
Tel: 020 7435 2062
[Rail: Hampstead Heath]
Visitors can see Keats's rooms and many of his
personal possessions.

Old Royal Naval College

2 Cutty Sark Gardens Greenwich London
SE10 9LW
Tel: 020 8269 4747 Fax: 020 8269 4757
www.oldroyalnavalcollege.org

*[J2, M25 then A2 & follow signs for Greenwich.
Rail: Greenwich. Tube: from Canary Wharf, take
the Docklands Light Railway to Cutty Sark]*
The Old Royal Naval College is one of London's
most famous riverside landmarks, and it stands
on the site of the Tudor palace where both
Henry VIII and Elizabeth I were born. The buildings were planned and designed by some of the
greatest architects of the seventeenth and eighteenth centuries (including Christopher Wren,
Nicholas Hawksmoor, and James "Athenian"
Stuart). Originally a hospital for wounded sea-
men, it became a training college for the Royal
Navy in 1873. The site was first opened to the
public in 1997, and today visitors can enjoy free
entry to its magnificent Painted Hall, the Chapel,
and the Visitor Centre (with its café and gift
shop). Guided tours run daily with exclusive
access to areas of the site not generally open to
the public, including the Nelson Room exhibition, and the Victorian Skittle Alley. Please visit
the website for more details and information on
the events programme. For disabled access
please phone ahead.
All year daily 10.00-17.00. Closed 24-26 Dec
Admission Free

PM Gallery and House

Walpole Park Mattock Lane Ealing London
W5 5EQ
Tel: 020 8567 1227
[Tube: Ealing Broadway]
PM Gallery and House comprises Pitzhanger
Manor House and a sympathetically designed
extension.

Queen's House

Romney Road Greenwich London SE10 9NF
Tel: 020 8858 4422 Fax: 020 8312 6522
www.nmm.ac.uk
*[J2 M25 then A2 & A206, follow signposts into
central Greenwich. Rail: Greenwich. DLR: Cutty
Sark]*

The first Palladian-style villa in England,
designed by Inigo Jones for Anne of Denmark
and completed for Queen Henrietta Maria, wife
of Charles I. Includes a loggia overlooking
Greenwich Park. Now the home of the fine art
collection of the National Maritime Museum with
additional displays on historic Greenwich.

All year daily 10.00-17.00. Closed 24-26 Dec
Admission Free

Royal Hospital Chelsea

Royal Hospital Road Chelsea London SW3 4SR
Tel: 020 7881 5305 Fax: 020 7881 5319
www.chelsea-pensioners.org.uk
*[Entrance London Gate. Tube: Sloane Square.
Coach party parking can be arranged if pre-
booked]*

The Royal Hospital Chelsea was established by
King Charles II for soldiers who were disabled or
worn out by long service. The buildings were
constructed by Sir Christopher Wren and the
first 'In-Pensioners' admitted in 1692. Currently
there are over 300 Chelsea Pensioners. Figure
Court is dominated by a statue of King Charles
II. On either side are the 'Long Ward's' where
the In-Pensioners live (not open to the public).
The Great Hall which is used for meals and
events is open to the public. It is dominated by
a mural commemorating the foundation of the
Royal Hospital and on the walls are listed the
Battle Honours of the British Army. Copies of
captured colours hang from the walls. Opposite
is the Chapel, with its original woodwork.
Museum, souvenir shop and post office on site.
The grounds are open to the public except during April/May when closed for the Chelsea
Flower Show.

*All year Mon-Sat 10.00-12.00 & 14.00-16.00,
Apr-Sept Sun 14.00-16.00. Closed 25, 26 Dec &
1 Jan*

Admission Free

Shakespeare's Globe Theatre Tour and Exhibition

21 New Globe Walk Bankside London SE1 9DT
Tel: 020 7902 1500 Fax: 020 7902 1515
www.shakespeares-globe.org

[Tube: London Bridge / Mansion House / Southwark / St Paul's]

The largest exhibition of its kind devoted to the world of Shakespeare, from Elizabethan times to the present day - situated beneath the Globe Theatre itself. Explore Bankside, the Soho of Elizabethan London, follow Sam Wanamaker's struggle to recreate an authentic Globe for the twentieth century and beyond, and take a fascinating guided tour of today's working theatre. Globe Education provides workshops, lectures, courses and online learning programmes for students of all ages and nationalities. For further information please call 020 7902 1433. Performances in the Globe Theatre: May-October. Box office 020 7401 9919. The Globe café offers light refreshments and main dishes. The Globe restaurant offers full á la carte dining as well as pre and post performance menus.

Shakespeare's Globe Exhibition: Oct-Apr daily 10.00-17.00, May-Sept (theatre season) 09.00-11.30 exhibition & guided tour into theatre, 12.00-17.00 exhibition, sword fighting & Elizabethan dressing demonstrations. Closed 24-25 Dec

A£9.00 Concessions£7.50 C(5-15)£6.50, Family Ticket £25.00. Admission includes a guided tour of Theatre and demonstrations. Group rates (15+) available on request

Discount Offer: One Child Free

Syon House and Gardens

Syon Park Brentford Middlesex TW8 8JF
Tel: 020 8560 0882 Fax: 020 8568 0936
www.syonpark.co.uk

[Approach via A310 (Twickenham Rd) into Park Rd. Plenty of on-site parking available]

Syon House is the London home of the Duke of Northumberland. The present house is Tudor in origin but famed for its splendid Robert Adam interiors. The Gardens contain the spectacular Great Conservatory. Member of the Historic Houses Association.
House: 21 Mar-28 Oct Wed, Thur, Sun & Bank Hol Mon (plus Good Fri & Easter Sat) 11.00-17.00. Gardens: Mar-Oct 10.30-17.00 or dusk, whichever is earlier. Nov-Feb weekends & New Years Day 10.30-16.00. Closed 25 & 26 Dec
House & Gardens: A£8.00 C£4.00 Concessions£7.00, Family Ticket £18.00. Gardens only: A£4.00 C&Concessions£2.50, Family Ticket £9.00. Group rates available on request

Discount Offer: Two for the Price of One

Landmarks

BA London Eye

Riverside Building County Hall Westminster Bridge Road London SE1 7PB
Tel: 0870 500 0600
[Tube: Waterloo]
One of the most dramatic additions to the London skyline.

Hyde Park
Tel: 020 7298 2100
[Tube: Knightsbridge]
Situated to the west of Park Lane, Hyde Park now consists of 340 acres of grass and trees with The Serpentine is at its centre.

Tower Bridge Exhibition
Tower Bridge Tower London SE1 2UP
Tel: 020 7940 3985
[Tube: London Bridge]
Over 100 years ago, the Victorians built a one of London's most famous landmarks.

Trafalgar Square
[Tube: Charing Cross]
In this famous meeting area stands Nelson's Column, built to commemorate Admiral Nelson, who was killed during his victorious battle against Napoleon's navy in 1805.

Literature & Libraries

British Library
96 Euston Road London NW1 2DB
Tel: 0870 444 1500
[Tube: Euston]
The British Library is the national library of the UK and one of the great libraries of the world.

Charles Dickens Museum
48 Doughty Street London WC1N 2LX
Tel: 020 7405 2127 Fax: 020 7831 5175
www.dickensmuseum.com
[Tube: Russell Square]

Discover the world of England's greatest novelist in his London home. The Charles Dickens Museum in London is the world's most important collection of material relating to the great Victorian novelist and social commentator. The only surviving London home of Dickens (1837 to 1839) was opened as a museum in 1925, and is still welcoming visitors from all over the world into its authentic and inspiring surroundings. Spread over four floors, visitors can see paintings, rare editions, manuscripts, original furniture and many items relating to the life of one of the most popular and beloved personalities of the Victorian age. Whilst living here, the author finished 'The Pickwick Papers,' wrote 'Oliver Twist' and 'Nicholas Nickleby,' and began work on 'Barnaby Rudge.' The museum offers a wide range of events and activities including handling sessions with original artefacts, and readings from Dickens' works. Introductory talks and private views can be arranged.
All year daily Mon-Sat 10.00-17.00, Sun 11.00-17.00
A£5.00 C£3.00 Concessions£4.00, Family Ticket £14.00

Dr Johnson's House

17 Gough Square London EC4A 3DE
Tel: 020 7353 3745
[Tube: Chancery Lane]

Built in 1700, this museum was once the home and workplace of Samuel Johnson from 1748-1759, and it was here that he compiled the first comprehensive English Dictionary.

Living History Museums

Age Exchange Reminiscence Centre

11 Blackheath Village Blackheath London SE3 9LA
Tel: 020 8318 9105
[Rail: Blackheath]

Small museum depicting everyday life from the 1920s-1940s. There is an old-fashioned shop set up to resemble a 1930s general store, where all exhibits can be handled. There are also changing exhibitions of memorabilia on different themes in social history.

Golden Hinde

St Mary Overie Dock Cathedral Street London SE1 9DE
Tel: 020 7403 0123 Fax: 020 7407 5908
www.goldenhinde.org
[Next to Southwark Cathedral on S side of Thames]

The Golden Hinde is an exact scale, fully operational reconstruction of Sir Francis Drake's sixteenth-century galleon. Guided tours for educational purposes are available all year round; public tours are available in the school holidays only. The Golden Hinde is a great venue for weddings, civil ceremonies, private hires, and children's birthday parties. Please call for information and opening times as sometimes the ship is closed for educational or private visits.
All year daily Shop 10.00-17.00, Ship 10.00-17.30, last tickets sold at 16.45
A£6.00 C&Concessions£4.50 Family Ticket(A2+C2)£18.00, Group rates available on request

Winston Churchill's Britain at War Experience

64-66 Tooley Street London SE1 2TF
Tel: 020 7403 3171 Fax: 020 7403 5104
www.britainatwar.co.uk
[Close to London Bridge]

A unique museum portraying the life of the British people living through WW2. This is an educational adventure for children and adults and an interesting trip down memory lane for seniors. Take the lift to the London Underground air-raid shelter to see where people spent sleepless nights. Just as they watched films, here visitors can watch a film about those dramatic years. The museum features the BBC radio studio, the dressing room of wartime stars, the Anderson shelter with the air-raid happening overhead, women working for the war effort, rationing, evacuation, the shops of Southwark, the Morrison shelter, bomb disposal, the Rainbow Room for G.I.'s and the full sized recreation of a bombed-out London street with the smouldering remains of a cinema, pub and people's homes. See it, feel it, breathe it!
All year Apr-Sept daily 10.00-18.00, Oct-Mar daily 10.00-17.00. Closed 24-26 Dec
A£9.50 C£4.85 Concessions£5.75, Family Ticket (A2+C2) £25.00 prices subject to change without prior notification

Discount Offer: Two for the Price of One

Maritime

National Maritime Museum

Greenwich London SE10 9NF
Tel: 020 8858 4422 / 8312 6565
Fax: 020 8312 6522
www.nmm.ac.uk

[J2 M25 then A2 & A206, follow signposts into central Greenwich. Rail: Greenwich. DLR: Cutty Sark]

See how the sea affects our daily lives in this impressive modern museum. Themes include exploration and discovery, Nelson, passenger shipping and luxury liners, maritime London, costume, art and the sea, the future of the sea and making waves.
All year daily 10.00-17.00 (18.00 July-Aug). Closed 24-26 Dec
Admission Free (except for special exhibitions)

Discount Offer: 20% off Adult Admissions to the 'Sailor Chic' Exhibition

Markets

Camden Lock

Chalk Farm Road London NW1
[Tube: Camden Town]
The markets of Camden are London's fourth biggest tourist attraction and the alleys and stalls apparently have the highest retail turnover in Europe. During the week, there are less stalls, but equally, less punters.

Covent Garden

Covent Garden London WC2
Tel: 020 7375 0441
[Tube: Covent Garden]
An excellent place to hang out with children. Covent Garden is one of London's few pedestrianised areas. Street entertainers, covered stalls and shops keep you all amused for hours.

Portobello Road Market

Portobello Road London
[Tube: Ladbroke Grove / Notting Hill]
The antiques stalls and shops are at Notting Hill end of Portobello Road (Saturdays only), while the vintage clothing is piled high under the Westway at the northern end.

Cross oceans, space and time, all in one day

ROYAL OBSERVATORY GREENWICH

NATIONAL MARITIME MUSEUM

GREENWICH · LONDON
Admission free
Bookings 0870 780 4264
bookings@nmm.ac.uk   www.nmm.ac.uk

Greenwich   Cutty Sark   Greenwich Pier   Welcome

Medical Museums

Alexander Fleming Laboratory Museum
St Mary's Hospital Praed Street W2 1NY
Tel: 020 7886 6528
[Tube: Paddington]
Leads you in the footsteps of Fleming.

Florence Nightingale Museum
St Thomas' Hospital 2 Lambeth Palace Road
London SE1 7EW
Tel: 020 7620 0374
[Tube: Waterloo]
A personal setting in which Florence's prized possessions, a lamp from the Crimean War and nursing artifacts are shown.

Museums of The Royal College of Surgeons of England
35-43 Lincoln's Inn Fields London WC2A 3PN
Tel: 020 7405 3474
[Tube: Holborn]
Boasts a host of enlightening, permanent and temporary, galleries and exhibitions.

Old Operating Theatre, Museum and Herb Garret
9a St Thomas St Southwark London SE1 9RY
Tel: 020 7188 2679
[Tube: London Bridge]
The oldest surviving operating theatre in Britain, with surgical paraphernalia and specimens.

Peter Pan Gallery and the Museum of the History of Geat Ormond Street Hospital
1st Floor 55 Great Ormond Street WC1 3JH
Tel: 020 7405 9200 X 5920
[Tube: Russell Square]
A small collection relating to the history of the renowned children's hospital and also a small section relating to Peter Pan and his creator J M Barrie.

Military & Defence Museums

Firepower! the Royal Artillery Museum
Royal Arsenal Woolwich London SE18 6ST
Tel: 020 8855 7755 Fax: 020 8855 7100
www.firepower.org.uk
[Rail : Woolwich Arsenal from Cannon St, Charing Cross, Waterloo East & London Bridge. 5min walk from Woolwich Arsenal to Firepower look for brown Firepower signage. National Rail Enquiries: 08457 484950. Bus routes 472, 161, 96, 180 stop in Plumstead Rd outside the Royal Arsenal. Bus routes 53, 54,422,380 stop in Woolwich town centre. Tube: Jubilee Line to North Greenwich, then 15min bus ride to Woolwich (161, 422, 472) to stops A & B. Car: The Royal Arsenal car park entrance is just off Beresford St/Plumstead Rd A206, E from Woolwich Ferry roundabout (A205). On-site parking available]
Located in the Historic Arsenal, the world's centre for munitions manufacture, Firepower takes you from slingshot to supergun, starting in the Field of Fire; where big screens, dramatic surround sound and moving eyewitness accounts illuminate the conflicts of the twentieth century. See and touch artillery from early cannon to modern missile systems. Learn how they work with touch-screen interactives. Get your hands on in the Real Weapon gallery to find out how ammunition reaches its target and what it does when it gets there. The Cold War Gallery section displays large self-propelled guns, from the Cold War era to the present day.
Apr-Oct Wed-Sun 10.30-17.00, Nov-Mar Fri-Sun 10.30-17.00, Open all School & Bank Hols
A£5.00 C£2.50 Concessions£4.50, Family Ticket £(A2+C2) or (A1+C3) £12.00. Special prices for groups (10+)

Guards Museum, The

Wellington Barracks Birdcage Walk London
SW1E 6HQ
Tel: 020 7414 3428 / 414 3271
Fax: 020 7414 3429
www.theguardsmuseum.com
[Tube: St. James Park. Walk up Queen Anne's Gate, turn L into Birdcage Walk & entrance is by Guards Chapel]
The Guards Museum is a superb facility covering the exciting, entertaining and interesting world of the Five Regiments of Foot Guards. Here you can find everything from the glory days of scarlet and gold to the mud and blood of two devastating World Wars. It traces the dangerous role of present-day soldiering in an increasingly volatile world. The cornucopia of weapons, paintings, uniforms and memorabilia includes personal items, not only of the Dukes of Marlborough and Wellington, but also of the equally heroic men who served them. The collection boasts a large number of artefacts belonged to members of the Royal Family, many of whom served in the Guards. There's also an inspiring exhibition of Victoria Crosses won by Guardsmen since it was first awarded 150 years ago, as well as numerous other gallantry awards. The museum is a hidden gem and well worth a visit.
All year daily 10.00-16.00 (occasionally closed for state ceremonies)
A£3.00 C£Free OAPs£2.00

Discount Offer: Two for the Price of One

Imperial War Museum

Lambeth Road London SE1 6HZ
Tel: 020 7416 5320
[Tube: Lambeth North]
Permanent exhibitions include First and Second World War Galleries, Conflicts since 1945 and

The Holocaust Exhibition.

Mills - Water & Wind

Wimbledon Windmill Museum

Windmill Road Wimbledon Common
Wimbledon London SW19 5NR
Tel: 020 8947 2825
www.wimbledonwindmillmuseum.org.uk

[Windmill Rd off Parkside (A219). Plenty of on-site parking available]

Have you ever visited a windmill and not understood how it worked? This is your opportunity to find out. The Windmill Museum is housed in the historic Wimbledon Windmill, built in 1817. It tells the story of windmills and milling in pictures, working models and the machinery and tools of the trade. Children can grind their own flour using a hand quern, saddle stone or mortar and have the working of the millstones explained. We have a collection of over 400 woodworking tools, donated by a millwright, and there are life size displays showing how the mill was built and what it was like to live in the mill after it stopped working in 1864. There is parking space for 300 cars and the mill is surrounded by Wimbledon Common with its 1,100 acres of heath, lakes and woodland. Our shop sells cut out model windmills, miniature millstones and querns!
Apr-end Oct Sat 14.00-17.00 Sun & Public Hol 11.00-17.00
A£1.00 C£0.50 Concessions£0.50. Group visits by arrangement only

Multicultural Museums

Horniman Museum and Gardens

100 London Rd Forest Hill London SE23 3PQ
Tel: 020 8699 1872 Fax: 020 8291 5506
www.horniman.ac.uk
*[On South Circular Rd (A205) Rail: Forest Hill.
Bus: 176 / 185 / 122 / P4 / P13 / 356 / 363]*
Situated in 16 acres of beautiful gardens, this
award winning south London museum has
unique exhibitions, events and activities to
delight adults and children alike. Housed in
Charles Townsend's landmark Arts and Crafts
style building, the Museum has outstanding collections that illustrate the natural and cultural
world. The museum dramatically doubled the
public space with the opening of the Centenary
Development in 2002, finally realising founder
Frederick Horniman's vision of re-orientating the
museum to take in the green oasis of the gardens. Visitors can discover African Worlds
showcasing the largest ceremonial mask in
Britain, celebrate world cultures in the
Centenary Gallery, experience the Victorian
time-capsule of the Natural History gallery with
original specimens and fossils, sound out the
Music Gallery with Britain's largest collection of
musical instruments from around the world, or
dive into the stunning new Aquarium featuring
jellyfish, seahorses, coastal rock pools, a man-
grove swamp and South American rainforest.
*All year daily 10.30-17.30. Closed 24-26 Dec.
Gardens close at sunset*
Admission Free

**Discount Offer: Two for the Price of
One**

Music & Theatre Museums

Handel House Museum

25 Brook Street Mayfair London W1K 4HB
Tel: 020 7495 1685 Fax: 020 7495 1759
www.handelhouse.org
*[Tube: Bond St (entrance to museum at rear in
Lancashire Ct)]*

Home to composer Handel from 1723 until his
death in 1759, the Handel House Museum celebrates Handel's music and life, through restored
Georgian interiors, eighteenth-century furniture
and art, displays, live music, events and special
exhibitions.
*All year Tue-Wed, Fri-Sat 10.00-18.00, Thur
10.00-20.00, Sun 12.00-18.00. Closed Bank
Hols & Mon*
A£5.00 C£2.00 Concessions£4.50, free for children on Sat

**Discount Offer: Two for the Price of
One**

Royal College of Music: Museum
of Instruments

Prince Consort Road South Kensington London
SW7 2BS
Tel: 020 7589 3643
[Tube: South Kensington]
Features over six hundred instruments, some of
which date from 1480.

V and A Theatre Museum

(Public Entrance) Russell Street Covent Garden
London WC2E 7PR
Tel: 020 7943 4700 Fax: 020 7943 4777
www.vam.ac.uk/theatre
[Tube: Covent Garden]

The Theatre Museum's galleries - which illustrate how theatre has evolved from 1550 to the present day through displays of costumes, props, models, paintings, playbill and programmes - are closed to general visitors while new performance displays and exhibitions are being developed at the Victoria and Albert Museum, South Kensington, for opening late 2007. Please check website before making a special visit.
All year Mon-Fri 10.00-18.00 for booked groups and guided tours only
Please telephone 020 7943 4806 or e-mail tmgroups@vam.ac.uk for group & tour prices & information

Natural History Museums

Natural History Museum

Cromwell Road London SW7 5BD
Tel: 020 7942 5000
[Tube: South Kensington]
Highlights include the huge roaring, breathing robotic Tyrannosaurus rex in 'Dinosaurs', an earthquake experience in 'The Power Within' and the beautiful Earth's Treasury, displaying the museum's famous collections of gems and minerals.

On the Water

Bateaux London and Catamaran Cruisers

Embankment Pier Victoria Embankment London
WC2N 6NU
Tel: 020 7695 1800 Fax: 020 7839 1034
www.bateauxlondon.com
[Tube: Embankment]
BATEAUX LONDON: London's premier operator of luxury lunch and dinner cruises on the River Thames. Guests indulge in a relaxing lunch cruise or experience the excitement of London by night with a dinner cruise onboard one of our elegant restaurant cruisers. A magical blend of fine food, friendly service and world-class entertainment combine to create this unique experience. Also available for private hire. CATAMARAN CRUISERS: Catamaran Cruisers operate daily sightseeing cruises, with full commentary from Westminster, Embankment, Waterloo, Bankside, Tower and Greenwich Piers. See all of London's sights including the London Eye, Shakespeare's Globe and the Tate Modern. Our multi-lingual, non-stop Thames Circular Cruise also offers an insight into London's history and encompasses London's best loved sights.
CATAMARAN CRUISERS: Hop-on-Hop-off Service - daily from Embankment, Waterloo, Bankside, Tower & Greenwich Piers every 45mins from 10.00-18.00. Thames Circular Cruise - daily from Westminster pier from 11.00-17.00. Please call for further timetable information. BATEAUX LONDON: Lunch cruises operate all year, Wed-Sat, apart from 1 Jan-31 Mar where they will only operate Thur-Sat. Departing Embankment Pier at 12.30 & Waterloo Pier at 12.45. Sunday Lunch Jazz Cruise: all year Sun, departs Embankment Pier at 12.30 & Waterloo Pier at 12.45. Dinner Cruises: all year every night apart from 1 Jan-31 Mar where operation is Tue-Sat, depart Embankment Pier at 20.00
CATAMARAN CRUISERS: Hop-on-Hop-off tickets start from A£3.40 C£1.70. Thames Circular

Cruise: A£9.50 C£4.95, Family Ticket (A2+C3) £23.00. BATEAUX LONDON: Lunch Cruise: £24.00 3 course set menu, £13.00 children's menu. Sunday Lunch Jazz Cruise: From £39.50, £22.00 children's menu. Dinner Cruises: Prices start from £69.00 per person. Prices and times subject to change from 1 Apr 2008.

Canal Cruises - Jenny Wren

250 Camden High Street London NW1 8QS
Tel: 020 7485 4433/6210 Fax: 020 7485 9098
www.walkersquay.com
[Tube: Camden Town]
Discover London's fascinating hidden water-ways aboard Jenny Wren, a traditionally decorated narrow boat, and enjoy the unique experience of passing through a canal lock. Our regular 90 minute tours take you past London Zoo and through picturesque Regent's Park, then by way of the 'haunted' Maida Hill tunnel to elegant Little Venice with its Regency style houses where you may alight for a short visit. An interesting commentary is provided by our crew. You may complement your cruise with refreshments, available from our restaurant. Jenny Wren is also available for Party Buffet Cruises and Children's Parties.
Mar-Oct daily all day
A£7.00 C£3.50
OAPs&Students(NUS/USI)£5.50, Family Ticket (A2+C2) £18.00. School Groups each £3.00. Other group rates available on request. Price increase due at Easter

Discount Offer: One Child Free

Canal Cruises - My Fair Lady Cruising Restaurant

250 Camden High Street London NW1 8QS
Tel: 020 7485 4433/6210 Fax: 020 7485 9098
www.walkersquay.com
[Tube: Camden Town]
Enjoy a leisurely dining cruise aboard the luxury Cruising Restaurant, 'My Fair Lady', where you are served an excellent three course á la carte meal freshly prepared in our on-board galley, whilst cruising London's fascinating hidden waterways. Our cruise takes you through the lock at Camden, past London Zoo and through the picturesque Regent's Park, then by way of the 'haunted' Maida Hill tunnel, to elegant Little Venice with its Regency style houses. 'My Fair Lady' offers evening dinner cruises and a family orientated traditional Sunday lunch cruise throughout the year. It is a unique venue for all occasions, both private and corporate, catering for all sizes of groups, up to 98 in number.
All year, cruise for lunch on Sunday, public cruise for dinner daily
Lunch £24.95, Dinner £39.95. Reduced prices available for children. Price increase due at Easter

Discount Offer: One free bottle of wine for every four full-paying adults

City Cruises

Cherry Garden Pier Cherry Garden Street
London SE16 4TU
Tel: 020 7740 0400 Fax: 020 7740 0495
www.citycruises.com

[Tube: Westminster (for Westminster Millennium Pier), Waterloo (for Waterloo Millennium Pier), Tower Hill (for Tower Millennium Pier) & Cutty Sark (DLR) (for Greenwich Pier)]

City Cruises plc, the largest operator of passenger services on the Thames, carries some 750,000 people annually on its extensive sightseeing, entertainment and charter services. The company offers a variety of boat services during the day and evening to suit all tastes. With City Cruises you can rest assured of a warm welcome and a friendly efficient service.
Westminster/Waterloo/Tower/Greenwich Sightseeing Service; a hop-on hop-off facility between the three major destination piers on the Thames. Passengers are able to travel in comfort on one of four new state of the art luxury Riverliners which offer on-board catering and bar services. A joint ticket is also available with the DLR. London Showboat; a unique floating entertainment experience with dinner and cabaret. Corporate and Private Charters; City Cruises has years of experience hosting important and memorable functions from Christmas and Birthday celebrations to corporate dinners and weddings. Our menus and staff make every occasion special. The company has an extensive fleet of 15 vessels catering for all budgets. City Cruises is the sole company on the Thames to possess its own catering facilities, including a dedicated floating kitchen at Cherry Garden Pier. Baby changing facilities, pushchair access and shelter available on some boats, please specify if you require these services when booking.
Westminster/Waterloo/Tower/Greenwich Sightseeing Service - operates every 40mins from 10.00. Boarding at either Westminster Millennium Pier, Waterloo Millennium Pier, Tower Millennium Pier or Greenwich Pier. London Showboat - Apr-Oct, Wed-Sun & Nov-Mar Thur-Sat. Corporate & Private Charters - please call for Charter information pack & further details
Westminster/Waterloo/Tower/Greenwich Sightseeing Service: A£10.00 C&Concessions£5.00, Family Ticket (A2+C3) £23.50 (these River Red Rover tickets offer unlimited travel throughout the day). Single & return tickets also available. London Showboat: £66.00 (inclusive of welcome drink, half bottle of wine, 4 course meal, cruise, cabaret & dancing). Corporate & Private Charters - please call for Charter information pack & further details

Discount Offer: One Child Free

London Ducktours

55 York Road London SE1 7NJ
Tel: 020 7928 3132 Fax: 020 7928 2050
http://www.londonducktours.co.uk

[Pick up point in Chicheley St, behind London Eye on South Bank]

London Duck Tours offer more than just a sightseeing tour; appealing to visitors of all ages! The name Duck Tours is actually drawn from the vehicles themselves, which is an important part of British history as they are the amphibious DUKWs used to take the troops ashore for the D-Day landings. This is no ordinary tour, as not only do you get a live guided tour of the City of Westminster by road, you also get to take a trip along the river, without ever leaving the comfort of your seat. Nothing compares to the thrill of literally driving from the road straight into the Thames. Why not also try London Duck tours for that special event, group hire or tailored made tour. London Duck Tours operates all year round, last tour dependant upon dusk. Pre-booking is recommended.

All year 10.00-dusk
A£18.00 C(under12)£12.00
Concessions£14.00, Family Ticket (A2+C2)
£55.00

London Waterbus Company
London NW1 8AF
Tel: 020 7482 2660
www.londonwaterbus.com/
[Camden Lock Location: West Yard, Camden Lock, off Camden High St, London, NW1, Camden Lock access: Bus: 24 / 27 / 29 / 31 /74 / 88 / 168 / 214 / 253. Tube: Camden Town / Chalk Farm. Little Venice location: Brownings Pool, Little Venice, Warwick Cres/Blomfield Rd, W9, Little Venice access: Bus: 6 / 8 / 16 / 18 / 31 / 46. Tube: Warwick Avenue/ Paddington]
Cruises on traditional canal narrow boats along the historic Regents Canal, through the green and leafy fringes of Regents Park in central London. From the point at Little Venice where Brownings Island is surrounded by elegant Regency architecture, through the dark and mysterious Maida Hill tunnel, past Marylebone and the park to the lively bustle of Camden Lock Market. On the way the boat stops at our canal gate into London Zoo. Trips one way, either way, or return. Make a stopover for a picnic at Little Venice or to shop and eat at Camden Lock. If you want to visit the Zoo, take the Waterbus from either end and pay our special low prices and miss out the queues at the Main Gate. No bookings necessary just turn up and pay on board. No dogs permitted.
Apr-Sept daily on the hour 10.00-17.00. Oct Thur-Sun 11.00-15.00, Nov-Mar Sat & Sun 11.00-15.00
Camden Lock or Little Venice One-way: A£6.00 C(3-15)&OAPs£4.30. Return: A£8.40 C(3-15)&OAPs£5.40. To London Zoo including admission A£16.50, OAPs£15.50 C(3-15)£13.50. All tickets on board - cash or cheques only. Group rates (for 20+) available on request and pre-booking is essential

Discount Offer: £0.80 off Adult Fares

Performing Arts

Barbican Centre
Silk Street London EC2Y 8DS
Tel: 020 7638 4141
[Tube: Barbican]
Huge, multifaceted arts, entertainment and education centre. Open 363 days a year, it offers the most diverse program of any London venue. Two theatres, three cinemas, the redeveloped Barbican Art Gallery, several exhibition spaces, shops, cafés, restaurants, bars and more.

BFI London IMAX Cinema
1 Charlie Chaplin Walk South Bank Waterloo London SE1 8XR
Tel: 0870 787 2525
[Rail/Tube: Waterloo]
Offers the biggest cinema screen in Europe housed inside a spectacular glass building.

Places of Worship

Southwark Cathedral
London Bridge London SE1 9DA
Tel: 020 7367 6700
[Tube: London Bridge]
For over 1,000 years Southwark Cathedral has been a centre for Christian worship.

St Paul's Cathedral
The Chapter House St Paul's Churchyard London EC4M 8AD
Tel: 020 7236 4128
[Tube: St Paul's]
Sir Christopher Wren's architectural masterpiece. Climb to the Whispering Gallery where your whisper can be heard on the other side.

Westminster Cathedral

Clergy House Victoria Street London
SW1P 1QW
Tel: 020 7798 9055 Fax: 020 7798 9090
www.westminstercathedral.org.uk

[300 yards from Rail: Victoria Station. Tube: Victoria]

Called 'A Series of Surprises' because of its architecture, mosaics and marble decorations, Westminster Cathedral was begun in 1895. Its origins go back much further, being designed in the early Christian Byzantine style by the Victorian architect, John Francis Bentley. Appointed by the third Archbishop of Westminster, Cardinal Herbert Vaughan, Bentley took much of his inspiration from the Italian churches and cathedrals he visited during the winter of 1894, particularly those in Ravenna, Pisa, Bologna and Venice where he undertook a detailed study of St Mark's Cathedral. His other inspiration was the Emperor Justinian's great church of Santa Sophia in Istanbul. The Cathedral was conceived to be built quickly with inside decorations added, as funds became available. The structure was completed in 1903. Brick built, the vast domed interior has the widest and highest nave in England and is decorated with mosaics plus 125 varieties of marble from around the world.

Cathedral: All year Mon-Fri 07.00-19.00, Sat 08.00-19.00 Sun closes 20.00. Tower: Apr-Nov daily 09.00-17.00. Dec-Mar Thur Sun 09.00-17.00
Admission Free, Tower lift charged

Police, Prisons & Dungeons

Clink Prison Museum

1 Clink Street Bankside London SE1 9DG
Tel: 020 7403 0900
[Tube: London Bridge]
The original site of the prison that gave its name to all others.

Roman Era

Crofton Roman Villa

Crofton Road Orpington Kent BR6 8AF
Tel: 01689 873826/020 8460 1442
www.the-cka.fsnet.co.uk
[J4 M25, A232 adjacent Orpington Railway station, signs on cover building. Rail: Orpington. Bus: 61, 208, 353]

The only Roman Villa in Greater London which is open to the public. The Crofton Villa house was inhabited from about AD140 to 400 and was the centre of a farming estate of about 200 hectares. Nearby would have been farm buildings, surrounded by fields, meadows and woods. The house was altered several times during its 260 years of occupation and at its largest probably had at least 20 rooms. The remains of 10 rooms can be seen today, with tiled floors and underfloor heating systems, within a modern cover building. Graphic displays, children's activity corner, schools service.
1 Apr-31 Oct Wed, Fri & Bank Hol Mon 10.00-13.00 & 14.00-17.00, Sun 14.00-17.00
A£0.80 C£0.50

Royal

Banqueting House
Whitehall London SW1A 2ER
Tel: 0870 751 5178
[Tube: Westminster]
Visitors will be enthralled by the history of this magnificent building.

Buckingham Palace, Royal Mews
London SW1A 1AA
Tel: 020 7766 7302
[Tube: Victoria]
Houses the State vehicles (cars, carriages and horses) used for official engagements.
24 Mar-31 Oct (Closed Fri)
Joint Ticket available for the State Rooms, Royal Mews and the Queen's Gallery

Buckingham Palace, State Rooms and Gardens
London SW1A 1AA
Tel: 020 7766 7300
[Tube: Victoria]
Used by The Royal Family to receive and entertain their guests on official occasions.
28 Jul-25 Sep 2007
Joint Ticket available for the State Rooms, Royal Mews and the Queen's Gallery

Buckingham Palace, The Queen's Gallery
London SW1A 1AA
Tel: 020 7766 7301
[Tube: Victoria]
Permanent space for the Royal Collection.
Open daily
Joint Ticket available for the State Rooms, Royal Mews and the Queen's Gallery

Changing of the Guard
Buckingham Palace London SW1A 1AA
[Tube: Victoria]
This intricate ceremony attracts thousands of tourists each year.
May-July daily 11.30. Please see www.army.mod.uk for Aug-Apr details

Clarence House
London SW1A 1AA
Tel: 020 7766 7303
[Tube: St James's Park]
The official residence of The Prince of Wales, The Duchess of Cornwall, Prince William and Prince Harry. Visitors are guided around where the family undertakes official engagements.
1 Aug-30 Sep daily (pre-booked guided tours only)

Hampton Court Palace
Hampton Court Palace East Molesey London KT8 9AU
Tel: 0870 752 7777 (info line)
[Rail: Hampton Court Station]
State Apartment and 60 acres of riverside gardens including the famous maze.
All year daily

Kensington Palace
Kensington Gardens London W8 4PX
Tel: 0870 751 5170 (info line)
[Tube: Kensington]
Explore the magnificent State Apartments and the Royal Ceremonial Dress Collection.
All year daily. Closed 24-26 Dec

Kew Palace and Queen Charlotte's Cottage
Royal Botanic Gardens Kew Richmond London TW9 3AB
Tel: 0870 751 5178
[Tube: Kew Gardens]
Kew Palace (once a merchant's home), was home to George III and Queen Charlotte from 1801-1818. Now, after a ten-year conservation project, the palace is open to the public.

Tower of London
Tower Hill London EC3N 4AB
Tel: 0870 756 6060 (info line)
[Tube: Tower Hill]
One thousand year-old prison, palace and place of execution. Includes the Royal Armouries and the Crown Jewels.
All year daily. Closed 24-26 Dec & 1 Jan

Grant Museum of Zoology and Comparative Anatomy

Darwin Building University College London
Gower Street London WC1E 6BT
Tel: 020 7679 2647
Dating back to 1828, the museum houses a
diverse natural history collection covering the
whole of the animal kingdon.

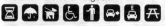

Royal Observatory Greenwich

Greenwich Park Greenwich London SE10 8XJ
Tel: 020 8858 4422/8312 6565
Fax: 020 8312 6652
www.rog.nmm.ac.uk

*[In Greenwich Park, off A2. Rail: Greenwich. DLR:
Cutty Sark]*

Stand on longitude zero - the Greenwich
Meridian, the home of time itself. See the
Astronomer Royal's apartments and Harrison's
amazing timekeepers in the charming Wren
building. The time ball falls daily at 13.00. See
our giant refracting telescope, our new astronomy galleries and the Planetarium (opening
Spring 2007). No wheelchair access to three
rooms.
*All year daily 10.00-17.00 (18.00 July-Aug).
Closed 24-26 Dec.*
Admission Free (but Planetarium shows are
charged)

Science Museum

Exhibition Road South Kensington London
SW7 2DD
Tel: 0870 870 4868
See, touch and experience the major scientific
advances of the last 30 years at the largest
museum of its kind in the world, with over 40
galleries, and 2,000 hands on exhibits.

Science Museum's Dana Centre

165 Queen's Gate London SW7 5HE
Tel: 020 7942 4040
The Dana Centre is a stylish, purpose-built
venue, complete with a cafebar, hosting exciting, informative and innovative debates about
contemporary science, technology and culture
for adults.

London's New
Peter Harrison Planetarium
& Space Galleries, Greenwich
Opening Spring 2007

ROYAL OBSERVATORY GREENWICH
at the National Maritime Museum

0870 780 4556
bookings@nmm.ac.uk

Sealife Centres & Aquariums

London Aquarium

County Hall Westminster Bridge Road London
SE1 7PB
Tel: 020 7967 8000 Fax: 020 7967 8029
www.londonaquarium.co.uk

*[Tube: Waterloo or Westminster. Across
Westminster Bridge from Houses of Parliament &
next to London Eye]*

Experience one of Europe's largest displays of
aquatic life. Just across the river Thames, opposite Big Ben, the award winning London
Aquarium has over 350 different species to discover. Visitors are even able to touch and stroke
the rays in the Touch pool. The one million litre
Pacific tank is home to several varieties of
shark, while a myriad of colourful fish can be
seen in the tropical tank, including the popular
clownfish.
All year daily 10.00-18.00
A£13.25 C(3-14)£9.75 Concessions£11.25,
Family Ticket (A2+C2) £44.00

Discount Offer: One Child Free

Social History Museums

Churchill Museum and Cabinet War Rooms

Clive Steps King Charles Street London SW1A
2AQ
Tel: 020 7930 6961 Fax: 020 7839 5897
www.iwm.org.uk

*[Tube: Westminster or St. James's Park. Bus: 3,
11, 12, 24, 53, 77a, 88, 109, 159, 184, 211]*

The world's first major museum dedicated to
the life of Sir Winston Churchill at the Cabinet
War Rooms, the top secret underground command centre that provided shelter for the British
Prime Minister and his government during the
Second World War. Take a step back in time in
the atmospheric rooms, which have been left
untouched since August 1945. In contrast, the
Churchill Museum is London's most technologically advanced and interactive visitor attraction
and explores the character and experiences of
the man behind the legend. The museum examines how Churchill achieved his iconic status not
just in Britain, but worldwide. It looks at the
changing world on which Churchill lived, the
successes and controversies of his long career
as a soldier, writer, politician, statesman, and
the conflicting opinions about him. Free personal sound guides are provided for every visitor.
All year daily 09.30-18.00. Closed 24-26 Dec
A£11.00 C£Free OAPs£9.00
Students(NUS/USI)£9.00 Unemployed (with
ES40) £6.00. Group rates available on request

Jewish Museum - Camden Town

Raymond Burton House 129-131 Albert Street
London NW1 7NB
Tel: 020 7284 1997 Fax: 020 7267 9008
www.jewishmuseum.org.uk

[Off Camden High St / Parkway. Tube: Camden Town]

Explores the history and religious life of the Jewish community in Britain and beyond. Its attractive galleries tell the story of the Jewish community from the Norman Conquest until recent times, and illustrate Jewish religious life with outstanding examples of Jewish ceremonial art. The Museum has been awarded Designated Status in recognition of the national importance of its collections. There are constantly changing temporary exhibitions, together with talks and lectures; as well as audio-visual programmes explaining Jewish faith, customs and history. Education programmes, group visits and refreshments by prior arrangement. A special exhibition: 'Champion of the Child - Janusz Korczak' runs until 8 April 2007. It tells the inspiring story of a Polish-Jewish doctor, educator and children's author who devoted his life to establishing the rights of the child, regardless of nationality or religion.
All year Mon-Thur 10.00-16.00, Sun 10.00-17.00. Closed: 24-26 Dec, 1 Jan, 2-4, 9-10 Apr
A£3.50 C£1.50 OAPs£2.50, Family Ticket £8.00

Discount Offer: Two for the Price of One

Jewish Museum - Finchley

80 East End Road London N3 2SY
Tel: 020 8349 1143 Fax: 020 8343 2162
www.jewishmuseum.org.uk
[On A504. Tube: Finchley Central. 12min walk via Station Rd / Manor View]

Social history displays tracing Jewish immigration and settlement in London including reconstructions of East End tailoring and cabinet-making workshops. Holocaust/Education gallery has special exhibition on Leon Greenman, British citizen and Holocaust survivor. Education programmes and group visits by prior arrangement. Changing exhibition, events and workshops available all year round. Currently showing: The Last Goodbye - The Rescue of children from Nazi Europe, until 2 September 2007. This extraordinary exhibition tells the remarkable story of 10,000 unaccompanied children rescued from Nazi Europe on the Kindertransport, using evocative photographs, documents and personal testimonies.
All year Mon-Thur 10.30-17.00, Sun 10.30-16.30. Closed 24 Dec-1 Jan, 2-4, 9-10 Apr & Bank Hol Weekends
A£2.00 C£Free Concessions£1.00

Discount Offer: Two for the Price of One

Library and Museum of Freemasonry

60 Great Queen Street London WC2B 5AZ
Tel: 020 7395 9257
[Tube: Covent Garden]
The world's largest collection of Masonic information and material.

Museum in Docklands

No 1 Warehouse West India Quay Hertsmere Road London E14 4AL
Tel: 0870 444 3855 Fax: 0870 444 3858
www.museumindocklands.org.uk
[Tube: Canary Wharf]
The Museum in Docklands unlocks the history of London's river, port and people in a nine-teenth-century warehouse at West India Quay. Explore London's connections with the world through an epic 2000-year story of trade, expansion and immigration.
Daily 10.00-18.00. Closed 24-26 Dec & 1 Jan
A£5.00 C(under16)&Students(NUS/USI)£Free Concessions £3.00

Discount Offer: Two for the Price of One

Museum of London

150 London Wall London EC2Y 5HN
Tel: 0870 444 3850 Fax: 0870 444 3853
www.museumoflondon.org.uk
[Entrance on pedestrian walk from Aldersgate St, London Wall or St Martins-le-Grand]
Officially opened in December 1976, the collections of the former London and Guildhall museums were brought together in one specially designed building. Step inside for an unforgettable journey through the turbulent years of the world's most fascinating city.

All year Mon-Sat 10.00-17.50 Sun 12.00-17.50. Closed 24-26 Dec & 1 Jan
Admission Free

Spectator Sports

Chelsea FC Stadium Tours

Stamford Bridge Ground Fulham Road London SW6 1HS
Tel: 0870 603 0005
www.chelseafc.com
[Tube: Fulham Broadway. On-site parking available]
The Chelsea FC Stadium Tour and Museum is the perfect football treat for all the family! Tour the home of one of the world's most famous sporting arenas and go behind-the-scenes into areas you'd only ever dreamed of seeing! Your guided tour will include the magnificent Home Dressing Room, the Away Dressing Room, the Press Room, the Players Tunnel, the Manager's Dug-Out and much, much more! After the guided tour, visit the club museum, and see an exhibition documenting over 101 years of football at Stamford Bridge. With sought after artifacts such as trophies, medals, shirts, boots and pennants, the Chelsea FC Museum has something for everybody. Guided tours run throughout the year and can be booked online at www.chelseafc.com/tours or by telephoning. Tours are subject to cancellation and alteration at short notice. Tours do not operate on Chelsea FC home matchdays. Pre-booking is advised.
Tours: All year daily. Mon-Fri: 11.00, 13.00, 15.00. Sat-Sun: 12.00, 13.00, 14.00.
A(17-64)£14.00 C(5-16)£8.00 C(under5)£Free OAPs(65+)£8.00

Kempton Park Racecourse

Kempton Park Sunbury-on-Thames Middlesex TW16 5AQ
Tel: 01932 782292
There is more to Kempton Park than horses! In addition to the very best in horse racing a wide range of events are held in the diverse and flexible facilities Kempton Park offers.

Sport & Recreation

Alexandra Palace Ice Rink

Alexandra Palace Way Wood Green London N22 7AY
Tel: 020 8365 2121
[Tube: Wood Green]
Opened in 1873, this majestic building is one of London's most famous landmarks and is renowned as the birthplace of television. It's now home to the biggest permanent ice rink in London, and is a great place to go skating. There are a wide range of activities on offer suitable for all ages and covering every aspect of ice sports.

Crystal Palace Park

Thicket Road Penge London SE20 8UT
Tel: 020 8778 9496 (Events-line)
[Rail: Crystal Palace Station]
The extensive grounds contain lakes, ancient oak trees, the National Sports Centre, a maze and an open air concert bowl. Most notable are the park's resident life-size (but anatomically inaccurate) dinosaur statues, first built in 1852.

ICANDO

17-19 Buckingham Palace Road London SW1W 0PT
Tel: 020 7592 1818
[Tube: Victoria]
What can you do at ICANDO? Come and experience our fully interactive activity centre for girl guides.

Sporting History Museums

Lord's Tour and MCC Museum

Lord's Ground St John's Wood London NW8 8QN
Tel: 020 7616 8595 / 6 Fax: 020 7266 3825
www.lords.org
[Tube: St John's Wood. Limited on-site parking available]
Lord's was established in 1787 and is the home of the MCC and cricket. When you tour this famous arena you follow in the footsteps of the 'greats' of the game, from W G Grace to Ian Botham. Daily guided tours take you behind the scenes at this venue. You will visit the Members' Pavilion including the hallowed Long Room and the Players' Dressing Room, the MCC Museum where the Ashes Urn is on display and many other places of interest including the newly constructed Grand Stand and futuristic NatWest Media Centre.

All year, tours normally 12.00 & 14.00, vary on cricket days, call to book. Apr-Sept 10.00
A£10.00 C£5.00 Concessions£7.00, Family Ticket £27.00

Discount Offer: One Child Free

Museum of Rugby and Twickenham Stadium Tours

Rugby Football Union Rugby Road Twickenham Middlesex London TW1 1DZ
Tel: 0870 405 2001 Fax: 0870 405 2002
www.rfu.com/microsites/museum
[On northern side of A316 as you head into London from SW. Plenty of on-site parking available]

Anyone for Twickers? Head to Twickenham Stadium's Museum of Rugby where the world's largest collection of rugby memorabilia helps tell the story of how a schoolboy game became an internationally renowned professional sport. Painting, archive match footage from around the globe and even a scrummaging machine that test your strength, bring the games vibrant history to life, promising an interactive experience for all the family. Fancy a peek inside the England dressing room? A Stadium Tour will get you there. Sit in the seat of your favourite player before finding out how it feels to run out of the players' tunnel-now that's something to shout about!
All year Tue-Sun & Bank Hol. Match Days: match ticket holders only. Closed on post match Sun, Mon (excluding Bank Hols), Easter Sun, 24-26, 31 Dec & 1 Jan
A£10.00 Concessions£7.00, Family Ticket £34.00

Discount Offer: Two for the Price of One

Wimbledon Lawn Tennis Museum and Tour

Museum Building All England Lawn Tennis & Croquet Club Church Road Wimbledon London SW19 5AE
Tel: 020 8946 6131 Fax: 020 8947 8752
www.wimbledon.org/museum

[Tube: Southfields. Car: from central London take A3 Portsmouth Rd to Tibbet's Corner, at underpass turn L towards Wimbledon, down Parkside. Entrance is in Church Rd, ample free parking from Aug-May. Bus: 493 from Wimbledon Station & Southfields Tube. Plenty of on-site parking available]

The all-new Wimbledon Museum is a state-of-the-art, fully interactive, multi-lingual tennis experience that traces the history of the once-Royal sport, right through to the modern game and the jet set lifestyles of the professional players on the ATP circuit. As well as numerous exhibits, our Audio-Visual Theatre explains and demonstrates the science of tennis with some unexpected special effects, there is also memorabilia and the world-famous Championships Trophies. Exclusive behind-the-scenes tour of the site available. Food is available from the Café Renshaw all-year round.
All year daily 10.30-17.00. Café Renshaw: As Museum but 10.00-17.00. Open to tournament visitors only during Championship 25 June-8 July
A£8.50 C£4.75 Concessions£7.50. Group rates available on request

Discount Offer: One Child Free

Superbreak Mini-Holidays - No 1 for UK short breaks

Theme & Adventure Parks

London Dungeon

28-34 Tooley Street London SE1 2SZ
Tel: 020 7403 7221 Fax: 020 7378 1529
www.thedungeons.com
[Rail/Tube: 100m from London Bridge Station]

The dungeons are a feast of fun with history's horrible bits. Live actors, shows, rides and interactive special effects take you back to those black, bleak times. Cower under the wrath of a vengeful sixteenth-century judge, face the resident torturer in his dark, dingy lair and try to find your way of the terrifying Labyrinth of the Lost… New for 2007 - Embark upon your last journey on the brand new Extremis: Drop Ride to Doom! Are you brave enough?
All year daily 10.00-17.00 varies in holiday periods please check website
Prices: Please call for information

Discount Offer: One Child Free

Namco Station

County Hall Riverside Building Westminster Bridge Road London SE1 7PB
Tel: 020 7967 1066
[Tube: Waterloo]
London's largest interactive entertainment venue. Encompassing a massive 35,000 sq-ft of bars, music, games, bowling, dodgems, pool and much much more.

Trocadero

1 Piccadilly Circus London W1V 7DD
Tel: 020 7439 1791
[Tube: Piccadilly Circus]
A grand centre of leisure, shopping and entertainment located in the heart of the West End.

Toy & Childhood Museums

V and A Museum of Childhood

Cambridge Heath Road London E2 9PA
Tel: 020 8983 5200 Fax: 020 8983 5225
www.museumofchildhood.org.uk
[Next to Bethnal Green tube station]
Recently transformed, the V&A Museum of Childhood opened in December 2006 and now features a stunning new entrance and front room gallery designed by award-winning architects. Part of the V&A family, the Museum and houses the national childhood collection. The galleries are designed to show the collections in a way which is accessible to adults and children of all ages. Visitors are encouraged to explore the themes of childhood past and present through the displays: Creativity; Moving Toys and the Childhood Galleries. As well as many hands-on activities including: dressing-up, indoor sandpit, Punch and Judy, ride-on rocking horses and role-play area. Highlights of the collection include the Nuremberg dolls' house, a rocking horse possibly owned by Charles I and Princess Daisy. We have a dynamic programme of temporary exhibitions, daily activities and seasonal events - please visit our website for more information.
Daily 10.00-17.45. Closed 25-26 Dec, 1 Jan
Admission free

For great hotel deals call Superbreak on 01904 679999 or visit www.superbreak.com

Transport Museums

London Canal Museum
12-13 New Wharf Road King's Cross London N1 9RT
Tel: 020 7713 0836
[Tube: Kings Cross]
The museum tells the story of the development of London's Canals. Visitors can learn about the people who strove to make a meagre livelihood by living and working on them.

Victorian Era

Leighton House Museum and Art Gallery
12 Holland Park Road London W14 8LZ
Tel: 020 7602 3316
[Tube: Kensington (Olympia)]
Built between 1864 and 1879 on the edge of Holland Park, the home of classical artist Lord Leighton also became home to the owner's extensive collection of Victorian paintings.

Linley Sambourne House
8 Stafford Terrace Kensington London W8 7BH
Tel: 020 7602 3316
[Tube: High St Kensington]
Step back in time into the best surviving middle-class Victorian town house in Britain. Weekend tours are led by an actor in period costume.
Pre-booking is advisable

Wax Works

Madame Tussauds
Marylebone Road London NW1 5LR
Tel: 020 7487 0200
[Tube: Baker St]
Experience what it is like to be famous as you join a host of the world's hottest celebrities. Includes London Planetarium.

Zoos

Battersea Park Children's Zoo
Battersea London SW11 4NJ
Tel: 020 7924 5826 Fax: 020 7350 0477
www.batterseaparkzoo.co.uk
[Rail: Battersea Park or Queenstown Rd. See website for public transport info]

So much to see and so much to do at Battersea Park Children's Zoo! Fun and enjoyment for the whole family… grandparents too! Come and visit the animals down on Barley Mow Farm and wander through the Mouse House with all its secrets. Then round the corner to the monkeys and lemurs who are waiting to show you how they can jump and swing. Say "Hello!" to the Mynah birds. Watch the otters swim and crawl down the tunnel to check on the meerkats. Any energy left? Then on to the Krazy Kids play area and move sand with a digger! Finally, need a drink? The Lemon Tree Café has light refreshments and excellent coffee.
Summer 10.00-17.30, Winter 10.00-16.30.
Guided tours by prior arrangement
A£5.95 C(2-15)£4.50, Family Ticket(A2+C2) £18.50

Discount Offer: One Free Child

London Zoo
Regents Park London NW1 4RY
Tel: 020 7722 3333
[Tube: Great Portland Street / Regents Park]
A vast array of amazing animals and beautiful gardens.

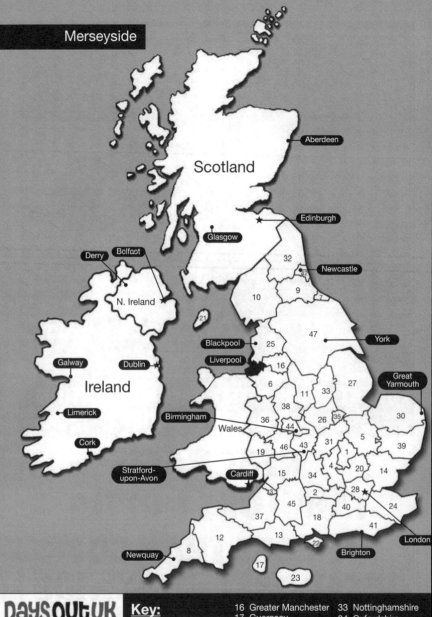

Merseyside

Aberdeen

Scotland

Edinburgh

Glasgow

Newcastle

Derry Belfast

N. Ireland

32
42
9
7

10

47 York

21

Blackpool
25

Liverpool

16

Great Yarmouth

Galway Dublin

6
11 33
27
30

Ireland

38

Limerick

36
44
26 35
5
39

Birmingham

Wales

19 46 43
31
1
20 14

Cork

Stratford-upon-Avon

15
4

Cardiff

34

28 London

13

2
24

45
40

37
18
41

12
13
22

Newquay

8
Brighton

17

23

Art Galleries

Lady Lever Art Gallery
Lower Road Port Sunlight Village Wirral
Merseyside CH62 5EQ
Tel: 0151 478 4136 Fax: 0151 478 4140
www.ladyleverartgallery.org.uk
[Plenty of on-site parking available]
Housing the collection of soap magnate William
Hesketh Lever, the first Lord Leverhulme. The
gallery is famous for its Pre-Raphaelite
paintings.
*All year daily. Closes 24 Dec at 14.00. Closed
25-26 Dec & 1 Jan*

Tate Liverpool
Albert Dock Liverpool Merseyside L3 4BB
Tel: 0151 702 7400 Fax: 0151 702 7401
www.tate.org.uk/liverpool
*[Rail: Lime St. Bus: Paradise St Station. Ample
Pay & Display parking at King's Dock, 5min walk
from Gallery]*
Tate Liverpool is home to the National Collection
of modern art in the North and is housed in a
beautiful converted warehouse in the historic
Albert Dock. Tate Liverpool displays work
selected from the Tate Collection and special
exhibitions which bring together artwork loaned
from around the world. The displays and exhibitions show modern and contemporary art from
1900s to the present day which includes photography, video, performance and installation as
well as painting and sculpture. There are a wide
range of events and family activities which
include free introductory tours, exhibition talks
and lectures as well as free family events which
take place every Sunday afternoon. Tate Shop
and Tate Café are open during gallery hours.
With stunning views across the River Mersey
Tate Liverpool is a great day out.
*All year, Galleries, Café & Shop: Sept-May Tue-
Sun, June-Aug daily 10.00-17.50*
Admission Free to Tate Collection. Charges for
special exhibitions, £5.00(£4.00 consessions)

Walker Art Gallery
William Brown Street Liverpool L3 8EL
Tel: 0151 478 4199 Fax: 0151 478 4190
www.thewalker.org.uk
The national gallery of the North, the Walker Art
Gallery is one of the finest galleries in Europe
housing outstanding collections of British and
European art from 1300s to the present day.
*All year daily. Closes 24 Dec at 14.00. Closed
25-26 Dec & 1 Jan*

Country Parks & Estates

Croxteth Hall and Country Park

Muirhead Avenue Liverpool Merseyside
L12 0HB
Tel: 0151 233 6910
Apart from the historic building itself, Croxteth
Hall also features a farm, a Victorian walled gar-
den and a country park.

Wirral Country Park Centre

Station Road Thurstatston Wirral Merseyside
L61 0HN
Tel: 0151 648 3884
Includes a 12 mile footpath through most of the
park. Guided walks, children's activities, boat
trips on Dee Estuary.

Exhibition & Visitor Centres

World of Glass

Chalon Way East St Helen's Merseyside
WA10 1BX

Tel: 08700 114466 Fax: 01744 616966
www.worldofglass.com

*[Just 30min from Manchester & Liverpool J7
M62. 5min walk from rail & bus stations Rail: St
Helen's Central. Plenty of on-site parking available]*

The World of Glass visitor centre in St.Helens
has all the ingredients for a great fun day trip for
families and kids of all ages. You can watch live
glassblowing demonstrations and see our resident experts transform molten glass into beautiful works of art. You'll be literally blown away by
our 3D multi-sensory special effects show,
which demonstrates how glass is used in technology as diverse as space exploration. Then
there's a fun-packed magic glass mirror maze
featuring distorting mirrors, kaleidoscopes and
periscopes as well as fascinating optical instruments. Visit our international museum collections and find out about the industries that
made St.Helens great then walk over a glass
bridge to the oldest glass-making tank furnace
in the world and explore a mysterious labyrinth
of underground tunnels. When your ready for a
break, there's the relaxing Kaleidoscope Café
while our superb new Artisan shop offers a
range of distinctive gifts - often hand made - at
down-to-earth prices. The range includes fur-
nishing items from our own in-house glassblowers. For more information telephone or visit our
website.
*Open all year Tue-Sun & Bank Hols 10.00-17.00.
Closed 25-26 Dec & 1st Jan*
A£5.30 Concessions£3.80, Family Ticket
(1A+2C) £10.80 or (2A+2C) £15.30

Festivals & Shows

Southport Flower Show

Victoria Park Southport Merseyside PR8 2BZ
Tel: 01704 547147 Fax: 01704 500750
www.southportflowershow.co.uk

Southport Flower Show is the UK's largest independent Flower Show. Set in 34 acres of parkland, visitors can expect to see spectacular
show gardens, water features and beautiful
blooms. It's the ideal opportunity to chat to gardening celebrities, enjoy shopping for gifts,
browse the arts and crafts and sample the best
produce in the fine foods marquee, with cookery demonstrations by celebrity chefs. For the
family there is non-stop live music, all day arena
entertainment and plenty for the children. It's a
fun day out for the whole family! Buy your ticket
early and save. Children under 16 are admitted
free when accompanied by a paying adult. For
more information visit our website.
16-19 August 2007
Please call 0870 44 44 226 for information &
tickets

Prescot Museum of Clock and Watch Making

34 Church Street Prescot Merseyside L34 3LA
Tel: 0151 430 7787
An attractive eighteenth-century town house contains exhibits pertaining to the clock, watch and tool-making industries of the area.

Port Sunlight Village and Heritage Centre

95 Greendale Road Port Sunlight Wirral
Merseyside CH62 4XE
Tel: 0151 644 6466
A garden village on the Wirral, purpose-built in 1888 by William Hesketh Lever to house the employees of Lever Brothers soap factory (now part of Unilever). The village is named after Lever's most popular brand of soap.

Williamson Tunnels Heritage Centre

The Old Stableyard Liverpool Merseyside
L7 3EE
Tel: 0151 709 6868
Joseph Williamson was one of the great eccentrics of the nineteenth century and (to this day) nobody knows why he built this strange underground kingdom beneath Liverpool.
Closed Mon-Wed in winter

Meols Hall

Botanic Road Churchtown Southport
Merseyside PR9 7LZ
Tel: 01704 228326
For one month of the year visitors to Meols Hall have the unique opportunity to take part in a full guided tour of Meols Hall, taking in all its amazing history and culture.

14 Aug-14 Sept

Mr Hardman's Photographic Studio

59 Rodney Street Liverpool L1 9EX
Tel: 0151 709 6107
www.nationaltrust.org.uk
[City centre]

Situated just below the Anglican Cathedral in the centre of Liverpool is this fascinating house, home, between 1947 and 1988, to Edward Chambré Hardman and his wife Margaret. The house contains a selection of photographs, the studio where most were taken, the darkroom where they were developed and printed, the business records and the rooms complete with all their contents and ephemera of daily life. The subject matter of the photographs - portraits of the people in Liverpool, their city and the land-scapes of the surrounding countryside - provide a record of a more prosperous time when Liverpool was the gateway to the British Empire and the world. Parallel to this is the quality of Hardman's work and his standing as a pictorial photographer.

21 Mar-28 Oct Wed-Sat 11.00-16.15. Admission by timed tickets & guided tour only including NT members, to avoid overcrowding and to preserve the fragile contents, no photography allowed inside property

A£4.95 C£1.40, Family Ticket (A2+C3) £12.60.
NT Members £Free

Discount Offer: One Child Free

Speke Hall

The Walk Speke Liverpool Merseyside L24 1XD
Tel: 08457 585702/0151 427 7231
Fax: 0151 427 9860
[8mi SE of Liverpool city centre, S of A561.
Signposted. Plenty of on-site parking available]
One of the most famous half-timbered houses
in the country set in varied gardens and an
attractive woodland estate. The Great Hall, Oak
Parlour and priest holes evoke Tudor times
while the small rooms, some with original
William Morris wallpapers, show the Victorian
desire for privacy and comfort. Fine plasterwork
and tapestries, plus a fully equipped Victorian
Kitchen and Servants' Hall. The restored garden
has spring bulbs, rose garden, Summer border
and stream garden; bluebell walks in the ancient
Clough Woodland, rhododendrons, spectacular
views of the grounds and Mersey Basin from a
high embankment - the Bund. Peaceful walks in
the wildlife oasis of Stocktons Wood. 1998 was
the 400th anniversary of Speke Hall and this
marks the four hundred years since the date of
1598 was carved over the front door during the
time of Edward Norris, the first owner of Speke
Hall, to mark the completion of the North Range
and the building we see today. Events and
activities reflect the different eras of the history
of Speke, its estate and the families who lived
and worked there, including open air theatre,
children's activities, and much more. Picnic area
by children's play area. Partial disabled access
please call before visit, 0151 427 7231.
Hall: 17 Mar-28 Oct Wed-Sun 13.00-17.30, 3
Nov-16 Dec Sat-Sun 13.00-16.30. Gardens: all
year daily 11.00-17.30 (or dusk). Closed 24-26,
31 Dec & 1 Jan
Hall & Gardens: A£6.70 C£3.70, Family Ticket
£20.50. Garden: A£4.00 C£1.90, Family Ticket
£11.00. NT Members £Free

Discount Offer: One Child Free

HM Customs and Excise National Museum

Merseyside Maritime Museum Albert Dock
Liverpool Merseyside L3 4AQ
Tel: 0151 478 4499
This museum tells the exciting story of the age-
old battle between smugglers and duty men.

Merseyside Maritime Museum

Albert Dock Liverpool Merseyside L3 4AQ
Tel: 0151 478 4499
Liverpool's seafaring heritage brought to life in
the historic Albert Dock.

Military & Defence Museums

Western Approaches

1-3 Rumford St Liverpool Merseyside L2 8SZ
Tel: 0151 227 2008 Fax: 0151 236 6913
[Town centre from M62 A5038]

Set beneath the streets of Liverpool, re-live the
times of 1940s Britain. See the life and work of
Wrens and Waafs working under constant pres-
sure in the original area command headquarters
for the battle of the Atlantic. Now open to the
public, visit the 50,000 sq.ft. labyrinth of audio
linked original rooms including main operations
room, Admirals office, Teleprinter station and
also a re-constructed Educational centre, with
Anderson shelter, and Bombed-out room.
1 Mar-31 Oct Mon-Thur & Sat 10.30-16.30
A£4.75 Concessions£3.45, Family Ticket £9.95.
Group rate (10+): £2.99

Colour section

DAYSOUTUK

Please see the relevant county section for further information on each of these attractions

The Forest Centre & Millennium Country Park
Station Road, Marston Moretaine, Bedford. MK43 0PR • 01234 767037 • www.marstonvale.org

The Forest Centre is a beautiful conservation centre set in the spectacular Millennium Country Park, just a few minutes drive from Milton Keynes & Bedford

The park & visitor centre are open all year round. Entry is free.

With easy free parking and trouble-free access for everyone,
The Forest Centre is a natural place for all your family to come and explore.

Lakeside Café & Bar · Gift Shop · Art Gallery
· Interactive Exhibition · Outdoor Children's Adventure Play Area
Sensory Wildlife Garden · Wetland Reserve & Trail
· 600 acres of Woodland · 8km surfaced footpaths & cycle paths
· 4km Horse trails · Cycle Hire Shop

ASCOT 👑
Back in the Saddle

Ascot Racecourse is synonymous with quality, style and excellence in providing both unparalleled racing and outstanding hospitality.

A day at Ascot Racecourse is not to be missed! Following a £200 million redevelopment programme, the racecourse has a modern, innovative stand within which they host the greatest racing events in the world.

Why not try Ascot for a great family day out? Children under the age of 16 can come racing for FREE, and on family days there is plenty of entertainment and fun activities for everyone.

For further information,
please call: 0870 727 1234
or visit our website: www.ascot.co.uk

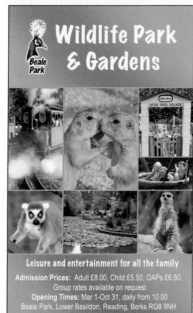

Wildlife Park & Gardens
Beale Park

Leisure and entertainment for all the family

Admission Prices: Adult £8.00, Child £5.50, OAPs £6.50,
Group rates available on request
Opening Times: Mar 1-Oct 31, daily from 10.00
Beale Park, Lower Basildon, Reading, Berks RG8 9NH

www.bealepark.co.uk

Please see the relevant county section for further information on each of these attractions

3

Please see the relevant county section for further information on each of these attractions

Vikings are invading LEGOLAND® Windsor!

There's a brand new land for 2007, and at its heart, the amazing new Vikings River Splash ride. Take a hilarious voyage through a Viking world built from thousands of LEGO bricks but try to avoid a soaking! All in all, LEGOLAND has over 50 rides, live shows and attractions set in 150 acres of parkland.

*Opens May 2007

Terms & Conditions:

Up to £25 off entry to LEGOLAND Windsor* - Excluding August

- This voucher entitles a maximum of five people to £5.00 off the full admission price per person at LEGOLAND Windsor.
- Entrance for children under three years of age is free.
- Voucher must be presented upon entrance into LEGOLAND Windsor and surrendered to the ticket booth operator. Discount vouchers cannot be used for pre-bookings. • Not to be used in conjunction with any other offer, reward/loyalty program, 2 Day Pass, Annual Pass, group booking, on-line tickets, rail inclusive offers or an exclusive event or concert. • Guests are advised that not all attractions and shows may be operational on the day of their visit. • Height, age and weight restrictions apply on some rides. Some rides will require guests who only just meet the minimum height requirements to be accompanied by a person aged 18 years or over. • Guests under the age of 14 must be accompanied by a person aged 18 or over. • This voucher is not for re-sale, is non-refundable and non-transferable.
- The park opens for the 2006 season on 17 March and closes on 3 November 2007. • This voucher is valid for admissions from 17 March to 3 November 2007, excluding the month of August and selected dates – please check www.LEGOLAND.co.uk in advance to confirm working dates. • This offer is limited to one per household. • This offer will apply irrespective of the entrance price at the time of use. • LEGOLAND Windsor will be closed on selected weekdays in March, April, May, September and October. • PLEASE visit www.LEGOLAND.co.uk in advance to confirm dates and prices.

For great hotel offers go to www.LEGOLANDhotels.co.uk

LEGO, the LEGO logo, the Brick and knob configurations, and LEGOLAND are trademarks of the LEGO Group. © 2007 The LEGO Group. SL2626

UP TO
£25 OFF

£5 per person
for up to 5 people

Cut out this coupon and take to LEGOLAND Windsor to receive up to £25 discount.

300709

Please see the relevant county section for further information on each of these attractions

7

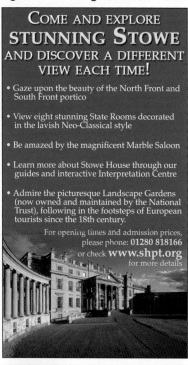

Please see the relevant county section for further information on each of these attractions

Please see the relevant county section for further information on each of these attractions

Please see the relevant county section for further information on each of these attractions

Please see the relevant county section for further information on each of these attractions

The Devil's Arse!

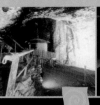

PEAK CAVERN

OPEN DAILY 10 am - 5 pm
Last Tour at 4pm (Times may vary)

NOV TO MARCH - weekdays 2 tours per day.
(Phone for timings) Open daily for school holidays.

Peak Cavern Ltd, Castleton
Tel: 01433 620285
Email: info@peakcavern.co.uk
www.devilsarse.com

Speedwell Cavern

SPEEDWELL CAVERN

OPEN DAILY
10 am - 3.30 pm low season
9.30 am - 5 pm high season

Speedwell Cavern Ltd, Winnats Pass, Castleton
Tel: 01433 620512
Email: info@speedwellcavern.co.uk
www.speedwellcavern.co.uk

PLEASE ASK ABOUT OUR JOINT TICKET

Home of Blue John Stone

Visit an underground wonderland of Stalactites, Stalagmites, Rocks, Minerals and Fossils

Home of the world famous
Blue John Stone

Special Events are held
throughout the year.

For further information contact:
T: 01433 620571
F: 01433 620519
E: treakcliff@bluejohnstone.com
www.bluejohnstone.com

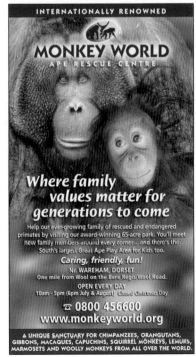

INTERNATIONALLY RENOWNED

MONKEY WORLD
APE RESCUE CENTRE

www.monkeyworld.org

Where family values matter for generations to come

Help our ever-growing family of rescued and endangered primates by visiting our award-winning 65-acre park. You'll meet new family members around every corner... and there's the South's largest Great Ape Play Area for Kids too.

Caring, friendly, fun!
Nr. WAREHAM, DORSET
One mile from Wool on the Bere Regis/Wool Road.
OPEN EVERY DAY
10am - 5pm (6pm July & August) Closed Christmas Day
☎ **0800 456600**
www.monkeyworld.org

A UNIQUE SANCTUARY FOR CHIMPANZEES, ORANGUTANS, GIBBONS, MACAQUES, CAPUCHINS, SQUIRREL MONKEYS, LEMURS, MARMOSETS AND WOOLLY MONKEYS FROM ALL OVER THE WORLD.

Please see the relevant county section for further information on each of these attractions

13

Please see the relevant county section for further information on each of these attractions

RHS GARDEN
Hyde Hall

A garden of inspirational beauty

Reg charity no.222879

Royal Horticultural Society

Shop • Plant Centre • Restaurant • Information Centre

Dry Garden • Australian Garden • Rose Garden • Ponds
Herbaceous Borders • Developing Woodland • & lots more!

Open daily from 10am (except Christmas Day)
Buckhatch Lane, Rettendon, Chelmsford, Essex CM3 8ET
Tel: 01245 400256 • Fax: 01245 402100

www.rhs.org.uk

BERKELEY CASTLE
BERKELEY, GLOUCESTERSHIRE

For group bookings, events,
and all openday information:
Tel: 01453 810332
www.berkeley-castle.com

Please see the relevant county section for further information on each of these attractions

15

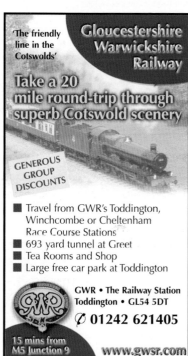

Please see the relevant county section for further information on each of these attractions

GALLERY OLDHAM
Greaves Street, Oldham, OL1 1AL

www.galleryoldham.org.uk

open monday~saturday 10am~5pm

admission free

for more information call
0161 911 4653

OLDHAM
Adult and Community Services

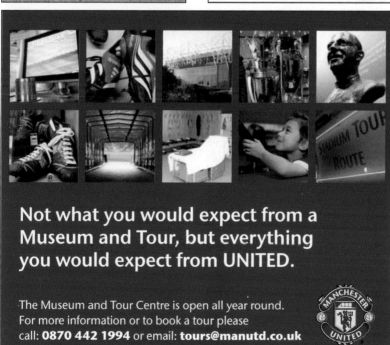

Not what you would expect from a Museum and Tour, but everything you would expect from UNITED.

The Museum and Tour Centre is open all year round. For more information or to book a tour please call: **0870 442 1994** or email: **tours@manutd.co.uk**

Please see the relevant county section for further information on each of these attractions

17

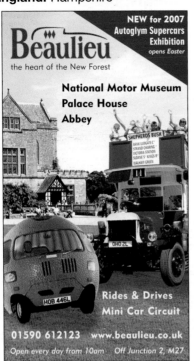
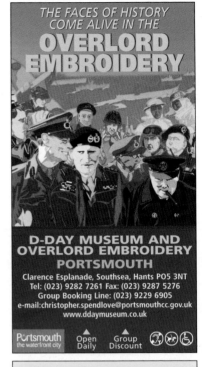
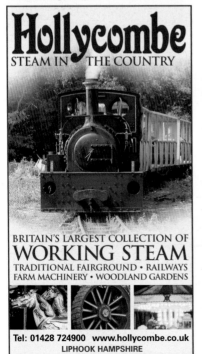

Please see the relevant county section for further information on each of these attractions

Please see the relevant county section for further information on each of these attractions

The Great Indoors...
...and Outdoors

Fairytale Georgian castle in magical surroundings, with Deer Park, Lake and Arboretum. Adventure Playground and Assault Course, Knight's Maze, Children's Fun Sheets, Tree Trail, Tearoom, Lakeside and Woodland Walks, Special Events.

For further details call
01531 633160 or visit
www.eastnorcastle.com

EASTNOR CASTLE

NEAR LEDBURY • HEREFORDSHIRE

THE NEEDLES PARK
Make a *point*
of visiting us.

You'll love our breathtaking Chairlift ride to the beach and back. Watch our craftsmen at work in our Glass Studio and Sweet Manufactory just some of the great attractions at The Needles Park.

THE Needles PARK
at ALUM BAY
ISLE OF WIGHT

Hotline **0870 458 0022**
www.theneedles.co.uk
The Needles Park, Alum Bay
Isle of Wight PO39 0JD

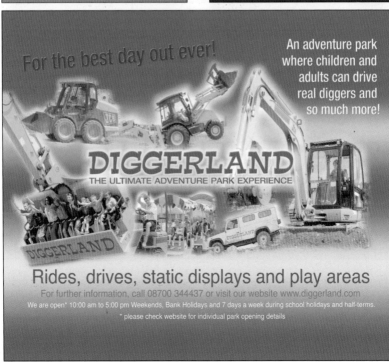

For the best day out ever!

An adventure park where children and adults can drive real diggers and so much more!

DIGGERLAND
THE ULTIMATE ADVENTURE PARK EXPERIENCE

Rides, drives, static displays and play areas

For further information, call 08700 344437 or visit our website www.diggerland.com

We are open* 10:00 am to 5:00 pm Weekends, Bank Holidays and 7 days a week during school holidays and half-terms.

* please check website for individual park opening details

Please see the relevant county section for further information on each of these attractions

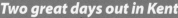

Please see the relevant county section for further information on each of these attractions

England: Kent - Lancashire

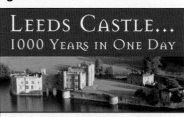

LEEDS CASTLE...
1000 YEARS IN ONE DAY

Leeds Castle is more than a journey through history. Whether you choose to tour the castle, picnic by the moat, enjoy the 500 acres of stunning parkland and gardens or lose yourself in the maze - make our castle your castle.

Events in 2007 include:

Spring Flower Festival	21-25 March
English Country Fair and Horse Show	28-29 April
Food and Drink Festival	12-13 May
Jousting Festival	1-3 June
1920s Weekend	8-9 September
Autumn Gold Flower Festival	3-7 October
Festive Fair	17-18 November

Visit www.leeds-castle.com for a full list of events, opening times and prices. Grounds open at 10am daily.

LEEDS & CASTLE
KENT, ENGLAND

www.leeds-castle.com

BLACKPOOL ZOO FUN

FABULOUS · UNDISCOVERED · NEAR YOU

Tel: 01253 830830
www.blackpoolzoo.org.uk

You will love a day out at
ILPH Penny Farm
a recovery & rehabilitation centre for rescued horses & ponies

FREE ENTRY

Guided tour of stables

Gift Shop

Coffee Shop & outside seating area

Come and meet our horses & ponies

Follow brown tourist signs on the A583, Preston New Road, Blackpool
Open all year Sat, Sun, Wed & Bank Hols
(except Christmas Day to New years Day)
11am - 4pm
Tel: 01253 766095
www.ilph.org/pennyfarm

ILPH
INTERNATIONAL LEAGUE FOR THE PROTECTION OF HORSES
Registered Charity No. 206658

AAAAAARRRRRGGGHH

HAVE A GREAT DAY
WWW.BLACKPOOLPLEASUREBEACH.COM
Days Out UK

Please see the relevant county section for further information on each of these attractions

Please see the relevant county section for further information on each of these attractions

a great family day out at butlins skegness!

Butlins
kids love it

One child for
£1
when accompanied by a full paying adult

For more information call Butlins on
☎ **01754 765567**
Quote: Days out UK

🖥 **www.butlins.com/dayvisitor**
Open daily 1 Apr - 4 Nov 2007 10am - 6pm

The Magical World of **FANTASY ISLAND**

The Magical World of Fantasy Island
Sea Lane, Ingoldmells, Skegness,
Lincolnshire PE25 1RH   01754 874668
www.fantasyisland.co.uk

Springfields Outlet Shopping & Festival Gardens

Springfields Outlet Shopping & Festival Gardens offers one of the best family days out in the country. Set in 38 acres of beautiful landscaped gardens, there are over 40 shopping outlets selling famous brands at up to 75% less than high street prices.

The beautiful Festival Gardens are designed and endorsed by famous horticulturalists such as Charlie Dimmock, Chris Beardshaw, Kim Wilde and Stephen Woodhams. There's free admission to the gardens, a massive Festival Garden Centre, cafés, restaurants and a family pub. Additional attractions include a children's Play Barn, an all-weather themed adventure golf course, and Fenscape – a free museum giving a modern interactive history of the Fens.

Charlie Dimmock   Chris Beardshaw   Stephen Woodhams   Kim Wilde

sowing the seeds for a great day out – tel 01775 760909

GARDEN CENTRE • 40 FAMOUS NAMED BRAND OUTLETS • FREE ENTRY • A16 SPALDING
OPENING TIMES: MON-FRI 10-6PM: LATE NIGHT THURS 10-8PM: SAT 9-6PM: SUN 11-5PM

Mexx   suitsyou   ex·Z   MARKS & SPENCER OUTLET   Clarks   festival   Reebok   Whittard   Springfields

Please see the relevant county section for further information on each of these attractions

Please see the relevant county section for further information on each of these attractions

CENTRAL HALL
Westminster

THE AFFORDABLE, VERSATILE, CENTRAL LONDON VENUE

• MEETING & CONFERENCES FROM 2 TO 2000

• EXHIBITIONS UP TO 1,400SQ METERS

• FILMING & PHOTO SHOOT LOCATIONS

• AUDIO VISUAL SERVICES

• CONCERTS & RECITALS

• SERVICED OFFICES

• BANQUETING

• ART GALLERY

• CAFÉ

Storey's Gate, Wesminster, London SW1H 9NH
T: 020 7222 8010
E: info@c-h-w.co.uk   W: www.c-h-w.com

River Red Rover

Unlimited river travel between: Westminster Waterloo, Tower Bridge and Greenwich for just £10.00

For details of our daily services aboard our quality riverliners:

☎ 02077 400 400
www.citycruises.com

CITY CRUISES
London's Premier Riverboat Operator

Explore Your World

HORNIMANMUSEUM

Set in 16 acres of beautiful Gardens, with stunning galleries and a new aquarium, the Horniman is full of discovery for adults and children alike.

Open daily 10.30am – 5.30pm Train Forest Hill (just 13 mins from London Bridge). Free car & coach parking nearby.

FREE admission
100 London Road • Forest Hill
London SE23
Tel 020 8699 1872 for further details

www.horniman.ac.uk

The
Houses of Parliament

Summer Opening 2007

Booking line opens January 2007
Please call 0870 906 3773 for further information
Groups call 020 7014 8444
Coaches call 020 7014 8440

Please see the relevant county section for further information on each of these attractions

Great.
Boys and
girls for lunch.
Hey, and a
grandma too

Come and watch us watching you at the London Aquarium

When it's time to dine I prefer a table next to the window. That way, I can enjoy a delicious meal and the humans on the other side can enjoy a hair-raising close-up.

Feeding time is just one of many reasons for coming to the London Aquarium. We're spread over 3 floors, we've got 14 fantastic zones and 350 different species. What's more we're just a short walk from Waterloo Mainline Station. So whatever you visit in London, remember, don't skip lunch.

LONDON AQUARIUM

**Tel: 020 7967 8000
londonaquarium.co.uk**

28

Please see the relevant county section for further information on each of these attractions

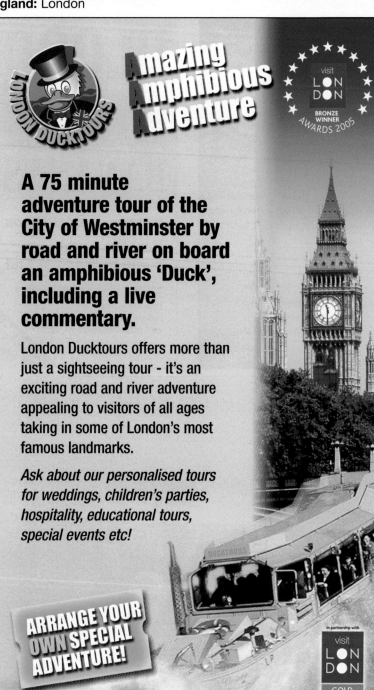

Amazing Amphibious Adventure

A 75 minute adventure tour of the City of Westminster by road and river on board an amphibious 'Duck', including a live commentary.

London Ducktours offers more than just a sightseeing tour - it's an exciting road and river adventure appealing to visitors of all ages taking in some of London's most famous landmarks.

Ask about our personalised tours for weddings, children's parties, hospitality, educational tours, special events etc!

ARRANGE YOUR OWN SPECIAL ADVENTURE!

In partnership with

visit **LONDON** GOLD

www.londonducktours.co.uk 020 7928 3132

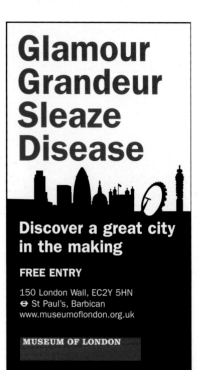

Please see the relevant county section for further information on each of these attractions

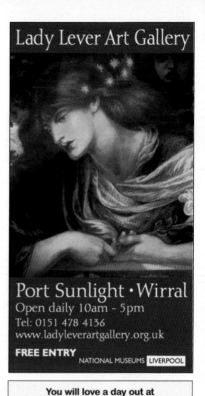

Please see the relevant county section for further information on each of these attractions

Oundle *International festival*

13 - 22 JULY 2007

Ten days of classical concerts, jazz, world music, children's events, film, open-air theatre, exhibitions, lunchtime recitals and more in this historic Nene Valley market town in Northamptonshire

Spectacular Fireworks Concert

Saturday 14 July 2007

featuring *Killer Queen* with Patrick Myers as Freddie Mercury

Please contact us for further information and a free brochure:

Tel: 01832 272026

email: information@oundlefestival.org.uk

www.oundlefestival.org.uk

Please see the relevant county section for further information on each of these attractions

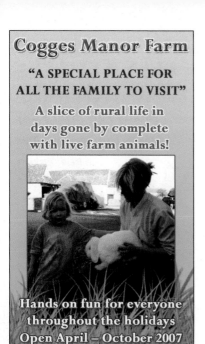

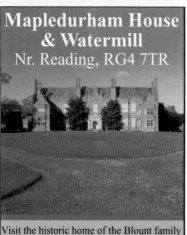

Please see the relevant county section for further information on each of these attractions

Barnsdale Gardens

Familiar to millions of BBC viewers as the home of Gardeners' World, Barnsdale consists of 37 individual gardens and features that all blend into an 8 acre garden, set in the heart of the beautiful Rutland countryside.

OPEN DAILY

9am-5pm:
March, April, May,
September and October

9am-7pm:
June, July and August

10am-4pm:
November to February

(Closed 24th & 25th December)

GENERAL ADMISSION

March to October:
Adults £6.00 • Concessions £5.00
• Children £2.00
• Family (2a + 3c) £15.00
November to February:
Reduced Admission

www.barnsdalegardens.co.uk

Tel: 01572 813200
Fax: 01572 813346
The Avenue, Exton,
Oakham, Rutland, LE15 8AH

discover with Tusker
the secrets of the hills

Family Fun - every day

○ Follow the Little Mammoth Trail

○ **NEW! Tusker's Ice Age Activities**

○ Geocaching trails-
Treasure hunting
with a GPS

○ Holiday
Activities
programme

Shropshire Hills Discovery Centre
Tel: 01588 676000
Just off the A49 at Craven Arms.
Open every day from 10am
www.shropshirehillsdiscoverycentre.co.uk

Shropshire
County Council

Shropshire Hills
Discovery Centre

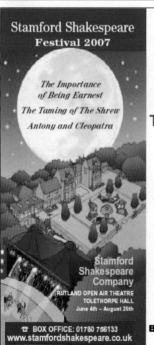

Stamford Shakespeare
Festival 2007

The Importance of Being Earnest

The Taming of The Shrew

Antony and Cleopatra

Stamford
Shakespeare
Company

RUTLAND OPEN AIR THEATRE
TOLETHORPE HALL
June 4th – August 25th

☎ BOX OFFICE: 01780 756133
www.stamfordshakespeare.co.uk

Rutland Open Air Theatre
Tolethorpe Hall

Just off the A1 near Stamford
(June 4th – August 25th 2007)

Presents

The Importance of Being Earnest
The Taming of The Shrew
Antony and Cleopatra

Come and enjoy a magical evening at one of Europe's finest Open Air Theatres.

On-site car park, picnic area, bar and restaurant in historic Tolethorpe Hall. 600 seat covered auditorium.

BOX OFFICE 01780 756133

Or book online at

www.stamfordshakespeare.co.uk

Brochure available from Libraries, TIC's or phone 01780 480216.

Please see the relevant county section for further information on each of these attractions

Please see the relevant county section for further information on each of these attractions

37

England: Somerset - Staffordshire

Dyrham Park, Nr Bath
- See the new landscaping and borders in the West Garden
- Fine 17th-century furnishings, paintings and Delftware reflecting the taste for Dutch fashions
- Tel: 01179 372501 Visit: www.nationaltrust.org.uk/dyrhampark

Prior Park Landscape Garden, Bath
- Walk over the famous Palladian Bridge
- Escape from the city and explore woodland paths
- Tel: 01225 833422 Visit: www.nationaltrust.org.uk/priorpark

www.nationaltrust.org.uk or call 0870 458 4000   THE NATIONAL TRUST

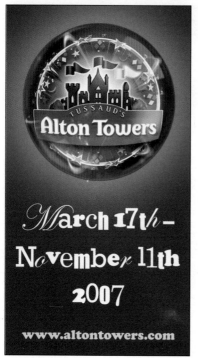

Caverswall Road | Blythe Bridge | Staffordshire
01782 396210 | enquiries@foxfieldrailway.co.uk
www.foxfieldrailway.co.uk

'Celebrating 40 years of steam'
Steaming through the decades!

A truly unique heritage steam railway winding you gently through beautiful Staffordshire country side.

A whole host of family and steam events held throughout the year from Postman Pat & Jess the Cat to Steam galas, Halloween & Santa Specials.

Open every Sunday, Bank holiday weekends & occasional Saturdays from 1st April - end of October.

Groups & coaches welcome, discounts available.

Facilities include: Tea Room • Station Bar Gift shop   Locomotive Display Area

Wheel Chair Access • Toilet Facilities
Induction Loop • Guide Dogs Welcome
Baby Changing • Free Car Park

Please phone or email for our 2007 leaflet!

Please see the relevant county section for further information on each of these attractions

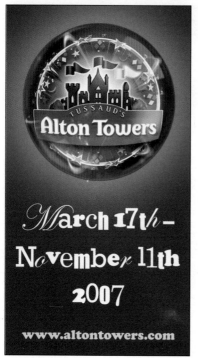

38

Enjoy a relaxing day in...

Stafford

Shop in the 'piazza-style' square adjacent to the Shire Hall Gallery and in the modern Guildhall Shopping Centre.

Wander away from the main street and discover picturesque streets and lanes... break for lunch at one of the many restaurants, bars, cafés or coffee shops.

TOURIST INFORMATION CENTRE
Market Street | Stafford | t. 01785 619 619
w. visitstafford.org | e. tic@staffordbc.gov.uk
OPEN Mon to Fri 9.30am - 5pm Sat 9am - 4pm

Stafford
BOROUGH COUNCIL

MOORCROFT
Factory Shop

With a vast selection of handmade Moorcroft giftware and table lamps. All pieces are sold at the factory shop are less than perfect.

With that comes the opportunity to make savings of up to 30% off the usual best quality retail price.

All stock is subject to availability.

Moorcroft Factory Shop
Nile Street, Burslem, Stoke-on-Trent, Staffordshire ST6 2BH
Telephone: 01782 820505 **Fax:** 01782 820501
Email: factoryshop@moorcroft.com **Web:** www.moorcroft.com

Open: Mon-Fri 10am-5pm, Sat 9.30am-4.30pm
Closed Sundays. Open for all Bank Holidays.

Made for over 100 years
MOORCROFT
Heritage Visitor Centre

There is something for everyone who comes to Moorcroft

Described as the world's leading art pottery made by the finest craftsmen offering a kaleidoscope of colour and quality

MOORCROFT

**Moorcroft Heritage Visitor Centre,
Shop, Museum and Bottle Oven**

Sandbach Road, Burslem, Stoke-on-Trent, Staffordshire ST6 2DQ
heritagevisitorcentre@moorcroft.com www.moorcroft.com
Telephone: 01782 207943
Open: Mon-Fri 10am-5pm Sat 9.30am-4.30pm
Closed Sundays. Open all Bank Holidays.
Guided Factory Tours: Booking in advance is advisable
Mon, Wed, Thurs (11am-2pm), Fridays (11am only)
Factory Tour Fee: Adults £4.50 Concessions £3.50

Please see the relevant county section for further information on each of these attractions

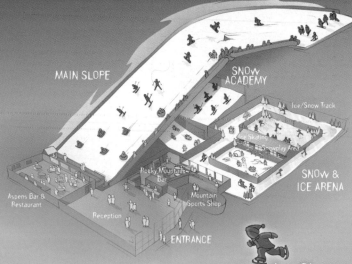

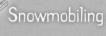

**The Ultimate Snow, Ice and Leisure Experience
Real Snow, Real Fun... For Everyone!**

**For more information, session times,
prices and bookings call 08705 000011**

info@snowdome.co.uk   www.snowdome.co.uk

Leisure Island, River Drive, Tamworth, Staffordshire B79 7ND

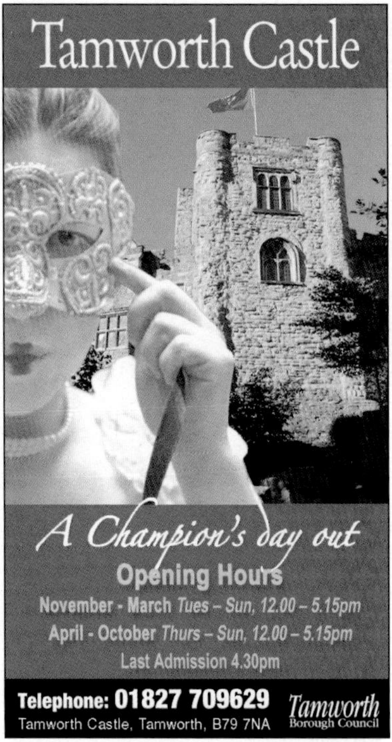
Tamworth Castle
A Champion's day out
Opening Hours
November - March Tues – Sun, 12.00 – 5.15pm
April - October Thurs – Sun, 12.00 – 5.15pm
Last Admission 4.30pm
Telephone: 01827 709629
Tamworth Castle, Tamworth, B79 7NA
Tamworth Borough Council

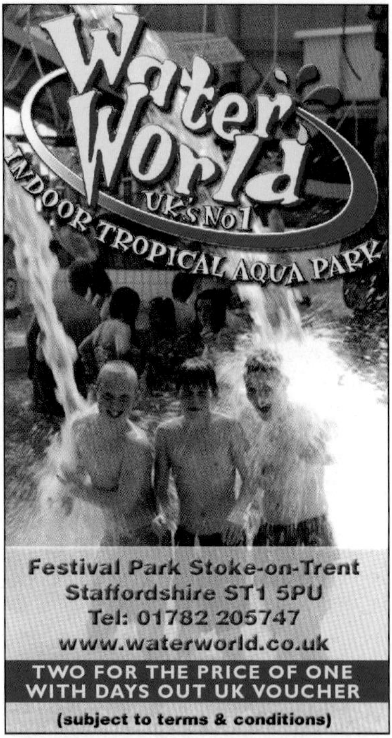
Water World
UK's No1
Indoor Tropical Aqua Park
Festival Park Stoke-on-Trent
Staffordshire ST1 5PU
Tel: 01782 205747
www.waterworld.co.uk
TWO FOR THE PRICE OF ONE
WITH DAYS OUT UK VOUCHER
(subject to terms & conditions)

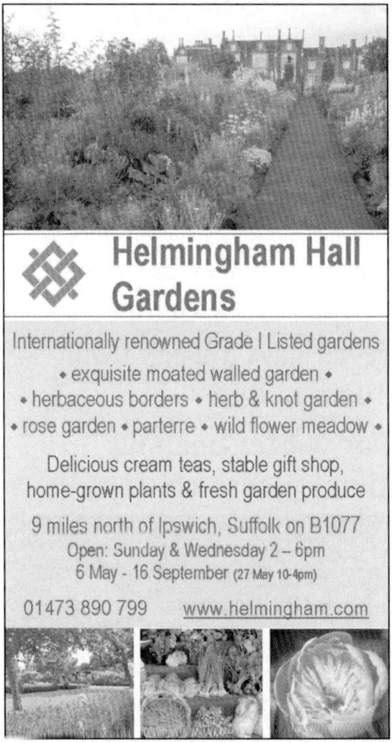
Helmingham Hall Gardens
Internationally renowned Grade I Listed gardens
• exquisite moated walled garden •
• herbaceous borders • herb & knot garden •
• rose garden • parterre • wild flower meadow •
Delicious cream teas, stable gift shop,
home-grown plants & fresh garden produce
9 miles north of Ipswich, Suffolk on B1077
Open: Sunday & Wednesday 2 – 6pm
6 May - 16 September (27 May 10-4pm)
01473 890 799
www.helmingham.com

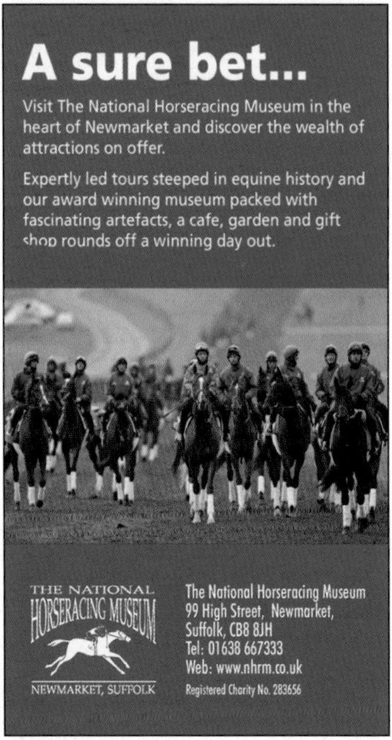
A sure bet...
Visit The National Horseracing Museum in the heart of Newmarket and discover the wealth of attractions on offer.
Expertly led tours steeped in equine history and our award winning museum packed with fascinating artefacts, a cafe, garden and gift shop rounds off a winning day out.
The National Horseracing Museum
Newmarket, Suffolk
The National Horseracing Museum
99 High Street, Newmarket,
Suffolk, CB8 8JH
Tel: 01638 667333
Web: www.nhrm.co.uk
Registered Charity No. 283656

Please see the relevant county section for further information on each of these attractions

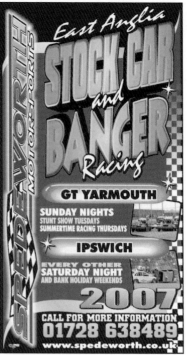

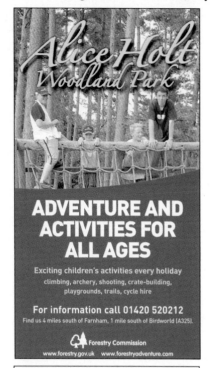

ADVENTURE AND ACTIVITIES FOR ALL AGES

Exciting children's activities every holiday
climbing, archery, shooting, crate-building,
playgrounds, trails, cycle hire

For information call 01420 520212

Find us 4 miles south of Farnham, 1 mile south of Birdworld (A325).

Forestry Commission
www.forestry.gov.uk   www.forestryadventure.com

Your great day out at
BIRDWORLD
The Bird Park and Gardens

- Parrots In Flight Aviary
- Children's Farm
- Penguin Island
- Gift Shops
- Play Areas
- Aquarium

www.birdworld.co.uk

Birdworld is on the A325, 3 miles south of Farnham
Holt Pound, Farnham, Surrey GU10 4LD Tel: 01420 22140

PAINSHILL PARK

Painshill Park is one of the most important 18th Century parks in Europe. It was created by the Hon. Charles Hamiton between 1738 and 1773 with its Ruined Abbey, working Vineyard, Gothic Temple, Crystal Grotto*, Hermitage, 18th Century plantings and much more.

American Roots (a major horticultural exhibition), recreates the 18th Century exchange of plants between Europe and America. The NCCPG has awarded Painshill Park full collection status for the John Bartram Heritage Plant Collection.

TEAROOM AND GIFT SHOP

OPEN ALL YEAR ROUND
(Closed Christmas Day & Boxing Day)

EXCITING RANGE OF EVENTS AT WEEKENDS AND DURING SCHOOL HOLIDAYS

*For Park and Grotto Opening Times and Admission Prices visit www.painshill.co.uk or telephone 01932 868113

PAINSHILL PARK, PORTSMOUTH ROAD, COBHAM, SURREY KT11 1JE

Please see the relevant county section for further information on each of these attractions

43

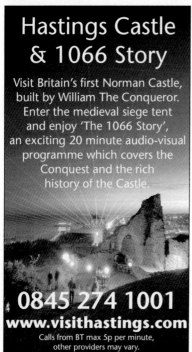
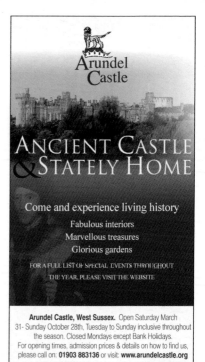

Please see the relevant county section for further information on each of these attractions

Looking for a great day out?

Knockhatch adventure Park

so much to see and do

- Giant Sky Leap
- Trampolines
- Birds of Prey
- Go-Karts
- Adventure Playground
- Bouncy Castle
- Boating Lake

and much much more!!

Don't forget to use your **One Child Free** discount voucher from the back of this guidebook!

A fun day out for all the family

www.knockhatch.com

Lancing College Chapel

Lancing, West Sussex
BN15 0RW

01273 465949

Magnificent Gothic chapel set in the South Downs

The chapel is open to visitors every day
Monday-Saturday 10.00-4.00
Sundays & Bank Holidays 12.00-4.00
Closed Christmas Day
Admission is free but donations are welcome

Arundel

WWT Wildfowl & Wetlands Centre

Pssst...!
Do you want to know a secret?

...WWT Arundel are running free water safaris everyday in 2007!

One of nine visitor centres run by the Wildfowl & Wetlands Trust

For more information:
T 01903 881530 www.wwt.org.uk
Registered charity no. 1030884

QUALITY ASSURED VISITOR ATTRACTION

The Heritage Motor Centre, New Look... New Experience...

Home to the world's largest collection of British cars. Come and visit the Centre in May 2007, with a striking new look, after its one million pound makeover. Discover the magical story of British cars with new and exciting exhibitions including 'Under the Skin' and 'The Making of British Cars'.

HERITAGE MOTOR CENTRE

MUSEUM I GUIDED TOURS I EVENTS
PICNIC & PLAY AREA I GROUP VISITS I CAFE
GIFT SHOP I OUTDOOR ACTIVITIES
TEL 01926 641188 www.heritage-motor-centre.co.uk

Please see the relevant county section for further information on each of these attractions

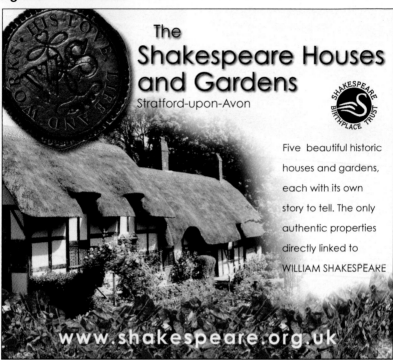

The Shakespeare Houses and Gardens
Stratford-upon-Avon

SHAKESPEARE BIRTHPLACE TRUST

Five beautiful historic houses and gardens, each with its own story to tell. The only authentic properties directly linked to WILLIAM SHAKESPEARE

www.shakespeare.org.uk

Don't worry, he's just a big pussycat.

Z Twycross Zoo
The World Primate Centre

Set in 50 acres of parkland, Twycross Zoo is alive with rare animals, exotic birds and strange reptiles. Pop in and meet them all in the flesh. For full prices and opening times call 01827 880250 or visit twycrosszoo.org

Atherstone, Warwickshire CV9 3PX

Please see the relevant county section for further information on each of these attractions

The Birmingham
Botanical Gardens
& Glasshouses

Open Daily (*except Christmas Day*)
9.00am (*10.00am Sundays*) - 7.00pm
(*or dusk if earlier*)

Adults: £6.50 **Concessions** £3.90

Westbourne Road, Edgebaston,
Birmingham B15 3TR
Tel: 0121 454 1860
www.birminghambotanicalgardens.org.uk
admin@birminghambotanicalgardens.org.uk

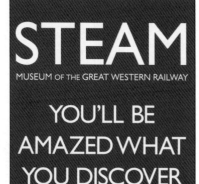

Please see the relevant county section for further information on each of these attractions

England: Worcestershire

THE NATIONAL TRUST

Do something unforgettable...

Come and visit **Coughton Court, Croome Park** and **Upton House & Gardens** for a great day out! Events and activities are held throughout the year and school holidays. Here is a taster of events for 2007.

For a full programme of events, visit www.nationaltrust.org.uk/thingstodo

Registered Charity No:205846

Coughton Court
Tel: 01789 400777
28 July
"Paint the Court" with Hans Holbein

Croome Park
Tel: 01905 371006
22 to 24 August
Kite Flying

Upton House and Gardens
Tel: 01295 670266
21 October
It's Civil War

Forge Mill Needle Museum

Discover the fascinating story of Victorian needlemaking in an old historic needle mill.

♦ *Temporary Textile Exhibitions.*
♦ *Enjoy expert guided tours for pre-booked groups.*
♦ *Gift shop specialising in unusual needles.*

Needle Mill Lane
Riverside, Redditch,
Worcs. B98 8HY
Located north of Redditch off A441, J2 M42

Tel: 01527 62509 REDDITCH BOROUGH COUNCIL

A Great Day Out

● Guided Tours ● World Famous Museum ● Paint a Plate Studio

● Factory Shopping

● Shopping Court ● Café

ROYAL WORCESTER

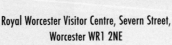

Royal Worcester Visitor Centre, Severn Street, Worcester WR1 2NE

Tel: 01905 746000. Email: siteshops@royal-worcester.co.uk www.royalworcester.co.uk

Open 7 days (Mon - Sat 9am - 530, Sun 11am - 5pm). 2 mins walk from cathedral/city centre. Easy access, 3 miles from junction 7 of M5

Open 7 days a week

Please see the relevant county section for further information on each of these attractions

Hartlebury
MUSEUM | CASTLE | EVENTS

There is something for everyone at Worcestershire's County Museum.

Visit historic Hartlebury, home to the Bishops of Worcester for over 1000 years.

Museum • Castle • Events • New Cafe & Shop • Nature Reserve

Open Tuesday-Friday 10am-5pm

Saturdays, Sundays & Bank Holidays 11am-5pm (closed Good Friday)
Hartlebury Castle is 4 miles south of Kidderminster and is signed from the A449.

For further details please call 01299 250416
or email museum@worcestershire.gov.uk

www.worcestershire.gov.uk/museums

worcestershire county council

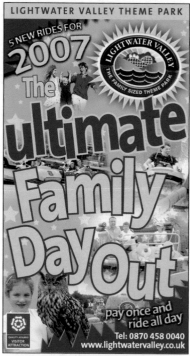

LIGHTWATER VALLEY THEME PARK

5 NEW RIDES FOR 2007

LIGHTWATER VALLEY
THE FAMILY SIZED THEME PARK

The **ultimate Family DayOut**

pay once and ride all day

Tel: 0870 458 0040
www.lightwatervalley.co.uk

QUALITY ASSURED VISITOR ATTRACTION

North Yorkshire Moors Railway — NYMR

Pickering – Levisham – Goathland – Grosmont

Running Daily:
11th - 25th February,
4th and 11th March
17th March to 3rd November
(plus some winter dates, please call for details)

Relive the Golden Age of Steam on one of Britain's most popular heritage railways.

Travel on the 18-mile line through the spectacular countryside of the North Yorkshire Moors National Park.

A GREAT FAMILY DAY OUT

Beautifully restored period stations, shops, refreshment rooms, locomotive viewing sheds, historical information, walks in the countryside - whatever you want from a day out you're sure to find it on the North Yorkshire Moors Railway.

Special Events & Dining Trains all year round:
Apr: *LNER Festival*, May: *Diesel Gala* and *Steam Gala*, Jun: *Moors 65*, Jul: *Vintage Vehicles*, Aug: *Music on the Moors*, Sep: *Day Out with Thomas*, Sep-Oct: *Autumn Steam Gala*, Oct: *Wartime Weekend* and *Wizard Weekend*

For Further Information Contact:
Customer Services: 01751 472508
Talking Timetable: 01751 473535
E: info@nymr.co.uk
www.nymr.co.uk

QUALITY ASSURED VISITOR ATTRACTION

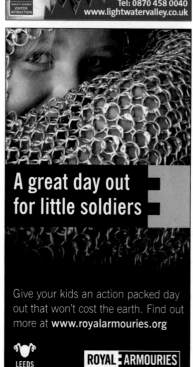

A great day out for little soldiers

Give your kids an action packed day out that won't cost the earth. Find out more at **www.royalarmouries.org**

LEEDS

ROYAL ARMOURIES

Please see the relevant county section for further information on each of these attractions

Visit...

The Saltburn Smugglers

HERITAGE CENTRE

STEP BACK INTO SALTBURN'S DARKEST PAST

Opening times

Easter–30th September, 10am – 6pm
(7 days a week)

October – Easter, groups and school
children by appointment only
Tel: 01642 496418

For further information please contact
The Saltburn Smugglers
Near the Ship Inn SALTBURN-BY-THE-SEA
TS12 1HF
Tel: 01287 625252 (24 hours)

SALTBURN

Come & explore

Skipton Castle

Guardian of the gateway to the
Yorkshire Dales for over 900 years.
This unique fortress is one of the
most complete and well-preserved
medieval castles in England.

Open every day from 10am(Sun 12noon)
Last admissions at 6pm (Oct–Feb 4pm)
Family tickets, Tearoom, Shop, Picnic Area
Free tour sheets in 9 languages.
High Street – large carpark nearby

Enquiries: 01756 792442

www.skiptoncastle.co.uk

*What
does your
brain
smell like?*

*Could a
donkey cure
whooping cough?*

**Experience history from horrendous
Victorian Slums to amazing surgery,
then travel through the human body
in Life Zone!**

THACKRAY
museum

TELLING THE STORY OF MEDICINE
*Near St James's Hospital, Beckett Street,
Leeds LS9 7LN   Tel: 0113 244 4343
www.thackraymuseum.org*

TROPICAL
BUTTERFLY
HOUSE

(Nr. Sheffield)
01909 569416

Handle creepy
crawlies, reptiles
and birds. Watch the
parrots performing their
tricks, the birds of prey flying display,
ferret racing and roulette. Feed the
friendly farm animals, then have
a tractor and trailer ride. Let off
steam in the activity and play centre.

Gift Shop
&
Café

www.butterflyhouse.co.uk

Please see the relevant county section for further information on each of these attractions

Hull Museums

Hull's key attraction in 2007 is Wilberforce House Museum, the world-famous birthplace of William Wilberforce (the famous slavery abolitionist). This 17th Century building was re-opened in March following an extensive redevelopment project. The museum explores the issue of slavery, abolition and human rights today, aiming to make slavery relevant to everyone in 2007. There are fascinating displays showcasing objects from West Africa, life on the plantation and the personal stories of enslaved African people.

Continue your discovery of historic Kingston upon Hull with a tour around its other free museums. Your journey begins with three more museums in the Museums Quarter (situated in the heart of the Old Town on the banks of the River Hull). Nearby warehouses, merchant dwellings, twisting lanes and old-world, offbeat pubs all lend their unique flavour to this historic district. Hull's four remaining free museums are just a short walk away.

- Ferens Art Gallery
- Hands-On History
- Hull and East Riding Museum
- Maritime Museum
- Spurn Lightship
- Streetlife Museum
- Wilberforce House Museum

Hull
Museums Tel: 01482 300300 Web: www.hullcc.gov.uk

Please see the relevant county section for further information on each of these attractions

Ireland

MEDIEVAL CASTLE BANQUET
OR
TRADITIONAL IRISH NIGHT

Bunratty Castle & Folk Park,
Bunratty, Co. Clare, Ireland
Tel: +353 61 360788
Email: reservations@shannondev.ie
www.shannonheritage.com

Mizen Head Signal Station
IRELAND'S MOST SOUTHWESTERLY POINT!

In any weather the Mizen is spellbinding.
Keeper's Quarters, The 99 Steps, The famous
Arched Bridge, Navigational Aids Simulator,
Mizen Cafe, Shop@TheMizen.

OPEN DAILY: Mid-march, April, May & Oct Daily 10.30-17.00
June to September Daily 10.00-18.00
OPEN WEEKENDS: November-Mid-March 11.00-16.00

PRICES

Adult	6.00 Euro
OAP/Student	4.50 Euro
Children Under12	3.50 Euro
Children Under 5	Free
Family Ticket: 2 Adults/3 Children	18.00 Euro
Groups 10+	Less 10%

IF YOU MISS THE MIZEN YOU HAVEN'T DONE IRELAND

Mizen Tourism Co-operative Society Ltd 028-35115 Goleen, West Cork, Ireland
www.mizenhead.net www.mizenhead.ie info@mizenhead.ie

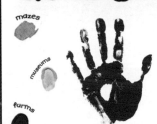

Please see the relevant section for further information on each of these attractions

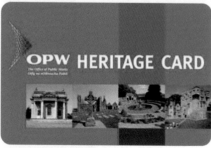

Northern Ireland

Please see the relevant section for further information on each of these attractions

It's a jungle in here!

TOTALLY UNIQUE IN SCOTLAND!

DISCOVER
AMAZONIA

Scotland's only
Indoor Tropical Rainforest,
packed full of exotic animals.

Strathclyde Park, Motherwell
0870 112 3777

www.discoveramazonia.co.uk

BO'NESS & KINNEIL RAILWAY

Enjoy a steam train journey along the banks of the Forth and visit the biggest Railway Exhibition in Scotland!

Open weekends: 31 Mar - 28 Oct and every day: 30 Jun - 26 Aug

For details of our special events, timetables and ticket prices visit our website www.srps.org.uk or call 01506 822298

You will love an afternoon out at
ILPH Belwade Farm
a recovery & rehabilitation centre
for rescued horses & ponies

FREE ENTRY

Guided tour of stables & paddocks

Gift Shop & Information Area

Outside Seating Areas

Country walks

Off the A93 between Kincardine O'Neil & Aboyne

Open all year Sat, Sun, Wed & Bank Hols
(except Christmas Day to New years Day)
2pm - 4pm
Tel: 01339 887186

ILPH www.ilph.org/belwadefarm

INTERNATIONAL LEAGUE FOR THE PROTECTION OF HORSES
Registered Charity No. 206658

THE **BIGGEST** FAMILY DAY OUT IN SCOTLAND

OVER 30
major rides and attractions! PLUS
MASSIVE indoor family entertainment complex!

M&D's
Scotland's Theme Park

Strathclyde Park, Motherwell
0870 112 3777
www.scotlandsthemepark.com

Please see the relevant section for further information on each of these attractions

57

Please see the relevant section for further information on each of these attractions

What treasures do we hold?

National Museum of Scotland
National Museum of Flight
National Museum of Costume
National Museum of Rural Life
National War Museum

find out more at
0131 225 7534
info@nms.ac.uk
www.nms.ac.uk

Please see the relevant section for further information on each of these attractions

Please see the relevant section for further information on each of these attractions

ORIEL YNYS MÔN

ANGLESEY HISTORY AND ART GALLERY

As a purpose built museum, arts and events gallery, Oriel Ynys Môn has so much to offer.

Visitors who wish to learn about the cultural history of Anglesey can enjoy the centre's atmospheric History Gallery which presents a vivid account of the island's past through sound, imagery, reconstructions and real artefacts.

In our Art Gallery, we hold up to eight exhibitions annually. The art gallery serves to allow artists, sculptors, craftworkers and performers to present their work on a local, regional and national level.

During the course of the year, the Oriel organises a variety of events – concerts, workshops for children and families as well as the odd specialised talk. School groups are welcome and often take advantage of the themes of the History Gallery and are given a talk. In the same way, societies or groups can enjoy a guided tour of the Oriel at any time.

WHATEVER THE PURPOSE OF YOUR VISIT, WE EXTEND A VERY WARM WELCOME TO YOU

Anglesey Heritage Gallery, Llangefni, Anglesey 01248 724444
www.angleseyheritage.co.uk

Mind your head!

ADMISSION:
Adult £1
Child (5yrs+) 50p

OPENING TIMES:
Apr-Early July
10.00-18.00
Late July-Aug
10.00-19.00
Sept-Oct
10.00-17.00

The Smallest House

Quay, Conwy, North Wales LL32 8DE

01492 593484

Situated on the Quayside at Conwy and measuring just 6ft wide, 8ft deep and 10ft high, the smallest house in the UK deserves its place in the *Guinness Book of Records*.

you'll be seeing SPOTS if you join our club!

Join the club and receive over

£2000

worth of discount vouchers for your favourite days out!
www.daysoutuk.com

Please see the relevant section for further information on each of these attractions

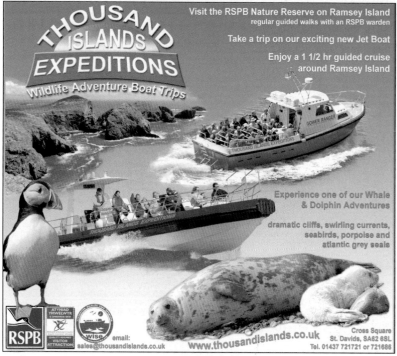

Multicultural Museums

World Museum Liverpool
William Brown St Liverpool Merseyside L3 8EN
Tel: 0151 478 4393
Extensive collections from the Amazonian Rain
Forest to the mysteries of outer space.

Music & Theatre Museums

Beatles Story
Britannia Vaults Albert Dock Liverpool
Merseyside L3 4AD
Tel: 0151 709 1963 Fax: 0151 708 0039
www.beatlesstory.com
*[Road: follow M62 into Liverpool, then follow
signs for Albert Dock. Large car park adjacent to
Dock. Rail: James Street Station, follow tourist
signs to Albert Dock, approx 10min walk. By foot:
10min walk from city centre, follow tourist signs.
The Beatles Story can be found between the
Holiday Inn Express & Premier Travel Inn]*
Located within Liverpool's historic Albert Dock,
the Beatles Story is a unique visitor attraction
that will transport you on an enlightening and
atmospheric journey into the life, times, culture
and music of the Beatles. See how four young
lads from Liverpool were propelled into the dizzy
heights of worldwide fame and fortune to
become the greatest band of all time, Hear the
story unfold through the "Living History" audio
guide narrated by John Lennon's sister, Julia.
Key highlights include: John Lennon's iconic
round spectacles; Brian Epstein describing his
first impressions of the Beatles; George
Harrison's first ever guitar; the world's only
'blue' white album, never heard before interview
with Paul McCartney and the emotional and
evocative white room.
All year daily 10.00-18.00. Closed 25-26 Dec

A£9.99 C£4.99 Concessions£6.99. Group rates
(for 10+) available on request

Discount Offer: One Child Free

Mendips and 20 Forthlin Road
Liverpool Merseyside
Tel: 0151 427 7231 / 0870 9000256
Fax: 0151 427 9860
www.nationaltrust.org.uk/beatles
*[Scheduled mini-bus tours from Liverpool city
centre in morning OR Speke Hall in afternoon.
Advance booking recommended. Tickets avail-
able on day subject to availability. Book tickets
on-line]*
Mendips was the childhood home of John
Lennon, he lived there with his Aunt Mimi and
Uncle George and composed early songs in the
front porch and in his bedroom. 20 Forthlin
Road is a 1950s terraced house and the former
home of the McCartney family, where the
Beatles met, rehearsed and wrote many of their
earliest songs. Displays include contemporary
photographs by Michael McCartney and early
Beatles memorabilia. The audio tour features
contributions from both Michael and Sir Paul
McCartney. We offer visitors a combined trip to
both 20 Forthlin Road and Mendips. There is
partial disabled access to Ground Floors only.
21 Mar-28 Oct Wed-Sun & Bank Hols
A£13.00 C£2.00 NT Members£7.00, Price
includes admission to garden & grounds of
Speke Hall, only applies to afternoon tours
departing from Speke Hall. Call for details of
combined ticket for Forthlin Road & Mendips

Nature & Conservation Parks

Eastham Country Park

Ferry Road Eastham Wirral Merseyside
CH62 0BH
Tel: 0151 327 1007
Once a Victorian pleasure garden, now a local
beauty spot. Superb views across the estuary
with its abundant birdlife and busy shipping
lanes. A network of surfaced paths provide
access throughout the woodland.

Formby Point

National Trust Victoria Road Freshfield, Formby
Liverpool L37 1LJ
Tel: 01704 878591 Fax: 01704 835378
www.nationaltrust.org.uk
*[15mi N of Liverpool, 2mi W of Formby, 2mi off
A565. Rail: Freshfield]*

202ha of dunes, sandy beaches and pinewoods
between the sea and the town of Formby. Red
squirrels can frequently be seen along the
woodland walks, and the site is a good starting
point for walks on the Sefton Coastal Path. The
shoreline attracts wading birds such as oyster-
catchers and sanderlings in the winter. Dogs
must be kept on a lead near wildlife, and under
control at all times. Learning Office fax/tel:
01704 874949.
Apr-Oct 09.00-18.00, Nov-Mar 09.00-16.30
£3.50 per car. Minibuses £10.00 & Coaches
£20.00 all year (must be pre-booked). School
groups must book in advance

National Wildflower Centre

Court Hey Park Roby Road Liverpool
Merseyside L16 3NA
Tel: 0151 738 1913 Fax: 0151 737 1820
www.nwc.org.uk

*[0.5mi from J5 M62. Rail: Broadgreen Station,
approx 10min walk. Take Bowring Park Rd exit,
follow rd under bridge & straight across traffic
lights. Continue down rd (keeping M62 on L) for
approx 0.5mi. Bus: Nos. 6 & 61 from Queens
Square, Liverpool city centre or Broadgreen
Station. Plenty of on-site parking available]*

The centre provides a national focus for promot-
ing new wildflower landscapes and the creation
of new wildlife habitats. Located in a 35 acre
park, once the home of the Gladstone family, a
former walled garden now produces the wildflower seeds and plants that help fund the charity. Nearby is a stunning and innovative 150
metre long visitor building, it features a café and
shop, outdoor exhibitions, the wildflower garden
centre and a children's area, whilst a roof top
walkway looks out across the complex. There
are seasonal wildflower demonstration areas.

1 Mar-1 Sept daily 10.00-17.00

A£3.00 C&Concessions£1.50, Family Ticket
(A2+C2) £7.50. Season Ticket available

**Discount Offer: Two for the Price of
One**

On the Water

Mersey Ferries Ltd

Victoria Place Wallasey Merseyside CH44 6QY
Tel: 0151 330 1444 Fax: 0151 639 0578
www.merseyferries.co.uk

*[Pier Head via M62 & Liverpool city centre, Wirral
via M56 / M53 or A41. Parking on site available
at Woodside & Seacombe. Park at Albert Dock
for Pier Head]*

A River Explorer Cruise on the famous Mersey
Ferries is an unforgettable day out for all the
family. There's no better way to learn the area's
fascinating history, see its spectacular sights
and discover its unique character. There's a full
commentary, the chance to stop at Seacombe
and visit Spaceport the space themed visitor
attraction, the Aquarium and 'Play Planet' children's play area. At Spaceport you can experience a fun and informative virtual journey
through space. You can become a virtual astronaut in the 180 degree Space Dome Cinema, fly
through space in a Space Explorer Craft, get
hands on with many interactive exhibits and see
real rockets that have recently flown. River
Explorer Cruises leave every day from Pier
Head, Liverpool and Seacombe or Woodside,
Wirral.
*All year daily Mon-Fri 07.30-19.30, Sat & Sun
09.00-19.20. Cruise Timetable: See special
events guide or call venue. Spaceport open Tue-
Sun 10.30-17.30 (open most Bank Hols & Mons
during school hols)*
Cruise A£5.10 C£2.85, Family Ticket £13.60.
Joint Ferry/Spaceport tickets are available (see
website)

Discount Offer: Save up to £1.00!

Yellow Duckmarine

Unit 32 Anchor Courtyard Atlantic Pavilion
Albert Dock Liverpool Merseyside L3 4AS
Tel: 0151 708 7799
www.theyellowduckmarine.co.uk

*[Albert Dock is easily accessible from rd, rail, & on
foot. Road: follow M62 into Liverpool, then follow
rd signs for Albert Dock. There is a car park adjacent to dock. Rail: James St, follow tourist signs
to Albert Dock (approx. 10min walk). By foot:
10min walk from city centre (follow tourist signs).
Ticket office is at Atlantic Pavilion, off Gower St]*
All aboard for this one-hour amphibious sightseeing tour of Liverpool's historic waterfront,
City and dockland areas. Travel in comfort on
one of our converted WWII DUKW vehicles,
which depart daily from the Albert Dock. From
the Albert Dock, the 'Duck's' first port of call is
to the magnificent Port of Liverpool building, the
Cunard building and the renowned Royal Liver
building, before heading up into the City Centre
where you will pass the Town Hall, Matthew
Street and St George's Hall. The tour then
heads north to both the impressive Metropolitan
and Anglican cathedrals, the Philharmonic Hall,
LIPA and China Town. The third section of the
tour takes in Liverpool's dockland waterways
with an exciting 'splashdown' into Salthouse
Dock, which will be loved by kids of all ages!
The Duck then visits Wapping Basin and Dock,
Queens and Coburg Dock before concluding
the tour in the world-famous Albert Dock. Live
commentary and fun throughout. Wa-ter way to
see Liverpool!
*All year daily from 10.00 (pre-booking advised).
Closed 24, 25 & 26 Dec. Please call for info*
Peak: A£11.95 C£9.95 Concessions£10.95,
Family Ticket (A2+C2) £34.00, extra C£7.00. Off
Peak: A£9.95 C£(?-15)£7.95 Concessions£8.95,
Family Ticket (A2+C2) £29.00, extra C£5.00.
Group rate (10+): 10% off, (advance booked)

**Discount Offer: Two for the Price of
One**

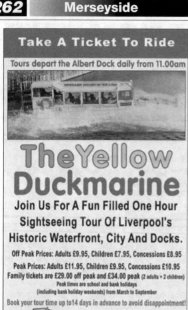
Performing Arts

Mathew Street

Mathew Street Liverpool Merseyside L2 6RE
*[Head for Albert Dock & follow signs for Paradise
St Car Park. Exit by foot from the rear, turn R into
North John St & Mathew St is on the R]*
Home to the Cavern Club (still a thriving music
venue), the Cavern Club's Wall of Fame, the
Mathew Street Gallery, the Liverpool Wall of
Fame, and a John Lennon statue.

Places of Worship

Birkenhead Priory and St Mary's Tower

Priory Street Birkenhead Merseyside CH41 5JH
Tel: 0151 666 1249
An interpretive centre traces the history and
development of the site.

Liverpool Cathedral

St James Mount Liverpool Merseyside L1 7AZ
Tel: 0151 709 6271 Fax: 0151 702 7292
www.liverpoolcathedral.org.uk

[Rail: Lime St. Plenty of on-site parking]

The largest cathedral in Britain and one of the
great buildings of the twentieth century. See
panoramic views from the famous vestey tower
and new for 2007 'The Great Space' film and
audio tour for children and adults with computer
interactive stations and a 'music experience' on
the high Nave Bridge. Check website for opening times and admission.

*All year daily. New mezzanine café bar & refecto-
ry, shop & visitor attractions open daily. Check
website for opening times*

Metropolitan Cathedral of Christ the King

Cathedral House Mount Pleasant Liverpool
Merseyside L3 5TQ
Tel: 0151 709 9222
Liverpool's dramatic, modern, circular, Roman
Catholic cathedral with its glorious multi-
coloured windows and modern works of art.

Spectator Sports

Aintree Racecourse

Ormskirk Road Liverpool Merseyside L9 5AS
Tel: 0151 523 2600
Aintree hosts five quality race meetings per year.

Sport and Recreation

Europa Pools
136 Conway Street Birkenhead Merseyside
CH41 6RN
Tel: 0151 647 4182
Offers an indoor tropical paradise where all the
family can relax and enjoy soaring temperatures
all year round.

Sporting History Museums

Everton Football Club Stadium Tour
Goodison Park Liverpool Merseyside
Tel: 0151 330 2305 (Bookings)
Your chance to see what goes on behind the
scenes at Goodison Park. Tours do not operate
on a matchday or on the afternoon before a first
team home fixture.

Liverpool Football Club Museum and Tour Centre

Anfield Road Liverpool Merseyside L4 0TH
Tel: 0151 260 6677 (Bookings)
Fax: 0151 264 0149
www.liverpoolfc.tv/club/tour.htm
*[From all major routes into Liverpool. Ground is
3mi from city centre, 4mi from M62 & 7mi from
end of M57 & M58. Well signposted from city
centre. Weekday - park in Main Stand or
Centenary Stand car parks, (except on mid-week
match-days). Rail: Lime St Railway Station 2mi
from Anfield. Match days: use Merseyrail network
to link with Soccerbus service from Sandhills*

*Station. Taxis available from Lime St. Bus: 26 / 27
from Paradise St. bus station or 17B, 17C, 17D,
or 217 from Queen Square bus station directly to
ground. 68 & 168 operate between Bootle &
Aigburth, 14 & 19 stop a short walk away. By Air:
Liverpool Airport approx 10mi from Ground. The
Soccerbus Service: Leave The Car At Home On
Match Day! A direct bus link from anywhere on
Merseyrail Network via Sandhills Station to Anfield.
Plenty of on-site parking available]*

Liverpool Football Club Museum & Stadium Tour
Liverpool's newest Five Star Attraction;
England's most successful football club has a
record 18 league Championships, 13 League
and F A Cups, plus 3 UEFA and European
Super Cups apiece. But it's the Five European
Trophies that place the club in an exclusive
group of just three, who have won the most
prestigious prize of all, five times or more.
Following "The Greatest football game ever" on
the 25th May 2005, Liverpool FC Museum has
added to it's collection the beautiful Champions
League trophy. Surrounded by the sights and
sounds of that night in Istanbul with many witty
banners created by fans, the Trophy has
brought in unprecedented numbers of adoring
fans. The stadium tour takes you behind the
scenes at Anfield, visiting the dressing rooms,
down the tunnel to the sound of the crowd,
touch the famous "This Is Anfield' sign and sit in
the team dug-out.
*All year daily 10.00-17.00. Match Days: 10.00-1
hr before kick-off. No stadium tours on Match
days*
Museum Centre: A£5.00 C&OAPs£3.00, Family
Ticket £13.00. Museum & Tours: A10.00
C&OAPs£6.00, Family Ticket £25.00. Group
rates available on request

Discount Offer: One Child Free

Wildlife & Safari Parks

Knowsley Safari Park
Prescot Merseyside L34 4AN
Tel: 0151 430 9009
A five-mile drive through the reserves enables
visitors to see lions, tigers, elephants, rhinos,
baboons, and many other animals.

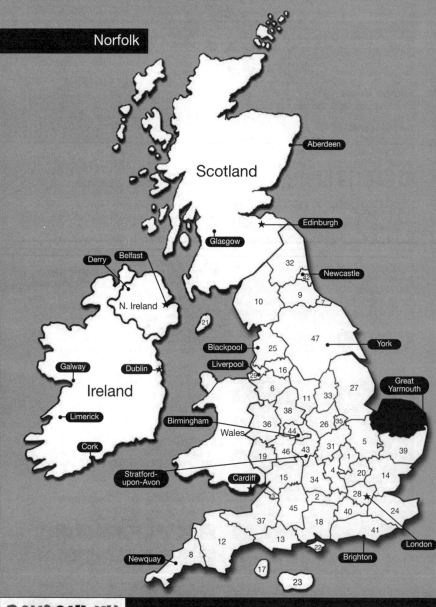

Norfolk

Aberdeen

Scotland

Edinburgh
Glasgow

Derry | Belfast
N. Ireland

Galway | Dublin
Ireland
Limerick
Cork

Newcastle

32
42
9
10
7

21

Blackpool
Liverpool

York

25
16
29
6 11 33
38
36 44
19 46 43
15 34
45
37 13
12
8
17 23

47

5 39
26 35
31 1 20 14
4 28
40 24
2 41
18 22

Great
Yarmouth

London

Brighton

Birmingham
Wales
Cardiff
Stratford-
upon-Avon
Newquay

DAYS OUT UK

The place to look for places to go

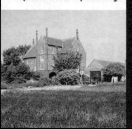

Key:

1 Bedfordshire
2 Berkshire
3 Bristol
4 Buckinghamshire
5 Cambridgeshire
6 Cheshire
7 Cleveland
8 Cornwall
9 County Durham
10 Cumbria
11 Derbyshire
12 Devon
13 Dorset
14 Essex
15 Gloucestershire

16 Greater Manchester
17 Guernsey
18 Hampshire
19 Herefordshire
20 Hertfordshire
21 Isle Of Man
22 Isle Of Wight
23 Jersey
24 Kent
25 Lancashire
26 Leicestershire
27 Lincolnshire
28 London
29 Merseyside
30 Norfolk
31 Northamptonshire
32 Northumberland

33 Nottinghamshire
34 Oxfordshire
35 Rutland
36 Shropshire
37 Somerset
38 Staffordshire
39 Suffolk
40 Surrey
41 Sussex
42 Tyne & Wear
43 Warwickshire
44 West Midlands
45 Wiltshire
46 Worcestershire
47 Yorkshire

Animal Attractions

Animal Ark

Fakenham Road Gt Witchingham Norfolk
NR9 5QS
Tel: 01603 872274
Adventure play and tiny tots adventure play.
Lots of green space to run off that excess energy. Feed the farm animals and cuddle the pets.

Redwings Caldecott Visitor Centre

Caldecott Hall Beccles Road Fritton Great
Yarmouth Norfolk NR31 9EY
Tel: 0870 040 0033 Fax: 0870 458 1942
www.redwings.org.uk

[1mi NE of Fritton village on A143. Plenty of on-site parking available]

Established in 1984, Redwings is now the largest horse charity in the UK, working to provide and promote the welfare, care and protection of horses, ponies, donkeys and mules. Redwings' Norfolk visitor centre has more than 70 acres of paddock and there is plenty for the whole family to enjoy. Residents include beautiful pony Darcey, Muffin the mule, cheeky donkey Denise and stunning Shire Victor. Visitors can meet the horses and ponies, watch equine care demonstrations, take a guided tour, shop in the gift shop or enjoy a light meal in the Nosebag café. There is even the chance to adopt one of the centre's special equines.
1 Apr-28 Oct daily 10.00-17.00
Admission Free

Discount Offer: Free Poster.

ILPH Hall Farm

Ada Cole Avenue Snetterton Norfolk NR16 2LP
Tel: 0870 870 1927/366 6911
Fax: 0870 904 1927
www.ilph.org/hallfarm

[0.5mi from A11 between Attleborough & Thetford. Approx 30min from Norwich & Newmarket. Plenty of on-site parking available]

Set in 250 acres of beautiful countryside, you can take one of the marked walkways around the paddocks (dogs on leads welcome) where you will meet some of the 150 or more rescued horses and ponies. We offer guided tours of Hall Farm and our visitor centre has information on the work we do in the UK and overseas. We also have equine related events on most weekends. You can spend time in our coffee shop, which provides a good range of hot and cold snacks and drinks.
All year Weds, Weekends & Bank Hols 11.00-16.00. Closed 25 Dec-1 Jan
Admission Free

Snettisham Park

Snettisham King's Lynn Norfolk PE31 7NQ
Tel: 01485 542425
Safari tours, visitor centre, crafts centre, art gallery, tearoom and souvenir shop. Indoor and outdoor activities include farm animals and pets.

Royal Norfolk Show and Showground

Dereham Road New Costessey NR5 0TT
Tel: 01603 748931 Fax: 01603 748729
www.norfolkshowground.com
[Off A47 southern bypass. Plenty of on-site parking available]

We are looking forward to yet another bumper Royal Norfolk Show for 2007. Major entertainment is planned for the Grand Ring and will be suitable for all age groups. Come along to the showground and enjoy two packed days of entertainment. The showground also hosts many other events throughout the year.
27-28 June 2007, 08.00
Tickets discounted if purchased in advance. A£15.00 C£5.00 OAP£13.00 Disabled£14.00 Carer£6.00, Family Ticket (A2+C3) £38.00. Group rate (20+): 20% discount

Gardens & Horticulture

Fairhaven Woodland and Water Garden

School Road South Walsham NR13 6DZ
Tel: 01603 270449 Fax: 01603 270449
www.fairhavengarden.co.uk

[9mi E of Norwich at South Walsham signposted on A47 at J with B1140. Plenty of on-site parking available]

This delightful woodland and water garden is a garden for all seasons. Only farmyard manure and the garden's leaf mulch is used to fertilise the soil and the fauna and flora are a testimony to an organic approach. Over three miles of wonderful woodland walks - all easy - with superb views across Fairhaven's private Broad. There are many ancient oaks and beech trees including the 950 year-old King Oak. Boat trips on our private Broad, Apr to end of Oct (additional charge) and a children's trail. Dogs on leads allowed. Programme of events throughout the year.
All year daily (except Christmas Day) 10.00-17.00 (10.00-16.00 winter months). Extended opening hours in May, June, July, & Aug. (Wed &Thu 10.00-21.00)
A£4.75 C(under5)£Free C(5+)£2.25 Concessions£4.25 Dog£0.25. Memberships: Single £17.50 Family £40.00 Dog£2.50

Discount Offer: Two for the Price of One

Mannington Gardens and Countryside

Mannington Hall Norwich Norfolk NR11 7BB
Tel: 01263 584175 Fax: 01263 761214
www.manningtongardens.co.uk
[2mi N of Saxthorpe nr B1149, 18mi NW of Norwich, 9mi from coast. On-site parking]
This moated manor house was built in 1460. Gardens to view and lovely countryside. Extensive country walks, Wildflower Meadow, Arboretum, Heritage Rose Gardens, shrubs, trees, scented and sensory gardens and events.
May-Sept Sun 12.00-17.00, June-Aug Wed-Fri 11.00-17.00
A£4.00 Concessions£3.00

Discount Offer: Two for the Price of One

Norfolk Lavender

Caley Mill Heacham King's Lynn PE31 7JE

Tel: 01485 570384 Fax: 01485 571176
www.norfolk-lavender.co.uk

[On A149 at J with B1454. On-site parking]

England's premier lavender farm. Home of the National Collection of Lavender. Tea room offering main meals, cream teas and snacks, gift shops, conservatory plant sales area, herb garden and fragrant meadow. Tours of grounds (including distillery and drying barn) from May to September. Minibus tours to lavender field and surrounding villages from July to end of harvest (pre-booking advisable). Please phone for info.
All year daily Apr-Oct 9.00-17.00, Nov-Mar 9.00-16.00. Closed 25-26 Dec & 1 Jan
Admission Free

Walsingham Abbey Grounds and Shirehall Museum

Estate Office Common Place Walsingham Norfolk NR22 6BP
Tel: 01328 820259 Fax: 01328 820098
[On B1105 between Wells / Fakenham]
Set in the picturesque medieval village of Little Walsingham, a place of pilgrimage since the eleventh century, the Abbey Grounds contain the remains of the famous Augustinian Priory. Although little now remains of the priory, the great east window is perhaps the most striking feature and along with the refectory walls, remains of the west tower and monks bath, give an impression of the size and scale of the original building. Visitors can enjoy the tranquil gardens and over the ancient packhorse bridge, the river and woodland walks lead into unspoilt natural woods and parkland. Entrance to the grounds in the summer is through the Shirehall Museum - a Georgian Magistrates court, now a 'hands-on' museum detailing the history of this interesting village. During the snowdrop season the Abbey Grounds are home to one of the most popular and impressive displays of snowdrops in the country. Member of the HHA.
Courthouse & Museum: Easter-end Oct.
Grounds: All year, call for more information
Combined Entrance: A£3.00 C&OAPs£2.00

Discount Offer: Two for the Price of One

Blickling Hall

Blickling Norwich Norfolk NR11 6NF

Tel: 01263 738030 Fax: 01263 738035
www.nationaltrust.org.uk/blickling

[On B1354. Plenty of on-site parking available]

Flanked by dark yew hedges and topped by pinnacles, the warm red brick front of Blickling makes a memorable sight. The house was built in the early seventeenth century, but the centrepiece of the house is the carved oak staircase which winds up in double flights from the hall. Dogs on lead are permitted in the park only. Facilities for visually impaired visitors are available. For special events, please call 0870 0104900.

Hall: 17 Mar-28 Oct Wed-Sun & Bank Hol Mons (Mon in local School Hols) 13.00-17.00. Gardens, 2nd hand Book Shop & Restaurant: 17 Mar-28 Oct Wed-Sun & Bank Hol Mon (Mon in local School Hols) 10.15-17.15, 1 Nov-8 Mar 2008 Thurs-Sun 11.00-16.00. Cycle hire: 6 Apr-28 Oct Sat-Sun & Bank Hol Mon (Wed-Mon in local School Hols) 10.15-17.00

Hall & Gardens: A£8.50 C£4.25. Gardens: A£5.50 C£2.75. Prices include 10% voluntary Gift Aid donations. Family & group rates available (Groups must book) free access to shop, restaurant, 2nd hand bookshop & plant centre

Wolterton Park

Erpingham Aylsham Norfolk NR11 7LY
Tel: 01263 584175 Fax: 01263 761214
www.manningtongardens.co.uk
[Nr Erpingham signposted from A140 Norwich to Cromer rd. Rail: Gunton. Plenty of on-site parking available]
Extensive historic park with lake, orienteering, adventure playground, walks. Hall built by diplomat brother of Sir Robert Walpole. Family portraits, fascinating history, special events; dinners, drama, music and textiles. Chair lift for disabled access.
Park: daily 9.00-dusk, Hall mid Apr-end Oct Fri 14.00-17.00
Cars£2.00 Hall£5.00

Discount Offer: Two for the Price of One

City of Norwich Aviation Museum

Old Norwich Road Horsham St. Faith Norwich Norfolk NR10 3JF
Tel: 01603 893080
The collection features a massive Vulcan bomber and some of the military and civil aircraft which have flown from Norfolk airfields.

Bircham Windmill

Bircham King's Lynn Norfolk PE31 6SJ
Tel: 01485 578393
www.birchamwindmill.co.uk

[Plenty of on-site parking available]

Bircham Windmill is one of the last remaining windmills in Norfolk. It has been fully restored to working order and the sails turn on windy days. There are lots on offer, a tearoom serving clotted cream teas, good coffee and homemade cakes. A working bakery making fresh bread six days a week (not Saturday), two gift shops, an art gallery, cycle hire, play area and animals. There are various events running most weekends throughout the summer.
1 Apr-end Sept daily 10.00-17.00
A£3.50 C£2.00 OAPs£3.00

Discount Offer: One Child Free

Model Towns & Villages

Merrivale Model Village

Wellington Pier Gardens Marine Parade
Great Yarmouth Norfolk NR30 3JG
Tel: 01493 842097
Set in attractive landscaped gardens, this comprehensive miniature village is built on a scale on 1:12.

Music & Theatre Museums

Thursford Collection

Thursford Fakenham Norfolk NR21 OAS
Tel: 01328 878477 Fax: 01328 878415
www.thursford.com

[1mi off A148 between Fakenham & Holt. Plenty of on-site parking available]

Mechanical organs, Wurlitzer organ, road engines, old-fashioned fairground rides and engines. Musical shows each day. Restaurant / coffee shop, Dickensian styled gift shops, including our famous Christmas shop, all housed in traditional Norfolk farm buildings.
1 Apr-30 Sept 12.00-17.00
A£6.00 C(4-14)£3.50 OAPs£5.70
Students(NUS/USI)&Groups£5.25

Discount Offer: Two for the Price of One

Nature & Conservation Parks

Pensthorpe Nature Reserve and Gardens

Pensthorpe Fakenham Norfolk NR21 0LN
Tel: 01328 851465 Fax: 01328 855905
www.pensthorpe.com
[1mi from Fakenham A1067. Plenty of on-site parking available]
The Natural Centre of Norfolk, an award winning must-visit attraction for all those who love nature, wildlife and the outdoors. Children love feeding the birds, pond dipping, completing their very own nature quiz and discovering minibeasts on our bug walk before letting off steam in the adventure play area. There is plenty for all the family; the red squirrels, walking with birds in the huge free-flight aviaries, the nature trails around seven beautiful lakes where you can spot some of the hundreds of wild bird species. Join the Wensum Discovery Tour an exciting guided nature expedition that takes in the beauty and importance of conservation while listening to tales of times gone by when woolly mammoths once roamed the land. You can also enjoy the stunning gardens designed by Chelsea Flower Show gold medallists, get closer to nature in the bird hides and find out about our conservation programmes. Then browse the large gift shop and have a delicious home-cooked meal in the courtyard café.
Jan-Mar 10.00-16.00, Apr-Dec 10.00-17.00. Closed 25-26 Dec
A£7.00 C(4-10)£3.50 OAPs£5.50, Family Ticket (A2+C2) £17.50

Discount Offer: £1.00 off Standard Admission Prices (for up to 6 people)

Places of Worship

Norwich Cathedral

12 The Close Norwich Norfolk NR1 4dH
Tel: 01603 218321 / 218324
A beautiful Norman building set in the largest close in England.

Railways

Bure Valley Railway

Aylsham Station Norwich Road Aylsham Norfolk NR11 6BW
Tel: 01263 733858 Fax: 01263 733814
www.bvrw.co.uk
[Mid-way between Norwich & Cromer on A140. Plenty of on-site parking available]

Travel through the Norfolk countryside on the 9 mile long, 15 inch Bure Valley Steam Railway. The Boat Train connects with cruises on the Broads - inclusive fares available. Regular services from Easter to end of September. Steam Locomotive driving courses are also available in off peak periods.
10-18 Feb, 31 Mar-30 Sept, 20-28 Oct (please call or visit website for detailed timetable)
Sample fares from A£10.00 C(5-15)£6.00 OAPs£9.00

Discount Offer: One Child Free

Sealife Centres & Aquariums

Great Yarmouth Sea Life Centre

Marine Parade Great Yarmouth Norfolk NR30 3AH
Tel: 01493 330631 Fax: 01493 330442
www.sealifeeurope.com

[A47 or A12 to Great Yarmouth, then head towards Sea Front]

Great Yarmouth Seal Life will be enhanced this year by the edition of some amazing sea turtles. Don't miss these beautiful creatures. Gliding silently by alongside a collection of amazing sharks and plenty of other incredible marine creatures you can't fail to be mesmerised. Walk through our underwater acrylic tunnel and spot these wonderful creatures all around you. Many of these creatures you will see come from the seas around our own coastline. Presentations and feeding demonstrations throughout the day provide a deeper insight into all of our fascinating creatures and how you can help to protect their future. Our younger visitors can explore the soft play area whilst you relax in the comfortable restaurant or browse in the themed gift shop, where there is something for everyone. Guided tours by prior arrangement.

All year daily from 10.00. Closed Christmas Day

Please call for prices

Discount Offer: One Child Free

Hunstanton Sea Life Sanctuary

Southern Promenade Hunstanton Norfolk
PE36 5BH
Tel: 01485 533576 Fax: 01485 533531
www.sealsanctuary.co.uk

[On seafront, signposted]

Situated on the West Coast, The Hunstanton
Sea Life Sanctuary offers visitors of all ages a
warm and friendly welcome. Combining a seal
and fish hospital, otter and penguin sanctuaries,
with the UK's first underwater tunnel, the
Sanctuary provides a real treat for everyone.
New for 2007: Shark Lagoon. Over 3 metres
deep and holding 187,500 litres of water complete with underwater walk-through tunnel. Here
in the amazing new shark lagoon, you can learn
while watching in awe, all about the most
graceful creature to swim in our oceans- The
Shark!
All year daily from 10.00. Closed Christmas Day
Please call for prices

Discount Offer: One Child Free

Spedeworth Motorsports

Yarmouth Stadium Yarmouth Road Caister on
Sea Great Yarmouth Norfolk NR30 5TE
Tel: 01493 720343
www.spedeworth.co.uk
[Plenty of on-site parking available]
Come and see World Class Racing in East
Anglia. Experience the thrill of wheel-to-wheel
action in non-stop racing. Here at Spedeworth
we aim to provide the spectator with great
sporting events throughout the year. With Stock
Cars and Bangers racing there's something for
everyone. We have drivers racing from all over
the UK and Europe, Oval Racing really is a thrill
a minute for spectators. The stadium has a fantastic wide tarmac oval (300mtrs) with a perimeter fence, which makes for very fast racing - up
to 70 mph with excellent viewing for spectators
all the way around the circuit. Following a major
refurbishment programme in 2006 Yarmouth
Stadium is fast becoming one of the most
glamorous short ovals. We have fully licensed
bars and a selection of catering outlets to suit
all tastes including a 4* viewing restaurant. Call
for a programme of events!
*Sunday night, Summer Holiday Tuesday Stunt
Show and Summertime Racing with fireworks on
Thursdays*
A£12.00 C(5-14)£6.00 OAPs£8.50
C(under5)£Free

Spectator Sports

Snetterton Circuit

Harling Road Snetterton Norfolk NR16 2JU
Tel: 0870 950 9000
Snetterton is one of the fastest race circuits in
the country.

Sport & Recreation

Sheringham Park

Upper Sheringham Norfolk NR26 8TB
Tel: 01263 823778
Llandscape park with mature woodlands.

Theme & Adventure Parks

Dinosaur Adventure Park

Weston Park Lenwade Norfolk NR9 5JW
Tel: 01603 876310
Dinosaur Trail and Secret Animal Garden.
Climb-a-Saurus and Assault-o-Saurus. Plus
woodland maze, raptor racers and crazy golf.

Pettitts Animal Adventure Park

Camphill Reedham Norfolk NR13 3UA
Tel: 01493 7000094 Fax: 01493 700933
www.pettittsadventurepark.co.uk
[Off A47 between Norwich / Great Yarmouth, fol-
low brown & white signs from Acle]
Pettitts is the top attraction to visit because it's
three parks in one. Superb fun rides includes
flying elephants, teacups, runaway train roller
coaster, half mile miniature train, Alice In
Wonderland, Toad of Toad Hall plus Robin
Hoods adventure play area. Animals galore, with
reindeer, lemurs, alpacas, racoons, reptile house
and a petting area where you can feed the animals and lots more to see. Live shows featuring, Bingo the clown and the park mascots,
Maxi mouse and Bobbi rabbit, three times a
day. We have large picnic areas as well as three
catering units. Palm's café, Maxi Snax and
Express Pizzas where hot and cold food and
snacks are available. Our gift and candy shops
offer a wide range of souvenirs and crafts. So,
spend a day not a fortune at Pettitts.
31 Mar-28 Oct daily 10.00-17.00/17.30
A&C£8.95 C(under3)£Free
OAPs/Disabled£6.85, Family Ticket (A2+C3)
£35.00. Group rates available on request

**Discount Offer: Two for the Price of
One**

Pleasure Beach, Great Yarmouth

Great Yarmouth Norfolk NR30 3EH

Tel: 01493 844585
Situated on the seafront, the Pleasure Beach is
a 9-acre leisure park featuring over 70 rides and
attractions. Entry is completely free.

Victorian Era

Strangers' Hall Museum

Station Yard Norwich Road North Walsham
Norfolk NR28 0DS
Tel: 01692 406266
We endeavor to keep the history of our engi-
neering world of motorcycles for future genera-
tions to study our heritage.

Wax Works

Louis Tussauds House of Wax

18 Regent Road Great Yarmouth Norfolk
NR30 2AF
Tel: 01493 844851

A waxworks exhibition with torture chambers, a
chamber of horrors, a hall of funny mirrors and
a family amusement arcade.

Zoos

Banham Zoo

The Grove Banham Norwich Norfolk NR16 2HE
Tel: 01953 887771
Set in 35 acres of parkland and gardens with
innovative enclosures, the zoo providing sanctuary for almost 1,000 animals.

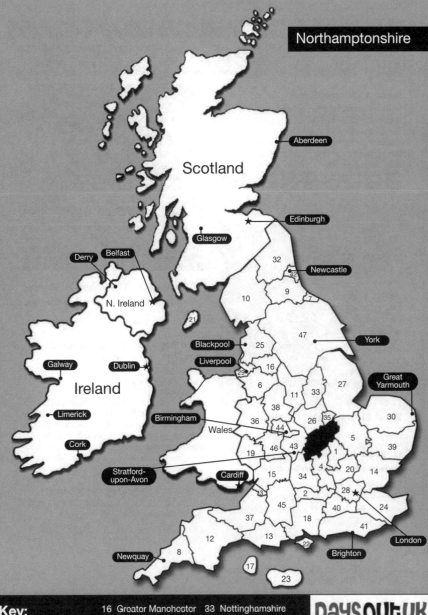

Northamptonshire

Scotland

Aberdeen

Edinburgh

Glasgow

32

Newcastle

Derry · Belfast

N. Ireland

10

9

7

Galway · Dublin

Ireland

21

Blackpool

25

47

York

Limerick

Liverpool

16

Great Yarmouth

Cork

29

6

11

33

27

30

38

Birmingham

36

44

26

35

5

39

Wales

46

43

19

Stratford-upon-Avon

Cardiff

15

34

1

4

20

14

3

2

28

24

45

40

41

London

Newquay

37

18

Brighton

8

12

13

22

17

23

Animal Attractions

Rookery Open Farm

Rookery Lane Stoke Bruerne Towcester
Northamptonshire NN12 7SJ
Tel: 01604 864855
A safe, clean environment has been created on
this commercial sheep farm for families and
schools to enjoy themselves whilst learning.

West Lodge Rural Centre

Back Lane Desborough Kettering
Northamptonshire NN14 2SH
Tel: 01536 760552 Fax: 01536 764862
www.westlodgeruralcentre.co.uk

*[Signposted off A6 from Desborough & Market
Harborough. From Kettering, Wellingborough or
Northampton, access A6 from A14 J3A. Plenty of
on-site parking available]*

One of the most spacious open family farms
with over 100 acres and 3.5 miles of walks to
explore. Encompassing rare breeds, cuddle corner, display barn, tractor rides, fantasy sculpture
trail, nature trails, play areas, play barn, licensed
restaurant and tea room. Many special events
held throughout the year.
*All year please call for specific times. Closed 25 &
26 Dec*
A£4.75 C£3.75 C(under2)£Free
Concessions£4.25

Arts, Crafts & Textiles

78 Derngate: The Charles Rennie Mackintosh House and Galleries

78 Derngate Northampton Northamptonshire
NN1 1UH
Tel: 01604 603407 Fax: 01604 603408
www.78derngate.org.uk

*[Close to town centre nr museum, gallery &
Northampton Theatres]*

The only house in England designed by Charles
Rennie Mackintosh: one of the most individual
and creative designers of the twentieth century.
Famous for his earlier works including the
Glasgow School of Art, The Hill House and the
Glasgow Tea Rooms, 78 Derngate features his
extraordinarily modern and striking interiors. 'To
the great museums of the world, there must
now be added one other. No 78 Derngate,
Northampton...this is the most delightful museum you will ever see'. Daily Telegraph.

*28 Mar- Christmas 2007, Weds-Sun 10.00-
17.00, Tues afternoon from 13.00. Closed Mon
(Except Bank Hols) & Tues morning. Guided
Tours: daily 10.30, 11.00, 12.00 & 12.30 approx
75mins*

A£5.50 Concessions£4.50, Family Ticket
£14.50. English Heritage Card holders £Free

Northampton Museum and Art Gallery

Guildhall Road Northampton NN1 1DP
Tel: 01604 838111 Fax: 01604 838720
www.northampton.gov.uk/museums
[M1, J15, signposted town centre]

The museum reflects Northampton's proud standing as Britain's shoe capital by housing a collection considered to be the world's finest. Two shoe galleries: 'Life & Sole' focuses on the industrial, commercial and health aspects of footwear giving visitors the opportunity to try out interactive exhibits and enjoy an audio-visual display. 'Followers of Fashion' is an Aladdin's cave of shoe delights spanning the centuries, which looks at shoe fashion and design featuring some of the most influential designers of the last 100 years. Also available is an art gallery featuring permanent and temporary exhibitions of fine art and a stunning display of Oriental and British ceramics. Two galleries show the town's history, from Stone Age times right up to the present day. There is a lively programme of talks, toddler afternoons, school holiday workshops and regular special themed activity days. The galleries and meeting room available for hire
All year Mon-Sat 10.00-17.00, Sun 14.00-17.00. Closed 25 Dec, 26 Dec & 1 Jan
Admission Free

Old Dairy Farm Craft Centre

Upper Stowe Weedon Northampton NN7 4SH
Tel: 01327 340525
Designer clothes, unusual gifts, delicatessen, needlecrafts, antiques, galleries and crafts.

Castle Ashby Country Fair

Horton Road Brafield on the Green
Northamptonshire NN7 1BJ
Tel: 01604 696521 / 07791 244161
Fax: 01604 696361
www.castleashbycountryfair.co.uk

[Off A428 nr Northampton. Plenty of on-site parking available]

At the 26th Castle Ashby Country Fair there'll be activities and entertainment for all the family, including: over 100 trade-stands, a craft-fair, a farmers' market, a regional food area and rural crafts. There'll also be over 6 hours of arena events including: falconry, pig racing, mountain and motorbikes, clowns, dog displays and a grand parade of vehicles. Other attractions include show-jumping, animal shows, gundog events, clay-shooting, off-road course, shooting clinic, model boats and aircraft, archery and air rifles, helicopter rides, chain saw carving, kites, plant societies, animals, tractor and trailer rides and free children's' shows. Licensed catering, free parking, disabled car parking and mobility scooters available for hire.

8 July 2007 (09.30-18.00)
A£6.00 C(5-16)£2.00 OAPs£3.00

For great hotel deals call Superbreak on 01904 679999 or visit www.superbreak.com

Northampton Balloon Festival

The Racecourse Kettering Road Northampton
Northamptonshire NN1 4LG
Tel: 01604 838222 Fax: 01604 838223
www.northamptonballoonfestival.com
[1mi N of town on Kettering Rd. Park & Ride:
Return from Sixfields Stadium, Delapre Park &
Nene College (Boughton Park). On-site parking]
Three action-packed days combining a mix of
hot air ballooning, live music, roadshows, entertainment, displays, exhibitions and trade stands.
The balloon races and evening glows all form
the centrepiece of this annual event that hosts
over 70 balloons of all shapes and sizes.
Alongside the balloons, the event offers all the
fun of the fair as well as a wide variety of food
and beverage and market stalls. Additional
entertainment takes the form of the arena entertainment, stage shows and family entertainment.
17-19 August 2007

Oundle International Festival

The Creed Chapel Ashton Oundle
Northamptonshire PE8 5LD

Tel: 01780 470297 Fax: 01780 470297
www.oundlefestival.org.uk

[12mi W of Peterborough, 7mi N of A14 (A1-M1
link rd). Rail: Peterborough. Plenty of on-site park-
ing available]

A chance to hear rising young stars and world-
class musicians performing at historic venues in
an around this lovely Nene Valley market town,
and to join 5,000 others for a massive party
under the stars at the annual festival fireworks
concert on Saturday 14 July. Ten days of classical music, jazz, open-air theatre, celebrity organ
recitals, films, exhibitions, children's events and
more.
12-22 July 2007
Range from £5.00-£20.00

Historical

Althorp

Northampton Northamptonshire NN7 4HQ
Tel: 01604 770107
The Spencers have lived and died here for near-
ly five centuries and twenty generations.

Deene Park

Deene Corby Northamptonshire NN17 3EW
Tel: 01780 450223 / 450278
House of great architectural importance and
historical interest. Extensive gardens with old-
fashioned roses, rare trees and shrubs.
Easter, May, Spring & Aug Bank Hol Sun & Mon
only, June-Aug Sun

Sulgrave Manor

Manor Road Sulgrave Banbury Oxfordshire
OX17 2SD
Tel: 01295 760205
Fine collection of sixteenth and eighteenth-cen-
tury furniture and artefacts, plus Washington
memorabilia.

Military & Defence Museums

Harrington Aviation Museums

Sunnyvale Farm and Nursery off Lamport Road
Harrington Northamptonshire NN6 9PF
Tel: 01604 686608
www.harringtonmuseum.org.uk
*[A14 W J2 on A508 to Kelmarsh. Turn R at
crossroads towards Harrington, follow museum
signs. A14 E J3, Rothwell, follow signs to
Harrington, go through village, then follow museum signs. Plenty of on-site parking available]*
The Harrington Aviation Museums comprise the
Carpetbagger Aviation and Secret War Museum
and the Northamptonshire Aviation Society
Museum. These museums offer a rare look at
life on this Top Secret base of the 801st/492nd
American Eighth Air Force Bombardment Group
during World War II. Photographs and exhibits
vividly present details of Operation
Carpetbagger and the secret war carried out by
the British Special Operations Executive (SOE)
and the American Office of Strategic Services
(OSS) in supplying resistance groups in
Occupied Europe with weapons, equipment
and secret agents from both Harrington and
Tempsford airfields during World War II; The
Thor IRBM nuclear armed rockets that were at
Harrington during the 1959-63 Cold War Period;
The history of the Harrington airfield; The Royal
Observer Corps from its inception in 1925
through to its stand down in 1991; air war and
the Home Front in Northamptonshire along with
other items of similar interest. Wheelchair
access to approximately 80% of exhibits.
*Weekend before Easter-end Oct Sat, Sun & Bank
Hol Mons 10.00-17.00. Closed Nov-1 Apr*
A£4.00 C(5-15)£2.00. No concessions. School
groups by arrangement only

**Discount Offer: Two for the Price of
One**

Nature & Conservation Parks

Barnwell Country Park
Barnwell Road Oundle Peterborough PE8 5PB
Tel: 01832 273435
A peaceful mixture of lakes and grassy meadow
and marsh, with adventure play area and shop.

Brixworth Country Park
Northampton Road Brixworth NN6 9DG
Tel: 01604 883920
The gateway to Pitsford Water and the Pitsford
Water Trail. Linked to the Brampton Valley Way.

Irchester Country Park
Gypsy Lane Little Irchester NN9 7DL
Tel: 01933 276866
Offers a wealth of experiences for everyone.

Social History Museums

Abington Park Museum

Abington Park Park Avenue South Northampton
Northamptonshire NN1 5LW
Tel: 01604 838110
www.northampton.gov.uk/museums

[Plenty of on-site parking available]

Abington Park Museum is a beautiful Grade 1
listed building in a picturesque setting of one of
Northampton's popular parks. Gaze at the ham-
mer beam roof in the Tudor hall and the intricate
carved panelling. Follow the Northamptonshire
Regiment and the Northamptonshire Yeomanry
round the world and through two world wars.
Look at life as it was for Northampton people
around one hundred years ago and stroll
around the fashions of the nineteenth century.
The museum also houses significant and interesting items from the Museum of Leather craft
collection. There is a lively programme of talks
at lunchtimes and for the over 60s mornings
together with the popular toddler afternoons. In
addition, look out for our school holiday workshops and special themed activity days. The
atmospheric courtyard and hall are available for
hire including wedding receptions.

*Mar-Oct Tue-Sun & Bank Hol Mon 13.00-17.00,
Nov-Feb Tue-Sun 13.00-16.00. Closed 25 + 26
Dec & 1 Jan*
Admission Free

Theme & Adventure Parks

Wicksteed Park

Barton Road Kettering NN15 6NJ
Tel: 01536 512475 Fax: 01536 518948
www.wicksteedpark.co.uk
*[On outskirts of Kettering. Follow signs from J10
off A14. Main Gate is on A6. On-site parking]*

With 147 acres of parkland and lakes and over
35 attractions (including one of the largest free
playgrounds in the UK), a double pirate ship,
roller coasters, bumper boats, fairground rides,
outdoor entertainment and an events programme throughout the year - Wicksteed Park
really is the all-round family day out. The
Wicksteed Railway is the busiest commercial
narrow gauge railway in the UK (carrying
250,000+ passengers a year). The Wicksteed
Pavilion hosts 'It's Showtime' daytime entertainment all year round (tickets must be booked in
advance). The pavilion is also licensed for weddings and is one of the largest banqueting
venues in Northamptonshire making it the perfect venue for your party, wedding, or corporate
event. Offers caravan/camping facilities, making
it 'The coastal experience in the heart of traditionally landscaped British countryside'.
*31 Mar-30 Sept, inclusive, opening times vary so
please telephone for more details*
No entry fee. Car-parking charged (£6.00 max.).
Buy wristbands/tickets as required. Wristbands:
A£10.00 C£15.00 OAPs£7.50. Tickets: 12 for
£10.00, 30 for £20.00, single ticket: £1.00.
Where applicable, children under 0.9m ride free!
Wristbands entitles the wearer to unlimited rides
only on the day of purchase. Does not include
coin-operated amusements or admission to certain special events. In the interests of safety,
certain rides have passenger height restrictions,
which are displayed by means of a colour code

**Discount Offer: Three Wristbands for the
Price of Two**

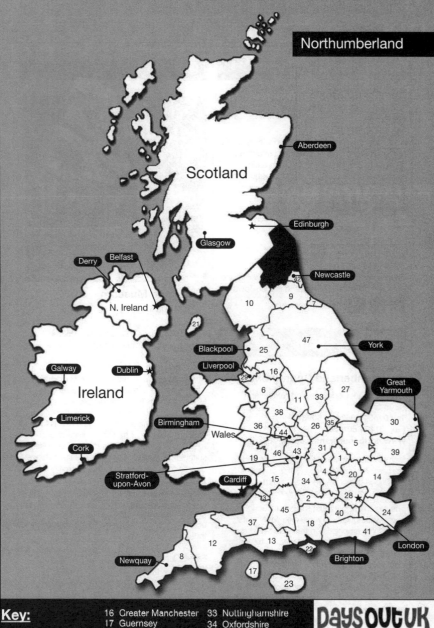

Northumberland

Aberdeen

Scotland

Edinburgh

Glasgow

Newcastle

Derry Belfast

N. Ireland

21

42

9

10

7

47

York

Blackpool

25

Liverpool

29

16

Great
Yarmouth

Galway Dublin

Ireland

6

11

33

27

Limerick

38

26

35

30

Cork

Birmingham

Wales

36

44

31

5

39

Stratford-
upon-Avon

19

46

43

1

20

14

Cardiff

15

34

4

28

London

13

2

24

Newquay

37

45

18

40

41

Brighton

12

13

22

8

17

23

Country Parks & Estates

Alnwick Garden

Denwick Lane Alnwick Northumberland
NE66 1YU
Tel: 01665 511350
An exciting, contemporary garden with beautiful
and unique gardens, features and structures
brought to life with water. Fantastic eating,
drinking and shopping. Events throughout the
year.

Hulne Park

Alnwick Northumberland NE66 1NQ
Tel: 01665 510777
Expansive parkland on the River Aln, containing
the ruins of Alnwick Abbey and Brizlee Tower.

Festivals & Shows

Northumberland County Show

Tynedale Park Corbridge Northumberland
NE45 5AY
Tel: 01434 604216 / 609533
Fax: 01434 601757
www.northcountyshow.co.uk

*[15mi W of Newcastle Upon Tyne & 4mi E of
Hexham. Tynedale Park on S side of river at
Corrbridge. Event AA signposted from A69 & A68
trunk rds. Plenty of on-site parking available]*

The regions single most successful agricultural
event with agriculture remaining firmly at its
heart. With emphasis on tradition e.g. sheep
shearing, hedge laying, heavy horse turnouts,
parade of hounds, grand parade and showing
classes for everything from Cattle to Alpacas
attracting exhibitors from as far as northern
Scotland to Lancashire. Intermingled with this
are some spectacular acts like Big Pete and his
monster trucks and the RAF parachute team to
thrill and entertain all members of the family
along with 300 trade stands.
28 May 2007 (09.00-18.00)
A£10.00 C(3-16)£2.50 OAPs£6.00

Folk & Local History Museums

Bailiffgate Museum

14 Bailiffgate Alnwick Northumberland
NE66 1LX
Tel: 01665 605847 Fax: 01665 605394
www.bailiffgatemuseum.co.uk

[Opposite main entrance to Alnwick Castle]

Attractively located in the former St Mary's
Church (which dates from 1836), Bailiffgate
Museum brings to life the people and places of
North Northumberland. Six specially themed
areas capture the unique heritage of this historic
region. A mixture of traditional displays and
exciting hands-on activities makes the Museum
suitable for all ages. Bailiffgate's Gallery stages a
diverse range of art and history exhibitions
throughout the year. Exhibitions include shows
by local and national artists and photographers,
costume and textile exhibitions and themed
local history exhibitions. A variety of workshops,
activities and special events for all ages are held
throughout the year.

*Easter-Oct daily 10.00-17.00, Nov-Easter 10.00-
16.00 (closed Mon). Closed 17 Dec 2007-08
Jan 2008*
A£2.75 C(under5)£Free OAPs£2.40
Concessions£2.00, Family Ticket (A2+C1) £6.40
or (A2+C2) £7.25

Food & Drink

Lindisfarne Mead

St.Aidans Winery Holy Island Berwick
Northumberland TD15 2RX
Tel: 01289 389230
Mead, fudge, preserves, fruit wines, British beer,
cider, malt whisky and famous Craster kippers.

Gardens & Horticulture

Howick Hall Gardens

Howick Alnwick Northumberland NE66 3LB
Tel: 01665 577285 (Estate office)
Fax: 01665 577285
www.howickhallgardens.org

[6mi NE of Alnwick off B1339 between Boulmer & Craster. Plenty of on-site parking available]

Howick Hall Gardens - Stunningly beautiful and an oasis of tranquillity. Located 6 miles from Alnwick, Northumberland the gardens are rated by BBC Gardeners World magazine as "One of the 'Top 5' coastal gardens in the UK." The extensive grounds boast a wealth of plant life to be explored and wildlife to be discovered. Stroll along the woodland walks covering some 65 acres, in an entirely wild collected arboretum, it's unique in the North East. And afterwards relax in the Earl Grey Tea House serving teas, coffee and light snacks set in beautiful, stately surroundings. Howick Hall Gardens - it's Northumberland's best-kept secret!
1 Apr-31 Oct 2007 daily 12.00-18.00
A£4.50 OAPs£3.50 C£Free

Historical

Alnwick Castle

Estates Office Alnwick NE66 1NQ
Tel: 01665 510777 Fax: 01665 510876
www.alnwickcastle.com
[33 mi N of Newcastle-upon-Tyne, 30 mi S of Berwick-upon-Tweed & 80 mi S of Edinburgh just off A1 in historic market town of Alnwick]
Best Large Visitor Attraction North East Tourism Awards 2006. A warm welcome awaits visitors to the mighty medieval fortress of Alnwick Castle - one of Europe's finest. Set in a stunning landscape this magnificent castle dominates the skyline and overlooks the historic market town of Alnwick. Alnwick Castle is home to the Duke and Duchess of Northumberland whose family have lived here for almost 700 years. This glorious castle has a wealth of history to be explored and treasures in abundance, a legacy of the Percy family who have been collecting for generations. Newly unveiled for this year is the refurbished and restored Dining Room which has beautiful silk walls, hand-woven carpet and intricately carved ceiling. Whether you wish to explore the fine collection of paintings and porcelain in the State Rooms or face the terrifying monster in the exciting and interactive activity area, Dragon's Quest, you are invited to experience the unique delights of Alnwick Castle for a magical visit. Exterior photography only.
2 Apr-28 Oct 10.00-18.00, (State Rooms 11.00-17.00)
Day Ticket: A£9.00 Concession£8.00 C£4.00, Family Ticket £24.00. Weekly Ticket: A£12.50 Concession£11.00 C£5.00, Family Ticket £32.00. Season Ticket: A£20.00 Concession£18.00 A&2C£35.00 Family Ticket £50.00

Discount Offer: One Child Free

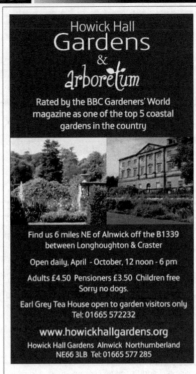

Howick Hall
Gardens
& arboretum

Rated by the BBC Gardeners' World magazine as one of the top 5 coastal gardens in the country

Find us 6 miles NE of Alnwick off the B1339 between Longhoughton & Craster

Open daily, April - October, 12 noon - 6 pm

Adults £4.50 Pensioners £3.50 Children free
Sorry no dogs.

Earl Grey Tea House open to garden visitors only
Tel: 01665 572232

www.howickhallgardens.org
Howick Hall Gardens Alnwick Northumberland
NE66 3LB Tel: 01665 577 285

Black Middens Bastle House

Bellingham Northumberland
Tel: 0191 261 1585
A sixteenth-century farmhouse, with ground floor accommodation for livestock and living quarters above.

Cherryburn

Station Bank Mickley Stocksfield
Northumberland NE43 7DD
Tel: 01661 843276
The birthplace of Thomas Bewick (1753-1828), Northumberland's greatest artist, wood engraver and naturalist.

Chillingham Castle and Gardens

Chillingham Alnwick Northumberland NE66 5NJ
Tel: 01668 215359   Fax: 01668 215463
www.chillingham-castle.com
[Plenty of on-site parking available]

This remarkable fortress with its alarming dungeons and torture chamber, has been owned by Earl Grey and his descendants continuously since about 1200.
Grounds & Tearoom 12.00, Castle 13.00
A£6.75 C£3.00 Concessions£5.50
C(under5)£1.00.

Discount Offer: One Child Free

Cragside House Gardens and Estate

Cragside Rothbury Morpeth Northumberland
NE65 7PX
Tel: 01669 620333 / 620150
Fax: 01669 620066
Crammed with gadgets, this was the first house in the world lit electrically.

Hadrian's Wall

Hexham Northumberland
Tel: 01434 322002
[West of Hexham, the Wall runs roughly parallel to A69 Carlisle to Newcastle rd, lying between 1-4mi N of it, close to the B6318. Bus:The Hadrian's Wall Bus Tel 01434 322002]
Stretching 73 miles from coast-to-coast across Northern England, Hadrian's Wall spans nearly 2,000 years of history.

Wallington

Cambo Morpeth Northumberland NE61 4AR
Tel: 01670 773600 Fax: 01670 774420
www.nationaltrust.org.uk
[12mi W of Morpeth on B6343. On-site parking]
Wallington, in the heart of the beautiful
Northumbrian countryside and yet only half an
hour from Newcastle, is the much loved home
of the Trevelyan family. With 13,000 acres of
farmland, and including Cambo village,
Wallington is the largest country estate protect-
ed by the National Trust. In the house, which
dates from 1688, see the wonderful dolls'
house collection and the famous paintings of
Northumbrian history by William Bell Scott.
Families can enjoy a picnic on the lawn, games
in the courtyard, and the adventure playground
in the woods. The wildlife hide gives everyone
the chance to see red squirrels and woodland
birds at close quarters. The enchanting walled
garden has it all, and in springtime is a blaze of
colour with bulbs and blossom. Finish your visit
to Wallington with some well-deserved tea and
cakes, browse through the gifts in the shop,
and buy your supper at the farm shop. Email
wallington@nationaltrust.org.uk for information.
*House: 17 Mar-30 Sept 13.00-17.30, 1 Oct-4
Nov 13.00-16.30. Closed Tue. Garden &
Grounds: Apr-Sept 10.00-19.00, Oct 10.00-
18.00, Nov-Mar 10.00-16.00*
A£8.80 C£4.40, Family Ticket £22.00. Walled
Garden & Grounds only: A£6.05 C£3.05, Family
Ticket £15.40

Barter Books

Alnwick Station Alnwick NE66 2NP
Tel: 01665 604888
The 'British Library of second hand bookshops'
is located in a listed Victorian station.

Music & Theatre Museums

Morpeth Chantry Bagpipe Museum

The Chantry Bridge Street Morpeth
Northumberland NE61 1PD
Tel: 01670 500717 Fax: 01670 500710
www.bagpipemuseum.org.uk

[Town Centre]

Most people think that all bagpipes are Scottish. They are not. Bagpipes are to be found all over Europe, Asia and North Africa and are one of the most ancient musical instruments. Morpeth Chantry Bagpipe Museum is devoted to bagpipes of all countries, but particularly those of Northumberland and the Borders. The Northumbrian pipes are a light, lilting and melodic instrument, made for playing indoors. They are played by inflating the bag with bellows held under one arm (rather than by blowing into the bag, like the Scottish bagpipes). The museum has a pre-recorded soundtrack, which allows visitors to hear how each set of pipes sounds. Live music is a feature of the museum - the Northumbrian Pipers Society holds Saturday afternoon meetings every month. Concerts throughout the year.
Mon-Sat 10.00-17.00, also Sun in Aug
Admission Free

Places of Worship

Lindisfarne Priory

Holy Island Berwick-Upon-Tweed
Northumberland TD15 2RX
Tel: 01289 389200
One of the most important early centres of Christianity in Anglo-Saxon England.

Police, Prisons & Dungeons

Cell Block Museum

Marygate Berwick-Upon-Tweed
Northumberland TD15 1BN
Tel: 01289 330900
A Georgian town hall and former town jail situated in the town centre.

Roman Era

Chesters Museum

Humshaugh Hexham NE46 4EP
Tel: 01434 681379
Roman inscriptions, sculpture, weapons, tools and ornaments from the forts at Chesters.

Sport & Recreation

Carlisle Park and Castle Wood

28 Bridge Street Morpeth Northumberland
NE61 1NL
Tel: 01670 535000
Formal park, riverside and woodland walks, aviary, tennis court, paddling pool and boating.

Wildlife & Safari Parks

Chillingham Wild Cattle Park

Wardens Cottage Chillingham Alnwick
Northumberland NE66 5NP
Tel: 01668 215250
www.chillingham-wildcattle.org.uk
[Plenty of on-site parking available]

Of all the 1200 million cattle in the world, the Chillingham Wild Cattle are the only ones to have remained free of any human interference or management, and are closest to their wild prehistoric ancestors in the way they live. They still roam in their natural surroundings, in the 134 hectares of Chillingham Park near Wooler in Northumberland. The existing herd are thought to have been enclosed at Chillingham for over 700 years. In recent years DNA samples have been prepared from hair roots collected from dead animals in the Park and sent to the Roslin Institute and Edinburgh University, which have revealed that the Wild Cattle are a natural clone, and are genetically identical. This is unique among animals, and arises from their very long history of inbreeding, together with occasional periods of very low numbers. No dogs allowed at all.
1 Apr-31 Oct Wed-Mon 10.00-12.00 & 14.00-17.00, Sun 14.00-17.00. Closed Tues
A£4.50 OAPs£3.00 C£1.50

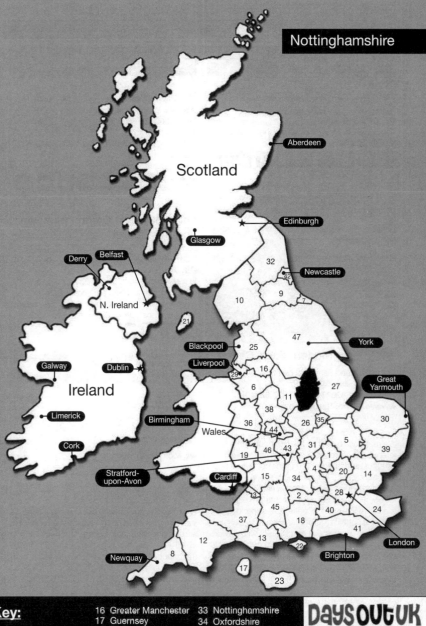

Nottinghamshire

Scotland

Aberdeen

Edinburgh

Glasgow

Newcastle

Derry
Belfast

N. Ireland

Galway
Dublin

Ireland

Limerick

Cork

Blackpool
Liverpool

Birmingham

Wales

Stratford-
upon-Avon

Cardiff

Newquay

York

Great
Yarmouth

London

Brighton

32

42

10

9

7

21

25

16

47

29

6

38

11

27

36

44

26

35

30

19

46

43

31

5

39

15

34

4

1

20

14

13

2

28

45

40

24

37

18

41

12

13

22

8

17

23

Animal Attractions

Sherwood Forest Farm Park

Lamb Pens Farm Edwinstowe Mansfield
Nottinghamshire NG21 9HL
Tel: 01623 823558
At Sherwood Forest Farm Park the lovely rare
breeds of farm animals are waiting.

White Post Modern Farm Centre

Mansfield Road Farnsfield Newark
Nottinghamshire NG22 8HL
Tel: 01623 882977 Fax: 01623 883499
www.whitepostfarmcentre.co.uk
[Plenty of on-site parking available]

Visit the White Post Farm Centre in 2007!
We're proud to offer a great day out with a difference, whatever the weather. With over 25
acres of attractive English farmland, over 3,000
animals and lots of indoor activities, a wonderful
day out is guaranteed. With llamas, cows, wallabies, reptiles and special events all-year round,
the White Post Farm Centre is exciting, dynamic
and most of all, fun! A great chance to learn
about farming heritage and interact with a wide
range of animals. With indoor and outdoor play
areas and a fantastic go-kart track, there's plenty of time for play. We cater for groups and offer
great deals on birthday parties and group tours
- please call for details.
All year daily from 10.00
A£7.50 C£6.95. Group rates on request

**Discount Offer: Two Free Bags of
Animal Feed**

Arts, Crafts & Textiles

Harley Gallery

Welbeck Worksop Nottinghamshire S80 3LW
Tel: 01909 501700
The Gallery was built in 1994 and displays
include contemporary art and craft, and a
museum showing historical objects from the
portland collections

Longdale Craft Centre, Museum and Restaurant

Longdale Lane Ravenshead Nottinghamshire
NG15 9AH
Tel: 01623 794858
Includes workshops, a museum, gallery and first
class restaurant. There are frequent demonstrations from local crafts people, whilst the restaurant plays host to regular Jazz Night Suppers.

Caverns & Caves

City of Caves

Upper Level Broad Marsh Shopping Centre
Nottingham Nottinghamshire NG1 7LS
Tel: 0115 952 0555

www.cityofcaves.com

*[M1 J26 from N, off M1 J25 from Derby & the W.
Situated beneath Broadmarsh Shopping centre.
There is plenty of public car parking nearby]*

An ancient and mysterious labyrinth of sandstone caves buried deep beneath the modern
and vibrant city of Nottingham. Enter and
explore a whole new world and descend into
the dark depths of the original Anglo Saxon tunnels, meeting real cave dwellers from its dramatic hidden past.
*All year daily 10.30-16.30. Please call for details
of Christmas opening times*
A£4.95 C£3.95 Concessions£3.95, Family
Ticket £14.95. Group rates available on request

Discount Offer: One Child Free

Country Parks & Estates

Rufford Abbey Country Park

Ollerton Newark Nottinghamshire NG22 9DF
Tel: 01623 822944 Fax: 01623 824840
www.nottinghamshire.gov.uk

[A614, 2mi S of Ollerton roundabout. 17mi N of Nottingham. For public transport details call Traveline on 0870 608 2 608. Plenty of on-site parking available]

Set in the heart of Robin Hood County and once one of North Nottinghamshire's great private estates, the picturesque remains of Rufford Abbey, Founded in the twelfth century by Cistercian monks and later transformed into a grand county house, are at the heart of the Country Park and house an exhibition on Cistercian life in the Undercroft. The Craft centre in the former stable block houses a nationally renowned gallery and a ceramic centre that traces the history of studio pottery as well as two shops-are featuring a selection of quality British crafts and they other variety of souvenirs and gifts. The nearby Coach House serves drinks and light refreshments while the Savile Restaurant offers traditional lunches. Enjoy the restored orangery and formal gardens before taking a stroll down to Rufford Lakes where you will find both the Lakeside Garden Shop and Outdoor Living store

All year, High Season (end Feb-end Oct) 10.30-17.00, Low Season (end Oct-end Feb) 10.30-16.30. Closed afternoon 24 Dec & reopens 26 Dec

Admission Free. Car Park charge at various times throughout the year

Sherwood Forest Country Park and Visitor Centre

Edwinstowe Mansfield Nottinghamshire NG21 9HN
Tel: 01623 823202 / 824490
Fax: 01623 823202
www.nottinghamshire.gov.uk/countryparks
[On B6034, N of Edwinstowe between A6075 & A616. For Public transport details to Park call Traveline on 0870 608 2 608. Minicom 0870 241 2 216 or email buses@nottscc.gov.uk. Plenty of on-site parking available]

Visit Sherwood Forest, the legendary home of England's most famous outlaw-Robin Hood, and now part of Nottinghamshire's only National Nature Reserve. Over 450 acres of ancient oak woodland, including the mighty major Oak, known world-wide as Robin Hood's tree. The visitor centre houses the Robyn Hode's Sherwode Exhibition which shows visitors what life was like in medieval times while, in the video studio, you can find out more about this former Royal Hunting Forest as well as two on-site shops where you can browse for souvenirs and gifts, and the Forest Table restaurant, where you can relax over a drink or meal. Explore woodland paths, picnic in the forest glades or enjoy some of the year round programme of events activities- including the Annual Robin Hood Festival which takes place the year from 30th July-5th August.

All year, High Season (Easter-Jan) 10.00-17.00, Low Season (Jan-Easter) 10.00-16.30. Closed afternoon 24 Dec & reopens 26 Dec

Admission Free, Car Park charge at various times throughout the year

Wollaton Hall and Park

Wollaton Nottingham Nottinghamshire NG8 2AE
Tel: 0115 915 3900 Fax: 0115 915 3932
www.nottinghamcity.gov.uk

[10min drive from Nottingham City Centre off A609, also accessible by bus. Plenty of on-site parking available]

Standing on a natural hill 3 miles west of Nottingham city centre, Wollaton Hall is a flamboyant sixteenth-century Robert Smythson building, set in a scenic, 500-acre historic deer park. Wollaton Hall houses a Natural History Museum, an Industrial Museum and the Yard Gallery, which houses exhibitions inspired by art and science. The park is home to herds of free-roaming red and fallow deer. Visitors have the choice of a variety of walks, or they can simply stroll around the lake, or relax in the formal gardens. New for 2007: Tudor kitchens, prospect room, salon, dining room, bird room and natural collections gallery. The hall and park have undergone a major programme of restoration and will be fully re-open to the public at Easter 2007.

Hall: Mar-Oct 11.00-17.00, Nov-Feb 11.00-16.00. Park: Sat-Sun 9.00-dusk, Mon-Fri 8.00-dusk
Mon-Fri Admission Free. Sat-Sun & Bank Hols A£1.50 C&Concession£1.00. C(under5)£Free. Group rates available on request. Parking: £2.00 per car. From Easter 2007 only guided tour, special event and car park charges will apply

Robin Hood Festival

Sherwood Forest Country Park and Visitor Centre Edwinstowe Nottinghamshire NG21 9HN
Tel: 01623 823202
www.robinhood.co.uk

[Off B6034, between A6075 & A616, 20mi from Nottingham, 35mi from Derby & 32mi from Sheffield. Plenty of on-site parking available]

The 23rd Annual Robin Hood Festival - Nottinghamshire's biggest celebration of the life and times of its legendary hero - will be taking place at Sherwood Forest Country Park this summer. During the week-long extravaganza, costumed entertainers will provide fun for all the family. These include jugglers, jesters, strolling minstrels, street theatre performers, archers and experts in medieval combat. No Robin Hood Festival would be complete without archery and costumed archers will offer visitors the chance to use a longbow. The festival also includes a Medieval Market and weekend jousting tournaments.

30 July-5 Aug 2007
Admission Free, small charge for some events. Parking charge for Cars £3.00

Folk & Local History Museums

Bassetlaw Museum
Amcott House 40 Grove Street Retford
Nottinghamshire DN22 6LD
Tel: 01777 713749
www.bassetlawmuseum.org.uk

[5min walk from Retford Market Place, next to Tourist Information Centre]

Set in the beautiful eighteenth-century Amcott House, the Bassetlaw Museum displays fascinating collections of archaeology, costume, local, social and farming history illustrating the life of Bassetlaw and its people. The Welchman collection of 20,000 images is an invaluable pictorial record of the period 1910-50. Supported by the Heritage Lottery Fund, these photographs, and many others, are available on computer in the museum and on the website. The museum and art gallery is a rich resource for schools, local and family historians. School parties are welcome by appointment. Contact the museum for details of our education service. The gift shop stocks a wide range of books, cards, jewellery and toys with something for every pocket.
Mon-Sat 10.00-17.00. Closed Sun. Please note venue closes from June 2007 until May 2008 for refurbishment
Admission Free

Mansfield Museum and Art Gallery
Leeming Street Mansfield NG18 1NG
Tel: 01623 463088
'Images of Mansfield past and present' uses objects and photographs to illustrate the history of the town.

Museum of Nottingham Life at Brewhouse Yard
Castle Boulevard Nottingham NG7 1FB
Tel: 0115 915 3600
www.nottinghamcity.gov.uk

[A short walk from Nottingham Castle]

Located at the base of the Castle Rock, this museum depicts the social history of Nottingham over the last 300 years. It contains a mixture of reconstructed room and shop settings, and gallery displays. Step into an air-raid shelter, experience being in a Victorian home, see inside a child's bedroom and look through the cupboards in the kitchen. See objects that were made or used by people in Nottingham and learn about the history of the area, through sight, touch and sound. Events are held regularly - from reminiscence sessions, talks and tours, to trails, dressing-up, plus seasonal and school-holiday activities. A 1940s extravaganza held every May celebrates the lighter side of WWII with song, dance and games. Schools are always welcome for both teacher-led and freelancer sessions.
All year daily 10.00-16.30
Joint Ticket with Nottingham Castle A£3.50 C&Concessions£2.00, Family Ticket (A2+C3) £8.00

Tales of Robin Hood
30-38 Maid Marian Way Nottingham NG1 6GF

Tel: 0115 948 3284
Be an outlaw for the day at this medieval adventure centre.

Heritage & Industrial

The Workhouse

Upton Road Southwell Nottinghamshire
NG25 0PT
Tel: 01636 817250
A formidable nineteenth-century institution with
a story to tell about the care of the poor.

Historical

Newstead Abbey

Newstead Abbey Park Ravenshead
Nottinghamshire NG15 8NA
Tel: 01623 455900 Fax: 01623 455904
www.nottinghamcity.gov.uk

*[J27 M1 12mi N of Nottingham on A60. Plenty of
on-site parking available]*

Beautiful historic house set in parklands, former
home of the poet Lord Byron. Byron's own
room and mementoes on display, and splendid-
ly decorated rooms from the Medieval to the
Victorian era. 40 acres of grounds to explore.
Disabled access limited to ground floor.
*Grounds only: All year daily 9.00-18.00 (except
last Fri in Nov & Christmas Day). House: 1 Apr-30
Sept daily 12.00-17.00*
House & Grounds: A£6.00 C£2.50
Concessions£4.00, Family Ticket (A2+C3)
£16.00. Group rate: £4.00. Grounds only:
A£3.00 C£1.50 Concessions£2.50
Cyclists£0.50 Group£2.50, Family Ticket
(A2+C2) £8.50

Nottingham Castle

Friar Lane Off Maid Marian Way Nottingham
Nottinghamshire NG1 6EL
Tel: 0115 915 3700 Fax: 0115 915 3653
www.nottinghamcity.gov.uk

*[From M1, follow signs for Nottingham City
Centre, then follow tourist signs. 5min walk from
Nottingham City Centre]*

Situated high above the city, Nottingham Castle
is a seventeenth-century mansion built over 300
years ago, on the site of a medieval castle originally built by William the Conqueror. Within the
castle a vibrant museum that houses a range of
collections including historic and contemporary
fine art, armour, china and silverware can be
found. The castle also exhibits many contemporary exhibitions ranging from local artist to touring shows. There are tours available to discover
the network of caves and hidden passageways
underneath the castle that is surrounded by
beautiful Victorian inspired gardens, and provides scenic views across the city and countryside beyond. The castle is a great place for children, with interactive displays and an activity-led
gallery bringing paintings to life, specifically for
the under 5s, plus a medieval-style playground
in the grounds with covered picnic area.

*All year daily Mar-Sept 10.00-17.00 Oct-Feb
10.00-16.00. Closed 24-26 Dec & 1 Jan*
Joint Ticket with Museum of Nottingham Life at
Brewhouse Yard: A£3.50 C&Concessions£2.00,
Family Ticket (A2+C3) £8.00. Group rates avail-
able on request

Living History Museums

NCCL Galleries of Justice

Shire Hall High Pavement Lace Market
Nottingham Nottinghamshire NG1 1HN
Tel: 0115 952 0555 Fax: 0115 993 9828
www.nccl.org.uk
[City centre, signposted both traffic & pedestrian, multi-storey parking signposted, 5-10min walk]
Travel with us on an atmospheric tour through three centuries of crime and punishment. Experience a real trial in the original Victorian Courtroom, put your friends and family in the dock, before being sentenced and 'sent down' to the original prison cells. But beware! You will not travel these layers of time alone - the dark corridors are haunted by characters that come to life before your very eyes! The NCCL Galleries of Justice is the new home for the HM Prison collection. This amazing and exciting exhibition is now on permanent display with never-before-seen artefacts from prisons across the country. Now you have the chance to experience some of Britain's most gruesome, yet touching reminders, of what prison life would have been like for inmates and prison staff. Visit our new family area, Narrow Marsh - Queen Victoria's backyard and experience what life was like for children in Nottingham's slums.
Wheelchair access: 85%
All year Tue-Sun, Bank Hol Mon & Mon throughout school hols, peak times 10.00-17.00, please call to confirm off peak times
A£7.95 C£5.95 Concessions£5.95, Family Ticket (A2+C2) £22.95. Tickets are valid for one visit to each exhibition over 12 months. Group rates available on request.

Discount Offer: Two for the Price of One

Science - Earth & Planetary

Green's Windmill and Science Museum

Windmill Lane Sneinton Nottingham
Nottinghamshire NG2 4QB
Tel: 0115 915 6878 Fax: 0115 915 6875
www.greensmill.org.uk

[1mi outside Nottingham City Centre. Bus: 23 & 24 from King St. Plenty of on-site parking available]

Green's Windmill is a working windmill that produces its own organic flour. You can see how the flour is made by climbing the different levels of the windmill. When the wind is blowing the experience is even better, you watch and hear the machinery turning the millstones. You can buy the award-winning organic flour from the shop. Children and adults can test their minds with fun, hands-on puzzles and experiments in the Science Centre, and for the under-5s, there's a special 'Mini Millers' area, where even the youngest scientists can start learning. Green's Windmill is a grade II listed building set in parkland, with a cobbled courtyard which provides an attractive space to sit and relax. It is the only inner-city windmill in the UK and the former home of the famous nineteenth-century mathematician George Green.

Wed-Sun 10.00-16.00 & most Bank Hols

Admission Free

Theme & Adventure Parks

Go Ape! High Wire Forest Adventure

Sherwood Pines Visitor Centre Sherwood Pines Forest Park Nr. Edwinstowe Mansfield Nottinghamshire NG21 9JL
Tel: 0870 420 7876
www.goape.co.uk

[Off B6030 between Old Clipstone & Ollerton. Plenty of on-site parking available]

Take to the trees and experience an exhilarating course of rope bridges, 'Tarzan Swings' and zip-slides up to 40 feet above the ground! Share approximately three hours of memorable fun and adventure, which you'll be talking about for days. Book online and watch people Go Ape! at www.goape.co.uk. Minimum height 1.4m. Maximum weight 130 kg (20.5 stone). Under-18s must be accompanied by a participating adult. One adult can supervise either two children (where one or both of them in under 16 years old) or up to five 16-17 year olds. Pre-booking is essential to avoid disappointment. Book online or by telephone (there is a £1.00 booking fee on all telephone bookings).
10-25 Feb, 23 Mar-2 Nov daily, Nov Sat-Sun. Closed Dec-Jan
Gorillas (18yrs+) £25.00, Baboons (10-17yrs) £20.00

Discount Offer: Two for the Price of One

Sundown Adventureland

Treswell Road Rampton Retford Nottinghamshire DN22 0HX
Tel: 01777 248274 Fax: 01777 248967
www.sundownadventureland.co.uk

[6mi from A1 Markham Moor. Plenty of on-site parking available]

The Theme Park especially designed for the under 10s. Your adventure is just beginning the moment you enter the park! Explore the Junglemania indoor play area, Fort Apache & Captain Sandy's play cove, ride aboard the Rocky Mountain Railroad, Santa's Sleigh ride, Robin Hood ride, and the Boozy Barrel Boat ride, a full day of fun awaits you! Adventure play areas, cafés, shops, plus lots lots more, Also don't forget, we're open at Christmas, so come along and visit Santa in his lovely home and receive a free gift for all children aged 2 to 10 years.
11 Feb-24 Dec daily from 10.00
A&C£8.00 C(under2)£Free. Group rates available on request

Toy & Childhood Museums

Vina Cooke Museum of Dolls and Bygone Childhood

The Old Rectory Great North Road Cromwell Newark Nottinghamshire NG23 6JE
Tel: 01636 821364
A large collection of dolls and toys dating from the eighteenth century to the present day. Also, dolls' hospital and Vina's portrait dolls.

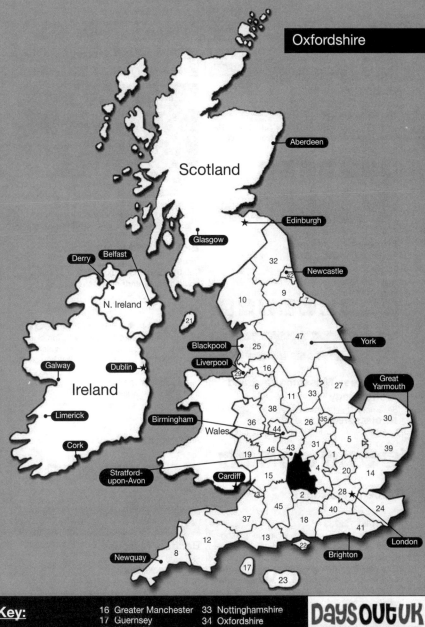

Oxfordshire

Scotland

Aberdeen

Edinburgh

Glasgow

Newcastle

Derry
Belfast

N. Ireland

Galway
Dublin

Ireland

Blackpool

Liverpool

York

Limerick

Birmingham

Great
Yarmouth

Cork

Wales

Stratford-
upon-Avon

Cardiff

London

Newquay

Brighton

Key:

1 Bedfordshire
2 Berkshire
3 Bristol
4 Buckinghamshire
5 Cambridgeshire
6 Cheshire
7 Cleveland
8 Cornwall
9 County Durham
10 Cumbria
11 Derbyshire
12 Devon
13 Dorset
14 Essex
15 Gloucestershire

16 Greater Manchester
17 Guernsey
18 Hampshire
19 Herefordshire
20 Hertfordshire
21 Isle Of Man
22 Isle Of Wight
23 Jersey
24 Kent
25 Lancashire
26 Leicestershire
27 Lincolnshire
28 London
29 Merseyside
30 Norfolk
31 Northamptonshire
32 Northumberland

33 Nottinghamshire
34 Oxfordshire
35 Rutland
36 Shropshire
37 Somerset
38 Staffordshire
39 Suffolk
40 Surrey
41 Sussex
42 Tyne & Wear
43 Warwickshire
44 West Midlands
45 Wiltshire
46 Worcestershire
47 Yorkshire

DAYS OUT UK
The place to look for places to go

Animal Attractions

Royal Oak Farm
Islip Road Beckley Oxfordshire OX3 9TY
Tel: 01865 351246
Animal garden with friendly goats, pigs, sheep, feed baby animals. Relax in the tearoom serving light lunches and teas.

Archaeology

Museum of Oxford
St. Aldates Oxford Oxfordshire OX1 1DZ
Tel: 01865 252761
Permanent displays depict the archaeology and history of the city.

Arts, Crafts & Textiles

Ashmolean Museum of Art and Archaeology
Beaumont Street Oxford Oxfordshire OX1 2PH
Tel: 01865 278000 / 278015
Collections of art from Europe, Japan, India and China.

Modern Art Oxford
30 Pembroke Street Oxford OX1 1BP
Tel: 01865 722733
Exhibitions include painting, sculpture, photography, film, performance and design.
Closed Mon

Birds, Butterflies & Bees

Waterfowl Sanctuary and Children's Animal Centre
Wigginton Heath Banbury OX15 4LQ
Tel: 01608 730252
A large selection of birds and rare farm breeds.

Festivals & Shows

Bicester and Finmere Show
Bicester Oxfordshire
Tel: 01869 253566 Fax: 01869 369064
www.bicesterandfinmereshow.co.uk

[1mi from Bicester town on the Buckingham rd A4421. Plenty of on-site parking available]

Raising funds for the Back Up Trust and Spinal Research. Main attractions include: Top class show jumping, featuring the country's leading riders, dog show, classic car display, horticultural show and crafts, trade stands, members tent, bars and refreshments and much more. Trade stand enquiries welcome please call 07973 543516. Horse show schedules please call venue number or see the website.
5 August 2007 (09.00 onwards)
A£5.00 (inc parking) C£Free

Folk & Local History Museums

Banbury Museum
Spiceball Park Road Banbury OX16 2PQ
Tel: 01295 259855
Museum on the history of Banbury and district. Plus innovative temporary exhibitions.

Oxfordshire Museum
Fletcher's House Park St Woodstock OX20 1SN
Tel: 01993 811456
An exhibition of the story of Oxfordshire and its people, from early times to the present day.

Gardens & Horticulture

Brook Cottage Garden

Well Lane Alkerton Banbury Oxfordshire
OX15 6NL
Tel: 01295 670303 / 670590
Fax: 01295 730362
www.brookcottagegarden.co.uk

[6mi NW Banbury, 0.5mi off A422 Banbury-Stratford upon Avon Rd. Limited on-site parking available]

This 4-acre hillside garden is set in exceptionally tranquil countryside. There is a wide variety of plants (some rare) to provide interest throughout the season. From the formal paved terrace (enclosed by weathered stonewalls and sharply symmetrical yew hedges), a wide sweep of steps form the start of a tour of imaginatively and richly planted areas of differing character. There are water and bog gardens, colour co-ordinating borders with themes of white/silver, purples/magentas and soft pinks/blues, a small gravel garden, handsome species trees and unusual flowering shrubs. There is a profusion of roses (species, old cultivars and modern) and clematis, from atrogenes to late summer flowering. The diversity of planting is supplemented by tender perennials in a variety of ornamental pots; while the handmade, designer wooden furniture offers resting places to pause and contemplate. Plants for sale. Evening, weekend and group visits by appointment only.
Easter Mon-31 Oct Mon-Fri (including Bank Hols) 09.00-18.00
A£4.00 C£Free OAPs £3.00

National Herb Centre

Banbury Road Warmington Banbury Oxfordshire
OX17 1DF
Tel: 01295 690999 Fax: 01295 690034
www.herbcentre.co.uk

[M40 from N J12 turn L at top of slip rd sign Gaydon 300yd. L onto B4100 about 6mi L at top of hill beyond the Church. M40 from S J11 turn L towards town centre straight across all roundabouts & pick up signs for Warmington. Passing General Foods factory on L & Tesco's on R about 800yd R at J with mini roundabouts, straight on for about 4.5mi on R. 5mi Banbury 11mi S of Warwick. Plenty of on-site parking available]

Visitors to the National Herb Centre can expect a warm welcome with a host of attractions for all the family. You can explore the Centre and sample the unique herbal flavours in our friendly Bistro and Deli Shop. Choose from over 500 varieties of culinary, medicinal and scented herbs. As well as plants, pots and other garden sundries, the shop offers a wide variety of gifts, books and cards. Many herbal lotions and toiletries, bouquets and confetti made from herbs and flowers.

Mon-Sat 9.00-17.30, Sun & Bank Hols 10.30-17.30

Discount Offer: 10% discount on all gift shop purchases (when you spend £10.00 or more)

Historical

Broughton Castle

Banbury Oxfordshire OX15 5EB
Tel: 01295 276070
www.broughtoncastle.com

[2mi W of Banbury on B4035 Shipston on Stour rd. Plenty of on-site parking available]

Historic fourteenth-century fortified manor house that was enlarged in the sixteenth century. Home of the family of Lord Saye and Sele for over 600 years, it contains its own medieval chapel, vaulted passages, fine panelling and splendid plaster ceilings and fireplaces. It was a centre of resistance to King Charles I during the Civil War and contains mementos of the period including armour and weapons. There are fine walled gardens with old roses, shrubs and herbaceous borders. The castle is surrounded by a broad moat and set in open parkland. It was a location for the filming of Shakespeare in Love and featured in many other films and TV programmes including the recently shown 'Elizabeth, The Virgin Queen' and Stephen Poliakoff's film 'Friends and Crocodiles.'

2 May-12 Sept Wed, Sun & Bank Hols 14.00-17.00, also Thurs in July-Aug. Groups welcome at any time by appointment

A£6.50 C£2.50 OAPs&Students(NUS/USI)£5.50

Discount Offer: Two for the Price of One

Mapledurham House and Watermill

Mapledurham Village Reading Oxfordshire RG4 7TR
Tel: 0118 972 3350 Fax: 0118 972 4016
www.mapledurham.co.uk

[Off A4074. Plenty of on-site parking available]

Mapledurham House, the historic home of the Blount family is an Elizabethan mansion full of history and intrigue, set in idyllic rural South Oxfordshire. Famous for the film, 'The Eagle has Landed,' the watermill is the last working watermill on the River Thames and still produces flour - excellent for bread making. Cream teas are served in the original Old Manor tea room together with a selection of handmade cakes to tempt you. Visitors may arrive by boat from near Caversham - a delightful cruise along a stunning stretch of river. We also have eleven self-catering cottages for visitors who wish to stay a little longer, full details of which can be found on our website.

Easter-end Sept Sat-Sun & Bank Hols from 14.00. Mid-week parties by arrangement
Please call for prices

Nuffield Place

Huntercombe, Nr Nettlebed Nuffield
Henley-On-Thames Oxfordshire RG9 5RY
Tel: 01491 641224
Built in 1914, the building retains the majority of the furniture and contents acquired by Lord and Lady Nuffield.

Literature & Libraries

Bodleian Library
Broad Street Oxford OX1 3BG
Tel: 01865 277000
The Divinity School and the Bodleian's exhibition room are open to the public, and receive a quarter of a million visitors each year.

Multicultural Museums

Pitt Rivers Museum
South Parks Road Oxford Oxfordshire OX1 3PP
Tel: 01865 270927
World famous museum of anthropology with a unique Victorian atmosphere. Audio tour provided by Sir David Attenborough.

Performing Arts

Creation Theatre Company
Oxford Oxfordshire
Tel: 01865 766266 (Box Office)
Fax: 01865 764677
www.creationtheatre.co.uk

[Oxford Castle, (City Centre, Summer). BMW Group Plant Oxford (Winter)]

"If you are a visitor in Oxford and you only have time for one cultural experience, make it this!" (The Oxford Times). Creation Theatre Company produces highly visual, energetic and accessible theatre in unusual spaces. Over the past 12 years, Creation has earned a reputation as

Oxfordshire's foremost producing theatre company, with their magical open-air productions of Shakespeare and many popular stories. Previous site-specific venues include an island in the River Cherwell, a ruined abbey, a beautiful arboretum, a car factory and a spectacular Mirror Tent. 2007 boasts Creation's most exciting season yet, with three fantastic open-air shows in the courtyards of the recently re-opened Oxford Castle (a visitor attraction in itself) and a return to the BMW Plant in the winter for a fabulous family Christmas show. These exceptional spaces provide the backdrop for a unique theatrical experience… come and see for yourself! "Energetic and imaginative" (The Independent)

Summer Season: June-Sept, Winter Season: Nov-Apr. Evenings 19.30/20.00, Matinees 14.30. Please visit website for more details
Prices range from £8.00-£22.50

Railways

Didcot Railway Centre

Didcot Oxfordshire OX11 7NJ
Tel: 01235 817200 Fax: 01235 510621
www.didcotrailwaycentre.org.uk
[On A4130 at Didcot Parkway Station signed from M4, J13 & A34]

Recreating the golden age of the Great Western Railway with a fine collection of over 20 steam locomotives, housed in the original engine shed, together with many passenger coaches and freight wagons. Other locomotives can be seen being overhauled in the Locomotive Works. There is a typical country station and signal box, and a recreation of Brunel's original broad gauge railway together with an impressive display of smaller items in the Relics Display. On Steamdays some of the locomotives come to life and you can ride the 1930s carriages and see the activities of a typical steam age depot. In 2007 we celebrate 75 years of the engine shed and 40 years since the Great Western Society saved it for preservation with a 40 75 Anniversary Gala on 5-7 May with many visiting steam engines and special displays.
All year Sat & Sun plus 10-18 Feb, 31 Mar-15 Apr, 26 May-3 June, 23 June-2 Sept 20-28 Oct & 27 Dec-1 Jan. Steamdays on Bank Hol weekends, all Sat-Sun 28 Apr-2 Sept, Wed 4 July-29 Aug, also 29-30 Sept 27-28 Oct, Day Out with Thomas 5-7 Oct & Thomas Santa Special 8-9, 14-16 & 21-24 Dec. Open 10.00-16.00 (Sat-Sun & Steamdays Mar-Oct 10.00-17.00)
A£4.00-£9.50 C£3.00-£7.50 OAPs£3.50-£8.00 (depending on event)

Discount Offer: Two for the Price of One

Pendon Museum of Miniature Landscape and Transport

High Street Long Wittenham Abingdon Oxfordshire OX14 4QD
Tel: 01865 407365
www.pendonmuseum.com
[Rail: Didcot. Please see website for further details. Limited on-site parking available]

Pendon Museum at Long Wittenham in Oxfordshire (near Abingdon and Didcot) is a delightful museum devoted to portraying parts of rural England as they were in the 1920s and 30s - in particular, it reflects how life was influenced by the transport infrastructure of the period. It achieves this through the medium of modelling - accurate, authentic and carried out to the highest standard at a 1:76 scale. Literally art in three dimensions, the models are built by a number of dedicated volunteers. If you are interested in rural social history, model railways, or are simply appreciative of superb craftsmanship, Pendon is well worth a visit. Open to the public at weekends, on bank holidays and on Wednesdays in school holidays. A special exhibition - "Go Great Western - Holiday Haunts" opens March 31. It will be a nostalgic look back at how people enjoyed their holidays over seventy years ago.

Jan-2 Dec Sat & Sun 14.00-17.30, 24-25 Feb, 6-9 Apr, 5-7 & 26-28 May, 21-22 July, 25-27 Aug, 13-14 Sept, Bank Hols & Special Event weekends 11.00-17.30, 14 Feb, 30 May, 1, 8, 15, 22 & 29 Aug & 24 Oct Wed 11.00-17.30. Closed 4-29 Dec

A£5.00 C(7-15)£3.00 C(0-6)£Free OAPs£4.00, Family Ticket (A2+C3) £16.00

Social History Museums

River and Rowing Museum

Mill Meadows Henley-on-Thames RG9 1BF
Tel: 01491 415600 Fax: 01491 415601
www.rrm.co.uk

[By Car: follow signs for Henley, then Museum & Mill Meadows, off A4130 Oxford to Maidenhead rd in Henley. Bus: regular bus services from High Wycombe, Marlow, Reading, Thame, Watlington & Lane End. Rail: hourly services from London (Paddington), Reading & Maidenhead. Henley station 5min walk. 3h free car-parking for visitors]

Visit the award-winning River & Rowing Museum with its stunning architecture and unique interpretation of the River Thames, the riverside town of Henley and the sport of rowing. History is brought to life with interactive displays and fascinating exhibits. Special exhibitions, family activities and events are held throughout the year and its Terrace Café offers excellent food in distinctive surroundings. In a spectacular permanent attraction, EH Shepard's illustrations from The Wind in the Willows are brought to life in an enchanting recreation of the classic book. You can walk along the river bank, through the wild wood, see into Badger's house and visit all 12 chapters of this delightful adventure story. Using theatrical and audio techniques, superb models, lighting and sets you are magically transported into the world of Ratty, Mole, Badger and of course, Mr Toad.

1 May-31 Aug daily 10.00-17.30, 1 Sept-30 Apr daily 10.00-17.00. Closed 24-25, 31 Dec-1 Jan
Museum Galleries only: A£3.50 C(under3)£Free C£2.50 Concessions£3.00, Family Ticket (4 people) £11.50, (5 people) £13.00, (6 people) £14.00. Galleries & Wind in the Willows. A£7.00 C(under3)£Free C£5.00 Concessions£6.00 Family Ticket (4 people) £18.00, (5 people) £23.00, (6 people) £25.00

Stately Homes

Blenheim Palace

Woodstock Oxfordshire OX20 1PX
Tel: 08700 602080
Birthplace of Sir Winston Churchill, with lake and formal gardens.

Kingston Bagpuize House

Kingston Bagpuize Abingdon OX13 5AX
Tel: 01865 820259 Fax: 01865 821659
www.kingstonbagpuizehouse.org.uk
[5.5mi W of Abingdon A415. Plenty of on-site parking available]

A Family home, this beautiful house originally built in the 1660s was remodelled in the early 1770s in red brick with stone facings. It has a fine-cantilevered staircase, well-proportioned panelled rooms with some good furniture and pictures. Surrounded by mature parkland the gardens, including large herbaceous border, shrub border and woodland garden contain a notable collection of trees, shrubs, perennials and bulbs planted for year round interest. A raised terrace walk leads to an eighteenth-century panelled pavilion with views of the house and gardens.

House & Garden: 4-5 & 18-19 Feb, 4-5 Mar, 1-2 & 8-10 Apr, 6-8 & 27-29 May, 3-4 June, 1-2 & 15-16 July, 5-6 & 26-28 Aug, 2-3 &16-17 Sept, Garden only: 1, 8, 15, 22, Feb, 15 Mar, 19 Apr, 17 May, 21 June, 19 July, 16 Aug, 20 Sept
House & Garden: A£5.00 Concession£4.50 C£2.50. Garden only: £3.00 C(under16)£Free

Stonor Park

Stonor Henley-On-Thames RG9 6HF
Tel: 01491 638587 Fax: 01491 639348
www.stonor.com

[Between M4 & M40 on B480. Approx 5mi N of Henley. 15min from M40 & 25min from J8/9 M4 Rail: Henley on Thames. On-site parking available]

A hidden treasure near London, "possibly the best setting for a country house in England". Visit Stonor, the home of Lord and Lady Camoys in the beautiful Chiltern countryside. This magnificent house set in 200 acres of parkland, has been home to the Stonor family for 850 years. Tour the house, where guides will be on-hand to unravel the fascinating history of this family and the house. Full of treasures, wonderful paintings, bronzes, furniture, tapestries and ceramics. 500 year-old books, (some illegal to own). Learn of the family struggle to hold true to the Catholic faith during the reformation. Visit the thirteenth-century chapel once occupied by some of Cromwell's army. Take refreshment and visit the souvenir shop in the mediaeval hall dating back to 1180. Stroll the formal Italianate gardens, see the pagan circle, picnic and walk in the park where fallow deer roam freely. Due to the location of the rooms, we are sorry; the tour is unsuitable for physically disabled visitors. Dogs permitted in the park only (and on a lead).
1 Apr-16 Sep: Sun (Closed Mon-Sat). July-Aug Wed only. Also open Bank Hols, 17 Apr & 28 Aug. Pre-booked private groups can be accommodated Tue & Thur as well as the normal open days Sun & Wed during season. Gardens: 13.00-17.30. House: 14.00-17.30. Last tour at 16.30. The house can host weddings, events & filming throughout the year - please see website for info
House & Gardens: A£7.00 1st C(5-16yrs)£3.00, 2 or more C£Free. Gardens only: A£3.50 1st C(5-16yrs)£1.50, 2 or more C£Free. C(under5)£Free

Upton House and Gardens

Upton Banbury Oxfordshire OX15 6HT
Tel: 01295 670266 Fax: 01295 671144
www.nationaltrust.org.uk
[On A422 (between Stratford-upon-Avon & Banbury). Plenty of on-site parking available]

The impressive mansion (built in the seventeenth century on an earlier site) was remodelled in the 1920s by the Second Viscount Bearsted, son of the founder of Shell Oil and later the company's Chairman. One of the great collectors of his age, he filled the house with stunning collections of art, tapestries and porcelain, and laid out magnificent gardens in the valleys below. Amongst the outstanding collection of English and Old Master paintings presented over three floors are works by Hogarth, Raeburn, Stubbs, El Greco, Bosch, Metsu, Canaletto and Breugel, whilst the porcelain collection includes fine examples of Sevres, Worcester tableware and figures by Bow, Chelsea and Derby. The magnificent Grade II gardens include wide lawns, woodland, a kitchen garden, dramatic terraces, water gardens, colourful borders, ornamental pools, orchards and the National Collection of Asters.
House: 3 Mar-31 Oct Sat-Wed 1200-17.00, 3 Nov-16 Dec Sat-Sun 12.00-16.00. Garden, Restaurant & Shop: 3 Mar-31 Oct Sat-Wed 11.00-17.00 (Aug: Gardens, Restaraunt & Shop only, Thu-Fri 11.00-17.00), 3 Nov-16 Dec Sat-Sun 12.00-16.00 (House Ground Floor & Upper Gardens only). Open Good Fri. Entry to House by timed tickets on Bank Hols
House & Gardens: A£8.00 C£4.00, Family Ticket £20.00. Gardens only: A£4.80 C£2.40. NT Members £Free. Group rate (15+): £6.20. Guided tours available by prior arrangement

Discount Offer: Two for the Price of One

Victorian Era

Cogges Manor Farm Museum

Church Lane Witney Oxfordshire OX28 3LA
Tel: 01993 772602 Fax: 01993 703056
www.cogges.org

[0.5mi SE of Witney off A40. Plenty of on-site parking available]

A special place to visit for all the family. Why not visit Cogges Manor Farm Museum and find out what life was like for the Victorians of rural Oxfordshire? Visitors take a step back in time when they enter the beautiful farmstead with its original Cotswold buildings and displays about farming in years gone by. In the Manor House you can talk to the Victorian maids and find out what their lives would have been like. Watch as they cook on the old range and if you are lucky, you might be able to sample some of their fresh baking. Upstairs, visitors can explore the history of the house and experience the activities room where children can try on replica Victorian clothes and play with the replica toys and games.

3 Apr-28 Oct, Mon-Fri 10.30-17.30 & Bank Hol Mon 12.00-17.30 (Oct 16.00), Sat & Sun 12.00-17.30 (Oct 16.00). Closed Good Fri
A£5.70 C(3-16)£2.45 C(under 3)£Free Concessions£4.85, Family Ticket (A2+C2) £14.50. Group rates available when pre-booked

Wildlife & Safari Parks

Cotswold Wildlife Park

Bradwell Grove Burford Oxfordshire OX18 4JP
Tel: 01993 823006 Fax: 01993 823807
www.cotswoldwildlifepark.co.uk

[2.5mi S of A40 on A361. Plenty of free on-site parking available]

The 160-acre landscaped zoological park, surrounding a Gothic-style Manor House, has a varied collection of animals from around the world. Many of these are endangered in the wild and are part of an international breeding programme, including Asiatic lions, Amur leopards and red pandas. There is a large Reptile House, Tropical House, children's farmyard and the ever-popular penguins and meerkats. Visitors are surprised and delighted at the beautiful gardens and wide range of planting to be seen as they walk around the Park, from the formal herbaceous borders and parterre by the Manor House to the exotic bananas, Daturas and Canna lilies in the walled garden. Other attractions include an adventure playground, animal brass-rubbing centre in the Manor House and the narrow-gauge railway which runs daily during the summer months, limited winter runs. The large self-service cafeteria serves hot and cold meals and snacks. There are also many picnicking areas and a well-stocked gift shop.

All year daily from 10.00. Closed 25 Dec
A£9.50 C(3-16)&OAPs£7.00. Group rates (20+): A£8.00 C£5.50 OAPs£6.00 (must be pre-booked). Season tickets (valid for 12 months) A£47.50 C&OAPs£35.00, Family Ticket (A2+C2) £155.00 - extra C£32.50

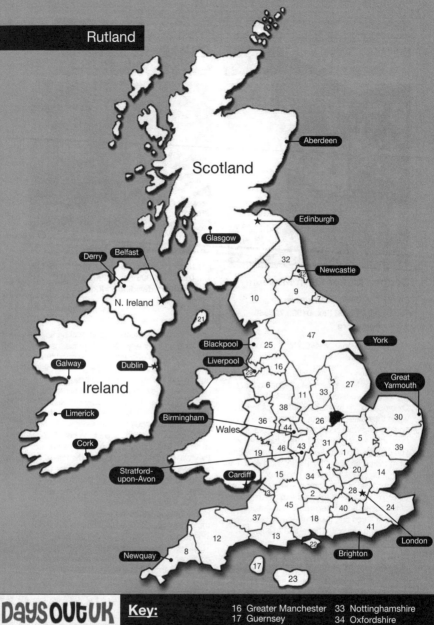

Rutland

Aberdeen

Scotland

Edinburgh

Glasgow

Newcastle

Derry
Belfast

N. Ireland

32

10

9

7

21

Blackpool

25

47

York

Liverpool

Galway
Dublin

16

Ireland

29

6

11

33

27

Great
Yarmouth

Limerick

38

30

Birmingham

36

44

26

5

39

Cork

Wales

19

46

43

31

1

Stratford-
upon-Avon

Cardiff

15

34

4

20

14

13

2

28

London

45

40

24

37

18

41

12

13

22

Brighton

Newquay

8

17

23

DAYS OUT UK
The place to look for places to go

Birds, Butterflies & Bees

Butterfly Farm and Aquatic Centre

Sykes Lane Car Park North Shore Oakham Rutland
Tel: 01780 460515
5,000 sq. ft. of walk-through jungle with free-flying butterflies and tropical birds. Ponds with Koi Carp and terrapins.

Folk & Local History Museums

Rutland County Museum

Catmos Street Oakham Rutland LE15 6HW
Tel: 01572 758440 Fax: 01572 758445
www.rutland.gov.uk/museum

[Nr town centre on A6003 signposted]

The museum tells the story of England's smallest county. The Welcome to Rutland gallery is a guide to the history of Rutland, and leads into displays of local archaeology, history and rural life collection. The site is remarkable as the museum is set in the old riding school of the Rutland Fencibles, a volunteer cavalry regiment around 1794. Changing exhibitions of the work of local artists are an added attraction.
All year Mon-Sat 10.30-17.00, Sun 14.00-16.00. Closed Good Fri, 25-26 Dec & 1 Jan
Admission Free

Gardens & Horticulture

Barnsdale Gardens

The Avenue Exton Oakham Rutland LE15 8AH
Tel: 01572 813200 Fax: 01572 813346
www.barnsdalegardens.co.uk
[Turn off A606 Oakham / Stamford rd at Barnsdale Lodge Hotel, then 1mi on L. Parking for cars & coaches free. Special parking spaces for disabled & people bringing dogs, (dogs not allowed in gardens). In event of car park filling up, spaces allocated for people with dogs will be used if needed. Tell us in advance you are bringing your dog & we will do our best to reserve parking for you]
Barnsdale Gardens are familiar to millions of BBC viewers as the home of Gardeners' World. The Gardens comprise 37 individual smaller gardens and features that all blend together by the linking borders into one 8 acre garden set in the heart of the beautiful Rutland countryside. There is not only a wealth of different plants to come and see in many different combinations but also a wealth of practical ideas for any garden with all gardeners, experienced or novice, leaving totally inspired. After strolling around the garden, why not relax in our friendly, licensed coffee shop that serves a very appetising range of hot and cold food and drink. Our large specialist nursery sells a wide range of choice and unusual garden plants, many initially propagated from the gardens. With our gift shop selling a range of exclusive Barnsdale gifts, all in all this makes for a memorable visit.
Garden, Gift Shop & Nursery: All year daily Mar-May 09.00-17.00, June-Aug 09.00-19.00, Sept-Oct 09.00-17.00, Nov-Feb 10.00-16.00. Closed 24 & 25 Dec. Coffee Shop: Mar-Oct daily 10.00-17.00 (stop serving 16.30), Nov-Feb daily 10.00-16.00 (stop serving 15.30)
A£6.00 Concessions£5.00 C£2.00, Family Ticket (A2+C3) £15.00. Season Tickets A£17.00 A(2) £30.00. Group rate (10+): A£4.50

Normanton Church Museum

Normanton South Shore Rutland Water Rutland
Tel: 01572 653026
Tells the story of this ancient valley.

Oakham Castle

Market Place Oakham Rutland LE15 6DX
Tel: 01572 758440
An examples of domestic Norman architecture.

Performing Arts

Stamford Shakespeare Festival

Rutland Open Air Theatre Tolethorpe Hall
Little Casterton Stamford Rutland PE9 4BH
Tel: 01780 754381/756133
Fax: 01780 481954
www.stamfordshakespeare.co.uk

[Just off A1, 90mi N of London. From Stamford take A6121 (Bourne Rd), after 2mi take first L signposted Tolethorpe, follow Heritage & RAC Shakespeare at Tolethorpe signs. On-site parking]

The finest open air theatre venue in Europe with 600 upholstered seats under a permanent covered auditorium, only the stage is in the open air in an enchanted wooded glade. Described in a national journal as one of England's premier alfresco venues. The theatre's historic Tolethorpe Hall houses a high class pre-performance restaurant (advance booking essential), seating up to 90 in two elegant dining rooms, a theatre bar, and a large new orangery used for serving interval coffee. There is a picnic area overlooking classic English parkland and free on site coach and car park. All facilities are within a minutes walk of each other on a compact site in an outstandingly beautiful garden setting. Tolethorpe attracts more than 30,000 worldwide patrons annually, many regular visitors. There is wheelchair access and disabled toilets. For a full colour brochure with booking details send SAE to the above address.

June-Aug, performances Mon-Sat 20.00, Grounds open for picnics from 17.00. 2007 Plays: 'The Importance of being Earnest', 'The Taming of the Shrew' & Antony and Cleopatra! please call box office on 01780 756133 for details/brochure or please visit our website
Seat prices: Mon-Tue £11.00, Wed-Thur £12.00, Fri £14.00, Sat £16.00, Preview Nights £9.00. Concessions £1.00 off except Fri-Sat. Group rates available on request

Railways

Rutland Railway Museum

Cottesmore Iron Ore Mines Sidings, Ashwell Road Cottesmore Oakham Rutland LE15 7BX
Tel: 01572 813203
The museum has an extensive collection of industrial locomotives and rolling stock.

Sport & Recreation

Rutland Water

Sykes Lane Empingham Rutland LE15 8PX
Tel: 01572 770651
One of the largest man-made reservoirs in Europe located in England's smallest county.

Stately Homes

Burghley House

Stamford Rutland PE9 3JY
Tel: 01780 752451
This magnificent house is famous for its remarkable collection of artworks.
House: 30 Mar-26 Oct daily.

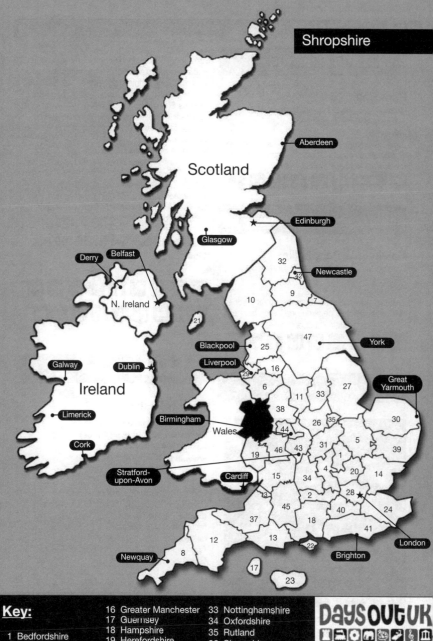

Shropshire

Scotland

Aberdeen

Edinburgh

Glasgow

Derry
Belfast

N. Ireland

Newcastle

32
42

10
9
7

21

Blackpool
25
47
York

Galway
Dublin

Liverpool
16

Ireland

Limerick

29
6
11
33
27
Great Yarmouth

Birmingham
38
26
35
30

Cork
Wales
44
31
5
39

19
46
43
1
20
14

Stratford-upon-Avon
Cardiff
15
4
28
London

34
2
24

45
40
41

Newquay
37
18
Brighton

8
12
13
22

17
23

Key:

1 Bedfordshire	16 Greater Manchester
2 Berkshire	17 Guernsey
3 Bristol	18 Hampshire
4 Buckinghamshire	19 Herefordshire
5 Cambridgeshire	20 Hertfordshire
6 Cheshire	21 Isle Of Man
7 Cleveland	22 Isle Of Wight
8 Cornwall	23 Jersey
9 County Durham	24 Kent
10 Cumbria	25 Lancashire
11 Derbyshire	26 Leicestershire
12 Devon	27 Lincolnshire
13 Dorset	28 London
14 Essex	29 Merseyside
15 Gloucestershire	30 Norfolk
	31 Northamptonshire
	32 Northumberland

33 Nottinghamshire
34 Oxfordshire
35 Rutland
36 Shropshire
37 Somerset
38 Staffordshire
39 Suffolk
40 Surrey
41 Sussex
42 Tyne & Wear
43 Warwickshire
44 West Midlands
45 Wiltshire
46 Worcestershire
47 Yorkshire

Park Hall

Burma Road Park Hall Whittington Oswestry
Shropshire SY11 4AS
Tel: 01691 671123
Pony grooming, new milking parlour, adventure
woodland, toy tractor circuit, electric cars, lan-
drovers for kids and quads.

Hawkstone Park Follies

Weston-under-Redcastle Near Shrewsbury
Shropshire SY4 5UY
Tel: 01939 200611
Created in the eighteenth century by the Hill
family, Hawkstone became one of the greatest
historic parklands in Europe.

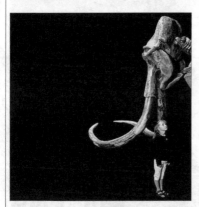

Secret Hills - The Shropshire Hills Discovery Centre

School Lane Craven Arms Shropshire SY7 9RS
Tel: 01588 676000 Fax: 01588 676030
www.shropshireonline.gov.uk/discover.nsf

*[On A49 in Craven Arms. 20mi S of Shrewsbury,
7mi N of Ludlow. Plenty of on-site parking avail-
able]*

Unfold the secrets of the Shropshire Hills in an
amazing grass roofed building. Enjoyable and
informative displays explore the heritage, wildlife
and traditions of this special area. Have fun in
the simulated hot air balloon ride and see the
famous Shropshire Mammoth. Admission to the
Centre is free (although there is an admission
charge to the exhibition) and visitors have free
access to 25 acres of attractive meadows slop-
ing down to the River Onny.
*All year Apr-Oct daily 10.00-17.30, Nov-Mar Tue-
Sun 10.00-16.30*
A£4.50 C£3.00 Concessions£4.00, Family
Ticket (A2+C3) £13.50. Group rates: A£4.00
C£1.00 Concessions£3.75. Prices stated are for
exhibition only

**Discount Offer: Two for the Price of
One**

Ludlow Festival

Ludlow Shropshire SY8 1AY
Tel: 01584 872150 (Box Office)
Fax: 01584 877673
www.ludlowfestival.co.uk

[Held in various venues throughout Ludlow]

For 2007, Ludlow Festival presents 'The
Comedy of Errors' by William Shakespeare
directed by Glen Walford and set inside the
medieval castle. Additionally, there will be a wide
range of musical and literary events and talks by
Andrew Motion, George Alagiah and George
Galloway. Music includes lunchtime concerts by
the Guillami Sting Quartet, Barber of Seville for
opera lovers and The Glenn Miller Orchestra led
by Ray McVay. The last night concert will feature
tributes to Robbie Williams and Kylie Minogue
and finish with the traditional Grand Firework
Display.
*23 June-8 July 2007. Box office opens in May.
General enquiries: 01584 875070 Email:
admin@ludlowfestival.co.uk*
Prices vary according to event attended

West Mid Show

The Showground Berwick Road Shrewsbury
Shropshire SY1 2PF
Tel: 0870 957 6444 Fax: 0870 957 6445
www.westmidshow.co.uk

*[Follow AA signs from any approach rd into
Shrewsbury. Free shuttle buses from Shrewsbury
Station. Plenty of on-site parking available]*

The West Mid Show is one of the major 2-day
shows in the UK. It's an excellent day out for
the whole family, with a varied programme of
events taking place. This year, the headline
attractions in the main ring will be the
Household Cavalry and the Bolddog freestyle
motocross display team. There is an excellent
range of trade stands with something for all the
family. Food Hall, 'Shropshire on Show' and a
wide range of agricultural machinery. There will
also be some of the finest livestock in the UK,
including cattle, horses and sheep.
Showjumping in the main ring on Saturday.
23-24 June 2007
In Advance A£10.00 C£2.00, Family Ticket
(2A+3C)£20.00

Ludlow Museum

Castle Street Ludlow Shropshire SY8 1AS
Tel: 01584 875384
Visit the fascinating museum and discover why
the rocks of Ludlow gained this reputation.

Mythstories Museum

The Morgan Library Aston Street Wem
Shropshire SY4 5AU
Tel: 01939 235500
Offers myths, legends and fables from around
the world and especially from Shropshire.
Apr-Oct Sun-Thur

Radbrook Culinary Museum

Radbrook College Radbrook Road Shrewsbury
Shropshire SY3 9BL

Tel: 01743 232686
A unique collection of domestic utensils and
examples of household crafts covering the late
Victorian and Edwardian era.

Shrewsbury Museum & Art Gallery

Barker Street Shrewsbury Shropshire SY1 1QH
Tel: 01743 361196
Major displays of the archaeology, geology, pre-
history, ceramics and local history of the region.

Heritage & Industrial

Ironbridge Gorge Museums

Coalbrookdale Telford Shropshire TF8 7DQ
Tel: 01952 884391 Fax: 01952 884391
www.ironbridge.org.uk

*[J4 M54, signposted. Parking available for visitors
with disabilities in marked bays close to entrance
of most sites. Central Ironbridge car parks are
'Pay & Display' but are free to Orange Badge*

holders. All Museum-owned car parks are free]

It has taken us over 200 years to create the perfect day out. The Ironbridge Gorge is one of Britain's great World Heritage Sites and is home to ten superb attractions set within six square miles of beautiful scenery. These include the world famous Iron Bridge, Blists Hill Victorian Town - where you can change your money into token Victorian coins to spend in the shops, Coalport China Museum - once one of the country's finest porcelain manufacturers, Jackfield Tile Museum - where you can now see a unique collection from the former world centre of the decorative tile industry, and Enginuity, a hands on interactive Design and Technology Centre. A great family day out.

Main sites: All year daily 10.00-17.00. Closed 24, 25 Dec & 1 Jan. Some sites close or reduce their opening hours in winter, please call for details

Passport tickets to all attractions: A£14.00 C&Students(NUS/USI)£9.50 OAPs£12.50, Family Ticket (A2+C3) £46.00. Tickets offer unlimited visits to all ten museums for 12 months. Group rates available on request. Discounts are not available on individual Passport Tickets. Prices valid until March 2008

Historical

Attingham Park

Attingham Park Shrewsbury Shropshire
SY4 4TP
Tel: 01743 708123
An elegant Neo-classical mansion of the late eighteenth century with magnificent state rooms, built for the 1st Lord Berwick.

Benthall Hall

Benthall Broseley Shropshire TF12 5RX
Tel: 01952 882159
Situated on a plateau above the gorge of the Severn, this sixteenth-century stone house has mullioned and transomed windows.

Dudmaston Hall

Quatt Nr Bridgnorth Shropshire WV15 6QN
Tel: 01746 780866 Fax: 01746 780744
www.nationaltrust.org.uk

[4mi SE of Bridgnorth on A442. Rail: Nearest station Hampton Loade, Severn Valley Railway 1.5mi, Kidderminster 10mi. Bus: 297 Bridgnorth-Kidderminster. Parking available all year at Hampton Loade car park]

Built in the late seventeenth century, Dudmaston Hall is a beautiful mansion house set in a lakeside garden. The house contains a fabulous collection of modern art, Dutch paintings and botanical drawings. Dudmaston Hall and Estate does not stand still, since Charles Babbage created the central heating system, innovation has been part of the character of the estate. More recent innovations include award-winning forestry techniques and environment heating on the estate. There are also miles of walks around the estate through the woods and beside the River Severn. Stiles inspired by modern designs, provide a point of interest throughout several of the walks. There are also links with the Severn Valley Railway at Hampton Loade.

1 Apr-27 Sept, House: Tue, Wed & Sun 14.00-17.30. Garden: Sun-Wed 12.00-18.00. Shop: Tue, Wed & Sun 13.00-17.30. Tea-room: Sun-Wed 11.30-17.30. Estate open daily. Open Bank Hol Mons

House & Garden: A£5.80 C£2.90 C(under5)£Free, Family Ticket £14.50. Group rate (15+): £4.60. Garden only: A£4.60 C£2.50 C(under5)£Free Family Ticket£11.50 Groups (15+) £3.50. NT Members £Free. Join the National Trust when you visit and you will be refunded your admission charge

Ludlow Castle

Castle Square Ludlow Shropshire SY8 1AY
Tel: 01584 873355
www.ludlowcastle.com

[0.75mi from A49, in centre of Ludlow, rd runs out at Castle]

Ludlow Castle dates from about 1086 and was greatly extended as ownership passed through the de Lacy and Mortimer families to the Crown. In 1473 Edward IV sent the Prince of Wales and his brother to Ludlow and Ludlow Castle became a seat of government with the establishment there of the Council for Wales and the Marches. Entry to shop is free of charge. Dogs welcome on leads. Audio guide available.
Apr-July & Sept daily 10.00-17.00, Aug 10.00-19.00, Oct-Dec & Feb-Mar 10.00-16.00, Jan Weekends only 10.00-16.00. Closed 25 Dec also 27 June & 4 July from 12.00, 30 June from 12.30, 8 & 9 July & 5, 6, 10 Sept closed all day Castle: A£4.00 C(under6)£Free C(6-16)£2.00 Concessions£3.50, Family Ticket £11.00. School parties by arrangement. All children must be accompanied by an adult

Shrewsbury Castle and Shropshire Regimental Museum

Castle Street Shrewsbury Shropshire SY1 2AT
Tel: 01743 358516
The museum is housed within the main surviving building of Shrewsbury Castle.

Weston Park

Weston-under-Lizard Shifnal TF11 8LE
Tel: 01952 852100
Built in 1671, this fine house stands in a vast park designed by Capability Brown.

Nature & Conservation Parks

Carding Mill Valley and Long Mynd

Chalet Pavilion Shropshire SY6 6JG
Tel: 01694 723068
An extensive area of historic upland heath, with stunning views across the Shropshire and Cheshire plains and Black Mountains.

Railways

Telford Steam Railway

Bridge Road Horsehay Telford TF4 2NF
Tel: 07765 858348
A preserved railway operated by a small and friendly team of volunteers.
Apr-Sep: Sun & Bank Hols only

Roman Era

Wroxeter Roman City

Wroxeter Shrewsbury Shropshire SY5 6PH
Tel: 01743 761330
The largest excavated Roman British city to have escaped development.

Theme & Adventure Parks

Mickey Miller's Playbarn and Maize Maze

Oakfield Farm Watling St Craven Arms SY7 8DX
Tel: 01588 640403
Massive indoor play area and maize maze for the whole family.

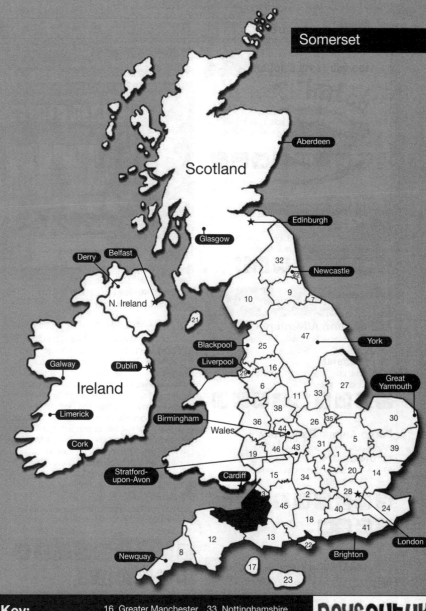

Somerset

Scotland

Aberdeen

Edinburgh

Glasgow

Newcastle

Derry Belfast

N. Ireland

York

Blackpool

Liverpool

Galway Dublin

Ireland

Great Yarmouth

Limerick

Birmingham

Wales

Cork

Stratford-upon-Avon

Cardiff

Norfolk

London

Newquay

Brighton

Key:

1 Bedfordshire	16 Greater Manchester	33 Nottinghamshire
2 Berkshire	17 Guernsey	34 Oxfordshire
3 Bristol	18 Hampshire	35 Rutland
4 Buckinghamshire	19 Herefordshire	36 Shropshire
5 Cambridgeshire	20 Hertfordshire	37 Somerset
6 Cheshire	21 Isle Of Man	38 Staffordshire
7 Cleveland	22 Isle Of Wight	39 Suffolk
8 Cornwall	23 Jersey	40 Surrey
9 County Durham	24 Kent	41 Sussex
10 Cumbria	25 Lancashire	42 Tyne & Wear
11 Derbyshire	26 Leicestershire	43 Warwickshire
12 Devon	27 Lincolnshire	44 West Midlands
13 Dorset	28 London	45 Wiltshire
14 Essex	29 Merseyside	46 Worcestershire
15 Gloucestershire	30 Norfolk	47 Yorkshire
	31 Northamptonshire	
	32 Northumberland	

Abbeys

Bath Abbey

Abbey Churchyard Bath BA1 1LT
Tel: 01225 422462
Fifteenth-century abbey church, built on site
where Edgar was crowned first King of England
in 973.

Cleeve Abbey

Washford Watchet Somerset TA23 0PS

Tel: 01984 640377
The Cistercian abbey was founded at the end of
the twelfth century and is now a ruin.

Animal Attractions

Animal Farm Adventure Park

Red Road Berrow Burnham-On-Sea Somerset
TA8 2RW
Tel: 01278 751628
All-weather play, friendly pets and Somerset's
biggest indoor slides.

Ferne Animal Sanctuary

Wambrook Chard Somerset TA20 3DH
Tel: 01460 65214
51 acres of lovely Somerset countryside with
over 300 animals.

Archaeology

Glastonbury Lake Village Museum

The Tribunal 9 High Street Glastonbury
Somerset BA6 9DP
Tel: 01458 832954
Collection of late prehistoric antiquities from
Glastonbury Lake Village, one of Europe's most
famous archaeological sites.

Arts, Crafts & Textiles

Holburne Museum of Art

Great Pulteney Street Bath Bristol and North
East Somerset BA2 4DB
Tel: 01225 466669 Fax: 01225 333121
www.bath.ac.uk/holburne

[Rail: Bath Spa. Limited on-site parking available]

The Holburne Museum is a beautiful building in
its own grounds at the top of the most impressive street in Georgian England. It houses
Bath's most exciting display of fine and decorative art assembled around the collection of Sir
William Holburne. Discover exquisite treasures
and old master paintings. The Holburne has a
busy exhibition, education and events calendar;
please see our website or contact us for further
details. Exhibitions for 2007 include: A Matter of
Life and Death, Drawing Comparisons:
Highlights from the Oppé Collection, An exhibition in partnership with Tate.
*All year daily Tue-Sat 10.00-17.00 Sun & Bank
Hols 11.00-17.00*
Admission varies with the temporary exhibition
programme, please check in advance

Museum of East Asian Art

12 Bennett Street Bath Somerset BA1 2QJ
Tel: 01225 464640
A wonderful insight into the art and cultures of
China, Japan, Korea and South-East Asia.

Caverns & Caves

Cheddar Caves and Gorge

Cheddar Somerset BS27 3QF
Tel: 01934 742343 Fax: 01934 744637
www.cheddarcaves.co.uk

[On A371 between Weston-Super-Mare & Wells. Follow brown signs on A38 from M5 J22. Plenty of on-site parking available]

Cheddar Caves and Gorge - 300 million years in the making. Limestone cliffs towering 450ft above a gorge 3 miles long. Underground cathedrals of stalactites and stalagmites, beautifully lit. The terrible secrets of our ancestors, who came here 40,000 years ago...The Gorge is an SSSI and a Special Conservation Area because of its karst limestone cliffs, beautiful caves and the rare plants and animals that live here. Six caves are scheduled as Ancient Monuments because they reveal the early history of our ancestors. Your Caves and Gorge Explorer ticket gives you first hand experience of this exciting world of nature, culture and adventure… and pays for our work to conserve and interpret Cheddar's geology, ecology and prehistory for you and future generations to enjoy. Look up and wonder….
All year daily, Sept-June 10.30-17.00, July & Aug 10.00-17.30
Please call or check website for admission prices

Discount Offer: £1.00 off per person

Wookey Hole Caves

Wookey Hole Wells Somerset BA5 1BB
Tel: 01749 672243 Fax: 01749 677749
www.wookey.co.uk

[J22 M5, A39, A38, A371. Plenty of on-site parking available]

Britain's most spectacular caves and legendary home of the infamous Witch of Wookey. The nineteenth-century Papermill houses a variety of fascinating attractions including a Cave Museum, Victorian Penny Arcade, Magical Mirror Maze, Haunted Corridor of Crazy Mirrors and Wizard's Castle play area. See paper being made in Britain's only surviving handmade papermill. Enjoy puppet theatre shows and live entertaining family shows, learn the art of magic with lessons in our Wizards Theatre (shows most weekends and school holidays). Relax in our Enchanted Fairy Garden, visit King Kong or stroll around the Valley of the Dinosaurs. Explore the Wookey Gorge and the wonderful views from the Mendip hills with our easy to follow Nature Trails. Self-service restaurant, gift shops, picnic areas and ample free parking. Please note, it may sometimes be necessary to close or restrict any attractions without prior notice.
All year daily Apr-Oct 10.00-17.00, Nov-Mar 10.30-16.00. Closed Christmas Day
A£12.50 C£9.50, Family Ticket £38.00

Discount Offer: Two for the Price of One

Costume & Jewellery Museums

Museum of Costume

Assembly Rooms Bennett Street Bath BA1 2QH
Tel: 01225 477173 Fax: 01225 477743
www.museumofcostume.co.uk

[Top of city just off Circus. Rail: Bath]

The Museum of Costume is one of the largest and most prestigious collections of original fashionable dress for men, women and children covering the late sixteenth century to the present day. It is housed in Bath's famous eighteenth-century Assembly Rooms designed by John Wood the Younger in 1771. Audio-guides in seven languages included in price. Special Exhibitions for 2007: 'Pick of the Bunch', celebrating Floral Frocks 17 July-27 August, in the ball room, Continuing; 'Pockets of history' until 2 September 2007, 'Corsets Uncovered' and 'Fashion and Bath'. See website for details.
All year daily Jan-Feb 11.00-16.00, Mar-Oct 11.00-17.00, Nov-Dec 11.00-16.00. Closed 25-26 Dec. Last exit one hour after closing
A£6.75C(6-16)£4.75 OAPs£5.75, Family Ticket (A2+C4) £19.00. Group rates (for 20+) available on request. Saver Ticket to Museum of Costume & Roman Baths A£13.50 C£8.00 OAPs£11.50 Family Ticket (A2+C4) £38.00

Country Parks & Estates

Yeovil Country Park

Yeovil Somerset

Tel: 01935 462462
88-acre country park including wooded hillsides, wetland habitats, waterfalls, lakes and grassland. Includes the areas also known as Ninesprings, Penn Hill Park, Summerhouse Hill, Wyndham Hill and Riverside Walk.

Festivals & Shows

Bath and West Showground

Shepton Mallet Somerset BA4 6QN
Tel: 01749 822200 Fax: 01749 823169
www.bathandwest.com

[A371. Rail: Castle Cary Station. Plenty of on-site parking available]

The Bath & West Showground offers visitors a huge range of events all year round. With several Exhibition Halls ranging from 500 to 2,787 square-metres in size, the showground hosts a wide variety of events from the smallest meeting to major conferences, antique fairs, dog shows, and national exhibitions, with plenty to interest people of all ages. All the facilities are based on the 240-acre showground - complete with car parks, toilets and permanent restaurant facilities. Major events for 2007 include 'The Bike Show: Southwest' (May 5th and 6th), 'The Royal Bath & West Show' (May 30th-June 2nd), 'The National Amateur Gardening Show' (August 31st - September 2nd), 'The Dairy Show' (October 3rd) and 'The Royal Smithfield Christmas Fair' (November 30th - December 1st). For full details of all events please call or visit our website.
Please visit our website for opening times

Bridgwater Guy Fawkes Carnival

Bridgwater Somerset TA6 5EJ
www.bridgwatercarnival.org.uk
[Nr J23/24 M5. Procession in town centre; rds closed to traffic from 18.00. Ample parking available, clearly signposted]
Bridgwater Carnival commemorates Guy Fawkes and his failed attempt to blow up the Houses of Parliament, and is commonly referred to as the world's largest illuminated winter carnival. The Carnival procession takes over two hours to pass any one point, and contains over 70 carnival floats - some 100ft long, 17ft high, 11ft wide and lit by over 25,000 light bulbs. Once the procession has finished, the Carnival is brought to a dramatic finale with an amazing squibbing firework display. Seeing is believing - don't miss this amazing Carnival.
9 November 2007, 19.00 start
Admission Free

Folk & Local History Museums

Bath Postal Museum

8 Broad Street Bath North East Somerset
BA1 5LJ
Tel: 01225 460333
Bath Postal Museum tells the story of 4,000 years of written communication.

Chard and District Museum

Godworthy House High Street Chard Somerset
TA20 1QL
Tel/Fax: 01460 65091
Chard Museum has displays illustrating the history of Chard and its surrounding area.

BRIDGWATER GUY FAWKES CARNIVAL

Bridgwater, Somerset
www.bridgwatercarnival.org.uk
Friday 9 November 07 (7pm start)
Near Junction 23 & 24 (M5).
Procession takes place in the town centre and is clearly signposted.
Roads are closed to traffic from 18.00hrs.
Ample parking available.
Bridgwater Carnival procession takes over two hours to pass any one point, and contains over 70 carnival floats - some 100ft long, 17ft high, 11ft wide and lit by over 25,000 light bulbs.

Shoe Museum

40 High Street Somerset BA16 0YA
Tel: 01458 842169 Fax: 01458 842226
[J23 M5. Bus: services run to High St]
The museum is in the oldest part of the shoe factory set up by Cyrus and James Clark in 1825. It contains shoes from Roman times to the present, buckles, engravings, fashion plates, machinery, hand tools and advertising material. One section illustrates the early history of the

shoe firm and its role in the town. Disabled access available.
All year Mon-Fri 10.00-16.45. Closed Bank Hols Admission Free

Food & Drink

Sheppy's Cider Farm Centre
Three Bridges Bradford on Tone Taunton Somerset TA4 1ER
Tel: 01823 461233
Traditional family run working cider farm. The Rural Life Museum shows a video of the cider making year.

Gardens & Horticulture

Barrington Court
Barrington Ilminster Somerset TA19 0NQ
Tel: 01460 241938
A formal garden influenced by Gertrude Jekyll and laid out in a series of walled rooms.

Prior Park Landscape Garden
Ralph Allen Drive Bath Somerset BA2 5AH
Tel: 01225 833422 Fax: 01225 833422
www.nationaltrust.org.uk/priorpark

[Prior Park is a green tourist heritage site, visitors need to use public transport or walk. Public transport runs every 30min. 30min walk from city centre. Call for a 'How to Get There' leaflet & events programme. There is disabled parking available]

A beautiful and intimate eighteenth-century landscape garden. Created by local entrepreneur Ralph Allen with advice from 'Capability' Brown and the poet Alexander Pope. The garden is set in a sweeping valley with magnificent views of the City of Bath. There are many interesting features including the Paladian Bridge, one of only four in the world. Look on as the wilderness area of the garden is restored to its former glory, supported by the Heritage Lottery Fund. The Tea Hut is open for light refreshments every Saturday and Sunday from March to October inclusive as well as for Bank Holidays and events. Explore the garden and its wildlife with free family tracker packs. Disabled parking available, please book in advance.
Refreshments available weekends March-October. Dogs permitted November-February only.

3 Mar-28 Oct Mon, Wed-Sun 11.00-17.30, 3 Nov-24 Feb 08 Sat-Sun 11.00-dusk
A£4.80 C£2.70, Family Ticket (A2+C2) £12.20. NT members £Free. Booking in advance for groups & guided walks

Tintinhull House Garden
Farm Street Tintinhull Yeovil Somerset BA22 9PZ
Tel: 01935 826357
Stands in two acres of beautiful formal gardens and orchard.
23 Mar-28 Sept Wed-Sun (open Bank Hol Mons)

Heritage & Industrial

Museum of Bath at Work
Camden Works Julian Road Bath North East Somerset BA1 2RH
Tel: 01225 318348
The museum houses the Bowler collection, the entire stock-in-trade of a Victorian brass founder, general engineer and aerated water manufacturer.

Historical

Clevedon Court

Tickenham Road Clevedon BS21 6QU
Tel: 01275 872257
Clevedon Court is a remarkably complete
manor house of around 1320. There is also a
beautiful eighteenth-century terraced garden.
Wed-Thu, Sun

Dunster Castle

Dunster Minehead Somerset TA24 6SL
Tel: 01643 821314 / 823004
This fortified storybook castle was the home of
the Luttrell family for 600 years.

Farleigh Hungerford Castle

Farleigh Hungerford Bath Somerset BA3 6RS
Tel: 01225 754026
The ruined fourteenth-century castle has a
chapel containing wall paintings, stained glass
and the fine tomb of Sir Thomas Hungerford.

Lytes Cary Manor

Kingsdon Charlton Mackrell Somerton
TA11 7HU
Tel: 01458 224471
A charming manor house refurbished in period
style and complemented by the attractive
hedged garden.
Easter-end Oct Wed, Fri-Sun

Montacute House

Montacute Somerset TA15 6XP
Tel: 01935 823289
A glittering Elizabethan house, adorned with ele-
gant chimneys, carved parapets and other
Renaissance features.

Sally Lunn's Refreshment House and Museum

4 North Parade Passage Bath BA1 1NX
Tel: 01225 461634
Sally Lunn's is the oldest house in Bath.

Military & Defence Museums

Fleet Air Arm Museum

Royal Naval Air Station Yeovilton Yeovil
Somerset BA22 8HT
Tel: 01935 840565 Fax: 01935 842630
www.fleetairarm.com

*[on B3151, close to J of A37 & A303. 7mi N of
Yeovil. Plenty of on-site parking available]*

The Fleet Air Arm museum is where Museum
meets theatre. You'll be 'transported by helicopter to the replica flight deck of the aircraft
carrier HMS ARK ROYAL where you'll see fighter aircraft and two enormous projection screens
showing a phantom strike fighter and a
Buccaneer fighter-bomber. You'll experience the
thrills and sounds of a flight deck, and feel the
wind in your hair and will even see a nuclear
bomb! The museum has the largest collection of
Naval aircraft anywhere in Europe and the first
British built Concorde, which you can go onboard, and visit the cockpit. Outside, there is a
children's adventure playground, a licensed
restaurant and a shop, ample parking and
excellent disabled access. The museum is
located alongside Europe's busiest military air
station RNAS Yeovilton.
*All year Apr-Oct daily 10.00-17.30, Nov-Mar
Wed-Sun 10.00-16.30. Closed 24-26 Dec, open
all public hols*
A£10.50 C(under5)£Free C(5-16)£7.50
Concessions£8.50, Family Ticket (A2+C3)
£32.00. Reduced rates for service personnel.
Group rates available on request

Discount Offer: One Child Free

Mills - Water & Wind

Dunster Working Watermill

Mill Lane Dunster Minehead Somerset
TA24 6SW
Tel: 01643 821759
Built on the site of a mill mentioned in the
Domesday Survey of 1086 the present mill
dates from the eighteenth century.

Stembridge Tower Mill

Mill Road High Ham Langport Somerset
TA10 9DJ
Tel: 01935 823289
The last thatched windmill in England dating
from 1822 and in use until 1910.

Nature & Conservation Parks

Fyne Court

Broomfield Bridgwater Somerset TA5 2EQ
Tel: 01823 652400
The former pleasure grounds of the now-demol-
ished home of the pioneer electrician Andrew
Crosse (1784-1855). Now managed as a nature
reserve.

Ham Hill Country Park

Stoke sub Hamdon Yeovil Somerset TA14 6RW
Tel: 01935 823617
Four-hundred acre open access country park.
Superb countryside walks with iron age and
roman earthworks. Panoramic views.

On the Water

Grand Pier

Marine Parade Weston-Super-Mare Somerset
BS23 1AL
Tel: 01934 620238
Filled with rides, attractions, amusements and
great food. Big wheel, ten-pin bowling, kids' ball
pool, children's adventure playground, video
games and slot machines.

Palaces

Bishop's Palace

The Bishop's Palace Wells Somerset BA5 2PD
Tel: 01749 678691 Fax: 01749 678691
www.bishopspalacewells.co.uk

[Top of Market Place]

More than simply a historic house and garden,
this splendid moated medieval Palace has been
the home of the Bishop of Bath and Wells for
800 years. There are 14 acres of gardens which
have been further enhanced with new planting.
Evening garden tours are available - please ring
for details. Visitors may also view the springs
from which the city takes its name. Visitors can
also see the Bishop's private Chapel, ruined
Great Hall and the Gatehouse with portcullis
and drawbridge beside which the famous mute
swans ring a bell for food. The oldest part of the
building is open to the public. The state rooms
are mainly decorated in the Victorian 'Italian
Gothic' style approached by a fine Jacobean
staircase. Morning coffee, lunches and teas are
served in the restaurant (which has wheelchair
access), and on the terrace.

*1 Apr-31 Oct Mon-Fri 10.30-18.00 (16.30 in
Oct), Sun 12.00-18.00 (16.30 in Oct). Guided
tours for groups available but must be booked in
advance*
A£5.00 C(0-11)£Free C(12-18)£2.00
Students(NUS/USI)&UB40£2.00 OAPs£4.00
Disabled£2.00. Group rate (10+): £4.00, addi-
tional charge of £30.00 for guide

Wells Cathedral

Chain Gate Cathedral Green Wells Somerset
BA5 2UE
Tel: 01749 674483
Walk around this cathedral church. Marvel at its
beauty. Think of the faith which built it and sustains it still. It tells its own story.

West Somerset Railway

The Railway Station Minehead Somerset
TA24 5BG
Tel: 01643 704996 Fax: 01643 706349
www.west-somerset-railway.co.uk

*[Leave M5 at J25 (Taunton) & follow brown tourist
signs. Plenty of on-site parking available]*

The West Somerset Railway recaptures the era
of the branch line country railway in the days of
steam. Enjoy 20 miles of glorious Somerset
scenery as the train gently rolls back the years
on its journey beside the Quantock Hills to the
Bristol Channel coast. Just sit back in your seat
and watch the steam and the countryside drift
past the window. The West Somerset Railway is
a wonderful day out for all the family, whatever
the weather. We look forward to welcoming you.
*First train from Bishop Lydeard (3m from Taunton)
at 10.25. First train from Minehead at 10.15*
Full Day Ticket: A£13.00 OAPs£11.60 C£6.50

Roman Baths

Abbey Church Yard Bath Somerset BA1 1LZ
Tel: 01225 477785 Fax: 01225 477743
www.romanbaths.co.uk
[J18 M4 then take A46, in Bath City centre]
This Great Roman Temple and bathing complex
is one of Britain's most spectacular ancient
monuments, built 2000 years ago around the
country's only hot springs and still flowing with
natural hot water. Free personal audio-guided
tours available in eight languages. Children's
audio guide and 'Bryson at the Baths' audio
guides included in admission price. Disabled
access is restricted. Please call for details.
*All year daily Jan-Feb 09.30-16.30, Mar-June
09.00-17.00, July-Aug 09.00-21.00, Sept-Oct
09.00-17.00, Nov-Dec 09.30-16.30. Closed 25-
26 Dec. Last exit 60mins after closing time. We
recommend you arrive early at peak holiday periods to avoid queues*
A£10.25 (A£11.25 July & Aug) C£6.50
Concessions£8.75, Family Ticket (A2+C4)
£29.00. Group rates (20+): A£7.50 C£4.50-
£4.75

William Herschel Museum

19 New King Street Bath BA1 2BL
Tel: 01225 446865
A Georgian townhouse that was home to the
astronomer and musician William Herschel.

Sealife Centres & Aquariums

SeaQuarium Ltd

Marine Parade Weston-Super-Mare Somerset
BS23 1BE
Tel: 01934 613361 Fax: 01934 613371
www.seaquarium.co.uk

*[J21 M5 follow A370 to Weston Super Mare &
follow rd signs for Aquarium or signs for Beach.
We are situated on beach infront of Beach
Lawns]*

The SeaQuarium features over 30 displays, from
British Marine Sharks and Rays to Tropical
Seahorses and Lionfish with our EvoZone
exhibit featuring Caiman and Bearded Dragons!
Walk under the waves with our Ocean Depths
Tunnel, watch as our resident sharks swim inch-
es above you! Don't miss our successful breeding programme within the Seahorse Family
Nursery, the Red-Bellied Piranhas and Puffer
Fish within our AmaZone and the Deadly Stone
Fish and Blue Spotted Ray in the Lethal Reef!
We have interactive touch screens throughout
the aquarium for further fun and learning. We
have daily feeding demonstrations and presentations with your ticket being valid all day! Don't
forget our tea room for light snacks and gift
shop for souvenirs for one and all!
*All year daily from 10.00 please call for closing
times. Closed 24-26 Dec*
A£5.75 C(under4)£Free C(4-16)&OAPs£4.75,
Family Ticket £19.99. Group rates (for 12+)
available on request

Discount Offer: One Child Free

Tropiquaria

Washford Cross Watchet Somerset TA23 0QB
Tel: 01984 640688
Indoor jungle with a waterfall, aquarium, tropical
plants and free flying birds. Downstairs is the
submarine crypt. Landscaped gardens, outdoor
aviaries, children's playgrounds with cafe.
Apr-Oct daily

Social History Museums

Blake Museum

Blake Street Bridgwater Somerset TA6 3NB
Tel: 01278 456127 Fax: 01278 456127
www.sedgemoor.gov.uk

[Bridgwater town centre, signposted]

Housed in the birthplace of Robert Blake (1598-
1657), General at Sea, the museum's displays
look at the history and archaeology of
Bridgwater and the surrounding area. From the
earliest settlements to the colourful excitement
of the annual Bridgwater Guy Fawkes Carnival,
from the drama of the 1685 Monmouth
Rebellion to the humour of John Chubb, eighteenth-century artist - there is plenty to interest
the whole family. There is also a lively programme of temporary exhibitions and events,
including holiday activities for children.
Wheelchair access limited to ground floor only.
Education service, guided tours and research
facilities also available.
*All year Tue-Sat 10.00-16.00. Closed all Bank Hol
Mon, Good Fri, Christmas & New Year*
Admission Free

Wimbleball Lake

Brompton Regis Dulverton Somerset
Tel: 01398 371372
Lakeside area with picnic areas, play area, cafe, walks and fishing.

Brean Leisure Park

Coast Road Brean Sands Somerset TA8 2QY
Tel: 01278 751595 Fax: 01278 752102
www.brean.com
[J22 M5, follow brown & white tourist signs from motorway towards Burnham On Sea & N heading for Berrow & Brean. Go past Resort & at mini roundabout turn R onto Park entrance Rd. Plenty of on-site parking available]

The south west's largest Fun Park with over 30 rides and attractions, with something for everyone, from roundabouts to rollercoasters. There's a choice of roller coasters, a Wild Water flume ride with two huge drops to get you soaked, and Wipeout, the 100ft swinging pendulum. Also the Super Looper Roller Coaster and many more.
Apr-Oct please call for specific times, from 16 July-4 Sept daily 11.00-22.00
Entrance free, wristband price depends on age, ranges from £9.99-£17.99. Alternatively, you can also purchase tokens

Discount Offer: Three for the Price of Two

Butlins

Warren Road Minehead Somerset TA24 5SH
Tel: 0870 145 0045 Fax: 01643 705264
www.butlins.com/dayvisitor
[From M5 follow A39. 0.5mi along Seafront Rd from Minehead town centre. Plenty of on-site parking available]

For a great day out, come on holiday for the day! With over 70 years experience entertaining holidaymakers, it's no wonder we know what makes the perfect day out. So come and see how much you can pack in! With wet n wild Splash Waterworld, adventure fort, indoor soft play zones, traditional funfair and fantastic entertainment in the Skyline Pavilion, there's more than enough to keep the whole family happy!
Dates vary please call for details
A£12.00 C(under2)£Free C£9.00, Family Ticket (A2+C2) £36.00. Group rates (20+) £6.00 & £5.00. School groups (20+): 1 in every 10 teacher free

Discount Offer: Kid For A Quid

Wildlife Park at Cricket St. Thomas

Cricket St. Thomas Chard Somerset TA20 4DB
Tel: 01460 30111
Over 600 animals from around the world.

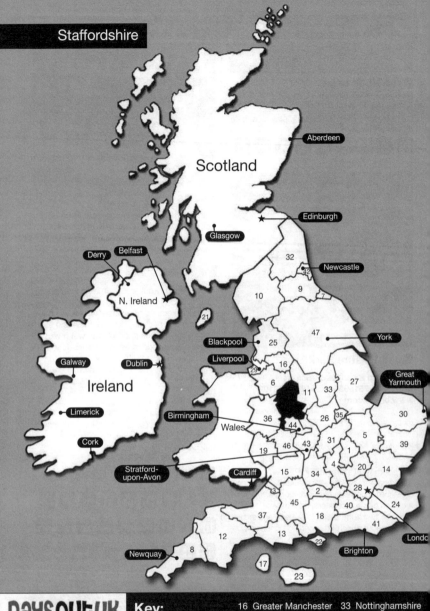

Staffordshire

Aberdeen

Scotland

Edinburgh

Glasgow

Newcastle

Derry
Belfast

N. Ireland

Galway
Dublin

Ireland

Blackpool

Liverpool

York

Great Yarmouth

Limerick

Birmingham

Wales

Cork

Stratford-upon-Avon

Cardiff

London

Newquay

Brighton

Key:

1	Bedfordshire
2	Berkshire
3	Bristol
4	Buckinghamshire
5	Cambridgeshire
6	Cheshire
7	Cleveland
8	Cornwall
9	County Durham
10	Cumbria
11	Derbyshire
12	Devon
13	Dorset
14	Essex
15	Gloucestershire
16	Greater Manchester
17	Guernsey
18	Hampshire
19	Herefordshire
20	Hertfordshire
21	Isle Of Man
22	Isle Of Wight
23	Jersey
24	Kent
25	Lancashire
26	Leicestershire
27	Lincolnshire
28	London
29	Merseyside
30	Norfolk
31	Northamptonshire
32	Northumberland
33	Nottinghamshire
34	Oxfordshire
35	Rutland
36	Shropshire
37	Somerset
38	Staffordshire
39	Suffolk
40	Surrey
41	Sussex
42	Tyne & Wear
43	Warwickshire
44	West Midlands
45	Wiltshire
46	Worcestershire
47	Yorkshire

Animal Attractions

Ash End House Children's Farm

Middleton Lane Middleton Tamworth
Staffordshire B78 2BL
Tel: 0121 329 3240 Fax: 0121 329 3240
www.childrensfarm.co.uk

[Signposted off A4091. Plenty of on-site parking available]

Ash End House Children's Farm is a fun filled family day out. Lots of undercover activities, ideal for rainy days! These include Chick chatting; sit on a pony; help bottle feed a lamb or goat kid (spring/summer); goat kid walking (weather permitting); meet Chirpy; make a memento to take home; Bunny brushing and Guinea pig grooming; Join in one of our Playlets (weekends/school holidays) and lots, lots more. We have three play areas, family games yard, crazy golf, toddler's tractor and trike barn, new gift shop, farmhouse café and picnic barns. Birthday parties are our speciality with 4 different themes to choose from; Traditional, Star in your party, Nursery Rhyme Tractor and Trike and Crafty Party. Come and join in our delightful Nativity Story and "wake up Santa in his cottage" from the last weekend of November until Christmas Eve.
Summer/Autumn 10.00-17.00. Winter 10.00-16.00. Closed 25 Dec until 2nd weekend in January.
A£4.50 C£4.90 (includes animal feed, farm badge & all activities) OAPs£4.50. Group rates available on request

Discount Offer: £1.00 off Child admission

Arts, Crafts & Textiles

Ceramica

Old Town Hall Burslem ST6 3DS
Tel: 01782 832001
Interactive displays and activities.

Gladstone Pottery Museum

Uttoxeter Road Longton Stoke-On-Trent
Staffordshire ST3 1PQ
Tel: 01782 237777 Fax: 01782 237076
www.stoke.gov.uk/museums
[On A50 signposted from A500 link with M6. Plenty of free on-site parking available]
Located at the heart of the Potteries, Gladstone Pottery Museum is the last remaining Victorian Pottery factory and perfectly presents the fascinating story of the pottery industry. In original workshops, potters can be found demonstrating traditional pottery skills. There are lots of opportunities for you to have a go at pottery making, throw your own pot on the potters wheel, make china flowers and decorate pottery items to take home. Now open, Flushed with Pride - the story of the toilet - remarkable new interactive galleries dedicated to the development of the humble loo.
All year daily 10.00-17.00. Limited opening Christmas & New Year
A£5.95 C£4.50 Concessions£4.95, Family Ticket (A2+C2) £18.00, Annual museum passport, A£8.50, Concessions£7.50, Family Tickets£20.50 (Free entry for a year & other local discounts)

Discount Offer: Two for the Price of One

Stoke-on-Trent
Museums

The Potteries Museum & Art Gallery

One of Britain's outstanding museums with impressive displays of the worlds finest ceramics, the National Minton Collection, a Mark XVI Spitfire and TV star 'Ozzy' the owl jug. Yours to discover!

Closed for refurbishment until 31st March 2007
Mar - Oct, Mon - Sat 10am - 5pm, Sun 2 - 5pm
Nov - Feb, Mon - Sat 10am - 4pm, Sun 1 - 4pm

Bethesda Street, City Centre,
Stoke-on-Trent ST1 3DW

Telephone: 01782 23 23 23

Gladstone Pottery Museum

The history of the Potteries all wrapped up in one unique museum! Step back in time and explore the last Victorian pottery factory complete with bottle ovens and original workshops where traditional pottery making skills are demonstrated daily.

Mon - Sun 10am - 5pm

Uttoxeter Road, Longton,
Stoke-on-Trent ST3 1PQ

Telephone: 01782 237777

Etruria Industrial Museum

Enjoying a canal-side location, this family-friendly Museum includes Jesse Shirley's Bone and Flint Mill, Britain's last surviving steam-powered potters' mill. See the historic machinery in action when the Mill is "in steam".

Apr - Dec, Wed - Fri, 12.00 - 4.30pm
(out of season visits are by appointment only)

Lower Bedford Street, Etruria,
Stoke-on-Trent ST4 7AF

Telephone: 01782 23 31 44

Ford Green Hall

Surrounded by a period garden, this 17th century timber-framed farmhouse offers a fascinating insight into life in the Stuart age. Rooms are furnished with an outstanding collection of textiles, ceramics and furniture.

Sun - Thur 1 - 5pm

Ford Green Road, Smallthorne,
Stoke-on-Trent ST6 1NG

Telephone: 01782 23 31 95

www.stoke.gov.uk/museums

Potteries Museum and Art Gallery

Bethesda Street City Centre Stoke-On-Trent
Staffordshire ST1 3DW
Tel: 01782 232323 Fax: 01782 232500
www.stoke.gov.uk/museums

[City centre, A50, A52, A53 all meet at Stoke-on-Trent]

The home of the World's finest collection of Staffordshire Ceramics. A family friendly welcome awaits at one of Britain's leading museums where the unique combination of 'product and place' is celebrated in its outstanding displays. With pottery that will win your heart, galleries that win awards and a Spitfire that won a war. Discover the story of Stoke-on-Trent's people, industry, products and landscapes through displays of pottery, community history, archaeology, geology and wildlife. Explore rich and diverse collections of paintings, drawings, prints, costume and glass. Relax in the tearoom with a light lunch or Staffordshire Oatcake. Teas, coffee and pastries. Try the Foyer Shop for unique and quality gifts, stationery and crafts. Ceramic and local history books and souvenirs of the Potteries. Experience our 300 seat Forum Theatre available for hire, for conferences, concerts and talks, not to mention a consistent programme of films for all the family at great prices. There is also lots to learn for all ages in our wide range of educational activities.

1 Mar-31 Oct Mon-Sat 10.00-17.00, Sun 14.00-17.00, 1 Nov-28 Feb Mon-Sat 10.00-16.00, Sun 13.00-16.00. Closed 25 Dec, call for Christmas opening times

Admission Free

Factory Outlets & Tours

Aynsley China Factory Shop

Sutherland Road Longton Stoke-on-Trent
Staffordshire ST3 1HS
Tel: 01782 339420 Fax: 01782 339401
[Signposted from main rd. Plenty of on-site parking available]

Aynsley China Visitor centre has many attractions including a wide selection of giftware and tableware on two floors, with exclusive pieces and extensive collections of Belleek Parian China and Galway Irish Crystal. Enjoy a snack in the Pembroke Coffee Shop.
All year Mon-Sat 09.00-17.00, Sun 11.00-16.00. Closed 25-26 Dec, 1 Jan & Easter Sun

Admission Free

Discount Offer: 10% discount on all Factory Shop purchases (when you spend £10.00 or more)

Portmeirion Factory Shop

London Road Stoke-on-Trent Staffordshire
ST4 7QQ
Tel: 01782 749131
Portmeirion produce tableware, giftware, candles, and decorative accessories in glass, metal, textile, and wood.

For great hotel deals call Superbreak on 01904 679999 or visit www.superbreak.com

Moorcroft Factory Shop

Nile Street Burslem Stoke-on-Trent ST6 2BH

Tel: 01782 820505 Fax: 01782 820501
www.moorcroft.com
[Plenty of on-site parking available]
The Factory Shop sells a selection of handmade
giftware and table lamps, which are all less than
perfect. With that comes the opportunity to
save up to 30% off the usual best-quality retail
price. All stock is subject to availability.
All year Mon-Fri 10.00-17.00, Sat 09.30-16.30.
Open Bank Hols. Closed Sun & 25 Dec.

Moorcroft Heritage Visitor Centre

Sandbach Road Burslem Stoke-on-Trent
Staffordshire ST6 2DQ
Tel: 01782 207943 Fax: 01782 283455
www.moorcroft.com
[Plenty of on-site parking available]
Visit the heritage centre shop where a wide
selection of hand made giftware and table
lamps awaits you. With a kaleidoscope of

colour, all pieces are displayed to breathtaking
effect in the shop. Our museum houses fascinating pieces of Moorcroft showing the rich and
colourful history of our unique company. Every
piece of Moorcroft is made by hand with no two
pieces the same. Moorcroft pieces are still
made using the traditional techniques, which
have remained virtually unchanged for over 100
years.
All year Mon-Fri 10.00-17.00, Sat 09.30-16.30.
Open Bank Hols. Closed Sun & 21 Dec-1 Jan
incl. Guided Factory Tours: Mon, Wed & Thurs
11.00 & 14.00, Fri 11.00 only
Admission free (to Shop, Museum & Bottle
Oven)

Spode Visitor Centre

Church Street Stoke-On-Trent ST4 1BX
Tel: 01782 744011 Fax: 01782 572505
www.spode.co.uk

[Plenty of on-site parking available]

Visit the birthplace of fine bone china. Come
with us behind closed doors and see traditional
craftsmen at work. Fully guided tours, museum
and licensed restaurant. There are bargains
galore in our Best shop, gift shop, cook shop
and Spode factory clearance shops.
All year daily Mon-Sat 09.00-17.30, Sun 10.00-
16.00. Closed 25-26 Dec & Easter Sun
Basic Tour: A£4.50 Concessions£4.00.
Connoisseur Tour: A£7.50 Concessions£6.50

**Discount Offer: Two for the Price of
One**

Wedgwood Visitor Centre
Barlaston Stoke-On-Trent ST12 9ES

Tel: 0870 606 1759 Fax: 01782 223063
www.thewedgwoodvisitorcentre.com
[J15 M6, signposted. On-site parking available]

Deciding on a family outing can be tricky. Some people want to delve into history, some want a little culture and for others, only retail therapy will do! The Wedgwood Visitor Centre meets all those needs and many more besides. Set in 200 acres of lush parkland (right in the heart of Staffordshire), visitors can take a fascinating trip behind-the-scenes of one of the world's most famous pottery companies. The award-winning tour allows visitors to enjoy the entire experience at their own pace. Hand-on activities (such as throwing your own pot or painting your own plate) are available in the demonstration area, where individual craft artisans demonstrate their skills, including a Coalport painter, a jewellery maker, a hand-painter and a flower maker. Add to this a superb restaurant, exhibition areas, film theatre, and an exclusive Wedgwood shop, the Wedgwood Visitor Centre offers an all-inclusive day out for all the family.
*All year daily Mon-Fri 09.00-17.00, Sat-Sun 10.00-17.00. Exclusive Wedgwood Shop closed 16.00 on Sun. Closed Christmas week*Weekdays: A£8.25 Concessions£6.25, Family Ticket£28.00, Weekends: A£6.25 Concessions£4.25, Family Ticket£20.00

Discount Offer: Two for the Price of One

A Great Day Out

- Factory Shopping • Shopping Court

Spode

- Guided Tours • Famous Museum
- Restaurant

Spode Visitor Centre, Church Street, Stoke-on-Trent. ST4 1BX

Tel: 01782 744011   Email: shop@spode.co.uk   www.spode.co.uk

Mon - Sat: 9am - 5pm. Sun: 10am - 4pm. Onsite car park. Easy access. 3 miles from J15 of M6 / 2 miles from J16 of M6.

Open 7 days a week

Festivals & Shows

Lichfield Festival

Lichfield Staffordshire WS13 7LD
Tel: 01543 412121 Fax: 01543 306274
www.lichfieldfestival.org
*[Held in Lichfield Cathedral, Lichfield Garrick
Theatre, country churches & other venues. From
S, M1 N, M6 J4 then follow signs on A446. From
N, M1 J28, A38 where signposted just after
Fradley J. From M6 N, J14 then A513 to Rugeley
where A51 to Lichfield]*

For ten days in July the elegant cathedral city of
Lichfield plays host to one of the UK's most
diverse arts festivals. Classical, jazz and world
music concerts form the backbone of celebration across the arts, including theatre, film, literature, workshops, talks and exhibitions. Free
events include the Medieval Fayre and Market
on 8 July which boasts over 100 stalls and
street entertainments. The festival climaxes with
a spectacular free fireworks display on 15 July.
5-15 July 2007
Prices range from £Free-£35.00

Folk & Local History Museums

Museum of Cannock Chase

The Valley Heritage Centre Cannock WS12 1TD
Tel: 01543 877666
A delightful museum illustrating the history of
Cannock Chase.

Gardens & Horticulture

Biddulph Grange Garden

Grange Road Biddulph Staffordshire Moorlands
Staffordshire ST8 7SD
Tel: 01782 517999
A number of small gardens designed to house
specimens from an extensive and wide-ranging
plant collection.

Heritage & Industrial

Etruria Industrial Museum

Lower Bedford Street Etruria Stoke-On-Trent
Staffordshire ST4 7AF
Tel: 01782 233144 Fax: 01782 233145
**www2002.stoke.gov.uk/museums/eim_mai
n.html**

*[J15 M6 onto A500 then B5045. Free parking off
Etruria Vale Rd]*

The Industrial Museum includes the Etruscan
Bone and Flint Mill which was built in 1857 to
grind materials for the agricultural and pottery
industries. It's Britain's sole surviving, steam-
powered potters' mill and contains an 1820s
steam-driven beam engine, 1903 coal fired boiler and original grinding machinery. Tea room
and shop, children's activities every school holiday, from April to December
*4 Apr-2 Dec Wed-Sun 12.00-16.30, Jan-Mar by
appointment*
A£2.50 Concessions£1.50, Family Ticket£5.95

Historical

Ancient High House

Greengate Street Stafford Staffordshire
ST16 2JA
Tel: 01785 619131 Fax: 01785 619132
www.staffordbc.gov.uk/heritage
[J14 & 14 M6]

Built in 1595 the Ancient High House is the largest timber framed town house in England. Room settings reflect the various periods in the history of the House; Tudor Bedroom, Civil War Room, Georgian Room and Edwardian Shop, and each has its own story to tell. With educational displays, art gallery with exhibition programme, gift shop and children's activities in each room - there's something for all the members of the family. The top floor houses the museum of the Staffordshire Yeomanry Regiment. Conveniently situated in the centre of Stafford, ideal for shopping, restaurants, theatre and other local attractions, the High House is a 'must visit' destination.

All year Tue-Sat 10.00-16.00
Admission Free. Events may be charged, please call for details

Croxden Abbey

Uttoxeter Staffordshire
Tel: 0121 625 6820
The impressive remains of an abbey of Cistercian 'white monks.

Erasmus Darwin House

Beacon Street Lichfield Staffordshire WS13 7AD
Tel: 01543 306260
www.erasmusdarwin.org
[1mi from Lichfield bus & train stations, accessed via Beacon St or Cathedral Close]

Erasmus Darwin (1731-1802) was more than just Charles Darwin's grandfather. Visit Erasmus Darwin House and learn about a genius of all trades! Erasmus was a highly regarded doctor, a critically acclaimed poet, a biologist, an inventor and a botanist. The museum is housed in a recently restored, grade-1 listed Georgian building and it hosts a range of special events throughout the year. The exhibitions include a film presented by our most vocal supporter, Adam Hart-Davis, and free audio-guides of the museum. You can also take a moment to look around the maturing herb garden, and enjoy all the culinary aromas of a secluded spot in this historical part of Lichfield. The museum is ideal for school visits, and there's a wide range of history and science activities that are linked to the National Curriculum. The Erasmus Darwin House is also a unique and stylish venue for business meetings, corporate events, wedding ceremonies and receptions (please telephone for more information).

Oct-Mar (Thu-Sun) & Apr-Sep (Tue-Sun): 12.00-17.00. Closed Mons, 25 & 31 Dec & Bank Hols
A£2.50 C&OAPs£2.00 C(under5)£Free, Family Ticket £6.00

Ford Green Hall

Ford Green Road Smallthorne Stoke-on-Trent
Staffordshire ST6 1NG
Tel: 01782 233195 Fax: 01782 233194
www.stoke.gov.uk

[NE of Stoke-on-Trent on B551 between Burslem / Endon. Signposted from A500. Situated next to a Nature Reserve. Plenty of on-site parking available]

Ford Green Hall is a seventeenth-century house, home of the Ford family for almost two centuries. Designated a museum with an outstanding collection the rooms are richly furnished with original and reproduction pieces according to inventories of the seventeenth century. Outside a garden has been reconstructed with Tudor and Stuart features including a knot garden, raised herb beds and a viewing mount. The museum has an award winning education service. Shop and tea room serving light refreshments. Children's activities held every holiday. Wheelchair access limited to ground floor only.

All year Sun-Thur 13.00-17.00. Please call to confirm Christmas opening times
A£2.50 Concessions£1.50. Wheelchair users & C(0-4)£Free. Groups & coaches by appointment only

Discount Offer: Two for the Price of One

Izaak Walton's Cottage

Worston Lane Shallowford Stafford Staffordshire ST15 0PA
Tel: 01785 760278 Fax: 01785 760278
www.staffordbc.gov.uk/heritage

[Shallowford off A5013 5mi N of Stafford, J14 M6. Plenty of on-site parking available]

Thatched timber-framed sixteenth-century cottage bequeathed to the people of Stafford by Izaak Walton, the celebrated church biographer and author of the 'Compleat Angler'. The cottage is decorated in period style and is home to a small angling museum. An entertaining events programme is available throughout the opening period and staff are on hand to give an insight into both this unique property and the great man himself. Wander around the rose and herb garden or linger over a pot of tea or refreshments from the tea-room. A gift shop is available to purchase souvenirs to remind you of your visit.
May-Aug Sat-Sun 13.00-17.00
Admission Free. Events may be charged, please call for details

Letocetum Roman Baths Site and Museum

Watling Street Wall Lichfield WS14 0AW
Tel: 01543 480768
Excavated Roman bathhouse, the finest excavated site of its kind as yet discovered. Home to an interesting museum of local archaeology and finds.

Samuel Johnson Birthplace Museum

Breadmarket Street Lichfield WS13 6LG
Tel: 01543 264972
The Johnson birthplace now houses a museum dedicated to this great man.

Shugborough Estate

Shugborough Milford Staffordshire ST17 0XB
Tel: 01889 881388 Fax: 01889 881323
www.shugborough.org.uk
[Off A513, well signed from J13 M6. Plenty of on-site parking available]

Leave the twenty-first century behind and step into the real working environments of The Complete Working Historic Estate of Shugborough, near Stafford. The elegant, eighteenth-century mansion house, Victorian Servants' quarters, homely working farm and walled garden are preserved just as they were centuries ago. At the walled garden meet the character gardeners as they work with authentic tools and seeds. The dairymaids at the farm will show you the very latest technology (early nineteenth-century, of course!) in our dairy where butter and cheese is produced. Our miller will gladly show you his pride and joy - the only working water mill of its kind in the country. After working up an appetite taste the delights of Shugborough's historically inspired dishes in the tearoom. Meet Mrs Stearn, the head cook, in the Victorian Servants' Quarters and discover what it was like to be a cook in the eighteenth century. Washdays in the laundry produce a flurry of activity as piles of linen are washed, scrubbed, rinsed, dried and then ironed using flat irons by our costumed laundry maids. Lord and Lady Anson greet visitors in the elegant Mansion House. Set in 900 acres of beautiful countryside with play area, walks and trails there's lots to do for all the family.

16 Mar-26 Oct daily 11.00-17.00, Nov-Mar pre-booked parties only
A£10.00 C£6.00 Concessions£8.00, Family Ticket(A2+C3) £25.00, (A1+C1) £12.50

Discount Offer: Two Children Free

Stafford Castle

off Newport Road Stafford ST16 1DJ
Tel: 01785 257698 Fax: 01785 257698
www.staffordbc.gov.uk/heritage
[Off A518 Newport Rd, SW of Stafford, J13 & 14 M6. Plenty of on-site parking available]

Crowning an important Norman archaeological site, Stafford Castle's ruined Gothic Revival Keep is built on the remains of an earlier medieval structure. The castle site consists of: Keep, motte and inner and outer baileys. The site also boasts commanding panoramic views over the surrounding countryside. The visitor centre, created to represent a Norman guard-house, has an audio-visual display, museum exhibits and a souvenir gift shop. Reproduction period arms and armour are available to try out - a fun hands-on experience for all the family. Limited wheelchair access is available to the visitor centre. A full events programme is planned and coaches and group tours are welcome.

Apr-Oct Tue-Sun & Bank Hol Mon 10.00-17.00, Nov-Mar Sat-Sun 10.00-16.00
Admission Free. Events may be charged, please call for details

Tamworth Castle

The Holloway Ladybank Tamworth B79 7NA
Tel: 01827 709629 Fax: 01827 709630
www.tamworthcastle.co.uk
[J10 M42, signposted off A51/A5. Rail: Tamworth Station 10min walk away]

Dramatic Norman motte and bailey castle set in attractive town centre park with floral terraces. Fifteen authentically furnished rooms open to the public, including Great Hall, Dungeon and Haunted Bedroom. Living Images of Baron Marmion and the Black Lady ghost. "The Tamworth Story" is a fascinating interactive exhibition telling the market town's history from Roman times to the present day using exhibits from the Museum Collection. Battlement wall-walks, gift shop, interactives and two free quizzes.
Spring/Summer: Tue-Sun 12.00-17.15, Autumn/Winter Thur-Sun 12.00-17.15
To 30th Sep 07: A£4.95 C£2.95 OAPs£3.95, Family Ticket (A2+C2) £13.65. Specially reduced rate for wheelchair users as access confined to the ground floor

Discount Offer: Two for the Price of One

Brindley Water Mill And Museum

Daintry Street Leek Staffordshire ST13 5PG
Operational corn mill built by James Brindley.

Lichfield Cathedral

The Close Lichfield Staffordshire WS13 7LD
Tel: 01543 306240
An 800 year-old gothic cathedral with three spires.

Foxfield Steam Railway

Blythe Bridge Road Caverswall Stoke-On-Trent Staffordshire ST11 9EA
Tel: 01782 396210 Fax: 01782 396210
www.foxfieldrailway.co.uk
[Off A50 (Stoke & Uttoxeter). Approx 1mi walk from Blythe Bridge train station (follow signs). Plenty of on-site parking available]

Take a nostalgic train journey on this unique heritage steam railway as it winds you gently through the beautifully scenic Staffordshire countryside. Afterwards, relax with a home-cooked meal or alcoholic refreshment in our station bar, 'The One Legged Shunter.' See our locomotive display area and visit our gift shop. Special events operate throughout the year from Postman Pat and Santa Specials to our Steam Gala event in July.
1 Apr-31 Oct Sun & Bank Hol weekends, 1-31 Dec Sat-Sun
Please call or visit website for admission prices

Discount Offer: One Child Free

Sport & Recreation

SnowDome

Leisure Island River Drive Tamworth B79 7ND
Tel: 08705 000011 Fax: 01827 62549
www.snowdome.co.uk
[5min from J10 M42. On-site parking available]

The SnowDome in Tamworth is the UK's premier real snow centre. The SnowDome complex
houses a 170m indoor slope, covered in real
snow all year round and two further real snow
nursery slopes, providing the perfect facilities for
learning new skills such as skiing and snowboarding. It's not only skiing and snowboarding
on the main slope, imagine racing your family
and friends down the snow in steerable tobog-
gans! Or hold on tight for the fastest experience
on snow-hurtling down the slope in specially
designed inflatable tubes! Also within the complex, there is a selection of bars, restaurants
and general amenities plus the snow and ice
arena. The snow and ice arena features an ice
rink, the UK's only ice track and 'mini' rink for
first timers, providing a unique and unparalleled
skating facility for all ages and abilities! The UK's
only children's Snowplay area is the place for
children to have fantastic fun with a game of
snowballs and slide around in the snow.
Meanwhile, you can command and manoeuvre
your very own snowmobile through the chicane,
corners and straights of the 250 metre real
snow track! If you are looking for a different and
exciting family outing...look no further. All you
need is warm clothes, gloves and a sense of
adventure!
All year daily 09.00-23.00

**Discount Offer: Two for the Price of
One**

Theme & Adventure Parks

Alton Towers

Alton Stoke-On-Trent Staffordshire ST10 4DB
Tel: 08705 204060 24hr Fax: 01538 704097
www.altontowers.com

*[Travelling N J23A M1 or J15 M6 travelling S J28
M1 or J16 M6 clearly signposted. Plenty of on-
site parking available]*

Escape to the extraordinary world of Alton
Towers, where the year round resort combines
theme park thrills with unlimited family fun,
unique hotels, waterpark and spa. Act your
shoe size not your age as you make it your very
own must do experience for 2007 - a celebration of all things family. New for 2007: Crawl into
the new Dung Heap playground; swing into
Extraordinary Golf or take a gravely spooky stroll
trough the new Haunted Hollow. All in the name
of unadulterated fun.

*17 Mar-11 Nov daily, rides open from 10.00,
Hotels, Waterpark & Spa are open all year round
(please note the park may be closed for special
events)*

A from £32.00, C from £22.00. Prices from
£24.00 if booked in advance through altontow-
ers.com or call 0870 444 44 55

Drayton Manor Theme Park

Tamworth Staffordshire B78 3TW
Tel: 08708 725252 Fax: 01827 288916
www.draytonmanor.co.uk
[M42, J9 or J10, M6 toll, exit T2. Plenty of on-site parking available]

Everyone's favourite theme park, packed with brilliant rides and attractions, set in 280 acres of lakes and parkland. Drayton Manor features some of the biggest, wettest and scariest rides around! 'Apocalypse' is the world's first stand-up tower drop. 'Shockwave' is Europe's only stand-up roller coaster. 'Stormforce 10' is the "best water ride in the country!" (The Daily Telegraph). 'Maelstrom is the only gyro-swing to make you face outwards! 'G-Force' is the only looping roller coaster in which you hang from the hip! New for 2007: 'The Bounty' - a massive ship that swings you high above the water for the ride of your life! There's fantastic family entertainment with 'Excalibur,' 'A Dragon's Tale' and 'The Pirate Adventure.' 'Robinson's Land' is packed with fun for the kids. Plus 'Drayton Manor Zoo,' 'Dinosaurland,' crazy golf, cafés, shops and restaurants. Voted 'Best UK Attraction' (Group Leisure Awards 2006) and 'UK Attraction of the Year' (Coach Tourism Awards 2006).
24 Mar-28 Oct daily, rides start at 10.30. Please see website or call for weekday opening times in Sep/Oct
Please call or visit our website for admission prices

Discount Offer: 20% off Admission Prices (when you purchase 4 tickets)

Waterworld

Festival Park Stoke-on-Trent Staffordshire
ST1 5PU
Tel: 01782 205747 Fax: 01782 201815
www.waterworld.co.uk

[On Festival Park Site at Etruria. 10min from M6 J15 & 16. Plenty of free on-site parking available]

If you are looking for a great day out for all the family then look no further! Waterworld's fantastic white knuckle ride, the 'Twister' is six seconds of thrills and spills combined with brilliant lighting and sound effects. In addition, there are many other exciting rides including the 'Nucleus', the 'Black hole', the 'Python', Super Flume and a family multi-slide. Alternatively you could relax in our spa and bubble pools, the lazy river in our outdoor pool, the dynamic wave pool and rapids. If you have energy to burn try the Aqua Assault Course and the Aqua Splash Jungle House for water babies taking their first steps into water. If splashing around is not for you then relax at the Waters Edge Restaurant. With full family changing and free parking Waterworld is the Number 1 Family Day Out! And new for 2007....New concept children's gym, amusement arcade and food court.
All year Peak: daily from 10.00, Off Peak: Wed-Fri from 14.00, Sat-Sun from 10.00

Peak (includes weekends): A&C£8.50 C(under1.1 metres)£5.00 Spectators£5.00. Off Peak: A&C£6.99 C(under1.1 metres)£4.00 Spectator£5.00. Group rates available on request

Discount Offer: Two for the Price of One

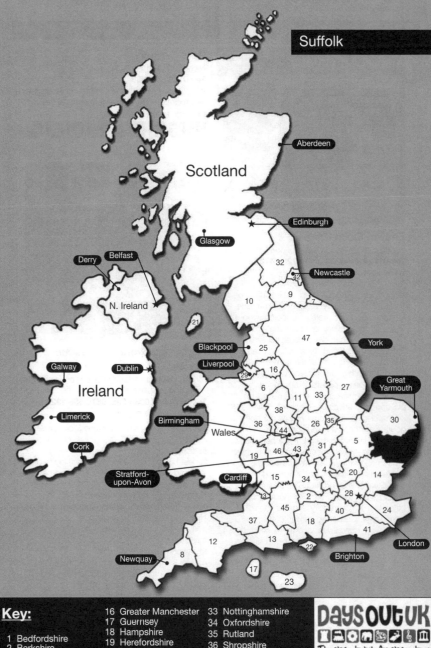

Suffolk

Aberdeen

Scotland

Edinburgh

Glasgow

Newcastle

Derry

Belfast

N. Ireland

32

42

9

7

10

21

47

York

Blackpool

25

Liverpool

16

29

6

33

27

Great
Yarmouth

11

30

38

Galway

Dublin

Birmingham

36

26

35

5

Ireland

Wales

44

31

Limerick

19

46

43

1

20

14

Stratford-
upon-Avon

Cardiff

15

34

4

28

London

Cork

3

2

40

24

45

18

41

Newquay

37

Brighton

12

13

8

22

17

23

Animal Attractions

Easton Farm Park
Pound Corner Easton Woodbridge IP13 0EQ
Tel: 01728 746475 Fax: 01728 747861
www.eastonfarmpark.co.uk
*[Signposted off A12 at Wickham
Market/Framlingham turn off. On-site parking]*
Set in 35 acres of idyllic Suffolk countryside,
Easton Farm Park offers an opportunity for the
whole family to learn about farming and its
development. Each day children can enjoy
FREE pony rides and pat-a-pet. You can feed
and make friends with all the farm animals,
ranging from big Suffolk Punch horses,
Shetland ponies, piglets, lambs, goats, calves,
rabbits and guinea pigs. Children's indoor soft
playbarn and adventure play area. Take a ride
on the electric diggers as well as our tractors,
go-karts and barrel train. Come and meet
Mildred, the milking cow. Enjoy a peaceful walk
down by the River Deben - there are a choice of
trails through the meadows and woods. If your
legs are tired, stop off at our Riverside café for a
bite to eat or a cream tea. The original Victorian
buildings at Easton Farm Park include our
octagonal Victorian dairy and working blacksmith forge. Converted holiday cottages are
available to rent all year and are decorated to 4
star Tourist Board marking. Caravan site with
electricity, gift shop (open daily). Farmers' markets held on the 4th Saturday of each month.
Anglian Business of the Year 2003/2004.
Outstanding Contribution to Suffolk Tourism 06.
*17 Mar-30 Sept daily 10.30-18.00, 20-28 Oct
daily 10.30-16.00, Dec Sat & Sun 11.00-15.00,
15-23 Dec daily 11.00-15.00*
A£6.25 C£4.75 OAPs£5.75, Family
Ticket(A2+C2) £20.00

Discount Offer: One Child Free

Pets Corner
Nicholas Everitt Park Oulton Broad NR33 9JU
Tel: 01502 563533
An ever-popular children's attraction where they
and their parents will love to meet and touch
the large range of animals.

Redwings Stonham Rescue Centre
Stonham Barns Pettaugh Road Stonham Aspal
Stowmarket Suffolk IP14 6AT
Tel: 0870 040 0033 Fax: 0870 458 1926
www.redwings.org.uk

*[On A1120 tourist route between Stowmarket &
Framlingham. Plenty of on-site parking available]*
Established in 1984, Redwings is now the
largest horse charity in the UK, working to provide and promote the welfare, care and protection of horses, ponies, donkeys and mules. At
the charity's Suffolk visitor centre you can meet
some of Redwings' resident equines including
Harry the Shetland, Finnegan the cob, Katy the
pony and Choccy the donkey. Many people
have been pleasantly surprised at the scale of
this twenty-acre site with over half a mile of
paddock walks. Visitors can meet the horses
and ponies, watch demonstrations, enjoy a
guided tour or shop in the gift shop and there is
even the chance to adopt one of the centre's
special equines.
1 Apr-28 Oct daily 10.00-17.00
Admission Free

Discount Offer: One Free Poster

Archaeology

Sutton Hoo
Woodbridge Suffolk IP12 3DJ
Tel: 01394 389700
The exhibition tells the story of the site and displays some original objects as well as replicas of the treasure.

West Stow Anglo-Saxon Village
West Stow Country Park Icklingham Road West Stow Bury St Edmunds Suffolk IP28 6HG
Tel: 01284 728718
Unique reconstructed Anglo-Saxon village built on an original settlement site.

Birds, Butterflies & Bees

Suffolk Owl Sanctuary
Stonham Barns Pettaugh Road Stonham Aspal Stowmarket Suffolk IP14 6AT
Tel: 01449 711425
Beautiful birds of prey flying free.

Country Parks & Estates

Alton Water
Holbrook Road Stutton Ipswich Suffolk IP9 2RY
Tel: 01473 589105
Water park with nature reserve, picnic area, footpaths, water sports and much more.

Clare Castle and Country Park
Visitor Centre Malting Lane Clare Sudbury Suffolk CO10 8NW
Tel: 01787 277491
A 33-acre site fronting the River Stour with the remains of a Norman motte and bailey castle.

Factory Outlets & Tours

Lowestoft Porcelain
Redgrave House 10 Battery Green Road Lowestoft Suffolk NR32 1DE
Tel: 01502 572940
Factory and retail shop are open to the public.

Folk & Local History Museums

Laxfield and District Museum
The Guildhall High Street Laxfield Woodbridge Suffolk IP13 8DU
Tel: 01986 798460 / 798421
Exhibits relate to rural domestic and working life in the nineteenth and early twentieth centuries including Victorian kitchen.

Easton Farm Park

Set in 35 acres of idyllic Suffolk countryside, Easton Farm Park offers a fun opportunity for the whole family to learn about farming and its development.

Easton,
Woodbridge,
Suffolk IP13 0EQ
T: 01728 746475
F: 01728 747861
W: www.eastonfarmpark.co.uk
E: info@eastonfarmpark.co.uk

Moyse's Hall Museum

Cornhill Bury St Edmunds Suffolk IP33 1DX
Tel: 01284 706183 Fax: 01284 765373
www.stedmundsbury.gov.uk
[A14]

Houses collections of local and social history relating to Bury St Edmunds and area, highlights of The Suffolk Regiment, crime and punishment including the famous William Corder 'Murder in the Red Barn' relics. New display of time-pieces, paintings and textiles. Events, workshops and children's' activities throughout the year.

All year Mon-Fri 10.30-16.30, Sat-Sun 11.00-16.00. Closed 25-26 Dec, 1 Jan & Good Fri & Bank hols

A£2.60 C&Concessions£2.10, Family Ticket £8.20 Residents£Free. Group rates available on request

Discount Offer: Two for the Price of One

Orford Museum

Orford Castle Castle Hill Orford Woodbrige Suffolk IP12 2NF
Tel: 01394 450295 / 45078
Local history and Orford Ness from World War I to the present day.
Apr-Sept

Food & Drink

Friday Street Farm Shop

Farnham Saxmundham Suffolk IP17 1JX
Tel: 01728 602783
Stocks a large selection of locally-grown (or produced) foods.

Greene King Brewery

Westgate Street Bury St Edmunds IP33 1QT
Tel: 01284 714382 / 714297
Start at the museum, tour the brewery then taste the different beers in our Brewery Tap.

Gardens & Horticulture

Helmingham Hall Gardens

The Events Office Helmingham Stowmarket Suffolk IP14 6EF
Tel: 01473 890799 Fax: 01473 890776
www.helmingham.com

[9mi N of Ipswich on B1077. Plenty of on-site parking available]

Helmingham Hall Gardens see a wide variety of visitors, groups and clubs, as well as tour operators, from all over the world visiting the captivating gardens each year. The Tollemache family, whose ancestors have lived at Helmingham Hall for the past 500 years, enjoy sharing their passion for the beautiful gardens. The gardens surround the impressive Tudor moated Hall set in a 400 year old ancient deer park. The rich traditional gardens are complimented by a wonderful balance of nature and the modern accents inspired by the current Lady Tollemache, a well-known garden designer and Chelsea Gold Medal Winner. A visit to the gardens makes a perfect afternoon out for everyone. There is a relaxed atmosphere for people to enjoy the serenity and tranquillity of the gardens, to lose themselves in the plethora of colour, scents and history. Most visitors take the opportunity to enjoy a delicious lunch or a cream tea in the Coach House and to visit the gift shop, produce and plant stall.

6 May-16 Sept Wed & Sun 14.00-18.00. Sun 27 May: Plant Sale 10.00-16.00

A£4.50 Concessions£4.00 C£2.50. Group rate (30+): £4.00

Heritage & Industrial

Long Shop Museum

Main Street Leiston Suffolk IP16 4ES
Tel: 01728 832189 Fax: 01728 832189
www.longshop.care4free.net
[Nr Aldeburgh, Snape & Saxmundham. Plenty of on-site parking available]

Enjoy a look back at Suffolk's amazing industrial past in this fascinating museum set in the original buildings of the Richard Garrett Engineering Works including six exhibition halls and Grade II listed Long Shop built in 1852. Discover Leiston's unique history. First production line to first woman doctor. See how Garretts developed from making hand tools in a forge to a world famous company producing steam engines, electric vehicles, diesel tractors, munitions, radio and radar equipment and plastics. Learn about 200 years of local, social and industrial history including Victorian Zeal and the Industrial Revolution, engineering, women's rights, agricultural machinery, WWII Leiston USAAF and Zeppelin L48 crash at nearby Theberton. There's something for all ages and interests with hands on puzzles, recently restored Victorian water tower, gift shop and picnic garden and special temporary exhibitions whatever the weather.
1 Apr-End Oct Mon-Sat 10.00-17.00 Sun 11.00-17.00
A£4.50 C£2.00 C(under5)£Free Concessions £4.00

Discount Offer: Two for the Price of One

Historical

Framlingham Castle

Castle Street Framlingham Woodbridge Suffolk IP8 9BT
Tel: 01728 724189
Walk the full length of the remarkable twelfth-century battlements that encircle the castle site.

Gainsborough's House

46 Gainsborough Street Sudbury Suffolk CO10 2EU
Tel: 01787 372958
Gainsborough's House is the birthplace of Thomas Gainsborough RA (1727-88).

Ickworth House Park and Gardens

The Rotunda Ickworth Bury St Edmunds Suffolk IP29 5QE
Tel: 01284 735270 Fax: 01284 735175
www.nationaltrust.org.uk/places/ickworth

[2mi SW of Bury St Edmunds on A143, signposted from A14. Plenty of on-site parking available]

Much to interest visitors with a wonderful collection of paintings including works by Titian, Gainsborough and Velasquez. Set in magnificent Italianate garden and parklands created by Capability Brown with many rare species of plants and trees. Waymarked walks and an adventure playground. Vineyard open days; family and special needs activity trail and exploration packs; handling collection and replica costumes for children. New visitor facilities in the West Wing of the House (not normally on visitor route). Dogs on leads and only in park.

House: 17 Mar-4 Nov daily 13.00-17.00 except Wed & Thur (closes 16.00 in Oct/Nov). Garden: 2 Jan-18 Mar 11.00-16.00, 19 Mar-1 Oct 10.00-17.00, 2 Oct-19 Mar 08 11.00-16.00.
Restaurant & Shop: as House but 10.00-17.00.
Park & Woods: All year dawn-dusk, except 25 Dec

A£7.50 C£3.00 Family discounts. Park & Garden: A£3.50 C£1.00 (includes access to Shop & Restaurant). Group rates available on request, pre-booking is essential & there will be no group discounts on Suns & Bank Hol Mons

Discount Offer: One Child Free

Kentwell Hall and Gardens

Long Melford Sudbury Suffolk CO10 9BA
Tel: 01787 310207 Fax: 01787 379318
www.kentwell.co.uk
[Off Suffolk/Essex border .On-site parking]
Kentwell Hall at Long Melford Suffolk, described by the writer Lucy Norton as 'a little great house of magical beauty, one of the loveliest of the Elizabethan houses that still remain to us, with an exterior that is quite unspoiled, a paradise on earth.' Subject of a unique restoration project since 1972. Extensive gardens, dominated by moats and mellow brickwork, enjoyable in every season. Renowned re-creations of sixteenth-century life. These take place on at least one weekend each month from April to September. Then anything from about 50 to, perhaps, 400 of Kentwell's 'Tudors' re-create aspects of daily life at the Hall over 400 years ago. Also occasional Re-creations of WWII daily life. 3 week season of Open Air Entertainments - Plays, Opera and Concerts (Classical, Jazz or Popular) - in late July/early August. Beautiful, peaceful

venue for weddings, dinners, conferences, Tudor banquets and corporate events of all kinds. We do have disabled access but this limited in some areas. Photography within the house is not allowed. Email us on info@kentwell.co.uk
Garden & Farm only: 11, 18, 25 Feb, 4, 11, 18, 25 Mar & half term daily 11.00-16.00. House, Gardens & Farm: 11.00-17.00 Sun-Wed, Apr-13 June & Easter Hols (2-14 Apr) & Summer half term (May 29-June 2), daily; July 11-end Aug, daily; Sept, Sun- Wed; Oct, Suns & half term (23-31 Oct) daily. Re-creation Days/WEs, 11.00-17.00: 6-9 Apr, 5-7 & 26-28 May, 17, 23-24, 30 June, 1, 6-8, 21-22 July, 4-5 & 24-27 Aug, 22-23 Sept & 20-21 Oct. There are occasional other Special Events & House may be closed, or close early for a function, so call before travelling any distance. Closed Nov-Jan
House, Garden & Farm on non-event days: A£7.75 C(under5)£Free C(5-15)£5.00 OAPs£6.75. Reductions for Gardens & Farm only on all Open Days when no event. Special prices may apply on all events days. Please phone for details

Discount Offer: One Child Free

Orford Castle

Castle Terrace Orford Woodbridge Suffolk IP12 2ND
Tel: 01394 450472
Visit the great keep of Henry II with its three huge towers rising 30 metres and providing commanding views over Orford Ness.

Living History Museums

Museum of East Anglian Life

Iliffe Way Stowmarket Suffolk IP14 1DL
Tel: 01449 612229
The extensive 70 acre all weather museum is set in an attractive river valley site.

Military & Defence Museums

Maritime Museum

Sparrow Nest Gardens Whapload Road
Lowestoft Suffolk NR32 1XG
Tel: 01502 561963
Models of ancient and modern fishing and commercial boats are exhibited.

Orford Ness

Orford Quay Orford Woodbridge IP12 2NU
Tel: 01394 450900 / 450057
[Accessed by ferry only from Orford Quay]
Described as 'half wilderness, half military junk-yard' Orford Ness was once the site of Britain's top-secret atomic weapons testing.
Boats cross regularly between 10.00-14.00. Last ferry leaves the Ness at 17.00

Natural History Museums

Amber Museum

15 Market Place Southwold Suffolk IP18 6EA
Tel: 01502 723394
A purpose-built museum dedicated to the story and history of amber.

Places of Worship

Bury St Edmunds Abbey

Bury St Edmunds Suffolk
Tel: 01284 764667
The impressive ruins of one of Europe's most powerful medieval monasteries.

St Edmundsbury Cathedral

Abbey House Angel Hill Bury St Edmunds
Suffolk IP33 1LS
Tel: 01284 754933
Built around 1500 for pilgrims visiting the Shrine of St. Edmund, St James' became a cathedral in 1914.

Railways

Mid-Suffolk Light Railway

Wetheringsett Stowmarket Suffolk IP14 5PW
Tel: 01449 766899
The 'Middy' as it was 90 years ago.
Closed Oct-Mar

Spectator Sports

Spedeworth International (EA) Ltd

Foxhall Stadium Foxhall Road Ipswich Suffolk
IP4 5TL
Tel: 01473 612 423 Fax: 01473 626 152
www.spedeworth.co.uk
[Plenty of on-site parking available]
Come and see World Class Racing in East Anglia. Experience the thrill of wheel-to-wheel action in non-stop racing. Here at Spedeworth we aim to provide the spectator with great sporting events throughout the year. With Stock Cars and Banger racing there's something for everyone. We have drivers racing from all over the UK and Europe, Oval Racing really is a thrill a minute for spectators. The stadium has a fantastic wide tarmac oval (400mtrs) with a concrete perimeter wall, which makes for very fast racing - up to 70 mph with excellent viewing for spectators all the way around the circuit. Every July Foxhall Stadium features the National Hot Rod World Final - the pinnacle of the racing diary. We have fully licensed bars and a selection of catering outlets to suit all tastes. Call for a programme of events!
Every other Saturday night & Bank Holiday Mons
A£12.00 C(5-14)£6.00 OAPs£8.50
C(under5)£Free

Sporting History Museums

National Horseracing Museum and Tours

99 High Street Newmarket Suffolk CB8 8JL I
Tel: 01638 667333 Fax: 01638 665600
www.nhrm.co.uk
[On High St in centre of Newmarket off A14. Ample car parking in the town]

The story of horseracing is told through the Museum's permanent collections that feature the horses, people, events and scandals that make the sport so colourful. Highlights include the head of Persimmon (a great Royal Derby winner in 1896), a special display about Fred Archer (a Victorian jockey who committed suicide after losing the struggle to keep his weight down), items associated with Red Rum, Lester Piggott, Frankie Dettori and other heroes of the turf. Learn all there is to know about the horse and jockey and experience the thrill of riding on the horse simulator in The Practical Gallery. Retired jockeys and trainers staff the Practical Gallery and make the world of racing come alive. New for 2007: 'The Life and Works of Alfred Munnings' exhibition. Daily minibus tours take visitors behind-the-scenes into a Trainer's yard, the Gallops and the Equine Pool.
Museum: 2 Apr-4 Nov daily including Bank Hols 11.00-16.30. Cafe & shop open all year but closed on Sun during winter period. Tours depart at 09.20 on Museum open days (except Sun).
A£5.50 C£3.00 Concessions£4.50 (includes temporary exhibitions), Family Ticket (A2+C2) £12.00. Group rate (20+): 10% discount (must be pre-booked). Pre-booked tours: A£22.00 Concessions£20.00 (includes entry to museum and exhibitions)

Discount Offer: Two for the Price of One

Theme & Adventure Parks

Go Ape! High Wire Forest Adventure

High Lodge Forest Visitor Centre Thetford Forest Nr. Brandon Suffolk IP27 0AF
Tel: 0870 420 7876
www.goape.co.uk

[On Norfolk/Suffolk border, off B1107 between Thetford & Brandon. Plenty of on-site parking available]

Take to the trees and experience an exhilarating course of rope bridges, 'Tarzan Swings' and zip-slides up to 40 feet above the ground! Share approximately three hours of memorable fun and adventure, which you'll be talking about for days. Book online and watch people Go Ape! at www.goape.co.uk. Minimum height 1.4m. Maximum weight 130 kg (20.5 stone). Under-18s must be accompanied by a participating adult. One adult can supervise either two children (where one or both of them in under 16 years old) or up to five 16-17 year olds. Pre-booking is essential to avoid disappointment. Book online or by telephone (there is a £1.00 booking fee on all telephone bookings).

10-25 Feb & 23 Mar-2 Nov daily, Nov Sat-Sun. Closed Dec-Jan
Gorillas (18yrs+) £25.00, Baboons (10-17yrs) £20.00

Discount Offer: Two for the Price of One

Pleasurewood Hills Theme Park

Leisure Way Corton Lowestoft Suffolk
NR32 5DZ
Tel: 01502 586000 Fax: 01502 567393
www.pleasurewoodhills.com

[Off A12 at Lowestoft. Plenty of on-site parking available]

Don't let the year slip by without a visit to the regions biggest and best theme park, Pleasurewood Hills. Set in 50 acres of beautiful coastal parkland just 10 minutes south of Gt. Yarmouth and only 5 minutes north of Lowestoft. Pleasurewood Hills has all the ingredients for a great day out and really does have something for all members of the family (whether young or young at heart). From adrenalin-fuelled white-knuckle thrill rides and coasters like Enigma, Wizzy Dizzy and Thunder Struck to white-water family favourites that are guaranteed to 'cool you off' including Mellow Yellow and the Wave Breaker. There's even a great selection of fun rides for the small adventures. You'll come for the rides and you'll stay for the shows...prepare to be entertained with a range of first class shows including the awesome Sea Lions, the hilarious Parrots and the breathtaking acrobatics in the Circus spectacular. See our website for specific opening dates, times and full price lists.
31 Mar-28 Oct (dates not inclusive), please see our website for specific opening dates
Over 1.4m £14.50, 1m-1.4m £12.50, under 1m £Free. Prices will increase during high season

Discount Offer: Three for the Price of Two

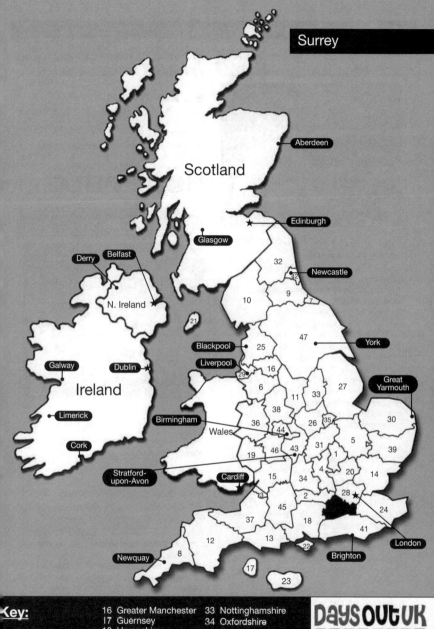

Surrey

Aberdeen

Scotland

Edinburgh

Glasgow

Derry Belfast

N. Ireland

Newcastle

32

42

9

10

7

21

47 York

Blackpool 25

Liverpool

16

29

Galway Dublin

Ireland

6

11 33

27

Great Yarmouth

Limerick

38

30

Birmingham

36 44

26 35

5

39

Wales

19 46 43

31

1

20 14

Cork

15

34

4

28 London

Stratford-upon-Avon

Cardiff

3

2

24

45

18

41

37

13

22

Brighton

Newquay

8

12

17

23

Birds, Butterflies & Bees

Birdworld, Underwater World and Jenny Wren Farm

Farnham Road Holt Pound Farnham Surrey
GU10 4LD
Tel: 01420 22140 Fax: 01420 23715
www.birdworld.co.uk

[By road: follow brown & white cockatoo sign boards. 3mi S of Farnham on A325. Well sign-posted from M3. Easily accessible from M25. Rail: train service runs from Waterloo through to Aldershot & Farnham. Buses run from Farnham Station. Aldershot to Birdworld: 6mi (using bus service). Farnham to Birdworld: 3mi (using a taxi or bus). Plenty of on-site parking available]

28 acres of garden and parkland are home to a wide variety of birds, from penguins to parrots, pelicans to peacocks. Meet some of the birds with their keepers at the Heron Theatre shows and learn more about them. Children will enjoy the special penguin feeding times and animal encounter sessions at the Jenny Wren children's farm. Shop and self-service restaurant. There are play areas and snack bars in the park. Underwater World contains a beautiful collection of marine and freshwater tropical fish, plus the alligators. There is also a link path to award winning Forest Lodge Garden Centre.
14 Feb-end Oct daily, Nov-mid Dec Sat-Sun, mid Dec-early Jan daily, early Jan-mid Feb Sat-Sun. Summer 10.00-18.00, Winter 10.00-16.30. Please call to confirm specific dates
A£11.95 C(3-14)&Concessions£9.95, Family Ticket(A2+C2) £39.95. Group rates available on request

Discount Offer: Two for the Price of One

Country Parks & Estates

Box Hill - The Old Fort

Box Hill Road Box Hill Tadworth Surrey
KT20 7LB
Tel: 01306 885502
Many beautiful walks and spectacular views towards the South Downs. On the summit there is an information centre, shop and a fort.

Festivals & Shows

Guilfest

Stoke Park Guildford Surrey GU1 1ER
Tel: 01483 454159 Fax: 01483 306551
www.guilfest.co.uk

[Rail: South West Trains run every 30min to Guildford from London Waterloo. Trains also run from Portsmouth. Festival is 10min walk from station. For coach tickets, please call 0115 912 9120. Plenty of on-site parking available]

A three day family outdoor festival with music, comedy, theatre, art and craft stalls, workshops, children's entertainment. You can also camp if you would like. Giant beer tent, cuisines from all around the world. Past acts have included Blondie, Simple Minds and Van Morrison.
13-15 July 2007 Fri 12.00-Midnight, Sat & Sun 10.00-Midnight
Prices vary, call for details

Hampton Court Palace Flower Show

Hampton Court Palace grounds East Molesey Surrey
Tel: 0870 842 2227
www.rhs.org.uk/flowershows

[Plenty of on-site parking available]

At the height of summer, the RHS hosts the Hampton Court Palace Flower Show - the world's largest annual flower show. In this spacious, historic location away from the hubbub of central London there is enough to fill your day from dawn till dusk. Admire 50 new gardens, explore 4 floral marquees where you can see, smell, touch and purchase an abundance of floral delights. Discover the Festival of Roses, picnic on the banks of the Long Water Canal and browse 100s of independent sellers of high-quality gifts - from hats to sundials and from trowels to lawnmowers.
5-8 July 2007, Thur-Sat 10.00-19.30 Sun 10.00-17.30
10.00-19.30: A£25.00, 15.00-19.30: A£16.00. C(5-15)£5.00 C(under5)£Free

Folk & Local History Museums

Bourne Hall Museum

Spring Street Ewell Epsom Surrey KT17 1UF
Tel: 020 8394 1734
A museum of Epsom & Ewell with relics of Henry VIII's Nonsuch Palace and the Epsom Spa visited by Samuel Pepys.

Elmbridge Museum

Church Street Weybridge Surrey KT13 8DE
Tel: 01932 843573
Elmbridge Museum tells the story of the Elmbridge area since prehistoric times.

Godalming Museum

109A High Street Godalming Surrey GU7 1AQ
Tel: 01483 426510
The museum is housed in a fifteenth-century town house. Displays relate to the local history of Godalming.

Guildford Museum

Castle Arch Guildford Surrey GU1 3SX
Tel: 01483 444750 Fax: 01483 532391
www.guildfordmuseum.co.uk

[200yds down Quarry St from High St, adjoining Castle grounds]

Guildford Museum is a beautiful seventeenth-century building adjoining the castle grounds in Guildford. Step into the world of prehistoric man, the Romans and Saxons, monks and friars, Lewis Carroll, the Victorians and local industries when you visit Guildford Museum. The archaeology gallery shows the development of life in Surrey from prehistoric times to the Middle Ages. The local history gallery displays the crafts and industries of the Guildford area and there is a fine collection of needlework on display. There is an Art Corner for children and children's activities, craft ideas and quiz trails available in the school holidays.
All year Mon-Sat 11.00-17.00. Closed Christmas through to New Year plus Good Fri
Admission Free

Food & Drink

Denbies Wine Estate

London Road Dorking Surrey RH5 6AA
Tel: 01306 876616 Fax: 01306 888930
www.denbieswineestate.com

[On A24, outskirts of Dorking. Rail: Dorking, 15min. Plenty of free on-site parking available]

Set in the spectacular scenery of the Surrey Hills, Denbies is one of the largest privately owned vineyards in Europe. The chateau-style visitor centre offers excellent facilities. Denbies is an all weather destination with wine experience tours which operate all year, a choice of restaurants, regularly changing art exhibitions, wine and gift shop and kitchen garden centre. 4-diamond farmhouse bed and breakfast accommodation for those wishing to extend their stay.

Wine & Gift Shop: Jan-Mar Mon-Fri 10.00-17.00 Sat 10.00-17.30 Sun 11.30-17.30. Apr-Dec Mon-Sat 10.00-17.30 Sun 11.30-17.30. Winery Tours & Tastings: Jan-Mar Mon-Fri on the hour from 11.00-15.00 (not 13.00) Sat 11.00-16.00 (not 13.00) Sun 12.00-16.00. Apr-Dec Mon-Sat on the hour from 11.00-16.00 (not 13.00) Sun 12.00-16.00. Vineyard Train Tour: Apr-Sept daily on the hour from 11.00-16.00. Oct 11.00-15.00-ring for confirmation

Winery Tours & Tastings: A£7.25 C(under5)£Free C(6-17)£3.00 (free grape juice) OAPs&Students(NUS/USI)£6.50, Family Ticket (A2+C2) £15.00 Group rates (20+) £6.25. Vineyard Train Tour: A£4.00 C(under5)£Free C(6-16)£3.00 OAPs&NUS/USI£3.50, Family Ticket (A2+C2) £12.00 Group rates (20+): £3.00. Dual Ticket Internal & External: A£10.25 OAPs&Students(NUS/USI)£9.25, Family Ticket (A2+C2) £25.00. Group rates available on request, please call 01306 742224

Discount Offer: Two for the Price of One

Forests & Woods

Alice Holt Woodland Park

Forestry Commission Bucks Horn Oak Farnham Surrey GU10 4LS
Tel: 01420 23666 / 520212 Fax: 01420 22082
www.forestry.gov.uk

[Off A325. Plenty of on-site parking available]

This ancient forest has a children's playground, the Timberline Trail (a mini assault course), the Habitat Trail (a series of large animal play structures), as well as an Easy Access Trail. Take part in the variety of holiday activities, such as den building and crafts, or go on the wildlife walks to see the deer, nightjar, bats and fungi. There are also outdoor programmes for mums and toddlers. Forestry Adventure, which organises bike hire, climbing, shooting and archery is located in the park and there is a visitor's centre serving refreshments and ice creams.

All year daily 08.00-17.00

Admission Free, car parking charges apply

Gardens & Horticulture

Claremont Landscape Garden

Portsmouth Road Esher Surrey KT10 9JG
Tel: 01372 467806
One of the earliest surviving English landscape gardens. Features include a lake, island with pavilion, grotto and turf amphitheatre.

Painshill Park

Portsmouth Road Cobham Surrey KT11 1JE
Tel: 01932 868113 Fax: 01932 868001
www.painshill.co.uk
*[By Road: Via M25 J10 & A3 Northbound or
Southbound. Exit A245 towards Cobham.
Entrance & free car park in between sts, 200m E
of A245/A307 roundabout. By Rail: From
Waterloo to Cobham/Stoke D'Abernon,
Weybridge or Walton-on-Thames then taxi. By
Bus: The Surrey Parks & Gardens Explorer Bus
Route 515/515A (Timetable Info: 0870 608 2608
or www.surreycc.gov.uk) available from Kingston,
Surbiton, Thames Ditton, Esher, Wisley &
Guildford or Bus Route 408 (Epsom Buses)
Epsom / Leatherhead / Stoke D'Abernon (No Sat,
Sun or BH Service)]*
Come and enjoy Painshill Park's eighteenth-cen-
tury Georgian landscape created by Hamilton as
a Living Work of Art. Discover 158 acres of
awarding winning authentically restored parkland and lake complete with fabulous vistas,
unusual follies and a magical Crystal Grotto*.
Our American Roots exhibition explores the
eighteenth-century exchange of plants between
Europe and America and includes the John
Bartram Heritage Collection of plants and
shrubs (National Collection Holders).
Throughout the year, especially at weekends
and during the school holidays, you can enjoy a
wide variety of exciting events for all the family
as well as a series of informative and entertaining adult talks. We offer a fantastic choice of
outdoor children's parties for age range 4 to 12
years set within our stunning landscape and the
conservatory situated within a private walled
garden offers you the perfect location for a truly
memorable wedding day or private party. Our
discovery centre offers a range of educational
programmes for colleges and schools covering
a variety of curriculum areas for all key stages.
The Hamilton Tea Room offers a range of light
refreshments and afternoon tea and our gift
shop has a lovely selection of unusual gifts to
purchase, including wine from our own vineyard.
Dogs on a lead are welcome.
*Mar-Oct 10.30-18.00 (or dusk); Nov-Feb 10.30-
16.00 (or dusk). Closed 25 & 26 Dec. Special*
*arrangements for school visits (all Key Stages
catered for). *Limited Grotto opening hours Sat,
Sun & Bank Hols only*
A£6.60 C(under5)£Free C(5-16)£3.85
Concessions£5.80, Family Ticket (A2+C4)
£22.00. Group rate (10+): £5.80, additional
£1.00 per person for optional guided tour (pre-
booking essential)

Ramster Gardens

Ramster Petworth Road Chiddingfold
Godalming Surrey GU8 4SN
Tel: 01428 654167 Fax: 01428 658345
*[On Surrey/Sussex borders, only 1h from London,
& within easy reach of Guildford, Farnham,
Godalming & Cranleigh. Haslemere & its excellent
train service to Waterloo is 5mi away. On A283
1.5mi S of Chiddingfold]*
A mature flowering shrub garden of over 20
acres (famous for its rhododendron and azalea
collection) that's open from 6th April to 24th
June. It's full of unusual and interesting plants
that flourish under a canopy of oaks and larch-
es. In April, sheets of daffodils, camellias, magnolias and early flowering rhododendrons cover
the ground. In May, the brilliant display of
rhododendrons and azaleas is at its best while a
carpet of bluebells fills the air with scent, and
the ever-changing colours of the garden are
reflected in the pond. The Tea House is open
daily for drinks, delicious homemade cakes and
sandwiches. There's also a small farm shop selling local produce. The biannual 'Ramster
Embroidery Exhibition' runs from 20th April to
1st May and features some of the UK's leading
embroidery.
*6 Apr-24 June daily 10.00-17.00 (Embroidery
Exhibition 20 Apr-1 May)*
Garden: £5.00 C(under16)Free OAPs £4.50

RHS Garden Wisley

Royal Horticultural Society

A fabulous garden for a fabulous day out

Something to see all year round

Open all year

- Shop
- Plant Centre
- Cafés
- Restaurant
- Coffee Shop

On the A3 in Surrey north of Guildford near J10 of the M25

RHS Garden Wisley
Woking, Surrey, GU23 6QB
Tel: 0845 260 9000 www.rhs.org.uk

RHS Garden Wisley

RHS Garden Wisley Woking Surrey GU23 6QB
Tel: 0845 260 9000 Fax: 01483 211750
www.rhs.org.uk
[J10 M25 on A3, London 22mi, Guildford 7mi]
Stretching over 240 acres, Wisley is the flagship of the Royal Horticultural Society demonstrating the very best in gardening practices. Highlights include the magnificent rock garden, rock pools and Alpine Houses, glories of the Mixed Borders and Rose Garden and 16 acre Fruit Field containing over 760 apple cultivars. Model gardens demonstrate design ideas on a realisable scale reflecting changing styles and new

techniques. Whatever the season, the Garden serves as a working encyclopedia for gardeners of all levels. Special events and activities take place throughout the year. New for 2007 the opening of the new Wisley Glasshouse. See spectacular plants from the Tropics, get amongst the canopy and see what happens in the root zone.
All year daily, Mon-Fri 10.00-18.00 (Nov-Feb 16.30), Sat & Sun 09.00-18.00 (Nov-Feb 16.30)
A£7.50 C(0-6)£Free C(6-16)£2.00. Group rate (10+): £5.50

Discount Offer: Two for the Price of One

Winkworth Arboretum

Hascombe Road Nr Godalming GU8 4AD
Tel: 01483 208477 Fax: 01483 208252
www.nationaltrust.org.uk
[SE of Guilford. Plenty of on-site parking available]
110 acres of native and exotic trees and shrubs. The arboretum is set in a valley in the rolling Surrey hillside woodland in an Area Of Oustanding Natural Beauty (AONB). The paths lead down to a lake with a boathouse and newly created wetland area. Winkworth is famous in Spring for its mass of bluebells, and also flowering shrubs such as azaleas and rhododendrons. Autumn though is equally impressive as the leaves on the trees and shrubs change colour in a riot of reds and golds and put on a show which is difficult to rival.
Dawn-Dusk
A£5.00 C£2.50

Discount Offer: Save £5.00! 2 Adults and 3 Children admitted for £12.50

Historical

Clandon Park

West Clandon Guildford Surrey GU4 7RQ
Tel: 01483 222482
A grand Palladian mansion built circa 1730 by
the Venetian architect Giacomo Leoni.

Claremont House

The Claremont Fan Court Foundation Ltd
Claremont Drive Esher Surrey KT10 9LY
Tel: 01372 467841
All the state rooms are open and you can see
Lord Clive's marble plunge bath and the unique
tunnel and turning circle entrance.

Guildford Castle and Grounds

Castle Grounds Castle Street Guildford Surrey
Tel: 01483 444750
www.guildfordmuseum.co.uk

[A3 signposted in Guildford town centre]

Set in the beautiful Castle grounds, stands the
Great Tower of Guildford Castle. The castle was
probably founded soon after 1066 by William
the Conqueror. Later a stone tower, or keep,
was built which may date largely from the time
of King Stephen and the battle for the throne
with his cousin Matilda. Later the Castle was
used as a courtroom and gaol, and the prisoners' graffiti can be seen on the walls. In Tudor
times, the Castle was no longer used as a gaol
and was given a make-over with new and fashionable brick windows and fireplaces. The
Castle has been extensively restored and was
re-opened to the public in June 2004. There is

a viewing platform on the roof of the castle,
accessed by a spiral staircase.
*Castle: Mar & Oct Sat-Sun 11.00-17.00, Apr-
Sept daily 10.00-17.00. Grounds: All year daily
dawn-dusk*
A£2.30 Concessions£1.00

Guildford House Gallery

155 High Street Guildford Surrey GU1 3AJ
Tel: 01483 444740 Fax: 01483 444742
www.guildfordhouse.co.uk

[N side of High St opposite Sainsbury]

Important features of the fascinating building are
the finely decorated plaster ceilings, panelled
rooms, wrought iron balcony and window
catches, together with the richly carved oak and
elm staircase. Guildford House dates from 1660
and has been Guildford's art gallery since 1957.
Changing art exhibitions throughout the year.
All year Tue-Sat 10.00-16.45
Admission Free

Hatchlands Park

East Clandon Guildford Surrey GU4 7RT
Tel: 01483 222482
A handsome house built in 1758 by Stiff
Leadbetter for Admiral Boscawen, and set in a
beautiful Repton park offering a variety of park
and woodland walks.

For great hotel deals call Superbreak on 01904 679999 or visit www.superbreak.com

Loseley Park

Guildford Surrey GU3 1HS
Tel: 01483 304440 Fax: 01483 302036
www.loseley-park.com

[Leave A3 at Compton on B3000 signposted. Rail: Guildford 2m. Bus: 1.25m. Plenty of on-site parking available]

Loseley Park, home of the More-Molyneux family for nearly 500 years, is set amid 1,400 acres of glorious parkland and rolling pastures. Built in 1562 by an ancestor of the present owner, the Elizabethan mansion features many fine works of art including paintings, tapestries and panelling from Henry VIII's Nonsuch Palace. The Walled Garden has been carefully restored and includes an award-winning rose garden with over 1,000 old fashioned rose bushes. The herb garden, planted with over 200 herbs (some dating back to ancient times), is divided into 4 separate sections: culinary, medicinal, household and ornamental. Other features include flower and white gardens, organic vegetable garden specialising in companion planting, with an area devoted to producing special seed for the National Seed Library (HDRA), an idyllic moat walk and new wild flower meadow. Member of the Historic Houses Association. Gift shop sells an exciting array of unusual and original gifts based on a gardening and historical theme. Photography permitted outside house only.
Gardens, Grounds, Shop & Tea room: May-Sept Tue-Sun & Bank Hol Mons 11.00-17.00. House: May-Aug Tue-Thur, Sun & Bank Hol Mons 13.00-17.00
House & Gardens: A£7.00 C£3.50 Concessions£6.50. Gardens & Grounds: A£4.00 C£2.00 Concessions£3.50. Group rates available on request, must be pre-booked

Polesden Lacey

Great Bookham Dorking Surrey RH5 6BD
Tel: 01372 458203 / 452048
The house is handsomely furnished with tapestries, porcelain, paintings and other artworks.

On the Water

Busbridge Lakes, Waterfowl and Gardens

Hambledon Road Busbridge Godalming Surrey GU8 4AY
Tel: 01483 421955 Fax: 01483 425903
www.busbridgelakes.co.uk

[1.5mi from Goldalming off B2130 Bus: to Home Farm Rd (6min walk). Rail: Milford 2mi, Godalming 1.5mi. Plenty of on-site parking available]

Busbridge Lakes is situated in a valley of some forty acres, with three spring fed lakes, home to over 150 species of wild waterfowl, pheasants, cranes, peafowl and fancy bantams, from all over the world, many endangered. It is a Heritage 2* Garden with follies and grottos; outstanding old specimen trees; nature trails. Much flora and fauna around the lakes and over the hills. Wander amongst the birds in the stunning landscaped gardens, many with their young babies. An ideal place for photography due to the wealth of colour and variety of scenery. A place of outstanding beauty.
6-15 Apr, 6-7 & 27-28 May, 19-27 Aug 10.30-17.30
A£5.00 C(5-13)£3.50 OAPs£4.00

*established in England.

River Wey Boat Houses

Millbrook Guildford Surrey GU1 3XJ
Tel: 01483 504494
Boating activities for all ages from Farncombe and Guildford Boat Houses.

Places of Worship

Guildford Cathedral

Stag Hill Guildford Surrey GU2 7UP
Tel: 01483 547860
The cathedral overlooks the University of Surrey beneath it. Its bricks are made from clay taken from the hill on which it stands.

Waverley Abbey

Farnham Surrey
Tel: 01483 252000
The first Cistercian Abbey to be established in England (founded in 1128).

Social History Museums

Rural Life Centre

The Reeds Tilford Farnham Surrey GU10 2DL
Tel: 01252 795571 Fax: 01252 795571
www.rural-life.org.uk

[Off A287 3mi S of Farnham halfway between Frensham / Tilford follow brown signposts. Plenty of on-site parking available]

The Rural Life Centre is a museum of past village life covering the years from 1750 to 1960. It is set in over ten acres of garden and wood-land and housed in purpose-built and recon-structed buildings including a chapel, village hall, cricket pavilion and schoolroom. Displays show village crafts and trades such as wheel-wrighting of which the centre's collection is probably the finest in the country. An historic village playground provides entertainment for chil-dren as does a preserved narrow gauge light railway which operates on Sundays. There is also an arboretum with over 100 species of tree from around the world. Indoor and outdoor pic-nic areas.

14 Mar-31 Oct Wed-Sun & Bank Hol Mons 10.00-17.00, Winter Wed & Sun only 11.00-16.00
A£5.50 C(5-16)£3.50 OAPs£4.50, Family Ticket(A2+C2) £16.00

Discount Offer: Two for the Price of One

Sport & Recreation

Campaign Paintball Park
Old Lane Cobham Surrey KT11 1NH
Tel: 01932 865999 Fax: 01932 865744
www.campaignpaintball.com
[Plenty of on-site parking available]

Campaign is situated in 100 acres of ancient forest and has enough space for over ten game zones. Through large investments these areas are not just 'trees and mud' but highly developed themed arenas. These include a film-set designed replica 'wild west' town, a WWII trench system and 'convoy' scenario with trucks, tanks, jeeps and a scud missile! For those really wet days Campaign also has a flood lit all weather speedball arena. Located near Cobham, Surrey, where the A3 meets the M25, Campaign Paintball Park is only 20 minutes from Central London. It is easily reached by train, with direct regular services from Waterloo or Clapham Junction. The site itself is just 5 minutes from Effingham Junction. Opened in 1998, this venue comes highly recommended for birthday parties, school and college trips, stags parties and office outings.
From £12.50

Discount Offer: 100 Free Paintballs (when you pay for a full game)

Theme & Adventure Parks

Chessington World of Adventures
Leatherhead Road Chessington KT9 2NE
Tel: 0870 444 7777
The park is full of great rides and attractions for under-12s including Land of the Dragons.

Go Ape! High Wire Forest Adventure
Alice Holt Woodland Park Nr Farnham Surrey GU10 4LS
Tel: 0870 420 7876
www.goape.co.uk

[Take A325 on A31 (heading S). Turn L after approx 3mi then follow signs to Woodland Park. Plenty of on-site parking available]

Take to the trees and experience an exhilarating course of rope bridges, 'Tarzan Swings' and zip-slides up to 40 feet above the ground! Share approximately three hours of memorable fun and adventure, which you'll be talking about for days. Book online and watch people Go Ape! at www.goape.co.uk. Minimum height 1.4m. Maximum weight 130 kg (20.5 stone). Under-18s must be accompanied by a participating adult. One adult can supervise either two children (where one or both of them in under 16 years old) or up to five 16-17 year olds. Pre-booking is essential to avoid disappointment. Book online or by telephone (there is a £1.00 booking fee on all telephone bookings).
30 Mar-2 Nov (plus Nov weekends). Closed Dec-Jan
Gorillas (18yrs+) £25.00, Baboons (10-17yrs) £20.00

Discount Offer: Two for the Price of One

Thorpe Park
Staines Road Chertsey Surrey KT16 8PN
Tel: 0870 444 4466
Home to some of the most exciting roller coaster experiences in Europe.

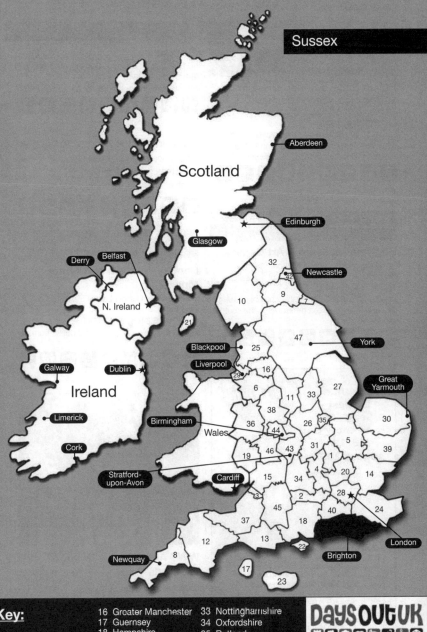

Sussex

Scotland

Aberdeen

Edinburgh

Glasgow

Derry Belfast

N. Ireland

Newcastle

32

42

9

7

10

47

York

21

Blackpool

25

Galway Dublin

Liverpool

29

16

Great
Yarmouth

Ireland

6

27

30

Limerick

11

33

Birmingham

38

26

35

5

39

Wales

36

44

31

Cork

19

46

43

1

20

14

Stratford-
upon-Avon

Cardiff

15

4

34

28

London

2

24

3

45

40

Newquay

37

18

Brighton

8

12

13

22

17

23

Key:

1 Bedfordshire	16 Greater Manchester	33 Nottinghamshire
2 Berkshire	17 Guernsey	34 Oxfordshire
3 Bristol	18 Hampshire	35 Rutland
4 Buckinghamshire	19 Herefordshire	36 Shropshire
5 Cambridgeshire	20 Hertfordshire	37 Somerset
6 Cheshire	21 Isle Of Man	38 Staffordshire
7 Cleveland	22 Isle Of Wight	39 Suffolk
8 Cornwall	23 Jersey	40 Surrey
9 County Durham	24 Kent	41 Sussex
10 Cumbria	25 Lancashire	42 Tyne & Wear
11 Derbyshire	26 Leicestershire	43 Warwickshire
12 Devon	27 Lincolnshire	44 West Midlands
13 Dorset	28 London	45 Wiltshire
14 Essex	29 Merseyside	46 Worcestershire
15 Gloucestershire	30 Norfolk	47 Yorkshire
	31 Northamptonshire	
	32 Northumberland	

DAYS OUT UK

The place to look for places to go

Animal Attractions

Seven Sisters Sheep Centre

The Fridays Gilberts Drive East Dean
Eastbourne East Sussex BN20 0DG
Tel: 01323 423207
Over 45 British breeds of sheep and all the
other farm favourites, tame enough to touch
and feed. Daily bottle feeding sessions.

Arts, Crafts & Textiles

Brighton Museum & Art Gallery

Royal Pavilion Gardens Brighton East Sussex
BN1 1EE
Tel: 01273 290900
Brighton Museum & Art Gallery has become
one of the most visited museums in the south-
east.

Fabrica

40 Duke Street Brighton East Sussex BN1 1AG
Tel: 01273 778646
Art gallery in the heart of Brighton town centre.

Worthing Museum and Art Gallery

Chapel Road Worthing West Sussex BN1 1HP

Tel: 01903 239999 / 221067
A rich collection of archaeological finds.

Birds, Butterflies & Bees

Bentley Wildfowl and Motor Museum

Harveys Lane Halland Lewes East Sussex
BN8 5AF
Fax: 01825 840573 / 841541
Hundreds of swans, geese and ducks from all
over the world.

WWT Arundel, The Wildfowl and Wetlands Trust

Mill Road Arundel West Sussex BN18 9PB
Tel: 01903 883355 Fax: 01903 884834
www.wwt.org.uk/visit/arundel

*[Close to A27 & A29, at Arundel follow brown
signs, 0.75mi along Mill Rd on R hand side. Rail:
Arundel 1.5mi. On-site parking available]*

Make a direct contribution to conservation.
WWT Arundel is a place to visit 364 days of the
year. Many hundreds of ducks, swans and
geese. Take a walk in beautiful scenery over-
looked by Arundel Castle, or watch birds from

our superb viewing gallery, or restaurant. No dogs except guide dogs.

All year daily, Summer: 09.30-17.30, Winter: 09.30-16.30. Closed 25 Dec

A£7.68 C(4-16)£3.75 OAPs£6.17, Family Ticket (A2+C2) £17.00. Group rates (for 12+) available on request & pre-booking is essential

Discount Offer: Two for the Price of One

Festivals & Shows

Airbourne: Eastbourne's International Airshow

Western Lawns and Seafront King Edwards Parade Eastbourne East Sussex BN21 4BY
Tel: 01323 415442 Fax: 01323 736373
www.visiteastbourne.com
[On Seafront & Western Lawns. A22 from London, A259 from Hastings, A27 from Brighton. Rail: Trains from London & Gatwick half-hourly]

Airbourne is a four-day international air show that takes place along Eastbourne's seafront. There are over 75 flying displays featuring the Red Arrows, the RAF, international aircraft and free-fall parachutists. Also features an RAF ground display, children's entertainment, trade stands and fireworks.
16-19 August 2007 10.00-18.00
Admission Free

Brighton Festival

Various Locations Brighton East Sussex BN1 1EE
Tel: 01273 709709
Brighton Festival is biggest and brightest mixed arts festival in England. Theatre, dance, music, books & debate, children's and family shows.
5-27 May 2007

Brighton Festival Fringe

Various Locations Brighton East Sussex
Tel: 01273 260804
The biggest open access, mixed arts event in England (an alternative programme to the Brighton Festival since 1966).
5-28 May 2007

Brighton Pride

Brighton East Sussex BN1 1EE
Tel: 01273 775939
The biggest and best free Pride festival in the UK, organised by LGBT groups and companies.
28 July-5 August 2007 (various locations). Parade & main event: Sat 4 Aug (Preston Park). Parade starts from Maderia Drive at 11.00. Main event runs 12.00-20.00

Eastbourne Beer Festival

Winter Garden Compton Street Eastbourne East Sussex BN21 4JJ
Tel: 01323 415442 Fax: 01323 736373
www.visiteastbourne.com

Eastbourne's 5th annual Beer Festival - Eastbourne Borough Council team up with

CAMRA's Sussex branch to offer over 120 real ales, ciders, perries, bottled beers and wines. Take your pick from over 120 cask real ales from across the UK. Will your pint be a 'Double Dragon Ale' from Felinfoel (West Wales), a 'Black Gold' from the Scottish Cairngorms or a 'Star of Eastbourne' from Harveys Brewery of Lewes? All weekend there will be live music, pub games and competitions 'on tap.' For further details, check out our website for what promises to be a weekend of fun, music, entertainment and lots of beer.

11-13 October 2007

Tickets available in advance from the Congress Theatre Box Office on 01323 412000 (from July 2007)

Discount Offer: £1.00 off individual admissions

Eastbourne Extreme

Eastbourne Seafront Royal Parade Eastbourne East Sussex BN21 7LQ
Tel: 01323 415442 Fax: 01323 736373
www.visiteastbourne.com
[A22 from London; A259 from Hastings; A27 from Brighton. Trains from London & Gatwick half-hourly. On Eastern Seafront opposite Princes Park]

Eastbourne goes 'Extreme' for the 3rd time! An extreme sports event incorporating the land, sea and air with windsurfing, kite-surfing, thundercat racing, skateboarding, inline skating, paragliding, sailing and rowing to mention a few. Check out the UK International Windsurfing Association freestyle and slalom trials. Across the range of sports there are a variety of demonstrations, displays and hands on 'have a go' sessions. Also features a 'Saturday Night

Skate' around town.
14-15 July 2007
Admission Free

Glyndebourne Festival Opera

Glyndebourne Lewes East Sussex BN8 5UU
Tel: 01273 812321
Glyndebourne Festival Opera is an opera festival held at Glyndebourne, a country house near Lewes. Under the supervision of the Christie family, the festival has been held annually since 1934. Please note, evening dress (black tie/dress) is customary.
19 May-26 August 2007

Hastings Old Town Festival and Carnival Week

Various venues Hastings East Sussex
Tel: 0845 274 1001
A series of festivities celebrating the traditions and myths of the historic Old Town with everything from a free beach concert to a spectacular carnival.
4-12 August 2007

Horsham Town Centre Festival

Horsham Town Centre The Carfax Horsham West Sussex RH12 1ER

Tel: 01403 215279 Fax: 01403 215268
www.horsham.gov.uk
[A24 / A264 / A281 all go to Horsham]

The Horsham Town Centre Festival, entering its
16th year, attracts thousands of visitors to the
town centre. Be delighted by a diverse range of
activities including arts workshops, live music,
wacky street entertainment, a traditional fun fair
as well as other fun treats. The feast of activities
will spread throughout the town and as usual,
the majority of entertainment will be absolutely
free, keeping youngsters and adults alike busy
for the latter part of the half-term week.
25-27 October 2007 10.00-21.00
Admission Free. Fair rides are charged

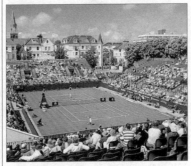

International Women's Open

Devonshire Park Eastbourne East Sussex
BN21 4JJ
Tel: 01323 415442 Fax: 01323 736373
www.visiteastbourne.com

This major international women's tennis tournament takes place in Eastbourne the week
before Wimbledon. See the world's top female
tennis players compete on the famous grass
courts at Devonshire Park. Last year's thrilling
final saw Justine Henin-Hardenne win against
Anastasia Myskina, and it is anticipated that
Justine will return to defend the title in 2007.
16-23 June 2007
Centre Court: 18 June £15.00, 19 June £18.00,
20 June £22.00, 21 June £24.00, 22 June
£26.00, 23 June 27.00 (Weekly Pass: £112.00).
Ground Pass: 16-21 June £6.00 (per day), 22
June £4.00, 23 June £2.00 (Weekly Ground
Pass: £36.00). Tickets are on sale from January
2007 - please call the Box Office on 01323
412000

Discount Offer: Save up to £8.00 off

Ticket Prices

Magnificent Motors

Western Lawns and Seafront King Edwards
Parade Eastbourne East Sussex BN21 4BY
Tel: 01323 415442 Fax: 01323 736373
www.visiteastbourne.com

*[On Seafront & Western Lawns. A22 from
London; A259 from Hastings; A27 from Brighton.
Rail: Trains from London & Gatwick half-hourly]*

Eastbourne's vintage vehicle spectacular, with
over 400 exhibitors. It takes place on the
seafront and includes displays of classic cars,
buses, motorbikes, cycles, cars, military and
commercial vehicles, steam and traction
engines. Vehicles range from 1899-1980 classics, with vintage vehicle rides, funfair, French
market and a cavalcade along the seafront.
5-6 May 2007 10.00-18.00
Admission Free

Paramount Comedy Festival

Brighton East Sussex BN1 1EE
Tel: 01273 709709
For two and a half weeks in October the
biggest and best standup comedians descend
in the city, including a mixture of well-known
acts and up and coming stars.
4-20 October 2007

For great hotel deals call Superbreak on 01904 679999 or visit www.superbreak.com

Rye Arts Festival

Various Venues Rye East Sussex
Tel: 01797 224442
Set against the stunning backdrop of the medieval town of Rye, festival-goers are treated to an array of music, literature, theatre and visual arts; many of which are staged in unusual venues and historic settings.
1-16 September 2007

South of England Show

The South of England Centre Ardingly West Sussex RH17 6TL
Tel: 01444 892700
www.seas.org.uk
[M23, J10 & take A264 towards East Grinstead. At first roundabout, continue straight on along A264. Follow signposts from next roundabout. Rail: East Grinstead & I laywards Heath. Plenty of on-site parking available]
The South of England Show is the highlight of the countryside calendar. Experience everything the countryside has to offer from the magnificent dairy cattle to the world-beating equestrian attractions. The three-day event is also a showcase for hundreds of trade and craft exhibitors. Visitors of all ages will enjoy a sparkling array of entertainment including The Young Craftsman of the Year competition and the fun Casablanca Steps- a superb day out for all!
7-9 June 2007, 09.00-18.00
On the gate: Thur A£13.00 C£5.00 Concessions£9.00 Family Ticket (A2+C2)£30.00; Fri-Sat A£12.00 C£5.00 Concessions£9.00 Family Ticket £30.00. In advance: Thurs, Fri & Sat A£11.00 C£4.00 Concessions£8.00 Family Ticket £25.00

Arundel Museum and Heritage Centre

61 High Street Arundel West Sussex BN18 9ST
Tel: 01903 885708
Exhibitions change regularly but focus on the life of the town of Arundel from Roman times to the twentieth century.
Mar-Sep

Chichester District Museum

29 Little London Chichester West Sussex PO19 1PB
Tel: 01243 784683 Fax: 01243 776766
www.chichester.gov.uk/museum
[From Portsmouth on A27, Museum is on E side of City, turning opposite McDonalds]

Housed in an eighteenth-century corn store, Chichester District Museum explores local history through displays and hands on activities. Start your journey back through time by finding out about local geology and pre-history. Discover what life was like in Roman, Saxon and Medieval Chichester. Upstairs you can find out about Chichester during the Civil War and see how the city changed from the eighteenth century onwards. The museum has a programme of changing exhibitions and events for all ages including talks, walks and children's activities. So come and visit Chichester District Museum and find out about local life in the past.
All year Tue-Sat 10.00-17.30. Closed Bank Hol, Good Fri, 25-26 Dec & 1 Jan
Admission Free

Marlipins Museum

36 High Street Shoreham-By-Sea BN43 5DA
Tel: 01273 462994
www.sussexpast.co.uk

The striking chequerboard facade on Shoreham High Street fronts one of the oldest lay buildings in Sussex, dating originally from the twelfth century. Towards the rear is one of the newest buildings, an award-winning purpose-built extension, with a gallery for temporary displays, education workshops, holiday activities and talks on subjects from Postal History to Pirates. Marlipins Museum (once a Customs House) now holds artefacts from the long history of the Shoreham area and our maritime past. It houses a fine collection of local archaeological material from prehistoric to medieval times. Upstairs are displays on the local silent film industry, the beach and transport from ferries and boat models to Shoreham Airport. Every month sees a new exhibition of paintings and photographs from the Museum's fine collections and temporary visiting shows, including Sussex Sculptors in June and Motor Memories in September. Also a venue for demonstrations and seminars.
1 May-31 Oct: Tue-Sat 10.30-16.30. Closed Sun-Mon & Bank Hols
A£2.50 C£1.50 Concessions£2.00

Discount Offer: Two for the Price of One

Old Town Hall Museum

High Street Hastings East Sussex TN34 1EW
Tel: 0845 274 1053
A walk back in time, covering all the key moments in the old town's history.

Priest House

North Lane West Hoathly near East Grinstead West Sussex RH19 4PP
Tel: 01342 810479
www.sussexpast.co.uk

This timber-framed hall house sits on the western edge of Ashdown Forest in the picturesque Wealden village of West Hoathly. Built in the fifteenth century for the Priory of St. Pancras in Lewes, the property was seized by Henry VIII in 1538 and belonged in turn to Thomas Cromwell, Anne of Cleves, Mary I and Elizabeth I. In the sixteenth century, central chimneys and a fine Horsham stone roof were added when it became a substantial yeoman farmer's house. The Priest House opened as a museum in 1908 and contains collections of seventeenth and eighteenth-century country furniture, ironwork, textiles and domestic objects displayed in furnished rooms. Standing in the colourful surroundings of a traditional cottage garden, the house is the only one of its kind open to the public in the Weald. The garden includes borders of herbaceous perennials, shrubs, wild flowers and over 170 culinary, medicinal and household herbs.
1 Mar-31 Oct Tue-Sat & Bank Hols: 10.30-17.30 Sun 12.00-17.30, 1-31 Aug daily 10.30-17.30
A£2.90 C£1.45 OAPs£2.60, Disabled/Carer £1.45

Discount Offer: Two for the Price of One

Winchelsea Museum

Court Hall High Street Winchelsea East Sussex TN36 4EA
Tel: 01797 226382
The court hall now houses the museum with the old prison cells underneath.

Gardens & Horticulture

Denmans Garden

Denmans Lane Fontwell West Sussex
BN18 0SU
Tel: 01243 542808 Fax: 01243 544064
www.denmans-garden.co.uk

[5mi E of Chichester on A27. Plenty of on-site parking available]

A beautiful garden designed for year round interest - through use of form, colour and texture. Individual plantings are allowed to self-seed and ramble. Nearly 4 acres in size and owned by Michael Neve and John Brookes MBE, renowned garden designer and writer, it is a garden full of ideas to be interpreted within smaller home spaces. Gravel is used extensively in the garden both to walk on and as a growing medium so that you walk through the plantings rather than past them. A dry gravel 'stream' meanders down to a large natural looking pond. There is a walled garden, a refurbished conservatory and a larger glass area for tender plants. The Plant Centre stocks over 1500 varieties of rare and unusual plants. The award winning Garden Café (Les Routiers Cafe of the year 2005 for London & South East) serves a selection of light lunches, coffees, teas and a variety of delicious cakes and is fully licensed.

All year daily 09.00-17.00 (dusk in winter)
A£4.25 C(0-4)£Free C(4+)£2.50 OAPs£3.80, Family Ticket £12.50. Group rate (15+): £3.60

Discount Offer: Two for the Price of One

High Beeches Gardens Conservation Trust

High Beeches Lane Handcross Haywards Heath West Sussex RH17 6HQ
Tel: 01444 400589 Fax: 01444 401543
www.highbeeches.com

[1mi E of A23 at Handcross, on B2110. Plenty of on-site parking available]

Twenty five acres of enchanting woodland and water gardens. Enjoy daffodils, magnolias, rhododendrons, bluebells and azaleas in spring. In autumn, the varied foliage makes a glorious display of scarlet and gold. In summer, four acres of natural Wildflower Meadows are at their best and August is the time to see the magnificent blue woodland gentians.

17 Mar-31 Oct Thur-Tue 13.00-17.00. Closed Weds. Groups by appointment
A£5.50 C(accompanied 0-13)£Free

Discount Offer: Two for the Price of One

Highdown Gardens

Ferring Worthing West Sussex
Tel: 01903 221441
These unique gardens were created out of a chalk pit overlooking the Downs. They are home to a collection of rare plants and trees (deemed a National Collection).

Holly Gate Cactus Garden and Nursery

Billingshurst Road Ashington West Sussex
RH20 3BB
Tel: 01903 892930
www.hollygatecactus.co.uk

[10mi equidistant between Horsham & Worthing on A24 0.5mi off B2133. Plenty of on site parking available]

This unique collection, exceeding 30,000 exotic plants, has accumulated over the years and is known worldwide. It features many rare plants from the more arid areas of the world, such as USA, Mexico, South America, Africa etc, also tropical jungle cactus of Central and South America. The Garden is attractively landscaped beneath 10,000 sq. ft. of glass, enabling visitors to wander leisurely amongst the eye-catching plants. Several plants have developed unusual forms. Some are majestically tall, others, tiny like pebbles. It is an ideal outing, whatever the weather, always with plants in flower and yes something of interest for everyone. Although featured on TV and radio and in various gardening magazines, the Cactus Garden must be visited, to appreciate the full effect of its natural splendour. Our well stocked sales house must also be visited, selling cactus and succulents in all sizes, as well as geraniums, patio plants, perennials, herbs and gift items.

All year daily Mar-Oct 09.00-17.00, Nov-Feb 09.00-16.00. Closed Christmas
A£2.00 C&OAPs£1.50. Group rates 20+ A£1.75 C£1.25

Discount Offer: Two for the Price of One

Leonardslee Lakes and Gardens

Lower Beeding Horsham West Sussex
RH13 6PP
Tel: 01403 891212 Fax: 01403 891305
www.leonardslee.com

[4mi SW of Handcross via B2110 at bottom of M23. BR: Horsham (5mi). Bus: 107. Plenty of on-site parking available]

Leonardslee, listed Grade I, has spectacular woodland gardens, containing world renowned rhododendrons, camellias, magnolias and azaleas. 240 acres nestling in a valley with seven lakes meandering through, Leonardslee provides a paradise for any visitor. In May it is described as one of Europe's most spectacular gardens, when spring flowers blossom they provide an incredible mosaic of colours and reflections. After spring spectacle the gardens calm down to more tranquil environment with softer, subtler, summer flowers, and ending with an exquisite display of autumn shades. There is an abundance of wildlife including wallabies, which help to cut the grass, and various duck, geese and swans. As well as the gardens see the amazing Victorian town in Miniature 1/12 scale called "Beyond the Dolls House"; a fine collection of working Victorian motorcars; and the new Sculpture for the Garden exhibition with exhibits by well known Sussex artists.

1 Apr-31 Oct daily 09.30-18.00
May weekends & Bank Hols: A£9.00, May weekdays: A£8.00, Apr & June-Oct: A£6.00 C(5-15yrs)£4.00 (all year)

Nymans Garden

Handcross Haywards Heath West Sussex
RH17 6EB
Tel: 01444 400321 / 405250
Set in the Sussex Weald, Nymans has flowering
shrubs and roses, a flower garden in the old
walled orchard, and a secret sunken garden.

Pashley Manor Gardens

Pashley Road Ticehurst Wadhurst TN5 7HE
Tel: 01580 200888 Fax: 01580 200102
www.pashleymanorgardens.com
*[On B2099 off A21 follow brown signposts. Plenty
of on-site parking available]*

'One of the finest gardens in England' Pashley
Manor Gardens offer a sumptuous blend of
romantic landscaping, imaginative plantings and
fine old trees, fountains, springs and large
ponds with interest and colour throughout the
season. This is a quintessential English garden
with a very individual character and exceptional
views to the surrounding valleyed fields. Many
eras of English history are reflected here, typify-
ing the tradition of the English Country house
and its garden. Delightful licensed Garden
Room Café offering light lunches and afternoon
teas, which can be enjoyed on the terrace overlooking the moat. Member of the Historic
Houses Association and a winner of the
HHA/Christie's 'Garden of the Year' Award.
*Gardens, Gift Shop & Café: 3 Apr-29 Sep Tue-
Thu, Sat & Bank Hol Mons 11.00-17.00.
Gardens Only: Oct Mon-Fri 10.00-16.00*
A£6.50 C(under6)£Free C(6-16)£5.00. Season
Tickets: £21.50. Admission for Tulip Festival &
Special Rose Weekend: £7.00 (for all). Group
rate (20+): £6.00

Sheffield Park Garden

Uckfield East Sussex TN22 3QX
Tel: 01825 790231 Fax: 01825 791264
www.nationaltrust.org.uk/sheffieldpark
*[Midway between East Grinstead & Lewes on E
Side of A275. Plenty of on-site parking available]*

This magnificent, informal landscape garden
was laid out in the eighteenth century by
'Capability' Brown and further developed in the
early years of the twentieth century by its owner,
Arthur G. Soames. The original four lakes form
the centrepiece. The garden is open all year
with dramatic shows of daffodils and bluebells
in spring, and spectacular rhododendrons and
azaleas in early summer. Throughout the summer water lilies dress the lakes whilst autumn
brings stunning colours from the many rare
trees and shrubs. Winter walks can also be
enjoyed, making Sheffield Park Garden truly a
garden for all seasons. Special events programme throughout the year including family fun
activities and garden walks, please call for info.
*6 Jan-11 Feb Sat-Sun 10.30-16.00, 13-25 Feb
Tue-Sun 10.30-16.00, 27 Feb-29 Apr Tue-Sun
10.30-17.30, 1 May-3 June daily 10.30-17.30, 5
June-30 Sep Tue-Sun 10.30-17.30, 1 Oct-4 Nov
daily 10.30-17.30, 6 Nov-23 Dec Tue-Sun
10.30-16.00, 27-30 Dec Thu-Sun 10.30-16.00,
5 Jan-2 Mar Sat-Sun 10.30-16.00. Also open
Bank Hols in Apr-Aug*
A£7.00* C£3.50*, Family Ticket £17.50*. Group
rate (15+): A£5.40 C£2.70. Joint Tickets (to
include Bluebell Railway): A£15.50 C£8.00
Family Ticket £40.00. Group rate (15+):
A£13.00. Free Admission for Great British
Heritage Pass holders & members of NT or
RHS. *Including a voluntary 10% donation, visitors can however choose to pay the standard
admission prices which are displayed at the
property and on the website

Wakehurst Place

Ardingly Haywards Heath Sussex RH17 6TN
Tel: 01444 894066
Vibrant ornamental plantings providing year round colour and interest.

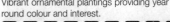

West Dean Gardens

West Dean Chichester West Sussex PO18 0QZ
Tel: 01243 818210 Fax: 01243 811342
www.westdean.org.uk
[On A286. 6mi N of Chichester & 6mi S of Midhurst. Plenty of on-site parking available]
A place of tranquillity and beauty in the rolling South Downs all year round, the award winning gardens at West Dean feature a restored walled kitchen garden with some of the finest Victorian glasshouses in the country. Over 200 varieties of carefully trained fruit trees, rows of vegetables and an array of exotic flowers and produce are produced in the walled garden. In the extensive grounds visit rustic summerhouses, a 300ft Edwardian pergola, ornamental borders and a pond. A circular walk through a 49-acre arboretum offers breathtaking views of the surrounding countryside and the fine flint mansion of West Dean College in its parkland setting. The visitor centre has a licensed restaurant and gift shop. The new Sussex Barn Gallery has an exciting programme of art exhibitions which showcase work by internationally renowned and emerging artists as well as students of West Dean College.
Mar-Oct daily 10.30-17.00, Nov-Feb Wed-Sun 10.30-16.00
Mar-Oct A£6.00 C£3.00 OAPs£5.50, Family Ticket (A2+C2) £15.00. Nov-Feb A£3.00 C£1.50 OAPs£2.75, Family Ticket £7.50

1066 Story in Hastings Castle

Castle Hill Road West Hill Hastings TN34 3RG
Tel: 0845 274 1001 Fax: 01424 781186
www.visithastings.com
[A259 or A21 into Hastings signposted]
Visit Britain's first Norman Castle built by William the Conqueror in 1067, after the Battle of Hastings. The ruins seen today are the remains of a stone fortress which was practically impregnable from three sides. Enter the medieval siege tent and enjoy an exciting audio-visual experience, 'The 1066 Story' which covers the Conquest and the history of the Castle through the centuries. Myths and Legends - to the east of the castle stands an area known as The Ladies Parlour where it's believed tournaments were held. A lady of distinction was always present at the events and it's said that the manifestation of a lady can still be seen on moonlit nights. The mysterious 'Whispering Dungeons' are also said to be haunted.
Easter-Sept daily 10.00-17.00, Oct-Easter daily 11.00-last show 15.30
A£3.65 C£2.60 Family Ticket(2A+2C) £11.00

Discount Offer: Two for the Price of One

Alfriston Clergy House

The Tye Alfriston Polegate BN26 5TL
Tel: 01323 870001
Half-timbered and thatched building with a medieval hall and exhibition room.
17 Mar-16 Dec Mon, Wed-Thu, Sat-Sun only (also closed 7-29 Oct)

Anne of Cleves House Museum

52 Southover High Street Lewes East Sussex BN7 1JA
Tel: 01273 474610 Fax: 01273 486990
www.sussexpast.co.uk/anneofcleves
The oldest part of this lovely timber-framed house was built in the fifteenth century. It was given to Henry VIII's fourth wife (Anne of Cleves) as part of her divorce settlement. The kitchen and bedroom are furnished in period. The Lewes Gallery tells the story of Lewes from the fifteenth century to modern times, the role of local resident Tom Paine, the Lewes Bonfire traditions and the sad story of the Snowdrop Inn. A further gallery illustrates the important Wealden iron industry and there are also displays of everyday domestic objects and children's toys from times past. The historic atmosphere and beautiful enclosed gardens give a very real feeling of stepping back into an earlier age. In October 2007, Anne of Cleves House Museum will host a Tudor Fair that's not to be missed!
1 Jan-28 Feb Tue-Sat 10.00-17.00, 1 Mar-31 Oct Tue-Sat 10.00-17.00 Sun-Mon & Bank Hols 11.00-17.00, 1 Nov-31 Dec Tue-Sat 10.00-17.00. Closed 24-26 Dec
A£3.50 C&Disabled/Carer£1.60 OAPs&Students(NUS/USI)£3.00, Family Ticket (A2+C2) £8.00 or (A1+C4) £6.50. Joint tickets (with Lewes Castle & Barbican House Museum) available

Discount Offer: Two for the Price of One

Arundel Castle

Arundel West Sussex
Tel: 01903 883136 / 882173
Fax: 01903 884581
www.arundelcastle.org
[Lower Lodge off Mill Rd]

Set high on a hill in West Sussex this great castle commands the landscape with magnificent views across the South Downs and the River Arun. Built at the end of the eleventh century it has been the home of the Dukes of Norfolk and their ancestors for nearly 1,000 years. Many of the original features such as the Crenellated Norman Keep, Gatehouse, Barbican and the lower part of the Bevis Tower survive. Between the 1870s and 1890s the house was almost completely rebuilt and the magnificent architecture in Gothic style is considered to be one of the great works of Victorian England. With finely preserved interiors, fascinating furniture, tapestries, rare art collections by renowned artists and beautiful well-stocked gardens - Arundel Castle provides the perfect day out.
Mar 31-28 Oct Tues-Sun 10.00-17.00. Closed Mon except Bank Hols
Castle Keep Gardens & Grounds: All £6.50. Full Visit: A£12.00 C(5-16)£7.50 Concessions£9.50, Family Ticket (A2+C5) £32.00

Bodiam Castle

Bodiam Robertsbridge East Sussex TN32 5UA
Tel: 01580 830436
One of the most famous and evocative castles in Britain, Bodiam was built in 1385, both as a defence and a comfortable home.

Gardens and Grounds of Herstmonceux Castle

Herstmonceux Hailsham East Sussex BN27 1RN
Tel: 01323 833816 Fax: 01323 834499
www.herstmonceux-castle.com
[Just outside village of Herstmonceux on A271, entrance on Wartling Rd. On-site parking]

Make time to visit this magnificent moated fifteenth-century castle set in beautiful parkland and superb Elizabethan gardens. Built originally as a country home in the mid fifteenth century, Herstmonceux Castle embodies the history of medieval England and the romance of renaissance Europe. Your experience begins with your first sight of the castle as it breaks into view. In the grounds you will find the formal gardens including a walled garden dating from 1570, a herb garden, the Shakespeare Garden, woodland sculptures, the pyramid, the water lily filled moat and the Georgian style folly. The woodland walks will take you to the remains of the three hundred year old sweet chestnut avenue, the rhododendron garden from the Lowther/Latham period, the waterfall (dependent on rainfall), and the 39 steps leading you through a woodland glade. Whilst you are here don't forget to visit the gift shop, tea room, visitor's centre, children's woodland play area and nature trail.

Gardens & Grounds: 14 Apr-28 Oct daily 10.00-18.00 (17.00 Oct). Closed 4 July & 5 Aug. Please call for confirmation of opening times

Gardens & Grounds: A£5.00 C(under15)£3.00 C(under5)£Free Concessions£4.00, Family Ticket (A2+C3 or A1+C4) £13.00. Joint ticket available with the Herstmonceux Science Centre. Castle Tours: A£2.50 C(under15)£1.00 C(under5)£Free. Group rates (for 15+) available on request, please call 01323 834457 for info

Discount Offer: One Child Free

Charleston

Firle Lewes East Sussex BN8 6LL
Tel: 01323 811265 (info line)
Fax: 01323 811628
www.charleston.org.uk
[6mi E of Lewes on A27 between Firle & Selmeston. Plenty of on-site parking available]

A seventeenth-century farmhouse, Charleston was transformed from 1916 onwards by the two Bloomsbury artists, Vanessa Bell and Duncan Grant. It is now a place of wonder and inspiration. They took painting beyond the canvas, decorating walls, doors and furniture in their unique style, influenced by post-impressionists like Picasso. They also created a painters' garden, filled with sculptures, mosaics and ponds. The flowers reflect their love of vibrant colour and appear in their still lives. Pioneering thinkers gathered here, like the writer Virginia Woolf, the economist Maynard Keynes, the art critics Roger Fry and Clive Bell and the irreverent biographer Lytton Strachey. Guided tours, on Wednesdays to Saturdays, offer illuminating insights into the bohemian lifestyles and experimental ideals of the Bloomsbury group, as well as the fine and decorative art in this very personal collection. On Sundays and Bank Holiday Mondays visitors can wander freely through this extraordinary house.

Apr-Oct Wed-Sun & Bank Hols. Wed & Sat 11.30-18.00 Thur-Fri 14.00-18.00 (11.30-18.00 July-Aug) Sun & Bank Hols 14.00-18.00

House & Garden: A£6.50 C£4.50 Disabled£4.50, Family Ticket £17.50 Concessions£5.50 Thurs only. Friday themed tour: £7.50. Garden only: A£2.50 C£1.50.

Gardens and Grounds of Herstmonceux Castle

Halisham, East Sussex BN27 1RN t: 01323 833816
www.herstmonceux-castle.com
Open daily 14th April - 28th October 10am - 6pm
(last admission 5pm) Closes at 5pm during
October, **Closed on 4th August 2007**

Make time to visit this magnificent moated 15th Century castle set in beautiful parkland and superb Elizabethan gardens. Built originally as a country home in the mid-15th Century, Herstmonceux Castle embodies the history of medieval England and the romance of renaissance Europe. Your experience begins with your first sight of the castle as it breaks into view. In the grounds you will find the formal gardens including a walled garden dating from 1570, a herb garden, the Shakespeare Garden, woodland sculptures, the pyramid, the water lily filled moat and the Georgian style folly. The woodland walks will take you to the remains of the three hundred year old sweet chestnut avenue, the rhododendron garden from the Lowther / Latham period, the waterfall (dependent on rainfall), and the 39 steps leading you through a woodland glade. The castle is not open to the public, however guided tours are conducted at an extra charge and subject to availability. We strongly advise you to telephone for confirmation of times before your visit. Whilst you are here don't forget to visit the Gift Shop, Tea Room, Visitor's Centre, Children's Woodland Play Area and Nature Trail.

Glynde Place

The Street Glynde Lewes East Sussex BN8 6SX
Tel: 01273 858224
Features fine architecture and interiors, paintings and extensive gardens.

Ham House

Ham Street Richmond Surrey TW10 7RS
Tel: 020 8940 1950
Famous for its lavish interiors and collections of fine furniture, textiles.

Lamb House

West Street Rye East Sussex TN31 7ES
Tel: 01372 453401
A delightful brick-fronted house, dating from the early eighteenth-century and typical of the attractive town of Rye.

Lewes Castle and Barbican House Museum

169 High Street Lewes East Sussex BN7 1YE
Tel: 01273 486290 Fax: 01273 486990
www.sussexpast.co.uk/lewescastle

Lewes Castle is one of the oldest castles in England (built shortly after the Norman Conquest) and is one of only two castles in England to be built on two mounds. Although never attacked, Lewes Castle played a part in the Battle of Lewes in 1264 and the Peasant's Revolt in 1381. The views over the county town of Lewes, the River Ouse and the surrounding Downs are worth the climb up the Keep. The Barbican House Museum (located opposite the Castle) tells the story of Sussex from the Stone Age to the end of the medieval period. Displays include flint tools, pottery, weapons, jewellery and other archaeological discoveries. It also houses a model of the town of Lewes during the Victorian period at around 1870. Special family sessions on archaeological and historical themes are run throughout the year. Other events include a Medieval Day in May and open-air theatre productions.

All year daily, Tue-Sat 10.00-17.30 Sun-Mon & Bank Hols 11.00-17.30. Closed Mon in Jan & 24-25 Dec

A£4.70 C£2.40 OAPs&Students(NUS/USI)£4.20 Disabled/Carer £2.40, Family Ticket (A2+C2) £12.20 or (A1+C4) £9.50. Joint tickets (with Anne of Cleves House Museum) available

Discount Offer: Two for the Price of One

Michelham Priory

Upper Dicker Nr Hailsham BN27 3QS
Tel: 01323 844224 Fax: 01323 844030
www.sussexpast.co.uk
[Plenty of on-site parking available]

The buildings at Michelham Priory have evolved over 800 years. The range of furniture and arte-facts on display trace the property's religious origins through its life as a working farm and its development as a country house. Objects include tapestries, furniture (including some made in the 1920s/1930s for the owner at that time), kitchen equipment and a fully furnished eighteenth-century child's bedroom. Seven acres of superb gardens are enhanced by a fourteenth-century gatehouse, fully restored medieval watermill, Kitchen, Physic Herb and Cloister Gardens, a working forge, rope muse-um and a dramatic Elizabethan Great Barn, now used for weddings, corporate functions and as exhibition space. See our website for special events including the Spring Garden Festival in mid-April, an exciting Celtic Weekend with Iron Age living history activities followed by a new event, an Antiques and Collectors Fair at the end of June. Mid-summer sees three popular events, the Game and Country Fair in July, Sussex Guild's Crafts in Action in August and the Medieval Market weekend held early September. There is a new event at the end of September for Falconry enthusiasts and the season ends with the sell-out Christmas Gift and Craft Fair at the end of November. Disabled access and wheelchair supplied.
1 Mar-31 Oct Tue-Sun (daily In Aug) from 10.00
A£6.00 C&Disabled/Carer£3.00
OAPs&Students(NUS/USI)£5.00, Family Ticket (A2+C2) £15.20

Discount Offer: Two for the Price of One

Monk's House

Rodmell Lewes East Sussex BN7 3HF
Tel: 01372 453401
This small village house was home of Leonard and Virginia Woolf from 1919.

Petworth House and Park

Petworth West Sussex GU28 0AE
Tel: 01798 342207 Fax: 01798 342963
www.nationaltrust.org.uk/petworth
[A272 / A283 centre of Petworth. Plenty of on-site parking available]
Magnificent mansion set in 700 acre deer park landscaped by 'Capability' Brown. State rooms contain the largest collection of paintings and sculpture in the care of the National Trust. To include works by Turner, Van Dyck, Blake and Claude. Intricate Grinling Gibbons carving in the Carved Room and beautiful Laguerre murals in the Grand Staircase. Fascinating servants' quar-ters to include Victorian kitchens and ancillary rooms. Guided tours by prior arrangement. Picnics allowed (no covered area). Events and exhibitions throughout the year.
House: 17 Mar-31 Oct Sat-Wed (open Good Fri) 11.00-16.30. Extra rooms shown weekdays (by kind permission of Lord & Lady Egremont), (not Bank Hol Mons): Mon - White & Gold Room and White Library Tue-Wed three bedrooms on first floor. Pleasure Ground & Car Park: as House but 11.00-18.00. Park: daily 08.00-dusk (closes 12.00 for open air concerts)
House, Pleasure Ground & Servants' Quarters: A£9.00 C(5-17)£4.50, Family Ticket (A2+C2) £22.50. Pleasure Grounds only: A£3.50 C£1.80. Park: Car park£2.00. NT Members £Free. Private Guided Tours for booked groups. Group rate (15+): A£7.00

Royal Pavilion

Brighton East Sussex BN1 1EE
Tel: 01273 290900
Former seaside residence of King George IV.
Decorated in Chinese and Indian styles.

Weald and Downland Open Air Museum

Singleton Chichester West Sussex PO18 0EU
Tel: 01243 811348 Fax: 01243 811475
www.wealddown.co.uk
[On A286 between Midhurst & Chichester. Discounted combined ticket on Stagecoach Coastline Bus. Free on-site parking available]
Situated in a beautiful downland setting, this museum displays more than 45 rescued historic buildings from south-east England. The buildings range from medieval houses to a nineteenth-century schoolhouse and Victorian labourers cottages. There is a medieval farmstead complete with animals, seven period gardens, a lakeside café, indoor and outdoor picnic areas, a working watermill, rural crafts, trade demonstrations and a working Tudor kitchen in an original Tudor service building. Shire horses and working cattle may be seen at seasonal tasks around the site. The first major timber gridshell building in Britain houses a conservation workshop and the Museum's collection of rural artefacts.
All year Jan-Feb, Sat, Sun & Wed 10.30-16.00, Feb half term & Mar daily 10.30-16.00, Apr-Oct daily 10.30-18.00, Nov-23 Dec plus 'A Sussex Christmas' 26 Dec-1 Jan daily 10.30-16.00
A£8.25 C(5+)£4.40 OAPs£7.25, Family Ticket(A2+C3) £22.65

Discount Offer: One Child Free

Military & Defence Museums

Tangmere Military Aviation Museum Trust

Tangmere Chichester West Sussex PO20 2ES
Tel: 01243 790090 Fax: 01243 789490
www.tangmere-museum.org.uk

[3mi E of Chichester on A27 well signposted. Limited on-site parking available]

Established in 1982, the museum tells the story of military flying from the earliest days to the present time, with emphasis on the RAF at Tangmere. Among several aircraft on display are the actual world speed record-breaking Meteor and Hunter jets. The Museum also has a full sized replica of the original Spitfire prototype and a special tribute to its designer, R.J. Mitchell. For the younger visitor there are many buttons to push, and the chance to 'fly' a Spitfire simulator. Essentially the museum is about people, their bravery, endurance and sacrifice. A unique feature is the Memorial Garden, where visitors can spend time in quiet and thoughtful reflection. You will find an intimate and friendly atmosphere so often lacking in other museums of this kind.

Mar-Oct daily 10.00-17.30, Feb & Nov daily 10.00-16.30
A£5.00 C£1.50 OAPs£4.00, Family Ticket £11.50

Discount Offer: One Child Free

Nature & Conservation Parks

Pulborough Brooks RSPB Nature Reserve

Wiggonholt Pulborough West Sussex RH20 2EL
Tel: 01798 875851 Fax: 01798 873816
www.rspb.co.uk

[Off A283, follow brown tourist signs from Pulborough. Plenty of on-site parking available]

Set in the sheltered Arun Valley, in the heart of West Sussex, Pulborough Brooks is a fantastic place for a day out for people of all ages. There is a superb nature reserve and trail with bird watching hides and viewpoints, a visitor centre with a gift shop and a tearoom with terrace, not to mention the play area! There is something of interest to see and hear throughout the year. Families can come and use the play area, look around the shop and enjoy lunch in the tea-room, without having to pay an entry charge. For those wishing to venture further, the reserve's nature trail offers a gentle walk with lots to see and do for just £7.00 for the whole family. A range of events run throughout the year and many are aimed at kids and families.
All year daily. Nature Trail: 09.00-21.00 or dusk if sooner. Visitor Centre: daily 9.30-17.00. Closed 25 & 26 Dec
A£3.50 C£1.00 Concessions£2.50, Family Ticket (A2+C4) £7.00

Discount Offer: 50% off One Family Ticket (A2+C4)

Places of Worship

Arundel Cathedral

Parsons Hill Arundel West Sussex BN18 9AY
Tel: 01903 882297
Built in 1873, the cathedral was constructed in the French Gothic style of 1300, with Romantic features such as pinnacles and gargoyles.

Chichester Cathedral

West Street Chichester West Sussex PO19 1PX
Tel: 01243 782595 Fax: 01243 812499
www.chichestercathedral.org.uk

[City centre]

In the heart of the city, this fine cathedral has been a centre of worship and community life for 900 years and is the site of the Shrine of St Richard. Its treasures range from Romanesque stone carvings to twentieth-century works of art by Feibusch, Benker-Schirmer, Chagall, Piper, Procktor, Skelton, Sutherland and Jackson. The delightful Cloisters Café on site offering a selection of homemade food, snacks and drinks. Shop situated next to café. Guided tours are available; general or specialist. Loop system during cathedral services; touch and hearing centre and Braille guide for the blind. Assistance dogs only.
End Mar-end Sept daily 07.15-19.00, end Sept-end Mar 07.15-18.00
Admission Free - Donations invited

Lancing College Chapel

Lancing West Sussex BN15 0RW
Tel: 01273 465949 Fax: 01273 464720
[Midway between Lancing & Shoreham, off A27 N of Shoreham Airport. Plenty of on-site parking]

Magnificent Gothic Chapel set on the South Downs. Founded in 1868 and dedicated in 1911. The Rose window which is 9.7m in diameter was dedicated in 1978. The dominant impression of the nave is its height 27.5m to the apex of the vault. Come and view the many other features including the stall canopies, the brass lectern and bronze candlesticks, and fine tapestries plus the newly installed stain glass window dedicated in memory of Bishop Trevor Huddleston, a pupil at Lancing in the late 1920s. Lancing College is a registered charity and senior school of the Woodard Corporation founded for the education of boys and girls aged between 13 to 18 years.
Mon-Sat 10.00-16.00, Suns & Bank Hols 12.00-16.00
Free Admission-Donations welcome

Railways

Bluebell Railway

Sheffield Park Station Uckfield East Sussex TN22 3QL

Tel: 01825 722370 / 720800
Fax: 01825 720804
www.bluebell-railway.co.uk
[A275 between Lewes & East Grinstead]

Here you will find the locomotive sheds, shop, museum and restaurant. Trains run between Sheffield Park, Horsted Keynes and Kingscote. An 18 mile round trip between Sheffield Park and Kingscote through open countryside.
All year Sat & Sun, Apr-Oct daily
A£9.80 C(3-15)£4.90, Family Ticket(A2+C3)£28.00

East and West Hill Cliff Railway

George Street Rock-a-Nore Hastings East Sussex TN34 3EG
Tel: 0845 274 1001 Fax: 01424 781186
www.visithastings.com
[West Hill lift entrance in George St Old Town, East Hill lift entrance in Rock-A-Nore]

The East Hill lift is the steepest funicular railway in Britain and provides spectacular views as it runs from Rock-A-Nore up the East Hill to the country park. The West Hill rises from George Street through the cliff itself to the Castle and Smugglers Adventure.
Winter: daily Oct-Mar 11.00-16.00, Summer: Mar-Sept 10.00-17.30. Closed 24-26 Dec
A£1.60 Concessions£1.00, Family Ticket £5.00

Lavender Line

Isfield Uckfield East Sussex TN22 5XB
Tel: 01825 750515
Operates a one-mile restored section of the Lewes-Uckfield Line that closed in 1969.

Roman Era

Fishbourne Roman Palace

Salthill Road Fishbourne Chichester West
Sussex PO19 3QR
Tel: 01243 785859 Fax: 01243 539266
www.sussexpast.co.uk/fishbourne
[Plenty of on-site parking available]

The remains of the late-first-century palace at
Fishbourne were first discovered in 1960. After
extensive archaeological excavations, a new
cover building protects the impressive remains
of one wing. Here you can see Britain's largest
collection of in-situ Roman floor mosaics. Other
everyday Roman objects found from the excavations are displayed in the museum gallery. A
new audio-visual presentation uses computer-
generated images to explain the site. Outside,
the garden has been replanted to its original
plan, using plants that may have been grown
then. A new 'Collections Discovery Centre' displays and houses yet more artefacts from both
Fishbourne and Chichester district. Join a
behind-the-scenes tour for an opportunity to
handle some of these ancient objects. Special
events throughout the year include a Celtic
Spring Festival in April, a Roman Gladiator re-
enactment weekend in September and a week
of Roman army activities for all the family in
October.
*22 Jan-15 Dec daily. 22 Jan-Feb 10.00-16.00,
Mar-July & Sep-Oct 10.00-17.00, Aug 10.00-
18.00, 1 Nov-15 Dec 10.00-16.00. Also open
Sat-Sun in Dec 10.00-16.00*
A£6.80 C£3.60 OAPs&Students(NUS/USI)£5.80
Disabled/Carer £5.00, Family Ticket (A2+C2)
£17.40

**Discount Offer: Two for the Price of
One**

Science - Earth & Planetary

Observatory Science Centre

Herstmonceux Hailsham East Sussex
BN27 1RN
Tel: 01323 832731 Fax: 01323 832741
www.the-observatory.org
*[2mi E of Herstmonceux village, on Boreham St to
Pevensey Rd. Look for sign to 'Herstmonceux
Castle & Science Centre' from A271. Plenty of
on-site parking available]*

The Royal Greenwich Observatory (RGO) was
founded at Greenwich in London in 1675 by
King Charles II but was moved just after the
second world war in order to escape the lights
and pollution of the city. The site at
Herstmonceux was chosen as the most suitable
in the UK. The existing telescopes were aug-
mented in 1967 by the giant 98-inch Isaac
Newton Telescope (INT). The domes, buildings
and telescopes are being renovated and the
centre is a major venue for exhibitions, lectures
and educational programmes. Events and activities programme.
All year daily 27 Jan-2 Dec also 8-9 Dec
A£6.80 C(under4)£Free C(4-15)£5.00
OAPs£5.25, Family Ticket (A2+C2 or A1+C3)
£20.50 or (A2+C3 or A1+C4) £23.40

Sealife Centres & Aquariums

Brighton Sea Life Centre

Marine Parade Brighton East Sussex BN2 1TB
Tel: 01273 604234 Fax: 01273 681840
www.sealifeeurope.com

[A23, M23]

The Brighton Sea Life Centre offers a fun and educational day out whatever the weather. With over 150 species and 57 displays, you will be hard pressed to find a more enjoyable day for the whole family! Watch in amazement as giant turtles and sharks glide above you in our underwater tunnel. Come and visit our Tropical Reef. Complete with a shark encircled wreak breath taking tropical coral, you can make it your own adventure! Opening March 2007 is the Victorian Explorer. Journey into the Oceans depths by stepping into a Submarine experience, taking you on a journey through the world's wondrous and restless Oceans. Travel along the seabed where you will encounter beautiful fish and stunning scenery, but beware the monstrous creatures of the deep who may not be happy to see you! Visit the Kingdom of the Seahorse and Marvel at the maternal male big bellies! Be prepared for a shock as you come face to face with giant spider crabs and watch out for the hungry piranhas. Enjoy holding crabs and learning about the shoreline at our rockpool display. Feeding the juvenile rays is also an unforgettable experience, but watch out for the lively sea bass! A showpiece of Victorian splendour and as the oldest operating aquarium in the world is considered to also be the best!
All year daily from 10.00. Closed Christmas Day
Please call for prices

Discount Offer: One Child Free

Underwater World Hastings

Rock-A-Nore Road Hastings TN34 3DW
Tel: 01424 718776
Rock-A-Nore Road, with its curious fishermen's huts and pebbly beach, is the ideal location for the resort.

Theme & Adventure Parks

Brighton Pier

Madeira Drive Brighton East Sussex BN2 1TW
Tel: 01273 609361
'Palace of Fun,' sideshows, kids' rides, funfair, 'Pleasurodome,' restaurant, cafés and bars.

Butlins

Bognor Regis West Sussex PO21 1JJ
Tel: 01243 822445 Fax: 01243 860591
www.butlins.com/dayvisitor
[From A259 coast rd. 1mi E of Bognor Regis on Littlehampton rd nr Felpham Village. Rail: Bognor Regis]

For a great day out, come to Butlins at Bognor Regis. With 'Splash Waterworld' (full of rides and slides), the 'Skyline Pavilion' (packed with live entertainment), a funfair, a huge indoor softplay area, go-karts, crazy-golf, a recording studio, plus a host of bars and restaurants, there's loads to keep the whole family entertained!
Daily 10.00-20.00. Closed some weekend breaks
A£15.00 C(under2)£Free C&OAPs£7.50, Family Ticket (A2+C2) £39.00

Eastbourne Pier

Eastbourne East Sussex BN21 3EL
Tel: 01323 410466
Victorian pier with pub/restaurant, family entertainment centres, nightclubs and much more

Harbour Park

Seafront Arun Parade Littlehampton
West Sussex BN17 5LL
Tel: 01903 721200 Fax: 01903 716663
www.harbourpark.com
[Littlehampton is on West Sussex coast, just off A27, on A284. Plenty of on-site parking available]

Harbour Park is situated right on the sandy beaches and adjacent to the working harbour and marina in Littlehampton, West Sussex. There are traditional rides like the Waltzer and Dodgems, and many juvenile rides for younger children. There are other attractions for the while family such as The Water Chute, Adventure Gold, Panning for Gold, Crazy Bikes and a Horror Hotel. When it comes to eating out there is plenty of choice from the maritime themed Galley Restaurant and Tea Rooms (where tea is served the traditional way with real tea leaves). If coffee is more your thing there is the newly refurbished Harbour Café which over looks the indoor skating rink. The arcade, skating rink and Harbour Café are open all year round.
All year daily. Closed 25 Dec
Admission Free

Discount Offer: Family Ride Books - 10 Rides for £12.00

Knockhatch Adventure Park

Hempstead Lane Hailsham East Sussex
BN27 3PR
Tel: 01323 442051 Fax: 01323 843035
www.knockhatch.com
[A22, to W of Hailsham. 8mi N of Eastbourne, 30min from Brighton, Hastings & Tunbridge Wells, 60min from London. Plenty of on-site parking available]

Exciting, yet relaxing - the most varied day out around. Bird of prey centre, Treetops indoor soft play, adventure playgrounds, trampolines, crazy golf, small childrens' area, sandpit, demon drop, bouncy castle play barn, reptile centre, boating lake, toboggan slide, ball games, giant astro slide, bungee trampoline, rock climbing wall plus for additional cost, burger bars, coffee corner, karting for children aged 3 years and over, laser adventure game, rodeo bull and corporate hospitality.
1-22 Apr, 7 & 28 May Sat & Sun, June-Aug & 1-9 Sept daily 10.00-17.30, Oct half term & weekends 10.00-17.00

A£7.50 C(under3)£Free C(3-16) £6.50 Students(NUS/USI)£5.50 OAPs£5.25, Family Ticket (4 people) £26.00, extra C£5.50. Season Tickets £20.00 per person. Group rate (16+paying people): 25% discount. Free pre-school visit for teachers, pre-booked C£3.99 + vat during term time through school

Discount Offer: One Child Free

Paradise Park

Avis Road Newhaven East Sussex BN9 0DH
Tel: 01273 512123 Fax: 01273 616000
www.paradisepark.co.uk
[A27 Brighton Lewes bypass & A26 give easy access to Paradise Park. Rail: regular services to Newhaven. Bus: regular services to Denton Corner. Plenty of on-site parking available]

The Heritage Trail and Gardens at Paradise Park are the ideal day out for all ages. Discover the fascinating world of animals and plants from millions of years ago to the present day. An extensive exhibition traces the history of Planet Earth. See fabulous collections of fossils, minerals and crystals. The life size moving dinosaurs provide an unforgettable experience. The Planthouses have a spectacular collection of the world's flora. The Dinosaur Garden reveals Sussex life millions of years ago. The gardens are one of Newhaven's hidden secrets with paths meandering through exquisite flowering shrubs, trees and plants that form a backdrop to waterfalls, fountains and small lakes. Follow the Sussex Heritage Trail through one of the finest water gardens in the South, with handcrafted models. Enjoy children's activities including crazy golf, miniature railway, indoor and outdoor play areas and amusements. Visit the unique garden centre with terrace café overlooking the gardens.
All year daily 09.00-18.00. Closed 25-26 Dec. Alternative tel no: 01273 616006
Combined Ticket to all 3 attractions: A£7.99 C£5.99, Family Ticket (A2+C2) £22.99. Any Pass purchased after 16.00 is valid the following day (subject to authorisation upon entry). Group rates available on request

Discount Offer: One Child Free

Tulleys Farm

Turners Hill Road Turners Hill Crawley
West Sussex RH10 4PD
Tel: 01342 718472 Fax: 01342 718473
www.tulleysfarm.com

[M23 J10. Rail: Three Bridges. Plenty of on-site parking available]

Tulleys Farm, with its shop stocked with top class food, tearoom serving light refreshments and lunches and bistro style Hayrack (open seasonally) is set in acres of outstanding natural beauty. There is much on offer; picnic, play areas and 'animal patch' to amuse the children. Quality bedding plants available from spring to autumn and we have extended our range of garden accessories and general giftware. Our renowned PYO strawberries and other soft fruit are available in season. There are several events during the year, including the Easter Eggstravaganza, a full day's fun for all ages at the A-Maze-ing adventure park from early July to early Sept which now includes Torch light evenings, October Festival packed with spooky goings-on, then finally at Christmas you can select your tree, gifts and produce and visit Santa in his Enchanted Forest. Corporate and children's parties can be booked at certain times. Pushchair access in most areas.
All year daily 10.00-18.00. Maze only: Early July-mid Sept. Tearoom: end Oct-end Mar daily 09.30-16.30, Apr-Sept 09.30-17.00. Shop: end Oct-end Mar daily 09.00-17.00, Apr-Sept 09.00-18.00
Prices vary, please call for further details

Toy & Childhood Museums

Brighton Toy and Model Museum

52-55 Trafalgar Street Brighton East Sussex
BN1 4EB
Tel: 01273 749494
Examples from top toy makers, priceless model
trains, plus and souvenirs to buy.
Closed Sun-Mon

Zoos

Drusillas Park

Alfriston East Sussex BN26 5QS
Tel: 01323 874100 Fax: 01323 874101
www.drusillas.co.uk *[Off A27 between*
Brighton / Eastbourne, 7mi from Seaford beach.
Plenty of on-site parking]

Award winning Drusillas Park is widely regarded
as the best small zoo in the country and is fast
becoming recognised as one of the most popular places for children in the south east of
England. With over 130 animal species in naturalistic environments there is plenty to enthral
everyone from the youngest to the oldest visitor.
Animals include the popular meerkats where
children can climb inside a dome to get really
close to the animals, as well as penguins,
otters, beavers, lemurs, gibbons, a splendid
range of monkeys and a walk-through bat
enclosure, to name but a few. However, animals
are only half the Drusillas experience. Playland,
including Monkey Kingdom, has masses of
climbing, sliding, jumping and swinging fun
thoughtfully separated for different age groups.
Indoors there is Amazon Adventure, a state-of-
the-art soft play complex, as well as the Toddler
Village and Toy Stables which are a hit with the

under 6s. And new for 2007 - Thomas the Tank
Engine, Annie and Clarabel, will be steaming
into Drusillas from Easter offering unlimited train
rides around the park 362 days a year! In addition to this there is also the Zoolympics
Challenge, Animal Spotter Books and Stamping
Trail, Jungle Adventure Golf, Panning for Gold,
Penguin Plunge, Vertical Limit, the Discovery
Centre and Wacky Workshop, Explorers
Restaurant, Oasis Café, five shops plus an interesting and varied event diary which runs
throughout the year.
All year daily Summer: 10.00-18.00, Winter:
10.00-17.00. Closed 24-26 Dec. Penguin feed-
ing takes place daily at 11.30 & 16.00. Email:
info@drusillas.co.uk
A&C(13+) from £10.70 C(under2)£Free C(2-12)
from £9.70, Family Tickets (2 people) from
£19.40, (3 people) from £29.10, (4 people) from
£38.80, (5 people) from £48.50

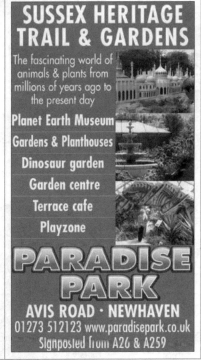

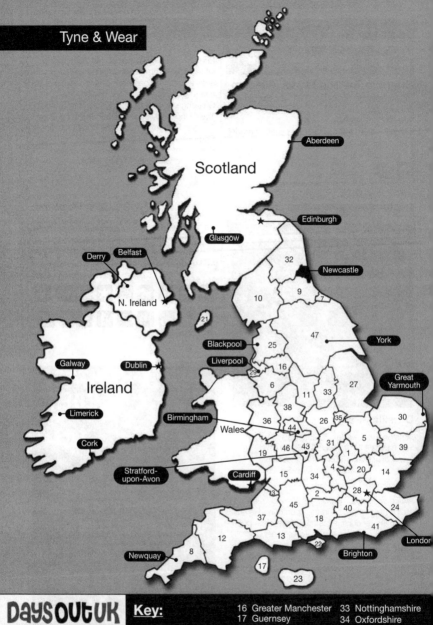

Tyne & Wear

Aberdeen

Scotland

Edinburgh

Glasgow

32

Newcastle

Derry Belfast

9

7

N. Ireland

10

21

Galway Dublin

Blackpool

25

47

York

Ireland

Liverpool

29

16

Limerick

6

11

33

27

Great Yarmouth

38

Birmingham

36

44

26

35

30

Cork

Wales

19

46

43

31

5

39

Stratford-upon-Avon

Cardiff

15

34

4

1

20

14

3

2

28

London

45

40

24

37

18

41

12

13

22

Brighton

Newquay

8

17

23

DAYS OUT UK
The place to look for places to go

Art Galleries

Baltic Centre for Contemporary Art

South Shore Road Gateshead Tyne & Wear NE8 3BA
Tel: 0191 478 1810
This converted Rank Hovis grain warehouse is one of the largest art centres in Europe.

Hatton Gallery

The Quadrangle University of Newcastle Newcastle Upon Tyne Tyne & Wear NE1 7RU
Tel: 0191 222 6059
Shows a changing programme of exhibitions, which include both historic and modern art.

Laing Art Gallery

New Bridge Street Newcastle Upon Tyne Tyne & Wear NE1 8AG
Tel: 0191 232 7734
The North of England's premier art gallery displays a stunning array of artistic works.

Country Parks & Estates

Derwent Walk Country Park

Lockhaugh Road Rowlands Gill Tyne & Wear NE39 1AU
Tel: 01207 545212
Track bed of the Derwent Valley Railway, suitable for walks, cycling, horses and wheelchairs.

Exhibition & Visitor Centres

National Glass Centre

Liberty Way Sunderland Tyne & Wear SR6 0GL
Tel: 0191 515 5555
Glass-making demonstrations plus a Glass Gallery with exhibitions from around the world.

Historical

Gibside

Estate Office Gibside Burnopfield Newcastle Upon Tyne Tyne & Wear NE16 6BG
Tel: 01207 541820 Fax: 01207 542741
www.nationaltrust.org.uk

[6mi SW of Gateshead, 20mi W of Durham, on B6314 between Burnopfield & Rowlands Gill, from A1 exit N of Metro Centre & follow brown property signs. Rail: Blaydon 5mi. Bus: Go North East Gateshead 611-3, 621. Newcastle 45,46A, 611. Picnic area adjacent to car park & on many of the walks. Plenty of on-site parking available]

One of the North's finest landscapes, much of which is SSSI (Site of Special Scientific Interest). There is a forest garden embracing many miles of riverside and forest walks, with fine views and abundant wildlife which is currently under restoration. Several outstanding buildings including a Palladian Chapel, Column of Liberty and others. The estate is the former home of the Queen Mother's family, the Bowes-Lyons. Disabled Access; some areas easier than others, please call Visitor Services Manager for details. Braille guide available.

5 Mar-28 Oct daily 10.00-18.00, 29 Oct-2 Mar 08 10.00-16.00

A£5.50 C(under5)£Free C(5+)£3.30, Family Ticket (A2+C4) £16.50 or (A1+C3) £11.00. NT Members £Free. Group rate (15+): A£4.50 these prices include a voluntary 10% gift aid donation

Maritime

Souter Lighthouse

Coast Road Whitburn Sunderland Tyneside
SR6 7NH
Tel: 0191 529 3161
Boldly painted in red and white stripes, this
rocket-like lighthouse opened in 1871 and was
the first to use electric light.

St Mary's Lighthouse and Visitor Centre

St. Marys Island Whitley Bay Tyne & Wear
NE26 4RS
Tel: 0191 200 8650
Three buildings open to the public, lighthouse,
bird watching hide and visitor centre. Exhibition,
shop and cafe.

Mills - Water & Wind

Path Head Water Mill

Summerhill Blaydon-On-Tyne Tyne & Wear
NE21 4SP
Tel: 0191 414 6288
Eighteenth-century Watermill restored by Vale
Mill Trust

Nature & Conservation Parks

Castle Eden Dene National Nature Reserve

Peterlee Tyne & Wear
Tel: 0191 586 0004 / 518 2403
The largest of Durham's wooded coastal
ravines, cut deep into limestone.

WWT Washington Wetland Centre

Pattinson Washington Tyne & Wear NE38 8LE
Tel: 0191 416 5454 Fax: 0191 416 5801
www.wwt.org.uk
[Plenty of on-site parking available]

Explore 103 acres of wetland, woodland and
wildlife reserve at Washington Wetland Centre -
one of the region's biggest conservation success stories. This vibrant, family-friendly, site
gives sanctuary to birds, insects and plant-life
alike. Its wildlife reserve is home to the North
East's largest nesting colony of Grey Herons;
while Hawthorn Wood feeding station offers
spectacular views of woodland birds such as
Great-spotted Woodpecker and Bullfinch. See
colourful Chilean Flamingos and watch as fluffy
ducklings take their first wobbly steps in the
Waterfowl Nursery (May-July). New developments include a stream channel, reedbed and
Close Encounters feeding area - bringing visitors nose to beak with some of the rarest water
birds on earth, many of which will eat corn from
an outstretched hand. Waterside Café, with its
sun terrace and BBQ area, offers a wide range
of delicious home-cooked food. Plus there's a
well-stocked gift shop, selling locally sourced
produce, the Discovery Centre and the early
years Splash Zone adventure play area for little
ones. Excellent disabled access and free wheelchair hire. Learn about the value of the UK's
diverse wetlands, their rich wildlife and the
importance of WWT's conservation programmes. WWT members get in free.
Summer: 09.30-17.00, Winter: 09.30-16.00
A£5.95 Concessions£4.95 C(4-16)£3.95
Family(A2+C2) £15.50

Discount Offer: Two for the Price of One

Arts Centre, Washington

Biddick Lane Fatfield Washington Tyne & Wear
NE38 8AB
Tel: 0191 219 3455
A converted nineteenth-century farm offering
performance spaces, art gallery and function
rooms with licensed bars.

St Nicholas Cathedral

St. Nicholas Churchyard Newcastle Upon Tyne
Tyne & Wear NE1 1PF
Tel: 0191 232 1939
Norman arch circa 1175. Unique lantern tower.
Guided tours by prior arrangement.

Tynemouth Priory and Castle

East Street Tynemouth North Shields
Tyne & Wear NE30 4BZ
Tel: 0191 257 1090
The castle, fortifications and priory are a testa-
ment to the vital strategic importance of the site
and its great religious significance.

Bowes Railway

Springwell Road Springwell Village Gateshead
Tyne & Wear NE9 7QJ
Tel: 0191 416 1847 (24 hrs)
Bowes Railway is the only rope hauled standard
gauge railway still working in the world today,
and is therefore of unique historical value.

Stephenson Railway Museum

Middle Engine Lane North Shields Tyne & Wear
NE29 8DX
Tel: 0191 200 7146
Re-live the glorious days of steam railway at
Stephenson Railway Museum.

Tanfield Railway

Old Marley Hill Nr Stanley Newcastle Upon Tyne
Tyne & Wear NE16 5ET
Tel: 0191 388 7545 Fax: 0191 387 4784
www.tanfield-railway.co.uk

*[Off A6076 (J63, A1). Plenty of on-site parking
available]*

The world's oldest existing railway, originally
opened in 1725. Three mile steam passenger
railway between Sunniside, Causey Arch and
East Tanfield.
*All year daily. Train times: all year Sun, plus
Summer School Hols Wed & Thur*
A£6.00 C(5-14)£3.00 C(under5)£Free
OAPs£4.00

Discount Offer: One Child Free

Arbeia Roman Fort and Museum

Baring Street South Shields Tyne & Wear
NE33 2BB
Tel: 0191 456 1369
Today, the excavated remains, stunning recon-
structions of original buildings and finds from
the Fort, show what life was like in Roman
Britain.

Sealife Centres & Aquariums

Blue Reef Aquarium

Grand Parade Tynemouth Tyne & Wear
NE30 4JF
Tel: 0191 258 1031 Fax: 0191 257 2116
www.bluereefaquarium.co.uk

[Signposted from A19/1058]

Take the ultimate undersea safari at the award winning Blue Reef Aquarium where there's a world of underwater adventure just waiting to be discovered. Over 30 living displays reveal the sheer variety of life in the deep; from native sharks, lobsters and adorable otters to seahorses, fascinating frogs and exotic fish. At the aquarium's heart is a giant ocean tank where an underwater walkthrough tunnel offers incredibly close encounters with the stunning beauty of a tropical coral reef - home of hundreds of colourful fish. Blue Reef is a great place for visitors of all ages to discover more about the wonders of the deep. There's a full programme of entertaining, informative talks and feeding displays throughout the day. Learn more about native sea creatures including crabs, anemones and starfish at our popular Rockpool Encounters where our experts will be on hand to answer all your questions. New for 2007 - Seal Cove A spectacular experience whatever the weather.
All year daily 10.00. Closed 25 Dec only
A£6.95 C£4.95 OAPs&Students(NUS/USI)£5.95

Discount Offer: One Child Free

Theme & Adventure Parks

New Metroland

39 Garden Walk Metrocentre Gateshead
Tyne & Wear NE11 9XY
Tel: 0191 493 2048 Fax: 0191 493 2904
www.metroland.uk.com

[Signposted for MetroCentre from A1/M. Plenty of on-site parking available]

Europe's largest indoor funfair theme park offers 12 major attractions. You can experience the thrills and spills of the new rollercoaster, test your driving skills on the Disco Dodgems, sail the high seas on the Swashbuckling Pirate Ship, Fly high on the Wonderful Waveswinger, Spin on the Whiling Waltzer, or take a leisurely journey round the park on the Terrific Train. The Children's Adventure Play Area is a great place for children to burn off all their energy while parents can sit and watch. There are four food outlets, MrB's Amusements and Prize Bingo and much more. Parties are a speciality for any occasion.
School hols: Mon-Sat 10.00-20.00, Sun 11.00-18.00. Term Time: Mon-Fri from 12.00
Standard All Day Pass: A&C£10.20. Gold All Day Pass: A&C£12.00. Evening passes available

Discount Offer: Two for the Price of One

Ocean Beach Pleasure Park

23 The Foreshore Sea Road South Shields
Tyne & Wear NE33 2LD
Tel: 0191 456 1617
www.oceanbeach.co.uk

[Plenty of on-site parking available]

Visit the exhilarating theme park and experience the fun and excitement of this family amusement park. With free admission enjoy our attrac tion all day long. New to the park is the first pirate-themed golf course within the North East region. Our rides range from traditional fun fair rides, such as waltzers, carousel, to rollercoasters, go karts and so much more, to ensure a fun filled day for all the family. For visitors who like to keep their feet on the ground, there are a number of amusement arcades, also there is a ten pin bowling tavern on site and a boating lake just across from the theme park.

Mar-Nov. See website for further details on opening times
Free Admission to park, although tokens must be purchased for the rides

Discount Offer: Get £25.00 worth of tokens for just £15.00

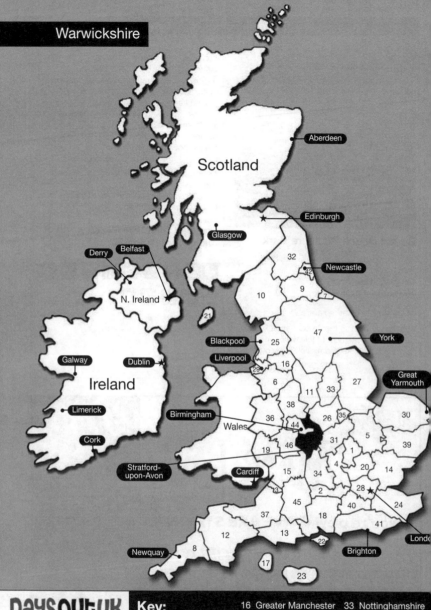

Warwickshire

Aberdeen

Scotland

Edinburgh

Glasgow

Newcastle

Derry · Belfast

N. Ireland

Galway · Dublin

Ireland

Limerick

Cork

Blackpool

Liverpool

Birmingham

Wales

Stratford-upon-Avon

Cardiff

Newquay

Brighton

York

Great Yarmouth

London

Key:

1	Bedfordshire	16	Greater Manchester	33	Nottinghamshire
2	Berkshire	17	Guernsey	34	Oxfordshire
3	Bristol	18	Hampshire	35	Rutland
4	Buckinghamshire	19	Herefordshire	36	Shropshire
5	Cambridgeshire	20	Hertfordshire	37	Somerset
6	Cheshire	21	Isle Of Man	38	Staffordshire
7	Cleveland	22	Isle Of Wight	39	Suffolk
8	Cornwall	23	Jersey	40	Surrey
9	County Durham	24	Kent	41	Sussex
10	Cumbria	25	Lancashire	42	Tyne & Wear
11	Derbyshire	26	Leicestershire	43	Warwickshire
12	Devon	27	Lincolnshire	44	West Midlands
13	Dorset	28	London	45	Wiltshire
14	Essex	29	Merseyside	46	Worcestershire
15	Gloucestershire	30	Norfolk	47	Yorkshire
		31	Northamptonshire		
		32	Northumberland		

Animal Attractions

Hatton Farm Village at Hatton Country World

Dark Lane Hatton Warwick Warwickshire CV35 8XA
Tel: 01926 843411 Fax: 01926 842023
www.hattonworld.com

[5min from J15 of M40. Take A46 towards Coventry, leave at first exit, turning L onto A4177. Follow brown tourist signs. Plenty of on-site parking available]

You'll find acres of fun for everyone in the Farm Village at Hatton Country World. Discover our Farmyard Favourites and Rare Breed Farm, experience our special events and demonstrations plus enjoy fun and adventure activities. Don't miss our Daft Duck Trials, Bird-o-batics Falconry Displays, Tristian the Runaway Tractor, Sheepstakes Sheep Racing and Guinea Pig Village. For fun there's bouncy castles and trampolines, an adventure playground, Country Fun Fair and giant puzzles. Children can pan for gold, peddle away in our mini tractors and enjoy the children's shows. There's also a special area just for the under-5s. A full day out for the whole family. Activities change throughout the season please call or visit the website for the latest information.

All year daily 10.00-17.00 (16.00 during winter). Closed 25 & 26 Dec
Please visit our website for admission prices

Discount Offer: One Child Free

Redwings Oxhill Rescue Centre

Banbury Road Oxhill Warwickshire CV35 0RP
Tel: 0870 040 0033 Fax: 0870 458 1942
www.redwings.org.uk

[On A422 between Stratford & Banbury. Plenty of on-site parking available]

Established in 1984, Redwings is now the largest horse charity in the UK, working to provide and promote the welfare, care and protection of horses, ponies, donkeys and mules. Redwings Oxhill Rescue Centre is the charity's first visitor centre established outside East Anglia. The site is home to more than 50 rescued horses, ponies and donkeys including cheeky pony Dylan, Will the former police horse and dinky Shetland Wensley. There is a brand new gift shop, information centre and café, and we hope the centre will serve to make more people aware of the charity's work and provide enjoyment and education for a new generation of supporters.

All year daily: 10.00-17.00. Closed 25-26 Dec & 1 Jan
Admission Free

Discount Offer: One Free Poster

Umberslade Children's Farm

Butts Lane Tanworth-In-Arden Nr Solihull Warwickshire B94 5AE
Tel: 01564 742251
Feeding, holding animals, milking, harnessing up and ferret racing.

Art Galleries

Compton Verney

Compton Verney Warwickshire CV35 9HZ
Tel: 01926 645500 Fax: 01926 645501
www.comptonverney.org.uk
*[9mi E of Stratford-upon-Avon, 10min from M40
J12. Entrance on B4086 Kineton to Wellesbourne
rd, just off Fosse Way B4455. Plenty of on-site
parking available]*

Compton Verney is an award winning art gallery.
Voted visitor attraction of the year and short-list-
ed for The Guardian Family Friendly Award. It
offers a great day out for all ages. The art on
display is housed in a Grade I listed Robert
Adam mansion, set in 120 acres of landscaped
parkland. The grounds offer a great place to
explore, relax, picnic or for children to let off
steam. Compton Verney offers fun and enjoyable ways to experience art whatever your age
or knowledge. The permanent collections are
drawn from Naples (1600-1800), Germany
(1450-1650). China - including the largest collection of Chinese bronzes outside London,
British portraits, British Folk Art and the Marx-
Lambert collection of popular art. There is also
an exciting exhibitions programme.
*24 Mar-9 Dec Tue-Sun 10.00-17.00 & Bank Hol
Mons*
A£7.00 C(under5)£Free C(5-16)£2.00
Concessions£5.00, Family Ticket (A2+C4)
£16.00. Season Tickets: A£24.00 Family Ticket
£50.00. Group rates available on request

**Discount Offer: Free children's lunch
box worth £3.50 with every main
course meal purchased in the Café**

Arts, Crafts & Textiles

Leamington Spa Art Gallery and Museum

The Royal Pump Rooms The Parade
Leamington Spa Warwickshire CV32 4AA
Tel: 01926 742700 Fax: 01926 742705
**www.royal-pump-
rooms.co.uk/gallery/index.html**

*[500m from Leamington Spa Railway Station.
2min walk from main shopping area]*

This award winning Leamington Spa Art Gallery
and Museum, Royal Pump Rooms has a fine art
collection, an exhibition on the history of Royal
Leamington Spa, cabinets of curiosities, gallery
of interactive exhibits, Hammam (restored
Turkish bath), history and local interest exhibitions. The fine art collection includes sixteenth
and seventeenth-century Dutch and Flemish,
eighteenth and twenty-first-century British
artists, local artists, sculpture, ceramics and
glassware. Recent acquisitions include works of
art by Mark Quinn, Damien Hirst and Catherine
Yass. Other key artists in the collection include
Stanley Spencer, L S Lowry, Gillian Wearing,
Vanessa Bell, Patrick Caulfield, Sir Terry Frost,
Walter Sickert and Graham Sutherland.

*All Year Tue, Wed, Fri & Sat 10.30-17.00 Thur
13.30-20.00 Sun 11.00-16.00. Closed Mon*
Admission Free

Rugby Art Gallery and Museum

Little Elborow Street Rugby Warwickshire
CV21 3BZ
Tel: 01788 533201 Fax: 01788 533204
www.ragm.org.uk

[Town centre. Plenty of on-site parking available]

The Art Gallery has a changing programme of
exhibitions of contemporary visual art and craft
including shows from the Rugby Collection of
twentieth-century British art. The Museum is
home to the Tripontium Collection of Roman
artefacts and a growing Social History
Collection reflecting on Rugby's industrial history, impact of war and the changing pattern of
family life. All exhibitions include interactive elements for families and children to enjoy together, we offer regular activities for children during
school holidays and special events for adults
linking into temporary exhibitions.

*All year Tue & Thu 10.00-20.00 Wed & Fri 10.00-
17.00 Sat 10.00-16.00 Sun & Bank Hols 12.00-
16.00. Closed Mons*
Admission Free

Warwick Arts Centre

University Of Warwick Coventry CV4 7AL
Tel: 024 7652 4524
T largest arts centre in the Midlands, attracting
around 280,000 visitors a year to over 2,000
individual events embracing music, drama,
dance, comedy, literature, films and visual art.

Stratford-upon-Avon Butterfly Farm

Swan's Nest Lane Stratford-upon-Avon
Warwickshire CV37 7LS
Tel: 01789 299288 Fax: 01789 415878
www.butterflyfarm.co.uk
[S bank of River Avon opposite RSC]

The UK's largest live Butterfly and Insect Exhibit.
Hundreds of the world's most spectacular and
colourful butterflies. Insect City has a huge col-
lection of strange and fascinating animals.
Arachnoland features the 'dealers in death'.
There is also an outdoor British butterfly garden
in the summer.
*All year, Summer daily 10.00-18.00, Winter
10.00-dusk. Closed 25 Dec*
A£5.25 C£4.25
OAPs&Students(NUS/USI)£4.75, Family Ticket
(A2+C2) £15.75, extra C£2.25. Special school
tours can be arranged

**Discount Offer: Two for the Price of
One**

Burton Dassett Hills Country Park

Northend Leamington Spa Warwickshire
Tel: 01827 872660
The country park, covering about 100 acres, is
situated on a spur of rugged hills projecting into
a relatively flat plain.

Coombe Country Park

Brinklow Road Binley Coventry Warwickshire
CV3 2AB
Tel: 024 7645 3720 Fax: 024 7663 5350
www.coventry.gov.uk

*[On B4027 between Coventry / Brinklow. Plenty
of on-site parking available]*

500 acres of historic parkland with a children's
playground, an adventure playground, and a
visitor centre with restaurant, souvenir shop and
exhibitions.
All year daily, dawn till dusk
Admission Free. Car parking charges apply

Draycote Water Country Park

Kites Hardwick Rugby Warwickshire
Tel: 01827 872660
Covers an area of 21 acres on the southern
side of Draycote Water.

Folk & Local History Museums

Nuneaton Museum and Art Gallery

Coton Rd Riversley Park Nuneaton CV11 5TU
Tel: 024 7635 0720
Features local history gallery focusing on the
development of the borough including Nuneaton
Priory.

Gardens & Horticulture

Garden Organic Ryton

Coventry Warwickshire CV8 3LG
Tel: 024 7630 3517
Gardens, visitor's centre, restaurant and shops.

Historical

Anne Hathaway's Cottage

Cottage Lane Shottery Stratford-Upon-Avon
Warwickshire CV37 9HH
Tel: 01789 292100 Fax: 01789 205014
www.shakespeare.org.uk
[Off A422, 1mi from town centre. On-site parking]
This world famous thatched cottage is the childhood home of Anne Hathaway, Shakespeare's
wife. It remained in the Hathaway family until the
late nineteenth century and still contains many
family items including the beautiful "Hathaway
Bed". Outside lies a beautiful cottage garden,
orchard, sculpture garden, maze and romantic
willow cabin. A virtual reality tour is available for
our visitors with restricted mobility.
*All year daily Apr-May Mon-Sat 09.30-17.00, Sun
10.00-17.00, June-Aug Mon-Sat 09.00-17.00,
Sun 09.30-17.00, Sept-Oct Mon-Sat 09.30-
17.00, Sun 10.00-17.00, Nov-Mar daily 10.00-
16.00. Times listed are opening time to last entry.
Closed 23-26 Dec. Cafe and refreshment facilities subject to seasonal opening*
A£5.50 C£2.00 Concession£4.50, Family Ticket
£13.00. Multiple Houses: A£14.00 C£6.50
Concessions£12.00, Family Ticket £29.00.
Group rates available on request, please call
01789 201806 for details

**Discount Offer: Two for the Price of
One**

Arbury Hall

Arbury Nuneaton Warwickshire CV10 7PT
Tel: 02476 382804
The sixteenth-century Elizabethan house,
Gothicised in the eighteenth century.

Charlecote Park

The National Trust Charlecote Warwick
Warwickshire CV35 9ER
Tel: 01789 470277 Fax: 01789 470544
www.nationaltrust.org.uk

Charlecote (with its mellow brickwork and great
chimneys) is a house with a fascinating history
and a Victorian presence that's set in the heart
of an ancient deer park (evoking the essence of
Tudor England). In Tudor times, both Elizabeth I
and William Shakespeare knew Charlecote well.
The Tudor Queen was staying here whilst a
young Shakespeare was allegedly caught
poaching on the estate. In 2007, visitors will
enjoy more access to the parkland as more
pathways are opened to the public.
*House: 11.00-17.00. Park & Gardens: 10.30-
18.00. Shop: 10.30-17.30. Restaurant: 10.30-
17.00. 3 Mar-28 Oct Fri-Tue. 3 Nov-22 Dec Sat-
Sun 11.00-16.00. House closed Nov. 1-22 Dec
Sat & Sun parts of house only 11.00-16.00. Park
& Gardens 3 Mar-29 Feb Fri-Tue 9.00-16.00*
Gift Aid admission* House: A£7.90 C£4.00,
Family Ticket £19.00 Groups £6.20. Grounds &
Gardens only: A£4.00 C£2.00. Grounds &
Gardens only (winter rates): A£2.50 C£1.50.
National Trust members & children under 5
£free. * Including a voluntary donation of at least
10%: Visitors can however, choose to pay the
standard admissions prices which are displayed
at the property and on the website

Coughton Court

Coughton Alcester Warwickshire B49 5JA
Tel: 01789 400777 Fax: 01789 765544
www.nationaltrust.org.uk
*[On A435, 2mi N of Alcester. Plenty of on-site
parking available]*
Coughton Court is one of England's finest Tudor
houses. Home of the Throckmorton family since
1409, the house has fine collections of furniture,
porcelain and family portraits, and a fascinating
exhibition on the Gunpowder Plot of 1605.
*House: 1 Apr-1 July Wed-Sun, 3 July-2 Sep
Tues-Sun, 5 Sep-30 Sep Wed-Sun, 6 Oct-28
Oct Sat-Sun 11.30-17.00.
Gardens/Restaurant/Shop/Plant Sales: 11.00-
17.30. Walled Garden: 11.30-16.45*
House & Garden: A£9.00 C£4.50, Family Ticket
£22.60. Garden Only: A£6.20 C£3.10, Family
Ticket £15.80. NT Members £Free (Walled
Garden: £2.50). Group rates (15+): House &
Garden £7.00, Garden Only £4.90

Hall's Croft

Old Town Stratford-Upon-Avon CV37 6BG
Tel. 01700 200107 Fax: 01789 266209
www.shakespeare.org.uk

[Town centre location]

This impressive seventeenth-century house was home to Shakespeare's eldest daughter Susanna and her husband, the physician Dr John Hall. Much is known of Dr Hall who is one of the best-documented provincial doctors of early modern England. Visit his consultation room and learn about early medicine, or simply enjoy the many elegant rooms designed to reflect John Hall's comparative wealth and status which are furnished with exquisite furnishings and paintings of the period. In the garden stands an ancient Mulberry Tree and formal herbal bed. Limited disabled access, please call for details.

All year Apr-May daily 11.00-17.00, June-Aug Mon-Sat 09.30-17.00, Sun 10.00 17.00, Sept-Oct daily 11.00-17.00, Nov-Mar daily 11.00-16.00. Times listed are opening times to last entry. Closed 23-26 Dec

A£3.75 C£1.75 Concessions£3.00, Family Ticket £10.00. Multiple Houses: A£11.00 C£5.50 Concessions£9.00, Family Ticket £23.00. All 5 Houses: A£14.00 C£6.50 Concessions£12.00, Family Ticket £29.00. Group rates available on request, please call 01789 201806 for details

Discount Offer: Two for the Price of One

Lord Leycester Hospital

60 High Street Warwick Warwickshire CV34 4BH
Tel: 01926 492797
These lovely half-timbered buildings were built in the late fourteenth century and adapted into almshouses by the Earl of Leycester in 1571.

Kenilworth Castle

Castle Green Kenilworth Warwickshire CV8 1NE
Tel: 01926 852078
The largest castle ruin in England - its massive walls tower over the peaceful Warwickshire landscape.

Mary Arden's

Feather Bed Lane Wilmcote Stratford-Upon-Avon Warwickshire CV37 9UN
Tel: 01789 293455 Fax: 01789 415404
www.shakespeare.org.uk
[3mi NW off A34 just 3.5mi from town centre. Plenty of on-site parking available]
Step back in to the 1570s and experience a normal day with a farming household from Shakespeare's time, lovingly recreated at Palmer's Farm in the heart of the Warwickshire countryside. A great day out for all the family at two historic houses. Mary Arden's house is the childhood home of Shakespeare's mother. A tour of the house and neighbouring Palmer's farm enables visitors to experience 500 years of rural life. A perfect place for a picnic in a gorgeous rural setting. Limited disabled access, please call for details.

All year daily Apr-May 10.00-17.00, June-Aug 09.30-17.00, Sept-Oct 10.00-17.00, Nov-Mar 10.00-16.00. Times listed are opening time to last entry. Closed 23-26 Dec

A£6.00 C£2.50 Concessions£5.00, Family Ticket £15.00. All 5 Houses: A£14.00 C£6.50 Concessions£12.00, Family Ticket £29.00. Group rates available on request, please call 01789 201806 for details

Discount Offer: Two for the Price of One

Middleton Hall

Middleton Tamworth Staffordshire B78 2AE
Tel: 01827 283095
Shows several architectural styles, circa 1300.

Nash's House and New Place

Chapel Street Stratford-Upon-Avon CV37 6EP
Tel: 01789 292325 Fax: 01789 266228
www.shakespeare.org.uk
[Town centre, next door to Shakespeare Hotel & opposite Falcon Hotel]

This property was once owned by Thomas Nash who married Shakespeare's granddaughter, Elizabeth. The rooms are decorated with original Tudor furniture, paintings and tapestries. It is also home to an exciting exhibition telling the remarkable story of Shakespeare's Complete Works as one of the best-loved and most influential books in the English language. Adjacent to Nash's House is the site of New Place, the property Shakespeare purchased in 1597 and where he died in 1616. Although only foundations remain, his original estate is now preserved as a picturesque garden space - the perfect spot for a poetry reading or picnic! Limited disabled access, please call for details.
All year Apr-May daily 11.00-17.00, June-Aug Mon-Sat 09.30-17.00, Sun 10.00-17.00, Sept-Oct daily 11.00-17.00, Nov-Mar daily 11.00-16.00. Times listed are opening times to last entry. Closed 23-26 Dec
A£3.75 C£1.75 Concessions£3.00, Family Ticket £10.00. Multiple Houses: A£11.00 C£5.50 Concessions£9.00, Family Ticket £23.00. All 5 Houses: A£14.00 C£6.50 Concessions£12.00, Family Ticket £29.00. Group rates available on request, please call 01789 201806 for details

Discount Offer: Two for the Price of One

Ragley Hall

Alcester Warwickshire B49 5NJ
Tel: 01789 762090
One of the earliest great Palladian Houses.
Apr-Sept Thur-Sun & Bank Hol Mons

Shakespeare's Birthplace

The Shakespeare Centre Henley Street Stratford-Upon-Avon Warwickshire CV37 6QW
Tel: 01789 201822 Fax: 01789 299132
www.shakespeare.org.uk
[J15 M40, A46 to Stratford upon Avon, in town centre]

A beautifully presented timber framed Town House where William Shakespeare was born in 1564 and home to the Shakespeare family until the nineteenth century. The house contains both original and replica artefacts depicting the house as Shakespeare would have known it as a child. To the rear is a traditional English garden featuring many plants and herbs mentioned in Shakespeare's plays. Explore the adjacent exhibition and learn about Shakespeare's life, work and times and see the first folio of 1623. Limited disabled access, please call for details.
All year daily Apr-May Mon-Sat 10.00-17.00, Sun 10.00-17.00, June-Aug Mon-Sat 09.00-17.00, Sun 09.30-17.00, Sept-Oct Mon-Sat 10.00-17.00, Sun 10.00-17.00, Nov-Mar Mon-Sat 10.00-16.00, Sun 10.30-16.00. Times listed are opening times to last entry. Closed 23-26 Dec
A£7.00 C£2.75 Concessions£6.00, Family Ticket £17.00. Multiple Houses: A£11.00 C£5.50 Concessions£9.00, Family Ticket £23.00. All 5 Houses: A£14.00 C£6.50 Concessions£12.00, Family Ticket £29.00. Group rates available on request, please call 01789 201806 for details

Discount Offer: Two for the Price of One

Warwick Castle

Warwick Warwickshire CV34 4QU
Tel: 0870 442 2000 Fax: 0870 442 2394
www.warwick-castle.com
[2mi from J15 of M40. Simply follow the signs. Plenty of on-site parking available]

You don't just visit Britain's Greatest Mediaeval Experience. You live it! Bursting to the towers with tales of treachery and torture, passion and power and above all fascinating people, times and events, Warwick Castle is so much more than simply a castle. See lavishly decorated State Rooms, watch as a household prepares for a Victorian party and discover how electricity was generated over 100 years ago to light up the castle. Explore the 60 acres of landscaped grounds and gardens, which include the beautiful Peacock Garden and Conservatory, the Victorian Rose Garden and Pageant Field. Throughout the year there is a fantastic programme of events including birds of prey, jousting and the world's largest trebuchet in action. Please visit our website for further information.
Apr-Sept 10.00-18.00, Oct-Mar 10.00-17.00
A£13.95-£17.95 C£8.95-£10.95
Concessions£9.95-£12.95, Family Ticket
£38.00-£48.00

Places of Worship

Coventry Cathedral and Treasury
Priory Street Coventry Warwickshire CV1 5EP
Tel: 024 7652 1200
Coventry's former cathedral was bombed during an air raid in November 1940.

Stratford-on-Avon Racecourse

Luddington Road Stratford-upon-Avon
Warwickshire CV37 9SE
Tel: 01789 267949 Fax: 01789 415850
www.stratfordracecourse.net

[J15 M40, J7 M5, on B439. Please allow plenty of time for your journey. Plenty of on-site parking available]

Steeplechasing has taken place at Stratford Racecourse since 1755. Today, we have sixteen meetings a year, most of which take place within the summer months. Equipped with a new Grandstand (opened in 1997) and having won a major award for the care of the racetrack, we are proud to be in the top flight of Britain's smaller courses. Our goal is to give everyone who comes to Stratford a wonderful day out. We will be very pleased to discuss our facilities with you, either for bringing groups large or small to the races, or for using the racecourse buildings for non-raceday events and functions. The flexibility of our restaurant facilities and the attractive rates that we are able to offer for their use have made Stratford Racecourse the place to hold a party. Dogs permitted, must be kept on a lead.
Race meetings between Feb-Nov
Club £18.00 Tattersalls £14.00 Course £7.00. Group rates (15+): Club £14.40 Tattersalls £11.20 Course £5.60 (must be pre-booked). Parking: Centre Course & Main Car Park £2.00, Public Car Park & Coaches £Free

Sport & Recreation

Mr Karting

The Hangers Harbury Lane Bishops Tachbrook
Leamington Spa Warwickshire CV33 9SA
Tel: 01926 833444 Fax: 01926 833456
www.mrkarting.co.uk
*[10min drive from J13 or J14 M40 near Bishop
Tachbook between Leamington Spa & Whitnash.
Plenty of on-site parking available]*
Mr Karting is an indoor Go Karting track situated outside Leamington Spa. Anyone can drive,
if over 8 years old and above 4' 4" tall. Every
driver has a safety briefing and helmet, gloves
and overalls supplied for your safety. At the end
of your session a print-out is supplied, showing
lap times etc. Family run company, with helpful
and knowledgeable staff to give you an unforgettable experience. All staff trained by National
Karting Association.
*All Year daily 10.00-18.00. Closed 25-26 Dec &
1 Jan*
A&C£15.00

**Discount Offer: Two for the Price of
One**

Toy & Childhood Museums

Coventry Toy Museum

Whitefriars Gate Much Park Street Coventry
Tel: 024 7623 1331
A collection of toys dating from 1740 to 1980,
housed in a fourteenth-century gatehouse.

Transport Museums

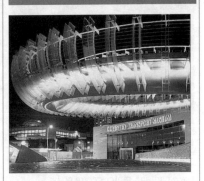

Coventry Transport Museum

Millennium Place Hales Street Coventry
Warwickshire CV1 1PN
Tel: 024 7623 4270 Fax: 024 7623 4284
www.transport-museum.com
[Follow signs for city centre; exit ring rd at J1]
It's hard to find places to visit that offer something that interests the whole family. But
Coventry Transport Museum is different. It's full
of inspiration, thrills and fun, and everyone in
the family will find something to keep them
happy. Visitors can explore over 150 years of
unique history with something different round
every corner. But its not just a place for the past
- you can design your own car, feel what it's like
to break the sound barrier at 763 miles an hour,
and even travel into the future. This is what
makes the museum one of the most popular
family days out in the West Midlands. What's
more admission is free for everyone and as it's
open every day of the week there really is no
excuse not to visit.
All year daily 10.00-17.00. Closed 24-26 Dec
Admission Free

**Discount Offer: 10% discount on all
gift shop purchases (when you spend
£10.00 or more)**

Heritage Motor Centre
Banbury Road Gaydon Warwickshire CV35 0BJ
Tel: 01926 641188 Fax: 01926 645103
www.heritage-motor-centre.co.uk

[J12 M40, 2-3min away on B4100, follow signs. Plenty of on-site parking available]

The Heritage Motor Centre is home to the world's largest collection of British cars. The museum launches in May 2007, with a striking new look, after its one million pound makeover. Discover the magical story of British cars with new and exciting exhibitions including 'Under the Skin' and 'The Making of British Cars', and see some hidden gems from our extensive archive and picture library collections. Experience the sights and sounds of the British Motor Industry, which you'll find fun, interactive and inspiring, and get up close to some amazing cars. Each year the centre hosts a variety of spectacular indoor and outdoor events, which will appeal to all the family. Take part in the centres fun-packed leisure facilities including the Land Rover 4x4 Experience, the go-karting track, miniature roadway and nature trail. Relax in our art deco café, which serves hot and cold meals and browse our museum gift shop to find a perfect memento from your visit. For a fun day out for all the family visit our website for more information.
Easter-31 Oct daily, 1 Nov-Easter Thur-Sun 10.00-17.00. Closed 24-26 Dec
A£8.00 C(0-4)£Free C(5-16)£6.00 OAPs£7.00, Family Ticket (A2+C3) £25.00

Discount Offer: Two for the Price of One

Twycross Zoo
Burton Road Atherstone Warwickshire CV9 3PX
Tel: 01827 880250 / 880440
Fax: 01827 880700
www.twycrosszoo.org

[A444 nr Market Bosworth on Burton to Nuneaton Rd, off J11 M4. Plenty of on-site parking]

Specialises in primates, and also includes gibbons, gorillas, orang-utans and chimpanzees. There is a huge range of monkeys from the tiny tamarins and spider monkeys to the large howler monkeys. Also various other animals such as lions, elephants and giraffes, with a pets' corner for younger children.
All year daily 10.00-17.30 (closes 16.00 in winter). Closed 25 Dec only
A£8.50 C(3-14)£5.00 OAPs£6.00. Group rates (25+): A£5.80 C(3-14)£4.30 C(1-3)£1.00. Special rates for school, college, university parties and physically handicapped/special needs

Discount Offer: One Child Free

Umberslade Children's Farm
Butts Lane Tanworth-In-Arden Nr Solihull Warwickshire B94 5AE
Tel: 01564 742251
Family-run working farm with delightful children's farm in authentic surroundings. Daily programme of feeding and holding animals.

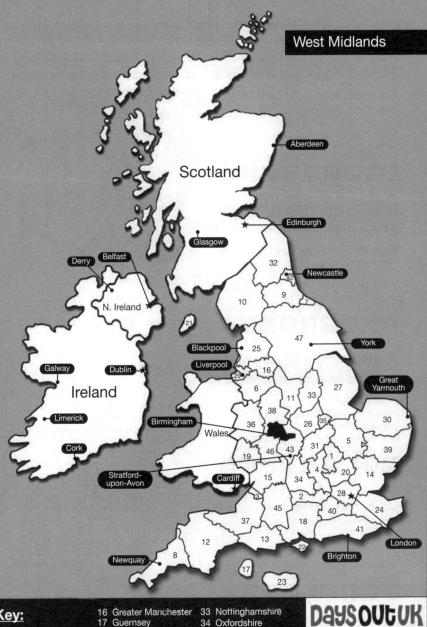

West Midlands

Aberdeen

Scotland

Glasgow

Edinburgh

Derry Belfast

N. Ireland

Newcastle

32

42

10 9 7

21

Blackpool

25

47

York

Galway Dublin

Liverpool

16

Great Yarmouth

Ireland

29

6

Limerick

38

11 33 27

Birmingham

36

26 35 30

Cork

Wales

19 46 43

31 1 5

39

Stratford-upon-Avon

15

4 20 14

Cardiff

34

28

London

13

2

24

45

40

18

41

Newquay

37

22

Brighton

8

12

13

17

23

Art Galleries

Birmingham Museum and Art Gallery
Chamberlain Square Birmingham B3 3DH
Tel: 0121 303 2834
Some of the finest art works, including the world's largest Pre-Raphaelite collection of art.

Arts Crafts and Textiles

Broadfield House Glass Museum
Compton Drive Kingswinford West Midlands DY6 9NS
Tel: 01384 812745
Permanent displays, temporary exhibitions and a programme of events for adults and children.

Country Parks & Estates

Himley Hall
Himley Park Himley Dudley DY3 4DF
Tel: 01902 326665
Extensive parkland offering a range of attractions including a golf course and coarse fishing.

Lickey Hills Country Park
Warren Lane Rednal Birmingham West Midlands
Tel: 0121 447 7106
Lickey Hills Country Park covers 524 acres and comprises of a mosaic of diverse habitats including deciduous and coniferous woodlands.

Sheldon Country Park
Ragley Drive off Church Road Sheldon Birmingham B26 3TU
Tel: 0121 742 0226
296 acres of mixed habitats. Includes an urban farm where a variety of animals can be seen.

Exhibition & Visitor Centres

Cadbury World
Linden Road Bournville Birmingham West Midlands B30 2LU
Tel: 0845 450 3599 Fax: 0121 451 1366
www.cadburyworld.co.uk

[1mi S of A38 Bristol Rd on A4040. Plenty of on-site parking available]

There's never been a better time to visit Cadbury World in Bournville, Birmingham. Come and experience the magic, making and history of Cadbury chocolate. In the new 'Essence,' you can travel back in time to witness the creation of Cadbury Dairy Milk. Create your own unique concoction by choosing a filling from popcorn to marshmallows. Warm liquid chocolate is then added to your cup of goodies for the most delicious taste sensation. In 'Purple Planet' you can chase a Cadbury Creme Egg, grow your own cocoa beans and see yourself moulded in chocolate! With the world's largest Cadbury shop, the 'Cadabra' ride, and much more, you couldn't ask for a more scrumptious day out. New for 2007: the Bournville Heritage Centre.

Please call for opening times
A£13.00 C(4-15)£9.95 Concessions£10.00 C(under4)£Free, Family Ticket (A2+C2) £40.00 or (A2+C3) £48.50

Discount Offer: £10.00 off One Family Ticket

Factory Outlets & Tours

Stuart Crystal
Wordsley Stourbridge West Midlands DY8 4AA
Tel: 01384 342701
Fine glass has been made in the area since the beginning of the seventeenth century.

Festivals & Shows

Three Great Shows, with One Amazing Ticket!
NEC Birmingham West Midlands
Tel: 0870 380 0143
www.bbcliveshows.com/summer

[Follow signs from M42 J6 or M6 J4. Rail: Birmingham International. On-site parking]

We bring you the biggest lifestyle show in the UK with the co-location of BBC Gardeners' World Live, BBC Good Homes Live and BBC Good Food Summer Festival giving you three great shows and one amazing event! These three shows blend together the ultimate day out with an array of beautiful show gardens, decorative home interiors and oodles of food glorious food. Plus tickets also give you entry in the all new Supertheatre where you'll find top celebrity experts including Alan Titchmarsh, Laurence Llewellyn-Bowen and Gordon Ramsay who'll be giving advice on everything you need for a perfect home. 2007 also sees the arrival of Music and Gardens for a Summer Evening, with four evenings of musical entertainment in the idyllic setting of our picturesque show gardens. One ticket gets you all this and a fantastic day out!
13-17 June 2007 09.00-18.00
Prices start from £16.00 (various packages)

Gardens & Horticulture

Birmingham Botanical Gardens and Glasshouses
Westbourne Road Edgbaston Birmingham
West Midlands B15 3TR
Tel: 0121 454 1860 Fax: 0121 454 7835
www.birminghambotanicalgardens.org.uk

[2mi W of city centre. Plenty of on-site parking]

The lush rainforest vegetation in the Tropical House includes many economic plants. Palms, tree ferns, orchids and insectivorous plants are displayed in the Subtropical House. The Mediterranean House features a wide variety of citrus plants, a pelargonium collection and seasonal displays of conservatory plants. A desert scene, with its giant agaves and opuntias, fills the Arid House. Outside there is colourful bedding on the terrace and a tour of the 15 acres of gardens includes rhododendrons and azaleas, herbaceous borders, an impressive Rock Garden and a collection of over 200 trees. There are Herb and Cottage Gardens, a Water Garden, Alpine Yard, Historic Gardens, Organic Garden and the National Bonsai Collection and Japanese Garden. Ferns, grasses and sensory plants all have their own areas. There is a children's adventure playground, Discovery Garden, aviaries, Gallery and Sculpture Trail. Shop at the Gardens and Plant Sales.
All year daily Mon-Sat 09.00-19.00 or dusk if sooner, Sun 10.00-19.00 or dusk if sooner. Closed 25 Dec
A£6.50 Concessions£4.00

Discount Offer: One Concession Free

For great hotel deals call Superbreak on 01904 679999 or visit www.superbreak.com

Birmingham EcoPark

Hob Moor Road Small Heath B10 9HH
Tel: 0121 785 0553
Wildflowers, woodland, wind power, solar
power, composting and water recycling.

Castle Bromwich Hall Gardens

Chester Road Castle Bromwich Birmingham
West Midlands B36 9BT
Tel: 0121 749 4100 Fax: 0121 749 4100
www.cbhgt.org.uk
[Plenty of on-site parking available]
This rare and enchanting late-seventeenth and
early eighteenth-century walled garden is set
within 10 acres of land, with very fine examples
of period planting, including Holly Walk, large
herbaceous borders, Archery Lawn, Parterres
and an interesting Holly Maze. Exceptional vegetable, herb and salad gardens (NEC - RHS
Silver Medal 2004). Walls lined with a wide variety of exotic fruits, Cordon and Espalier pears.
More than 120 varieties of apples and pears in
two large orchards, together with Quince,
Medlar and Walnut etc. Ornamental ponds
attract interesting wildlife. Eighteenth-century
green house/orangery and summer house
where interesting displays are on show at various times. An oasis of historical peace and tranquillity in the centre of the modern urban sprawl
of the Midlands. Tearoom available or bring a
picnic. Many events of special interest held
throughout the year.
Apr-Sept Tue-Thur 11.00-16.30, Fri 11.00-15.30,
Sat-Sun & Bank Hol Mon 13.30-17.30
A£3.50 Concessions£3.00 C£0.50. Groups by
appointment.

**Discount Offer: Two for the Price of
One**

Heritage & Industrial

Birmingham Railway Museum

Warwick Road Tyseley Birmingham B11 2HL
Tel: 0121 707 4696
Working railway museum and workshop.

Lock Museum

54 New Road Willenhall West Midlands
WV13 2DA
Tel: 01902 634542
In gas-lit rooms, experience the everyday life of
a locksmith. Collection of locks and keys.

Walsall Leather Museum

Littleton Street West Walsall WS2 8EQ
Tel: 01922 721153
Visitors can see how traditional leather goods
have been made.

Historical

Baddesley Clinton

Rising Lane Baddesley Clinton Village Knowle
Solihull West Midlands B93 0DQ
Tel: 01564 783294
A romantic manor house, dating from 1634.

Kinver Edge and the Rock Houses

The Warden's Lodge The Compa Kinver
Stourbridge DY7 6HU
Tel: 01384 872553
Unique rock houses carved into a contorted
sandstone ridge. Inhabited till the 1950s, they
were restored to their nineteenth-century glory.

Packwood House

Packwood Lane Lapworth Solihull B94 6AT
Tel: 01564 783294
A fascinating twentieth-century evocation of
domestic Tudor architecture.

Selly Manor Museum

Maple Road Bournville Birmingham B30 2AE
Tel: 0121 472 0199 Fax: 0121 415 6410
[Maple Rd, next to Bournville Village Green]

One of Birmingham's oldest buildings, Selly
Manor was saved from demolition by the
chocolate manufacturer, George Cadbury,
almost a hundred years ago. Originally a mile
from its present site, it was dismantled then
moved to the heart of historic Bournville and
opened as a museum in 1917. The building
dates back to at least 1327 and is an excellent
example of a Tudor manor house. Selly Manor
contains a superb collection of sixteenth and
seventeenth-century furniture and artefacts collected by Laurence Cadbury, George's son.
Alongside Selly Manor stands the 750-year-old
Minworth Greaves, a cruck-framed medieval
hall. These impressive buildings are surrounded
by beautiful gardens, accurately recreated from
the Tudor period. Please call for information on
tours, talks, events, school visits and civil ceremonies.

*All year Tue-Fri 10.00-17.00 Easter-Sept Sat, Sun
& Bank Hol Mons 14.00-17.00*
A£3.50 C£1.50 Concessions £2.00, Family
Ticket (A2+C3) £9.00

Wightwick Manor

Wightwick Bank Wolverhampton WV6 8EE
Tel: 01902 761400
One of only a few surviving examples of a
house built and furnished under the influence of
the Arts & Crafts movement.

Black Country Living Museum

Tipton Road Castle Hill Dudley West Midlands
DY1 4SQ
Tel: 0121 557 9643
Friendly costumed demonstrations bring recon-
structed, original cottages, shops and work-
shops to life on a 26-acre site.

Nature & Conservation Parks

Birmingham Nature Centre

Pershore Road Edgbaston Birmingham B5 7RL
Tel: 0121 472 7775
Otters, foxes, lynxes, fallow deer, harvest mice
and snowy owls are among 134 species of
mainly British and European wildlife.

On the Water

Edgbaston Reservoir

The Rangers Lodge 115 Reservoir Road
Ladywood Birmingham B16 9EE
Tel: 0121 454 1908
Large expanse of water, lots of wildfowl.
Windsurfing lessons available. 1.5mi path and a
trim trail around reservoir.

Places of Worship

Birmingham Cathedral

Colmore Row Birmingham B3 2QB
Tel: 0121 262 1840
Birmingham Cathedral, designed by Thomas
Archer, is one of the most notable eighteenth-
century church buildings in the country and
stands at the heart of the city.

Science - Earth & Planetary

Thinktank

Millennium Point Curzon Street Birmingham
West Midlands B4 7XG
Tel: 0121 202 2222
Four floors of fun and exploration, 10 themed
galleries containing over 200 interactive games.

Sealife Centres & Aquariums

National Sea Life Centre

The Waters Edge Brindleyplace Birmingham
B1 2HL
Tel: 0121 633 4700 Fax: 0121 633 4787
www.sealifeeurope.com
[Rail: New Street Station]
The National Sea Life centre in Birmingham
turned tropical in 2005, and takes the transfor-
mation a step further in 2006 with the addition
of a magical AmaZonia exhibition. There will be
a slightly 'sinister' slant to this feature, with several hazardous creatures like piranhas and poison dart frogs among its inhabitants. And it will
create a convincing illusion of a genuine journey
into the dense rainforest, with authentic foliage,
jungle sounds and perpetual mist. An amazing
360° acrylic tunnel allows all round viewing of a
fantastic collection of marine life including
sharks, sea turtles and beautiful colourful tropical fish. Meet our cheeky short-clawed otters
and see the graceful movements of the rays.
Talks and feeding presentations throughout the
day provide visitors with a deeper insight into
the marvels of the undersea world.
All year daily from 10.00. Closed Christmas Day
Please call for admission prices

Discount Offer: One Child Free

Social History Museums

Blakesley Hall

Blakesley Road Yardley Birmingham B25 8RN
Tel: 0121 464 2193
Delightfully restored, Blakesley Hall is one of the
last surviving examples in Birmingham of a timber framed farmhouse.

Spectator Sports

Wolverhampton Racecourse

Dunstall Park Centre Dunstall Park
Wolverhampton West Midlands WV6 0PE
Tel: 0870 220 2442 Fax: 0870 220 0107
www.wolverhampton-racecourse.co.uk
*[Rail: Wolverhampton. Plenty of on-site parking
available]*

As the first floodlit racecourse in Britain,
Wolverhampton features racing throughout the
year on their all-weather track. There is also a
Holiday Inn Hotel on site, but book early to
avoid disappointment. Pre-book for the
Grandstand Value Package and restaurants for
evening race meetings.
Dependent of fixture - contact us for details
From £12.00 (From £15.00 Boxing Day)

**Discount Offer: Three for the Price of
Two**

Sport & Recreation

Solihull Ice Rink

Hobs Moat Road Solihull West Midlands
B92 8JN
Tel: 0121 742 5561 Fax: 0121 742 4315
www.solihullicerink.co.uk

*[M6 J4/4A take M42 S exit J6, take A45
Birmingham. L lane into Hobs Moat Rd B425.
Follow brown tourist sign. To enter free car park
go past Solihull Ice Rink & turn R into Ulleries Rd
& next R by Fitness First. M42 J5 on A41 Solihull
bypass turn R into B425 Lode Lane & follow
brown tourist sign. Continue past Land Rover factory on your R, straight ahead at island into Hobs
Moat Road. Ice rink is second L. R by Fitness
First. Rail: Solihull. Bus: 71, 72 & 57a & to
Coventry Rd 57, 58, 60 & 900. Plenty of free on-
site parking available]*

Welcome to Solihull Ice Rink @ Blue Ice Plaza.
The venue also incorporates Fitness First Health
Club, Riley's pool and snooker and three restaurants to include Spicewood's, Pizza by Goli and
Woks Hall. Solihull Ice Rink has its very own
skate shop within the ice rink. The shop sells a
wide variety of recreational ice skates and skating accessories. Also specialises in ice hockey
equipment and figure skates for both juniors
and adults. We are also proud to offer cool
birthday parties, skating lessons, café, function
rooms for hire as well as a variety of hockey, fig-
ure/dance and speed skating clubs for adults
and children.
*All year round. Sessions: Mon 13.45-15.45, Tue
10.00-12.00 & 13.45-15.45 & 19.30-21.30,
Wed 10.00-12.00 & 13.45-15.00 & 19.30-21.30
(speed garage and funky-house disco), Thu
10.00-15.45 & 19.30-21.30, Fri 10.00-12.00 &
13.45-15.45 & 17.00-18.30 & 20.00-22.30 (live
DJ), Sat 11.00-16.00 & 20.00-22.30 (live DJ),
Sun 11.00-16.00 & 20.30-22.30, Local School
Hols (excluding teacher-training days) 11.00-
16.00 & evenings as normal*
Prices valid until 30 Nov 2007. Spectators

£1.50. C(under4)£2.00 A(over60)£2.80. Mon-Fri
Daytime Sessions: A(+skate-hire)£6.00
C(+skate-hire)£5.80, Family Ticket (+skate-hire)
£17.80. Sat-Sun Daytime Session: A(+skate-
hire)£7.20 C(+skate-hire)£7.00, Family Ticket
(+skate-hire) £21.50. Local School Hols
(Daytime Sessions): A(+skate-hire)£7.00
C(+skate-hire)£6.80, Family Ticket (+skate-hire)
£21.00. Tue-Thu & Sun Evening Sessions:
A(+skate-hire)£6.00 C(+skate-hire)£5.85, Family
Ticket (+skate-hire) £17.80. Fri & Sat Evening
Sessions (Disco): A(+skate-hire)£7.20 C(+skate-
hire)£7.00. Group rates, Off Peak: £3.50 Peak:
£4.50. Skating lessons available on request

Discount Offer: Save up to £5.00

Transport Museums

Jaguar Daimler Heritage Trust

Jaguar Cars Ltd Browns Lane Alesbury
Coventry West Midlands CV5 9DR
Tel: 024 7620 2141
Portraying over a century of outstanding auto-
motive design.
*Last Sunday of every month (Subject to
availability). Other times by appointment only*

National Motorcycle Museum

Coventry Road Bickenhill Solihull B92 0EJ
Tel: 01675 443311
Recognized as the finest and largest motorcycle
museum in the world. It is a place where
'Legends Live On.'

Zoos

Dudley Zoological Gardens

2 The Broadway Dudley DY1 4QB
Tel: 01384 215313
The wooded grounds of Dudley Castle make a
wonderful setting for this traditional zoo, which
has animals from all continents.

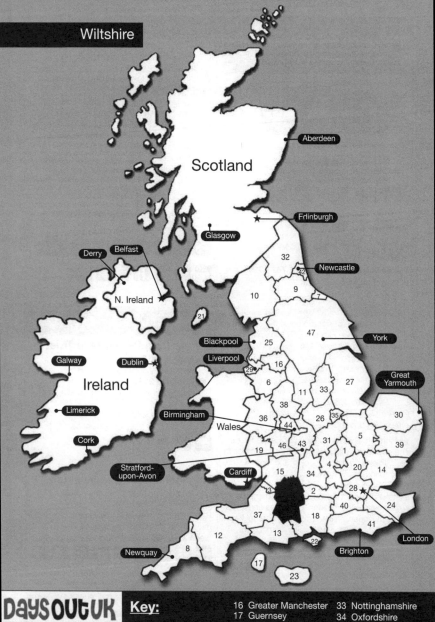

Wiltshire

Aberdeen

Scotland

Frlinburgh

Glasgow

Derry
Belfast

N. Ireland

Newcastle

Galway
Dublin

Ireland

Blackpool
Liverpool

Limerick

Birmingham

Cork

Wales

Stratford-upon-Avon

Cardiff

Newquay

Brighton

London

York

Great Yarmouth

Key:

1 Bedfordshire
2 Berkshire
3 Bristol
4 Buckinghamshire
5 Cambridgeshire
6 Cheshire
7 Cleveland
8 Cornwall
9 County Durham
10 Cumbria
11 Derbyshire
12 Devon
13 Dorset
14 Essex
15 Gloucestershire

16 Greater Manchester
17 Guernsey
18 Hampshire
19 Herefordshire
20 Hertfordshire
21 Isle Of Man
22 Isle Of Wight
23 Jersey
24 Kent
25 Lancashire
26 Leicestershire
27 Lincolnshire
28 London
29 Merseyside
30 Norfolk
31 Northamptonshire
32 Northumberland

33 Nottinghamshire
34 Oxfordshire
35 Rutland
36 Shropshire
37 Somerset
38 Staffordshire
39 Suffolk
40 Surrey
41 Sussex
42 Tyne & Wear
43 Warwickshire
44 West Midlands
45 Wiltshire
46 Worcestershire
47 Yorkshire

Animal Attractions

Bush Farm Bison Centre

West Knoyle Mere Wiltshire BA12 6AE
Tel: 01747 830263 (phone/fax)
www.bisonfarm.co.uk
[Follow the brown signs from A350. 1mi from A303. Plenty of on-site parking available]
Bush Farm is tucked away in a great Oak Wood. Visitors will see herds of bison, elk and Red deer as they follow the trail through 100 acres of meadows, lakes and woodlands. There is a gallery and shop selling art, native American artefacts, bison meat and venison. We also have a children's farmyard and playground.
2 Apr-26 Sept Wed-Sun 10.00-17.00. Winter: Shop & Gallery Thur & Fri only
Farmyard & Woodland Walks: A£5.50 C(under4)£Free C£3.00. Camping & Caravanning £6.00 per night, Woodland Camping £6.00 per person

Discount Offer: One Child Free

Cholderton Rare Breeds Farm

Amesbury Road Cholderton Salisbury SP4 0EW

Tel: 01980 629438 Fax: 01980 629594
www.rabbitworld.co.uk

[4 mi E of Stonehenge. Plenty of on-site parking available]

A farm park in the Wiltshire countryside close to the A303, boasts a superb collection of rare breed farm animals, visitor centre, café, picnic area (undercover) Rabbitworld, adventure play area and a new soft play area in a massive barn. A good family day out!
All year daily, Summer 10.00-18.00, Winter 10.00-16.00
A£5.50 C(2-16)£4.95 Concessions£4.50 Family Ticket (A2+C2)£19.00, Season Tickets available

Discount Offer: One Child Free

Farmer Giles Farmstead Ltd

Teffont Salisbury Wiltshire SP3 5QY
Tel: 01722 716338 Fax: 01722 716993
www.farmergiles.co.uk
[Follow brown signs from A303. On-site parking]

Enjoy a great day out at this fun family attraction! Bottle-feed the lambs and the kids-goats, groom the donkeys, ride the ponies and cuddle the rabbits, before browsing the gift shop and enjoying one of the best tractor rides in Wiltshire! Alternatively, just relax and take it easy in the beautiful surroundings. There are huge indoor play areas, including a bouncing castle, pedal tractors, a ball pool and a special play area for toddlers. The kids can enjoy our children's menu whilst the adults can sample our selection of fine wines (produced right here on the farm!). School trips, and birthday parties are our specialities. There's also excellent disabled access and catering for special-needs groups. Please call for further information.
Summer: 10.00-18.00, Winter: 10.00-16.00
A£4.99 C(2-14)£3.99 OAPs£4.50, Family Ticket (A2+C2) £16.00. Group rates available on request

Discount Offer: One Child Free

Archaeology

Alexander Keiller Museum

Avebury Wiltshire SN8 1RF
Tel: 01672 539250
Exciting displays illustrate the world of the Neolithic in the Avebury area.

Avebury Stone Circles

Avebury Wiltshire
[in Avebury, 7m W of Marlborough]
Complex, gigantic and mysterious, the Circles were constructed 4,000 years ago.

Old Sarum

Castle Road Salisbury Wiltshire SP1 3SD
Tel: 01722 335398
A great earthwork with huge banks and ditches. It was created by Iron Age people and later occupied by Romans and Saxons. Today, you can see the remains of the prehistoric fortress, the Norman palace, castle and cathedral.

Silbury Hill

West Kennet Avebury Wiltshire
Tel: 0117 975 0700
The largest man-made mound in Europe, Silbury Hill is a similar size to the Egyptian pyramids (which were built around the same time). However, its purpose remains a mystery.

Stonehenge

Amesbury Salisbury Wiltshire SP4 7DE
Tel: 01980 624715 infoline
A prehistoric monument of unique importance. Known throughout the world, for over 5,000 years these enigmatic stones have fascinated the millions of people who have visited them. Why they were put here remains a mystery.

Wiltshire Heritage Museum

41 Long Street Devizes Wiltshire SN10 1NS
Tel: 01380 727369
World-famous collections from Wiltshire, including unique finds from barrows near Stonehenge.

Woodhenge

Amesbury Wiltshire
Tel: 0117 975 0700
A Neolithic ceremonial monument consisting of six concentric rings of timber posts (now marked by concrete piles).

Gardens & Horticulture

Flower Farms

Carvers Hill Farm Shalbourne Marlborough Wiltshire SN8 3PS
Tel: 01672 870782 Fax: 01672 870782
www.wildflowerfarms.com

[Rail: Great Bedwyn. Road: follow signs from A338 3mi S of Hungerford. Plenty of on-site parking available]

Spectacular displays of wild flowers that you thought you would never see again, attracting hundreds of butterflies. With nature trails, picnic area, children's playground. Guided tours or countryside workshops available.

12 May-9 Sept 10.00-17.00
Admission Free

Peto Garden at Iford Manor

Ilford Bradford-on-Avon Wiltshire BA15 2BA
Tel: 01225 863146
This Grade I Italian-style garden is famous for its tranquil beauty and was the home of architect and landscape gardener, Harold A. Peto from 1899 to 1933. This unique and romantic hillside garden is characterised by steps, terraces, sculpture and magnificent rural views.

Crofton Beam Engines 2007

**1812 Boulton & Watt
and 1843 Harvey Beam Engines
regularly steamed from
a hand stoked, coal fired
Lancashire Boiler**

Open Daily
10:30 - 17:00
April 6 - September 30

In Steam
April 7-8-9
May 5-6-7, 26-27-28,
June 30-July 1, July 28-29
Aug 25-26-27, Sept 29-30

Gift Shop, Refreshments etc.

Crofton Pumping Station, Crofton,
Marlborough, Wilts SN8 3DW
01672 870300
www.croftonbeamengines.org

Heritage & Industrial

Crofton Beam Engines

Crofton Pumping Station Crofton Marlborough
Wiltshire SN8 3DW
Tel: 01672 870300
www.croftonbeamengines.org

*[6mi SE of Marlborough, follow brown signs from
Burbage, then follow the brown 'Beam Engine'
signs. 6mi SW of Hungerford, proceed towards
Salisbury on A338. Turn R to Shalbourne following signs to Great Bedwyn, then follow brown
'Beam Engine' signs. From Salisbury direction, follow signs to Hungerford on A338, then turn L at
East Grafton, following brown 'Beam Engine'
signs. Plenty of on-site parking available]*

Amazing industrial archaeology situated in the
beautiful Wiltshire countryside. This Grade I listed building house two magnificent Cornish
Beam Engines, - the 1812 Boulton and Watt is
the oldest working beam engine in the world still
in its original engine house and capable of doing
the job for which it was installed - which it does
on steaming days. Crofton Pumping Station
was built in 1807 to provide water to the summit of the Kennet and Avon Canal. The 1812
Boulton and Watt, and the 1846 Harvey engine
are in working condition, and are regularly
steamed publicly through the summer months
from a coal fired Lancashire boiler - please see
our website for dates. The station is also open
for static viewing on non-steaming days. Also of
interest are a number of stationary engines
housed in the boiler room, which are run when
the station is in steam. Guided tours available
on static days. Please note we have limited disabled access.
*Easter-end Sept daily 10.30-17.00. Closed Oct-
Easter*
In Steam: A£6.50 C£1.50 OAPs£5.50, Family
Ticket (A2+C2) £14.00 C(Under5)£Free. Static:
A£4.50 C£1.50 OAPs£4.00, Family Ticket
(A2+C2) £9.00 C(Under5)£Free

Historical

Avebury Manor and Garden

High Street Avebury Marlborough SN8 1RF
Tel: 01672 539250
Avebury Manor has a monastic origin, and has
been much altered since then. The present
buildings date from the early sixteenth century.

Bowood House and Gardens

Estate Office Bowood Calne Wiltshire SN11 0LZ
Tel: 01249 812102
Outstanding eighteenth-century house with
remarkable collection of family heirlooms including fine paintings and water-colours. 100 acre
park landscaped by Capability Brown.

Bratton Camp and White Horse

Westbury Wiltshire
Tel: 01225 776655
Below an Iron Age hillfort stands the Westbury White Horse. Cut into the hillside in 1778, it replaced a much older horse (that commemorated King Alfred's victory over the Vikings).

Ludgershall Castle and Cross

Lydiard Tregoze Swindon Wiltshire SN5 9PA
Tel: 0117 975 0700
The visitor can see large earth works of the Norman motte-and-bailey castle and the flint walling of the later hunting palace.

Lydiard House

Lydiard Park Lydiard Tregoze West Swindon Wiltshire SN5 3PA
Tel: 01793 770401
Character figures and audio guides bring the story of Lydiard Park to life.

Mompesson House

The Close Salisbury Wiltshire SP1 2EL
Tel: 01722 335659
This Queen Anne house makes an impressive addition to the elegant Cathedral Close in Salisbury. Film location for 'Sense and Sensibility' (1995).
Mar-Oct (Closed Thu & Fri)

Old Wardour Castle

Old Wardour Tisbury Salisbury Wiltshire SP3 6RR
Tel: 01747 870487
Built in the late fourteenth century, this six-sided castle was unique in medieval architecture.

Wilton House

Wilton Salisbury Wiltshire SP2 0BJ
Tel: 01722 746716
Contains an art collection, introductory film, recreated Tudor kitchen and Victorian laundry. Extensive parkland with Palladian bridge, plus an adventure playground.

Places of Worship

Salisbury Cathedral

33 The Close Salisbury Wiltshire SP1 2EJ
Tel: 01722 555120 Fax: 01722 555116
www.salisburycathedral.org.uk
[A30, M3, M27 signposted locally]

Salisbury is Britain's finest thirteenth-century Cathedral - with the highest spire (123 metres/404 ft), the best preserved Magna Carta (AD 1215), a unique thirteenth-century frieze of bible stories in the octagonal Chapter House and Europe's oldest working clock (AD 1386). Boy and girl choristers sing daily services, continuing a tradition of worship that dates back nearly 800 years. Set within the Cathedral Close, surrounded by eight acres of lawns and eight centuries of beautiful houses, Salisbury Cathedral has been the source of inspiration to generations of artists and writers. Volunteers provide guided tours highlighting the Cathedral's many fine treasures, including tours of the roof and tower. The city of Salisbury, Stonehenge and Old Sarum are all within easy reach.

All year Mon-Sat, 1 Jan-10 June 07.15-18.15, 11 June-24 Aug 07.15-19.15, 25 Aug-31 Dec 07.15-18.15, Sun 07.15-18.15
Suggested Donations: A£5.00 C(5-17)£3.00 OAPs&Students(NUS/USI)£4.25, Family Ticket £12.00. Tower Tour: A£5.50 Concessions£4.50

Transport Museums

Atwell-Wilson Motor Museum
Downside Stockley Road Calne SN11 0NF
Tel: 01249 813119
Contains over 120 exhibits, including a seven-teenth-century water-meadow walk.

STEAM - Museum of the Great Western Railway
Kemble Drive Swindon Wiltshire SN2 2TA
Tel: 01793 466646 Fax: 01793 466615
www.swindon.gov.uk/steam
[Adjacent to Great Western Designer Outlet Centre. From M4 & other major routes, follow brown tourist signs to 'Outlet Centre']
STEAM - Museum of the Great Western Railway tells the story of the men and women who built, operated and travelled on the Great Western Railway. Hands on displays, world famous loco-motives, archive film footage and the testi-monies of ex-railway workers bring the story to life. A reconstructed station platform, posters and holiday memorabilia recreate the glamour and excitement of the golden age of steam. Located next door to the McArthurGlen Designer Outlet Great Western, STEAM offers a great day out for all. With excellent value group packages, special events and exhibitions, shop and refreshments. Photography permitted for private use only.
All year daily 10.00-17.00. Closed 25-26 Dec & 1 Jan
A£5.95 C(under5)£Free C£3.80 OAPs£3.90, Family Ticket (A2+C2) £14.70 or (A2+C3) £17.50. Group rates (15+): A£5.00 C£3.20. Prices subject to change

Wildlife & Safari Parks

Longleat
Warminster Wiltshire BA12 7NW
Tel: 01985 844400 Fax: 01985 844885
www.longleat.co.uk
[A36 between Bath & Salisbury, A362 Warminster to Frome. Plenty of on-site parking available]
The star of BBC's hugely popular Animal Park series invites you to discover the magnificent animals which roam the first Safari Park outside Africa from the comfort of your own car…see how you measure up to the giraffe, watch out for the zebra's crossing, wander amongst the wallabies in wallaby wood and be enthralled by the majestic lions and tigers! Continue your adventure aboard the Safari Boats for a sea lion escorted cruise to Gorilla Island, find yourself lost in the Longleat Hedge Maze and enjoy a fun packed railway ride before discovering the treasures and priceless heirlooms within Longleat House and much, much more…your day at Longleat will never be long enough! Longleat's great value Passport Ticket offers access to over 11 amazing Longleat attractions.
All Attractions: 3 Mar-25 Mar Sat-Sun, 31 Mar-4 Nov daily. Longleat Safari Park: 10.00-16.00 (17.00 Sat-Sun, Bank Hols & state school hols). Other Longleat Attractions: 11.00-17.00 (10.30-17.30 Sat-Sun, Bank Hols & state school hols). Longleat House: All year daily Easter-Sept 10.00-17.00 (17.30 on Sat-Sun, Bank Hols & state school hols). Closed 25 Dec, All other times guid-ed tours only 11.00-15.00, tours subject to change, please call for up to date info
Make huge savings by purchasing the 'Great Value' Passport & seeing all 11 of the Longleat attractions! Visit Longleat in a day or come back at any time before the end of the season to see those attractions previously missed... the choice is yours! Each attraction may be visited only once. A£20.00 C(3-14)&OAPs£16.00

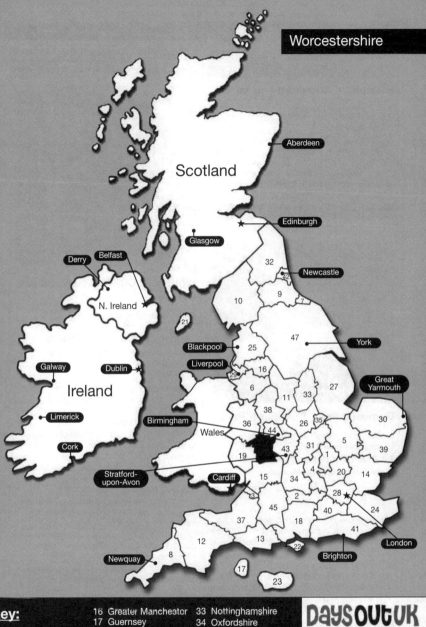

Worcestershire

Aberdeen

Scotland

Edinburgh

Glasgow

32

Newcastle

42

9

Derry Belfast

10

Newcastle

N. Ireland

21

47

York

Blackpool

25

Great Yarmouth

Galway

Dublin

Liverpool

29

16

Ireland

6

11 33

27

30

Limerick

38

Birmingham

36

44

26 35

Wales

Cork

19

43

31 1

5

39

Stratford-upon-Avon

Cardiff

15

34

4

20

14

2

28

London

45

18

40

24

37

13

41

12

22

Brighton

Newquay

8

17

23

Animal Attractions

Bodenham Aboretum and Earth Centre

Wolverley Kidderminster DY11 5SY
Tel: 01562 852444
Bodenham Arboretum is a collection of over 2,700 trees set in 156 acres of Worcestershire countryside with 11 pools, four miles of footpaths and a working farm. In addition there is an award-winning Visitor Centre set in the hillside overlooking the Big Pool.

Domestic Fowl Trust Farm Park

Station Road Honeybourne Evesham Worcestershire WR11 7QZ
Tel: 01386 833083 Fax: 01386 833364
www.domesticfowltrust.co.uk

[Rail: Honeybourne. Plenty of on-site parking available]

Conservation centre for pure breeds of poultry and rare breeds of farm animals. The shop has a wide range of poultry equipment, books, feedstuff, poultry housing and birds, as well as gifts for children and chicken-lovers. There is an indoor play area for the under-7s, and a playground suitable for older children. There is also an interpretation centre and museum.
Daily 9.30-17.00
A£3.75 C(3-15)£2.50 OAPs£3.25

Discount Offer: One Child Free

Arts, Crafts & Textiles

Worcester City Museum and Art Gallery

Foregate Street Worcester Worcestershire WR1 1DT
Tel: 01905 25371 Fax: 01905 616979
www.worcestercitymuseums.org.uk/

[City centre J6 or J7 M5]

Housed in a beautiful Victorian building in the heart of Worcester, the City Art Gallery & Museum runs a lively programme of exhibitions, activities and events for all the family. The gallery presents a changing programme of contemporary art and craft exhibitions. Current displays also include the Spirit of Enterprise tracing the history of Worcester's industrial past, displays of geology and natural history as well as a selection of nineteenth and twentieth-century paintings, prints, and photographs. Visitors can also discover the colourful collections of uniforms, medals and pictures from the independent museums of the Worcestershire Regiment and the Yeomanry Cavalry. The museum has an activity space and runs a regular programme of art and craft workshops for children, as well as artist led events for schools and adults. Visit the gallery shop, which has a superb selection of cards, books and gifts, or relax in the Balcony Café.
All year Mon-Fri 09.30-17.30, Sat 09.30-17.00. Closed Sun & Bank Hols
Admission Free

Factory Outlets & Tours

Royal Worcester Visitor Centre

Severn Street Worcester Worcestershire
WR1 2NE
Tel: 01905 21247 Fax: 01905 619503
www.royalworcester.com

[2min walk from cathedral/city centre easy access, 3mi from J7 of M5. Plenty of on-site parking available]

Established in 1751 along the banks of the River Severn The Royal Worcester Visitor Centre is a great day out for everyone. Nestles amidst Victorian factory buildings, just 2 minutes walk from the cathedral & historic city centre, the Royal Worcester visitor centre offers something of interest for everyone whether you take a guided tour and see skilled craftsmen at work or try your hand at paint a plate. Our Royal Worcester bestware and seconds shops offer an extensive range of quality bone china, porcelain and giftware with great savings and special offers throughout the year. The Shopping Court, home to a many famous names, offers an unrivalled array of home accessories, cookware, linens, luggage, glassware and cutlery.

Daily Mon-Sat 09.00-17.30, Sun 11.00-17.00)
Guided Tour A£5.00 Concessions£4.25, Family Ticket £12.00

Discount Offer: Two for the Price of One

Folk & Local History Museums

Almonry Heritage Centre

Abbey Gate Evesham WR11 4BG
Tel: 01386 446944
www.evesham.uk.com

[Centre of Evesham opposite Merstow Green car park]

The fourteenth-century stone and timber building was the home of the Almoner of the Benedictine Abbey in Evesham. It now houses exhibitions relating to the history of Evesham Abbey, the battle of Evesham, and the culture and trade of Evesham. A perfect introduction to the town and Vale of Evesham which will appeal to all the family. (Evesham Tourist Information Centre is also located here.)

All year Mon-Sat & Bank Hol Mon 10.00-17.00, Sun 14.00-17.00. Closed Sun Nov, Dec, Jan & Feb
A£2.50 C(0-16)£Free OAPs£1.50

Avoncroft Museum of Historic Buildings

Redditch Road Stoke Heath Bromsgrove
Worcestershire B60 4JR
Tel: 01527 831363 / 831886
Fax: 01527 876934
www.avoncroft.org.uk
[Off A38. Plenty of on-site parking available]

Avoncroft is a fascinating collection of historic buildings, rescued and restored on a scenic 15-acre open-air site in north Worcestershire. Explore the fifteenth-century Tudor Merchant's House, Victorian Mission Church, 1940s 'prefab' or the wonderful nineteenth-century working windmill, meet volunteers in the buildings and experience live interpretations of historic life. On event days, craftsmen can be seen working in workshops and on machinery. There's also a gift shop, tearoom and picnic site. With an outdoor children's play area, a miniature railway (subject to availability) and a National Telephone Kiosk Collection. Come along and join us for a fun day out for all the family.

Mar Tue-Thur, Sat-Sun 10.30-16.00, Apr-June & Sep-Oct Tue-Sun 10.30-17.00, July-Aug daily 10.00-17.00

A£6.00 C£3.00 Concessions£5.00, Family Ticket (A2+C3) £15.00

Discount Offer: One Child Free

Forests & Woods

Wyre Forest Visitor Centre

Wyre Forest Callow Hill Bewdley Kidderminster Worcestershire DY14 9XQ
Tel: 01299 266944
Tranquil woodland walks and deer at dusktime.

Gardens & Horticulture

Croome Park

National Trust Estate Office The Builders' Yard High Green Severn Stoke WR8 9JS
Tel: 01905 371006 Fax: 01905 371090
www.nationaltrust.org.uk
[9mi S of Worcester off A38. 6mi NW of Pershore off B4084. Exit 1 off M50, Exit 7 off M5. Rail:

Pershore. Plenty of on-site parking available]
Croome Park was the first commissioned landscape by Capability Brown who went on to revolutionise the world of garden and landscape design. The restoration project, the largest of its kind undertaken by the National Trust, has included the replanting of thousands of trees, creation of wetlands, replacement of shrubberies, the lake and river cleared and re-creation of pastureland. The planting now appears as it would have done in the 1760s. Gentle paths take visitors around the Pleasure Garden, to the river and lake and through the meadows. Be inspired by the Classical Temple Greenhouse or lakeside garden with its bridges, grotto, urn and temple. Or admire the parkland as you walk along the river to the Park Seat. A full programme of events takes place year-round.

2 Mar-29 Apr Wed-Sun 10.00-17.30, 30 Apr-2 Sep daily 10.00-17.30, 5 Sep-28 Oct Wed-Sun 10.00-17.30, Nov & Dec Sat-Sun 10.00-16.00
A£4.40 C£2.20, Family Ticket £10.80. NT Members £Free. Group rate: £3.40. Out of hours tours: £6.00

Whit Lenge Gardens and Nurseries

Whit Lenge Lane Hartlebury DY10 4HD
Tel: 01299 250720 Fax: 01299 251259
www.whit-lenge.co.uk
[S of Kidderminster off A442 Kidderminster-Droitwich Rd. Look for Brown Whitlenge Garden signs. Plenty of on-site parking available]

Wander through the three-acre show garden of professional designer Keith J Southall, set around his eighteenth-century cottage. Walk the 'Twisted Brick Pergola' with its fan trained apples and pears, sit in the 'Verdigris Gazebo' see the water gardens with their split-level waterfalls. Listen to the 'bubblers' and marvel at the size of the Gunnera in the bog garden,

against the compactness of the 'Scree Gardens.' Walk into the manmade cave and fernery, dwell upon the mystic of the 'Green Man' and the 'Sword in the Stone' features. Explore our Labyrinths. A plantsmans delight with over 800 varieties. Come and be inspired.
All year Mon-Fri 09.00-17.00, Sun 10.00-17.00
A£1.50 C£Free

Discount Offer: Two for the Price of One

meadows next to the Museum. Adult and children's audio tours for both the Needle Museum and Bordesley Abbey. The pleasant grounds with picnic tables enhance the visit.
Easter-Sept Mon-Fri 11.00-16.30 Weekends 14.00-17.00, Feb-Easter & Oct-Nov Mon-Thur 11.00-16.00 Sun 14.00-17.00
A£3.80 C£0.65 OAPs£2.80

Discount Offer: Two for the Price of One

Heritage & Industrial

Forge Mill Needle Museum and Bordesley Abbey Visitor Centre

Needle Mill Lane Riverside Redditch Worcestershire B98 8HY
Tel: 01527 62509
www.redditchbc.gov.uk/pagemaster/page-manager/Arts&Leisure/ForgeMill.asp

[N side of Redditch off A441 / J2 M42. Plenty of on-site parking available]

Forge Mill Museum is a unique museum about the Redditch needle industry. Redditch supplied needles throughout the British Empire. Part of the Museum is a needle scouring mill, which was working until 1958, and still has original water-powered machinery. See how needles were made from the initial metal coil to the packets sold in the shops. The Museum also has fishing tackle displays and holds contemporary textile exhibitions. The Bordesley Abbey Visitor Centre is an archaeological site museum telling the story of the Cistercian Abbey in the

Historical

Harvington Hall

Harvington Hall Lane Harvington Kidderminster Worcestershire DY10 4LR
Tel: 01562 777846 Fax: 01562 777190
www.harvingtonhall.com
[3mi SE of Kidderminster. On-site parking]

Moated medieval and Elizabethan manor-house containing secret hiding-places and rare wall-paintings. Georgian Chapel in garden. Tearoom serving light lunches and afternoon teas, gift shop, picnic area and free parking. Events such as outdoor plays, musical evenings, living history weekends and candlelight tours.
Mar & Oct Sat-Sun, Apr-Sept Wed-Sun 11.30-16.30. Occasionally the Hall may be closed for a function, please ring for up-to-date information
A£5.00 C(5-16)£3.50 OAPs£4.30, Family Ticket £14.50

Discount Offer: One Child Free

Worcestershire County Museum

Hartlebury Castle Stourport Road Hartlebury
Nr Kidderminster Worcestershire DY11 7XZ
Tel: 01299 250416 Fax: 01299 251890
www.worcestershire.gov.uk/museum

*[4mi S of Kidderminster on A449 rd to Worcester.
Plenty of on-site parking available]*

Worcestershire County Museum is housed in
historic Hartlebury Castle, home to the Bishops
of Worcester since 850. The museum collection
ranges from toys and domestic items to beautiful costume and ancient archaeological finds.
There are also room sets to explore such as the
Victorian schoolroom as well as a Transport
Gallery showing a wide range of vehicles including a fire engine, a hearse and a fascinating collection of gypsy caravans. Visitors can also see
some of the Bishops State Rooms, usually the
Great Hall and the Saloon. The site also
includes a new café area in the historic Castle
Kitchen and two picnic areas and a newly
opened shop. There is also an annual events
programme including historic re-enactments,
family activity days and weekends when the
Blacksmith's Forge and Cider Mill are brought to
life.
*1 Feb-23 Dec Tue-Fri 10.00-17.00, Sat-Sun &
Bank Hol Mon 11.00-17.00. Closed Mon & Good
Fri*
A£4.00 Concessions £2.00, Family Ticket
(A2+C2) £10.00

**Discount Offer: Two for the Price of
One**

Elgar Birthplace Museum

Crown East Lane Lower Broadheath WR2 6RH
Tel: 01905 333224
The cottage where the composer was born,
and the modern Elgar Centre.

Places of Worship

Pershore Abbey

Church Street Pershore WR10 1DT
Tel: 01386 552071
The Abbey Church of the Holy Cross, Pershore
has been a centre for Christian Worship for over
1300 years. The present Abbey celebrated its
Millennium in 1972.

Worcester Cathedral

10a College Green Worcester WR1 2LH
Tel: 01905 28854 Fax: 01905 611139
www.worcestercathedral.co.uk
[M5 J6/J7, then follow signs to city centre]

Worcester Cathedral is one of England's most
interesting cathedral's, with Royal tombs,
medieval cloisters, an ancient crypt and Chapter
House, and magnificent Victorian stained glass.
The Tower is open in the summer on Saturdays
and school holidays. We welcome families,
groups and individuals, with refreshments, a gift
shop, disabled access and gardens. We also
offer Conference facilities, with rooms catering
for 6-60. There is nearby parking, bus and train
stations. Services three times daily. "Turn up for
a tour" available after Easter until the end of
October.
*All year daily 07.30-18.00. Tower open in summer
from 10.00-16.00 Sat & School Hols "Turn up for*

a tour" Mon-Sat at 11.00 &14.30 after Easter to end Oct
Admission Free: Invite donation of A£3.00 C£1.50. Guided Tours: A£4.00 Concessions£3.50 C£1.50, Prebooked Group: £3.00

Railways

Severn Valley Railway
The Railway Station Bewdley DY12 1BG
Tel: 01299 403816 Fax: 01299 400839
www.svr.co.uk

[Rail: Kidderminster. Town station is adjacent to railway station. On Comberton Hill on A448]

The leading standard gauge steam railway, with one of the largest collections of locomotives and rolling stock in the country. Services operate from Kidderminster and Bewdley to Bridgnorth through 16 miles of picturesque scenery along the River Severn. Events throughout the year include: 1960s Transport Day, Diesel and Steam Gala Weekends, Day Out With Thomas Weekends, 1940s Weekends, Severn Valley in Bloom, Bridgnorth Beer Festival, Classic Car and Bike Day, Wizard Weekend, Remembrance Day Service, Santa Specials and Festive Season Specials. Full details can be found on the website.
Weekends throughout year, 5 May-30 Sept daily plus school holidays
Prices depend on journey, call for details

Spectator Sports

Worcester Racecourse
Pitchcroft Worcester Worcestershire WR1 3EJ
Tel: 0870 220 2772 Fax: 0870 220 2882
www.worcester-racecourse.co.uk

[Rail: Worcester Foregate St. Plenty of on-site parking available]

Worcester Racecourse is set in idyllic surroundings. There are race meetings with special themes including Family Fun Days from March to October. Book in advance for Grandstand Value Package.
Mar-Oct

Adults and Concessions Grandstand £12.00 (02 June, 11 July & 09 Sept £16.00)

Wildlife & Safari Parks

West Midlands Safari and Leisure Park
Spring Grove Bewdley Worcestershire DY12 1LF
Tel: 01299 402114
Drive through safari park, pets corner, reptile house, hippo lakes, tiger world, goat walk, live shows and train ride to amusement area.

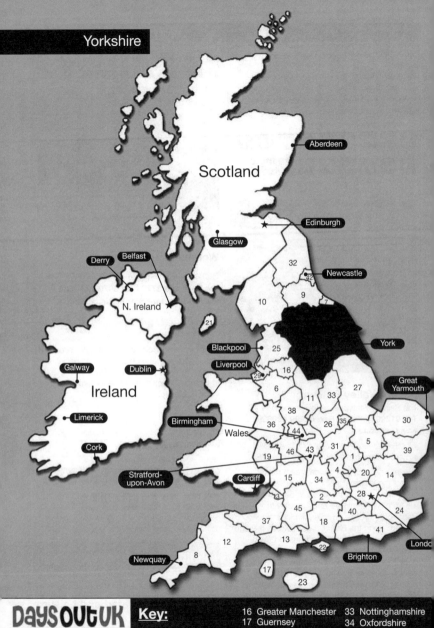

Yorkshire

Scotland

Aberdeen

Edinburgh

Glasgow

Newcastle

Derry
Belfast

N. Ireland

Galway
Dublin

Ireland

Limerick

Cork

Blackpool

Liverpool

York

Great
Yarmouth

Birmingham

Wales

Stratford-
upon-Avon

Cardiff

London

Newquay

Brighton

DAYS OUT UK

The place to look for places to go

Abbeys

Fountains Abbey and Studley Royal Water Garden

Visitor Centre Ripon North Yorkshire HG4 3DY
Tel: 01765 608888
Sheltered in a secluded valley, Fountains Abbey and Studley Royal Water Garden, is one of the most remarkable sites in Europe.

Whitby Abbey

Whitby North Yorkshire YO22 4JT
Tel: 01947 603568
Set high on a North Yorkshire hilltop, Whitby Abbey's gaunt and moving remains overlook a picturesque town and harbour.

Archaeology

DIG - An Archaeological Adventure

St Saviour's Church St. Saviourgate York North Yorkshire YO1 8NN
Tel: 01904 543403 Fax: 01904 627097
www.digyork.co.uk

[M62 / A1041 / A19 to city centre]

York Attraction of the Year. Never before have you been able to experience an authentic interactive archaeological adventure like this! Visitors of all ages are invited to grab their trowels and go on a fascinating archaeological exploration to unearth the secrets of York's past. This world first offers the latest in 3D audio-visual and IT interactive experiences! The concept, development and management of DIG are brought to

visitors by the team who created JORVIK Viking Centre, The York Archaeological Trust.
Open every day Mon-Fri 10.00-17.00. Opening times may vary over the Christmas period. Please call to check opening & availability & to pre-book your visit
A£5.50 C(5-15)£4.50, Family Ticket (A2+C2) £16.00 or (A2+C3) £19.50

Discount Offer: One Child Free

Hull and East Riding Museum

36 High Street Hull East Riding of Yorkshire HU1 1NE
Tel: 01482 300300 Fax: 01482 613710
[M62 A63 to town centre]

The Hull and East Riding Museum is located in the attractive Museums Quarter and boasts some of the most spectacular archaeology and natural history displays in Britain. See a life-size model of a woolly mammoth; investigate the meaning of the mysterious Bronze Age warriors and marvel at the beautiful Roman mosaics. You can even stroll through an Iron Age village and visit a Roman bath-house. From ammonites to civil war armoury, visitors can look forward to an experience that is unique, fascinating and - above all - fun.
All year daily, Mon-Sat 10.00-17.00, Sun 13.30-16.30. Closed Good Fri, Christmas week & 1st Jan
Free Admission

Agriculture / Working Farms

Cruckley Animal Farm

Foston on the Wolds Driffield East Riding of Yorkshire YO25 8BS
Tel: 01262 488337
Cruckley is a working family farm with many kinds of modern and rare breeds of cows, sheep and pigs with their young.

Art Galleries

1853 Gallery, Salt's Mill

Victoria Road Shipley Saltaire West Yorkshire BD18 3LA
Tel: 01274 531163
Salt's Mill is an art gallery, shopping and restaurant complex located in Saltaire. It is home to a permanent exhibition of more than 300 pieces of David Hockney's work.

Batley Art Gallery

Market Place Batley West Yorkshire WF17 5DA
Tel: 01924 326021
A series of changing exhibitions feature contemporary art in a variety of media by local and regional artists.

Beverley Art Gallery

Champney Road Beverley
East Riding of Yorkshire HU17 9BQ
Tel: 01482 392780
Good collection of paintings by well known Beverley artist Fred Elwell RA (1870-1958).

Cartwright Hall Art Gallery

Lister Park Bradford West Yorkshire BD9 4NS
Tel: 01274 431212
Built in dramatic baroque style in 1904, features permanent collections of nineteenth and twentieth-century British art.

Ferens Art Gallery

Monument Buildings Queen Victoria Square Hull
East Riding of Yorkshire HU1 3RA
Tel: 01482 300300   x4 Fax: 01482 613710
[M62 A63 to town centre]

Built in 1927, the Ferens was extended in 1991
to provide additional space for a lively temporary programme and cafe. Extensive permanent
collection displays are complemented by thriving exhibition and education programmes. A
multi-sensory children's gallery opened in 2000.
The internationally renowned permanent collection of paintings and sculpture spans the
medieval period to the present day. European
Old Masters, particularly Dutch and Flemish,
portraiture, marine paintings, modern and contemporary British art are amongst the strengths.
The gallery has also been developed as a
'Centre of Excellence' in the collection and display of contemporary art through a partnership
with the Contemporary Art Society and the Arts
Council Lottery.
All year daily, Mon-Sat 10.00-17.00, Sun 13.30-
16.30. Closed Good Fri, Christmas week & 1st
Jan
Admission Free

Graves Art Gallery

Surrey Street Sheffield South Yorkshire S1 1XZ
Tel: 0114 278 2600
Home to Sheffield's impressive collection of
British and European late nineteenth and twentieth-century art. The main trends and movements are traced through key works by notable
artists of the period.

Henry Moore Institute

74 The Headrow Leeds Yorkshire LS1 3AH
Tel: 0113 246 7467 Fax: 0113 246 1481
www.henry-moore-fdn.co.uk
[In centre of Leeds, adj to Leeds City Art Gallery.
Rail: approx 10min walk from Leeds railway sta-
tion. Leeds is equidistant from London &
Edinburgh & just 2hr by train from King's Cross]

The Henry Moore Institute, an award winning,
architecturally designed gallery, is a centre for
the study of sculpture, with exhibition galleries,
a reference library and archive, and an active
research programme. The four gallery spaces
on the ground floor show temporary sculpture
exhibitions of all periods and nationalities. It is
advisable to ring the recorded information line
(0113 234 3158) prior to a visit for up-to-date
information. Wheelchair access is from
Cookridge Street and a lift serves all floors.
Induction loops are sited at ground floor and
library reception areas. Information is available in
braille and large print.
All year daily 10.00-17.30, Wed 10.00-21.00.
Closed Bank Hols. Free guided tours require pre-
booking (0113 246 7467). Library / Collection
enquiries, 0113 246 9469
Admission Free

**Discount Offer: 15% discount on all
publications, plus one free poster**

Leeds City Art Gallery

The Headrow Leeds West Yorkshire LS1 3AA
Tel: 0113 247 8248
An outstanding collection of paintings, from
English watercolours to Pre-Raphaelites.

Rotherham Art Gallery

Central Library & Arts Centre Walker Place
Rotherham South Yorkshire S65 1JH
Tel: 01709 382121
The Gallery hosts a continuous programme of
temporary exhibitions covering a wide range of
artistic subjects.

University of Hull Art Collection

Cottingham Road Hull East Yorkshire HU6 7RX
Tel: 01482 465192 Fax: 01482 465192
www.hull.ac.uk/artcoll
[Plenty of on-site parking available]

The Hull University Art Collection is a small but
outstanding collection specialising in paintings,
sculpture, drawings and prints produced in
Britain 1890-1940. Displayed in two purpose-
built galleries in Sir Leslie Martin's Middleton
Hall, it includes works by Beardsley, Sickert,
Steer, Lucien Pissarro, Augustus John, Stanley
Spencer, Wyndham Lewis and Ben Nicholson
as well as sculpture by Epstein, Gill, Gaudier-
Brzeska and Henry Moore. The Camden Town
Group and Bloomsbury artists are particularly
well-represented. Also on display are two collections of Chinese ceramics, on long loan from
Dr. & Mrs. Peter Thompson, of Hong Kong. One
is an important collection of seventeenth-centu-
ry works. The second provides choice examples
from the Tang to the Qing dynasties (c.618-
1850). Regular loan exhibitions are also shown.
Mon-Fri 10.00-16.00 except Bank Hols
Admission Free

Wakefield Art Gallery

Wentworth Terrace Wakefield WF1 3QW
Tel: 01924 305796
An important collection of twentieth-century
paintings and sculptures.

York Art Gallery

Exhibition Square York YO1 7EW
Tel: 01904 687687
700 years of European painting, from early
Italian gold-ground panels to the art of the
twentieth century.

Arts, Crafts & Textiles

Bankfield Museum

Boothtown Road Akroyd Park Halifax HX3 6HG
Tel: 01422 354823 / 352334
Built by Edward Akroyd in the 1860s, it has an
outstanding collection of costumes and textiles.

Colour Museum

Perkin House PO Box 244 1 Providence Street
Bradford West Yorkshire BD1 2PW
Tel: 01274 390955
The exhibits are lots of fun with interactive
opportunities at every turn. Regular workshops
suitable for adults or children.
*Open by appointment only - please call in
advance*

Millennium Galleries

Arundel Gate Sheffield South Yorkshire S1 2PP
Tel: 0114 278 2600
Visit Yorkshire's premier art venue and adjacent
Winter Garden. See the best craft and design.

Yorkshire Sculpture Park

Bretton Hall West Bretton Wakefield WF4 4LG
Tel: 01924 830302
Set in the beautiful grounds of the eighteenth-
century Bretton Estate.

Birds, Butterflies & Bees

Tropical Butterfly House, Wildlife and Falconry Centre

Woodsetts Road North Anston Nr Sheffield
South Yorkshire S25 4EQ
Tel: 01909 569416 Fax: 01909 564025
www.butterflyhouse.co.uk
*[J31 M1, then A57 towards Worksop & follow
brown signs. Free on-site parking available]*

Wander among exotic butterflies, birds and
plants in the tropical rainforest environment,
where you will find unusual residents from all
over the world, with creepy crawly hissing cock-
roaches, leaf cutting ants, slithering snakes and
glow in the dark scorpions. Meet the snappy
crocodile while he basks by his pool, watch the
interactive displays from performing parrots to
magnificent birds of prey, being flown in the
open air arena. Come along to meet the skunk
and feed the farm animals along with the
cheeky marmoset monkeys. Take a tractor trailer ride around the nature trail, let the kids let off
steam in the activity centre were they will find
arts and crafts, badge making, brass rubbing
and pot painting to air hockey, table football,
pool and shooting cannons. Delicious meals,
snacks and refreshments can be purchased
from the café, the gift shop stocks a wide range
of interesting souvenirs. Come and enjoy a
great day out, whatever the weather.
*All year daily. Apr-Oct Sat & Sun 10.00-17.30
Mon-Fri 10.00-16.30, Oct-Apr Sat & Sun 10.00-
17.30 Mon-Fri 11.00-16.30. Closed 1/-26, 31
Dec & 1 Jan*
A£6.99 C£5.99, Family Ticket £25.99

Discount Offer: One Child Free

Yorkshire Dales Falconry and Conservation Centre

Crows Nest Austwick via Lancaster North
Yorkshire LA2 8AS
Tel: 01729 822832 / 825164
Fax: 01729 825160
www.falconryandwildlife.com

*[A65 bypass from Settle to Kendal, 2nd L after
Giggleswick railway station. Plenty of on-site parking available]*

Since the centre's creation in 1991, its role has
been to demonstrate birds of prey to the public,
while educating the public that many of these
birds are now endangered species. To assist
the re-population of the birds of prey, the centre
is now part of a worldwide breeding and conservation programme. The displays at the centre
take place in a purpose built display area allowing the public to observe dramatic fly-bys,
swoops, and the awesome gracefulness of flight
that these birds can achieve. Birds that are not
on flying duty are viewable in purpose built
aviaries and cave dwellings. Members of staff
are on hand to answer any questions that you
may have and to make sure your visit is a most
enjoyable one. We have a gift shop, a tearoom
and a video room should the weather turn
nasty. There are also picnic areas and a children's play area. All areas are suitable for wheelchair visitors.
*Mar-Sept 10.00-17.00, Sept-Feb 10.00-15.30.
Mar-Sept three displays during the day at 12.00,
13.30 & 15.00, Sept-Feb two displays during the
day. Closed 25-26 Dec & 1 Jan*
A£5.80 C£3.80 OAPs£4.50, Family Ticket
(A2+C2) £18.00. Group rate: A£4.80 C£3.50

Discount Offer: One Child Free

Caverns & Caves

Mother Shipton's Cave and the Petrifying Well

Prophecy House High Bridge Knaresborough North Yorkshire HG5 8DD
Tel: 01423 864600
Learn about Yorkshire's sixteenth-century prophetess at England's oldest tourist attraction.
Mar-Oct daily

White Scar Cave

Ingleton North Yorkshire LA6 3AW
Tel: 015242 41244 Fax: 015242 41700
www.whitescarcave.co.uk
[1.5mi from Ingleton on B6255 rd to Hawes. Plenty of on-site parking available]
White Scar Cave, in the Yorkshire Dales National Park, is the longest show cave in Britain. There are underground waterfalls and streams, and thousands of stalactites. The curious cave formations include the Devil's Tongue, the Arum Lily, and the remarkably lifelike Judge's Head. Guides lead visitors along the well-lit paths and explain the features. The highlight of the tour is the 200,000-year-old Battlefield Cavern. Over 330 feet long, with its roof soaring in places to 100 feet, this is one of the largest caverns in Britain. The visitor centre has an eco-friendly turf roof, and an alpine-style café with views over the Dales to the sea. The cave shop stocks fine rock and mineral specimens, jewellery, and much more besides.
All year, Feb-Oct daily, Nov-Jan Sat-Sun from 10.00, weather permitting. Closed 25-26 Dec
A£7.50 C£4.50, Family Ticket (A2+C2) £21.00. Group rate (12+): A£6.20 C£3.50

Country Parks & Estates

Goathland and Mallyan Spout

Nr. Whitby North Yorkshire
Tel: 01723 383637 (TIC)
A picturesque village in the North Yorkshire Moors National Park. Surrounded by open moorland and farms, the village provides the setting for the television series 'Heartbeat'. Tame, black-faced sheep roam the village at leisure. The train station is located on the North Yorkshire Moors steam railway line, and was recently used to represent Hogwarts Station in a recent Harry Potter film. There are several waterfalls around Goathland, the best known is Mallyan Spout. There are interesting walks in virtually every direction that will take you through some stunning scenery.

Rother Valley Country Park

Mansfield Road Wales Bar Sheffield South Yorkshire S26 5PQ
Tel: 0114 247 1452
This 750-acre country park offers woods and parkland, a visitor centre, craft centre, watersports, cafe and shop. Cycles for hire. Golf. Nature reserve, working mill, coarse fishing, footpaths, orienteering and cycle routes.

Sandall Beat Wood

Sandall Beat Community Enviroment Centre Off Leger Way Doncaster Yorkshire DN2 5QB
Tel: 01302 737411
[Next to Doncaster Racecourse. On-site parking]

Explore woodland walks, fascinating displays, fun activities, our brand new woodland garden and exciting playground. Set in the heart of Sandall Beat Wood Local Nature Reserve, next to Doncaster Racecourse. Re-opening after redevelopment Spring 2007. 'Wildthings' is a summer holiday fun-filled, activity packed play scheme for children aged 8-11 years old, where they can explore the secrets of the wood. Phone or email to book your child's place.
Nature Reserve: All year daily. Wildthings: 23, 25, 27 & 30 July, 1 & 3 August
Admission Free: Wildthings playscheme: £10 per day

Factory Outlets & Tours

Freeport Hornsea Retail and Leisure Outlet Village

Rolston Road Hornsea Yorkshire HU18 1UT
Tel: 01964 534211
An outlet village where you'll find everything at up to 50% off high street prices.

Festivals & Shows

Hull Fair

Walton Street Hull East Yorkshire
Tel: 01482 300300
The largest travelling fair in Europe recieves over a million visitors every year and dates back to 1293.
5-13 October 2007 12.00-00.00 (Closed Sun)

JORVIK Viking Festival 2008

York North Yorkshire YO1 9WT
Tel: 01904 543403
www.jorvik-viking-centre.com

[Various venues throughout York city centre]

The JORVIK Viking Festival attracts thousands of visitors from around the world. Events will include children's activities, famous battle re-enactments, sagas and songs. Please call for full programme of events or check the website for further details.
13-17 February 2008

Nidderdale Festival

Various venues Pateley Bridge Nr Harrogate North Yorkshire HG3
Tel: 078 3715 0844
www.nidderdalefestival.org.uk
[Various venues in & around Pateley Bridge. Bus: from Harrogate. Plenty of parking]

A rich and varied programme of events celebrates the heritage and culture of this beautiful part of Yorkshire. From Ripley at the eastern end of Nidderdale to Middlesmoor at the head of the dale, from 'walks and talks' to rock-climbing, from folk to classical concerts, drama, exhibitions, craft demonstrations, the Festival offers something for everyone - local and visitor, young and not so young alike.
6-22 July 2007
Prices vary, please call for details

Whitby Gothic Weekends

Spa Pavilion Whitby North Yorkshire
Tel: 01947 602124
One of the most popular international gothic events, attracting attendees from across the UK and around the world.
27-28 April & 26-27 Oct 2007

Folk & Local History Museums

Bagshaw Museum

Wilton Park Batley West Yorkshire WF17 0AS
Tel: 01924 326155
The museum is housed in a nineteenth-century building with displays of local history, Oriental arts, natural history and a gallery of Egyptology.

Beside the Seaside

34-35 Queen Street Bridlington East Riding of Yorkshire YO15 2SP
Tel: 01262 608890
Join the holidaymakers for tea in the beach side bathing bungalow for a taste of life 'Beside the Seaside' at Bridlington.

Thirsk Museum

14/16 Kirkgate Thirsk North Yorkshire YO7 1PQ
Tel: 01845 527707
www.thirskmuseum.org
[From clock tower in Market Place: Kirkgate is rd leading to your R as you look towards NatWest bank. As you follow this rd, Museum is on your R, just past Electroworld & opposite The Zillah Bell Art Gallery. From car park in Marage Rd: Follow Marage Rd towards church. Turn L into Kirkgate. Museum on L]

Set in the 1755 birthplace of Thomas Lord, founder of the London cricket ground that bears his name, Thirsk Museum offers eight rooms that take visitors on a nostalgic trip back through time, tracing the story of this ancient market town made famous in the 'James Herriot' books written by local vet Alf Wight. See the bones of our Saxon Giant and shiver at the dreadful legend of the Busby Stoop Chair! Admire the fine china on display in the Edwardian Sitting Room and take time to browse among the workaday objects in our newly refurbished Victorian Kitchen. Upstairs you will find memorabilia of two World Wars and a special feature in honour of the Canadian airmen who flew Halifax and Lancaster bombers from local airfields. View the displays of period costume while the children enjoy our 'Happy Families' challenge quiz - there are prizes to be won.
Easter-31 Oct Mon-Wed, Fri & Sat 10.00- 16.00. Closed Thurs & Sun
A£1.50 C£Free Students(NUS/USI)£0.75

World of James Herriot

23 Kirkgate Thirsk North Yorkshire YO7 1PL
Tel: 01845 524234
Combines history, humour, nostalgia, science and education in a tribute to the author.

Black Bull in Paradise Theakston Brewery Visitor Centre

The Brewery Masham North Yorkshire HG4 4YD
Tel: 01765 680000 Fax: 01765 684330
www.theakstons.co.uk
Visit this famous brewery located in the beautiful Yorkshire Dales town of Masham and home of the legendary Old Peculier! Experience the wonderful aromas of hops and malted barley whilst learning about the traditional brewing techniques still in use today. The visitor centre named 'Black Bull in Paradise' after the original Black Bull Inn where Robert Theakston first began brewing in 1827 and Paradise fields where the present brewery now stands. Within the Black Bull in Paradise you will find the heritage centre with a collection of historical brewery artefacts, a virtual tour of the brewery hosted by Simon Theakston and of special interest is the Cooper's workshop and display of tools. The Brewery Tap is the perfect opportunity to sample the legendary ales fresh from the brewery and the gift shop is stocked full of Peculierly Fine souvenirs, Theakston merchandise and other Yorkshire delights.
16 Jan-30 Mar 10.30-15.00, 31 Mar-24 July 10.30-16.00, 24 July-2 Sept 10.30-17.00, 03 Sept-31 Oct 10.30-16.00, 1 Nov-23 Dec 10.30-15.00. Heritage Centre, Brewery Tap & Gift Shop are open daily from 10.30. Regular guided tours of the brewery are available. For-up-to-date information on tour times please call the Visitor Centre
Tours: A£4.95 C£2.75 OAPs£4.25 Students(NUS/USI)£4.50, Family Ticket (A2+C2) £12.95. Prices include complimentary drink. We regret for health and safety reasons, no children under 10 years are allowed on brewery tours

Black Sheep Brewery

Wellgarth Masham Ripon North Yorkshire
HG4 4EN
Tel: 01765 680101 / 680100
Fax: 01765 689746
www.blacksheepbrewery.com
[Plenty of on-site parking available]

Situated at the gateway to Wensleydale,
Masham is the home of the Black Sheep
Brewery. Established in the early nineties by
Paul Theakston, 5th generation of Masham's
famous brewing family, the brewery now produces a staggering 17 million pints of beer each
year. The Black Sheep Visitor Centre is the ideal
place for an interesting and alternative day out.
Regular 'shepherded' tours of the brewery allow
guests to experience the traditional brewing
process from the aroma and taste of English
hops and malted barley, through to sampling
Black Sheep's award-winning ales in the comfort and relaxation of the Baa...r. The spacious
split-level bistro provides a variety of culinary
delights throughout the day and the shop is full
of 'ewe-nique' delights for the perfect gift.

*Opening times vary, please telephone prior to
your visit*
Prices vary, Please call for detail

Forests & Woods

Chevin Forest Park

Johnny Lane
Otley West Yorkshire LS21 3JL
Tel: 01943 465023
A wooded escarpment overlooking Otley.

Dalby Forest Drive and Visitor Centre

Low Dalby Pickering North Yorkshire YO18 7LT
Tel: 01751 472771
A 9-mile scenic drive with car parks, picnic
places, waymarked walks (up to 4.5 miles)
including a Habitat Trail and an orienteering
course. Visitor centre in Low Dalby village.

Gardens & Horticulture

Constable Burton Hall Gardens

Constable Burton Leyburn North Yorkshire
DL8 5LJ
Tel: 01677 450428
Large romantic garden surrounded by eigh-
teenth-century parkland, with superb John Carr
house (not open).

Forbidden Corner

Tupgill Park Estate Coverham Middleham
Leyburn North Yorkshire DL8 4TJ
Tel: 01969 640638
A unique labyrinth of tunnels, chambers, follies
and surprises created in a four acre garden in
the heart of the Yorkshire Dales. A day out with
a difference which will challenge and delight
adults and children of all ages.

RHS Garden Harlow Carr

Crag Lane Beckwithshaw Harrogate
North Yorkshire HG3 1QB
Tel: 01423 565418
Beautiful 58-acre gardens, streamside, scented,
grasses and foliage gardens, woodland and
arboretum, vegetable and flower trials.

Sheffield Botanical Gardens

Clarkehouse Road Sheffield South Yorkshire
S10 2LN
Tel: 0114 267 6496
The gardens have been developed with many
themed plantings; either horticultural or geo-
graphical to provide a place of pleasure and
education for families of all ages.

Historical

Bar Convent

17 Blossom Street York North Yorkshire
YO24 1AQ
Tel: 01904 643238 Fax: 01904 631792
www.bar-convent.org.uk
*[From city centre head out of Micklegate Bar,
down Blossom St. The convent is just on your L,
after traffic lights. Park & Ride buses stop immediately outside or opposite at Odeon cinema]*

The Bar Convent Museum is located in an elegant Georgian building close to the historic centre of York. The museum outlines the early history of Christianity in the North of England, and
tells the story of Mary Ward, (1585-1645)
foundress of a world-wide institute known as
the Congregation of Jesus and the Institute of
the Blessed Virgin Mary. Mary Ward was a pioneer of education for women and fought, life-
long, for the right of nuns to pursue a variety of
ministries outside the convent walls. A community of the Congregation of Jesus still lives and
works at the Bar Convent. As well as the museum the Bar Convent also has a card and gift
shop, café and an 18-bed guest house, and is
able to offer conferencing facilities in a choice of
4 meeting rooms all set in the tranquil grounds
of this modern, bustling convent.
All year Mon-Sat. Closed Easter & Christmas
A£3.00 (includes free tea/coffee in the Bar
Convent Café) C(under16)&OAPs£Free. Meeting
delegates & residents of the guest house also
have free admission

Brontë Parsonage Museum

Church Street Haworth Keighley West Yorkshire
BD22 8DR
Tel: 01535 642323 Fax: 01535 647131
www.bronte.info
*[On A6033 from A629 extensively signposted,
museum is at top of Main St behind Parish
Church]*
Charlotte, Emily and Anne Brontë were the
authors of some of the greatest books in the
English language. Haworth Parsonage was their
much loved home, and Jane Eyre, Wuthering
Heights and The Tenant of Wildfell Hall were all
written here. Set between the unique village of
Haworth and the wild moorland beyond, this
homely Georgian house still retains the atmosphere of the Brontës' time. The rooms they
once used daily are filled with the Brontes' furniture, clothes and personal possessions. Here
you can marvel at the handwriting in their tiny
manuscript books, admire Charlotte's wedding
bonnet and imagine meeting Emily's pets from
her wonderfully lifelike drawings. Gain an insight
into the place and objects that inspired their
work.
*All year daily Apr-Sept 10.00-17.30, Oct-Mar
11.00-17.00. Closed 24-27 Dec & 2-31 Jan*
A£5.50 C£2.00
OAPs&Students(NUS/USI)£4.00, Family Ticket
(A2+C3) £13.00

**Discount Offer: Two for the Price of
One**

Burton Agnes Hall

Burton Agnes Driffield Yorkshire YO25 4NB
Tel: 01262 490324 Fax: 01262 490513
www.burton-agnes.co.uk
[On A614 between Driffield / Bridlington. Plenty of on site parking available]

A beautiful Elizabethan Hall with award-winning gardens. The same family has lived in the hall since it was built four hundred years ago. They have filled it with treasures, ranging from magnificent Elizabethan carvings and plasterwork to modern French Impressionist paintings, contemporary furniture and tapestries. Lawns, clipped ewe bushes and beautiful woodland gardens surround the hall. The old Elizabethan walled garden is a unique wonderland containing over four thousand different plants, a potager (vegetable garden) filled with herbs and vegetables, giant board games, herbaceous borders, a maze, fruit beds, a jungle garden, and a national collection of campanulas. In our courtyard you'll find plants and dried flowers from the walled garden, imaginative gifts, and a children's play area. Our 'Farmers Food Store' is packed with seasonal Yorkshire produce including our own game, fruit and vegetables. Enjoy freshly prepared meals in the Impressionists' Café and indulgent treats in our ice cream parlour.

All facilities: 1 Apr-31 Oct & 14 Nov-23 Dec daily 11.00-17.00. Café, shops & gardens only: Jan-Mar & Nov-Dec Thu-Sun 11.00-16.00
Hall & Gardens: A£6.00 C£3.00 OAPs£5.50.
Gardens only: A£3.00 C£1.50 OAPs£2.75.
Group rate (30+): 10% discount

Burton Constable Hall

Burton Constable Hull East Yorkshire HU11 4LN
Tel: 01964 562400
The ancestral home of the Constable family,

Castle Howard

York North Yorkshire YO60 7DA
Tel: 01653 648333
Magnificent eighteenth-century house and park.

Fairfax House

Castlegate York North Yorkshire YO1 9RN
Tel: 01904 655543
An outstanding mid eighteenth-century house.

Fort Paull

Battery Road Paull Nr Hull East Riding of Yorkshire HU12 8FP
Tel: 01482 896236 Fax: 01482 896236
www.fortpaull.com
[3mi past Hull Docks off A1033 Hull-Hedon Rd. Plenty of on-site parking available]

10 acre Napoleonic Fortress with 500 years of Military History. Underground tunnels and chambers with fantastic exhibits and waxworks plus the world's only Blackburn Beverley Transport aircraft. bar and cafés. Children's play areas and events throughout the summer.
Apr-Oct 10.00-18.00, Nov-Mar 11.00-16.00. Closed Dec & Jan
A£4.50 Concessions£3.00, Family Ticket(A2+C2) £12.00

Discount Offer: Two for the Price of One

Harewood House and Bird Garden

Harewood Leeds West Yorkshire LS17 9LG
Tel: 0113 218 1010 Fax: 0113 218 1002
[7mi between Leeds & Harrogate, A61. Plenty of on-site parking available]

Harewood, home of the Earl and Countess of Harewood, is renowned for its stunning architecture, exquisite Adam interiors, Chippendale furniture, fine porcelain, and outstanding art collections. Visit 'Below Stairs' and explore the old kitchen, servant's hall and corridors - discover fascinating stories of servants who lived and worked there. Enjoy glorious grounds and Yorkshire in Bloom Gold award winning gardens - the elaborate terrace parterre, sub tropical archery border, Himalayan garden and of course the popular lakeside bird garden and adventure playground. Harewood hosts an exciting and varied programme of outdoor events - from car rallies and dog shows to open air concerts and theatre.
16 Mar-28 Oct 2007. Grounds: 10.00-18.00. House & Below Stairs: 12.00-16.00

Discount Offer: Two for the Price of One

Helmsley Castle

Helmsley North Yorkshire YO6 5AB
Tel: 01439 770442
The ruined castle dated from the twelfth century and later.

JORVIK Viking Centre

Coppergate York North Yorkshire YO1 9WT
Tel: 01904 543403/643211 (24hr)
Fax: 01904 627097
www.jorvik-viking-centre.com
[In centre of York. Can be reached from A1 via A64 or A19 or A1079 Park & Ride service call 01904 613161]

Explore York's Viking history on the very site where archaeologists uncovered remains of the Viking-Age City of 'Jorvik'. Get face-to-face with our expert Viking residents, see over 800 artefacts, excavated between 1976-1981 magically brought to life by talking Viking ghosts in our new exhibition - 'Artefacts Alive!' and learn what life was really like in our special exhibitions. New for 2007, 'Are you a Viking?' brings together bio-scientific and artefact evidence to determine if visitors could have Viking ancestors. 'Unearthed' tells how the people of York lived - and died - as revealed by real bone material. JORVIK also takes visitors through a reconstruction of the actual Viking-Age streets which stood here 1,000 years ago, faithfully recreated following twenty years of archaeological and historical research. A programme of special events runs throughout the year, including the JORVIK Viking Festival every February - check the website for further details.
All year daily, Apr-Oct 10.00-17.00, Nov-Mar 10.00-16.00. Closed 25 Dec. Opening hours may vary over Christmas & New Year, please call to confirm
A£7.95 C(under5)£Free C(5-15)£6.60 OAPs&Students(NUS/USI) £6.60, Family Ticket (A2+C2) £21.95 or (A2+C3) £26.50

Discount Offer: One Child Free

Newby Hall and Gardens

Newby Hall Ripon North Yorkshire HG4 5AE
Tel: 01423 322583 Fax: 01423 324452
www.newbyhall.com

*[2mi off A1(M) at Ripon exit (signposted). 40min
(23mi) from York. 45min (27mi) NE of
Leeds/Bradford Airport. 30min (15mi) from
Harrogate. Plenty of on-site parking available]*

Designed under the guidance of Sir Christopher
Wren, this graceful country house epitomizes
the Georgian 'Age of Elegance'. Its beautifully
restored interior presents Robert Adam at his
very best. The contents of the house include a
rare set of Gobelins tapestries, a renowned
gallery of classical statuary and some of
Chippendale's finest furniture. The 25 acres of
award winning gardens are a haven for both the
specialist and amateur gardener alike. They
include a miniature railway, an adventure garden
for children, a woodland discovery walk and a
new contemporary sculpture park. Newby also
has an irresistible shop and well stocked plant
centre.

*31 Mar-30 Sept Tue-Sun plus Bank Hols & Mon
in July-Aug 12.00-17.00 (Gardens: 11.00-17.30)*

House & Garden: A£9.50 C(under4)£Free
C£6.60 OAPs£8.50. Gardens only: A£7.00
C(under4)£Free C£5.50 OAPs£6.00

Discount Offer: One Child Free

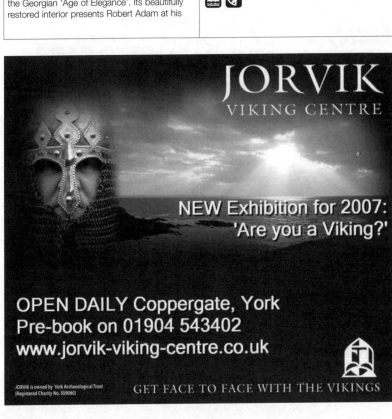

Ripley Castle

Ripley Harrogate North Yorkshire HG3 3AY
Tel: 01423 770152 Fax: 01423 771745
www.ripleycastle.co.uk
[Off A61 3.5mi N of Harrogate. Plenty of on-site parking available]

An extraordinary castle with 700 years of history. It is an amazing place to visit, and it's open all year round. Ripley is one of Yorkshire's great visitor attractions and is something the whole family will enjoy. You will learn of kings and queens, civil war and plagues, secrets concealed in the Knight's Chamber, Oliver Cromwell held at gunpoint in the library, and the Gunpowder Plot - to name but a few. Tours are enthralling for all ages. There are acres of formal gardens, woodland and parkland to explore. Within the beautiful walled gardens in late April you will find the National Hyacinth Collection. The kitchen garden contains a rare collection of fruit and vegetables, herbs and spices. Deer park and lakes. Children's play trail. Superb facilities including tearooms and wonderful shops. Boar's Head Hotel serves restaurant and bar meals daily and beer garden is very popular in the summer months.

Castle: Guided Tours only - First Tour 11.00, Last Tour 15.00 June-Sept daily. Oct-Nov & Mar-May Tue, Thur, Sat & Sun, Dec-Feb Sat-Sun, Good Friday, Easter & May Bank Hols. Please call prior to visit as opening times may vary without prior notice. Gardens: Daily 09.00-17.00. Except Christmas Day

Castle & Gardens: A£7.00 C(5-16)£4.50 OAPs&Groups£6.00. Gardens only: A£4.50 C£3.00 OAPs&Groups£4.00

Discount Offer: One Child Free

Sewerby Hall and Gardens

Church Lane Sewerby Bridlington
East Riding of Yorkshire YO15 1EA
Tel: 01262 673769
Set in 50 acres of early nineteenth-century parkland, the hall contains the orangery, art galleries, period rooms, and an Amy Johnson room. There is also a children's zoo.

Skipton Castle

Skipton North Yorkshire BD23 1AW
Tel: 01756 792442 Fax: 01756 796100
www.skiptoncastle.co.uk

[Located in Skipton centre]

Skipton Castle is one of the best preserved, most complete medieval castles in England. Dating from Norman times with a charming Tudor Courtyard, it withstood a three year siege in the Civil War. Explore this exciting castle and relax in the peaceful grounds. Guided tours for pre-booked groups only.
All year daily Mar-Sept Mon-Sat 10.00-18.00, Sun 12.00-18.00, Oct-Feb Mon-Sat 10.00-16.00, Sun 12.00-16.00. Closed 25 Dec A£5.60* C(0-4)£Free C(5+)£3.00 OAPs£5.00 Students(NUS/USI)£5.00, Family Ticket (A2+C3) £16.90. Group rate (15+): £4.60. *Cost includes illustrated tour sheet in choice of 9 languages (English, French, German, Dutch, Italian, Spanish, Chinese, Japanese or Esperanto)

Discount Offer: Two for the Price of One

Treasurer's House

Minster Yard York North Yorkshire YO1 7JL
Tel: 01904 624247
This elegant house stands within the tranquil
surroundings of the Minster Close.

Wilberforce House

23-24 High Street Hull East Yorkshire HU1 1NE
Tel: 01482 300300 Fax: 01482 613710
[M62 A63 situated in town centre]

Wilberforce House will open to the public on the
afternoon of the 25th March 2007, exactly 200
years since the passing of the abolition of the
Slave Trade Act in Parliament. Contemporary
forms of slavery, human rights and the transatlantic slavery will be explored through exciting
new displays and interactives. Visitors will be
able to explore the history of the Transatlantic
Slave Trade through African narratives for the
first time in Wilberforce House exploring the
lives of enslaved people through human voices
and stories. These hidden histories will be
revealed in the new displays to engage with visitors to the museum in new ways. William
Wilberforce, the famous abolitionist's private
library will be on show in its entirety for the first
time. Find out what books he likes and why his
eldest son gave Wilberforce much grief in his
latter years.
*All year daily, Mon-Sat 10.00-17.00, Sun 13.30-
16.30. Closed Good Friday, Christmas week &
1st Jan*
Admission Free

York Castle Museum

The Eye of York York North Yorkshire YO1 9RY
Tel: 01904 687687
Venture into the prison cell of notorious high-
wayman Dick Turpin. Wander through Victorian
and Edwardian streets.

Maritime

Maritime Museum

Queen Victoria Square Hull Yorkshire HU1 3RA

Tel: 01482 300300 Fax: 01482 613710
[M62 A63 town centre or A1079 from York]

Hulls maritime story from the eighteenth century
to the present. Relics of the hunt for the
Greenland whale in the far north far beyond the
Artic Circle; pursuit with the hand harpoon in
open boats half the size of the whale. An outstanding collection of 'scrimshaw' the folk art of
the whaler, carved in his spare time from bone
and whales teeth. The North Sea fishing in sail
and steam and the development of the modern
deep sea fishery. Hull docks and trading
throughout the world and the history of the
Wilson line, once the biggest privately owned
shipping company in the world. Paintings, ship
models, figureheads, nautical instruments etc.
Shop with books and souvenirs. Disabled
access throughout.
*All year daily, Mon-Sat 10.00-17.00, Sun 13.30-
16.30. Closed Good Friday, Christmas week &
1st Jan*
Admission Free

Saltburn Smugglers Heritage Centre

Old Saltburn Saltburn-by-the-Sea North Yorkshire TS12 1HF
Tel: 01287 625252 Fax: 01287 625252
[Next to Ship Inn]

The Saltburn Smugglers recreates the eighteenth-century Ship Inn using a series of authentic room settings with sound and lighting effects to tell the story of smuggling on the Cleveland coast. There is a tourist information centre and a souvenir shop.
1 Apr-30 Sept daily 10.00-18.00
A&OAPs£1.95 C£1.45, Family Ticket (A2+C2) £5.80. Prices due to increase

Discount Offer: One Child Free

Spurn Lightship

Marina Hull East Riding of Yorkshire
Tel: 01482 300300 Fax: 01482 613710
Spurn Lightship, moored in Hull Marina, is one of Hull's historical maritime treasures. Built in 1927, it served as bleak home to a small crew posted at the mouth of the River Humber to warn passing ships of danger. The Lightship operated for almost 50 years and is now a museum. We welcome you to climb aboard and discover what life was like onboard. Take a trip back in time and see the living quarters of the people who worked here. Compare the comfort of the master's cabin with the basic bunks slept in by the ordinary seaman! Learn about the types of equipment these men used to keep others safe in the Humber's busy and treacherous waters. Spurn Lightship is open between April and October. We apologise that for health and safety reasons the vessel is not suitable for wheelchair users or people with mobility problems.
Apr-Oct Mon-Sat 10.00-17.00, Sun 13.30-16.30. Closed Oct-March
Admission Free

Markets

Darley Mill Centre

Darley Nr. Harrogate North Yorkshire HG3 2QQ
Tel: 01423 780857
[11mi from Harrogate / 17mi from Skipton. Head W on A59 & take B6451. Plenty of on-site parking available]

Shop, dine and relax during your Darley Mill Experience! The Darley Mill Centre is set around a beautiful seventeenth-century corn mill, complete with one of the largest water wheels in Yorkshire. The Darley Mill Centre is set in the idyllic Yorkshire Moors and will provide a truly breath-taking day out for all the family. There are three floors of the finest quality linens, country clothing, exclusive gifts, a traditional sweet shop and a magnificent picture gallery. When you tire of shopping there is a beautiful duck pond to see and the traditional Miller's Cottage licensed restaurant where you can choose from homemade cakes and snacks to a full lunch and wine. You'll also find a children's play area for your children to explore. So whatever you do, visit The Darley Mill Centre for the perfect day out for all the family, an outstanding experience that's beyond the high street for quality and value.

All Year Daily, Mon-Sat 09.30-17.30 Sun 11.00-17.00. Closed 25 Dec & Easter Sun
Admission Free

Medical Museums

Ponden Mill

Colne Road Stanbury Keighley West Yorkshire BD22 0HP
Tel: 01535 643500 Fax: 01535 645744
[5mi from Keighley / 9mi from Colne on B6142. Plenty of on-site parking available]

Ponden Mill (Stanbury) is the original mill shopping experience and is known as 'the country home of linens'. There's a big difference between Ponden Mill and the typical factory shops you've probably visited. To begin with, Ponden Mill was one of the first and is now on everyone's essential destination when visiting Brontë country. With three floors packed full of unbeatable bargains on linens, clothing, toys, gifts and accessories, you may think it's all shopping and no relaxing... far from it. You'll find the delights of the traditional sweet shop to explore and the Weavers Buttery licensed restaurant. Here you can enjoy a coffee and a snack, or even a full meal with wine. If you enjoy a relaxed atmosphere, traditional surroundings and (above all) a bargain, then a visit to Ponden Mill is a must.
All Year Daily, Mon-Sat 09.30-17.30 Sun 11.00-17.00. Closed 25 Dec & Easter Sun
Admission Free

Thackray Museum

Beckett Street Leeds West Yorkshire LS9 7LN
Tel: 0113 244 4343 Fax: 0113 247 0219
www.thackraymuseum.org
[From M621 follow signs for York, then follow brown signs. From N, take A58. Next to St James Hospital. On-site parking available]

An award winning interactive museum offering a great day out for all. From a Victorian operating theatre to the wonders of modern surgery, the museum's galleries, collections and interactive displays bring to life the history of medicine. Experience the sights and sounds of a Victorian slum, discover the incredible lotions and potions once offered as treatments. Experience pregnancy by trying on an empathy belly and have fun exploring the workings of the human body in the Life Zone. Please call the information line on 0113 245 7084 for further details on school holiday activities.

All year daily 10.00-17.00. Closed 24-26, 31 Dec & 1 Jan
A£5.50 C£4.00 OAPs&Concessions£4.50, Family Ticket £18.00. Group rates available on request

Discount Offer: Two for the Price of One

Military & Defence Museums

Duke of Wellington's Regiment Museum

Bankfield Museum Akroyd Park Boothtown Road Halifax West Yorkshire HX3 6HG
Tel: 01422 354823
The collections cover the history of the regiment from 1702 to the present day. Emphasis is on the uniforms, equipment and relics, often displayed in period settings.

Eden Camp

Eden Camp Old Malton Malton North Yorkshire YO17 0SD
Tel: 01653 697777
A former winner of the Museum of the Year Award, Eden Camp recreates the experience of life in WWII Britain in original p-o-w huts.

Royal Armouries Museum

Armouries Drive Leeds Yorkshire LS10 1LT
Tel: 08700 344344
www.royalarmouries.org

[Off J4 of M621. Follow brown signs to Royal Armouries Museum. A multi-storey car park is located 100m from museum entrance plus coach parking. 15min walk from centre of Leeds]

Experience the excitement of reliving some of the most important moments in our history - from the Dark Ages to the present day. Costumed demonstrations, authentic re-enactments, entertaining films and interactive technol-ogy all give you a true sense of how it felt to be involved. Throughout the year, live performances put you in the midst of the action. From April to October we recreate jousting tournaments, and let you get close to the falcons and horses that are part of the pageant. And for 2007, there's even more with a calendar of special events including a fantastic free exhibition in the summer - "Horrible Histories" There are also over 8,000 exhibits to see - and some you can touch - in our five themed galleries: War, Tournament, Oriental, Hunting and Self Defence. Discover what it was like to hold a fifteenth-century poleaxe or a powder-firing musket, and take a good look at the armour Henry VIII actually wore. Even if you've been here before, there are plenty of new objects to see. The Royal Armouries Museum spans 3,000 years of history - and is still relevant to the issues of power, conflict and protection we live with today. Come along with the whole family, for a truly memorable, fun-packed day out.
All year daily 10.00-17.00. Closed 24-25 Dec
Museum Admission Free. Some activities/events charged for

Yorkshire Air Museum and Allied Air Forces Memorial

Halifax Way Elvington York North Yorkshire YO41 4AU
Tel: 01904 608595
Restored control tower, Air Gunners museum, archives, Airborne Forces display, Squadron memorial rooms and gardens.

Mills - Water & Wind

Skidby Mill and Museum of East Riding Rural Life

Beverley Rd Skidby Cottingham HU16 5TF
Tel: 01482 848405
The last working windmill north of the Humber, lhousing the Museum of East Riding Rural Life.

Mining

National Coal Mining Museum For England

Caphouse Colliery New Road Overton Wakefield West Yorkshire WF4 4RH
Tel: 01924 848806 Fax: 01924 844567
www.ncm.org.uk
[On A642 between Wakefield / Huddersfield. Plenty of on-site parking available]

A great day out for all the family. Don't miss the unique opportunity to travel 140 metres underground down one of Britain's oldest working mines, where models and machinery depict methods and conditions of mining from the early 1800s to the present. An experienced local miner will guide your party around the underground workings. Above ground, find out more about the development of mining in the exhibitions around the site. Visit the pit ponies and the Shire horse. Take a train ride right across the site, and see the second colliery, Hope Pit. See the steam winder and the pithead baths. Visit the museum's well-stocked shop where you can get your very own mining memorabilia. Children under 5 years are not allowed underground. Disabled facilities include level parking, ramp and disabled toilets.
Underground tours are also available with prior arrangement. We strongly recommend warm, practical clothing and sensible, flat shoes. Photography permitted above ground only. Free audio tour available.
All year daily 10.00-17.00. Closed 24-26 Dec & 1 Jan. During Bank Hols we recommend you arrive early to ensure a place on an underground tour
Admission Free

Nature & Conservation Parks

Aysgarth Falls

Wensleydale North Yorkshire
Tel: 01969 662910
Aysgarth Falls are a triple flight of waterfalls, carved out by the River Ure over an almost one-mile stretch on its descent to Wensleydale. The Upper-Falls featured in the film, 'Robin Hood, Prince of Thieves.'

Performing Arts

Hull Truck Theatre

Spring Street Hull East Riding of Yorkshire HU2 8RW
Tel: 01482 323638
Home of internationally acclaimed playwright, John Godber - Hull Truck hosts a diverse programme and showcases new talent.

National Museum of Photography, Film & Television

Bradford West Yorkshire BD1 1NQ
Tel: 0870 701 0200
Take a voyage of discovery at the National Museum of Photography, Film & Television.

Places of Worship

Bradford Cathedral

Church Bank Bradford West Yorkshire BD1 4EH
Tel: 01274 777720
Fifteenth-century building with additions and works of art from the fifteenth to the twentieth century. Bookstall within the cathedral.

York Minster

Deangate York North Yorkshire YO1 2JN
Tel: 01904 557216
From 1220 to 1472 the present church was built to replace the Romanesque one.

Railways

Kirklees Light Railway

Park Mill Way Clayton West Huddersfield West
Yorkshire HD8 9XJ
Tel: 01484 865727
www.kirkleeslightrailway.com

*[M1 J 39, then A636 towards Denby Dale follow-
ing the brown tourist signs. Plenty of on-site parking available]*

Steam along on Hawk, Owl, Fox or Badger, our
four friendly steam engines here at Kirklees
Light Railway the home of Yorkshires great little
steam trains. Take an enchanting 50-minute
return trip on narrow gauge rail through the
superb scenery of the lovely South Pennine
foothills to our new family area at the top of our
line complete with a large train themed play
area, sand pit, picnic site and bouncy castle
(seasonal) not forgetting the facilities back at the
main station with a large play area, café and
miniature railway round the pond, this all weather attraction is hugely popular with all the family.
Also make sure you catch one of our exciting
events from our busy fun packed yearly calendar from 'Days out with Thomas the Tank
Engine' to 'Spooky Halloween Ghost Trains'.
Please call for further details and dates.
*All year Sept-May Sat, Sun & School Hols 10.00-
17.00, May-Sept daily 10.00-17.00. Trains:
11.00-16.00*
A£6.00 C£4.00 C(under3's)£Free OAPs£5.00,
Family Ticket (A2+C2) £18.00. Special event
prices may vary

Discount Offer: One Child Free

Middleton Railway Leeds

Moor Road Hunslet Leeds Yorkshire LS10 2JQ
Tel: 0113 271 0320
The first railway authorised by an Act of
Parliament (1758) and the first to succeed with
steam locomotives (1812).

North Yorkshire Moors Railway

Pickering Station Pickering North Yorkshire
YO18 7AJ
Tel: 01751 472508 Fax: 01751 476970
www.nymr.co.uk

[In Pickering off A170]

Operating through the heart of the North York
Moors National Park between Pickering and
Grosmont, steam trains cover a distance of 18
miles. Beautiful Newtondale Halt gives walkers
easy access to forest and moorland. The locomotive sheds al Grosmont are open to the public. Special events throughout the year and during 2007 regular services now operate to
Whitby.
*Mar-Nov daily plus some further winter dates,
please call for details*
All line return A£14.00 C£7.00 OAPs£12.00,
Family Ticket(A2+ up to C4)£30.00 please telephone for further details. Group rates available
on request

York Model Railway

Tearoom Square York Station York North
Yorkshire YO24 1AY
Tel: 01904 630169
One of the biggest model railways in Britain,
with two intricate railway layouts.

Science - Earth & Planetary

Eureka! The Museum for Children

Discovery Road Halifax Yorkshire HX1 2NE
Tel: 01422 330069 Fax: 01422 330275
www.eureka.org.uk
[M62 J24, follow A629 to Halifax. Plenty of on-site parking available]

Eureka! The Museum for Children is the first and foremost hands-on children's museum in the UK designed especially for under 12s. With more than 400 must touch exhibits and a full programme of events and activities, you'll be amazed at the fun things you can do! Find out how your body and senses work, discover the realities of daily life, explore the science behind sound, rhythm and performance and travel from your backyard to some amazing, faraway places across the globe.
All year daily 10.00-17.00. Closed 24-26 Dec
A&C(3+)£7.25 C(1-2)£2.25 C(under1)£Free
Donation inclusive prices

Discount Offer: Two for the Price of One

Museum of Victorian Science

Woodberry Glaisdale Whitby YO21 2QL
Tel: 01947 897440
A fascinating collection of Victorian scientific instruments.

Sealife Centres & Aquariums

Scarborough Sea Life and Marine Sanctuary

Scalby Mills Road Scarborough North Yorkshire YO12 6RP
Tel: 01723 376125
Fax: 01723 376285
www.sealifeeurope.com

[Scarborough North Bay]

New For 2007: Great Barrier Reef. Explore the magical recreation of the most amazing natural wonder of the world and dive beneath the bright, awe inspiring phenomenon, which is the Great Barrier Reef. Take the journey through the reef discovering an amazing array of tropical sharks, beautiful rays and colourful coral deep beneath the oceans surface. Our seal hospital is busy all year round caring for sick and injured seal pups until, whenever possible, they are well enough to be returned to the wild. Other highlights include an incredible otter sanctuary where visitors can see the playful Asian short-clawed otters, a collection of comical Humbolt penguins and a whole host of other incredible marine creatures. Presentations and feeding demonstrations throughout the day make this a memorable day out for the whole family. Guided tours by prior arrangement.

All year daily from 10.00. Closed Christmas Day
Please call for admission prices

Discount Offer: One Child Free

The Deep - The World's Only Submarium

Hull East Riding of Yorkshire HU1 4DP
Tel: 01482 381000 Fax: 01482 381018
www.thedeep.co.uk
[From N take A1/M, M62/A63. From S take A1/M, A15/A63. From P&O North Sea Ferry Terminal take A1033/A63 for 2mi. Rail: Hull, 4 direct trains from London daily, regular services from Manchester, Sheffield, York & East Coast. 15min walk or taxi ride from station. Regular local buses run to The Deep]

The Deep, the world's only submarium is a unique award winning attraction. It tells the amazing story of the world's oceans using a blend of stunning aquaria and the latest interactives. It is home to over 3,000 fish and 40 sharks. Now featuring the Twilight Zone - bringing you face to face with weird and wonderful creatures including wolf eels and giant Japanese spider crabs.
All year daily 10.00-18.00. Closed 24-25 Dec.
A£8.50 C£6.50 OAPs£7.00. Family tickets available. Group rates (for 10+ or schools) available on request

Discount Offer: One Child Free

Social History Museums

Courthouse Museum

Minster Road Ripon North Yorkshire HG4 1QT
Tel: 01765 690799
Stand in the dock where prisoners were sentenced to transportation to Australia.

Hands on History

South Church Side Market Place Hull East Riding of Yorkshire HU1 1RR
Tel: 01482 300300 Fax: 01482 613710
[M62, situated in the town centre. Rail: Kingston-upon-Hull]

Housed in the old Grammar School 'Hands on History' is a curriculum resource centre for schools. The ground floor houses 'Victorian Britain' a themed hands on interactive exhibition examining aspects of Victorian Britain.
All year daily, Mon-Sat 10.00-17.00, Sun 13.30-16.30. Closed Good Fri, Christmas week & 1st Jan
Admission Free

Pontefract Museum

Salter Row Pontefract West Yorkshire WF8 1BA
Tel: 01977 722740
Previously a Carnegie free library, the small, compact museum situated in the town centre next to the library is packed full of life, history and artefacts from the town's earliest beginnings to the present day.

Prison and Police Museum

St Marygate Ripon North Yorkshire HG4 1LX
Tel: 01765 690799
Imagine confinement in a cell and the harsh conditions of a Victorian prison where hard labour meant the treadmill, the 'crank' or oakum picking.

Workhouse Museum of Poor Law

Allhallowgate Ripon North Yorkshire HG4 1LE
Tel: 01765 690799
Situated in the men's casual wards of the former Ripon Union workhouse, which has been refurbished to portray the treatment of vagrants one hundred years ago.

Yorkshire Museum and Gardens

Museum Gardens York Yorkshire YO1 7FR
Tel: 01904 687687
Set in ten acres of botanical gardens, the museum displays some of the finest Roman, Anglo-Saxon, Viking and Medieval treasures.

Spectator Sports

Catterick Bridge Racecourse

Catterick Bridge Richmond Yorkshire DL10 7PE
Tel: 01748 811478
The first recorded race meeting at Catterick took place on 22nd April 1783. It was not until 1906 that a stand was built and in 1923 the first Race Company was formed.

Doncaster Racecourse

The Grandstand Leger Way Doncaster South Yorkshire DN2 6BB
Tel: 01302 304200 Fax: 01302 323271
www.doncaster-racecourse.com

[M1 (J32), M18 (J3 or J4), A1M (J36) & M62. Plenty of on-site parking available]

At the home of the world's oldest Classic (the Ladbrokes St Leger), the festivities are sure to be more colourful than ever before. A £32m refurbishment enables race-goers to enjoy a whole new experience at one of the UK's most prestigious racecourses. At the heart of the new development is an impressive five storey-grandstand, which includes a wide range of excellent catering outlets, bars and luxury dining areas - all with spectacular views over the racecourse. For a day out with family and friends, the new-look Doncaster racecourse has it all - colour excitement, comfort and convenience, with race meetings through out the year.
Open 2 hours before 1st race of the day
A£5.00-£50.00 depending on enclosure and raceday, C(under16)£Free. Group discounts available on request

Ripon Races

Boroughbridge Road Ripon Yorkshire HG4 1UG
Tel: 01765 602156 Fax: 01765 690018
www.ripon-races.co.uk
[Plenty of on-site parking available]

Known as the 'Garden Racecourse', Ripon Racecourse is a family friendly place to experience racing from as little as £12 per car with four occupants in the course enclosure. With children's playgrounds, giant screen showing the racing and a cross section of catering facilities it's a great family day out. Fixtures run from April to August. Please see our website events section for fixtures.
Apr-Aug. Course opens 2 hrs before first race
£12.00 for car plus 4 occupants in the course enclosure

Thirsk Racecourse

Station Road Thirsk North Yorkshire YO7 1QL
Tel: 01845 522276 Fax: 01845 525353
www.thirskracecourse.net

[A61 Thirsk/Ripon Rd, 0.5mi W of Thirsk Rail:
Thirsk. Helicopter landing by prior arrangement.
Plenty of on-site parking available]

Thirsk is one of Yorkshire's most beautiful country courses, set between the North Yorkshire Moors and the Dales with easy access from road or rail. Thirsk is a friendly racecourse with compact, well maintained enclosures. Facilities for entertainment have continuously been improved and upgraded in recent years. Hospitality options are available for all sizes of party in either viewing boxes overlooking the winning post or private banqueting suites. Marquees are also an option. Facilities available on non racedays for private functions.
Race meetings Apr-Sept
Club£18.00 Paddock£12.00 Family Ring £5.00 Cars(+4 people)£16.00 OAPs(proof of age required): Paddock£7.00 Family Ring £4.00 Cars(+4 people)£8.00

Sport & Recreation

Xscape: Castleford

Colorado Way Glasshoughton Castleford
Tel: 0871 200 3221
Adventure sports, cinema, 20 bars and restaurants and 10 urban retail outlets.

Cleethorpes Leisure Centre

Kingsway Cleethorpes Yorkshire DN35 0BY
Tel: 01472 323200
Visit the region's most exciting heated indoor water attraction.

Theme & Adventure Parks

Go Ape! High Wire Forest Adventure

Dalby Forest Visitor Centre Nr Thornton-le-Dale North Yorkshire
Tel: 0870 420 7876
www.goape.co.uk
[Adjacent to Low Dalby. Access is via Thornton-le-Dale on A170. Follow brown tourist signs. Plenty of on-site parking available]
Take to the trees and experience an exhilarating course of rope bridges, 'Tarzan Swings' and zip-slides up to 40 feet above the ground! Share approximately three hours of memorable fun and adventure, which you'll be talking about for days. Book online and watch people Go Ape! at www.goape.co.uk. Minimum height 1.4m. Maximum weight 130 kg (20.5 stone). Under-18s must be accompanied by a participating adult. One adult can supervise either two children (where one or both of them in under 16 years old) or up to five 16-17 year olds. Pre-booking is essential to avoid disappointment. Book online or by telephone (there is a £1.00 booking fee on all telephone bookings).
23 Mar-2 Nov (plus Nov w/e). Closed Dec-Jan
Gorillas (18yrs+) £25.00, Baboons (10-17yrs) £20.00

Discount Offer: Two for the Price of One

Lightwater Valley Theme Park

North Stanley Ripon North Yorkshire HG4 3HT
Tel: 0870 458 0040 Fax: 0870 300 4440
www.lightwatervalley.co.uk

[Lighwater is well signposted, turn off A1 onto A61 towards Ripon, then take A6108 for 2.5mi. Manchester approx 2h drive, Preston approx 90min drive, Hull approx 90min drive. Plenty of on-site parking available]

Action packed value for all the family… experience the fun and thrills of this family theme park. Pay once and enjoy the fun all day. Five new rides and attraction for 2007. The Ultimate, Europe's longest roller coaster, the Sewer Rat, the mighty Eagle's Claw, Skyrider and the Trauma Tower all makes for a fantastic fun filled day for everyone. For budding grand prix drivers who want to experience real excitement try our go-karts. There's also a traditional carousel, Flying Camels, and much more for younger children. Or why not retreat to the calm Swan Lake, or perhaps visit Lightwater Shopping Village where value never goes out of fashion. There's also the Bird of Prey Centre where you can get up close to some of the world's most exciting and dramatic birds. Be amazed by world class flying shows and meet real pythons, tarantulas and bugs in our Creepy Crawly Cave.
31 Mar-15 Apr 2007, 21-22, 28-29 Apr, 5-7, 12-13, 19-20 & 26 May-3 Jun, 6-10, 13-17 & 20 June-4 Sept, 8-9,15-16, 22-23, 29-30 Sept, 6-7, 13-14, 20-28 Oct. Gates open at 10.00 & park closes at 16.30 depending on the time of the year, please our website for further details

Pay once & ride all day: Over 1.3m £15.95, Under 1.3m £14.50, Under 1m £Free. Family Ticket(4 people) £58.00, (5 people) £72.50, (6 people) £87.00, (Family Ticket admits 2 adults + up to 4 children under 16 or 1 adult and up to 5 children under 16). OAPs£7.95. Single Season Ticket £48.00, Family Season Ticket(4 people) £160.00. Group rates available on request

Discount Offer: One Child Free

Hemsworth Waterpark and Playworld

Hoyle Mill Road Kinsley Pontefract West Yorkshire WF9 5JB
Tel: 01977 617617
Fax: 01977 610494
www.hemsworthcouncil.co.uk

[Plenty of on-site parking available]

Hemsworth Water Park has two lakes; the largest lake is available for pedalo rides and has sandy beaches; the smallest lake is in a more secluded area to attract wildlife. Both lakes are stocked for fishing, which is available all year round. There are also plenty of grassed areas for picnics and games. Playworld is an outdoor adventure playground within the water park and is suitable for children of all ages with a tower slide, climbing frames and a toddler's sandpit area. A miniature railway operates in Playworld. The Windsurfer licensed premises, set in the grounds of the water park, provides good quality, value for money refreshments. There is also Windy's café, which opens during busy periods where light snacks can be obtained. The Windsurfer has a function room overlooking the lake and can be booked for private parties or conferences. A catering service is also available.

Water Park & Windsurfer: All year daily. Playworld: Easter-Sept most Sat, Sun & School Hols

Playworld: A£Free C£1.50, Miniature Train Rides: £1.00. Easter-Sept most Sat, Sun & School Hols Pedalo Rides: £1.50, Car Parking: £1.00

Magna Science Adventure Centre

Sheffield Road Templeborough Rotherham
South Yorkshire S60 1DX
Tel: 01709 720002
Fax: 01709 820092
www.visitmagna.co.uk

[M1, J33/ J34, close to Meadowhall shopping centre. Plenty of on-site parking available]

Magna, the UK's first Science Adventure Centre explores the elements earth, air, fire and water. Inside you can have fun firing a giant water cannon, launching rockets, exploding rock faces, working real JCBs and experience the roar of the Big Melt show. Also explore Sci-Tek, Europe's largest high tech playground. New exhibitions opening in 2007 include: Torchquest and Lovesport. For more details visit our website.
All year daily 10.00-17.00. Closed 24-27 Dec & 1 Jan
A£9.95 C£(4-15)&Concessions£7.95, Family Ticket (A2+C2)£31.50, (A2+C3)£35.00. Group rates & annual Centre & Sci-Tek passes available

Discount Offer: One Child Free

York Dungeon

12 Clifford Street York North Yorkshire YO1 9RD
Tel: 01904 632599 Fax: 01904 612602
www.thedungeons.com
[York Centre]

The York Dungeon invites you to a unique feast of fun with history's horrible bits. Live actors, shows and special effects transport you back to those black, bleak times. Are you brave enough to delve into the darkest chapters of history? You know you'll love it! Meet the notorious Viking leader Erik Bloodaxe, wander through the plague ravaged streets, and come face to face with Dick Turpin. The seventeenth-century judge knows exactly what you have been up to…. The court isn't impressed and the punishment will be harsh! New for 2007 - Ghosts of York. Experience the presence of ghosts that will chill your bones. Will you hold your nerve as you enter the paranormal world and be confronted by the vengeful ghostly presence…or will it leave you paralysed with fear?
All year daily. Closed 25 Dec
Please call for admission prices

Discount Offer: One Child Free

Transport Museums

Immingham Museum
Resource Centre Margaret Street Immingham DN40 1LE
Tel: 01469 577066
The main theme of the museum is the part played by the Great Central Railway in the development of the docks.

Museum of Rail Travel

Ingrow Railway Centre Keighley West Yorkshire
BD21 5AX
Tel: 01535 680425
Multiple award winning museum that has provided restored carriages for film and TV.

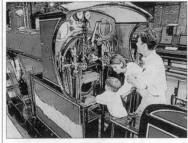

National Railway Museum

Leeman Road York North Yorkshire YO26 4XJ
Tel: 0870 421 4001 Fax: 0870 421 4011
www.nrm.org.uk
[A64 from Scarborough, Malton & Pickering. A64 from Tadcaster, Leeds, M62, M1 & A1. A19 from Selby. A19 from Teesside & Thirsk. A59 from Harrogate. A1079 from Hull. Outer ring rd A1237. On Leeman Rd, just outside city centre, behind railway station. Limited on-site parking available]
Nowhere tells the story of the train better than the world's largest railway museum. From Stephenson's Rocket and giant steam engines to Eurostar, the Bullet Train and the Flying Scotsman, rail travel is brought dramatically to life with interactive displays and lavish exhibitions. Discover it all in one fun-packed family day out where everyone gets in free (excludes certain special events). Picnic facilities available both in and outdoors. Also located at the museum, is York's newest landmark 'must see' attraction, The Norwich Union Yorkshire Wheel. Ride the wheel, rise 60 metres into the sky and be amazed at the beautiful city of York and some of the best views in the county. It's an unforgettable experience for all the family (charges apply).
All year daily 10.00-18.00. Pre-booked guided tours (prices on application)
Admission Free (excludes certain special events)

Streetlife Museum of Transport

High Street Hull East Yorkshire HU1 1NE
Tel: 01482 300300 Fax: 01482 613710
[M62 A63 or A1079 from York in city centre. Rail: Kingston-upon-Hull]
Treat your family to a journey spanning two-hundred years of transport history. Our award-winning themed galleries will inspire your eyes, ears and nose! This family friendly museum has something to offer everyone. On the first floor, the carriage Gallery takes you back to the hey-day of coaching with one of the finest collections of horse-drawn carriages in the north of England. You can also explore the history of cycling in the region, with a 1818 Hobby Horse the highlight of the Bicycle Gallery. How do you want to power your car - petrol, steam or electricity? Our Motor Show lets you see cars from the very early days of motoring when these decisions were made. Check out Hull's local transport heritage and step aboard our double-deck tram and experience more of our motor vehicles in our changing Streetscene display.
All year daily, Mon-Sat 10.00-17.00 Sun 13.30-16.30. Closed Good Fri, Christmas week & 1st Jan
Admission Free

Zoos

Flamingo Land

The Rectory Kirby Misperton Malton
North Yorkshire YO17 6UX
Tel: 0870 752 8000
Come and brave the many white knuckle rides and meet our zoo animals.

For great hotel deals call Superbreak on 01904 679999 or visit www.superbreak.com

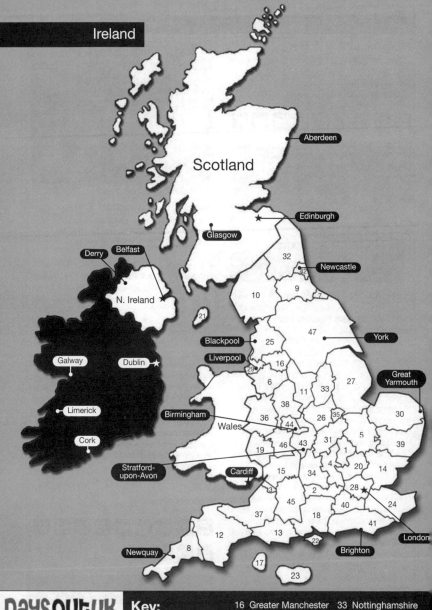

Ireland

Scotland

Aberdeen

Edinburgh

Glasgow

Derry
Belfast

Newcastle

N. Ireland

Galway

Dublin

Blackpool

Liverpool

York

Great Yarmouth

Limerick

Birmingham

Wales

Cork

Stratford-upon-Avon

Cardiff

London

Newquay

Brighton

DAYS OUT UK
The place to look for places to go

Key:

1 Bedfordshire
2 Berkshire
3 Bristol
4 Buckinghamshire
5 Cambridgeshire
6 Cheshire
7 Cleveland
8 Cornwall
9 County Durham
10 Cumbria
11 Derbyshire
12 Devon
13 Dorset
14 Essex
15 Gloucestershire

16 Greater Manchester
17 Guernsey
18 Hampshire
19 Herefordshire
20 Hertfordshire
21 Isle Of Man
22 Isle Of Wight
23 Jersey
24 Kent
25 Lancashire
26 Leicestershire
27 Lincolnshire
28 London
29 Merseyside
30 Norfolk
31 Northamptonshire
32 Northumberland

33 Nottinghamshire
34 Oxfordshire
35 Rutland
36 Shropshire
37 Somerset
38 Staffordshire
39 Suffolk
40 Surrey
41 Sussex
42 Tyne & Wear
43 Warwickshire
44 West Midlands
45 Wiltshire
46 Worcestershire
47 Yorkshire

Caverns & Caves

Aillwee Cave

Ballyvaughan County Clare Ireland
Tel: 00 353 65 707 7036 / 707 7067
A whole labyrinth of caves, pot holes, underground lakes and streams.

Dunmore Cave

Ballyfoyle County Kilkenny Ireland
Tel: 00 353 56 776 7726
Fax: 00 353 56 776 7262
[10km from Kilkenny off N78. Plenty of on-site parking available]

History and geology blend at Dunmore Cave to give an interesting and unique situation. Consisting of a series of chambers formed over millions of years, the cave contains some of the finest calcite formations found in any Irish cave. The cave has been known to man for many centuries and is first mentioned in the ninth-century Irish triads. The most interesting reference however, comes from the Annals which tells of a Viking massacre at the cave in the year 928 A.D. Archaeological finds within the cave confirm Viking activity. Exhibitions and displays in the centre. The cave is inaccessible for wheelchair users. Visitors are advised to wear suitable footwear.
Mar Mid June & Mid Sept-end Oct daily 09.30-17.00, Mid June-Mid Sept daily 09.30-18.30, Nov-Mar Fri-Sun & Bank Hols 10.00-17.00. Access by guided tour only, max 50 duration 60mins
A€2.90 Groups&OAPs€2.10
C&Students(NUS/USI)€1.30, Family Ticket €7.40

Country Parks & Estates

Castletown

Celbridge County Kildare Ireland
Tel: 00 353 1 628 8252
Fax: 00 353 1 627 1811
www.heritageireland.ie

[20km from centre of Dublin on N4/R403. Plenty of on-site parking available]

Castletown is the largest and most significant Palladian style country house in Ireland. Built c. 1722 for the speaker of the Irish House of Commons, William Conolly (1662-1729) the designs of a number of important architects were used, notably Alessandro Galilei, Sir Edward Lovett Pearce and later Sir William Chambers. The entire estate was sold by the Conolly-Carew family in 1965 to a property developer and in 1967 the house and some parkland were purchased by the Hon. Desmond Guinness. Both Mr. Guinness and subsequently the Castletown Foundation, who acquired the house in 1979, devoted considerable effort and resources to maintaining the house and restoring the principal rooms to a high standard. Castletown was transferred to State care on 1 January 1994. Ask the guide on site about discounts to other heritage sites in the area. Restricted access for visitors with disabilities.
Easter Sun-Oct Mon-Fri 10.00-18.00 (17.00 in Oct) Sat-Sun & Bank Hols 13.00-18.00 (17.00 in Oct). Access by guided tour only, max 20 duration 45mins
A€3.70 Groups&OAPs€2.60
C&Students(NUS/USI)€1.30, Family Ticket €8.70

Folk & Local History Museum

Donegal County Museum

High Road Letterkenny County Donegal Ireland
Tel: 00 353 74 912 4613
Based in a fine old stone building, which was once part of the Letterkenny Workhouse, built in 1846. The museum houses a fascinating range of artefacts covering all aspects of life in Donegal.

Forests & Woods

Phoenix Park Visitor Centre and Ashtown Castle

Phoenix Park Dublin 8 Ireland
Tel: 00 353 1 677 0095
A lively and entertaining exhibition on the history and the wildlife of the Phoenix Park is on display in the Visitor Centre.

Gardens & Horticulture

Glanleam Subtropical Gardens

Glanleam Estate Valentia Island County Kerry Ireland
Tel: 00 353 66 947 6176
Created over 150 years ago. Towering woodlands sweep down to the sea, overlooking the spectacular scenery of Valentia Harbour.

Japanese Gardens and St Fiachra's Garden

Tully Kildare County Kildare Ireland
Tel: 00 353 45 521617 / 522963
Irish National Stud - home to some of the world's finest stallions, mares and foals. Irish Horse Museum, housing the skeleton of the Arkle.

Heritage & Industrial

Brú na Bóinne Visitor Centre

Newgrange and Knowth Donore County Meath Ireland
Tel: 00 353 41 988 0300
Fax: 00 353 41 982 3071

[S of River Boyne on L21, 2km W of Donore. Signposted from Drogheda (off N1), from Slane (off N2) & from M1 also]

Brú na Bóinne Visitor Centre interprets the Neolithic monuments of Newgrange, Knowth and Dowth. The extensive exhibition includes a full-scale replica of the chamber at Newgrange as well as a full model of one of the smaller tombs at Knowth. All admission to Newgrange and Knowth is through the Visitor Centre, there is no direct access to these monuments. Visitors are brought from the Visitor Centre to the monuments by shuttle bus.

Daily Mar-Apr & Oct 09.30-17.30, May & Mid Sept-End Sept 09.00-18.30, June-Mid Sept 09.00-19.00, Nov-Feb 09.30-17.00. Newgrange open all year. Knowth opens from Easter. Guided tours, Newgrange: max 25 duration 45mins, Knowth: max 40 duration 45mins

Exhibition: A€2.90 Groups&OAPs€2.10 C&Students(NUS/USI)€1.60, Family Ticket €7.40. Exhibition & Newgrange: A€5.80 Groups&OAPs€4.50 C&Students(NUS/USI)€2.90, Family Ticket €14.50. Exhibition & Knowth: A€4.50 Groups&OAPs€2.90 C&Students(NUS/USI)€1.60, Family Ticket €11.00. Exhibition & Newgrange & Knowth: A€10.30 Groups&OAPs€7.40 C&Students(NUS/USI)€4.50, Family Ticket €25.50

Connemara Heritage and History Centre and Dan O'Hara's Homestead

Lettershea Clifden County Galway Ireland
Tel: 00 353 95 21246/21808
Fax: 00 353 95 22098
www.connemaraheritage.com

[Approx. 10min from Clifden or 1h from Galway City on N59. Plenty of on-site parking available]

Nestling beneath the Twelve Bens mountain range is an award-winning heritage centre that offers a unique insight into nineteenth century Connemara life and the hardship endured by tenant farmers. Enjoy our presentation, 'Connemara through the ages', which is available in both Irish and English. Experience our authentic reconstructions of a pre-Famine farm, a crannóg (an island used as a settlement), a ringfort (a fortified settlement from the Early Medieval Period) and a clochaun (an Early Christian place of prayer). See the restored homestead of Dan O'Hara (a man made famous in song and story). Guided tours with turf-cutting and sheep-shearing demonstrations are available for groups by prior arrangement. Visit our craft shop with its large selection of knitwear, marble, jewellery and other high-quality gifts, and our restaurant with fresh seafood. Farmhouse and self-catering accommodation is also available (please call or visit our website for more information).
Apr Oct daily
A€7.50 C€4.00

Discount Offer: Two for the Price of One

Jameson Experience (The)

The Old Distillery Midleton County Cork Ireland
Tel: 00 353 21 461 3594
Fax: 00 353 21 461 3704
www.jamesonwhiskey.com

[Midleton town is off N25, Cork to Waterford route. Plenty of free on-site parking available]

A tour of the Jameson Experience, Midleton consists of a 15 minute audio-visual presentation, a 35 minute guided tour of the Old Distillery and then back to the Jameson Bar for a whiskey tasting - minerals are available for children. Visitors can see the largest Pot Still in the world with a capacity of 32,000 gallons and the Old Waterwheel manufactured in 1825 to provide motive power prior to the days of electricity and still turning today. The guided tour and audio-visual aids are available in six languages. After the tour why not relax in the centre's elegant restaurant specialising in country farmhouse fare or perhaps browse through the gift and craft shop.
All year daily 10.00-18.00. Tours during the day
A€9.75 C€6.50 OAPs€7.00, Family Ticket (A2+C3) €23.00. Group rate: €8.00

Scattery Island Centre

Merchant's Quay Kilrush County Clare Ireland
Tel: 00 353 65 682 9100
Interprets the history, flora and fauna of the island on which a monastery is situated.

Historical

Ballyhack Castle
Ballyhack Waterford County Wexford Ireland
Tel: 00 353 51 389468
Located on a steep slope in a commanding position overlooking Waterford Estuary.

Barryscourt Castle
Carrigtwohill County Cork Ireland
Tel: 00 353 21 488 2218 / 488 3864
The seat of the Barry family from the twelfth to the seventeenth centuries.

Blarney Castle
Blarney County Cork Ireland
Tel: 00 353 21385669
A partial ruin that dates back to 1446. At the top of the castle lies the Blarney Stone.

Bunratty Castle and Folk Park
Bunratty County Clare Ireland
Tel: 00 353 61 360788 Fax: 00 353 61 361020
www.shannonheritage.com

[Just off N18 Limerick-Ennis Rd (10mins from Shannon Airport). Plenty of on-site parking available]

Bunratty Castle is the most complete and authentic medieval fortress in Ireland. This magnificently restored castle contains fifteenth and sixteenth-century furnishings and tapestries. Within its grounds is Bunratty Folk Park where nineteenth-century Irish Life is tellingly recreated. The Folk Park, set on 26 acres, features a watermill, a church, a village street, a magical walled garden, a playground and various farm animals. By night, Bunratty Castle hosts unique Medieval Castle Banquets which feature music and song by the Bunratty Castle entertainers and the evening is complemented by a delicious 4 course meal with wine (reservations necessary). The Corn Barn venue within the Folk Park hosts an Irish night from April to October and this is also complemented by delicious home cooked food and wine, (reservations necessary). *Jan-Mar & Nov-Dec 09.30-17.30 (last admission 16.15), Apr-May & Sept-Oct 09.00-17.30 (last admission 16.15), June-Aug 09.00-18.00 (last admission 17.15). Closed Good Friday & 24-26 Dec. Medieval Banquets nightly (reservations necessary). Bunratty Folk Park Traditional Irish Night Apr-Oct (reservations necessary)*
A€14.00 C€9.00 OAPs€7.95
Students(NUS/USI)€9.50, Family Ticket (A2+C2) €30.50, or (A2+C4) €32.50, or (A2+C6) €33.50

Casino Marino

Cherrymount Crescent Marino Dublin 3 Dublin
Region Ireland
Tel: 00 353 1 833 1618
Fax: 00 353 1 833 2636
www.heritageireland.ie
*[5 km from City Centre, off the Malahide Rd, after
J with Griffith Avenue, turn L at pedestrian lights
after Dublin Fire Brigade Training HQ. Plenty of
on-site parking available]*

The Casino was designed by Sir William
Chambers as a pleasure house for James
Caulfeild, First Earl of Charlemont. It is one of
the finest eighteenth-century neo-classical buildings in Europe. The Casino, meaning "small
house", surprisingly contains sixteen finely decorated rooms, endlessly rich in subtlety and
design. It is a remarkable building-both in terms
of structure and history. The Casino is located
at Marino, just off the Malahide Road and only
three miles north of the centre of Dublin. Ask
the guide on site about discounts to other heritage sites in Dublin. The interior is accessed by
a stairway. In order to protect the inlaid floor visitors will not be permitted to wear shoes, dis-
posable foot coverings will be provided free of
charge.

*Nov-Mar Sat & Sun only 12.00- 16.00, Apr Sat &
Sun only 12.00-17.00, May-Oct daily 10.00-
17.00 (18.00 in June-Sept). Access by guided
tour only, max 16 duration 45mins*
A€2.90 Groups&OAPs€2.10
C&Students(NUS/USI)€1.30, Family Ticket
€7.40

Charles Fort

Summer Cove Kinsale County Cork Ireland
Tel: 00 353 21 477 2263
Fax: 00 353 21 477 4347
A classic example of a star-shaped fort.

Clonmacnoise

Athlone County Offaly Ireland
Tel: 00 353 90 967 4195
Fax: 00 353 90 967 4273
*[21km from Athlone signposted from N62 or
20km from Ballinasloe signposted from R357.
Plenty of on-site parking available]*

An early Christian site founded by Saint Ciaran
in the sixth century on the banks of the River
Shannon. The site includes the ruins of a cathedral, seven churches (ranging from the tenth to
the thirteenth century), two round towers, three
high crosses and the largest collection of early
Christian graveslabs in Ireland. The original high
crosses and a selection of graveslabs are on
display in the visitor centre. The long and varied
history of Clonmacnoise is recounted in an
audio visual presentation shown in the visitor
centre. There are also exhibitions that deal with
the flora, fauna and landscape of the region.
The visitor centre is fully accessible for visitors
with disabilities. Please note this is a very busy
site and visitors may experience a delay during
the summer months.
*Nov-Mar 10.00-17.30, Mid Mar-Mid May &
Mid Sept-Oct 10.00-18.00, Mid May-Mid Sept
09.00-19.00. Closed 25 Dec. Guided tours available max 40 duration 45mins*
A€5.30 Groups&OAPs€3.70
C&Students(NUS/USI)€2.10, Family Ticket
€11.50

Cork City Gaol

Sunday's Well Cork City County Cork Ireland
Tel: 00 353 21 430 5022
Fax: 00 353 21 430 7230
This castle like prison once housed nineteenth-
century prisoners, often in wretched conditions.

Craggaunowen - The Living Past

Kilmurry Sixmilebridge Near Quin County Clare Ireland
Tel: 00 353 61 360788 Fax: 00 353 61 361020
www.shannonheritage.com

[Off R469]

Visit Ireland's original award winning pre-historic park. Situated on 50 acres of wooded grounds, the park interprets Ireland's pre-historic and early Christian eras. It features a stunning recreation of some of the homesteads, animals and artefacts that existed in Ireland over 1,000 years ago. Explore the Crannog (lake dwelling), the Ring Fort, the Medieval Castle and the 'Brendan Boat' - a leather hulled boat built by Tim Severin who sailed across mid-Atlantic and thus reenacted the voyage of St. Brendan and the early Christian monks reputed to have discovered America centuries before Columbus. Visit Craggaunowen Castle, built in 1550 standing defiantly on a crag overlooking the lake. See rare animal breeds - specimens of the pre-historic era. Enjoy the fresh air and lake walks in a most enjoyable rural setting. Savour the wonderful home-made fare in the charming farmhouse tearoom.

Early Apr-Sep 10.00-18.00
A€8.50 C€5.00 OAPs€6.20, Family Ticket (A2+C2) €19.50, or (A2+C4) €20.50, or (A2+C6) €21.50

Derrynane House, National Historic Park

Caherdaniel County Kerry Ireland
Tel: 00 353 66 947 5113
Derrynane is the ancestral home of Daniel O'Connell, lawyer, politician and statesman.

Desmond Castle (French Prison)

Cork Street Kinsale County Cork Ireland
Tel: 00 353 21 477 4855 / 2263
[600 metres from Guard Well along Cork Street- close to Carmelite Friary]

Desmond Castle was built by Maurice Bacach Fitzgerald, the Ninth Earl of Desmond (c.1500). A good example of an urban tower house, the castle consists of a keep with storehouses to the rear and domestic offices on the first and second floors. Originally built as the Kinsale Customs House, Desmond Castle has also served as an ordnance store, prison and during the Great Irish Famine, as a workhouse. In 1601 during the Battle of Kinsale, Desmond Castle was used by the Spanish forces under Don Juan Del Aguila. By the early decades of the twentieth century, the Castle had fallen into disrepair. It was declared a National Monument in 1938. Today Desmond Castle is host to the international Museum of Wine. This exhibition documents the intriguing story of Ireland's wine links with Europe and the wider world. Access to Castle by steps.

Mid Apr-Oct daily 10.00-18.00. Regular guided tour, max 20 duration 30mins
A€2.90 Groups&OAPs€2.10 C&Students(NUS/USI)€1.30, Family Ticket €7.40

Desmond Hall (Banqueting Hall)

The Square Newcastlewest County Limerick Ireland
Tel: 00 353 69 77408
West Limerick preserves many of Ireland's surviving spacious medieval halls.

Donegal Castle

Donegal Town County Donegal Ireland
Tel: 00 353 74 972 2405
Fax: 00 353 74 972 2436
www.heritageireland.ie

[Located in the centre of town. Plenty of on-site parking available]

Built by the O'Donnell chieftain in the fifteenth century (beside the River Eske), the castle has extensive seventeenth-century additions by Sir Basil Brooke. The castle is furnished throughout and includes Persian rugs and French Tapestries. Information panels chronicle the history of the castle owners from the O'Donnell chieftains to the Brooke family. Limited access for visitors with disabilities to the ground floor
Mid Mar-End Oct daily 10.00-18.00, 1 Nov-6 Mar Fri-Sun 9.30-16.30. Guided tours available every hour, max 25, duration 30mins. Acess to the site is available for group bookings in the off-season by prior arrangement Tel 00 353 87 270 4032
A€3.70 Groups&OAPs€2.60 C&Students(NUS/USI)€1.30, Family Ticket €8.70

Drimnagh Castle

Long Mile Road Drimnagh Dublin 12 Ireland
Tel: 00 353 1 450 2530
Drimnagh Castle was, until 1954, one of the oldest continually inhabited Castles in Ireland, and is an outstanding example of an old feudal stronghold. It is the only Irish castle still to be surrounded by a flooded moat.

Dublin Castle, State Apartments

Dame Street Dublin 2 Dublin Region Ireland
Tel: 00 353 1 677 7129
Fax: 00 353 1 679 7831
www.dublincastle.ie/state_apartments.html

[Situated in the City Centre off Dame St behind City Hall. 5min walk from Trinity College en-route to Christchurch]

Originally built in the thirteenth century (on a site previously settled by the Vikings) Dublin Castle functioned as a military fortress, a prison, treasury, courts of law and the seat of English Administration in Ireland for 700 years. Rebuilt in the seventeenth, eighteenth, nineteenth and twentieth centuries. Dublin Castle is now used for important State receptions and Presidential Inaugurations. The State Apartments, Undercroft, Chapel Royal, craft shop, heritage centre and restaurant are open to visitors. Access for visitors with disabilities to State Apartments, Chapel Royal and restaurant.
All year Mon-Fri 10.00-16.45, Sat-Sun & Bank Hols 14.00-16.45. Closed 24-27 Dec, 31 Dec, 1 Jan & Good Friday. Access by guided tour only, max 40 duration 1hr. (On occasions the State Apartments only may be closed for state purposes)
A€4.50 OAPs&Students(NUS/USI)€3.50 C(under12)€2.00 Groups rates (20+) available on request

Dún Aonghasa

Kilmurvey Inishmore Aran Islands
County Galway Ireland
Tel: 00 353 99 61008 Fax: 00 353 99 61009
www.heritageireland.ie

[7km W of Kilronan. Local ferry boat service from Galway & Rossaville to Kilronan. Bicycle traffic on Island]

Perched spectacularly on a cliff overlooking the Atlantic Ocean, this is the largest of the prehistoric stone forts of the Aran Islands. It is enclosed by three massive dry-stone walls and a "chevaux-de-frise" consisting of tall blocks of limestone set vertically into the ground to deter attackers. The fort is about 900m from the visitor centre and is approached over rising ground. Access for visitors with disabilities to the visitor centre. As much of the tour is outdoors, visitors are advised to weather protective clothing and shoes suitable for walking over uneven terrain.

Mar-Oct 10.00-18.00, Nov-Feb 10.00-16.00
A€2.10 Groups&OAPs€1.30
C&Students(NUS/USI)€1.10, Family Ticket
€5.80

Duncannon Fort

Duncannon County Wexford Ireland
Tel: 00 353 51 389454
The Fort is a star shaped fortress on a strategically important promontory in Waterford Harbour.

Dwyer McAllister Cottage

Derrynamuck County Wicklow Ireland
Tel: 00 353 404 45325/45352
Nestling in the shade of Kaedeen mountain at the top of a grassy lane.

Ennis Friary

Abbey Street Ennis County Clare Ireland
Tel: 00 353 65 682 9100
Fax: 00 353 65 684 1020
www.heritageireland.ie
This thirteenth-century Franciscan friary, founded by the O'Briens, has numerous fifteenth and sixteenth century sculptures carved in the local hard limestone. The visitor can see the figure of St. Francis displaying the stigmata, an elaborately ornamented screen, a representation of the Virgin and Child and the Ecce Homo. The Chancel is lit by the magnificent east window. Limited access for visitors with disabilities by prior arrangement. (Conservation works are ongoing on site).

Apr-Oct daily 10.00-17.00 (18.00 May-Sept). Guided tours available on request, max 30 duration 45mins
A€1.60 Groups&OAPs€1.10
C&Students(NUS/USI)€1.00, Family Ticket
€4.50

Ferns Castle

Ferns County Wexford Ireland
The castle was built in the thirteenth century, possibly by William, Earl Marshall.

Gallarus Castle

Ballydavid Kerry County Kerry Ireland
Tel: 00 353 66 915 6444 / 915 6371
Gallarus Castle was built by the Knight of Kerry before 1600 and is one of the few surviving castles on the Dingle peninsula.

Glendalough Visitor Centre

Glendalough Bray County Wicklow Ireland
Tel: 00 353 404 45325/45352
Fax: 00 353 404 45626
[Plenty of on-site parking available]

This early Christian monastic site was founded by St. Kevin in the sixth century and is set in a glaciated valley with two lakes. The monastic remains include a superb round tower, stone churches and decorated crosses. The visitor centre has an interesting exhibition and an audio-visual show. French, Italian and Spanish guided tours are available all year by advance booking. The visitor centre is fully accessible for visitors with disabilities. Access to the site is very difficult for wheelchair users.
Mid Oct-Mid Mar daily 09.30-17.00, Mid Mar-Mid Oct daily 09.30-18.00. Guided tours available on request, max 50 duration 40mins
A€2.90 Groups&OAPs€2.10
C&Students(NUS/USI)€1.30, Family Ticket
€7.40

Kilkenny Castle

The Parade Kilkenny County Kilkenny Ireland
Tel: 00 353 56 772 1450
A twelfth-century castle remodelled in Victorian times and set in extensive parklands.

Killruddery House and Gardens

Bray County Wicklow Ireland
Tel: 00 353 1 286 3405 / 286 2777
The core of the garden is a pair of canals which focus on the house at one end and on an avenue of lime trees at the other.
Gardens; Apr-Sept daily. House: May, June and Sept daily

King House

Boyle County Roscommon Ireland
Tel: 00 353 71 966 3242
Visitors can explore the colourful history of the house and surrounding area through a range of interactive exhibitions.
May-Sept daily. Apr & Oct weekends only

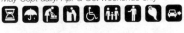

King John's Castle

Nicholas Street King's Island Limerick County Limerick Ireland
Tel: 00 353 61 360788 Fax: 00 353 61 361020
www.shannonheritage.com

[Situated on King's Island in Limerick City]

King John's Castle is situated in the heart of Limerick's Medieval Heritage Precinct, 'Kings Island'. The Castle was built between 1200 and 1210 and was repaired and extended many times in the following centuries. King John's Castle remains a most impressive Anglo-Norman Fortification. It retains many of the pioneering features which made its construction unique for its day. Its massive gatehouse, battlements and corner tower await exploration! Features include; an imaginative historical exhibition on the history of the castle featuring two-multi vision shows and archaeological excavations featuring amongst other things the earliest evidence of settled life in Limerick. Enjoy scenic battlement walks and views of the surrounding hinterland.
Jan-Feb & Nov-Dec 10.00-16.30, Mar-Apr & Oct 09.30-17.00. May-Sept 09.30-17.30. Closed Good Friday & 24-26 Dec
A€9.00 C€5.25 OAPs€6.65
Students(NUS/USI)€6.65, Family Ticket
(A2+C2) €20.60, or (A2+C4) €21.60, or
(A2+C6) €22.75

Knappogue Castle

Quin County Clare Ireland
Tel: 00 353 61 360788
Built in 1467, it has over five troubled but colourful centuries of Irish history, succoured friend and foe alike within its keep.
May-early Oct

Ormond Castle

Castle Park off Castle Street Carrick-on-Suir County Tipperary Ireland
Tel: 00 353 51 640787/56 772 4623 Fax: 00 353 56 775 4003
Ormond Castle is the best example of an Elizabethan manor house in Ireland. It was built by Thomas, the 10th Earl of Ormond in the 1560s. Closely integrated into the manor house are two fifteenth-century towers. It is the country's only major unfortified dwelling from that turbulent period. The 'state rooms' contain some of the finest decorative plasterwork in the country and include plasterwork portraits. Restricted access for visitors with disabilities.
Mid June-early Sept daily 10.00-18.00. Winter: please call for details. Access by guided tour only, max 20 duration 40mins
Admission Free

Pearse Museum and St Enda's Park

St Enda's Park Grange Road Rathfarnham Dublin 16 Ireland
Tel: 00 353 1 493 4208
A former school run by Patrick Pearse, now a museum in beautiful grounds.

Rock of Cashel

Cashel County Tipperary Ireland
Tel: 00 353 62 61437 Fax: 00 353 62 62988
[500 metres from centre of Cashel town, off the Dublin rd]

A spectacular group of Medieval buildings set on an outcrop of limestone in the Golden Vale including the twelfth-century round tower, High Cross and Romanesque Chapel, thirteenth-century Gothic cathedral, fifteenth-century castle and the restored Hall of the Vicars Choral. Attractions include an audio-visual show and exhibitions. Access for visitors with disabilities by prior arrangement. Please note that this is a very busy site and visitors may experience a delay during the summer months.
Daily Mid Sept-Mid Oct & Mid Mar-Early June 09.00-17.30, Mid Oct-Mid Mar 09.00-16.30, Early June-Mid Sept 09.00-19.00. Closed 24-26 Dec. Guided tours available, max 50 duration 45mins
A€5.30 Groups&OAPs€3.70 C&Students(NUS/USI)€2.10, Family Ticket €11.50

Shaw Birthplace

33 Synge Street Dublin 8 Ireland
Tel: 00 353 1 475 0854 / 872 2077
The first home of George Bernard Shaw's family has been restored to its Victorian elegance.

Ross Castle

Ross Road Killarney County Kerry Ireland
Tel: 00 353 64 35851
This Castle may be considered a typical example of the stronghold of an Irish Chieftain during the Middle Ages.

Literature & Libraries

Dublin Writers Museum

18 Parnell Square Dublin 1 Ireland
Tel: 00 353 1 872 2077
The Irish literary tradition is one of the most illustrious in the world, famous for four Nobel prize winners and for many other writers of international renown. In 1991 the Dublin Writers Museum was opened to house a history and celebration of literary Dublin. Situated in a magnificent eighteenth century mansion in the north city centre, the collection features the lives and works of Dublin's literary celebrities over the past three hundred years. Swift and Sheridan, Shaw and Wilde, Yeats, Joyce and Beckett are among those presented through their books, letters, portraits and personal items.

James Joyce Museum

Joyce Tower Sandycove County Dublin Ireland

Tel: 00 353 1 280 9265 / 872 2077
The Joyce Tower is one of a series of Martello Towers build to withstand an invasion by Napoleon, and now holds a museum devoted to the life and works of James Joyce, who made the tower the setting for the first chapter of his masterpiece, Ulysses.

Marsh's Library

St Patrick's Close Dublin 8 Ireland
Tel: 00 353 1 454 3511
The first public library in Ireland dating from 1701. It was designed by William Robinson and the interior has been unchanged for nearly 300 years.

National Library of Ireland

Kildare Street Dublin 2 Ireland
Tel: 00 353 1 603 0200
The National Library of Ireland, which was founded in 1877, has many associations with famous figures in Irish history.

Maritime

Mizen Head Signal Station

Harbour Road Goleen West Cork Ireland
Tel: 00 353 28 35115/35225
Fax: 00 353 28 35422
www.mizenhead.net
[Leave N71 at Ballydehob, through Schull & Goleen to Mizen Head or leave N71 at Bantry, through Durrus on R591 to Goleen & Mizen Head. Plenty of on-site parking available]
Mizen Head Signal Station is open to the public for the first time since it was completed in 1910. The award winning Mizen Head Visitor Centre in the Keeper's House and the Engine Room, the famous Arched Bridge, the 99 Steps, the Fastnet Hall Navigational Aids Simulator and the views up the South and West Coasts guarantee a unique and authentic experience.
Shop@theMizen and Mizen Café. A different experience every time you visit.
Mid Mar-May & Oct daily 10.30-17.00, June-end Sept 10.00-18.00, Nov-mid Mar Sat & Sun 11.00-16.00
A€6.00 C(0-4)€Free C(5-11)€3.50 OAPs&Students(NUS/USI)€4.50, Family Ticket (A2+C3) €18.00. Group rate: 10% discount

Mills - Water & Wind

Water Wheels

Abbey Assaroe Rossnowlagh Road
Bally Shannon County Donegal Ireland
Tel: 00 353 71 985 1580
The Cistercians canalised the river to turn water wheels for mechanical power.

West Cork Model Railway Village
Inchydoney Road Clonakilty County Cork
Ireland
Tel: 00 353 2 333224
See exhibitions of the railways and industries
which once linked six West Cork towns.
Feb-Oct daily

Burren Way
The Burren Way is a 26 mile signposted walking
trail between Liscannor and Ballyvaughn in
North Clare. The route brings the walker from
Liscannor, along by the Cliffs of Moher, on to
Doolin and Ballinalacken. It then continues,
mostly, along the Green Roads across the
Burren landscape to Ballyvaughan.

Cliffs of Moher and O'Brien's Tower
Liscannor County Clare Ireland
Tel: 00 353 61 711269
Situated in County Clare and bordering the
Burren Area, the Cliffs of Moher are one of
Ireland's most spectacular sights.

Connemara National Park
Letterfrack Galway County Galway Ireland
Tel: 00 353 95 41054 / 41006
The park covers some 2,000 hectares (4,942
acres) of scenic countryside (rich in wildlife) on
the slopes of the Twelve Bens.

Glenveagh National Park and Castle
Churchill Letterkenny County Donegal Ireland
Tel: 00 353 74 91 37090
Fax: 00 353 74 91 37072
*[24km NW of Letterkenny, Kilmacrennan/Termnon
to Dunlewy rd (or Churchill to Dunlewy rd). Plenty
of on-site parking available]*

16,540 hectares (40,873 acres) of mountains,
lakes, glens and woods, with a herd of red deer.
A Scottish style castle is surrounded by one of
the finest gardens in Ireland, which contrast with
the rugged surroundings. The visitor centre
houses exhibitions and an audio-visual show.
The visitor centre is accessible for visitors with
disabilities. Glenveagh Castle: Built in the years
1870-1873, the castle consists of a four storey
rectangular keep. Access to the interior is by
tour only. Morning and afternoon teas are
served in the castle tearooms all season. The
ground floor of the castle is partially accessible
for visitors with disabilities.
*1 Feb-30 Nov 10.00-18.30. Access to Castle by
guided tour only, max 20 duration 45mins*
A€2.60 Groups&OAPs€2.00
C&Students(NUS/USI)€1.25, Family Ticket
€6.60

Wexford Wildfowl Reserve
North Slob Wexford County Wexford Ireland
Tel: 00 353 53 912 3129
The Wexford Slobs are internationally famous
for wild geese which spend the winter months
here.

Places of Worship

Ardfert Cathedral
Ardfert Kerry County Kerry Ireland
Tel: 00 353 66 713 4711
A monastery was reputedly founded here by St
Brendan 'The Navigator' in the sixth century.

St Patrick's Cathedral
Saint Patrick's Close Dublin 8 Dublin Region
Ireland
Tel: 00 353 1 453 9472
St. Patrick's Cathedral is the the largest church
in Ireland and was built between 1191 and
1270. It is considered the National Cathedral for
the whole island.

Police, Prisons & Dungeons

Kilmainham Gaol
Inchicore Road Kilmainham Dublin 8 Dublin
Region Ireland
Tel: 00 353 1 453 5984
Fax: 00 353 1 453 2037
www.heritageireland.ie

[3.5 km from centre of Dublin]

One of the largest unoccupied gaols in Europe,
covering some of the most heroic and tragic
events in Ireland's emergence as a modern
nation from the 1780s to the 1920s. Attractions
include a major exhibition detailing the political
and penal history of the prison and its restoration. Tours may be arranged for visitors with
special needs by prior arrangement. Please
note that this is a very busy site and visitors
may experience a delay during the summer
months. During winter months the interior of the
gaol is very cold please dress appropriately.
*Apr-Sept daily 09.30-18.00, Oct-Mar Mon-Sat
09.30-17.30 Sun 10.00-18.00. Closed 24-26
Dec. Access by guided tour only, max 50 duration 1hr 10mins*
A€5.30 Group&OAPs€3.70
C&Students(NUS/USI)€2.10, Family Ticket
€11.50

Wicklow's Historic Gaol
Kilmantin Hill Wicklow County Wicklow Ireland
Tel: 00 353 404 61599
Wicklow's historic gaol tells the story of eighteenth and nineteenth-century social and political history through various forms of interpretation.

Railways

Donegal Railway Heritage Centre
The Old Station Donegal Town County Donegal
Ireland
Tel: 00 353 74 972 2655
Bringing back the 'Wee Donegal'! Come along
and step back in time!

Fry Model Railway
Malahide Castle Demesne Malahide County
Dublin Ireland
Tel: 00 353 1 846 3779 / 2184
A unique collection of handmade models of Irish
trains, from the beginning of rail travel to mod-
ern times.

Sealife Centres & Aquariums

National Sea Life Centre

Strand Road Bray County Wicklow Ireland
Tel: 00 353 1 286 6939
Fax: 00 353 1 286 0562
www.sealife.ie

[Rail: Bray. Bus: 45, 84 & 145]

Dive into a magical marine world at the National Sea Life centre, Bray, where you will encounter strange and beautiful creatures from around the globe. March 2007 the launch of an amazing new feature called Weird and Wonderful Creatures of the Deep. Also see the mesmerising effects of beautifully coloured shoals of tropical fish swimming around our mythical sea god, and be enchanted by our majestic black-tipped reef sharks. There are also many creatures on display around our own coastline. Informative talks and feeding presentations throughout the day provide a deeper insight into the world beneath the waves and help us to understand why it is so important to protect these wonderful creatures. Ireland's leading marine conservation experience has something for the whole family. Guided tours by prior arrangement.
All year daily from 10.00. Closed 25 & 26 Dec
Please call for prices

Discount Offer: One Child Free

Spectator Sports

Naas Racecourse

Tipper Road Naas County Kildare Ireland
Tel: 00 353 45 897391
There has never been a better time to go racing at Naas Racecourse, located in the heart of the Thoroughbred County of Kildare.

Sport & Recreation

Connemara Trail

Aille Cross Loughrea County Galway Ireland
Tel: 00 353 91 841 216
Come ride with us on The Connemara Trail where we will be riding deep into the mountains overlooking the lakes and sea, along bays, rivers and beaches.

Transport Museums

Flying Boat Museum

Foynes County Limerick Ireland
Tel: 00 353 6 965416
The museum recalls the era of the flying boats during the 1930s and the early 1940s.

Steam Museum and Lodge Park Walled Garden

Lodge Park Straffan Nr Dublin County Kildare Ireland
Tel: 00 353 1 627 3155
Collection of historic prototype locomotive models. Full size live steam stationary engines. The Hands-on Area is provided for children and adds an imaginative and inventive arena.

Zoos

Dublin Zoo

Phoenix Park Dublin 8 Ireland
Tel: 00 353 1 474 8900
Explore the African Plains, which is home to giraffes, zebras, hippos, rhinos, cheetahs, lions and chimpanzees.

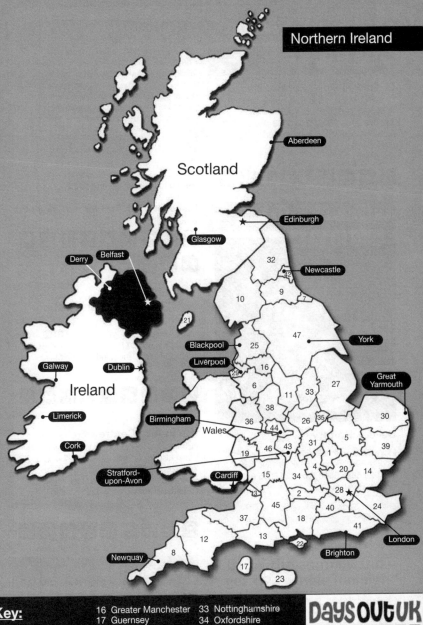

Northern Ireland

Scotland

Aberdeen

Edinburgh

Glasgow

Newcastle

Derry Belfast

Galway

Dublin

Ireland

Limerick

Cork

Blackpool

Liverpool

Birmingham

Wales

Stratford-
upon-Avon

Cardiff

Newquay

York

Great
Yarmouth

London

Brighton

Animal Attractions

Leslie Hill Open Farm

Leslie Hill Macfin Road Ballymoney County
Antrim BT53 6QL
Tel: 028 2766 6803/2766 3109
A Georgian house, magnificent period farm
buildings, and fine grounds with paths, lakes
and trees.

Arts, Crafts & Textiles

Belleek Pottery

Main Street Rathmore Belleek, Enniskillen
County Fermanagh Northern Ireland BT93 3FY
Tel: 028 6865 9300 Fax: 028 6865 8625
www.belleek.ie

*[A46 from Enniskillen, follow signs to Belleek.
Pottery is signposted. Plenty of on-site parking
available]*

Belleek Pottery has a very special place in the
cultural and commercial heritage of Ireland. It is
also one of the country's top-five visitor attractions! The award-winning Visitor Centre features
a museum, tearoom, video theatre and
Showroom (shop). This is an especially exciting
time to visit Belleek, as Ireland's oldest pottery
celebrates its 150th anniversary. Explore one of
the most authentic museums in the country
where the Pottery's heritage is illustrated with
magnificent creations from every Belleek period,
including one-off masterpieces like the
'Exhibition Centrepiece' and the exquisite
'Prisoner of Love'. The Belleek Showroom is an
Aladdin's Cave where you can browse and buy
an array of must-have items including special

giftware for weddings, new babies and
Christmas. The Belleek Factory Tour offers a
fascinating and enjoyable insight into the inner-
workings of a company that has become a
global icon for Irish design. Meet the craftspeo-
ple and observe the intricate production
process… you might even get the chance to
join in!
*Mon-Fri 09.00-17.30, Sat 10.00-18.00, Sun
14.00-18.00. Tours Mon-Fri every 30min 09.30-
12.15 & 13.45-15.30 last tour on Fri leaving at
15.00. Please check for opening times in winter*
Guided tours (every 30min): £4.00

**Discount Offer: Two for the Price of
One**

Irish Linen Centre and Lisburn Museum

Market Square Lisburn Co. Antrim BT28 1AG
Tel: 028 9266 3377
The Irish Linen Centre and Lisburn Museum is
established in the town's seventeenth-century
market house.

Island Arts Centre

Lisburn City Council Lagan Valley Island The
Island Lisburn County Antrim BT27 4RL
Tel: 028 92 509509
Nestled by the banks of the River Lagan at
Lagan Valley Island, Island Arts Centre is
Lisburn City Council's visually stunning new arts
base.

Birds, Butterflies & Bees

Castle Espie Wildfowl and Wetland Centre

78 Ballydrain Road Comber Newtownards
County Down BT23 6EA
Tel: 028 9187 4146
Located on the shores of Strangford Lough,
Castle Espie is home to the largest collection of
wildfowl in Ireland.

Caverns & Caves

Marble Arch Caves and Cuilcagh Mountain Park

Marlbank Scenic Loop Florencecourt
Fermanagh County Fermanagh BT92 1EW
Tel: 028 6634 8855
Explore a fascinating natural underworld.

Country Parks & Estates

Carnfunnock Country Park

Drains Bay Coast Road Larne County Antrim
BT40 2QG
Tel: 028 2827 0541
A maze in the shape of Northern Ireland! Walled
garden, BBQ, picnic sites and golf.

Castle Archdale Country Park

Irvines Town Nr Enniskillen County Fermanagh
BT94 1PP
Tel: 028 6862 1588
Marina, access to White Island, natural history
exhibits, old agricultural machinery.

Colin Glen Forest Park

163 Stewartstown Road Dunmurry Belfast
County Antrim BT17 0HW
Tel: 028 9061 4115
A wooded glen at the foot of Black Mountain
that gives a taste of the countryside.

Crawfordsburn Country Park

Bridge Road South Helen's Bay County Down
BT19 1LD
Tel: 028 9185 3621
Beaches, wooded glens, waterfalls, meadows,
a fort, the country centre and much more.

Delamont Country Park

Downpatrick County Down
Tel: 028 4482 8333
Boat trips, playground, tea room/gardens, visi-
tor centre, woods/park, wildlife and mini railway.

Exhibition & Visitor Centres

Palace Stables Heritage Centre

The Palace Demense Armagh County Armagh
Northern Ireland BT60 4EL
Tel: 028 3752 1801 Fax: 028 3751 0180
www.visitarmagh.com

[Armagh City. Plenty of on-site parking available]

The Palace Stables Heritage Centre is a
restored Georgian stable block located on the
Palace Demesne situated next to the impressive
Primate's Palace, formerly the home of the
Archbishops of the Church of Ireland from 1770
until the 1970s. Guided tours are available that
tell the story of the Demesne and through Living
History costumed interpreters recreate both the
grandeur and the squalor of the Georgian peri-
od. These tours also give you access to the
Chapel, School Room, Withdrawing Room,
Tack Room Coachman's Kitchen, Servant's tun-
nel, Ice House and at weekends into the
Demesne.

*Apr, May & Sept Sat 10.00-17.00 Sun 12.00-
17.00, June-Aug Mon-Sat 10.00-17.00 Sun
12.00-17.00. Grounds open all year*

A£4.75 C£3.75 OAPs£3.00, Family Ticket
£14.00

**Discount Offer: Two for the Price of
One**

Saint Patrick's Trian Visitor Complex

40 English Street Armagh County Armagh
Northern Ireland BT61 7BA
Tel: 028 3752 1801 Fax: 028 3751 0180
www.visitarmagh.com
[City Centre. Plenty of on-site parking available]

An exciting visitor complex located in the heart
of Armagh City, Saint Patrick's Trian, (pro-
nounced Tree-an) derives its name from the
ancient division of Armagh City into three distinct districts, or 'Trians'. The complex features
three major exhibitions: Armagh Story - Step
back in time and visit historic Armagh - from the
massive stone monuments of pre-history, with
its myths and legends, to the coming of Saint
Patrick and Celtic Christianity. Francis Johnston,
the renowned Armagh architect relates the history of Georgian buildings in the city in a most
unusual manner. A thought provoking audio-
visual presentation portrays 'belief' throughout
the world, with particular emphasis on Armagh,
as the Ecclesiastical Capital of Ireland. Saint
Patrick's Testament takes its title from Saint
Patrick's Confession, and examines the life and
work of our patron Saint and his connections
with Armagh as found in the ancient manuscript
- the 'Book of Armagh'. The Land of Lilliput. -
Jonathan Swift, author and clergyman spent
time in the district, and his most famous work
'Gullivers Travels' is encapsulated in the fantasy
'Land of Lilliput' where the adventures of
Gulliver are narrated with the help of a 20 foot
giant!
All year Mon-Sat 10.00-17.00, Sun 14.00-17.00
A£4.75 C£3.00 OAPs£3.75, Family Ticket
£14.00

Discount Offer: Two for the Price of One

Ballydougan Pottery

Bloomvale House, 171 Plantation Road
Portadown Craigavon Co. Armagh BT63 5NN
Tel: 028 3834 2201
Bloomvale House, dating from 1785, is the
home to award-winning Ballydougan Pottery.

Armagh County Museum

The Mall East Armagh County Armagh Northern
Ireland BT61 9BE
Tel: 028 3752 3070 Fax: 028 3752 2631
www.armaghcountymuseum.org.uk

Located near the centre of St Patrick's cathedral city, a visit to Armagh County Museum is an
ideal way to experience a flavour of the orchard
country. Discover a rich and varied legacy
revealed in objects ranging from prehistoric artefacts to household items from a bygone age. An
impressive collection of paintings includes
works by many well known Irish artists. With a
range of changing exhibitions throughout the
year, the Museum is an ideal place to see and
explore the fair county of Armagh.
*All year Mon-Fri 10.00-17.00, Sat 10.00-13.00 &
14.00-17.00*
Admission Free

Ulster American Folk Park

2 Mellon Road Castletown Omagh County
Tyrone Northern Ireland BT78 5QY
Tel: 028 8224 3292 Fax: 028 8224 2241
www.folkpark.com
*[N of Omagh on A5 Omagh to Strabane rd.
Plenty of free on-site parking available]*

The Ulster American Folk Park is an outdoor
museum of emigration which tells the story of
millions of people who emigrated from these
shores throughout the eighteenth and nineteenth centuries. The Old World and New World
layout of the park illustrates the various aspects
of emigrant life on both sides of the Atlantic.
Traditional thatched buildings, American log
houses and a full-scale replica emigrant ship
and dockside gallery help to bring a bygone era
back to life. Costumed demonstrators go about
their everyday tasks including spinning, open
hearth cookery, printing and textiles. The museum also includes an indoor Emigrants Exhibition
and a Centre for Migration Studies / Library that
is accessible to all visitors if they wish to find
further information on the history of emigration
and the place of their families in it. A full programme of special events is organised throughout the year.
*Apr-Sept Mon-Sat 10.30-18.00, Sun & Bank
Hols 11.00-18.30, Oct-Mar Mon-Fri 10.30-
17.00. Closed Weekends & Bank Hols*
A£5.00 C(5-16)£3.00 Concessions£3.00, Family
Ticket (A2+C4)£13.00, (A1+C3)£10.00 Group
rates available on request

Discount Offer: Two for the Price of One

Ulster Folk and Transport Museum

Bangor Road Cultra Holywood County Down
Northern Ireland BT18 0EU
Tel: 028 9042 8428 Fax: 028 9042 8728
www.uftm.org.uk
*[On A2 at Cultra, 7mi E of Belfast. On main
Belfast to Bangor Rd, close to Belfast City Airport
& Belfast Harbour. Plenty of on-site parking]*
The Ulster Folk and Transport Museum, is one
of Ireland's foremost visitor attractions, illustrat-
ing the way of life and the traditions of the people of the north of Ireland. At the open air Folk
Museum, 60 acres are devoted to illustrating
the way of life of people in the early 1900s.
Costumed visitor guides, working buildings and
exhibits all bring our stories to life. Indoors the
Folk Gallery features a number of interesting
exhibitions including Farming and Food and
Meet the Victorians. The Transport Museum
boasts the most comprehensive transport collection on Ireland. The Irish Railway Collection is
displayed in an award-winning gallery. Alongside
the Irish Railway Collection are the Road
Transport Galleries. These Galleries house a fine
collection of vehicles ranging from cycles,
motorcycles, trams, buses, fire engines and
cars. Also, the 'Titanic' exhibition and the two
new, exciting and interactive x2 'Flight' exhibitions located in the General Transport Galleries.
Events programme includes Easter Celebration,
May Day, Halloween and Christmas Past.
*All year Mar-June Mon-Fri 10.00-17.00, Sat
10.00-18.00, Sun 11.00-18.00, July-Sept Mon-
Sat 10.00-18.00, Sun 11.00-18.00, Oct-Feb
Mon-Fri 10.00-16.00, Sat 10.00-17.00, Sun
11.00-17.00. Please call for Xmas opening times*
Folk or Transport: A£5.50 C£3.50, Family Ticket
£15.50. Group rate (15+): 10% discount

Discount Offer: Two for the Price of One

Historical

Carrickfergus Castle

Marine Highway Carrickfergus County Antrim
Northern Ireland BT38 7BG
Tel: 028 9335 1273 Fax: 028 9336 5190
www.ehsni.gov.uk

A striking feature of the landscape from land,
sea and air, Carrickfergus Castle greets all visitors with its strength and menace. It represents
over 800 years of military might. Besieged in
turn by the Scots, Irish, English and French, the
Castle saw action right up to World War II.
Today it is maintained by the Environment and
Heritage Service and can be enjoyed by visitors
wanting to learn more about its history or just
looking for a fun day out in a unique setting. As
you walk around the Castle you will find model
historic figures that bring its stormy history to
life. From the Norman knight, John de Courcy
and his wife Lady Affreca to guards at their
posts keeping watch over the Castle, these life
size models portray the characters that make
up the Castle's history. For further information,
please refer to the website.
*Winter: Mon-Sat 10.00-16.00 Sun 14.00-16.00,
Apr, May & Sept Mon-Sat 10.00-18.00 Sun
14.00-18.00, June-Aug Mon-Sat 10.00-18.00
Sun 12.00-18.00*
A£3.00 C&OAPs£1.50 Family
Ticket(A2+C2)£8.00. Group rates available: 10+
must be pre-booked

Dunluce Castle

87 Dunluce Road Bushmills County Antrim
Northern Ireland BT57 8UY
Tel: 028 2073 1938
www.ehsni.gov.uk
[Plenty of on-site parking available]
This late-medieval and seventeenth-century
castle is dramatically sited, on a headland drop-
ping sheer into the sea on the north Antrim
Coast. It creates an exciting image of danger
and adventure backed up by its history. It was
first documented in McQuillan hands, in 1513,
and later became the stronghold of the
McDonnells, Earls of Antrim and Lords of the
Isles. The seventeenth-century mainland court
contains domestic buildings leading downhill to
the narrow crossing to the rock, formerly pro-
tected by a drawbridge to the Gatehouse. The
buildings on the rock are almost all of six-
teenth/early-seventeenth century date. Slight
earthworks, visible to the west of the castle, are
remains of a formal garden and part of the long-
deserted town, whose ruined church stands in
the graveyard south of the castle, separated
from it by the modern Coast Road.
*Winter: 1 Oct-31 Mar daily 10.00-16.30,
Summer: 1 Apr-30 Sept daily 10.00-17.00*
Admission: A£2.00 C&OAPs-£1.00
C(under4)£Free, Group Rate (10+): £1.00 per-
person

Florence Court

Florence Court Demesne Enniskillen
County Fermanagh BT92 1DB
Tel: 028 6634 8249 (for opening times)
Exquisite rococo plasterwork and Irish furniture
collection. 'Living History' tours give an insight
into 1920s Florence Court.

Greencastle
Kilkeel County Down
Tel: 028 9054 3145
A Norman castle with massive keep, gatehouse and curtain wall, this thirteenth-century royal fortress stands on the shores of Carlingford Lough.

Grey Abbey
Ballywalter County Down
Tel: 028 9054 3145
Cistercian abbey founded in 1193 by John de Courcey's wife Affreca, it was dissolved in 1541 but in the early seventeenth century was granted to Sir Hugh Montgomery.

Jordan's Castle
Ardglass County Down
Tel: 028 9054 3145
A fifteenth-century reactangular tower house, four storeys high and vaulted above the ground floor. The entrance is at the bottom of the north-west tower and leads to a spiral stairway to roof level. It was built to defend the port.

Malone House-Barnett Demesne
Barnett Park Upper Malone Road Belfast
County Antrim BT9 5PB
Tel: 028 9068 1246
An early nineteenth-century Georgian mansion overlooking the River Lagan, beautifully restored in 1983 after fire gutted the interior.

Mount Stewart House, Garden and Temple of the Winds
Mountstewart Portaferry Road Newtownards
County Down BT22 2AD
Tel: 028 4278 8387
A fascinating eighteenth-century house with nineteenth-century additions, the childhood home of Lord Castlereagh and famous for its magnificent garden.

Navan Centre and Fort
81 Killylea Road Armagh County Armagh
Northern Ireland BT60 4LD
Tel: 028 3752 1800 Fax: 028 3751 0180
www.visitarmagh.com
[A28 2.5 mi from Armagh City. On-site parking]

Visit the Navan Centre, which interprets one of Ireland's most important ancient monuments, Navan Fort! This was the royal seat of the Kings of Ulster and the Province's ancient capital. Start your tour in the 'Vanished World' of lost myths, travel into the 'Real World' of archaeology and then enter the 'Other World' to hear the legends of the Ulster Cycle. Visit the Iron Age/Early Christian period dwelling and through Living History interpretation, learn about that way of life. Multi-Lingual facilities available. Finally, walk the path of history to the great Ancient Seat of Kings, Navan Fort.

June-Aug Mon-Sat 10.00-17.00, Sun 12.00-17.00, Apr, May & Sept (Weekends only) Sat 10.00-17.00, Sun 12.00-17.00. Closed 12 July. Other times by arrangement for Tour Groups or Educational visits

A£4.75 C£3.00 OAPs£3.75, Family Ticket £14.00

Discount Offer: Two for the Price of One

Scrabo Country Park
Scrabo Rd Newtownards Co. Down BT23 4SJ
Tel: 028 9181 1491
The park is centred upon the tower built on the summit of Scrabo Hill. It includes the woodlands of Killynether, disused quarries, a pond and a prehistoric hill fort.

Places of Worship

Down Cathedral

English Street Downpatrick County Down
BT30 6AB
Tel: 028 4461 4922
Cathedral Hill in Down has been a focus of
Christian worship for almost as long as
Christianity has been in Ireland.

St Columb's Cathedral

London Street Londonderry County
Londonderry BT48 6RQ

Tel: 028 7126 7313
Stained glass depicts heroic scenes from the
great siege of 1688/89.

Sealife Centres & Aquariums

Exploris

Exploris Aquarium The Rope Walk Castle Street
Portaferry, Newtownards County Down
Northern Ireland BT22 1NZ
Tel: 028 4272 8062 Fax: 028 4272 8396
www.exploris.org.uk
*[From Belfast take A20 through Newtownards to
Portaferry. From Downpatrick take A25 following
signs for Strangford Ferries (ferries every 30min).
Exploris is well signposted. Plenty of on-site park-
ing available]*

Exploris - The Northern Ireland Aquarium and
seal sanctuary is ideally sited on the shores of a
marine nature reserve and area of specific scientific interest - Strangford Lough. A visit to
Exploris enables the visitor to learn about the
species indigenous to Strangord Lough and the
coastline of the island. The seal sanctuary lets
visitors view the valuable work carried with
rehabilitating sick and injured seal pups. A
rolling programme of events, guided tours and
demonstrations make Exploris fun for all the
family.
*Peak: Apr-Sept Mon-Fri 10.00-18.00, Sat 11.00-
18.00, Sun 12.00-18.00. Off Peak: Oct-Mar
Mon-Fri 10.00-17.00, Sat 11.00 17.00, Sun
13.00-17.00*
Peak: A£6.70 Concessions£3.80. Off Peak:
A£5.40, Concession£3.30

Social History Museums

Ballycastle Museum

59 Castle Street Ballycastle County Antrim
BT54 6AS
Tel: 028 2076 2024 (TIC)
Folk social history of the Glens in the town's
eighteenth-century courthouse. Exhibits include
the Glen Taisie banner.

Causeway School Museum

52 Causeway Road Bushmills County Antrim
BT57 8SU
Tel: 028 2073 1777
Take your desk in a 1920s classroom with
inkwells and splodgy pens. Whip 'peeries', play
with yo-yos, marbles and skipping ropes.

Sport & Recreation

Lagan Valley Leisureplex

Lisburn Leisure Park Lisburn County Antrim
BT28 1LP
Tel: 028 9267 2121
The LeisurePlex boasts the largest leisure pool
of its kind in Northern Ireland, with some of the
fastest, longest and wettest water rides in
Ireland.

Portstewart Strand

Portstewart County Londonderry
Tel: 028 7083 6396
Magnificent two-mile stretch of dunes and a
sandy beach, popular with holiday makers in
summer and walkers throughout the year.

W5

Odyssey 2 Queens Quay Belfast County Antrim
Northern Ireland BT3 9QQ
Tel: 028 9046 7700 Fax: 028 9046 7707
www.w5online.co.uk
*[From Belfast City Centre follow signs for A2
Bangor onto Queen Elizabeth Bridge. Keep in L
lane & immediately after crossing River Lagan turn
L onto Queen's Island. Follow road for 0.25mi car
park on R. Plenty of on-site parking available]*

W5 is Ireland's first and only purpose-built interactive discovery centre and offers an entertaining day out that will appeal to visitors of all
ages. The centre has 160 innovative hands-on
exhibits, which are housed in five action packed
exhibition areas with attractions including animation stations, cloud rings, a giant race track
and a lie detector! In addition to the exhibits W5
also present live floorshows and run a changing
programme of special events. Image copyright:
whowhatwherewhenwhy-W5.
*All year daily Mon-Sat 10.00-18.00, Sun 12.00-
18.00. During school term time W5 will close at
17.00 Mon-Thur (last admission 16.00)*
A£6.50 C£4.50 Concessions£5.00, Family
Ticket (A2+C2) £19.00

Waterworld

The Harbour Portrush Northern Ireland
BT56 8DR
Tel: 028 7082 2001
Massive waterslides, childrens' play pool, and a
health suite (with sauna and steam room).

Transport Museums

Coach and Carriage Museum

Blessingbourne Fivemiletown County Tyrone
BT75 0QS
Tel: 028 8952 1221
Among the numerous coaches on display is an
1825 London to Oxford stagecoach.

Larne Interpretive Centre

Narrow Gauge Road Larne County Antrim
BT40 1XB
Tel: 028 2826 0088 (TIC)
Model of the famous Antrim Coast Road and
crafts.

Victorian Era

Workhouse Museum and Library

23 Glendermott Road Waterside Londonderry
County Derry BT47 6BG
Tel: 028 7131 8328
Set in a restored nineteenth-century workhouse,
the museum features dormitories and the mas-
ter's quarters. It also has exhibitions on the
Great Famine and the Battle of the Atlantic.

Zoos

Belfast Zoological Gardens

Antrim Road Newtownabbey County Antrim
BT36 7PN
Tel: 028 9077 6277
Attractions include the primate house, penguin
enclosure, African enclosure and underwater
viewing of sea-lions and penguins.

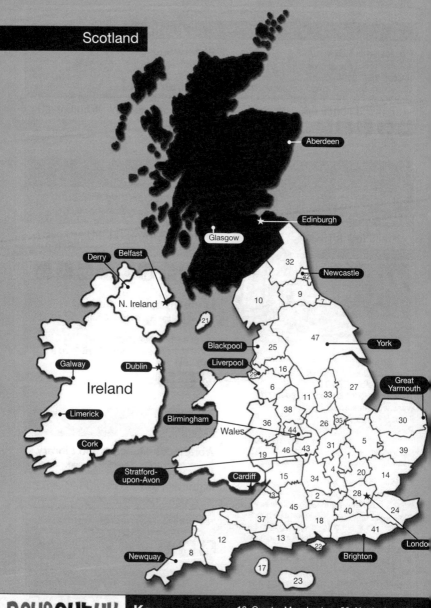

Scotland

Aberdeen

Edinburgh

Glasgow

Derry Belfast

N. Ireland

Galway Dublin

Ireland

Limerick

Cork

Blackpool

Liverpool

Birmingham

Wales

Stratford-upon-Avon

Cardiff

Newquay

Newcastle

York

Great Yarmouth

Brighton

London

Key:

DaysOUT UK
The place to look for places to go

1 Bedfordshire	16 Greater Manchester	33 Nottinghamshire
2 Berkshire	17 Guernsey	34 Oxfordshire
3 Bristol	18 Hampshire	35 Rutland
4 Buckinghamshire	19 Herefordshire	36 Shropshire
5 Cambridgeshire	20 Hertfordshire	37 Somerset
6 Cheshire	21 Isle Of Man	38 Staffordshire
7 Cleveland	22 Isle Of Wight	39 Suffolk
8 Cornwall	23 Jersey	40 Surrey
9 County Durham	24 Kent	41 Sussex
10 Cumbria	25 Lancashire	42 Tyne & Wear
11 Derbyshire	26 Leicestershire	43 Warwickshire
12 Devon	27 Lincolnshire	44 West Midlands
13 Dorset	28 London	45 Wiltshire
14 Essex	29 Merseyside	46 Worcestershire
15 Gloucestershire	30 Norfolk	47 Yorkshire
	31 Northamptonshire	
	32 Northumberland	

Abbeys

Arbroath Abbey
Abbey Street Arbroath Angus DD11 1EG
Tel: 01241 878756
The substantial ruins of a Tironensian
monastery, founded by William the Lion in 1178,
who is buried in the Abbey.

Dunfermline Abbey and Palace
Pittencrieff Park St. Margaret Street Dunfermline
Fife KY12 7PE
Tel: 01383 739026
The great abbey of Dunfermline was founded in
the eleventh century by Queen Margaret.

Melrose Abbey
Melrose Borders
Tel: 01896 822562
Melrose Abbey is a magnificent ruin on a grand
scale with lavishly decorated masonry.

Sweetheart Abbey
New Abbey Dumfriesshire DG2 8BU
Tel: 01387 850397
Splendid ruin of a late thirteenth-century and
early fourteenth-century Cistercian abbey found-
ed in 1273 by Lady Devorgilla of Galloway.

Agriculture / Working Farms

Aberdeenshire Farming Museum
Aden Country Park Peterhead Mintlaw
Aberdeenshire AB42 5FQ
Tel: 01771 624590
Explore North East farming heritage and estate
life at this Museum set in the beautiful surround-
ings of Aden Country Park.

National Museum of Rural Life Scotland
Wester Kittochside Philipshill Road East Kilbride
Scotland G76 9HR
Tel: 0131 247 4377 Fax: 01355 571290
www.nms.ac.uk
*[By car: just off A727, approx 10 mi S of
Glasgow. Plenty of on-site parking available. For
detailed directions, please visit our website. By
bus: First Bus Service 31 from Glasgow to East
Kilbride. Rail: East Kilbride (approx 3 mi from
museum), then by taxi or bus]*

A change of scenery? Get a healthy dose of
fresh country air! Take in the sights, sounds and
smells as you explore Wester Kittochside Farm.
Discover what life was like for country people in
the past and how this has shaped Scotland's
countryside today. Would you cope working on
a 1950s farm? Try milking cows by hand! Hitch
a ride on our tractor-trailer. Meet the horse,
sheep, cows and hens. Get back to nature at
the National Museum of Rural Life Scotland.
*All year daily 10.00-17.00. Closed 25-26 Dec &
1 Jan*
A£5.00 C(under12)£Free Concessions£4.00.
National Museums Scotland Members receive
free or reduced entry to all five National
Museums Scotland. The National Trust for
Scotland Members receive free admission
although there may be a charge for some special events

**Discount Offer: Two for the Price of
One**

Airfields / Flight Centres

National Museum of Flight Scotland

East Fortune Airfield North Berwick East Lothian Scotland EH39 5LF
Tel: 01620 897240 Fax: 01620 880355
www.nms.ac.uk
[By car: 20mi E of Edinburgh, off B1347. For detailed directions, please visit our website. Bus: First Bus service 121, between Haddington & North Berwick, stops at museum. Plenty of on-site parking available]
Ready for take off? Our historic airfield is home to a collection of key aircraft that chronicle the story of flight, from the daunting early days to the sleek sophistication of Concorde. How difficult were each of them to fly? What speeds did they reach? What would it have been like to actually build and fly them? Seek out the answers at the National Museum of Flight Scotland.
Apr-Oct daily 10.00-17.00, July & Aug 10.00-18.00, Nov-Mar Sat & Sun 10.00-16.00
Museum including The Concorde Experience: A£5.00 C(under12)£Free Concessions£4.00. Museum including Concorde Experience & Concorde Boarding Pass: A£8.00 C(under12)£2.00 Concessions£6.00. Telephone 0870 421 4299 to book your Concorde Booking Pass or book online. Members receive free or reduced entry to all five National Museums Scotland

Discount Offer: Two for the Price of One

Animal Attractions

Amazonia

Strathclyde County Park Motherwell Lanarkshire Scotland ML1 3RT
Tel: 0870 112 3777 Fax: 01698 338733
www.discoveramazonia.co.uk

[Plenty of on-site parking available]
Amazonia is Scotland's only tropical indoor rainforest attraction, packed full of exotic animals. This offers a new fun and educational experience for all ages. It's a unique place to learn and explore, giving insight into the life in a tropical forest. Learn about the secret life of some of our rainforest inhabitants. Our reptiles, rare birds, insects, monkeys, amphibians and fish. Marvel at our rare tropical plants, waterfalls and ponds. Amazonia is packed full of exotic animals including, poison dart frogs, tarantulas, pythons, fruit bats, assassin, beetles, geckos, chameleons, marmoset monkeys, toucans, parrots, leaf cutter ants and tropical fish. Visitors are given the opportunity to take part in our daily animal handling sessions, where we try to dispel some of the 'Hollywood myths' surrounding creatures such as tarantulas and pythons. Keep up to date by visiting our new web site.
All year daily 10.00-18.00
A(16+)£4.95 C£3.95

Discount Offer: One Child Free

Cairngorm Reindeer Centre

Aviemore Inverness-Shire PH22 1QU
Tel: 01479 861228
Britain's only herd of reindeer, found free ranging in the Cairngorm mountains in Scotland.

Edinburgh Butterfly and Insect World

Dobbies Garden World Melville Nursery
Lasswade Midlothian Scotland EH18 1AZ
Tel: 0131 663 4932 Fax: 0131 654 2774
www.edinburgh-butterfly-world.co.uk
*[Located at Dobbies Gardening World off
Edinburgh City Bypass at Gilmerton exit or from
Sheriffhall Roundabout - just follow signs. Bus:
Lothian Region Transport 3 from Princes St
(Shops Side) Mon-Sun. Plenty of free on-site
parking available]*

Walk through a tropical paradise and observe
stunning exotic butterflies flying around you.
Iguanas roam free and quail and a hummingbird
can be spotted darting through the jungle flora.
There are tarantulas, stick insects, leaf-cutting
ants, scorpions and frogs! You can get up close
and personal at twice daily 'Meet the Beasties'
handling sessions. We can even help cure your
phobias! In the Reptile Room you'll find lizards,
chameleons, giant pythons and yellow anacon-
das! The nocturnal zone displays bugs and
beasties that can be seen going about their
night time activities, with the leaf cutter ants
nest and glow in the dark scorpions! Every
Friday afternoon you can view the Snake Pit,
where our royal pythons will be fed! With
monthly themes throughout the year, there will
always be a new weird and wonderful creature
to come and see!
*All year daily, summer 09.30-17.30, winter 10.00-
17.00*
A£5.00 C£3.85, Family Tickets from £16.50.
Group rates (for 10+) available on request,
please call for details

Discount Offer: One Child Free

Heads of Ayr Farm Park

Dunure Road Ayr Ayrshire KA7 4LD
Tel: 01292 441210
Large selection of rare and exotic animals, birds
and pets. Try out the Quad Biking. Fly down the
sledge slope or bounce on trampolines.

ILPH Belwade Farm

Aboyne Aberdeenshire Scotland AB34 5DJ
Tel: 01339 887186
www.ilph.org/belwadefarm

*[Signposted off A93 between Aboyne &
Kincardine Oneil. Plenty of on-site parking avail-
able]*

When you follow the signs off the A93, down
the mile-long wooded road, no one expects to
find the haven that is the Scottish home of the
ILPH. Belwade Farm has around 65 horses and
ponies at any one time - from Shetland ponies
to Clydesdales and Shires - which came into
our care for many different reasons. Many of the
horses have been through hard times and it is
at the ILPH that they receive the attention they
so rightly deserve. Some just need TLC whilst
others are undergoing intensive rehabilitation to
restore their quality of life. You will be able to
see and meet the horses in work or out in their
fields, while enjoying the views that Belwade
has to offer. Take an enjoyable walk around our
picturesque centre to take in the wonderful
scenery and watch the wildlife in the natural
habitats. ILPH Belwade Farm has so much to
offer so why not come and see for yourself.
*All year Weds, Weekends & Bank Hols 14.00-
16.00. Closed 25 Dec-1 Jan*
Admission Free

Jedforest Deer and Farm Park

Mervinslaw Estate Camptown Jedburgh
Roxburghshire TD8 6PL
Tel: 01835 840364
Discover the farm animals of yesteryear within
our large conservation collection of rare breeds.

Oban Rare Breeds Farm Park

Glencruitten Oban Argyll PA34 4QB
Tel: 01631 770608
Conservation centre breeding and exhibiting
rare breeds of farm animals.
Mid Mar-Oct

Scottish Deer Centre

Bow of Fife Cupar Fife KY15 4NQ
Tel: 01337 810391
Nine species of deer and you can even feed
them yourself.

Scottish Wool Centre

Off Main Street Aberfoyle Stirlingshire Scotland
FK8 3UQ
Tel: 01877 382850
Sheep shearing and the opportunity to feed the
centre's cute little spring lambs.

Art Galleries

Burrell Collection

2060 Pollokshaws Road Glasgow G41 1AT
Tel: 0141 287 2550
A world-famous collection of textiles, furniture,
ceramics, stained glass, silver and pictures.

Centre for Contemporary Arts

350 Sauchiehall Street Glasgow G2 3JD
Tel: 0141 352 4900
One of Europe's leading contemporary galleries,
with a range of artforms including visual arts,
performance, live art, dance, music and events.
Closed Sun & Mon

City Art Centre

2 Market Street Edinburgh Midlothian EH1 1DE
Tel: 0131 529 3993
Houses the city's permanent fine art collection
and stages temporary exhibitions drawn from all
over the world. Six floors of display galleries.

Dundee Contemporary Arts (DCA)

152 Nethergate Dundee Scotland DD1 4DY
Tel: 01382 909900/909252
Outstanding exhibitions from British and international artists, the best of world cinema, shop,
print studio and café bar.

Gallery of Modern Art

Queen Street Glasgow Lanarkshire G1 3AZ
Tel: 0141 229 1996
A new gallery right in the heart of the city, four
floor spaces, each with its own distinct style.

Gracefield Arts Centre

28 Edinburgh Road Dumfries Dumfriesshire
DG1 1JQ
Tel: 01387 262084
Collection of over 400 Scottish paintings, con-
temporary art exhibitions, craft shop, darkroom,
printmaking studio, all set in beautiful grounds.

House For An Art Lover

Bellahouston Park 10 Dumbreck Road Glasgow
G41 5BW
Tel: 0141 353 4770
Designed by (and dedicated to) Rennie
Mackintosh, offers hospitality and events.
Features a cafe and Mackintosh gift shop.

Lighthouse (The)

Scotland's Centre for Architecture, Design and
the City 11 Mitchell Lane Glasgow G1 3NU
Tel: 0141 221 6362
Spanning six floors, The Lighthouse provides an
opportunity to experience architecture and
design through a programme of exhibitions.

National Gallery of Scotland
The Mound Edinburgh Scotland EH2 2EL
Tel: 0131 624 6200
Widely regarded as one of the finest smaller galleries in the world, the National Gallery of Scotland contains an outstanding collection.

Scottish National Gallery of Modern Art
75 Belford Road Edinburgh Scotland EH4 3DR
Tel: 0131 624 6200
The Scottish National Gallery of Modern Art houses Scotland's finest collection of twentieth and twenty-first-century paintings, sculpture and graphic art.

Scottish National Portrait Gallery
1 Queen Street Edinburgh Midlothian EH2 1JD
Tel: 0131 624 6200
The Scottish National Portrait Gallery provides a unique visual history of Scotland, told through portraits of the figures who shaped it.

St Mungo Museum of Religious Life and Art
2 Castle Street Glasgow Lanarkshire G4 0RH
Tel: 0141 553 2557
This unique museum, opened in 1993, explores the universal themes of life and death and the hereafter.

Arts, Crafts and Textiles

Paisley Museum and Art Galleries
High Street Paisley Renfrewshire PA1 2BA
Tel: 0141 889 3151
Pride of place here is given to a world-famous collection of Paisley shawls. Other collections illustrate local industrial and natural history, while the emphasis of the art gallery is on nineteenth-century Scottish artists and an important studio ceramics collection.

Communication Museums

Orkney Wireless Museum
Kiln Corner Kirkwall Orkney
Tel: 01856 871400
Large, unique collection showing the development of communication equipment from its early beginnings.

Costume & Jewellery Museums

National Museum of Costume Scotland
Shambellie House New Abbey Dumfries Scotland DG2 8HQ

Tel: 01387 850375 Fax: 01387 850461
www.nms.ac.uk
[7mi S of Dumfries on A710. Bus: 372 from Whitesands. Plenty of on-site parking available]

Dressed for success? Clothes have always defined a period in history or even a time of day. From strait-laced Victorian dress to wartime utility wear, put yourself in the shoes of those who wore the trends of their time. What was it like wearing a corset? Try one on for size! Enjoy a fitting tribute to past fashions at the National Museum of Costume Scotland.
Apr-Oct daily 10.00-17.00
A£3.00 C(under12)£Free Concessions £2.00. Members receive free or reduced entry to all five National Museums Scotland

Discount Offer: Two for the Price of One

KELBURN *The natural place to go*

CASTLE & COUNTRY CENTRE

Kelburn is the home of the Earls of Glasgow, famous for its Castle, historic gardens, unique trees and romantic glen.

Waterfalls, deep gorges, attractive woodland and spectacular views over the Firth of Clyde make it a place of great natural beauty. There's a 'History of Kelburn' cartoon exhibition, history trail, family museum, ranger and falconry centre, pony trekking and riding school, stockade, adventure course, pets corner, gift shop and licenced cafe. The 'Secret Forest' is Scotland's most unusual attraction, where you can discover the Giant's Castle, the crocodile swamp, the secret grotto, the gingerbread house, the Chinese garden, the maze of the Green Man, a 40 foot high pagoda and a hundred other surprises.

OPENING TIMES
Castle open in Summer for afternoon guided tours
Please telephone for details and availability

Adult £7   Conc. £4.50   Family ticket £22

Family ticket for 2 adults and 3 children or 1 adult and 4 children. It be used again discounting the next visit to £15.00

Country Parks & Estates

Kelburn Castle and Country Centre

South Offices Fairlie Largs Ayrshire KA29 0BE
Tel: 01475 568685 Fax: 01475 568121
www.kelburncountrycentre.com
[A78 2mi S of Largs. Rail: Largs. Plenty of on-site parking available]

Home of the Earls of Glasgow, Kelburn enjoys spectacular views over the Firth of Clyde. Explore its historic gardens and romantic glen, waterfalls and unique trees. There is also a rid-

ing centre, birds of prey, pottery, adventure playgrounds including new indoor play area, gift shop, licensed café, exhibitions and Scotland's most unusual attraction - the 'Secret Forest'. *Apr-Oct daily 10.00-18.00, Nov-Mar 11.00-17.00. Castle open July & Aug for afternoon guided tours (3 per day)*
A£7.00 Concessions£4.50, Family Ticket (A2+C3 or A1+C4) £22.00. (Family tickets may be used again, discounting the next visit to £15.00)

Discount Offer: Two for the Price of One

Mugdock Country Park
Milngavie Glasgow Lanarkshire G62 8EL
Tel: 0141 956 6100
750 acres of stunning countryside (lochs, rivers, woods, heaths and moors) with lovely views over Glasgow and to the Highlands.

Exhibition & Visitor Centres

Loch Lomond and the Trossachs National Park Gateway Centre
Loch Lomond Shores Ben Lomond Way
Balloch, Alexandria Dunbartonshire G83 8LQ
Tel: 01389 722 199
This state-of-the-art visitor centre on the shores of Loch Lomond is staffed by National Park and Tourist Board experts who can offer information, guided walks, nature trails and maps of the park.

Loch Ness 2000 Exhibition Centre
Drumnadrochit Inverness IV63 6TU
Tel: 01456 450573
Takes you from the pre-history of Scotland through the Ice Age and Viking times onto the 50 year controversy that surrounds Loch Ness. *Easter-Oct*

Festivals & Shows

Braemar Gathering

The Princess Royal and Duke of Fife Memorial
Park Braemar Aberdeenshire Scotland
AB35 5YX
Tel: 013397 55377
www.braemargathering.org
*[On the A93, 50mi from Perth, 60mi from
Aberdeen. All outside car parking is free, with
exception of the reserved area on Chapel Brae for
buses. Limited on-site parking available]*
The Gathering is a must for tourists; there is
Highland dancing, solo piping events, tug of
war, running and jumping events, a hill race,
and all the heavy events. Twelve pipe bands
play in the arena individually and three times as
a massed band - a tremendous spectacle.

1 September 2007 09.30-17.00

A£7.00 C£2.00. Seats bookable in advance,
standing room available on the day

Edinburgh Festival Fringe

Various Locations Edinburgh Scotland
Tel: 0131 226 0026
The Edinburgh Festival Fringe is the world's
greatest celebration of live art and performance.
With up to 1,000 different shows a day including theatre, music, circus, dance, comedy, children's shows and street entertainment, for just
over three weeks in August, the whole of
Scotland's most majestic city becomes a stage.
5-27 August 2007

Edinburgh International Festival

Various Locations Edinburgh Scotland
Tel: 0131 473 2000
One of the world's most prestigious arts festival,
the Edinburgh International Festival celebrates
the drama of live performance in Scotland's
capital city.
10 August-2 September 2007

Scottish Traditional Boat Festival

Various Venues Portsoy Aberdeenshire Scotland
Tel: 01261 842951
www.scottishtraditionalboatfestival.co.uk
*[Portsoy Harbour lies in middle of southern shore
of Moray Firth. It sits N of A98, about 50mi W of
Aberdeen & about 60mi E of Inverness]*

The 14th Scottish Traditional Boat Festival
includes the largest collection of traditional
boats in Scotland; a great range of craft and
heritage demonstrators and displays; non-stop
music, dance and theatre on the harbour side
stage; a Food Fayre with all that's best in the
region's food and Adventure Land with fun for
children of all ages. In 2007 the Portsoy event
will be the final port of call of the Moray Firth
Flotilla, a unique week long project in which the
finest traditional craft from all over the UK will
sail from Wick, round the coast to Portsoy. In
addition to providing an opportunity to see a
great fleet of craft, on Saturday night, the
Portsoy Festival will feature a dramatic finale
with great music and spectacular fireworks. All
this means that as you wander round Portsoy's
historic harbour and lovely town your senses will
be assailed by the sound of great music from
Scotland, England, Ireland and Scandinavia; the
smells of delicious food and the sight of fabulous sailing craft. A great weekend not to be
missed!
29 June-1 July 2007
Prices vary according to event

Folk & Local History Museums

Andrew Carnegie Birthplace Museum

Moodie Street Dunfermline Fife KY12 7PL
Tel: 01383 724302
The museum tells the story of the humble hand-loom weaver's son who was born here in 1835.
Apr-Oct

Angus Folk Museum

Kirkwynd Glamis Angus DD8 1RT
Tel: 01307 840288
The museum presents six charming eighteenth-century cottages contain the domestic section, and the agricultural collection in the farm steading opposite.

Arbroath Museum

Signal Tower Ladyloan Arbroath Angus
DD11 1PU
Tel: 01241 875598
Through sights, sounds and smells, the museum introduces visitors to the extraordinary history of the lighthouse.

Baird Institute History Centre and Museum

Lugar Street Cumnock Ayrshire KA18 1AD
Tel: 01290 421701
A local history museum and history centre featuring local pottery, Mauchline ware in conjunction with a programme of temporary exhibitions.

Black House Complex

Arnol Barvas Isle Of Lewis HS2 9DB
Tel: 01851 710395
A traditional, fully furnished, Lewis thatched house, which provides a unique insight into island life.

Breadalbane Folklore Centre

Killin Perthshire Scotland FK21 8XE
Tel: 01567 820254 Fax: 01567 820764
www.breadalbanefolklorecentre.com
[Off A85]

Come and find out what makes this part of Scotland so fascinating. Here's the perfect place to stop during your day in the country - The Breadalbane Folklore Centre. At The Falls of Dochart, the river splashes and tumbles past a beautiful old waterside mill. Spend a while in this enchanting spot - and you'll find out what makes Scotland's 'High Country' so special. Trace the story of famous Highland clans, and admire their treasures. Listen to the story of St. Fillan, see his famous healing stones, and discover some of the mythical tales and legends of The Scottish Highlands. Souvenir, gift and book shop. Also see the 'Living Legends' presentations with Scotty Wilson, revealing the secrets of Breadalbane - regular performances from June to September.
Apr-Oct daily 10.00-17.00. Closed Nov-Mar
A£2.75 C£1.80-£2.20 OAPs£2.20, Family
Ticket £7.30

Fife Folk Museum

High Street Ceres Cupar Fife KY15 5NF
Tel: 01334 828180
The history of everyday rural life in this area.

Inverness Museum and Art Gallery

Castle Wynd Inverness IV2 3EB
Tel: 01463 237114
An extravaganza of archaeology, art, natural and local history.

Low Parks Museum

129 Muir Street Hamilton Lanarkshire ML3 6BJ
Tel: 01698 328232 Fax: 01698 328412
www.southlanarkshire.gov.uk

[J6 M74 Nr Hamilton's Palace Grounds Retail Park Nr Asda Superstore. Plenty of on-site parking available]

A visit to Low Parks will make you look again at this unique part of the Clyde Valley. Entertaining and informative displays will take you on a fascinating journey around South Lanarkshire. Interesting objects tell their own tales of local life and industries, which have shaped the land and people. We are also the home of the Cameronians (Scottish Rifles) Regimental Museum. The Cameronians were unique as the only Scottish rifle regiment. We tell their colourful story from their covenanting origins in 1689 to their defiant disbandment in 1968.

All year daily Mon-Sat 10.00-17.00, Sun 12.00-17.00
Admission Free

Museum of Edinburgh

142 Canongate Royal Mile Edinburgh EH8 8DD
Tel: 0131 529 4143
This is one of the best-preserved sixteenth-century buildings in the old town.

North Berwick Museum

School Road North Berwick East Lothian EH39 4JU
Tel: 01620 828203
The former Burgh School contains a local history museum with various displays.

Orkney Museum

Tankerness House Broad Street Kirkwall Orkney KW15 1DH
Tel: 01856 873535
A laird's town house which dates from the sixteenth century, with a fine walled garden.

People's Palace

Glasgow Green Glasgow Scotland G40 1AT
Tel: 0141 271 2962
This museum looks at the work and leisure of the ordinary people of Glasgow.

People's Story

163 Canongate Edinburgh Midlothian EH8 8BN
Tel: 0131 529 4057
Tells the story of the ordinary people of Edinburgh from the late eighteenth century.

Perth Museum and Art Gallery

George Street Perth Perthshire PH1 5LB
Tel: 01738 632488
One of the oldest museums in Britain, found in the centre of the fair city of Perth.

Shetland Museum

Lower Hillhead Lerwick Shetland ZE1 0EL
Tel: 01595 695057
A range of items recovered from shipwrecks, and houses a permanent collection of artefacts.

St Andrews Museum

Kinburn Park Double Dykes Road St. Andrews Fife KY16 9DP
Tel: 01334 412690 / 412933
St Andrews Museum tells the story of the historic city of St Andrews.

Stirling Old Town Jail

St John Street Stirling Stirlingshire FK8 1EA
Tel: 01786 450050 Fax: 01786 471301
www.oldtownjail.com

*[On St John St (main route to Stirling Castle).
Plenty of on-site parking available]*

Can you imagine what it was like to be locked
up in prison - 150 years ago? Come and find
out! Are you ready to explore the historic heart
of Stirling? Then get your day off to a great start
by visiting an authentic Victorian jail! Step inside
for a fascinating live prison tour - the warden
himself will welcome you, and the hangman just
can't wait to meet you! Who knows who else
you'll encounter - perhaps a convict desperately
trying to escape? When you reach the Rooftop
Viewpoint you'll get a totally different view of the
old city and the countryside stretched out
beneath you, and make sure you visit the exhibition area for a chilling reminder of the life
faced by today's prisoners in Scotland.
Especially for children - join the Prison Beastie
Hunt! Audio tour, souvenir and gift shop.

*All year daily 10.30-16.30, extended opening
Mar-Sept. Closed 25-26 Dec & 1 Jan*
A£5.00-£5.95 C&OAPs£3.20-£4.50, Family
Ticket £13.25-£15.70

Tweeddale Museum

Chambers Institute High Street Peebles
Tweeddale EH45 8AG
Tel: 01721 724820
Museum of local history covering memorabilia,
natural history and the story of Peebles.

Vikingar

Greenock Road Largs Ayrshire KA30 8QL
Tel: 01475 689777
Vikingar is an amazing multi-media experience
which takes you from the first Viking raids in
Scotland to their defeat at the Battle of Largs.

West Highland Museum

Cameron Square Fort William Inverness-Shire
PH33 6AJ
Tel: 01397 702169
The displays illustrate traditional Highland life
and history, with numerous Jacobite relics.

World Famous Old Blacksmith's Shop Centre

Gretna Green Dumfries & Galloway Scotland
DG16 5EA
Tel: 01461 338441
Runaway couples have raced here to marry
under Scottish law since 1754. See the world-
famous marriage anvil and enjoy the excellent
shopping and great places to eat.

Food & Drink

Famous Grouse Experience

Glenturret Distillery The Hosh Crieff Perthshire
PH7 4HA
Tel: 01764 656565
Set in Scotland's oldest, most visited and
award-winning distillery The Famous Grouse
Experience opened in July 2002.

Glen Grant Distillery and Garden

Elgin Road Rothes Aberlour Banffshire
AB38 7BS
Tel: 01340 832118
Visitors can go on a guided tour of the distillery,
followed by a walk in the garden where you can
enjoy a sample of Glen Grant Pure Malt Whisky
in Major Grant's dram hut.

Glenfiddich Distillery
Dufftown Keith Banffshire AB55 4DH
Tel: 01340 820373
The distillery was founded in 1887 by William
Grant and has remained in the hands of the
family ever since.

Glenmorangie Distillery
Glenmorangie Visitor Centre Coy Tain
Ross-shire IV19 1PZ
Tel: 01862 892477
Tour the distillery with one of the guides who will
explain the whisky-making process and intro-
duce you to the Sixteen Men of Tain.

Scotch Whisky Heritage Centre
354 Castlehill The Royal Mile Edinburgh
Scotland EH1 2NE
Tel: 0131 220 0441
Brings the story of whisky to life in an entertain-
ing and informative way.

Forests & Woods

Galloway Forest Park
21 King Street Castle Douglas Dumfries
Scotland DG7 1AA
Tel: 01671 402420
Almost 300 sq miles of largely coniferous forest,
wild moorland, lochs and mountains make up
this forest park in Scotland's little visited southwest corner.

Queen Elizabeth Forest Park
David Marshall Lodge, Visitor Centre Trossachs
Road (Dukes Pass) Aberfoyle Stirling
Stirlingshire FK8 3UX
Tel: 01877 382258
Queen Elizabeth Forest Park welcomes visitors
all year round and offers forest walks, mountain
paths, spectacular views, car parks and picnic
areas

Gardens & Horticulture

David Welch Winter Gardens
Duthie Park Polmuir Road Aberdeen
Aberdeenshire Scotland AB11 7TH
Tel: 01224 585310
Temperate House, Corridor of Perfumes, Fern
House, Victorian Corridor, Japanese Garden,
Tropical House and the Arid House.

Royal Botanic Garden, Edinburgh
20a Inverleith Row Edinburgh Scotland
EH3 5LR
Tel: 0131 552 7171
Home to over 6% of all known plants. Discover
some of the world's oldest plants, plus other the
well known and economically important plants.

The Pineapple
N of Airth Falkirk
Tel: 01324 831137
A bizarre structure in the shape of a pineapple,
14 metres (45ft) high, built in 1761 as a garden
retreat. The architect is unknown.

Guided Tours

Edinburgh Bus Tours
Waverley Bridge Edinburgh Scotland
Tel: 0131 220 0770
See Edinburgh Castle, the Palace of
Holyroodhouse, Princes Street, the Royal Mile,
New Town and the Scottish Parliament.
*Tours: Every 20-30min between 09.30-17.00.
Tickets can be bought from the drivers at any
stop on the route, from Waverley Bridge or in
advance.*

Mercat Tours Ltd
Mercat House 28 Blair Street Edinburgh Lothian
Scotland EH1 1QR
Tel: 0131 225 5445
Specialises in historically accurate tours of
Edinburgh's spookiest locations, including the
South Bridge Vaults,

Isle of Arran Heritage Museum

Rosaburn Brodick Isle of Arran KA27 8DP
Tel: 01770 302636
An eighteenth-century croft farm, with a cottage restored to its pre-1920 state and a smiddy where a blacksmith worked until the late 1960s.

Motherwell Heritage Centre

High Road Motherwell North Lanarkshire Scotland ML1 3HU
Tel: 01698 251000 Fax: 01698 268867
http://motherwellheritage.freeservers.com
[From S J6 M74 from N J6 M74. Limited on-site parking available]

Motherwell Heritage Centre is situated in High Road, just off the top of the A723 Hamilton Road. It has a Visit Scotland '4 Star' award. The centre's main feature is the multi-media 'Technopolis' interactive facility. This takes the visitor from the arrival of the Romans, through the rise and fall of heavy industry to the present day regeneration of the district. The use of 'hands on' technology with recreated streets and foundry scenes really brings history of the area to life. The centre also has an exhibition gallery, the focus of many fascinating displays and community projects. There is also a family history research room, with staff available to advise on tracing family and local histories. A fifth floor viewing platform gives an outlook over the Clyde Valley and, on the ground floor, a small shop sells books, postcards and gifts with local heritage flavour.
All year Mon-Sat 10.00-17.00 Sun 12.00-17.00
Admission Free

New Lanark Visitor Centre

New Lanark Mills Lanark Strathclyde ML11 9DB
Tel: 01555 661345
There are a range of visitor attractions on offer at New Lanark. The village is a UNESCO World Heritage Site.

Scottish Mining Museum

Lady Victoria Colliery Newtongrange Edinburgh Scotland EH22 4QN
Tel: 0131 663 7519 Fax: 0131 654 1618
www.scottishminingmuseum.com
[In Newtongrange, 9mi S of Edinburgh on A7. Regular bus services connect museum with central Edinburgh. Plenty of on-site parking available]

Set in the Lady Victoria Colliery on the A7 this '5 Star' visitor attraction houses the story of coal for Scotland. This vital way of life can be discovered through exhibitions, interactivities, film theatres, a recreated underground and coalface and the Magic Helmet Tour. Also, on Wednesdays and Sundays take our Big Stuff Tour - see the huge pieces of machinery and transportation which were used underground! As well as our tours we also have a gift shop, licensed coffee shop serving hot meals and cold snacks, a picnic and play area and a large free car park. Credit cards not accepted in restaurant.
All year daily Mar-Oct 10.00-17.00, Nov-Feb 10.00-16.00. Closed 24-26, 31 Dec & 1-2 Jan
A£5.95 C&Concessions£3.95. Group rates: A£4.95 C&Concessions£3.50

Discount Offer: One Child Free

Historical

Armadale Castle Gardens and Museum of the Isles

Armadale Castle Armadale Sleat Isle of Skye
Scotland IV45 8RS
Tel: 01471 844305/844227
Fax: 01471 844275
www.clandonald.com

*[16mi S of Broadford on scenic A851. Easily
reached either by Skye Bridge or from Mallaig /
Arnadale, Glenelg / Kylerhea ferry points. Plenty
of on-site parking available]*

Skye's award-winning visitor centre is situated
at the south end of the island. Armadale Castle
and Gardens were built in 1815 as the home of
Lord Macdonald. Museum of the Isles, with an
exhibition, a library and study centre. 40 acre
gardens and nature trails. Adventure play area.
*Apr-Oct daily 09.30-17.30. Limited winter open-
ing*
A£4.90 C(5-15)&Concessions£3.80, Family
Ticket (A2+C4) £14.00. Group rate (8+): A£3.40

Discount Offer: Two for the Price of One

Balmoral Castle Grounds and Exhibition

Balmoral Ballater Aberdeenshire AB35 5TB
Tel: 013397 42534
Queen Victoria and Prince Albert first rented the
property in 1848 and it remains the Royal
Family's highland residence.

Bowhill House and Country Park

Bowhill Selkirk Scottish Borders TD7 5ET
Tel: 01750 22204
Art collection, furniture, porcelain, silver and
tapestries. Visitors' centre, picnic areas, gift
shop and licensed tearoom. Adventure playground and Victorian treasure trail. Woodland,
loch and riverside walks.

Culzean Castle and Country Park

Maybole Ayrshire Scotland KA19 8LE
Tel: 01655 884455
Noted for oval staircase, circular drawing room
and plasterwork. Scotland's first country park,
woodland walks cover 563 acres to shoreline.

Duff House

Banff Banffshire AB45 3SX
Tel: 01261 818181
Duff House is a Treasure House with an extraordinary history containing masterpieces from the
National Galleries of Scotland. The outstanding
collections consist of furniture including chairs
by Chippendale, tapestries and paintings by
artists such as El Greco.

Edinburgh Castle

Castle Hill Edinburgh Scotland EH1 2NG
Tel: 0131 225 9846
The castle houses the Honours (Crown Jewels)
of Scotland, the Stone of Destiny, the famous
fifteenth-century gun Mons Meg, the One O'
Clock Gun and the National War Museum of
Scotland.

Eilean Donan Castle

Dornie by Kyle of Lochalsh Scotland IV40 8DX
Tel: 01599 555202
Discover the history, see the stunning views,
walk on the ramparts and catch whispers in the
wind; they carry a myriad of tales of MacRaes,
MacKenzies and much more.
Easter-Oct

Glamis Castle

Estates Office Glamis Forfar Angus DD8 1RJ
Tel: 01307 840393
The splendid turreted castle is the family home
of the Earls of Strathmore, and was the child-
hood home of HM The Queen Mother.
Mar-Oct

Jedburgh Castle Jail

Castle Gate Jedburgh Roxbroughshire TD9 6BD
Tel: 01835 864750
On the original site of Jedburgh's mediaeval
castle this is the one of the only remaining
examples of a Howard Reform Prison, built in
the 1820s.

John Knox House

45 High Street Edinburgh Midlothian EH1 1SR
Tel: 0131 556 9579 / 556 2647
John Knox is said to have died in the house,
which contains an exhibition about his life and
times.

MacLellan's Castle

Kirkcudbright Dumfries & Galloway
Tel: 01557 331856
This handsome structure has been a ruin since
the mid eighteenth century.

Maes Howe Chambered Cairn

Finstown Orkney
Tel: 01856 761606
Maes Howe is the finest chambered tomb in
north-west Europe and more than 500 years
old.

Mount Stuart House and Gardens

Rothesay Isle Of Bute Strathclyde PA20 9LR
Tel: 01700 503877
The ancestral home of the Marquess of Bute;
one of Britain's most spectacular High Victorian
Gothic houses.

National Wallace Monument

Abbey Craig Hillfoots Road Stirling Stirlingshire
Scotland FK9 5LP
Tel: 01786 472140
www.nationalwallacemonument.com

[Off A907. Plenty of on-site parking available]

A national hero - a national landmark. Come
and discover one of Scotland's most magnificent sights, packed with fascinating exhibits
and displays, including the magnificent battle
sword once wielded by Sir William Wallace. You
will come face to face with the martyr and patri-
ot whose victory at The Battle of Stirling Bridge
in 1297 inspired generations of Scots the world
over. Listen in on a recreation of the trial 700
years ago in London which led to his brutal execution, and visit The Hall of Heroes. Trace the
story of Building The Monument, and then when
you reach The Crown enjoy one of the most
stunning views in Scotland - across those same
fields which witnessed so many fearsome
encounters, to the beautiful scenery of The
Ochil Hills and The Trossachs. Audio tour in 5
languages, picnic area, coffee shop, souvenir
and gift shops.
*All year daily 10.30-16.00, extended opening
Mar-Oct. Closed 25-26 Dec & 1 Jan*
A£6.50 C&OAPs£4.00-£4.90, Family Ticket
£17.00

Paxton House and Country Park

Paxton Berwick Upon Tweed Northumberland
TD15 1SZ
Tel: 01289 386291 Fax: 01289 386660
www.paxtonhouse.com
[Signposted 3mi from A1 Berwick upon Tweed
bypass on B6461. Rail: Berwick upon Tweed
(5mi). Plenty of on-site parking available]

Scottish Tourist Board 5-Star Historic House,
2006. Paxton House is one of the finest eighteenth-century Palladian country houses in
Britain. It was built in 1758 to the design of
John Adam. The twelve period rooms hold the
finest collections of Chippendale and Trotter furniture. The restored Regency Picture Gallery
houses over seventy paintings from the National
Gallery of Scotland. Stroll around 80 acres of
gardens, woodlands, and riverside walks. Enjoy
a family competition on the croquet lawn or the
9-hole putting green. The adventure playground,
picnic areas, nature trails-every day and 'Paxton
Ted's Tuesday Fundays' throughout July and
August make Paxton House a fun place for children. See many changing exhibitions throughout the year and visit the now permanent exhibition of 'The Ellem Fishing Club' the oldest net
fishing club in the world. And after all that, visit
our gift shop and enjoy a home-cooked lunch
or tea in our licensed tearoom.
1 Apr-31 Oct House: daily 11.00-17.00.
Grounds: daily 10.00-sunset
House: A£6.00 C£3.00, Family Ticket £16.00.
Grounds only: A£3.00 C£1.50, Family Ticket
£8.00

Discount Offer: One Child Free

Rough Castle

Bonny Bridge Falkirk
Tel: 0131 668 8800
The impressive earthworks of a large Roman
fort on the Antonine Wall can be seen here. The
buildings have disappeared, but the mounds
and terraces are the sites of barracks, granary
and bath buildings.

St Andrews Castle and Visitor Centre

The Scores St. Andrews Fife KY16 9AR
Tel: 01334 477196
The ruins of the castle of the Archbishops of St
Andrews, dating from the thirteenth century.

Stirling Castle

Upper Castle Hill Stirling Stirlingshire Scotland
FK8 1EJ
Tel: 01786 450000
Without doubt one of the grandest of all
Scottish castles, both in its situation on a com-
manding rock outcrop and in its architecture.

Strome Castle

Lochcarron Highlands

Tel: 01599 566325
The ruined castle is romantically situated on a
rocky promontory jutting into Loch Carron,
commanding fine views westwards to Skye.
First recorded in 1472 when it was a stronghold
of the Lords of the Isles, it later belonged to the
MacDonells of Glengarry. Following a quarrel
with Kenneth MacKenzie, Lord of Kintail, it fell in
1602 after a long siege and was blown up. All
that remains of the tower is a heap of rubble
but substantial sections of the enclosing wall
still stand.

Thomas Carlyle's Birthplace

The Arched House High Street Ecclefechan
Lockerbie Dumfriesshire DG11 3DG
Tel: 01576 300666
The Arched House in which Thomas Carlyle
was born on 4th December 1795, was built in
1791.

Traquair House

Innerleithen Peeblesshire Scotland EH44 6PW
Tel: 01896 830323 Fax: 01896 830639
www.traquair.co.uk
[On B709 off A72 at Peebles. Plenty of on-site parking available]

Visit romantic Traquair where Alexander I signed a charter over 800 years ago and where the 'modern wings' were completed in 1680. Once a pleasure ground for Scottish kings in times of peace, then a refuge for Catholic priests in times of terror, the Stuarts of Traquair supported Mary, Queen of Scots and the Jacobite cause without counting the cost. Imprisoned, fined and isolated for their beliefs, their home, untouched by time, reflects the tranquillity of their family life. Enjoy the unique atmosphere and history. See the secret stairs, spooky cellars, books, embroideries and letters from former times. Visit the ancient brewery and inhale the delicious aroma, then sample the potent liquor in the brewery museum. Browse through the gift shop and then enjoy a relaxed lunch in the Old Walled Garden. Finally, search for the centre of the maze, explore the enchanted woods and look out for the Grey Lady... a truly magical day out for all the family.
Apr & May 12.00-17.00, June-Aug 10.30-17.00, Sept 12.00-17.00, Oct 11.00-16.00. Guided Tours Apr & outside opening hours (please book in advance). Also open Nov Sat-Sun 12.00-16.00 (for guided tours only)
House & Grounds: A£6.30 C£3.40 OAPs£5.70, Family Ticket (A2+C3) £17.70. Grounds only: A£3.50 C£2.00. Group rates available on request. Guided tours (book in advance, minimum 20 people) £7.00 per-person. Personal guided tour by Catherine Maxwell Stuart (21st Lady of Traquair): £15.00 per-person

Discount Offer: One Child Free

Urquhart Castle

Drumnadrochit Highlands Scotland
Tel: 01456 450551
Magnificently sited, overlooking Loch Ness. Urquhart is one of the largest castles in Scotland, with a long and colourful history.

Burns National Heritage Park

Murdoch's Lone Alloway Ayr Ayrshire KA7 4PQ
Tel: 01292 443700
Explore Burns Cottage and museum, Burns Monument, the Brig O'Doon and the haunted Kirk Alloway. Relax at the Tam O' Shanter Experience visitor centre.

Innerpeffray Library

Crieff Perthshire Scotland PH7 3RF
Tel: 01764 652819
http://innerpeffraylibrary.co.uk

[5mi from A9 at Gleneagles/Auchterarder on B8062 via Kinkell bridge. 4mi from A85 at Crieff on B8062. Tourist Board sign on main rd, look for flag. On most road atlas. Plenty of on-site parking available]

Innerpeffray: Early complete, very important group of religious and educational buildings, built by the Drummond family of Strathearn, in continuous use for 500 years. Pre 1680 David Drummond, 3rd Lord Madertie, built and endowed his school and library. All the knowledge of his world in 400 books in English, Latin, French, German, and Italian etc. Library: 1762, built Bishop Robert Hay Drummond re-opened

1763 - Scotland's oldest free public lending library, continuous borrowing record 1747 - 1969. Bishop's collection on law, history/geography, maths (Newton), the enlightenment and social comment added similar breadth. Chapel: rebuilt by John 1st Lord Drummond 1508, renaissance triple cube, paintings, hatchments, medieval altar, upper room for library. Free access. Weddings etc. Historic Scotland. Events - Schools and Library friends. School: (rebuilt 1847) six sash windows, bell-cote, and passed 1889 inspection with 29 pupils. Innerpeffray Castle: private, built 1st Lord Madertie, admirable from a distance (countryside access code) - beautiful, if roofless, fortalice.

Mar-Oct Wed-Sat 10.00-12.45 & 14.00-16.45, Sun 14.00-16.00. Closed Sun am. Groups are welcome anytime by arrangement. Nov-Feb only open by appointment

A£5.00 C£Free. Group rates available on request. Special rates for researchers, school parties: charge for worksheets etc

J M Barrie's Birthplace
9 Brechin Road Kirriemuir Angus Strathclyde DD8 4BX
Tel: 01575 572646
In this two-storeyed house J M Barrie (1860-1937), the creator of Peter Pan, was born.

Macbeth Experience
Perthshire Visitor Centre Bankfoot Perth Perthshire PH1 4EB
Tel: 01738 787696
Witchcraft, tyranny, murder! All the key elements of Macbeth's story.

Writers' Museum
Lady Stair's Close Lawnmarket (Royal Mile) Edinburgh Midlothian EH1 2PA
Tel: 0131 529 4901
Dedicated to the lives and works of Scotland's great literary figures, in particular Robert Burns, Sir Walter Scott and Robert Louis Stevenson.

Callendar House
Callendar Park Falkirk Stirlingshire Scotland FK1 1YR
Tel: 01324 503770 Fax: 01324 503771
www.falkirk.gov.uk/cultural/museums/callho.htm

[E of Falkirk town centre on A803. Rail: Falkirk High / Grahamstone. Plenty of on-site parking available]

Imposing mansion within attractive parkland. Facilities include a working kitchen of 1825, where costumed interpreters carry out daily chores including cooking based on 1820s recipes. Exhibition area and 'Story of Callendar House' plus two temporary galleries, regularly changing exhibitions, a history research centre, gift shop and Georgian tea shop at the Stables. Major permanent exhibition 'William Forbes Falkirk' and working 1820s Store, Clockmaker and Printer, also the new Roman exhibition.

All year Mon-Sat 10.00-17.00, Apr-Sept Sun & Bank Hols 14.00-17.00
Admission Free

Discount Offer: 10% discount on all gift shop purchases (when you spend £10.00 or more)

Maritime

Britannia - The Royal Yacht

Ocean Terminal Leith Edinburgh EH6 6JJ
Tel: 0131 555 5566 Fax: 0131 555 8835
www.royalyachtbritannia.co.uk

[10min drive from Edinburgh city centre in Leith, signposted, or No. 22 bus from Princes St. Plenty of on-site parking available]

"Scotland's leading visitor-friendly attraction" BBC News. Visit The Royal Yacht Britannia, now in Edinburgh's historic port of Leith. The experience starts in the visitor centre where you can discover Britannia's fascinating story. Then step aboard for your complimentary self-led audio handset tour (available in 21 languages, children's handset available in English) which takes you around five decks giving you a unique insight into what life was like for the Royal Family, Officers and Yachtsmen. Highlights include the State Dining Room, the Drawing Room, the Sun Lounge, the Wardroom and the Chief Petty Officers' Mess. Good access for pushchairs and wheelchairs.

Daily Apr-Oct 9.30-16.30 (last admission), Nov-Mar 10.00-15.30 (last admission). Closed 25 Dec & 1 Jan

A£9.50 C(under5)£Free C(5-17)£5.50 OAPs£7.50 Family Ticket (A2+C3) £26.50

Discount Offer: 15% off Admission Prices

Scottish Fisheries Museum

St Ayles East Shore Harbour Head Anstruther Fife Scotland KY10 3AB
Tel: 01333 310628 Fax: 01333 310628
www.scotfishmuseum.org
[10mi S of St Andrews, signposted on A95]

The Scottish Fisheries Museum overlooks the ancient fishing harbour in Anstruther - in the old Kingdom of Fife. It is at the heart of the East Neuk fishing villages of St. Monans, Pittenweem, Cellardyke and Crail (the centre of local crab and lobster fishing). The museum researches (and tells the story of) the Scottish fishing industry and its people from its earliest recorded times to the present. The comprehensive collection includes ships, models, paintings, photographs, equipment and the written word. The museum occupies 27,600 square-feet around a cobbled courtyard. It is housed within a group of attractive buildings that are of historical and architectural interest. These include the eighteenth-century Merchant's Dwelling, the nineteenth-century Storehouse on the foundations of the Mediaeval Chapel of St Ayles and also the sixteenth-century Abbot's Lodging.
Apr-Sept Mon-Sat 10.00-17.30 Sun 10.00-16.30, Oct-Mar Mon-Sat 10.00-16.30 Sun 12.00-16.30
A£5.00 Concessions£4.00

Discount Offer: Accompanied Children Free

Scottish Maritime Museum

Laird Forge Gottries Road Irvine KA12 8QE
Tel: 01294 278283
Relive the heyday of Scotland's shipping.

Stromness Museum

52 Alfred Street Stromness Orkney Scotland
KW16 3DF
Tel: 01856 850025 Fax: 01856 871560
www.orkneyheritage.com

[0.5mi walk (or drive) S from Stromness Pier Head]

If you want a glimpse into Orkney's Natural History and Maritime Past, or to study it in more detail, Stromness Museum is a must. Since 1837 the museum has amassed a unique and fascinating collection which has something for everyone. Learn how to survive in the arctic through displays about Dr John Rae, Sir John Franklin and the Arctic Whalers. Find out about local connections with The Hudson Bay Company and the Canadian Fur Trade. On show are artefacts salvaged from the German fleet which was scuttled in Scapa Flow in 1919, in sight of Stromness. The recently refurbished Victorian Natural History Gallery has a magnificent bird collection complemented by displays of eggs, fossils, sea creatures, mammals, butterflies and moths. Also available are kids activities and a photographic archive. You will enjoy your visit, all you have to do is get here! Changing summer exhibition: Hands Across the Sea and Orkney's History Links with Canada.
Apr-Sept daily 10.00-17.00, Oct-Mar Mon-Sat 11.00-15.30. Closed mid Feb-mid Mar
A£3.00 C(school age)£0.50 Concessions£2.00, Family Ticket (A2+C2) £6.00, Entry ticket is valid for 1 week

Discount Offer: 10% discount on all gift shop purchases (when you spend £10.00 or more)

Military & Defence Museums

Gordon Highlanders Museum

St Luke's Viewfield Road Aberdeen Grampian
AB15 7XH
Tel: 01224 311200
At the Gordon Highlanders Museum, you can re-live the compelling and dramatic story of one of the British Army's most famous regiments.

National War Museum Scotland

Edinburgh Castle Edinburgh Scotland EH1 2NG
Tel: 0131 247 4413 Fax: 0131 225 3848
www.nms.ac.uk
[Follow signs for Edinburgh Castle throughout central Edinburgh]

A force to be reckoned with? War and military service have touched the lives of countless Scots, leaving their mark on Scotland's history, image and reputation abroad. Here, in the magnificent setting of Edinburgh Castle, explore over 400 years of the Scottish military experience. Uncover stories of courage and determination, victory and defeat, heroics and heartbreak.
All year daily, Nov-Mar 09.45-16.45, Apr-Oct 09.45-17.45
Entry to the Museum is free with admission to Edinburgh Castle. A£11.00 C£4.50 Concessions£9.00, Members receive free or reduced entry to all five National Museums Scotland

Scotland's Secret Bunker

Crown Buildings Troywood St. Andrews Fife
Scotland KY16 8QH
Tel: 01333 310301 Fax: 01333 312040
www.secretbunker.co.uk
*[7mi from St Andrews, signposted off B9131 &
B940. Plenty of on-site parking available]*

Scotland's Secret Bunker has been Scotland's
best kept secret for over 40 years. An innocent
looking farmhouse conceals the entrance to an
amazing labyrinth built 100 feet below ground.
Government Command Control Centre, radar
rooms, BBC broadcast rooms, operations
room, dormitories, two cinemas, a café... a
legacy of the Cold War. Take the opportunity to
discover how they would have survived and you
wouldn't! One of Scotland's deepest and best
kept secrets.
27 Mar-31 Oct daily 10.00-18.00
A£7.20 C£4.50 OAPs£5.95, Family Ticket
£22.00

Discount Offer: One Child Free

Museum of Lead Mining

Wanlockhead Dumfrieshire ML12 6UT
Tel: 01659 74387
Explore over 300 years of mining history.
1 Apr-31 Oct

National Museum of Scotland

Chambers Street Edinburgh Scotland EH1 1JF
Tel: 0131 247 4422 Fax: 0131 220 4819
www.nms.ac.uk

*[In heart of Old Town, a few min walk from
Princes St & Royal Mile. By bus: Number of
buses go via city & stop at George IV Bridge or
South Bridge. Rail: nearest Edinburgh Waverley,
few min walk. Road: Follow signs for city centre.
Pay & display parking on Chambers St with off-
street car parking nearby]*

Our collections cover life, the universe and
everything in it. From science and art to nature
and outer space. What influence has the rest of
the world had on Scotland and Scotland on it?
How has the face of the nation changed over
the centuries? Find the answers to all the big
questions (and some tricky little ones as well) at
the National Museum of Scotland. You can also
enjoy special exhibitions, free tours and events
for all ages, throughout the year.
All year daily 10.00-17.00. Closed 25 Dec
Admission Free. There may be a charge for
special exhibitions/events. Members receive free
or reduced entry to all five National Museums
Scotland and some charging exhibitions

Natural History Museums

Bute Museum
Stuart Street Rothesay Isle of Bute PA20 OEP
Tel: 01700 505067
The contents are all from the Isle of Bute, and
are housed in two galleries.

Nature & Conservation Parks

Grey Mare's Tail
Moffat Valley Dumfries and Galloway
Tel: 0844 493 2249
A spectacular 61-metre (200-ft) waterfall in a
hillside near Moffat. A visitor centre offers CCTV
views of a peregrine falcon nest and a
panoramic view of hillside features.

Scottish Seabird Centre
The Harbour North Berwick East Lothian
Scotland EH39 4SS
Tel: 01620 890202 Fax: 01620 890222
www.seabird.org
*[From Edinburgh follow A1 to North Berwick, fol-
low tourist signs to Scottish Seabird Centre]*

Escape to another world at this stunning five
star wildlife visitor centre! Exhilarating sea air
and breathtaking panoramic views over the sea
and beautiful sandy beaches. See wildlife really
close up with the amazing live interactive 'Big
Brother' cameras. Puffins spring cleaning their
burrows, gannets with fluffy white chicks, seals
sunning themselves and sometimes dolphins
and whales. Wildlife theatre, films, talks and a
packed programme of festivals and events. A
great day out - whatever the weather. Licensed
cafe/bistro with deck overlooking the sea. Boat
trips to the islands. Well-stocked shop. Full disabled facilities including on-site parking.
Environment Zone and Migration Flyway!
*All year daily: Apr-Sep 10.00-18.00, Feb-Mar &
Oct Mon-Fri 10.00-17.00 Sat & Sun 10.00-
17.30, Nov-Jan Mon-Fri 10.00-16.00 Sat & Sun
10.00-17.30. Closed 25 Dec*
A£6.95 C&OAPs£4.50, Family Tickets from
£13.95. Group rates available on request

Discount Offer: One Child Free

On the Water

Falkirk Wheel, The
Lime Road Tamfourhill Falkirk Stirlingshire
Scotland FK1 4RS
Tel: 08700 500208
As the world's only rotating boatlift, The Falkirk
Wheel towers above everything.

Jacobite Cruises, Loch Ness
Tomnahurich Bridge Glenurquhart Road
Inverness Invernes-shire IV3 5TD
Tel: 01463 233999
Company ships sail along the Caledonian Canal
and on to Loch Ness.
Mar-Oct trips daily

Palaces

Bishop's Palace and Earl's Palace
Watergate Kirkwall Orkney KW15 1PD
Tel: 01856 871918
The Bishop's Palace is a half-house of twelfth-
century date, later much altered, with a round
tower built by Bishop Reid in 1541-48.
Open Summer only

Linlithgow Palace

Linlithgow Lothian EH49 7AL
Tel: 01506 842896
The magnificent ruin of a great Royal Palace.

Scone Palace

Scone Perth Perthshire Scotland PH2 6BD
Tel: 01738 552300 Fax: 01738 552588
www.scone-palace.co.uk

[2mi N of Perth on A93. Plenty of on-site parking available]

Family home of the Earl of Mansfield, Scone Palace houses a magnificent and varied collection of works of art. Scone Palace is set in mature and historic grounds, with an adventure playground and the Murray Star Maze. Once the crowning place of the Kings of Scots, Scone offers a fascinating day out for all the family. Also features 'I' Spy for children and a children's grounds trail. Exterior photography permitted.

1 Apr-31 Oct daily 09.30-17.30. Grounds close at 18.00. Special groups at other times and winter by arrangement
Palace & Grounds: A£7.50 C£4.50 Concessions£6.50. Grounds only: A£4.00 C£2.75 Concessions£3.65. Group rates available on request. Guidebooks: £4.00

Discount Offer: Two for the Price of One

Places of Worship

Dunblane Cathedral

The Cross Dunblane Fife and Central
Tel: 01786 825388
One of Scotland's noblest medieval churches. The lower part of the tower is Romanesque, but the larger part is of the thirteenth century. It was restored in 1889-93 by Sir Rowand Anderson. The museum contains a collection of artefacts, archives and pictures concerning the history of Dunblane and it's cathedral. There is a library also.

Elgin Cathedral

North College Street Elgin Morayshire IV30 1EL
Tel: 01343 547171
The superb ruin of what many think was Scotland's most beautiful cathedral.

Glasgow Cathedral

Cathedral Square Glasgow Lanarkshire G4 0QZ
Tel: 0141 552 6891
Glasgow Cathedral is built on the site where St Kentigern, or Mungo, the first bishop within the ancient British kingdom of Strathclyde.

St Andrews Cathedral and St. Rule's Tower

St. Andrews Fife and Central
Tel: 01334 472563
The remains of what was Scotland's largest and most magnificent church still show how impressive St Andrew's Cathedral must have been.

St Magnus Cathedral

Broad Street Kirkwall Orkney
Tel: 01856 874894
Contains some of Britain's finest medieval grave markers and beautiful Oscar Paterson stained glass.

Police, Prisons & Dungeons

Inveraray Jail

Church Square Inveraray Argyll Scotland
PA32 8TX
Tel: 01499 302381 Fax: 01499 302195
www.inverarayjail.co.uk

[From Glasgow: A82 N along Loch Lomond to Tarbert then the A83 round the head of Loch Fyne to Inveraray (allow 90min). From Oban: A85 N to Connel, Taynuilt & Loch Awe - turn R onto A819 to Inveraray (allow 1h)]

Inveraray Jail is an award winning living nine-teenth-century jail and museum. It was the original jail for the Argyll area, and has now been developed into one of the most popular visitor attractions in the west of Scotland. The Jail contains the imposing Courthouse, where you can listen to the actual trials from its own records; the original prison dating back to 1820 where men and women were held in over-crowded, damp conditions, the new prison, built in 1848, and the airing yards. There is also an interesting exhibition on 'Torture, Death and Damnation' over the previous four hundred years, and finally a visitor shop selling a wide variety of souvenirs. Visitors have the opportunity to meet a 'prisoner', 'warder' and 'matron', all dressed in authentic costume, who will be happy to answer any questions as well as giving a lively insight into life in the prison.
All year Apr-Oct 09.30-18.00 Nov-Mar 10.00-17.00
A£6.50 C£3.50 OAPs£4.95 Groups rates are available on request

Discount Offer: One Child Free

Railways

Bo'ness and Kinneil Railway

Bo'ness Station Union Street Bo'ness
West Lothian Scotland EH51 9AQ
Tel: 01506 822298 Fax: 01506 828766
www.srps.org.uk/railway/

[Rail: Linlithgow, Falkirk Grahamston]

Welcome to the living museum of Scotland's Railways! There's so much to see and do, but one of the highlights of your visit must be the thrill of travelling in a train behind a lovingly restored historic locomotive from the collection of listed buildings that make up Bo'ness Station. This is a journey that runs along the shores of the Forth and delivers you to Birkhill, with its lovely woodlands and fascinating fireclay mine. When you get back to Bo'ness, why not visit the Scottish Railway Exhibition? It contains a large selection from our collection of locomotives, carriages and wagons, as well as models and displays that tell the history of railways in Scotland. There are a few surprises too - particularly the signs that encourage you to climb onto and explore some of the exhibits! Throughout the season we have special events for all the family - please see our website for details.
Apr-Oct Sat-Sun, 1 July-26 Aug daily - see website for further details
A£5.00 C£2.50 Concessions£4.00, Family Ticket (A2+C2) £13.00

Discount Offer: One Free Child Fare

CairnGorm Mountain Railway

Aviemore Inverness-shire Scotland PH22 1RB
Tel: 01479 861261
The CairnGorm Funicular is the country's highest and fastest mountain railway. Panoramic views, exhibition and shop.

Keith and Dufftown Railway

Dufftown Station Dufftown Banffshire Scotland
AB55 4BA
Tel: 01340 821181
Eleven-mile heritage line operating in the summer months. The line passes through some of Scotland's most picturesque scenery, with forest and farmland, lochs and glens, castles and distilleries.

Strathspey Steam Railway

Aviemore Station Dalfaber Road Aviemore
Inverness-shire Scotland PH22 1PY
Tel: 01479 810725 Fax: 01479 812220
www.strathspeyrailway.co.uk
[Off B970, signposted. Plenty of on-site parking available]

This steam railway runs the 9.5 miles between Aviemore, Boat of Garten and Broomhill, near the villages of Nethybridge and Dulnain Bridge. Broomhill is also the location for station scenes in 'Monarch of The Glen'. A round trip takes approximately ninety minutes. You can join the train at any of the stations. The railway runs through heather moorland between Aviemore and Boat of Garten. From there onwards the 'strath' opens out into rolling farmland. The Cairngorm Mountains provide a backdrop throughout. Refreshments are available on most trains. Sunday lunch, served at your seat, booking advisable, also available on Fridays 1 June-28 September. Evening Diner trains run Wednesdays and Fridays from 1 June-14 September, pre-booking required. On most Saturdays the train is made up to resemble a branch line operation and no catering is available on such trains.

Trains run June-Sept daily, Apr, May & Oct Wed-Thur, Sat-Sun & Bank Hol Mon. Call for a timetable
Round Trip: A£9.50 C£4.75, Family Ticket (A2+C3) £24.00. Day Rover Tickets: A£12.00 C£6.00, Family Ticket (A2+C3) £30.00

Roman Era

Bearsden Bathhouse

Bearsden South Strathclyde
Tel: 0131 668 8600
The well preserved remains of a bathhouse and latrine, built in the second century AD to serve a small fort.

Roman Bath-House

Roman Road Bearsden Glasgow Lanarkshire
G61 2SG
Tel: 0131 668 8800
Considered to be the best surviving visible Roman building in Scotland, the bath-house was discovered in 1973 during excavations for a construction site. It was originally built for use by the Roman garrison at Bearsden Fort, which is part of the Antonine Wall defences.

Seabegs Wood

Bonny Bridge Fife and Central
Tel: 0131 668 8600
Part of Antonine Wall Monuments; The wall, Rome's north-west frontier, ran for 37 miles from Bo'ness to Old Kilpatrick. It consisted of a turf rampart fronted by a ditch; there were forts about every 2 miles. The wall was built in the 140s AD and occupied for about 20 years.

Royal

Palace of Holyroodhouse
Edinburgh Scotland EH8 8DX
Tel: 0131 556 5100
An official residence of Her Majesty The Queen.
Exhibitions from the Royal Collection.

Science - Earth & Planetary

Camera Obscura and World of Illusions
Castlehill Royal Mile Edinburgh EH1 2LZ
Tel: 0131 226 3709
A magical 1850s 'cinema' giving a unique experience of Edinburgh.

Glasgow Science Centre
50 Pacific Quay Glasgow Scotland G51 1EA
Tel: 0141 420 5010
With hundreds of interactive exhibits based over 3 floors, the Science Mall also offers live science shows, workshops and demonstrations.

Our Dynamic Earth
Holyrood Road Edinburgh Scotland EH8 8AS
Tel: 0131 550 7800
Our Dynamic Earth is a fantastic journey of discovery suitable for visitors of all ages and abilities.

Satrosphere
The Tramsheds 179 Constitution Street
Aberdeen Aberdeenshire AB24 5TU
Tel: 01224 640340
Exhibits, shows and events. Step inside a bubble; meet Mac, the robotic dog; make a skeleton ride a bike; or see some really disgusting demonstrations in Urgghh! Science.

Sealife Centres & Aquariums

Deep Sea World, Scotland's Shark Capital
Forthside Terrace Queensferry Fife KY11 1JR
Tel: 01383 411880
Boasts a large collection of sand tiger sharks.

Macduff Marine Aquarium
11 High Shore Macduff Aberdeenshire
AB44 1SL
Tel: 01261 833369 Fax: 01261 831052
www.macduff-aquarium.org.uk
[1hr N Aberdeen on A947, 90min E of Inverness on A98. Plenty of on-site parking available]
Situated on Aberdeenshire's scenic north coast, Macduff Marine Aquarium offers a fascinating view into the underwater world of the Moray Firth. The aquarium's central exhibit contains a living community of seaweeds, fish and invertebrates normally only seen by scuba divers. Visitors come face to face with hundreds of local fishy characters, from fearsome wolf fish to ancient lobsters, and can watch them from several viewing windows. Several times a week divers hand feed the fish in the main tank. Other innovative displays include a ray pool, rock pools, a splash tank, estuary and deep reef displays. Visitors get a chance to get a feel for seashore life at the touch pools. There are also special talks, videos and feeding shows throughout the week, and quizzes for kids. The aquarium is great fun for people of all ages. Tickets valid all day.
All year daily 10.00-17.00. Closed 25-26 & 31 Dec, 1-2 Jan
A£5.20 C£2.60 OAP£3.20, Family Ticket £14.25

Scottish Sea Life Sanctuary

Barcaldine Oban Argyll Scotland PA37 1SE
Tel: 01631 720386 Fax: 01631 720529
www.sealsanctuary.co.uk

[On A828. Plenty of on-site parking available]

The Scottish Sea Life Sanctuary near Oban on the west coast of Scotland unveils in 2007 Seal Experience - an exciting chance to learn more about the Rescue Rehabilitation and Release of seals back into the wild. See them playing through our underwater observation area and learn more about their amazing lives at daily feeding demonstrations. Meet our resident seals and find out how they found a home at our Sanctuary. The chance to see our playful North American River Otters Fingal and Sula, the diverse native marine aquarium, the opportunity to get close to some of the curious creatures that reside in the local waters at the Loch Creran are more than enough incentive for any potential visitor. Presentation visitors. Presentations and feeding demonstrations throughout the day provide a deeper insight into all of our fascinating creatures and how you can protect their future. Enjoy a woodlands walk or relax in our café to truly appreciate the nature and wildlife of the area will truly complete your day. Scotland's leading marine conservation experience has something for everyone. Guided tours can be organised by prior arrangement.
All year daily from 10.00, 12.00 on New Years Day. Closed Christmas Day
Please call for admission prices

Discount Offer: One Child Free

St Andrews Aquarium

The Scores St. Andrews Fife KY16 9AS
Tel: 01334 474786
From shrimp to sharks, octopus to eels, rays to seals - and now our Amazonian displays including the deadly piranha.
Easter-Oct

Social History Museums

Auchindrain Township - Open Air Museum

Furnace Inveraray Argyll PA32 8XN
Tel: 01499 500235
Auchindrain is an original West Highland township, or village, of great antiquity.

Highland Folk Museum

Aultlarie Croft Newtonmore Inverness-Shire PH20 1AY
Tel: 01540 661307
This award winning museum has transformed 300 years of history by recreating a thriving township from the 1700s, a working croft with old breed horses, cattle, ducks and farm machinery and an old, tin highland school where the teacher rules!

Highland Folk Museum

Duke Street Kingussie Inverness-Shire PH21 1JG
Tel: 01540 661307
This unique and extensive collection of everyday domestic objects, together with major exhibits of furniture, machinery and implements connected with the countryside.

Ullapool Museum and Visitor Centre

7 & 8 West Argyle Street Ullapool Ross-Shire IV26 2TY
Tel: 01854 612987
An audio-visual presentation and exhibitions on natural history, social history, emigration, fishing, religion, education with touch screens.

Spectator Sports

Perth Racecourse

Scone Palace Park Perth Perthshire Scotland
PH2 6BB
Tel: 01738 551597 Fax: 01738 553021
www.perth-races.co.uk

[2mi from city centre off A93. Rail: Perth. Nearest airports are Glasgow or Edinburgh. Plenty of free on-site parking available]

Get your heart racing... Race days at Perth are more than just great horse racing, Perth Races are a great day out for all the family. The new Nelson Stand opened in April 2005 with a unique dining experience overlooking the course. Perth is one of the most beautiful race-courses in the UK. Horses have been racing at Scone Palace Park since 1908. Come and experience the special atmosphere at Perth and be part of it's future. Superb hospitality pack-ages and a wide range of restaurant and licensed bar facilities make the racecourse a perfect venue for group entertainment. Additional pre-race entertainment features on major racedays. Best small racecourse in Scotland and North East 2006.
Race meetings Apr-Sept every year. The commit-ments - playing live after racing on 31st July 2007 Grandstand Enclosure £15.00. Centre Course £10.00. C(under16)£Free. Discounts available for advance bookings of 15+, please call for more details at least one week before race date. Book tickets on the website for any race meet-ing in 2007

Sport & Recreation

Craigluscar Activities

The Cottage Craigluscar Farm Dunfermline Fife
Scotland KY12 9HT
Tel: 01383 738429 Fax: 01383 738429
www.craigluscar.co.uk

[Plenty of on-site parking available]

We offer various activities for large or small par-ties. Quad Biking - trail ride over hill and forest tracks with spectacular views over the Forth val-ley. Hovercraft - try your hand at flying a single seat hovercraft. Clay Target Shooting - after some tuition start hitting moving targets. Snowcat - have a trip in the ultimate off-road vehicle.
All year

Holyrood Park

Edinburgh Lothian SC1
Tel: 0131 652 8150
Within the park is a wealth of history and archaeology spanning thousands of years.

Nevis Range

Torlundy Fort William Inverness-shire PH33 6SW
Tel: 01397 705825 / 705855
Scotland's highest ski area is a winter wonder-land for enthusiasts and sightseers alike.

Scotkart Indoor Karting Centre

Westburn Rd Cambuslang Glasgow G72 7UD
Tel: 0141 641 0222
Challenge your friends to a full throttle race to the chequered flag!

XScape: Braehead

Kings Inch Road Braehead Renfrew
Renfrewshire Scotland PA4 8XQ
Tel: 0871 200 3222
Features real snow slopes, urban retailers, bars
and restaurants, a cinema, family attractions
and extreme sports all under one roof.

Sporting History Museums

British Golf Museum

Bruce Embankment St. Andrews Fife KY16 9AB
Tel: 01334 460046
The British Golf Museum uses diverse displays
to explore the history of the game.

Scottish Football Museum

Hampden Park Letherby Drive Glasgow
G42 9BA
Tel: 0141 616 6139
Scotland's football heritage, remembering the
legends. Include the Hampden Stadium Tour.

Theme & Adventure Parks

Cairnie Mega Maze

Cairnie Lodge Cupar Fife Scotland KY15 4QD
Tel: 01334 655610
A Mega Maze ticket holder will have unlimited
use of the 'funyard' which will feature go-karts,
a huge sand pit with diggers, a straw bale
climbing fortress, trampolines, hammock and
other dino surprises! 'Pick Your Own' strawberries, raspberries or other soft fruit.

David Livingstone Centre

165 Station Road Blantyre Glasgow Lanarkshire
G72 9BT
Tel: 01698 823140
Scotland's most famous explorer and mission-
ary was born here in Shuttlerow in 1813.

Edinburgh Dungeon

31 Market Street Edinburgh Scotland EH1 1QB
Tel: 0131 240 1000 Fax: 0131 240 1002
www.thedungeons.com

[Next to Waverley Bridge]

The Edinburgh Dungeon invites you to a unique
feat of fun with history's horrible bits. Live
actors, an eerie ride, shows and special effects
transport you back to those black bleak times.
Are you brave enough? You'll be exposed to
torture, witchcraft, grave robbing, the plague,
cannibalism and of course murder! Your journey
into the dungeon begins in a seventeenth-century court of law where an eccentric judge will
haul you into the dock! Visitors are accused of a
range of heinous crimes where the verdict is
always 'guilty' and the punishment is always
harsh! A scary new Ghost feature is coming to
the Edinburgh Dungeon from Easter 2007! Will
you hold your nerve as you enter the paranormal world and be confronted by a vengeful
ghostly presence…or will it leave you paralysed
with fear? With all this and more, the Edinburgh
Dungeon is the scariest attraction in Scotland,
where you're never quite sure what's behind
you and things have a nasty habit of coming
back to life!
*Nov-Mid Mar 11.00-16.00, Sat & Sun 10.30-
16.30, Mid Mar-June 10.00-17.00, July-Aug
10.00-19.00, Sept-Oct 10.00-17.00*
A£11.95 Concessions£9.95 C£8.95

Discount Offer: One Child Free

Go Ape! High Wire Forest Adventure

Queen Elizabeth Forest Park Aberfoyle
Stirlingshire Scotland FK8 3UX
Tel: 0870 420 7876
www.goape.co.uk
[From Glasgow follow signs on M8 for Aberfoyle. From Stirling/Callander follow A81 to Aberfoyle via Dukes Pass. Plenty of on-site parking available]
Take to the trees and experience an exhilarating course of rope bridges, 'Tarzan Swings' and zip-slides up to 40 feet above the ground! Share approximately three hours of memorable fun and adventure, which you'll be talking about for days. Book online and watch people Go Ape! at www.goape.co.uk. Minimum height 1.4m. Maximum weight 130 kg (20.5 stone). Under-18s must be accompanied by a participating adult. One adult can supervise either two children (where one or both of them in under 16 years old) or up to five 16-17 year olds. Pre-booking is essential to avoid disappointment. Book online or by telephone (there is a £1.00 booking fee on all telephone bookings).
23 Mar-2 Nov (plus Nov weekends). Closed Dec-Jan
Gorillas (18yrs+) £25.00, Baboons (10-17yrs) £20.00

Discount Offer: Two for the Price of One

Landmark Forest Theme Park

Carrbridge Inverness-Shire PH23 3AJ
Tel: 0800 7313446
Fun, discovery and adventure for all ages

M and D's Scotland's Theme Park

Strathclyde Country Park Motherwell
Lanarkshire Scotland ML1 3RT
Tel: 0870 112 3777
Fax: 01698 303034 / 338733
www.scotlandsthemepark.com

[Plenty of on-site parking available]

At Scotland's biggest and best value Theme Park there is something for everyone. With over 40 major rides and attractions it really is "Too much fun for just one day". This season M&D's is home to the roller coaster, with white knuckle coasters, the Tsunami and the Tornado and the kids get their very own coaster too the Big Apple. If that's not enough this season M&D's have invested millions of pound in a brand new coaster, The Run Away Mine Train! There are also the old favorites, The Wave Swinger, Flying Carpet, White Water Rapids, three in one water slide, Moby's Revenge and much much more. There are loads for our younger visitors too including, the Crazy Boot, Seastorm, Pony Express, Dropzone, Flying Bees and many more. There's also our 18 hole mini adventure golf, fun for all the family. Don't forget our multi million pound indoor complex including, indoor bowling, softplay, Amazonia, tropical rainforest, American Pools hall, bars, restaurants, coffee shop and the list goes on. Keep up to date with our new website.
Admission Free. Unlimited Ride Band: Over 1.35m £14.95, Under 1.35m £10.95

Discount Offer: £5.00 off One Unlimited Ride Wristband (for a famlly of 4)

Wildlife & Safari Parks

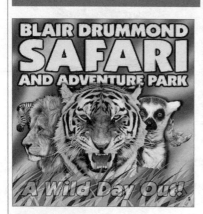

Blair Drummond Safari and Adventure Park

Blair Drummond By Stirling Scotland FK9 4UR
Tel: 01786 841456 Fax: 01786 841491
www.blairdrummond.com

[J10 M9 4mi along A84 towards Callander signposted on M9 & A84. On-site parking available]

Drive through our wild animal reserves and see rhinos, giraffes, elephants, lions, tigers, bears, zebra, bison and much more. Wander through Pets' Farm and see donkeys, llamas, ponies, pigs, penguins, lemurs, otters and meerkats. Sit back, relax and enjoy our sea lion shows and birds of prey displays. Take a boat Safari to visit our chimps on their island. Barbecues are available on request with undercover area if required. Enjoy a meal in our restaurant or cafes but if you prefer to bring your own we have picnic tables and benches. The kids will enjoy our adventure playground which includes its very own pirate ship with buried treasure!! Finish off your day with a souvenir from one of our gift shops. Facilities are available for Special Needs and visitors with young children.

24 Mar-22 Oct daily 10.00-17.30

A£10.00 C(under3)£Free C/OAPs&Special Needs £6.50 Carers £2.00. Free kennels at entrance for dogs

Discount Offer: One Child Free

Galloway Wildlife Conservation Park

Lochfergus Plantation Kirkcudbright
Dumfries and Galloway DG6 4XX

Tel: 01557 331645 Fax: 01557 331645
www.gallowaywildlife.co.uk
[1mi from Kirkcudbright on B727. Turn up hill at Royal Hotel. Signposted from A75. Plenty of on-site parking available]

A varied collection of over 120 animals from all over the world can be seen within the peaceful and natural settings in the woodlands. Endangered species to be seen at the park including red pandas, maned wolves, otters, lemurs and, of course, our famous Scottish wildcats! Woodland walk and close animal encounters.

Dec-Jan Fri-Sun 10.00-16.00, Feb-Nov daily 10.00-18.00

A£5.00 C(4-16)£3.00 C(under4)£Free
OAPs£4.00

Discount Offer: One Child Free

Zoos

Edinburgh Zoo

Corstorphine Road Edinburgh Scotland
EH12 6TS
Tel: 0131 334 9171
Scotland's largest and most exciting wildlife attraction!

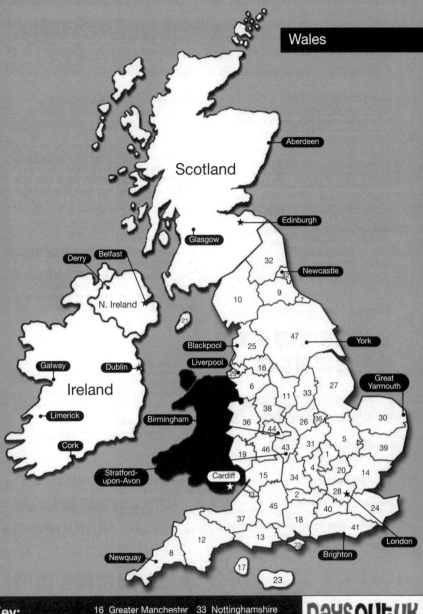

Wales

Aberdeen

Scotland

Edinburgh

Glasgow

Derry
Belfast

N. Ireland

Newcastle

32
42
9
7
10
47 York

21

Blackpool
25
16
Liverpool
29
27 Great Yarmouth
6
11 33
30
38
26 35
36
44
5
43
19 46
31
39
15
34
20 14
13
2
28 London
45
40
24
37
18
41
22
Brighton
12
13

Galway
Dublin
Ireland
Limerick
Cork

Birmingham

Stratford-upon-Avon

Cardiff

Newquay

8

17

23

Agriculture / Working Farms

Greenmeadow Community Farm

Greenforge Way Cwmbran Gwent NP44 5AJ
Tel: 01633 862202 Fax: 01633 489332

[1mi W of Cwmbran town centre. Bus: Nos 5 or 63. Plenty of on-site parking available]

Just four miles from the M4, this is one of Wales' leading farm attractions - milking demonstrations, tractor and trailer rides, dragon adventure play area, farm trail, nature trail and lots more. Phone for details of lambing weekends, shearing, country fair and agricultural shows, Halloween and Christmas events.
All year daily, summer 10.00-18.00, winter 10.00-16.30. Closed 23 Dec-1 Feb
A£4.50 C&Concessions£3.50, Family Ticket (A2+C3) £16.00. Group rates available on request

Discount Offer: One Child Free

Animal Attractions

Haulfre Stables

Haulfre Gardens Llangoed Beaumaris Anglesey Wales LL58 8RY
Tel: 01248 490709 / 724444
Fax: 01248 750282
www.angleseyheritage.co.uk
[Plenty of on-site parking available]
Haulfre is a small equestrian museum and restored stables. This modest but fascinating museum has an interesting collection of Victorian harness and saddlery, carts and carriages and other equestrian and transport material dating from an earlier age when horses were vital for transport, for agriculture and for haulage of heavy goods. Haulfre also offers an insight into the work of the grooms, coachmen and stable boys, who cared for the horses and the leisure pursuits of a country gentleman. Everything is housed in a historic stable block.

Easter-Sept (by appointment only)
Please telephone for admission prices

Art Galleries

Aberystwyth Arts Centre

Penglais Aberystwyth Ceredigion SY23 3DE
Tel: 01970 623232
Situated on the university campus and has panoramic views over Cardigan Bay. The centre offers busy year long programme of live events, cinema, exhibitions and courses.

Chapter

Market Road Canton Cardiff CF5 1QE
Tel: 02920 304400
Chapter has an international reputation for excellence, innovation and collaboration.

g39

Wyndham Arcade Mill Lane Cardiff CF10 1FH
Tel: 029 2025 5541
An artist-run initiative providing exhibiting opportunities for unestablished artists and graduates.

Model House Craft and Design Centre

Bull Ring Llantrisant Pontyclun Mid Glamorgan CF72 8EB
Tel: 01443 237758
A superb, contemporary craft centre. The Craft Council listed Gallery Shop sells quality work from top UK makers.

National Museum: Cardiff

Cathays Park Cardiff Cardiff County CF10 3NP
Tel: 029 2039 7951
Discover art, archaeology, natural history and geology. With a busy programme of exhibitions and events, there is something for everyone.

Arts, Crafts and Textiles

Makers' Guild: Craft in the Bay

The Flourish Lloyd George Avenue Cardiff Bay
Wales CF10 4QH
Tel: 029 2048 4611
A retail gallery that hosts exhibitions, demonstrations and activities all year round.

National Wool Museum

Dre-Fach Felindre Llandysul Carmarthenshire
Wales SA44 5UP
Tel: 01559 370929
A comprehensive display tracing the evolution of
the industry.

Newport Museum and Art Gallery

John Frost Square Newport Gwent NP9 1PA
Tel: 01633 656656
[Newport town centre]

Natural science displays including geology; fine
and applied art, specialising in early English
watercolours, teapots and contemporary crafts;
prehistoric finds from Gwont and Romano-
British remains from Caerwent; local history
including the Chartist movement. Regular exhibitions and associated activities.
*All year Mon-Thur 09.30-17.00 Fri 09.30-16.30
Sat 09.30-16.00*
Admission Free

Oriel Ynys Môn History and Art Gallery

Rhosmeirch Llangefni Anglesey LL77 7TQ
Tel: 01248 724444 Fax: 01248 750282
www.angleseyheritage.co.uk
[Plenty of on-site parking available]

Anglesey's premier purpose built museum and
art gallery. History Gallery: a fascinating insight
into the island's culture, history and environment. Art Gallery: a dynamic and changing programme of exhibitions, encompassing art, craft,
drama, sculpture and social history. Concerts,
events, workshops for adults and children, open
days, courses for all ages, shop and café.
Mon-Sun & Bank Hol Mon 10.30-17.00
Admission Free

Rhiannon Welsh Gold Centre

Main Square Tregaron Ceredigion SY25 6JL
Tel: 01974 298415
A unique collection of fine and unusual gifts,
gathered together from all the Celtic countries,
that reflect our rich cultural heritage.

Ruthin Craft Centre

Park Road Ruthin Denbighshire LL15 1BB
Tel: 01824 704774
The main gallery at Ruthin Craft Centre is listed
on the Crafts Council's national list of Craft
Shops and Galleries.

Welsh Royal Crystal

5 Brynberth Industrial Estate East Street
Rhayader Powys LD6 5EN
Tel: 01597 811005
Visit the Welsh Masters of Fire and Glass.

Wrexham Arts Centre

Rhosddu Road Wrexham Wales LL11 1AU
Tel: 01978 292093
A centre for excellence for contemporary visual
arts. Programme of temporary exhibitions.

For great hotel deals call Superbreak on 01904 679999 or visit www.superbreak.com

FELINWYNT RAINFOREST CENTRE

A glimpse into a miniforest with tropical butterflies and the sounds of the Peruvian-Amazon.

- Cafe • Gift Shop • Exhibition • Video Room • Picture Colouring for the Gallery
- **Wales Tourist Board Quality Assured Visitor Attraction**
- National Category ~ Winner Loo of the Year

Open everyday Easter to October 10.30am-5pm (11am-4pm during October) - Suitable for disabled
Felinwynt Rainforest Centre is in West Wales, 6 miles north of Cardigan. Follow signs from the A487
**Tel: 01239 810250 / 810882
www.butterflycentre.co.uk**

Birds, Butterflies & Bees

Felinwynt Rainforest Centre

Felinwynt Cardigan Ceredigion Wales SA43 1RT
**Tel: 01239 810250 / 810882
Fax: 01239 810465
www.butterflycentre.co.uk**

[From A487 (Cardigan-Aberystwyth) turn onto B4333 at Airfield, follow Rainforest signposts.

Plenty of on-site parking available]

Felinwynt Rainforest Centre has become one of Ceredigion's chief attractions with thousands of visitors every year. The highlight of any visit is the mini-rainforest created by owner John Devereux. Wander through a jungle among tropical plants, exotic butterflies, waterfalls, pools and fish, with the soothing sounds of the Peruvian Rainforest. The video room shows films of rainforests and butterflies and is free to all customers. The visitor centre houses the gift shop with an extensive range of gifts for everyone, the café where you can have freshly cooked meals and snacks all day, including Dorothy's homemade cakes, and the exhibition based on the Tambopata region of Peru. All facilities are suitable for disabled visitors. Entrance charge applies to Tropical House only. A warm welcome awaits at this Wales Tourist Board Quality Assured visitor attraction. National Winner of Loo of the Year 2005/2006.
Easter-31 Oct daily 10.30-17.00 (11.00-16.00 Oct)
A£3.95 C(3-14)£1.95 C(under 2)£Free OAPs£3.75

Discount Offer: Two for the Price of One

Red Kite Feeding Centre and Nature Trail

Gigrin Farm South Street Rhayader Powys LD6 5BL
Tel: 01597 810243
Wild red kites are fed at Gigrin Farm every day of the year. With breathtaking feats of aerial piracy, red kites compete with buzzards and ravens for choice pickings.

Welsh Hawking Centre

Weycock Road Barry South Glamorgan CF62 3AA
Tel: 01446 734687
There are over 200 birds of prey here, including eagles, owls and buzzards as well as hawks and falcons.

WWT National Wetland Centre Wales

Llwynhendy Llanelli Carmarthenshire Wales
SA14 9SH
Tel: 01554 741087 Fax: 01554 744101
www.wwt.org.uk
*[Off A484 10min from J47 or J48 M4 follow
brown-duck signs. On-site parking available]*
The award-winning National Wetlands Centre
Wales (one of the world-famous WWT centres)
is situated on the northern shore of the Bury
Inlet, with stunning views over the estuary and
Gower. Whether you're a serious bird-watcher
or just looking for family fun and relaxation, you
can enjoy a day of discovery all year round,
whatever the weather. Bring your own binoculars or hire them at the centre - you'll want a
closer look at the amazing wildlife that inhabits
this important national site. The landscape
grounds with acres of pond, lakes, streams and
reed-beds provide a picturesque home for hundreds of the world's most spectacular ducks,
geese, swans and flamingos - many of which
are so tame, they'll feed from your hand. During
summertime be sure to see lots of ducklings,
cygnets, goslings and flamingo chicks. There's
also a hands-on 'Discovery Centre' and outdoor
play areas for the children.
*All year daily 9.30-17.00. Closed 24-25 Dec.
Centre closes 17.00, Grounds close 18.00 in
Summer*
A£5.50 C£3.50 OAPs£4.50, Family Ticket
£14.50. Group rates (10+): A£4.50 C£2.75
OAPs£4.00

**Discount Offer: Two for the Price of
One**

King Arthur's Labyrinth

Corris Craft Centre Corris Machynlleth Powys
Wales SY20 9RF
Tel: 01654 761584 Fax: 01654 761575
www.kingarthurslabyrinth.com

*[Off A487, between Machynlleth & Dolgellau.
Plenty of on-site parking available]*

Take an exciting boat ride along an underground river and through the great waterfall into
a labyrinth of tunnels and spectacular caverns.
Welsh tales of King Arthur and other ancient
Welsh legends unfold with tableaux and stunning sound and light effects. Back above
ground, join the Bards' Quest to search for the
ancient legends lost in the maze of time.
Fascinating stories from across the ages come
back to life as you discover their hiding places.
The starting point for King Arthur's Labyrinth
and Bards' Quest is the Corris Craft Centre,
home to ten craft workshops. See the talented
crafters at work and buy their unique items;
woodcraft, toymaking, pottery, jewellery, leather
work, hand made candles, patchwork and quilting, glassware, rustic furniture and hand made
designer cards.

31 Mar-4 Nov daily 10.00-17.00
A£5.75 C£4.10 OAPs£5.20

**Discount Offer: 20% off Adult
Admissions to the Labyrinth**

Llechwedd Slate Caverns

Blaenau Ffestiniog Gwynedd Wales LL41 3NB
Tel: 01766 830306 Fax: 01766 831260
www.llechwedd-slate-caverns.co.uk
[Beside A470, 25mi from A55 Expressway. Plenty of on-site parking available]

Llechwedd offers two underground rides and free surface attractions. The 'Deep Mine Tour' begins with a ride on Britain's steepest passenger railway for a walk through ten sound-and-light sequences, lead by the ghost of a Victorian miner! The 'Miners Tramway' is a guided tour with demonstrations of Victorian mining skills. In the 'Victorian Village', re-minted Victorian coins are available from the 'Old Bank,' so you can buy a penn'orth of boiled sweets at the 'Corner Shop' or a pint at the 'Village Pub'.
All year daily 10.00-17.00. Closed 25-26 Dec & 1 Jan
Both Tours: A£14.75 C£11.25 OAPs£12.50. Group rate (15+): A£13.25 C£9.50 OAPs£11.50

Country Parks & Estates

Portmeirion

Penrhyndeudraeth Gwynedd LL48 6ET
Tel: 01766 770000
Built by Welsh architect Sir Clough Williams-Ellis between 1926-1976. The 1960s television series, The Prisoner was filmed on location at this surreal 'candy-coloured' village.

Dylan Thomas Centre

Somerset Place Swansea Wales SA1 1RR
Tel: 01792 463980
A permanent exhibition on Dylan and his life.

Egypt Centre

University of Wales Swansea Singleton Park Swansea SA2 8PP
Tel: 01792 295960
The Egypt Centre is based at the University of Wales and features hands-on activities as well as an exciting display of Egyptian artefacts including weapons, jewellery, coffins and more.

Gower Heritage Centre

Parkmill Gower Swansea West Glamorgan Wales SA3 2EH
Tel: 01792 371206 Fax: 01792 371471
www.gowerheritagecentre.co.uk
[In village of Parkmill, 8mi W of Swansea on A4118, South Gower Rd. On-site parking]

Last year the Gower celebrated its 50th year as the first designated Area of Outstanding Natural Beauty. Still with breath taking unspoilt scenery what better place to come and see its Heritage than at the Gower Heritage Centre, a working water powered corn and saw mill museum, with its superb range of activities and events. In addition to the normal weekend and holiday time heritage tours, we have our outstanding fun days, inspirational crafts, mystical ghost nights and we host a variety of musical events. New for 2007 is our fully operational woollen mill, making authentic Gower shawls and blankets. Also this year we will have a selection of talks by local historians. Recently nominated as the 2nd most important place to visit on the Gower after Worms Head. For further information please call or visit our website.

10.00-17.00

A£4.10 C£3.10, Family Ticket £13.50

Discount Offer: One Child Free

Ocean Lab, Deep Sea Time Adventure

The Parrog Goodwick Fishguard SA64 OPE
Tel: 01348 874737
Takes the visitor back in time to see marine creatures that lived in the distant past.
Apr-Oct daily

Festivals & Shows

Fishguard Folk Festival / Gwyl Werin Abergwaun

Royal Oak Fishguard Various Venues Fishguard Pembrokeshire Wales SA64
Tel: 01348 875183
www.pembrokeshire-folk-music.co.uk
[In & around historic town of Fishguard, scene of the last ever invasion of Britain]

Make a date in your diary for this friendly festival, now extended to four days. Hear live music at its very best, featuring TANNA (Tom Leary, Peter Knight and Kevin Dempsey), Máire Ní Chathasaigh and Chris Newman, Alan Burke and Paul Bradley, plus many more (please see website). There will also be concerts, sessions,

workshops, 'meet the artists', open mic slots, street performers and a 'Smugglers and Pirates' guided walk around the historic town of Fishguard (located on the Pembrokeshire coastal path). Based mainly in The Royal Oak, the festival is town-wide.
25-28 May 2007
Prices to be confirmed

Gwyl Gregynog Festival

The Music Room Gregynog Hall Tregynon, Nr Newtown Powys Wales SY16 3PW
Tel: 01686 625007 (Box Office)
Fax: 01686 650656
www.gwylgregynogfestival.org
[5mi N of Newtown, signposted from A483 & B4389 via Bettws Cedewain. Bus & rail: Newtown (taxis operating). On-site parking available]

Visit magnificent Gregynog for its annual international arts festival. Picnic beneath the rhododendrons and stroll in the beautiful grounds before enjoying the music of world-class artists. Special events for 2007 include a free 'At Home', featuring music, storytelling, tours and refreshments (16 June) and an Elgar Day (24 June). Families will love the Fathers' Day concert, 'Red Priest: Pirates of the Baroque' (17 June) and the final of our 'Young Musician Competition' (23 June). Art exhibitions run throughout the Festival. Limited accommodation is available in the historic Hall. The purpose built Music Room seats 200 maximum so please book promptly!
15-24 June 2007
Ticket prices vary, please call or visit our website for full details

Gwyl Ifan 2007

Various venues Cardiff Wales CF1
Tel: 029 2056 3989
www.gwylifan.org
[Central Cardiff, M4 A48(M) A470. Plenty of on-site parking available]

Gwyl Ifan is the festival of Welsh folk dancing to celebrate summer, and 2007 will be the 31st festival. It is held at various locations throughout the city and surrounding area, such as Cardiff Bay, with evening activities being held in the Angel Hotel and the historic Coal Exchange in the Bay. Dance teams come to the festival from all over Wales and beyond. Come to Cardiff and see a folk dance procession, displays on the streets, 'taplas' (feast and festivities), barn dance and various workshops.
22-24 June 2007

Llangollen International Musical Eisteddfod

Royal International Pavillion Abbey Road
Llangollen Denbighshire Wales LL20 8SW
Tel: 01978 862000 Fax: 01978 862005
www.international-eisteddfod.co.uk
[From Shrewsbury follow A5 signs from Chester A483 onto A529. Plenty of on-site parking avail-

able. Disabled parking available]
Beautiful North Wales hosts the International Music festival in Llangollen with International choirs, folk dancers, folk groups and much more. 3 Outdoor stages- for live entertainment and non-stop colourful costume and competition in the Royal Pavilion. Themed days with Wednesday-folk song and dance, Thursday-Youth Day, Friday - Celtic Day and Saturday-International Family Day with international folk performers, entertainers and crafts. Enjoy shopping for souvenirs and the wide range of food and drink from around the world. All you have to do is soak up the atmosphere and enjoy the experience. Celebrity concerts every evening. Visit our website for details.
10-15 July 2007 Wed-Sat, 09.00-17.00. Evening outdoor concerts from 18.00, Celebrity concerts from 19.45
Day Ground Admission: A£8.00 C£5.00 (Sat C£1.00). Pavilion Prices: Seats from £12.00

RHS Spring Flower Show, Cardiff

Bute Park Cardiff Wales
Tel: 08700 667799
www.rhs.org.uk/flowershows

Set in Bute Park against the magnificent backdrop of Cardiff Castle, the RHS Spring Flower Show marks the beginning of the Royal Horticultural Society's flower show season. Alongside two floral marquees (brimming with award-winning nurseries) are inspiring feature gardens, talks, demonstrations, opportunities to buy plants (direct from the growers) and gardening accessories, bandstand entertainment and the 'Experience Wales' marquee, which is packed with locally produced fine food, produce and crafts. With children under 16 gaining free entry (with an accompanying adult) the RHS Spring Flower Show, Cardiff is a great day out for all the family.

20-22 April 2007 Fri & Sat 10.00-17.30, Sun 10.00-16.30

A£10.00 (A£9.00 if booked in advance)
C(under16)£Free with accompanying adult

Royal Welsh Agricultural Winter Fair

The Showground Llanelwedd Builth Wells Powys Wales LD2 3SY
Tel: 01982 553683 Fax: 01982 553563
www.rwas.co.uk

[Rail: Builth Rd or Llandrindod Wells station. Plenty of on-site parking available]

The Royal Welsh Agricultural Winter Fair a prime stock show for cattle, sheep, pigs and carcases also features horses, hounds, poultry, tradestands and crafts. Over 24,000 visitors attend.
26-27 November 2007. Please call for futher information
A£10.00 C(under16)£2.00
Concessions(60+)£8.00

Royal Welsh Show

The Showground Llanelwedd Builth Wells Powys Wales LD2 3SY
Tel: 01982 553683 Fax: 01982 553563
www.rwas.co.uk
[Rail: Builth Rd or Llandrindod Wells station]
The Royal Welsh Show provides a prime shop window for farming in Wales. It attracts more than 200,000 visitors, up to 8,000 entries of livestock and over 1,000 tradestands together with sections covering the whole of farming and rural life in Wales.
23-26 July 2007. Please call RWAS office for further information
Gate: Mon-Wed A£18.00 Thur A£16.00. Gate: C(under16)£4.00 Concessions(60+)£15.00

Royal Welsh Smallholder and Garden Festival

The Showground Llanelwedd Builth Wells Powys Wales LD2 3SY
Tel: 01982 553683 Fax: 01982 553563
www.rwas.co.uk

[Rail: Builth Rd or Llandrindod Wells station. Plenty of on-site parking available]

The Royal Welsh Smallholder and Garden Festival features livestock, crafts, lectures and advice on countryside issues; displays and auctions of poultry and vintage machinery, display gardens, trade-stands, farmers markets and Wonderwool exhibition. Over 24,000 visitors attend.

19-20 May 2007. Please call 01982 554408/09 for further information

A£7.00 C(under16)£3.00

Tenby Arts Festival

Tenby Pembrokeshire Wales SA70 7ET
Tel: 01834 875341
www.tenbyartsfest.co.uk
[Festival held at various venues]

Visit this picturesque walled town when it is enlivened by a splendid feast of music, dance, poetry, film, drama, talks, art, and family fun at the seaside. Tenby Arts Festival presents performances by local, national and international artistes packed into a delightful eight days of entertainment, culture, information, education and relaxation. There will be something for everyone from the beach bum to the culture vulture and all those in between. The Festival opens with a vibrant and colourful procession of street entertainers at the harbour followed by activities on south beach which will occupy and amuse children of all ages. The remainder of the week will provide a cultural repast.

22-29 September 2007

Prices vary according to event attended, range from £Free-£12.00

Swansea Museum

Victoria Road Maritime Quarter Swansea West Glamorgan SA1 1SN
Tel: 01792 653763
Archaeology, natural history and local history exhibits are on show including a 'Cabinet of Curiosities'.

Forests & Woods

Cwmcarn Forest Drive, Visitor Centre and Campsite

Cwmcarn Crosskeys Newport Gwent Wales NP11 7FA
Tel: 01495 272001 Fax: 01495 271403
www.caerphilly.gov.uk/visiting

[Plenty of on-site parking available]

This spectacular 7-mile forest drive is a great family day out, set amongst rolling hills and green forests, the drive offers seven car parks where visitors can enjoy cycling and walking whilst absorbing the breathtaking views across the Bristol Channel. Many car parks have picnic and BBQ spots, and children will enjoy the adventure playground and Cwmcarn's magical woodcarvings throughout the forest. During 2007 Cwmcarn will have a new visitor centre constructed which will offer more facilities to visitors, during this time temporary facilities will be in place, a takeaway café facility will be onsite along with an information/booking area, small gift shop and toilet facilities. Access to the Forest Drive will be unaffected. For dedicated mountain bikers, the Twrch Trail offers almost 15.5km of pure single track ensuring riders have an adrenaline filled descent. Riders can now enjoy the newly opened downhill track, both trails are free to ride and open all year, there is a daily charge for a downhill car pass.

Temporary Visitor Centre: Easter-Sept Mon-Thur 09.00-17.00 Fri-Sun 09.00-18.00, June-Aug call for extended opening times, Oct-Mar Sat-Thur 09.00-17.00 Fri 09.00-16.30. Forest Drive: Nov-Feb 11.00-16.00 (Weekends only), Mar & Oct daily 11.00-17.00, Apr-June & Sept daily 11.00-19.00, July-Aug daily 11.00-21.00

Visitor Centre & Bike Trails: Free, Forest Drive £3.00 per car

Llyn Brenig Visitor Centre

Cerrigydrudion Corwen Conwy LL21 9TT
Tel: 01490 420463
Exhibition telling the story of Brenig's evolution from primeval Silurian seas to modern river regulating dam.
Mar-Oct

Gardens & Horticulture

Bodnant Garden

Tal-y-Cafn Colwyn Bay Conwy LL28 5RE
Tel: 01492 650460 Fax: 01492 650448
[Off A470. Rail: Tal-y-Cafn]

One of the finest gardens in Britain with magnificent rhododendrons, camellias and magnolias in the spring followed by herbaceous borders, roses and water lilies.
Mar-Oct daily

National Botanic Garden of Wales

Llanarthne Carmarthenshire Wales SA32 8HG
Tel: 01558 668768 Fax: 01558 668933
www.gardenofwales.org.uk

[Off A48 dual carriageway nr Carmarthen, less than 1h from Cardiff. Plenty of on-site parking available]

The No. 1 'Modern Wonder of Wales' boasts the largest single-span glasshouse in the world and is set in more than 500 acres of fantastic, unspoilt, rolling Welsh countryside. The Great Glasshouse is home to some of the most endangered plants on the planet from six Mediterranean climate regions: Western Australia, Chile, the Canaries, California, southern Africa, and the Mediterranean basin. There is a unique and historic double-walled garden, lakes, ponds and walks, a theatre, licensed restaurant, shop, gallery, bog garden and bee garden, Physicians of Myddfai Exhibition and Apothecaries' Garden, children's farm, children's play area and discovery centre. Whatever your age, there is something for you at the most visited garden in Wales. Whatever time of year it is, the stunning views and remarkable sights and smells have to be experienced to be believed. But, be warned, you may not be able to see and do it all in a day. A new Tropical Glasshouse is currently under construction.
All year daily Summer 10.00-18.00, Winter 10.00-16.30. Closed Christmas Day
A£8.00 C(5-16)£3.00 C(under5)£Free Concessions£6.00, Family Ticket (A2+C4) £17.00

Heritage & Industrial

Drenewydd Museum

26-27 Lower Road Bute Town Rhymney
Caerphilly NP2 5QH
Tel: 01685 843039
This museum recreates life for an iron-working household. Play with Victorian toys, make a rag mat or visit the Ty Bach and period gardens.
Easter-Oct Sat, Sun & Bank Hol

Electric Mountain

Llanberis Caernarfon Gwynedd LL55 4UR
Tel: 01286 870636
Between 1976 and 1982, the heart of a mountain was tunnelled away and a pumped storage power station - the largest in Europe - built inside.

Inigo Jones and Co Ltd

Tudor Slate Works Y Groeslon Caernarfon
Gwynedd Wales LL54 7UE
Tel: 01286 830242 Fax: 01286 831247
www.inigojones.co.uk

[Rail: Bangor & Porthmadog. Bus: 1, 2 & 80.
Plenty of on-site parking available]

Witness the various processes as craftsmen use
age old skills and working machinery to cut,
shape and polish raw slate slabs into practical
products such as cills, coping, flooring, steps,
kitchen worktops, hearths and a multitude of
craft items. A self guided tour starts with an
informative film in our new video room on how
slate is mined and quarried before arriving at
our Works. In our Historical Exhibition you are
able to learn about the development of the
Welsh slate industry and of Inigo Jones in particular. The visitor centre houses a range of original top quality slate ware produced by Inigo
Jones. In addition, slate product for both inside
use and for the garden are displayed in a contemporary setting. Our Welsh Rock Café, features the history of Welsh music right up to the
present. It serves morning coffee, lunches and
Welsh afternoon tea. Secure website.
All year daily 9.00-17.00. Closed 25, 26 Dec & 1
Jan

A4.00 C&Concessions£4.00, Family Ticket
(A2+C2) £15.00 Group rate (10+): 20% discount (must be pre-booked)

Discount Offer: Two for the Price of
One

National Slate Museum

Gilfach Ddu Padarn Country Park Llanberis
Gwynedd LL55 4TY
Tel: 01286 870630
See the story of slate unfold before your eyes.
Watch skilled craftsmen as they deftly split and
dress the slate by hand, visit the largest working
waterwheel on mainland Britain and enjoy a
unique glimpse into the lives of the quarrymen
and their families.
Easter-Oct

National Waterfront Museum

Oystermouth Road Maritime Quarter Swansea
West Glamorgan Wales SA1 3RD
Tel: 01792 638950 Fax: 01792 638956
www.waterfrontmuseum.co.uk

The National Waterfront Museum tells the story
of how industry and innovation have affected
the lives of people in Wales over the last three
hundred years. The latest interactive multi media
and original everyday objects bring the industrial
revolution to life. The museum building combines a late Victorian dockside warehouse with
striking, purpose-built galleries right in the heart
of Swansea's historic maritime quarter. You can
be plunged into poverty, wallow in wealth or
even dabble in danger! Experience noise, high
finance, upheaval and social change. You can
also look to the future and discover how people
across Wales are breaking new ground. Also in
the vicinity are other cultural attractions, cafés,
shops and bars.
All year daily 10.00-17.00
Admission Free

Historical

Beaumaris Castle
Castle Street Beaumaris Isle of Anglesey
LL58 8AP
Tel: 01248 810361
The last of the great castles built by Edward I
around the coast of North Wales.

Bodelwyddan Castle
Ymddiriedolaeth Castell Bodelwyddan
Denbighshire LL18 5YA
Tel: 01745 584060
Set in rolling parkland against the impressive
background of the Clwydian Hills.

Caernarfon Castle
Castle Ditch Caernarfon Gwynedd LL55 2AY
Tel: 01286 677617
In 1283 Edward I began building work on the
castle and extensive town walls after defeating
Llyelyn ap Gruffyd.

Caerphilly Castle
Caerphilly Mid Glamorgan CF83 1JD
Tel: 029 2088 3143
The concentrically planned castle was begun in
1268 by Gilbert de Clare.

Caldicot Castle and Country Park
Church Road Caldicot Monmouthshire
NP26 4HU
Tel: 01291 420241
Discover its romantic and colourful history with
a taped tour, relax and enjoy the grounds and
explore the hands-on activities.

Cardiff Castle
Castle Street Cardiff CF10 3RB
Tel: 029 2087 8100
Decorated with carved and painted animals,
themed fireplaces, gilded ceilings and glorious
stained glass.

Carew Castle and Tidal Mill
Carew Tenby Pembrokeshire Wales SA70 8SL
Tel: 01646 651657/651782
Fax: 01646 651782
www.carewcastle.com
*[On A4705 5mi E of Pembroke. Plenty of on-site
parking available]*

Carew is one of the few castles to display the
development from Norman fortification to
Elizabethan country house. Archaeological
excavation has revealed a much earlier settlement dating back perhaps some 2000 years. A
mile long round walk, with delightful views,
takes in the castle, the Celtic cross, the mill, the
causeway, the 23 acre millpond and a medieval
bridge. Also part of the historic site is the only
restored tidal mill in Wales, with all its original
machinery. An introductory slide-tape programme is complemented by automatic 'talking
points' explaining the milling process and a special exhibition on milling through the ages. A
wide range of events are held every year at
Carew, including theatre interpretation, holiday
activities, battle re-enactments, country fairs
and concerts. A special schools programme
enables children to dress in period costume and
experience life in the castle in times past.
1 April-End Oct 10.00-17.00
Castle & Mill: A£3.00 C&OAPs£2.00, Family
Ticket £8.00. Please be aware that prices are
currently under review

Chepstow Castle
Bridge Street Chepstow Gwent NP6 5EZ
Tel: 01291 624065
Chepstow Castle stands guard over a strategic
crossing point into Wales. In a land of castles,
Chepstow can rightly claim special status.

Conwy Castle

Rosehill Street Conwy Conwy LL32 8LD
Tel: 01492 592358
The castle is a magnificent fortress, built from 1283-7 by Edward I. There is an exhibition on castle chapels on the ground floor of the Chapel Tower.

Harlech Castle

Castle Square Harlech Gwynedd LL46 2YH
Tel: 01766 780552
Harlech Castle was built in 1283-89 by Edward I, with a sheer drop to the sea on one side.

Llanfairpwllgwyngyllgogerychwyr ndrobwllllantysiliogogogoch

Anglesey Wales
Tel: 01248 750057
[From the South: use the A5/A55 to cross the Britannia Bridge then follow the signs]
The tiny village with the big name. It translates to English as 'St Mary's church in the hollow of the white hazel near to the rapid whirlpool and the church of St Tysilio of the red cave'.

Pembroke Castle

Main Street Pembroke Pembrokeshire Wales SA71 4LA
Tel: 01646 684585/681510
[10mi W of Tenby]

This early Norman castle houses many fascinating displays and exhibitions. Enjoy a picnic, in the beautifully kept grounds, or on the roof of St. Anne's Bastion and take in the views along the estuary. As the birthplace of Henry VII, Pembroke can be seen as a pivotal place in history. Henry was the founder of the Tudor dynasty, and the Crown of England has remained ever since in the line of his heirs. Pembroke Castle occupies a strong position high on a ridge between two tidal inlets. Its fortifications were continually extended throughout its history and it displays stonework from many periods.
All year daily. Closed 24-26 Dec & 1 Jan

Penrhyn Castle

Bangor Gwynedd LL57 4HN
Tel: 01248 353084/371337
The splendid castle with its towers and battlements was commissioned in 1827 as a sumptuous family home.

Powis Castle and Gardens

Welshpool Powys Wales SY21 8RF
Tel: 01938 551929 Fax: 01938 554336
www.nationaltrust.org.uk

[1mi S of Welshpool off A483. Bus: Arriva North Midlands 71. Rail: Welshpool 1.75mi. Plenty of on-site parking available]

The world-famous garden, overhung with enormous clipped yews, shelters rare and tender plants. Laid out under the influence of Italian and French styles, the garden retains its original lead statues, an orangery and an aviary on the terraces. In the eighteenth century an informal woodland wilderness was created on the opposing ridge. Perched on a rock above the garden terraces, the medieval castle contains one of the finest collections in Wales. It was originally built c.1200 by Welsh princes and was subsequently adapted and embellished by generations of Herberts and Clives, who furnished the castle with a wealth of fine paintings and furniture. A beautiful collection of treasures from India is displayed in the Clive Museum.

Garden: 17, 18, 24, 25 & 31 Mar. Castle & Gardens: 1 Apr-28 Oct Thu-Mon, July-Aug Wed-Mon. Please phone for more details

Castle & Garden: A£9.90 C(under5)£Free C(under17)£4.95, Family Ticket (A2+C3) £24.75. Garden only: A£6.90 C(under5)£Free C(under17)£3.45, Family Ticket (A2+C3) £17.25. NT Members £Free

Smallest House in Great Britain

Quay Conwy Wales LL32 8DE
Tel: 01492 593484
[Take Conway rd off A55, signposted in town]

The 'Guinness Book of Records' lists this as the smallest house in Britain. Just 6ft wide by 10ft high, it is furnished in the style of a mid-Victorian Welsh cottage.
Apr-Oct 10.00-18.00
A£1.00 C£0.50 C(under5)£Free

Discount Offer: One Child Free

Tredegar House and Park

Coedkernew Newport Gwent Wales NP10 8YW
Tel: 01633 815880 Fax: 01633 815895
[2mi W signposted from A48/M4 J28. Rail: Newport. Bus: local services 15 & 30 stop nearby. Plenty of on-site parking available]

Set in ninety acres of award winning Gardens and Parkland, Tredegar House is one of the finest examples of Restoration Architecture in Wales, and was the ancestral home of the Morgans for over five hundred years. Visitors today can discover what life was like for those who lived 'above and below' stairs. A stunning sequence of Staterooms, elaborately decorated with carvings, gilding, and fine paintings contrast with the fascinating and extensive domestic quarters. Lakeside walks, beautiful walled gardens, orangery and spectacular stable block complete the 'Country House' picture. Gift shop, tea room, craft workshops together with special events in the house and park throughout the year.
Good Fri-end Sept Wed-Sun & Bank Hol 11.30-16.00. Special Christmas & Halloween opening. Group visits at other times
Please call for admission prices, information on weddings & Victorian school tours

Wern Isaf (Formerly Rosebriers)

Penmaen Park Llanfairfechan Gwynedd LL33 0RN
Tel: 01248 680437
Built by H.L. North, one of the leading Arts and Crafts Architects in Wales.

Literature & Libraries

Living History Museums

Dylan Thomas Boat House

Dylan's Walk Laugharne Carmarthenshire Wales SA33 4SD
Tel: 01994 427420 Fax: 01994 427420
www.dylanthomasboathouse.com

[14mi W of Carmarthen A40-A4066]

The waterside house, set on the heron priested shore of the Taf estuary, contains much original furniture, family photographs, an art gallery and displays on the life and works of Dylan Thomas.
May-Oct & Easter weekend 10.00-17.30, Nov-Apr 10.30-15.30
A£3.50 OAPs£3.00

Discount Offer: One Child Free

National Library of Wales

Penglais Hill Aberystwyth Ceredigion SY23 3BU
Tel: 01970 632800
Fax: 01970 615709
[On A487]
The huge library is one of Britain's six copyright libraries, and specialises in Welsh and Celtic literature. It has maps, manuscripts, prints and drawings, as well as books in all languages.

Llancaiach Fawr Manor

Nelson Treharris Mid Glamorgan CF46 6ER
Tel: 01443 412248 Fax: 01443 412688
www.caerphilly.gov.uk/visiting
[12mi from A470, from J32 M4 follow A470 N to Merthyr Tydfil follow signs from roundabout at Ystrad Mynach. Plenty of on-site parking available]
A 'timely' greeting from costumed interpreters welcomes visitors to this manor house in the year of 1645. Colonel Prichard's servants will be pleased to discuss with you the troubled times of the Civil War in which they live. The tour around the house promises to entertain with gossip, customs and traditions of the lives of ordinary people over 350 years ago. A daytime tour of the manor will take visitors just over one hour and special events throughout the year offer extra insight on specific topics. Take a look at the events pages on the website for a full calendar of events including ghost tours, garden tours, musical entertainment, king's day and murder mystery evenings. The conservatory café has a great selection of refreshments and the popular Sunday lunch menu is available every week on a pre-bookable basis. Whilst at the manor you can browse the well-stocked gift shop, which has a range of unusual gifts, visit the exhibition, which gives a brief history of the manor from the time of restoration in 1991 back to 1645.
All year daily 10.00-17.00. Closed Mon Nov-Feb, open at various times for pre-bookable evening tours & events
A£5.50 Concession£4.50 C£4.00, Family Ticket(A2+C2) £16.50

Discount Offer: One Child Free

Maritime

Moelfre Seawatch

Moelfre Anglesey Wales LL72 8LG
Tel: 01248 410277
www.angleseyheritage.co.uk
[Plenty of on-site parking available]

The Seawatch Centre in the small, picturesque
harbour village of Moelfre is a reminder of the
island's rich maritime history and importance of
the ever present sea for the people of Anglesey.
Learn about the wonderful array of marine
wildlife to be found in the coastal waters. Learn
about the bravery of Coxswain Richard Evans
who was awarded two gold medals for saving
the lives of the crew of two ships.
*Easter-Sept Tues-Sun & Bank Hol Mon 11.00-
17.00. Other times by appointment*
Admission free

Porthmadog Maritime Museum

Oakley Wharf No.1 The Harbour Porthmadog
Gwynedd LL49 9LU
Tel: 01766 513736
Situated on one of the old wharves of
Porthmadog harbour, the last remaining slate
shed houses a display on the maritime history
of Porthmadog and district.

South Stack

Holyhead Anglesey Wales
Tel: 01407 763207
www.angleseyheritage.co.uk
[Plenty of on-site parking available]

One of Wales' most spectacular lighthouses.
South Stack lighthouse was constructed in
1809 on the north west coast of Anglesey act-
ing as a waymark for coastal traffic and a landmark and orientation light for vessels crossing
the Irish Sea to and from the ports of Holyhead
and Dun Laoghaire. Live performances based
on the history of the lighthouse run every weekend July-September.
*Easter-Sept Mon-Sun & Bank Hol Mon 10.30-
17.30. At other times by appointment*
Please telephone for admission prices

Thousand Islands Expeditions

Cross Square St. Davids Pembrokeshire Wales
SA62 6SL
Tel: 01437 721721 or 721686
Fax: 01437 721698
www.thousandislands.co.uk
[On the Cross Square in middle of St. Davids]
Join us on one of our Wildlife Adventure Boat
Trips to experience the beautiful scenery and
wildlife of this unspoilt island wilderness. Caves,
bays, gorges, swirling currents and white water,
magnificent high cliffs with hundreds of nesting
seabirds, Atlantic Grey Seals, Harbour Porpoise,
Whales and Dolphins. Take a fast, exhilarating
Jet Boat trip or a traditional leisurely cruise. All
our vessels have a wildlife guide onboard. Get
on the ferry and visit the RSPB Nature Reserve
on Ramsey Island, guided walks are available.
Our offshore trips go in search of whales and
dolphins and visit the gannet colony on
Grassholm Island, over 32000 pairs of breeding
gannets. There is a Puffin and Shearwater
Cruise in the evening or a 2 hour Spectacular
Jet Boat trip around Ramsey and the offshore
islands. We can accommodate groups or individuals. Call or see our website for more info
1 Apr-31 Oct daily 09.00-17.00
For a large selection of Boat trips see our website or ring for a brochure

**Discount Offer: 10% off all Full-Priced
Fares**

Military & Defence Museums

South Wales Borderers (24th Regiment) Museum

The Barracks Brecon Powys LD3 7EB
Tel: 01874 613310
This museum tells the 300-year history of the
24th Regiment.

Mills - Water & Wind

Llynnon Mill
Llanddeusant Anglesey Wales LL65 4AB

Tel: 01407 730797 / 724444
www.angleseyheritage.co.uk

[Plenty of on-site parking available]

The only working windmill in Wales. The mill produces stoneground wholemeal flour for sale using organic wheat. Built at the time of the Napoleonic Wars at one time there were more than 50 working mills on the island. A unique impression of Anglesey's rural life. Shop, tea-room (offering traditional home-cooking), workshops, traditional events and the Anglesey Mills Trail.
Easter-Sept Mon-Sun & Bank Hol Mon 11.00-17.00. At other times by appointment
Please telephone for admission prices

Mining

Big Pit: National Coal Museum
Blaenafon Torfaen NP4 9XP
Tel: 01495 790311
'Big Pit' closed as a working coalmine in 1980, but today visitors can don safety helmets and lamps, and go 300ft underground to a different world.
Mar-Nov daily

Llywernog Silver Lead Mine
Llywernog Mine Llywernog Ponterwyd Aberystwyth Ceredigion SY23 3AB
Tel: 01970 890620
Explore tunnels and chambers and see veins of silver lead ore running through the rocks. Pan for silver and 'fools gold'.
Easter-Oct daily

Multicultural Museums

Welsh Christian Heritage Centre
Laura Place Aberystwyth Ceredigion SY23 2AU
Tel: 01970 617184
Located in a historic church which is still the focus for a living community of Christians.

Natural History Museums

St Fagans National History Museum
St Fagans Cardiff Glamorgan Wales CF5 6XB
Tel: 029 2057 3500
The museum tells the story of everyday life in Wales during the last 500 years.

Nature & Conservation Parks

Breacon Beacons National Park
Brecon Powys Wales
Tel: 01874 624437
To the west are the wild black mountains, to the east is the broad valley of the UK, south is a landscape again of limestone and millstone grit.

Garwnant Visitor Centre
Forest Enterprise Cwm Taff Merthyr Tydfill Mid Glamorgan Wales CF48 2HT
Tel: 01685 723060
A variety of beautiful walks starting from the visitor centre.

RSPB Nature Reserve Ynys-hir
Eglwysfach Machynlleth Powys SY20 8TA
Tel: 01654 700222
With a mixture of Welsh oak woodland, estuary, reedbeds and pools, this reserve is attractive all year.

Taf Fechan Nature Reserve

Taf Fechan South Wales
[Start from Owl's Grove car park]
Ancient broadleaved woodlands, calcareous grasslands, river and cliffs. The Taf Fechen LNR comprises of about 2.5 km of river with steep valley sides of Carboniferous limestone. The river has eroded the limestone into a narrow gorge in the centre of the site.

Snowdonia National Park

National Park Office Penhryndendraeth Gwynedd Wales LL48 6LS
Tel: 01766 770274 Fax: 01766 771211
www.eryri-npa.gov.uk

[Plenty of on-site parking available]

Snowdonia National Park covers an area of 840 square miles and boasts Snowdon as its main attraction and highest peak.

Welsh Wildlife Centre

Teifi Marshes Nature Reserve Cilgerran Cardigan Ceredigion SA43 2TB
Tel: 01239 621600
One of Wales' top nature reserves home to otters, birds, wildflowers and butterflies in their natural habitats.

On the Water

Horse Drawn Boats and Narrowboat Aqueduct Trips

The Wharf Wharf Hill Llangollen Denbighshire Wales LL20 8TA
Tel: 01978 860702 Fax: 01978 860702
www.horsedrawnboats.co.uk
[From Llangollen town centre, cross river & continue up hill]

Llangollen Wharf is home to the famous horse-drawn boats. Enjoy the peace and tranquillity of the Llangollen Canal on a 45-minute boat trip (pulled by one of our gorgeous heavy horses). Boats are covered and are therefore suitable for all-weather trips. Enjoy a 2-hour cruise (on our fully weatherproofed, centrally-heated boat) over the Pontcysllte Aqueduct. Commentary, licensed bar and snacks available. You can also enjoy home-cooked food in the Wharf Tearooms (famous for delicious cakes!), where you can watch our beautiful boats pass by, or admire views of Llangollen from the terrace.
Mid Mar-end of Oct daily 9.30-17.00
Horse-Drawn Boat Trips: A£5.00 C£2.50, Family Ticket £12.50. Aqueduct Cruises: A£10.00 C£8.00. Group rates available on request

Performing Arts

Wales Millennium Centre

Bute Place Cardiff Bay Cardiff CF10 5AL
Tel: 08700 402000
An international receiving house for world class ballet, musicals, dance and opera.

Places of Worship

Llandaff Cathedral

The Cathedral Green Cardiff CF5 2LA
Tel: 029 2056 4554
This restored twelfth-century cathedral features significant works by Medieval, pre-Raphaelite and Victorian artists alongside groundbreaking work by more contemporary artists.

St Davids Cathedral

The Close St Davids Pembrokeshire SA62 6RH
Tel: 01437 720199 Fax: 01437 721885
www.stdavidscathedral.org.uk
[A487]

Begun in 1181 on the site reputed to be where St David founded a monastic settlement in the sixth century. The present building was altered during the twelfth to the fourteenth centuries and again in the sixteenth. It also has an extension added in 1993, so the architecture is varied. The ceilings - oak, painted wood and stone vaulting are of considerable interest. The floor of the nave slopes a metre over its length while over the entire length of the cathedral the difference is four metres. In addition to services there are organ recitals on Wednesdays from late July through to early September. Last year a splendid new refectory opened offering fresh local food.
All year daily 08.30-18.00
Suggested donation of £3.00

Police, Prisons & Dungeons

Beaumaris Courthouse

Castle Street Beaumaris Anglesey LL58 8BP
Tel: 01248 811691 / 724444
www.angleseyheritage.co.uk
Beaumaris Courthouse is one of Anglesey's most fascinating buildings. Now restored and refurbished to its past splendour, it is a place that to this day almost orders you to get up and proclaim out loud '...Not Guilty' Prisoners of all descriptions have faced trial in this unique courtroom since it was built in 1614. For many of them the outcome of their case was a matter of life or death. Live performances based on the history of the courthouse from July to September daily.
Easter-Sept Mon-Sun & Bank Hol Mon 10.30-17.00. At other times by appointment
Please telephone for admission prices

Beaumaris Gaol

Steeple Lane Beaumaris Anglesey LL58 8EP
Tel: 01248 810921 Fax: 01248 750282
www.angleseyheritage.co.uk
This building is full of sad memories and secrets. Bars and locks. Dark and dusty corridors. Darkness, Cold and despair. Beaumaris Gaol will live in your memory for a long time. Not for the faint hearted; call and see for your-

self. It will give you a fascinating insight into the world of the prisoner in Victorian times. Live performances based on the History of the gaol from July-Sept.

Easter-Sept Mon-Sun & Bank Hol Mon 10.30-17.00. At other times by appointment
Please call for admission prices.

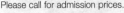

Railways

Bala Lake Railway

Llanuwchllyn Bala Gwynedd Wales LL23 7DD
Tel: 01678 540666 Fax: 01678 540535
www.bala-lake-railway.co.uk
[Off A494. Adequate car parking at Llanuwchllyn Station, roadside parking at Bala Station with large car parks in town centre]

Narrow gauge steam trains with views of Llyn Tegid (Bala Lake). Look for the buzzards that are frequently seen along the railway. Picnic by the lake at Llangower. Visit the signal box at Llanuwchllyn and see how trains are signalled in and out of the station. We recommend you join the train at Llanuwchllyn where there is on-site car parking.
Easter-end Sept daily except some Mon & Fri, please call to confirm. Trains leave from Llanuwchillyn: 11.15, 12.50, 14.25 & 16.00. Trains leave from Bala: 11.50, 13.25, 15.00 & 16.35
Return Tickets: A£7.30 C(5-15)£2.00 C(0-5)£Free, Family Ticket (A1+C1) £8.50 - extra C£2.00 or (A2+C2) £17.00 OAPs£6.50. Single Tickets: A£4.50 C(5-15)£2.00 C(0-5)£Free
Unaccompanied C: return £3.00, single £2.00

Ffestiniog Railway

Harbour Station Porthmadog Gwynedd Wales LL49 9NF
Tel: 01766 516000 Fax: 01766 516006
www.festrail.co.uk
[Porthmadog: A487 station well signposted. Blaenau Ffestiniog: A470 - station signposted. Plenty of on-site parking available]

The Ffestiniog Railway is the oldest independent railway company in the world. We have been operating steam trains for over 140 years. It was founded in 1823 to carry slate to the harbour at Porthmadog from the quarries of Blaenau Ffestiniog and was an important part of the social and industrial culture of the area. Nowadays, the little steam trains climb over 700 feet from sea level, carrying visitors through the stunning scenery of the Snowdonia National Park. There is much to see and do along the line and a day Rover ticket gives you the opportunity to make the most of your day, perhaps with a walk through the woodlands at Tan-y-Bwlch station or a visit to Portmeirion village only a mile away. Trains run daily between Easter and the end of October with limited services during the winter months. Please phone or visit our website for details of services. Public car parks are available in Porthmadog and Blaenau Ffestiniog. For car users we suggest starting your journey from Blaenau Ffestiniog during the summer. Alternatively take advantage of combined Rail / Bus Rover tickets, some of which give discounts on the Ffestiniog Railway.
Trains run daily from 24 Mar-4 Nov plus on other dates. See timetable for details
A£16.95 C£8.50 OAPs£15.25, Family Ticket (A2+C2) £33.90

Discount Offer: One Child Free

Llanberis Lake Railway

Padarn Country Park Gilfach Ddu Llanberis,
Caernarfon Gwynedd Wales LL55 4TY

Tel: 01286 870549 Fax: 01286 870549

www.lake-railway.co.uk

[Off A4086 in Llanberis. 15min from A55 J11 follow Llanberis tourist signs. Plenty of on-site parking available]

Sit back and enjoy a more leisurely way to travel. Let our little steam trains take you on a journey through spectacular scenery right in the heart of Snowdonia. The journey takes you past the thirteenth-century Dolbadarn Castle, across rivers and streams and along part of the old slate railway route following the shores of beautiful Lake Padarn. Enjoy magnificent views of Snowdon and the surrounding high peaks from the comfort of your carriage. The five-mile return journey takes around 60 minutes, and the trains stop briefly at Cei Llydan (midway along the lake). Here we have a very pleasant lakeside picnic site, and there's an independently operated children's play area nearby. All our trains are scheduled to be hauled by one of our historic narrow-gauge steam engines that spent their earlier career working the nearby slate quarries. Souvenir shop and café at Gilfach Ddu Station.

Easter-late Oct trains run frequently Sun-Fri. June-Aug daily

Return Fares: A£6.50 C£4.50, Family discounts available

Llangollen Railway Plc

The Station Abbey Road Llangollen
Denbighshire Wales LL20 8SN
Tel: 01978 860951/860979
Fax: 01978 869247
www.llangollen-railway.co.uk

Welcome to the Llangollen Railway in North Wales. We offer 7 ¼ miles of beautiful scenery between the stations of Llangollen and Carrog. The line side follows the River Dee, past such features as the Horseshoe Falls. This weir was built to provide water for the Llangollen canal, and along with the Aqueduct between Trevor and Froncysyllte, is an example of the engineering skills of Thomas Telford. The River Dee has been designated a Site of Special Scientific Interest, this area being the habitat for a variety of species, which have seen a decline in numbers during recent years. Steam locomotives mainly operate the railway timetable, but during some of the earlier and later times in the season, one of our heritage Railcars provides the train service. The town of Llangollen offers a good selection of hostelries, accommodation and shops, to suit all tastes and budgets. Come and visit Llangollen, where Wales welcomes the World.

4, 10-25 Feb, 3, 4, 10, 11, 16-18, 24-31 Mar, 1-15, 17-22, 24-26 28, 29 Apr, 1-3, 5-31 May, 1-30 June, 1-31 July, 1-31 Aug, 1-30 Sept, 1-14, 16-18, 20-31 Oct, 1-4 Nov, 1, 2, 8, 9, 15, 16, 20-24, 26-31 Dec, 1, 5, 6 Jan

Standard Return: A£8.00 C(3-16)£4.00 OAPs£6.00. Bicycles & dogs £1.00 per journey. Group rates available on request - please call 01978 860979. Concessionary tickets are not available on Gala, Thomas or Santa Trains. Thomas the Tank Engine prices: A£10.00 C£6.00 OAPs£7.00, Family Ticket (A2+C2) £20.00

Snowdon Mountain Railway

Llanberis Caernarfon Gwynedd Wales LL55 4TY
Tel: 0870 458 0033 Fax: 01286 872518
www.snowdonrailway.co.uk

[Railway operates from Llanberis Station on A4086, 7.5mi from Caernarfon. Less than 15min drive from main A55/A5 J at Bangor. Rail: Bangor 9mi. Regular buses direct from Bangor & Caernarfon & in Summer months from Llandudno, Beddgelert & Betws-y-Coed]

Travel by the UK's only rack and pinion railway up Snowdon - the highest mountain in Wales. Majestic Mount Snowdon dominates the glorious, ancient landscape of North Wales. At 3,560ft (1,085m) it is a true place of legend - said to be the burial place of the giant ogre Rhita, vanquished by King Arthur. Some believe that King Arthur's knights still lie beneath. Clogwyn Station at 2,556ft (779m) is the destination for 2007 where the views across the Menai Strait to the island of Anglesey are fantastic. Due to the redevelopment of the Summit facility, trains will be running to Clogwyn in 2007. The journey is packed with adventure, dramatic scenery and will peak at 2500 feet above sea level. If you wish to pre-book tickets please call or for further information visit our website. Please note bookings cannot be taken on the day of travel.

Late March-1st Week of Nov Inc 09.00-17.00 (Trains will only run subject to carrying a minimum number of passengers)

Return Fare: A£15.00 C£11.00 OAP&Student£12.00 Disabled A£12.00 Disabled C£8.00 Privilege (ATOC pass holders)£7.50, Early Bird: A£7.50 C£5.50. Single Fare: A£11.00 C£8.00 OAP&Student£7.00 Disabled A£8.00 Disabled C£4.50 Privilege (Atoc pass holders)£5.50, Early Bird A£7.50 C£5.50. Telephone bookings will be subject to a £2.50 administration charge per transaction

Welsh Highland Railway (Caernarfon)

St Helen's Road Caernarfon Gwynedd Wales LL55 2YD
Tel: 01766 516000 Fax: 01766 516006
[From A55 follow signs to Caernarfon, then 'brown signs' to station. Plenty of on-site parking]

The Welsh Highland Railway is Snowdonia's newest railway offering you the best of narrow gauge steam and beautiful scenery. This exciting project to restore the old railway line that linked the towns of Porthmadog and Caernarfon has been backed by the Millennium Commission and the Welsh Assembly Government. At the moment, trains run between Caernarfon, right beside the famous castle, and Rhyd Ddu, at the foot of Snowdon, a distance of 13 miles. However, there is much to be seen as work is in fill swing. Why not catch an open top bus onwards to Beddgelert or Porthmadog? It makes a great day out. Ideal as well for using as your transport into the Snowdonia National Park with excellent walks from the line and places to eat along the way. Trains run daily between Easter and October with limited services during the winter months. Please phone or visit our website for more info

Trains run daily from 25 Mar-31 Oct, plus other dates. See timetable for details

A£16.95 C£8.50 OAPs£15.25, Family Ticket (A2+C2) £33.90

Discount Offer: One Child Free

Welshpool and Llanfair Railway

The Station Llanfair Caereinion Welshpool Powys SY21 0SF
Tel: 01938 810441
Offers and 8-mile trip through glorious scenery by narrow-gauge steam train.

Science - Earth & Planetary

Centre for Alternative Technology
Pantperthog Machynlleth Powys SY20 9AZ
Tel: 01654 705950
Exciting interactive displays that demonstrate
the incredible power of wind, water and sun.

Techniquest
Stuart Street Cardiff Wales CF10 5BW
Tel: 029 2047 5475 Fax: 029 2048 2517
www.techniquest.org
*[M4, J33, follow A4232 until signposted. Limited
on-site parking available (reserved for disabled
visitors) but plenty of parking nearby]*
Techniquest Science Discovery Centre, in the
heart of Cardiff Bay, is where science and technology are brought to life. There are over 150
hands-on exhibits that will keep the whole family
entertained and the ever-changing programme
of special events means that there is always
something new to discover. Take part in one of
the fascinating science theatre shows, experi-
ment and investigate in a laboratory workshop
or explore the universe in Techniquest's
Planetarium where the stars appear before your
very eyes.
*All year Mon-Fri 09.30-16.30, Sat-Sun & Bank
Hols 10.30-17.00, (open 09.30-17.00 during
local school hols). Closed 24-27 Dec*
A£6.90 C(under4)£Free C&Concessions£4.80,
Family Ticket £20.00. Events in Planetarium &
Laboratory are chargeable in addition to main
admission, please call for details

**Discount Offer: Two for the Price of
One**

Sport & Recreation

Rhyl Sun Centre
East Parade Rhyl Denbighshire LL18 3AQ
Tel: 01745 344433
Rides, slides, pools and fun for all the family.
Enjoy the tropical climate whatever the weather.

Theme & Adventure Parks

GreenWood Forest Park
Y Felinheli Gwynedd Wales LL56 4QN
Tel: 01248 670076 Fax: 01248 670069
www.greenwoodforestpark.co.uk
[Rail: Bangor. Plenty of on-site parking available]
Family adventure and forest fun! Ride our eco-
friendly family roller coaster, zoom down our 70
metre sledge slide. Enjoy the Jungle Boat
Adventure, drive mini-tractors, shoot traditional
longbows and build dens in the woods. Tackle
the challenge of our treetop Towers and find a
crocodile in our maze, adventure playgrounds,
puzzle barn and Toddlers Village, big indoor
interactive exhibition. Gift shop, café and snack
bars. New for 2007: Tunnel Warren - tunnels,
slides, ropes and towers for the under 7s, plus
the new Giant Jumper - the Biggest Bouncing
Pillow ever and the first one in Wales! Award -
winning attraction with lots to do, whatever the
weather. Plus fantastic entertainment - see website for our events details.
*12 Feb-24 Feb daily 11.00-17.00, 14 Mar-3 Sept
daily 10.00-17.30, 4 Sept-3 Nov daily 11.00-
17.00*
For prices please call or see our website

Oakwood Theme Park

Canaston Bridge Narberth Pembrokeshire
Wales SA67 8DE
Tel: 01834 861889
Features over 30 rides and attractions set in 80
acres of beautiful Pembrokeshire countryside.

Victorian Era

Judge's Lodging

Broad Street Presteigne Powys LD8 2AD
Tel: 01544 260650
Explore the fascinating world of the Victorian
judges, their servants, and felonious guests at
this award-winning historic house.

Zoos

The Animalarium

Borth Ceredigion Wales SY24 5NA
Tel: 01970 871224
www.animalarium.co.uk/
*[In Borth a short walk from Cardigan Bay beach.
Plenty of on-site parking available]*

The Animalarium is a small zoo set in the pretty
seaside town of Borth, near Aberystwyth. Many
of the animals are rescued or re-homed pets,
including large snakes, iguana and monkeys.
Visitors can see at close quarters breeding
colonies of lemurs, monkeys, wallabies and
rheas, and a wide selection of wild cats. Even
the leopard is an ex-pet! You may feed the animals in the petting barn, pots of feed are on
sale at the shop. Twice a day you may have the

opportunity of stroking or handling a snake, of
having a pony ride (summer only). Crocodile
feeding time is a twice weekly feature. There are
outdoor children's play areas and an indoor ball
pool. The whole area is disabled friendly and
there is a tea room, picnic areas, souvenir shop
and free car park.
*All year daily Easter-Oct daily 10.00-18.00, Nov-
Easter daily 11.00-16.00*
A£7.50 C£5.50 Concessions£6.50, Family
Ticket (A2+C3) £24.00

Discount Offer: One Child Free

Welsh Mountain Zoo

Colwyn Bay North Wales LL28 5UY
Tel: 01492 532938
Set in lovely garden surroundings.

1066 Story in Hastings Castle

Castle Hill Road West Hill Hastings East Sussex

Two for the Price of One

with a full-paying adult

Cannot be used in conjunction with other offers. One voucher per party. Not valid on Bank Hols or special event days.

Expires end Feb 2008 (unless otherwise specified)

Adventure Island

Western Esplanade Southend-On-Sea Essex SS1 1EE

3 Wristbands for the Price of 2

Free wristband to be of equal or lesser value; cannot be used in half price wristband times

Cannot be used in conjunction with other offers. One voucher per party. Not valid on Bank Hols or special event days.

Valid until 4th November 2007

Alnwick Castle

Estates Office Alnwick Northumberland NE66 1NQ

One Child Free

with full-paying adult

Cannot be used in conjunction with other offers. One voucher per party. Not valid on Bank Hols or special event days.

valid 2 April - 28 October 2007

Amazonia

Strathclyde County Park Motherwell Lanarkshire ML1 3RT

One Child Free

with a full-paying adult

Cannot be used in conjunction with other offers. One voucher per party. Not valid on Bank Hols or special event days.

valid for 2007 season only

Anne Hathaway's Cottage

Cottage Lane Shottery Stratford-Upon-Avon Warwickshire CV37 9HH

Two for the Price of One

Voucher entitles one Adult or Child to be admitted free of charge when accompanied by a full paying adult

Cannot be used in conjunction with other offers. One voucher per party. Not valid on Bank Hols or special event days.

Expires end Feb 2008 (unless otherwise specified)

Anne of Cleves House Museum

52 Southover High Street Lewes East Sussex BN7 1JA

Two for the Price of One

with a full-paying adult

Cannot be used in conjunction with other offers. One voucher per party. Not valid on Bank Hols or special event days.

Expires end Feb 2008 (unless otherwise specified)

1. Each voucher entitles the holder to the discount specified by the selected attraction.
2. Valid for use until 28/02/08 (unless otherwise specified, or if attraction season finishes prior to this). Vouchers are subject to the terms, conditions and restrictions of the selected attraction.
3. One voucher per party will be accepted, cannot be used in conjunction with any other offer, photocopies will not be accepted.
4. All attractions offering a discount have confirmed their willingness to participate. All information is subject to change without notice and should any attraction close or decline to accept a voucher for any reason, Days Out UK are not liable and cannot be held responsible.
5. Days Out UK shall not accept liability for any loss, accident or injury that may occur at a participating attraction and any dispute arising must be settled direct with the attraction concerned.
6. Cash redemption value of each voucher is 0.001p.
7. You are advised to check all relevant information with your chosen attraction before commencing your journey.

Days Out UK, PO Box 427, Northampton NN1 3YN. Tel: 01604 622445

1. Each voucher entitles the holder to the discount specified by the selected attraction.
2. Valid for use until 28/02/08 (unless otherwise specified. or if attraction season finishes prior to this). Vouchers are subject to the terms, conditions and restrictions of the selected attraction.
3. One voucher per party will be accepted, cannot be used in conjunction with any other offer, photocopies will not be accepted.
4. All attractions offering a discount have confirmed their willingness to participate. All information is subject to change without notice and should any attraction close or decline to accept a voucher for any reason, Days Out UK are not liable and cannot be held responsible.
5. Days Out UK shall not accept liability for any loss, accident or injury that may occur at a participating attraction and any dispute arising must be settled direct with the attraction concerned.
6. Cash redemption value of each voucher is 0.001p.
7. You are advised to check all relevant information with your chosen attraction before commencing your journey.

Days Out UK, PO Box 427, Northampton NN1 3YN. Tel: 01604 622445

1. Each voucher entitles the holder to the discount specified by the selected attraction.
2. Valid for use until 28/02/08 (unless otherwise specified, or if attraction season finishes prior to this). Vouchers are subject to the terms, conditions and restrictions of the selected attraction.
3. One voucher per party will be accepted, cannot be used in conjunction with any other offer, photocopies will not be accepted.
4. All attractions offering a discount have confirmed their willingness to participate. All information is subject to change without notice and should any attraction close or decline to accept a voucher for any reason, Days Out UK are not liable and cannot be held responsible.
5. Days Out UK shall not accept liability for any loss, accident or injury that may occur at a participating attraction and any dispute arising must be settled direct with the attraction concerned.
6. Cash redemption value of each voucher is 0.001p.
7. You are advised to check all relevant information with your chosen attraction before commencing your journey.

Days Out UK, PO Box 427, Northampton NN1 3YN. Tel: 01604 622445

1. Each voucher entitles the holder to the discount specified by the selected attraction.
2. Valid for use until 28/02/08 (unless otherwise specified, or if attraction season finishes prior to this). Vouchers are subject to the terms, conditions and restrictions of the selected attraction.
3. One voucher per party will be accepted, cannot be used in conjunction with any other offer, photocopies will not be accepted.
4. All attractions offering a discount have confirmed their willingness to participate. All information is subject to change without notice and should any attraction close or decline to accept a voucher for any reason, Days Out UK are not liable and cannot be held responsible.
5. Days Out UK shall not accept liability for any loss, accident or injury that may occur at a participating attraction and any dispute arising must be settled direct with the attraction concerned.
6. Cash redemption value of each voucher is 0.001p.
7. You are advised to check all relevant information with your chosen attraction before commencing your journey.

Days Out UK, PO Box 427, Northampton NN1 3YN. Tel: 01604 622445

1. Each voucher entitles the holder to the discount specified by the selected attraction.
2. Valid for use until 28/02/08 (unless otherwise specified, or if attraction season finishes prior to this). Vouchers are subject to the terms, conditions and restrictions of the selected attraction.
3. One voucher per party will be accepted, cannot be used in conjunction with any other offer, photocopies will not be accepted.
4. All attractions offering a discount have confirmed their willingness to participate. All information is subject to change without notice and should any attraction close or decline to accept a voucher for any reason, Days Out UK are not liable and cannot be held responsible.
5. Days Out UK shall not accept liability for any loss, accident or injury that may occur at a participating attraction and any dispute arising must be settled direct with the attraction concerned.
6. Cash redemption value of each voucher is 0.001p.
7. You are advised to check all relevant information with your chosen attraction before commencing your journey.

Days Out UK, PO Box 427, Northampton NN1 3YN. Tel: 01604 622445

1. Each voucher entitles the holder to the discount specified by the selected attraction.
2. Valid for use until 28/02/08 (unless otherwise specified, or if attraction season finishes prior to this). Vouchers are subject to the terms, conditions and restrictions of the selected attraction.
3. One voucher per party will be accepted, cannot be used in conjunction with any other offer, photocopies will not be accepted.
4. All attractions offering a discount have confirmed their willingness to participate. All information is subject to change without notice and should any attraction close or decline to accept a voucher for any reason, Days Out UK are not liable and cannot be held responsible.
5. Days Out UK shall not accept liability for any loss, accident or injury that may occur at a participating attraction and any dispute arising must be settled direct with the attraction concerned.
6. Cash redemption value of each voucher is 0.001p.
7. You are advised to check all relevant information with your chosen attraction before commencing your journey.

Days Out UK, PO Box 427, Northampton NN1 3YN. Tel: 01604 622445

1. Each voucher entitles the holder to the discount specified by the selected attraction.
2. Valid for use until 28/02/08 (unless otherwise specified, or if attraction season finishes prior to this). Vouchers are subject to the terms, conditions and restrictions of the selected attraction.
3. One voucher per party will be accepted, cannot be used in conjunction with any other offer, photocopies will not be accepted.
4. All attractions offering a discount have confirmed their willingness to participate. All information is subject to change without notice and should any attraction close or decline to accept a voucher for any reason, Days Out UK are not liable and cannot be held responsible.
5. Days Out UK shall not accept liability for any loss, accident or injury that may occur at a participating attraction and any dispute arising must be settled direct with the attraction concerned.
6. Cash redemption value of each voucher is 0.001p.
7. You are advised to check all relevant information with your chosen attraction before commencing your journey.

Days Out UK, PO Box 427, Northampton NN1 3YN. Tel: 01604 622445

1. Each voucher entitles the holder to the discount specified by the selected attraction.
2. Valid for use until 28/02/08 (unless otherwise specified. or if attraction season finishes prior to this). Vouchers are subject to the terms, conditions and restrictions of the selected attraction.
3. One voucher per party will be accepted, cannot be used in conjunction with any other offer, photocopies will not be accepted.
4. All attractions offering a discount have confirmed their willingness to participate. All information is subject to change without notice and should any attraction close or decline to accept a voucher for any reason, Days Out UK are not liable and cannot be held responsible.
5. Days Out UK shall not accept liability for any loss, accident or injury that may occur at a participating attraction and any dispute arising must be settled direct with the attraction concerned.
6. Cash redemption value of each voucher is 0.001p.
7. You are advised to check all relevant information with your chosen attraction before commencing your journey.

Days Out UK, PO Box 427, Northampton NN1 3YN. Tel: 01604 622445

1. Each voucher entitles the holder to the discount specified by the selected attraction.
2. Valid for use until 28/02/08 (unless otherwise specified, or if attraction season finishes prior to this). Vouchers are subject to the terms, conditions and restrictions of the selected attraction.
3. One voucher per party will be accepted, cannot be used in conjunction with any other offer, photocopies will not be accepted.
4. All attractions offering a discount have confirmed their willingness to participate. All information is subject to change without notice and should any attraction close or decline to accept a voucher for any reason, Days Out UK are not liable and cannot be held responsible.
5. Days Out UK shall not accept liability for any loss, accident or injury that may occur at a participating attraction and any dispute arising must be settled direct with the attraction concerned.
6. Cash redemption value of each voucher is 0.001p.
7. You are advised to check all relevant information with your chosen attraction before commencing your journey.

Days Out UK, PO Box 427, Northampton NN1 3YN. Tel: 01604 622445

Biddenden Vineyards and Cider Works

Little Whatmans Gribble Bridge Lane Biddenden Kent

One Free Cup of Tea or Coffee in the Café
(one free beverage per voucher and transaction)

Cannot be used in conjunction with other offers. One voucher per party. Not valid on Bank Hols or special event days.

Expires end Feb 2008 (unless otherwise specified)

DISCOUNT VOUCHER

Big Sheep

Abbotsham Bideford Devon EX39 5AP

One Child Free

with every full-paying adult

Cannot be used in conjunction with other offers. One voucher per party. Not valid on Bank Hols or special event days.

Expires end Feb 2008 (unless otherwise specified)

DISCOUNT VOUCHER

Bircham Windmill

Bircham King's Lynn Norfolk PE31 6SJ

One Child Free

with every full-paying adult

Cannot be used in conjunction with other offers. One voucher per party. Not valid on Bank Hols or special event days.

Expires end Feb 2008 (unless otherwise specified)

DISCOUNT VOUCHER

Bird of Prey and Conservation Centre

Old Warden Park Biggleswade Bedfordshire SG18 9EA

One Child Free

with a full-paying adult

Cannot be used in conjunction with other offers. One voucher per party. Not valid on Bank Hols or special event days.

Expires end Feb 2008 (unless otherwise specified)

DISCOUNT VOUCHER

Birdland

Rissington Road Bourton on the Water Cheltenham
Gloucestershire GL54 2BN

One Child Free
with a full-paying adult

Cannot be used in conjunction with other offers. One voucher per party. Not valid on Bank Hols or special event days.

Expires end Feb 2008 (unless otherwise specified)

DISCOUNT VOUCHER

Birdworld, Underwater World
and Jenny Wren Farm
Farnham Road Holt Pound Farnham Surrey GU10 4LD

Two for the Price of One
with a full-paying adult
not valid for Santa events; not valid for groups

Cannot be used in conjunction with other offers. One voucher per party. Not valid on Bank Hols or special event days.

Expires end Feb 2008 (unless otherwise specified)

DISCOUNT VOUCHER

1. Each voucher entitles the holder to the discount specified by the selected attraction.
2. Valid for use until 28/02/08 (unless otherwise specified. or if attraction season finishes prior to this). Vouchers are subject to the terms, conditions and restrictions of the selected attraction.
3. One voucher per party will be accepted, cannot be used in conjunction with any other offer, photocopies will not be accepted.
4. All attractions offering a discount have confirmed their willingness to participate. All information is subject to change without notice and should any attraction close or decline to accept a voucher for any reason, Days Out UK are not liable and cannot be held responsible.
5. Days Out UK shall not accept liability for any loss, accident or injury that may occur at a participating attraction and any dispute arising must be settled direct with the attraction concerned.
6. Cash redemption value of each voucher is 0.001p.
7. You are advised to check all relevant information with your chosen attraction before commencing your journey.

Days Out UK, PO Box 427, Northampton NN1 3YN. Tel: 01604 622445

1. Each voucher entitles the holder to the discount specified by the selected attraction.
2. Valid for use until 28/02/08 (unless otherwise specified, or if attraction season finishes prior to this). Vouchers are subject to the terms, conditions and restrictions of the selected attraction.
3. One voucher per party will be accepted, cannot be used in conjunction with any other offer, photocopies will not be accepted.
4. All attractions offering a discount have confirmed their willingness to participate. All information is subject to change without notice and should any attraction close or decline to accept a voucher for any reason, Days Out UK are not liable and cannot be held responsible.
5. Days Out UK shall not accept liability for any loss, accident or injury that may occur at a participating attraction and any dispute arising must be settled direct with the attraction concerned.
6. Cash redemption value of each voucher is 0.001p.
7. You are advised to check all relevant information with your chosen attraction before commencing your journey.

Days Out UK, PO Box 427, Northampton NN1 3YN. Tel: 01604 622445

1. Each voucher entitles the holder to the discount specified by the selected attraction.
2. Valid for use until 28/02/08 (unless otherwise specified, or if attraction season finishes prior to this). Vouchers are subject to the terms, conditions and restrictions of the selected attraction.
3. One voucher per party will be accepted, cannot be used in conjunction with any other offer, photocopies will not be accepted.
4. All attractions offering a discount have confirmed their willingness to participate. All information is subject to change without notice and should any attraction close or decline to accept a voucher for any reason, Days Out UK are not liable and cannot be held responsible.
5. Days Out UK shall not accept liability for any loss, accident or injury that may occur at a participating attraction and any dispute arising must be settled direct with the attraction concerned.
6. Cash redemption value of each voucher is 0.001p.
7. You are advised to check all relevant information with your chosen attraction before commencing your journey.

Days Out UK, PO Box 427, Northampton NN1 3YN. Tel: 01604 622445

1. Each voucher entitles the holder to the discount specified by the selected attraction.
2. Valid for use until 28/02/08 (unless otherwise specified, or if attraction season finishes prior to this). Vouchers are subject to the terms, conditions and restrictions of the selected attraction.
3. One voucher per party will be accepted, cannot be used in conjunction with any other offer, photocopies will not be accepted.
4. All attractions offering a discount have confirmed their willingness to participate. All information is subject to change without notice and should any attraction close or decline to accept a voucher for any reason, Days Out UK are not liable and cannot be held responsible.
5. Days Out UK shall not accept liability for any loss, accident or injury that may occur at a participating attraction and any dispute arising must be settled direct with the attraction concerned.
6. Cash redemption value of each voucher is 0.001p.
7. You are advised to check all relevant information with your chosen attraction before commencing your journey.

Days Out UK, PO Box 427, Northampton NN1 3YN. Tel: 01604 622445

Birmingham Botanical Gardens
and Glasshouses
Westbourne Road Edgbaston Birmingham West Midlands B15 3TR

One Concession Free
with a full-paying adult

Cannot be used in conjunction with other offers. One voucher per party. Not valid on Bank Hols or special event days.

Expires end Feb 2008 (unless otherwise specified)

DISCOUNT VOUCHER

Blackpool Sea Life Centre

Golden Mile Centre Promenade Blackpool Lancashire

One Child Free with one full-paying adult

1. This voucher entitles free admission to the Blackpool Sea Life Centre for one child when accompanied by one full paying adult.
2. Offer expires 31 December 2007.
3. Cannot be used in conjunction with any other offer.
4. A "child" is classed as a person aged 3-14 inclusive (under 3s go free anyway).
5. No cash alternative, non-refundable; and non-exchangeable.
6. All children must be accompanied by an adult.
7. Only one voucher per party and per transaction.
8. Photocopies not accepted.
9. SEA LIFE/Sanctuaries reserve the right to alter, close or remove details/exhibits without prior notice for technical, operational or other reasons, and no refunds can be given in these circumstances.
10. SEA LIFE/Sanctuaries reserve the right to refuse entry without explanation.
Voucher Ref: DOUK.

Cannot be used in conjunction with other offers. One voucher per party. Not valid on Bank Hols or special event days.

Expires 31 December 2007

DISCOUNT VOUCHER

Blair Drummond Safari
and Adventure Park

Blair Drummond By Stirling FK9 4UR

One Child Free per vehicle

Cannot be used in conjunction with other offers. One voucher per party. Not valid on Bank Hols or special event days.

valid 24 March - 22 October 2007

DISCOUNT VOUCHER

Blue Reef Aquarium
Towan Promenade Newquay Cornwall TR7 1DU

One Child Free
with one full-paying adult

Cannot be used in conjunction with other offers. One voucher per party. Not valid on Bank Hols or special event days.

valid until 31 March 2008

DISCOUNT VOUCHER

Blue Reef Aquarium
Clarence Esplanade Southsea Portsmouth Hampshire

One Child Free
with one full-paying adult

Cannot be used in conjunction with other offers. One voucher per party. Not valid on Bank Hols or special event days.

valid until 31 March 2008

DISCOUNT VOUCHER

1. Each voucher entitles the holder to the discount specified by the selected attraction.
2. Valid for use until 28/02/08 (unless otherwise specified, or if attraction season finishes prior to this). Vouchers are subject to the terms, conditions and restrictions of the selected attraction.
3. One voucher per party will be accepted, cannot be used in conjunction with any other offer, photocopies will not be accepted.
4. All attractions offering a discount have confirmed their willingness to participate. All information is subject to change without notice and should any attraction close or decline to accept a voucher for any reason, Days Out UK are not liable and cannot be held responsible.
5. Days Out UK shall not accept liability for any loss, accident or injury that may occur at a participating attraction and any dispute arising must be settled direct with the attraction concerned.
6. Cash redemption value of each voucher is 0.001p.
7. You are advised to check all relevant information with your chosen attraction before commencing your journey.

Days Out UK, PO Box 427, Northampton NN1 3YN. Tel: 01604 622445

1. Each voucher entitles the holder to the discount specified by the selected attraction.
2. Valid for use until 28/02/08 (unless otherwise specified, or if attraction season finishes prior to this). Vouchers are subject to the terms, conditions and restrictions of the selected attraction.
3. One voucher per party will be accepted, cannot be used in conjunction with any other offer, photocopies will not be accepted.
4. All attractions offering a discount have confirmed their willingness to participate. All information is subject to change without notice and should any attraction close or decline to accept a voucher for any reason, Days Out UK are not liable and cannot be held responsible.
5. Days Out UK shall not accept liability for any loss, accident or injury that may occur at a participating attraction and any dispute arising must be settled direct with the attraction concerned.
6. Cash redemption value of each voucher is 0.001p.
7. You are advised to check all relevant information with your chosen attraction before commencing your journey.

Days Out UK, PO Box 427, Northampton NN1 3YN. Tel: 01604 622445

1. Each voucher entitles the holder to the discount specified by the selected attraction.
2. Valid for use until 28/02/08 (unless otherwise specified, or if attraction season finishes prior to this). Vouchers are subject to the terms, conditions and restrictions of the selected attraction.
3. One voucher per party will be accepted, cannot be used in conjunction with any other offer, photocopies will not be accepted.
4. All attractions offering a discount have confirmed their willingness to participate. All information is subject to change without notice and should any attraction close or decline to accept a voucher for any reason, Days Out UK are not liable and cannot be held responsible.
5. Days Out UK shall not accept liability for any loss, accident or injury that may occur at a participating attraction and any dispute arising must be settled direct with the attraction concerned.
6. Cash redemption value of each voucher is 0.001p.
7. You are advised to check all relevant information with your chosen attraction before commencing your journey.

Days Out UK, PO Box 427, Northampton NN1 3YN. Tel: 01604 622445

Blue Reef Aquarium

Grand Parade Tynemouth Tyne & Wear NE30 4JF

One Child Free

with one full-paying adult

Cannot be used in conjunction with other offers. One voucher per party. Not valid on Bank Hols or special event days.

valid until 31 March 2008

Bo'ness and Kinneil Railway

Bo'ness Station Union Street Bo'ness West Lothian

One Free Child Fare

with a full-paying adult or concession
not valid on 'Days Out with Thomas' or 'Santa Special' trains

Cannot be used in conjunction with other offers. One voucher per party. Not valid on Bank Hols or special event days.

Expires end Feb 2008 (unless otherwise specified)

Bowes Museum (The)

Barnard Castle County Durham DL12 8NP

Two for the Price of One

with a full-paying adult
(lowest priced tickets go free)

Cannot be used in conjunction with other offers. One voucher per party. Not valid on Bank Hols or special event days.

Expires end Feb 2008 (unless otherwise specified)

Bramall Hall

Bramhall Park Bramhall Cheshire SK7 3NX

Two for the Price of One

one free adult or child with one full-paying adult

Cannot be used in conjunction with other offers. One voucher per party. Not valid on Bank Hols or special event days.

Expires end Feb 2008 (unless otherwise specified)

Breamore House

and Countryside Museum

Breamore Fordingbridge Hampshire SP6 2DF

Two for the Price of One

with a full-paying adult

Cannot be used in conjunction with other offers. One voucher per party. Not valid on Bank Hols or special event days.

Expires end Feb 2008 (unless otherwise specified)

Brean Leisure Park

Coast Road Brean Sands Somerset TA8 2QY

Three for the Price of Two

full-paying adults
(not valid on Bank Holiday weekends Sat-Mon)

Cannot be used in conjunction with other offers. One voucher per party. Not valid on Bank Hols or special event days.

Expires end Feb 2008 (unless otherwise specified)

1. Each voucher entitles the holder to the discount specified by the selected attraction.
2. Valid for use until 28/02/08 (unless otherwise specified, or if attraction season finishes prior to this). Vouchers are subject to the terms, conditions and restrictions of the selected attraction.
3. One voucher per party will be accepted, cannot be used in conjunction with any other offer, photocopies will not be accepted.
4. All attractions offering a discount have confirmed their willingness to participate. All information is subject to change without notice and should any attraction close or decline to accept a voucher for any reason, Days Out UK are not liable and cannot be held responsible.
5. Days Out UK shall not accept liability for any loss, accident or injury that may occur at a participating attraction and any dispute arising must be settled direct with the attraction concerned.
6. Cash redemption value of each voucher is 0.001p.
7. You are advised to check all relevant information with your chosen attraction before commencing your journey.

Days Out UK, PO Box 427, Northampton NN1 3YN. Tel: 01604 622445

1. Each voucher entitles the holder to the discount specified by the selected attraction.
2. Valid for use until 28/02/08 (unless otherwise specified, or if attraction season finishes prior to this). Vouchers are subject to the terms, conditions and restrictions of the selected attraction.
3. One voucher per party will be accepted, cannot be used in conjunction with any other offer, photocopies will not be accepted.
4. All attractions offering a discount have confirmed their willingness to participate. All information is subject to change without notice and should any attraction close or decline to accept a voucher for any reason, Days Out UK are not liable and cannot be held responsible.
5. Days Out UK shall not accept liability for any loss, accident or injury that may occur at a participating attraction and any dispute arising must be settled direct with the attraction concerned.
6. Cash redemption value of each voucher is 0.001p.
7. You are advised to check all relevant information with your chosen attraction before commencing your journey.

Days Out UK, PO Box 427, Northampton NN1 3YN. Tel: 01604 622445

1. Each voucher entitles the holder to the discount specified by the selected attraction.
2. Valid for use until 28/02/08 (unless otherwise specified. or if attraction season finishes prior to this). Vouchers are subject to the terms, conditions and restrictions of the selected attraction.
3. One voucher per party will be accepted, cannot be used in conjunction with any other offer, photocopies will not be accepted.
4. All attractions offering a discount have confirmed their willingness to participate. All information is subject to change without notice and should any attraction close or decline to accept a voucher for any reason, Days Out UK are not liable and cannot be held responsible.
5. Days Out UK shall not accept liability for any loss, accident or injury that may occur at a participating attraction and any dispute arising must be settled direct with the attraction concerned.
6. Cash redemption value of each voucher is 0.001p.
7. You are advised to check all relevant information with your chosen attraction before commencing your journey.

Days Out UK, PO Box 427, Northampton NN1 3YN. Tel: 01604 622445

1. Each voucher entitles the holder to the discount specified by the selected attraction.
2. Valid for use until 28/02/08 (unless otherwise specified, or if attraction season finishes prior to this). Vouchers are subject to the terms, conditions and restrictions of the selected attraction.
3. One voucher per party will be accepted, cannot be used in conjunction with any other offer, photocopies will not be accepted.
4. All attractions offering a discount have confirmed their willingness to participate. All information is subject to change without notice and should any attraction close or decline to accept a voucher for any reason, Days Out UK are not liable and cannot be held responsible.
5. Days Out UK shall not accept liability for any loss, accident or injury that may occur at a participating attraction and any dispute arising must be settled direct with the attraction concerned.
6. Cash redemption value of each voucher is 0.001p.
7. You are advised to check all relevant information with your chosen attraction before commencing your journey.

Days Out UK, PO Box 427, Northampton NN1 3YN. Tel: 01604 622445

1. Each voucher entitles the holder to the discount specified by the selected attraction.
2. Valid for use until 28/02/08 (unless otherwise specified, or if attraction season finishes prior to this). Vouchers are subject to the terms, conditions and restrictions of the selected attraction.
3. One voucher per party will be accepted, cannot be used in conjunction with any other offer, photocopies will not be accepted.
4. All attractions offering a discount have confirmed their willingness to participate. All information is subject to change without notice and should any attraction close or decline to accept a voucher for any reason, Days Out UK are not liable and cannot be held responsible.
5. Days Out UK shall not accept liability for any loss, accident or injury that may occur at a participating attraction and any dispute arising must be settled direct with the attraction concerned.
6. Cash redemption value of each voucher is 0.001p.
7. You are advised to check all relevant information with your chosen attraction before commencing your journey.

Days Out UK, PO Box 427, Northampton NN1 3YN. Tel: 01604 622445

1. Each voucher entitles the holder to the discount specified by the selected attraction.
2. Valid for use until 28/02/08 (unless otherwise specified, or if attraction season finishes prior to this). Vouchers are subject to the terms, conditions and restrictions of the selected attraction.
3. One voucher per party will be accepted, cannot be used in conjunction with any other offer, photocopies will not be accepted.
4. All attractions offering a discount have confirmed their willingness to participate. All information is subject to change without notice and should any attraction close or decline to accept a voucher for any reason, Days Out UK are not liable and cannot be held responsible.
5. Days Out UK shall not accept liability for any loss, accident or injury that may occur at a participating attraction and any dispute arising must be settled direct with the attraction concerned.
6. Cash redemption value of each voucher is 0.001p.
7. You are advised to check all relevant information with your chosen attraction before commencing your journey.

Days Out UK, PO Box 427, Northampton NN1 3YN. Tel: 01604 622445

Brighton Sea Life Centre

Marine Parade Brighton East Sussex BN2 1TB

One Child Free with a full-paying adult

1. This voucher entitles free admission to the Brighton Sea Life Centre for one child when accompanied by one full paying adult.
2. Offer expires 28 February 2008.
3. Cannot be used in conjunction with any other offer.
4. A "child" is classed as a person aged 3-14 inclusive (under 3s go free anyway).
5. No cash alternative, non-refundable; and non-exchangeable.
6. All children must be accompanied by an adult.
7. Only one voucher per party and per transaction.
8. Photocopies not accepted.
9. SEA LIFE/Sanctuaries reserve the right to alter, close or remove details/exhibits without prior notice for technical, operational or other reasons, and no refunds can be given in these circumstances.
10. SEA LIFE/Sanctuaries reserve the right to refuse entry without explanation.
Voucher Ref: DOUK.

Cannot be used in conjunction with other offers. One voucher per party. Not valid on Bank Hols or special event days.

Expires end Feb 2008 (unless otherwise specified)

DISCOUNT VOUCHER

Bristol Zoo Gardens

Clifton Bristol BS8 3HA

One Child Free

with a full-paying adult

Cannot be used in conjunction with other offers. One voucher per party. Not valid on Bank Hols or special event days.

Expires end Feb 2008 (unless otherwise specified)

DISCOUNT VOUCHER

Britannia - The Royal Yacht

Ocean Terminal Leith Edinburgh EH6 6JJ

15% off Admission Prices

(A£8.07 C£4.67 OAPs£6.37, Family Ticket £22.52)

Cannot be used in conjunction with other offers. One voucher per party. Not valid on Bank Hols or special event days.

Expires end Feb 2008 (unless otherwise specified)

DISCOUNT VOUCHER

Broadview Gardens

Hadlow College Tonbridge Road Hadlow Tonbridge Kent

Two for the Price of One

with a full-paying adult

Cannot be used in conjunction with other offers. One voucher per party. Not valid on Bank Hols or special event days.

Expires end Feb 2008 (unless otherwise specified)

DISCOUNT VOUCHER

Brontë Parsonage Museum

Church Street Haworth Keighley West Yorkshire BD22 8DR

Two for the Price of One

with a full-paying adult

Cannot be used in conjunction with other offers. One voucher per party. Not valid on Bank Hols or special event days.

Expires end Feb 2008 (unless otherwise specified)

DISCOUNT VOUCHER

1. Each voucher entitles the holder to the discount specified by the selected attraction.

2. Valid for use until 28/02/08 (unless otherwise specified, or if attraction season finishes prior to this). Vouchers are subject to the terms, conditions and restrictions of the selected attraction.

3. One voucher per party will be accepted, cannot be used in conjunction with any other offer, photocopies will not be accepted.

4. All attractions offering a discount have confirmed their willingness to participate. All information is subject to change without notice and should any attraction close or decline to accept a voucher for any reason, Days Out UK are not liable and cannot be held responsible.

5. Days Out UK shall not accept liability for any loss, accident or injury that may occur at a participating attraction and any dispute arising must be settled direct with the attraction concerned.

6. Cash redemption value of each voucher is 0.001p.

7. You are advised to check all relevant information with your chosen attraction before commencing your journey.

Days Out UK, PO Box 427, Northampton NN1 3YN. Tel: 01604 622445

1. Each voucher entitles the holder to the discount specified by the selected attraction.
2. Valid for use until 28/02/08 (unless otherwise specified. or if attraction season finishes prior to this). Vouchers are subject to the terms, conditions and restrictions of the selected attraction.
3. One voucher per party will be accepted, cannot be used in conjunction with any other offer, photocopies will not be accepted.
4. All attractions offering a discount have confirmed their willingness to participate. All information is subject to change without notice and should any attraction close or decline to accept a voucher for any reason, Days Out UK are not liable and cannot be held responsible.
5. Days Out UK shall not accept liability for any loss, accident or injury that may occur at a participating attraction and any dispute arising must be settled direct with the attraction concerned.
6. Cash redemption value of each voucher is 0.001p.
7. You are advised to check all relevant information with your chosen attraction before commencing your journey.

Days Out UK, PO Box 427, Northampton NN1 3YN. Tel: 01604 622445

1. Each voucher entitles the holder to the discount specified by the selected attraction.
2. Valid for use until 28/02/08 (unless otherwise specified, or if attraction season finishes prior to this). Vouchers are subject to the terms, conditions and restrictions of the selected attraction.
3. One voucher per party will be accepted, cannot be used in conjunction with any other offer, photocopies will not be accepted.
4. All attractions offering a discount have confirmed their willingness to participate. All information is subject to change without notice and should any attraction close or decline to accept a voucher for any reason, Days Out UK are not liable and cannot be held responsible.
5. Days Out UK shall not accept liability for any loss, accident or injury that may occur at a participating attraction and any dispute arising must be settled direct with the attraction concerned.
6. Cash redemption value of each voucher is 0.001p.
7. You are advised to check all relevant information with your chosen attraction before commencing your journey.

Days Out UK, PO Box 427, Northampton NN1 3YN. Tel: 01604 622445

1. Each voucher entitles the holder to the discount specified by the selected attraction.
2. Valid for use until 28/02/08 (unless otherwise specified, or if attraction season finishes prior to this). Vouchers are subject to the terms, conditions and restrictions of the selected attraction.
3. One voucher per party will be accepted, cannot be used in conjunction with any other offer, photocopies will not be accepted.
4. All attractions offering a discount have confirmed their willingness to participate. All information is subject to change without notice and should any attraction close or decline to accept a voucher for any reason, Days Out UK are not liable and cannot be held responsible.
5. Days Out UK shall not accept liability for any loss, accident or injury that may occur at a participating attraction and any dispute arising must be settled direct with the attraction concerned.
6. Cash redemption value of each voucher is 0.001p.
7. You are advised to check all relevant information with your chosen attraction before commencing your journey.

Days Out UK, PO Box 427, Northampton NN1 3YN. Tel: 01604 622445

1. Each voucher entitles the holder to the discount specified by the selected attraction.
2. Valid for use until 28/02/08 (unless otherwise specified, or if attraction season finishes prior to this). Vouchers are subject to the terms, conditions and restrictions of the selected attraction.
3. One voucher per party will be accepted, cannot be used in conjunction with any other offer, photocopies will not be accepted.
4. All attractions offering a discount have confirmed their willingness to participate. All information is subject to change without notice and should any attraction close or decline to accept a voucher for any reason, Days Out UK are not liable and cannot be held responsible.
5. Days Out UK shall not accept liability for any loss, accident or injury that may occur at a participating attraction and any dispute arising must be settled direct with the attraction concerned.
6. Cash redemption value of each voucher is 0.001p.
7. You are advised to check all relevant information with your chosen attraction before commencing your journey.

Days Out UK, PO Box 427, Northampton NN1 3YN. Tel: 01604 622445

Broughton Castle
Banbury Oxfordshire OX15 5EB
Two for the Price of One
with a full-paying adult

Cannot be used in conjunction with other offers. One voucher per party. Not valid on Bank Hols or special event days.

Expires end Feb 2008 (unless otherwise specified)

Buckinghamshire Railway Centre
Quinton Road Station Quainton Aylesbury Buckinghamshire
Two for the Price of One
with a full-paying adult
(not valid for 'Days Out with Thomas' or 'Steaming Santa' events)

Cannot be used in conjunction with other offers. One voucher per party. Not valid on Bank Hols or special event days.

Expires end Feb 2008 (unless otherwise specified)

Bure Valley Railway
Aylsham Station Norwich Road Aylsham Norfolk NR11 6BW
One Child Free
with every full-paying adult
(excludes combined Train/Boat trips, 'Santa Specials' and 'Day Out with Thomas')

Cannot be used in conjunction with other offers. One voucher per party. Not valid on Bank Hols or special event days.

Expires end Feb 2008 (unless otherwise specified)

Bush Farm Bison Centre
West Knoyle Mere Wiltshire BA12 6AE
One Child Free
with a full-paying adult

Cannot be used in conjunction with other offers. One voucher per party. Not valid on Bank Hols or special event days.

Expires end Feb 2008 (unless otherwise specified)

Butlins
Skegness Lincolnshire PE25 1NJ
Two for the Price of One
with a full-paying adult

Cannot be used in conjunction with other offers. One voucher per party. Not valid on Bank Hols or special event days.

Expires end Feb 2008 (unless otherwise specified)

Butlins
Warren Road Minehead Somerset TA24 5SH
Kid For A Quid
(One Child enters for £1.00)

Cannot be used in conjunction with other offers. One voucher per party. Not valid on Bank Hols or special event days.

Expires end Feb 2008 (unless otherwise specified)

1. Each voucher entitles the holder to the discount specified by the selected attraction.
2. Valid for use until 28/02/08 (unless otherwise specified, or if attraction season finishes prior to this). Vouchers are subject to the terms, conditions and restrictions of the selected attraction.
3. One voucher per party will be accepted, cannot be used in conjunction with any other offer, photocopies will not be accepted.
4. All attractions offering a discount have confirmed their willingness to participate. All information is subject to change without notice and should any attraction close or decline to accept a voucher for any reason, Days Out UK are not liable and cannot be held responsible.
5. Days Out UK shall not accept liability for any loss, accident or injury that may occur at a participating attraction and any dispute arising must be settled direct with the attraction concerned.
6. Cash redemption value of each voucher is 0.001p.
7. You are advised to check all relevant information with your chosen attraction before commencing your journey.

Days Out UK, PO Box 427, Northampton NN1 3YN. Tel: 01604 622445

1. Each voucher entitles the holder to the discount specified by the selected attraction.
2. Valid for use until 28/02/08 (unless otherwise specified. or if attraction season finishes prior to this). Vouchers are subject to the terms, conditions and restrictions of the selected attraction.
3. One voucher per party will be accepted, cannot be used in conjunction with any other offer, photocopies will not be accepted.
4. All attractions offering a discount have confirmed their willingness to participate. All information is subject to change without notice and should any attraction close or decline to accept a voucher for any reason, Days Out UK are not liable and cannot be held responsible.
5. Days Out UK shall not accept liability for any loss, accident or injury that may occur at a participating attraction and any dispute arising must be settled direct with the attraction concerned.
6. Cash redemption value of each voucher is 0.001p.
7. You are advised to check all relevant information with your chosen attraction before commencing your journey.

Days Out UK, PO Box 427, Northampton NN1 3YN. Tel: 01604 622445

1. Each voucher entitles the holder to the discount specified by the selected attraction.
2. Valid for use until 28/02/08 (unless otherwise specified, or if attraction season finishes prior to this). Vouchers are subject to the terms, conditions and restrictions of the selected attraction.
3. One voucher per party will be accepted, cannot be used in conjunction with any other offer, photocopies will not be accepted.
4. All attractions offering a discount have confirmed their willingness to participate. All information is subject to change without notice and should any attraction close or decline to accept a voucher for any reason, Days Out UK are not liable and cannot be held responsible.
5. Days Out UK shall not accept liability for any loss, accident or injury that may occur at a participating attraction and any dispute arising must be settled direct with the attraction concerned.
6. Cash redemption value of each voucher is 0.001p.
7. You are advised to check all relevant information with your chosen attraction before commencing your journey.

Days Out UK, PO Box 427, Northampton NN1 3YN. Tel: 01604 622445

1. Each voucher entitles the holder to the discount specified by the selected attraction.
2. Valid for use until 28/02/08 (unless otherwise specified, or if attraction season finishes prior to this). Vouchers are subject to the terms, conditions and restrictions of the selected attraction.
3. One voucher per party will be accepted, cannot be used in conjunction with any other offer, photocopies will not be accepted.
4. All attractions offering a discount have confirmed their willingness to participate. All information is subject to change without notice and should any attraction close or decline to accept a voucher for any reason, Days Out UK are not liable and cannot be held responsible.
5. Days Out UK shall not accept liability for any loss, accident or injury that may occur at a participating attraction and any dispute arising must be settled direct with the attraction concerned.
6. Cash redemption value of each voucher is 0.001p.
7. You are advised to check all relevant information with your chosen attraction before commencing your journey.

Days Out UK, PO Box 427, Northampton NN1 3YN. Tel: 01604 622445

1. Each voucher entitles the holder to the discount specified by the selected attraction.
2. Valid for use until 28/02/08 (unless otherwise specified, or if attraction season finishes prior to this). Vouchers are subject to the terms, conditions and restrictions of the selected attraction.
3. One voucher per party will be accepted, cannot be used in conjunction with any other offer, photocopies will not be accepted.
4. All attractions offering a discount have confirmed their willingness to participate. All information is subject to change without notice and should any attraction close or decline to accept a voucher for any reason, Days Out UK are not liable and cannot be held responsible.
5. Days Out UK shall not accept liability for any loss, accident or injury that may occur at a participating attraction and any dispute arising must be settled direct with the attraction concerned.
6. Cash redemption value of each voucher is 0.001p.
7. You are advised to check all relevant information with your chosen attraction before commencing your journey.

Days Out UK, PO Box 427, Northampton NN1 3YN. Tel: 01604 622445

Cadbury World

Linden Road Bournville Birmingham West Midlands B30 2LU

£10.00 off One Family Ticket

(A2+C2) or (A2+C3)

Cannot be used in conjunction with other offers. One voucher per party. Not valid on Bank Hols or special event days.

Expires end Feb 2008 (unless otherwise specified)

DISCOUNT VOUCHER

Callendar House

Callendar Park Falkirk Stirlingshire FK1 1YR

10% discount on all gift shop purchases

(when you spend £10.00 or more)

Cannot be used in conjunction with other offers. One voucher per party. Not valid on Bank Hols or special event days.

Expires end Feb 2008 (unless otherwise specified)

DISCOUNT VOUCHER

Camelot Theme Park

Park Hall Road Charnock Richard Chorley Lancashire

Two for the Price of One

with a full-paying adult

Cannot be used in conjunction with other offers. One voucher per party. Not valid on Bank Hols or special event days.

Expires end Feb 2008 (unless otherwise specified)

DISCOUNT VOUCHER

Campaign Paintball Park

Old Lane Cobham Surrey KT11 1NH

100 Free Paintballs

(when you pay for a full game)

Cannot be used in conjunction with other offers. One voucher per party. Not valid on Bank Hols or special event days.

Expires end Feb 2008 (unless otherwise specified)

DISCOUNT VOUCHER

Canal Cruises - Jenny Wren

250 Camden High Street London NW1 8QS

One Child Free

with every full-paying adult

Cannot be used in conjunction with other offers. One voucher per party. Not valid on Bank Hols or special event days.

Expires end Feb 2008 (unless otherwise specified)

DISCOUNT VOUCHER

Canal Cruises - My Fair Lady

Cruising Restaurant

250 Camden High Street London NW1 8QS

One free bottle of wine for every four full-paying adults
(valid for lunch or dinner cruises)

Cannot be used in conjunction with other offers. One voucher per party. Not valid on Bank Hols or special event days.

Expires end Feb 2008 (unless otherwise specified)

DISCOUNT VOUCHER

Caring Parent Show with Noddy
Kent Showground Detling Kent ME14 3JF
Two for the Price of One
with a full-paying adult

Cannot be used in conjunction with other offers. One voucher per party. Not valid on Bank Hols or special event days.

Expires end Feb 2008 (unless otherwise specified)

Castle Bromwich Hall Gardens
Chester Road Castle Bromwich Birmingham West Midlands
Two for the Price of One
with a full-paying adult

Cannot be used in conjunction with other offers. One voucher per party. Not valid on Bank Hols or special event days.

valid until 30 September 2007

Catalyst: Science Discovery Centre
Mersey Road Widnes Cheshire WA8 0DF
One Child Free
with a full-paying adult

Cannot be used in conjunction with other offers. One voucher per party. Not valid on Bank Hols or special event days.

Expires end Feb 2008 (unless otherwise specified)

Cattle Country Adventure Park
Berkeley Heath Farm Berkeley Gloucestershire GL13 9EW
10% Discount on Admission Prices
& Gift Shop Purchases

(one voucher per person and per transaction; cannot be used for food and drink purchases)
Cannot be used in conjunction with other offers. One voucher per party. Not valid on Bank Hols or special event days.

valid until 31 December 2007

Charles Dickens' Birthplace
393 Old Commercial Road Portsmouth Hampshire PO1 4QL
20% off Adult Admissions (A£2.80)

not valid on events days; maximum 2 discounted adults per transaction
Cannot be used in conjunction with other offers. One voucher per party. Not valid on Bank Hols or special event days.

Expires end Feb 2008 (unless otherwise specified)

Cheddar Caves and Gorge
Cheddar Somerset BS27 3QF
£1.00 off per person
on full admission price
(not valid with any other discount or offer)

Cannot be used in conjunction with other offers. One voucher per party. Not valid on Bank Hols or special event days.

Expires end Feb 2008 (unless otherwise specified)

Chillingham Castle and Gardens

Chillingham Alnwick Northumberland NE66 5NJ

One Child Free

with one full-paying adult

Cannot be used in conjunction with other offers. One voucher per party. Not valid on Bank Hols or special event days.

Expires end Feb 2008 (unless otherwise specified)

Chislehurst Caves

Old Hill Chislehurst Kent BR7 5NB

One Child Free

with a full-paying adult

Cannot be used in conjunction with other offers. One voucher per party. Not valid on Bank Hols or special event days.

Expires end Feb 2008 (unless otherwise specified)

Cholderton Rare Breeds Farm

Amesbury Road Cholderton Salisbury Wiltshire SP4 0EW

One Child Free

with a full-paying adult

Cannot be used in conjunction with other offers. One voucher per party. Not valid on Bank Hols or special event days.

Expires end Feb 2008 (unless otherwise specified)

City Cruises

Cherry Garden Pier Cherry Garden Street London SE16 4TU

One Child Free

with a full-paying adult

Cannot be used in conjunction with other offers. One voucher per party. Not valid on Bank Hols or special event days.

Expires end Feb 2008 (unless otherwise specified)

City of Caves

Upper Level Broad Marsh Shopping Centre Nottingham Nottinghamshire NG1 7LS

One Child Free

with a full-paying adult

Cannot be used in conjunction with other offers. One voucher per party. Not valid on Bank Hols or special event days.

Expires end Feb 2008 (unless otherwise specified)

Clearwell Caves Ancient Iron Mines

Royal Forest of Dean Coleford Gloucestershire GL16 8JR

One Child Free

with a full-paying adult

not valid for 'Christmas Fantasy' event

Cannot be used in conjunction with other offers. One voucher per party. Not valid on Bank Hols or special event days.

Expires end Feb 2008 (unless otherwise specified)

1. Each voucher entitles the holder to the discount specified by the selected attraction.
2. Valid for use until 28/02/08 (unless otherwise specified, or if attraction season finishes prior to this). Vouchers are subject to the terms, conditions and restrictions of the selected attraction.
3. One voucher per party will be accepted, cannot be used in conjunction with any other offer, photocopies will not be accepted.
4. All attractions offering a discount have confirmed their willingness to participate. All information is subject to change without notice and should any attraction close or decline to accept a voucher for any reason, Days Out UK are not liable and cannot be held responsible.
5. Days Out UK shall not accept liability for any loss, accident or injury that may occur at a participating attraction and any dispute arising must be settled direct with the attraction concerned.
6. Cash redemption value of each voucher is 0.001p.
7. You are advised to check all relevant information with your chosen attraction before commencing your journey.

Days Out UK, PO Box 427, Northampton NN1 3YN. Tel: 01604 622445

1. Each voucher entitles the holder to the discount specified by the selected attraction.
2. Valid for use until 28/02/08 (unless otherwise specified. or if attraction season finishes prior to this). Vouchers are subject to the terms, conditions and restrictions of the selected attraction.
3. One voucher per party will be accepted, cannot be used in conjunction with any other offer, photocopies will not be accepted.
4. All attractions offering a discount have confirmed their willingness to participate. All information is subject to change without notice and should any attraction close or decline to accept a voucher for any reason, Days Out UK are not liable and cannot be held responsible.
5. Days Out UK shall not accept liability for any loss, accident or injury that may occur at a participating attraction and any dispute arising must be settled direct with the attraction concerned.
6. Cash redemption value of each voucher is 0.001p.
7. You are advised to check all relevant information with your chosen attraction before commencing your journey.

Days Out UK, PO Box 427, Northampton NN1 3YN. Tel: 01604 622445

1. Each voucher entitles the holder to the discount specified by the selected attraction.
2. Valid for use until 28/02/08 (unless otherwise specified, or if attraction season finishes prior to this). Vouchers are subject to the terms, conditions and restrictions of the selected attraction.
3. One voucher per party will be accepted, cannot be used in conjunction with any other offer, photocopies will not be accepted.
4. All attractions offering a discount have confirmed their willingness to participate. All information is subject to change without notice and should any attraction close or decline to accept a voucher for any reason, Days Out UK are not liable and cannot be held responsible.
5. Days Out UK shall not accept liability for any loss, accident or injury that may occur at a participating attraction and any dispute arising must be settled direct with the attraction concerned.
6. Cash redemption value of each voucher is 0.001p.
7. You are advised to check all relevant information with your chosen attraction before commencing your journey.

Days Out UK, PO Box 427, Northampton NN1 3YN. Tel: 01604 622445

1. Each voucher entitles the holder to the discount specified by the selected attraction.
2. Valid for use until 28/02/08 (unless otherwise specified, or if attraction season finishes prior to this). Vouchers are subject to the terms, conditions and restrictions of the selected attraction.
3. One voucher per party will be accepted, cannot be used in conjunction with any other offer, photocopies will not be accepted.
4. All attractions offering a discount have confirmed their willingness to participate. All information is subject to change without notice and should any attraction close or decline to accept a voucher for any reason, Days Out UK are not liable and cannot be held responsible.
5. Days Out UK shall not accept liability for any loss, accident or injury that may occur at a participating attraction and any dispute arising must be settled direct with the attraction concerned.
6. Cash redemption value of each voucher is 0.001p.
7. You are advised to check all relevant information with your chosen attraction before commencing your journey.

Days Out UK, PO Box 427, Northampton NN1 3YN. Tel: 01604 622445

1. Each voucher entitles the holder to the discount specified by the selected attraction.
2. Valid for use until 28/02/08 (unless otherwise specified, or if attraction season finishes prior to this). Vouchers are subject to the terms, conditions and restrictions of the selected attraction.
3. One voucher per party will be accepted, cannot be used in conjunction with any other offer, photocopies will not be accepted.
4. All attractions offering a discount have confirmed their willingness to participate. All information is subject to change without notice and should any attraction close or decline to accept a voucher for any reason, Days Out UK are not liable and cannot be held responsible.
5. Days Out UK shall not accept liability for any loss, accident or injury that may occur at a participating attraction and any dispute arising must be settled direct with the attraction concerned.
6. Cash redemption value of each voucher is 0.001p.
7. You are advised to check all relevant information with your chosen attraction before commencing your journey.

Days Out UK, PO Box 427, Northampton NN1 3YN. Tel: 01604 622445

DAYSOUTUK
The place to look for places to go

Combe Martin Wildlife
and Dinosaur Park
Combe Martin Ilfracombe Devon EX34 0NG
One Child Free
with every two full-paying adults
Cannot be used in conjunction with other offers. One voucher per party. Not valid on Bank Hols or special event days.
Expires end Feb 2008 (unless otherwise specified)

DAYSOUTUK
The place to look for places to go

Compton Acres Gardens
164 Canford Cliffs Road Poole Dorset BH13 7ES
Two for the Price of One
with a full-paying adult
not valid on pre-booked events
Cannot be used in conjunction with other offers. One voucher per party. Not valid on Bank Hols or special event days.
valid 1 Mar-31 Oct 2007

DAYSOUTUK
The place to look for places to go

Compton Verney
Compton Verney Warwickshire CV35 9HZ
Free children's lunch box worth £3.50
with every main course meal purchased in the Café
Cannot be used in conjunction with other offers. One voucher per party. Not valid on Bank Hols or special event days.
valid 27 March - 7 December 2007 (Tue-Fri only)

DAYSOUTUK
The place to look for places to go

Connemara Heritage and History Centre
and Dan O'Hara's Homestead
Lettershea Clifden County Galway Ireland
Two for the Price of One
with a full-paying adult
Cannot be used in conjunction with other offers. One voucher per party. Not valid on Bank Hols or special event days.
Expires end Feb 2008 (unless otherwise specified)

DAYSOUTUK
The place to look for places to go

Cornwall's Crealy Great Adventure Park
Tredinnick Newquay Cornwall PL27 7RA
One Free Ice-Cream
one voucher per party and per transaction. Code: DOUK07C
Cannot be used in conjunction with other offers. One voucher per party. Not valid on Bank Hols or special event days.
Expires 30 September 2007

DAYSOUTUK
The place to look for places to go

Cotswold Farm Park
Guiting Power Stow on the Wold Cheltenham
Gloucestershire GL54 5UG
One Child Free
with a full-paying adult
Cannot be used in conjunction with other offers. One voucher per party. Not valid on Bank Hols or special event days.
Expires end Feb 2008 (unless otherwise specified)

1. Each voucher entitles the holder to the discount specified by the selected attraction.
2. Valid for use until 28/02/08 (unless otherwise specified, or if attraction season finishes prior to this). Vouchers are subject to the terms, conditions and restrictions of the selected attraction.
3. One voucher per party will be accepted, cannot be used in conjunction with any other offer, photocopies will not be accepted.
4. All attractions offering a discount have confirmed their willingness to participate. All information is subject to change without notice and should any attraction close or decline to accept a voucher for any reason, Days Out UK are not liable and cannot be held responsible.
5. Days Out UK shall not accept liability for any loss, accident or injury that may occur at a participating attraction and any dispute arising must be settled direct with the attraction concerned.
6. Cash redemption value of each voucher is 0.001p.
7. You are advised to check all relevant information with your chosen attraction before commencing your journey.

Days Out UK, PO Box 427, Northampton NN1 3YN. Tel: 01604 622445

1. Each voucher entitles the holder to the discount specified by the selected attraction.
2. Valid for use until 28/02/08 (unless otherwise specified, or if attraction season finishes prior to this). Vouchers are subject to the terms, conditions and restrictions of the selected attraction.
3. One voucher per party will be accepted, cannot be used in conjunction with any other offer, photocopies will not be accepted.
4. All attractions offering a discount have confirmed their willingness to participate. All information is subject to change without notice and should any attraction close or decline to accept a voucher for any reason, Days Out UK are not liable and cannot be held responsible.
5. Days Out UK shall not accept liability for any loss, accident or injury that may occur at a participating attraction and any dispute arising must be settled direct with the attraction concerned.
6. Cash redemption value of each voucher is 0.001p.
7. You are advised to check all relevant information with your chosen attraction before commencing your journey.

Days Out UK, PO Box 427, Northampton NN1 3YN. Tel: 01604 622445

1. Each voucher entitles the holder to the discount specified by the selected attraction.
2. Valid for use until 28/02/08 (unless otherwise specified. or if attraction season finishes prior to this). Vouchers are subject to the terms, conditions and restrictions of the selected attraction.
3. One voucher per party will be accepted, cannot be used in conjunction with any other offer, photocopies will not be accepted.
4. All attractions offering a discount have confirmed their willingness to participate. All information is subject to change without notice and should any attraction close or decline to accept a voucher for any reason, Days Out UK are not liable and cannot be held responsible.
5. Days Out UK shall not accept liability for any loss, accident or injury that may occur at a participating attraction and any dispute arising must be settled direct with the attraction concerned.
6. Cash redemption value of each voucher is 0.001p.
7. You are advised to check all relevant information with your chosen attraction before commencing your journey.

Days Out UK, PO Box 427, Northampton NN1 3YN. Tel: 01604 622445

1. Each voucher entitles the holder to the discount specified by the selected attraction.
2. Valid for use until 28/02/08 (unless otherwise specified, or if attraction season finishes prior to this). Vouchers are subject to the terms, conditions and restrictions of the selected attraction.
3. One voucher per party will be accepted, cannot be used in conjunction with any other offer, photocopies will not be accepted.
4. All attractions offering a discount have confirmed their willingness to participate. All information is subject to change without notice and should any attraction close or decline to accept a voucher for any reason, Days Out UK are not liable and cannot be held responsible.
5. Days Out UK shall not accept liability for any loss, accident or injury that may occur at a participating attraction and any dispute arising must be settled direct with the attraction concerned.
6. Cash redemption value of each voucher is 0.001p.
7. You are advised to check all relevant information with your chosen attraction before commencing your journey.

Days Out UK, PO Box 427, Northampton NN1 3YN. Tel: 01604 622445

1. Each voucher entitles the holder to the discount specified by the selected attraction.
2. Valid for use until 28/02/08 (unless otherwise specified, or if attraction season finishes prior to this). Vouchers are subject to the terms, conditions and restrictions of the selected attraction.
3. One voucher per party will be accepted, cannot be used in conjunction with any other offer, photocopies will not be accepted.
4. All attractions offering a discount have confirmed their willingness to participate. All information is subject to change without notice and should any attraction close or decline to accept a voucher for any reason, Days Out UK are not liable and cannot be held responsible.
5. Days Out UK shall not accept liability for any loss, accident or injury that may occur at a participating attraction and any dispute arising must be settled direct with the attraction concerned.
6. Cash redemption value of each voucher is 0.001p.
7. You are advised to check all relevant information with your chosen attraction before commencing your journey.

Days Out UK, PO Box 427, Northampton NN1 3YN. Tel: 01604 622445

1. Each voucher entitles the holder to the discount specified by the selected attraction.
2. Valid for use until 28/02/08 (unless otherwise specified, or if attraction season finishes prior to this). Vouchers are subject to the terms, conditions and restrictions of the selected attraction.
3. One voucher per party will be accepted, cannot be used in conjunction with any other offer, photocopies will not be accepted.
4. All attractions offering a discount have confirmed their willingness to participate. All information is subject to change without notice and should any attraction close or decline to accept a voucher for any reason, Days Out UK are not liable and cannot be held responsible.
5. Days Out UK shall not accept liability for any loss, accident or injury that may occur at a participating attraction and any dispute arising must be settled direct with the attraction concerned.
6. Cash redemption value of each voucher is 0.001p.
7. You are advised to check all relevant information with your chosen attraction before commencing your journey.

Days Out UK, PO Box 427, Northampton NN1 3YN. Tel: 01604 622445

1. Each voucher entitles the holder to the discount specified by the selected attraction.
2. Valid for use until 28/02/08 (unless otherwise specified, or if attraction season finishes prior to this). Vouchers are subject to the terms, conditions and restrictions of the selected attraction.
3. One voucher per party will be accepted, cannot be used in conjunction with any other offer, photocopies will not be accepted.
4. All attractions offering a discount have confirmed their willingness to participate. All information is subject to change without notice and should any attraction close or decline to accept a voucher for any reason, Days Out UK are not liable and cannot be held responsible.
5. Days Out UK shall not accept liability for any loss, accident or injury that may occur at a participating attraction and any dispute arising must be settled direct with the attraction concerned.
6. Cash redemption value of each voucher is 0.001p.
7. You are advised to check all relevant information with your chosen attraction before commencing your journey.

Days Out UK, PO Box 427, Northampton NN1 3YN. Tel: 01604 622445

1. Each voucher entitles the holder to the discount specified by the selected attraction.
2. Valid for use until 28/02/08 (unless otherwise specified, or if attraction season finishes prior to this). Vouchers are subject to the terms, conditions and restrictions of the selected attraction.
3. One voucher per party will be accepted, cannot be used in conjunction with any other offer, photocopies will not be accepted.
4. All attractions offering a discount have confirmed their willingness to participate. All information is subject to change without notice and should any attraction close or decline to accept a voucher for any reason, Days Out UK are not liable and cannot be held responsible.
5. Days Out UK shall not accept liability for any loss, accident or injury that may occur at a participating attraction and any dispute arising must be settled direct with the attraction concerned.
6. Cash redemption value of each voucher is 0.001p.
7. You are advised to check all relevant information with your chosen attraction before commencing your journey.

Days Out UK, PO Box 427, Northampton NN1 3YN. Tel: 01604 622445

1. Each voucher entitles the holder to the discount specified by the selected attraction.
2. Valid for use until 28/02/08 (unless otherwise specified, or if attraction season finishes prior to this). Vouchers are subject to the terms, conditions and restrictions of the selected attraction.
3. One voucher per party will be accepted, cannot be used in conjunction with any other offer, photocopies will not be accepted.
4. All attractions offering a discount have confirmed their willingness to participate. All information is subject to change without notice and should any attraction close or decline to accept a voucher for any reason, Days Out UK are not liable and cannot be held responsible.
5. Days Out UK shall not accept liability for any loss, accident or injury that may occur at a participating attraction and any dispute arising must be settled direct with the attraction concerned.
6. Cash redemption value of each voucher is 0.001p.
7. You are advised to check all relevant information with your chosen attraction before commencing your journey.

Days Out UK, PO Box 427, Northampton NN1 3YN. Tel: 01604 622445

1. Each voucher entitles the holder to the discount specified by the selected attraction.
2. Valid for use until 28/02/08 (unless otherwise specified, or if attraction season finishes prior to this). Vouchers are subject to the terms, conditions and restrictions of the selected attraction.
3. One voucher per party will be accepted, cannot be used in conjunction with any other offer, photocopies will not be accepted.
4. All attractions offering a discount have confirmed their willingness to participate. All information is subject to change without notice and should any attraction close or decline to accept a voucher for any reason, Days Out UK are not liable and cannot be held responsible.
5. Days Out UK shall not accept liability for any loss, accident or injury that may occur at a participating attraction and any dispute arising must be settled direct with the attraction concerned.
6. Cash redemption value of each voucher is 0.001p.
7. You are advised to check all relevant information with your chosen attraction before commencing your journey.

Days Out UK, PO Box 427, Northampton NN1 3YN. Tel: 01604 622445

Dartington Crystal

Linden Close Torrington Devon EX38 7AN

Two for the Price of One

with a full-paying adult

Cannot be used in conjunction with other offers. One voucher per party. Not valid on Bank Hols or special event days.

Expires end Feb 2008 (unless otherwise specified)

Denbies Wine Estate

London Road Dorking Surrey RH5 6AA

Two for the Price of One

with a full-paying adult

Cannot be used in conjunction with other offers. One voucher per party. Not valid on Bank Hols or special event days.

Expires end Feb 2008 (valid Mon-Fri only)

Denby Pottery Visitor Centre

Derby Road Denby Ripley Derbyshire DE5 8NX

Two for the Price of One

with a full-paying adult

applies to Factory Tours; lowest priced ticket goes free; one per party

Cannot be used in conjunction with other offers. One voucher per party. Not valid on Bank Hols or special event days.

Expires end Feb 2008 (unless otherwise specified)

Denmans Garden

Denmans Lane Fontwell West Sussex BN18 0SU

Two for the Price of One

with a full-paying adult

(excluding weekends and Bank Holidays; no cash alternative)

Cannot be used in conjunction with other offers. One voucher per party. Not valid on Bank Hols or special event days.

Expires end Feb 2008 (unless otherwise specified)

Devon's Crealy Great Adventure Park

Sidmouth Road Clyst St Mary Exeter Devon EX5 1DR

One Free Go-Kart Ride

only valid before 12.00 (noon)

one voucher per party and per transaction. Code: DOUK07D

Cannot be used in conjunction with other offers. One voucher per party. Not valid on Bank Hols or special event days.

Expires 30 September 2007

Didcot Railway Centre

Didcot Oxfordshire OX11 7NJ

Two for the Price of One

with a full-paying adult

(not valid for 'Days Out with Thomas' or 'Santa Specials')

Cannot be used in conjunction with other offers. One voucher per party. Not valid on Bank Hols or special event days.

Expires end Feb 2008 (unless otherwise specified)

1. Each voucher entitles the holder to the discount specified by the selected attraction.
2. Valid for use until 28/02/08 (unless otherwise specified, or if attraction season finishes prior to this). Vouchers are subject to the terms, conditions and restrictions of the selected attraction.
3. One voucher per party will be accepted, cannot be used in conjunction with any other offer, photocopies will not be accepted.
4. All attractions offering a discount have confirmed their willingness to participate. All information is subject to change without notice and should any attraction close or decline to accept a voucher for any reason, Days Out UK are not liable and cannot be held responsible.
5. Days Out UK shall not accept liability for any loss, accident or injury that may occur at a participating attraction and any dispute arising must be settled direct with the attraction concerned.
6. Cash redemption value of each voucher is 0.001p.
7. You are advised to check all relevant information with your chosen attraction before commencing your journey.

Days Out UK, PO Box 427, Northampton NN1 3YN. Tel: 01604 622445

1. Each voucher entitles the holder to the discount specified by the selected attraction.
2. Valid for use until 28/02/08 (unless otherwise specified. or if attraction season finishes prior to this). Vouchers are subject to the terms, conditions and restrictions of the selected attraction.
3. One voucher per party will be accepted, cannot be used in conjunction with any other offer, photocopies will not be accepted.
4. All attractions offering a discount have confirmed their willingness to participate. All information is subject to change without notice and should any attraction close or decline to accept a voucher for any reason, Days Out UK are not liable and cannot be held responsible.
5. Days Out UK shall not accept liability for any loss, accident or injury that may occur at a participating attraction and any dispute arising must be settled direct with the attraction concerned.
6. Cash redemption value of each voucher is 0.001p.
7. You are advised to check all relevant information with your chosen attraction before commencing your journey.

Days Out UK, PO Box 427, Northampton NN1 3YN. Tel: 01604 622445

1. Each voucher entitles the holder to the discount specified by the selected attraction.
2. Valid for use until 28/02/08 (unless otherwise specified, or if attraction season finishes prior to this). Vouchers are subject to the terms, conditions and restrictions of the selected attraction.
3. One voucher per party will be accepted, cannot be used in conjunction with any other offer, photocopies will not be accepted.
4. All attractions offering a discount have confirmed their willingness to participate. All information is subject to change without notice and should any attraction close or decline to accept a voucher for any reason, Days Out UK are not liable and cannot be held responsible.
5. Days Out UK shall not accept liability for any loss, accident or injury that may occur at a participating attraction and any dispute arising must be settled direct with the attraction concerned.
6. Cash redemption value of each voucher is 0.001p.
7. You are advised to check all relevant information with your chosen attraction before commencing your journey.

Days Out UK, PO Box 427, Northampton NN1 3YN. Tel: 01604 622445

1. Each voucher entitles the holder to the discount specified by the selected attraction.
2. Valid for use until 28/02/08 (unless otherwise specified, or if attraction season finishes prior to this). Vouchers are subject to the terms, conditions and restrictions of the selected attraction.
3. One voucher per party will be accepted, cannot be used in conjunction with any other offer, photocopies will not be accepted.
4. All attractions offering a discount have confirmed their willingness to participate. All information is subject to change without notice and should any attraction close or decline to accept a voucher for any reason, Days Out UK are not liable and cannot be held responsible.
5. Days Out UK shall not accept liability for any loss, accident or injury that may occur at a participating attraction and any dispute arising must be settled direct with the attraction concerned.
6. Cash redemption value of each voucher is 0.001p.
7. You are advised to check all relevant information with your chosen attraction before commencing your journey.

Days Out UK, PO Box 427, Northampton NN1 3YN. Tel: 01604 622445

1. Each voucher entitles the holder to the discount specified by the selected attraction.
2. Valid for use until 28/02/08 (unless otherwise specified, or if attraction season finishes prior to this). Vouchers are subject to the terms, conditions and restrictions of the selected attraction.
3. One voucher per party will be accepted, cannot be used in conjunction with any other offer, photocopies will not be accepted.
4. All attractions offering a discount have confirmed their willingness to participate. All information is subject to change without notice and should any attraction close or decline to accept a voucher for any reason, Days Out UK are not liable and cannot be held responsible.
5. Days Out UK shall not accept liability for any loss, accident or injury that may occur at a participating attraction and any dispute arising must be settled direct with the attraction concerned.
6. Cash redemption value of each voucher is 0.001p.
7. You are advised to check all relevant information with your chosen attraction before commencing your journey.

Days Out UK, PO Box 427, Northampton NN1 3YN. Tel: 01604 622445

1. Each voucher entitles the holder to the discount specified by the selected attraction.
2. Valid for use until 28/02/08 (unless otherwise specified, or if attraction season finishes prior to this). Vouchers are subject to the terms, conditions and restrictions of the selected attraction.
3. One voucher per party will be accepted, cannot be used in conjunction with any other offer, photocopies will not be accepted.
4. All attractions offering a discount have confirmed their willingness to participate. All information is subject to change without notice and should any attraction close or decline to accept a voucher for any reason, Days Out UK are not liable and cannot be held responsible.
5. Days Out UK shall not accept liability for any loss, accident or injury that may occur at a participating attraction and any dispute arising must be settled direct with the attraction concerned.
6. Cash redemption value of each voucher is 0.001p.
7. You are advised to check all relevant information with your chosen attraction before commencing your journey.

Days Out UK, PO Box 427, Northampton NN1 3YN. Tel: 01604 622445

1. Each voucher entitles the holder to the discount specified by the selected attraction.
2. Valid for use until 28/02/08 (unless otherwise specified, or if attraction season finishes prior to this). Vouchers are subject to the terms, conditions and restrictions of the selected attraction.
3. One voucher per party will be accepted, cannot be used in conjunction with any other offer, photocopies will not be accepted.
4. All attractions offering a discount have confirmed their willingness to participate. All information is subject to change without notice and should any attraction close or decline to accept a voucher for any reason, Days Out UK are not liable and cannot be held responsible.
5. Days Out UK shall not accept liability for any loss, accident or injury that may occur at a participating attraction and any dispute arising must be settled direct with the attraction concerned.
6. Cash redemption value of each voucher is 0.001p.
7. You are advised to check all relevant information with your chosen attraction before commencing your journey.

Days Out UK, PO Box 427, Northampton NN1 3YN. Tel: 01604 622445

1. Each voucher entitles the holder to the discount specified by the selected attraction.
2. Valid for use until 28/02/08 (unless otherwise specified, or if attraction season finishes prior to this). Vouchers are subject to the terms, conditions and restrictions of the selected attraction.
3. One voucher per party will be accepted, cannot be used in conjunction with any other offer, photocopies will not be accepted.
4. All attractions offering a discount have confirmed their willingness to participate. All information is subject to change without notice and should any attraction close or decline to accept a voucher for any reason, Days Out UK are not liable and cannot be held responsible.
5. Days Out UK shall not accept liability for any loss, accident or injury that may occur at a participating attraction and any dispute arising must be settled direct with the attraction concerned.
6. Cash redemption value of each voucher is 0.001p.
7. You are advised to check all relevant information with your chosen attraction before commencing your journey.

Days Out UK, PO Box 427, Northampton NN1 3YN. Tel: 01604 622445

1. Each voucher entitles the holder to the discount specified by the selected attraction.
2. Valid for use until 28/02/08 (unless otherwise specified, or if attraction season finishes prior to this). Vouchers are subject to the terms, conditions and restrictions of the selected attraction.
3. One voucher per party will be accepted, cannot be used in conjunction with any other offer, photocopies will not be accepted.
4. All attractions offering a discount have confirmed their willingness to participate. All information is subject to change without notice and should any attraction close or decline to accept a voucher for any reason, Days Out UK are not liable and cannot be held responsible.
5. Days Out UK shall not accept liability for any loss, accident or injury that may occur at a participating attraction and any dispute arising must be settled direct with the attraction concerned.
6. Cash redemption value of each voucher is 0.001p.
7. You are advised to check all relevant information with your chosen attraction before commencing your journey.

Days Out UK, PO Box 427, Northampton NN1 3YN. Tel: 01604 622445

1. Each voucher entitles the holder to the discount specified by the selected attraction.
2. Valid for use until 28/02/08 (unless otherwise specified, or if attraction season finishes prior to this). Vouchers are subject to the terms, conditions and restrictions of the selected attraction.
3. One voucher per party will be accepted, cannot be used in conjunction with any other offer, photocopies will not be accepted.
4. All attractions offering a discount have confirmed their willingness to participate. All information is subject to change without notice and should any attraction close or decline to accept a voucher for any reason, Days Out UK are not liable and cannot be held responsible.
5. Days Out UK shall not accept liability for any loss, accident or injury that may occur at a participating attraction and any dispute arising must be settled direct with the attraction concerned.
6. Cash redemption value of each voucher is 0.001p.
7. You are advised to check all relevant information with your chosen attraction before commencing your journey.

Days Out UK, PO Box 427, Northampton NN1 3YN. Tel: 01604 622445

1. Each voucher entitles the holder to the discount specified by the selected attraction.
2. Valid for use until 28/02/08 (unless otherwise specified, or if attraction season finishes prior to this). Vouchers are subject to the terms, conditions and restrictions of the selected attraction.
3. One voucher per party will be accepted, cannot be used in conjunction with any other offer, photocopies will not be accepted.
4. All attractions offering a discount have confirmed their willingness to participate. All information is subject to change without notice and should any attraction close or decline to accept a voucher for any reason, Days Out UK are not liable and cannot be held responsible.
5. Days Out UK shall not accept liability for any loss, accident or injury that may occur at a participating attraction and any dispute arising must be settled direct with the attraction concerned.
6. Cash redemption value of each voucher is 0.001p.
7. You are advised to check all relevant information with your chosen attraction before commencing your journey.

Days Out UK, PO Box 427, Northampton NN1 3YN. Tel: 01604 622445

Donington Grand Prix Collection
Donington Park Castle Donington Derby Derbyshire
Two for the Price of One
with a full-paying adult
(buy one full-price adult admission and receive another one free)

Cannot be used in conjunction with other offers. One voucher per party. Not valid on Bank Hols or special event days.

Expires end Feb 2008 (unless otherwise specified)

DISCOUNT VOUCHER

Doone Valley Holidays:
Cloud Farm and the Doone Valley
Cloud Farm Oare Lynton Devon EX35 6NU
One Child Rides Half-Price
with each full-paying adult
(offer applies to riding only)

Cannot be used in conjunction with other offers. One voucher per party. Not valid on Bank Hols or special event days.

Expires end Feb 2008 (unless otherwise specified)

DISCOUNT VOUCHER

Drayton Manor Theme Park
Tamworth Staffordshire B78 3TW
20% off Admission Prices
when you purchase 4 tickets

Conditions: offer only applies to Adult (12+) and Child (4-11) tickets, and at least one Adult ticket must be purchased; present this voucher at the ticket booth at the park entrance before you make the transaction; offer not valid on Bank Holidays (Fri-Mon); One voucher per party and per transaction; cannot be used in conjunction with any other offer or promotion; no refunds and no cash alternatives; only original vouchers accepted (no photocopies); applies to individual visitors only (cannot be used by groups, schools or parties); subject to availability.
Code: 51

Cannot be used in conjunction with other offers. One voucher per party. Not valid on Bank Hols or special event days.

valid 24 March-26 October 2007

DISCOUNT VOUCHER

Dulwich Picture Gallery
Gallery Road Dulwich London SE21 7AD
Two for the Price of One
with a full-paying adult

Cannot be used in conjunction with other offers. One voucher per party. Not valid on Bank Hols or special event days.

Expires end Feb 2008 (unless otherwise specified)

DISCOUNT VOUCHER

Dylan Thomas Boat House
Dylan's Walk Laugharne Carmarthenshire SA33 4SD
One Child Free
with a full-paying adult

Cannot be used in conjunction with other offers. One voucher per party. Not valid on Bank Hols or special event days.

Expires end Feb 2008 (unless otherwise specified)

DISCOUNT VOUCHER

1. Each voucher entitles the holder to the discount specified by the selected attraction.
2. Valid for use until 28/02/08 (unless otherwise specified, or if attraction season finishes prior to this). Vouchers are subject to the terms, conditions and restrictions of the selected attraction.
3. One voucher per party will be accepted, cannot be used in conjunction with any other offer, photocopies will not be accepted.
4. All attractions offering a discount have confirmed their willingness to participate. All information is subject to change without notice and should any attraction close or decline to accept a voucher for any reason, Days Out UK are not liable and cannot be held responsible.
5. Days Out UK shall not accept liability for any loss, accident or injury that may occur at a participating attraction and any dispute arising must be settled direct with the attraction concerned.
6. Cash redemption value of each voucher is 0.001p.
7. You are advised to check all relevant information with your chosen attraction before commencing your journey.

Days Out UK, PO Box 427, Northampton NN1 3YN. Tel: 01604 622445

1. Each voucher entitles the holder to the discount specified by the selected attraction.

2. Valid for use until 28/02/08 (unless otherwise specified. or if attraction season finishes prior to this). Vouchers are subject to the terms, conditions and restrictions of the selected attraction.

3. One voucher per party will be accepted, cannot be used in conjunction with any other offer, photocopies will not be accepted.

4. All attractions offering a discount have confirmed their willingness to participate. All information is subject to change without notice and should any attraction close or decline to accept a voucher for any reason, Days Out UK are not liable and cannot be held responsible.

5. Days Out UK shall not accept liability for any loss, accident or injury that may occur at a participating attraction and any dispute arising must be settled direct with the attraction concerned.

6. Cash redemption value of each voucher is 0.001p.

7. You are advised to check all relevant information with your chosen attraction before commencing your journey.

Days Out UK, PO Box 427, Northampton NN1 3YN. Tel: 01604 622445

1. Each voucher entitles the holder to the discount specified by the selected attraction.
2. Valid for use until 28/02/08 (unless otherwise specified, or if attraction season finishes prior to this). Vouchers are subject to the terms, conditions and restrictions of the selected attraction.
3. One voucher per party will be accepted, cannot be used in conjunction with any other offer, photocopies will not be accepted.
4. All attractions offering a discount have confirmed their willingness to participate. All information is subject to change without notice and should any attraction close or decline to accept a voucher for any reason, Days Out UK are not liable and cannot be held responsible.
5. Days Out UK shall not accept liability for any loss, accident or injury that may occur at a participating attraction and any dispute arising must be settled direct with the attraction concerned.
6. Cash redemption value of each voucher is 0.001p.
7. You are advised to check all relevant information with your chosen attraction before commencing your journey.

Days Out UK, PO Box 427, Northampton NN1 3YN. Tel: 01604 622445

1. Each voucher entitles the holder to the discount specified by the selected attraction.
2. Valid for use until 28/02/08 (unless otherwise specified, or if attraction season finishes prior to this). Vouchers are subject to the terms, conditions and restrictions of the selected attraction.
3. One voucher per party will be accepted, cannot be used in conjunction with any other offer, photocopies will not be accepted.
4. All attractions offering a discount have confirmed their willingness to participate. All information is subject to change without notice and should any attraction close or decline to accept a voucher for any reason, Days Out UK are not liable and cannot be held responsible.
5. Days Out UK shall not accept liability for any loss, accident or injury that may occur at a participating attraction and any dispute arising must be settled direct with the attraction concerned.
6. Cash redemption value of each voucher is 0.001p.
7. You are advised to check all relevant information with your chosen attraction before commencing your journey.

Days Out UK, PO Box 427, Northampton NN1 3YN. Tel: 01604 622445

East Lancashire Railway

Bolton Street Station Bolton Street Bury Lancashire BL9 0EY

Two for the Price of One

with a full-paying adult

Cannot be used in conjunction with other offers. One voucher per party. Not valid on Bank Hols or special event days.

Expires end Feb 2008 (unless otherwise specified)

Eastbourne Beer Festival

Winter Garden Compton Street Eastbourne East Sussex

£1.00 off individual admissions

valid for evening session on the 11th & lunchtime session on the 13th October; not valid on the 12th October 2007; one voucher per transaction; voucher to be presented at time of purchase;

Cannot be used in conjunction with other offers. One voucher per party. Not valid on Bank Hols or special event days.

Valid evening of 11th or lunchtime on 13th Oct 07

Eastnor Castle

Eastnor Ledbury Herefordshire HR8 1RL

Two for the Price of One

with a full-paying adult

Cannot be used in conjunction with other offers. One voucher per party. Not valid on Bank Hols or special event days.

Expires end Feb 2008 (unless otherwise specified)

Easton Farm Park

Pound Corner Easton Woodbridge Suffolk IP13 0EQ

One Child Free

with one full-paying adult

Cannot be used in conjunction with other offers. One voucher per party. Not valid on Bank Hols or special event days.

valid until 30 September 2007

Edinburgh Butterfly and Insect World

Dobbies Garden World Melville Nursery Lasswade Midlothian

One Child Free

with a full-paying adult

Cannot be used in conjunction with other offers. One voucher per party. Not valid on Bank Hols or special event days.

Expires end Feb 2008 (unless otherwise specified)

Edinburgh Dungeon

31 Market Street Edinburgh EH1 1QB

One Child Free

with every full-paying adult

Cannot be used in conjunction with other offers. One voucher per party. Not valid on Bank Hols or special event days.

Expires end Feb 2008 (unless otherwise specified)

1. Each voucher entitles the holder to the discount specified by the selected attraction.
2. Valid for use until 28/02/08 (unless otherwise specified, or if attraction season finishes prior to this). Vouchers are subject to the terms, conditions and restrictions of the selected attraction.
3. One voucher per party will be accepted, cannot be used in conjunction with any other offer, photocopies will not be accepted.
4. All attractions offering a discount have confirmed their willingness to participate. All information is subject to change without notice and should any attraction close or decline to accept a voucher for any reason, Days Out UK are not liable and cannot be held responsible.
5. Days Out UK shall not accept liability for any loss, accident or injury that may occur at a participating attraction and any dispute arising must be settled direct with the attraction concerned.
6. Cash redemption value of each voucher is 0.001p.
7. You are advised to check all relevant information with your chosen attraction before commencing your journey.

Days Out UK, PO Box 427, Northampton NN1 3YN. Tel: 01604 622445

1. Each voucher entitles the holder to the discount specified by the selected attraction.
2. Valid for use until 28/02/08 (unless otherwise specified, or if attraction season finishes prior to this). Vouchers are subject to the terms, conditions and restrictions of the selected attraction.
3. One voucher per party will be accepted, cannot be used in conjunction with any other offer, photocopies will not be accepted.
4. All attractions offering a discount have confirmed their willingness to participate. All information is subject to change without notice and should any attraction close or decline to accept a voucher for any reason, Days Out UK are not liable and cannot be held responsible.
5. Days Out UK shall not accept liability for any loss, accident or injury that may occur at a participating attraction and any dispute arising must be settled direct with the attraction concerned.
6. Cash redemption value of each voucher is 0.001p.
7. You are advised to check all relevant information with your chosen attraction before commencing your journey.

Days Out UK, PO Box 427, Northampton NN1 3YN. Tel: 01604 622445

1. Each voucher entitles the holder to the discount specified by the selected attraction.
2. Valid for use until 28/02/08 (unless otherwise specified, or if attraction season finishes prior to this). Vouchers are subject to the terms, conditions and restrictions of the selected attraction.
3. One voucher per party will be accepted, cannot be used in conjunction with any other offer, photocopies will not be accepted.
4. All attractions offering a discount have confirmed their willingness to participate. All information is subject to change without notice and should any attraction close or decline to accept a voucher for any reason, Days Out UK are not liable and cannot be held responsible.
5. Days Out UK shall not accept liability for any loss, accident or injury that may occur at a participating attraction and any dispute arising must be settled direct with the attraction concerned.
6. Cash redemption value of each voucher is 0.001p.
7. You are advised to check all relevant information with your chosen attraction before commencing your journey.

Days Out UK, PO Box 427, Northampton NN1 3YN. Tel: 01604 622445

1. Each voucher entitles the holder to the discount specified by the selected attraction.
2. Valid for use until 28/02/08 (unless otherwise specified, or if attraction season finishes prior to this). Vouchers are subject to the terms, conditions and restrictions of the selected attraction.
3. One voucher per party will be accepted, cannot be used in conjunction with any other offer, photocopies will not be accepted.
4. All attractions offering a discount have confirmed their willingness to participate. All information is subject to change without notice and should any attraction close or decline to accept a voucher for any reason, Days Out UK are not liable and cannot be held responsible.
5. Days Out UK shall not accept liability for any loss, accident or injury that may occur at a participating attraction and any dispute arising must be settled direct with the attraction concerned.
6. Cash redemption value of each voucher is 0.001p.
7. You are advised to check all relevant information with your chosen attraction before commencing your journey.

Days Out UK, PO Box 427, Northampton NN1 3YN. Tel: 01604 622445

1. Each voucher entitles the holder to the discount specified by the selected attraction.
2. Valid for use until 28/02/08 (unless otherwise specified, or if attraction season finishes prior to this). Vouchers are subject to the terms, conditions and restrictions of the selected attraction.
3. One voucher per party will be accepted, cannot be used in conjunction with any other offer, photocopies will not be accepted.
4. All attractions offering a discount have confirmed their willingness to participate. All information is subject to change without notice and should any attraction close or decline to accept a voucher for any reason, Days Out UK are not liable and cannot be held responsible.
5. Days Out UK shall not accept liability for any loss, accident or injury that may occur at a participating attraction and any dispute arising must be settled direct with the attraction concerned.
6. Cash redemption value of each voucher is 0.001p.
7. You are advised to check all relevant information with your chosen attraction before commencing your journey.

Days Out UK, PO Box 427, Northampton NN1 3YN. Tel: 01604 622445

DAYS OUT UK
The place to look for places to go

Escot Gardens, Maze
and Fantasy Woodland
Escot Fairmile Nr Ottery St Mary Devon EX11 1LU
One Child Free
with a full-paying adult
Cannot be used in conjunction with other offers. One voucher per party. Not valid on Bank Hols or special event days.
Expires end Feb 2008 (unless otherwise specified)

DAYS OUT UK
The place to look for places to go

Eureka! The Museum for Children
Discovery Road Halifax West Yorkshire HX1 2NE
Two for the Price of One
with a full-paying adult
one discount per transaction; cheapest ticket goes free; Code 437
Cannot be used in conjunction with other offers. One voucher per party. Not valid on Bank Hols or special event days.
Expires end Feb 2008 (unless otherwise specified)

DAYS OUT UK
The place to look for places to go

Exbury Gardens and Steam Railway
Exbury Southampton Hampshire SO45 1AZ
One Child Free
with a full-paying adult
(for garden entry only)
Cannot be used in conjunction with other offers. One voucher per party. Not valid on Bank Hols or special event days.
valid July, August & September 2007

DAYS OUT UK
The place to look for places to go

Explosion! The Museum of Naval Firepower
Priddy's Hard Heritage Way Gosport Hampshire PO12 4LE
Two for the Price of One
with a full-paying adult
Cannot be used in conjunction with other offers. One voucher per party. Not valid on Bank Hols or special event days.
Expires end Feb 2008 (unless otherwise specified)

DAYS OUT UK
The place to look for places to go

Fairhaven Woodland and Water Garden
School Road South Walsham Norwich Norfolk NR13 6DZ
Two for the Price of One
with a full-paying adult
Cannot be used in conjunction with other offers. One voucher per party. Not valid on Bank Hols or special event days.
Expires end Feb 2008 (unless otherwise specified)

DAYS OUT UK
The place to look for places to go

Fan Museum
12 Crooms Hill Greenwich London SE10 8ER
Two for the Price of One
with a full-paying adult
Cannot be used in conjunction with other offers. One voucher per party. Not valid on Bank Hols or special event days.
Expires end Feb 2008 (unless otherwise specified)

1. Each voucher entitles the holder to the discount specified by the selected attraction.
2. Valid for use until 28/02/08 (unless otherwise specified, or if attraction season finishes prior to this). Vouchers are subject to the terms, conditions and restrictions of the selected attraction.
3. One voucher per party will be accepted, cannot be used in conjunction with any other offer, photocopies will not be accepted.
4. All attractions offering a discount have confirmed their willingness to participate. All information is subject to change without notice and should any attraction close or decline to accept a voucher for any reason, Days Out UK are not liable and cannot be held responsible.
5. Days Out UK shall not accept liability for any loss, accident or injury that may occur at a participating attraction and any dispute arising must be settled direct with the attraction concerned.
6. Cash redemption value of each voucher is 0.001p.
7. You are advised to check all relevant information with your chosen attraction before commencing your journey.

Days Out UK, PO Box 427, Northampton NN1 3YN. Tel: 01604 622445

1. Each voucher entitles the holder to the discount specified by the selected attraction.
2. Valid for use until 28/02/08 (unless otherwise specified. or if attraction season finishes prior to this). Vouchers are subject to the terms, conditions and restrictions of the selected attraction.
3. One voucher per party will be accepted, cannot be used in conjunction with any other offer, photocopies will not be accepted.
4. All attractions offering a discount have confirmed their willingness to participate. All information is subject to change without notice and should any attraction close or decline to accept a voucher for any reason, Days Out UK are not liable and cannot be held responsible.
5. Days Out UK shall not accept liability for any loss, accident or injury that may occur at a participating attraction and any dispute arising must be settled direct with the attraction concerned.
6. Cash redemption value of each voucher is 0.001p.
7. You are advised to check all relevant information with your chosen attraction before commencing your journey.

Days Out UK, PO Box 427, Northampton NN1 3YN. Tel: 01604 622445

1. Each voucher entitles the holder to the discount specified by the selected attraction.
2. Valid for use until 28/02/08 (unless otherwise specified, or if attraction season finishes prior to this). Vouchers are subject to the terms, conditions and restrictions of the selected attraction.
3. One voucher per party will be accepted, cannot be used in conjunction with any other offer, photocopies will not be accepted.
4. All attractions offering a discount have confirmed their willingness to participate. All information is subject to change without notice and should any attraction close or decline to accept a voucher for any reason, Days Out UK are not liable and cannot be held responsible.
5. Days Out UK shall not accept liability for any loss, accident or injury that may occur at a participating attraction and any dispute arising must be settled direct with the attraction concerned.
6. Cash redemption value of each voucher is 0.001p.
7. You are advised to check all relevant information with your chosen attraction before commencing your journey.

Days Out UK, PO Box 427, Northampton NN1 3YN. Tel: 01604 622445

1. Each voucher entitles the holder to the discount specified by the selected attraction.
2. Valid for use until 28/02/08 (unless otherwise specified, or if attraction season finishes prior to this). Vouchers are subject to the terms, conditions and restrictions of the selected attraction.
3. One voucher per party will be accepted, cannot be used in conjunction with any other offer, photocopies will not be accepted.
4. All attractions offering a discount have confirmed their willingness to participate. All information is subject to change without notice and should any attraction close or decline to accept a voucher for any reason, Days Out UK are not liable and cannot be held responsible.
5. Days Out UK shall not accept liability for any loss, accident or injury that may occur at a participating attraction and any dispute arising must be settled direct with the attraction concerned.
6. Cash redemption value of each voucher is 0.001p.
7. You are advised to check all relevant information with your chosen attraction before commencing your journey.

Days Out UK, PO Box 427, Northampton NN1 3YN. Tel: 01604 622445

1. Each voucher entitles the holder to the discount specified by the selected attraction.
2. Valid for use until 28/02/08 (unless otherwise specified, or if attraction season finishes prior to this). Vouchers are subject to the terms, conditions and restrictions of the selected attraction.
3. One voucher per party will be accepted, cannot be used in conjunction with any other offer, photocopies will not be accepted.
4. All attractions offering a discount have confirmed their willingness to participate. All information is subject to change without notice and should any attraction close or decline to accept a voucher for any reason, Days Out UK are not liable and cannot be held responsible.
5. Days Out UK shall not accept liability for any loss, accident or injury that may occur at a participating attraction and any dispute arising must be settled direct with the attraction concerned.
6. Cash redemption value of each voucher is 0.001p.
7. You are advised to check all relevant information with your chosen attraction before commencing your journey.

Days Out UK, PO Box 427, Northampton NN1 3YN. Tel: 01604 622445

Farmer Giles Farmstead Ltd

Teffont Salisbury Wiltshire SP3 5QY

One Child Free

with a full-paying adult

(not valid on Bank Holiday weekends)

Cannot be used in conjunction with other offers. One voucher per party. Not valid on Bank Hols or special event days.

Expires end Feb 2008 (unless otherwise specified)

DISCOUNT VOUCHER

Felinwynt Rainforest Centre

Felinwynt Cardigan Ceredigion SA43 1RT

Two for the Price of One

with a full-paying adult

Cannot be used in conjunction with other offers. One voucher per party. Not valid on Bank Hols or special event days.

Expires end Feb 2008 (unless otherwise specified)

DISCOUNT VOUCHER

Ffestiniog Railway

Harbour Station Porthmadog Gwynedd LL49 9NF

One Child Free

with every full-paying adult

Cannot be used in conjunction with other offers. One voucher per party. Not valid on Bank Hols or special event days.

Expires end Feb 2008 (unless otherwise specified)

DISCOUNT VOUCHER

Finchcocks Living Museum of Music

Finchcocks Museum Riseden Goudhurst Kent TN17 1HH

Two for the Price of One

with a full-paying adult

Cannot be used in conjunction with other offers. One voucher per party. Not valid on Bank Hols or special event days.

Expires end Feb 2008 (unless otherwise specified)

DISCOUNT VOUCHER

Fishbourne Roman Palace

Salthill Road Fishbourne Chichester West Sussex PO19 3QR

Two for the Price of One

with a full-paying adult

Cannot be used in conjunction with other offers. One voucher per party. Not valid on Bank Hols or special event days.

Expires end Feb 2008 (unless otherwise specified)

DISCOUNT VOUCHER

Flambards Experience

Helston Cornwall TR13 0QA

One Child Free

when accompanied by a full-paying adult

(maximum 2 children per transaction; not valid 24 October 2007)

Cannot be used in conjunction with other offers. One voucher per party. Not valid on Bank Hols or special event days.

Valid 31 March - 27 October 2007

DISCOUNT VOUCHER

1. Each voucher entitles the holder to the discount specified by the selected attraction.
2. Valid for use until 28/02/08 (unless otherwise specified, or if attraction season finishes prior to this). Vouchers are subject to the terms, conditions and restrictions of the selected attraction.
3. One voucher per party will be accepted, cannot be used in conjunction with any other offer, photocopies will not be accepted.
4. All attractions offering a discount have confirmed their willingness to participate. All information is subject to change without notice and should any attraction close or decline to accept a voucher for any reason, Days Out UK are not liable and cannot be held responsible.
5. Days Out UK shall not accept liability for any loss, accident or injury that may occur at a participating attraction and any dispute arising must be settled direct with the attraction concerned.
6. Cash redemption value of each voucher is 0.001p.
7. You are advised to check all relevant information with your chosen attraction before commencing your journey.

Days Out UK, PO Box 427, Northampton NN1 3YN. Tel: 01604 622445

1. Each voucher entitles the holder to the discount specified by the selected attraction.
2. Valid for use until 28/02/08 (unless otherwise specified, or if attraction season finishes prior to this). Vouchers are subject to the terms, conditions and restrictions of the selected attraction.
3. One voucher per party will be accepted, cannot be used in conjunction with any other offer, photocopies will not be accepted.
4. All attractions offering a discount have confirmed their willingness to participate. All information is subject to change without notice and should any attraction close or decline to accept a voucher for any reason, Days Out UK are not liable and cannot be held responsible.
5. Days Out UK shall not accept liability for any loss, accident or injury that may occur at a participating attraction and any dispute arising must be settled direct with the attraction concerned.
6. Cash redemption value of each voucher is 0.001p.
7. You are advised to check all relevant information with your chosen attraction before commencing your journey.

Days Out UK, PO Box 427, Northampton NN1 3YN. Tel: 01604 622445

1. Each voucher entitles the holder to the discount specified by the selected attraction.
2. Valid for use until 28/02/08 (unless otherwise specified, or if attraction season finishes prior to this). Vouchers are subject to the terms, conditions and restrictions of the selected attraction.
3. One voucher per party will be accepted, cannot be used in conjunction with any other offer, photocopies will not be accepted.
4. All attractions offering a discount have confirmed their willingness to participate. All information is subject to change without notice and should any attraction close or decline to accept a voucher for any reason, Days Out UK are not liable and cannot be held responsible.
5. Days Out UK shall not accept liability for any loss, accident or injury that may occur at a participating attraction and any dispute arising must be settled direct with the attraction concerned.
6. Cash redemption value of each voucher is 0.001p.
7. You are advised to check all relevant information with your chosen attraction before commencing your journey.

Days Out UK, PO Box 427, Northampton NN1 3YN. Tel: 01604 622445

1. Each voucher entitles the holder to the discount specified by the selected attraction.
2. Valid for use until 28/02/08 (unless otherwise specified, or if attraction season finishes prior to this). Vouchers are subject to the terms, conditions and restrictions of the selected attraction.
3. One voucher per party will be accepted, cannot be used in conjunction with any other offer, photocopies will not be accepted.
4. All attractions offering a discount have confirmed their willingness to participate. All information is subject to change without notice and should any attraction close or decline to accept a voucher for any reason, Days Out UK are not liable and cannot be held responsible.
5. Days Out UK shall not accept liability for any loss, accident or injury that may occur at a participating attraction and any dispute arising must be settled direct with the attraction concerned.
6. Cash redemption value of each voucher is 0.001p.
7. You are advised to check all relevant information with your chosen attraction before commencing your journey.

Days Out UK, PO Box 427, Northampton NN1 3YN. Tel: 01604 622445

1. Each voucher entitles the holder to the discount specified by the selected attraction.
2. Valid for use until 28/02/08 (unless otherwise specified, or if attraction season finishes prior to this). Vouchers are subject to the terms, conditions and restrictions of the selected attraction.
3. One voucher per party will be accepted, cannot be used in conjunction with any other offer, photocopies will not be accepted.
4. All attractions offering a discount have confirmed their willingness to participate. All information is subject to change without notice and should any attraction close or decline to accept a voucher for any reason, Days Out UK are not liable and cannot be held responsible.
5. Days Out UK shall not accept liability for any loss, accident or injury that may occur at a participating attraction and any dispute arising must be settled direct with the attraction concerned.
6. Cash redemption value of each voucher is 0.001p.
7. You are advised to check all relevant information with your chosen attraction before commencing your journey.

Days Out UK, PO Box 427, Northampton NN1 3YN. Tel: 01604 622445

Fleet Air Arm Museum

Royal Naval Air Station Yeovilton Yeovil Somerset BA22 8HT

One Child Free

with every full-paying adult

Cannot be used in conjunction with other offers. One voucher per party. Not valid on Bank Hols or special event days.

Expires end Feb 2008 (unless otherwise specified)

Ford Green Hall

Ford Green Road Smallthorne Stoke-on-Trent Staffordshire

Two for the Price of One

with a full-paying adult
(excludes evening events and children's activities)

Cannot be used in conjunction with other offers. One voucher per party. Not valid on Bank Hols or special event days.

Expires end Feb 2008 (unless otherwise specified)

Forest Centre
and Millennium Country Park

Station Road Marston Moretaine Bedford Bedfordshire

Free One-Day Family Wetland Pass

Please validate this voucher at the Forest Centre reception on the day of use

Cannot be used in conjunction with other offers. One voucher per party. Not valid on Bank Hols or special event days.

Expires end Feb 2008 (unless otherwise specified)

Forge Mill Needle Museum
and Bordesley Abbey Visitor Centre

Needle Mill Lane Riverside Redditch Worcestershire

Two for the Price of One

with a full-paying adult

Cannot be used in conjunction with other offers. One voucher per party. Not valid on Bank Hols or special event days.

Expires end Feb 2008 (unless otherwise specified)

Fort Paull

Battery Road Paull Nr Hull East Riding of Yorkshire

Two for the Price of One

with a full-paying adult

Cannot be used in conjunction with other offers. One voucher per party. Not valid on Bank Hols or special event days.

Expires end Feb 2008 (unless otherwise specified)

Foxfield Steam Railway

Blythe Bridge Road Caverswall Stoke-On-Trent Staffordshire

One Child Free

with every two full-paying adults

Cannot be used in conjunction with other offers. One voucher per party. Not valid on Bank Hols or special event days.

Expires end Feb 2008 (unless otherwise specified)

1. Each voucher entitles the holder to the discount specified by the selected attraction.
2. Valid for use until 28/02/08 (unless otherwise specified, or if attraction season finishes prior to this). Vouchers are subject to the terms, conditions and restrictions of the selected attraction.
3. One voucher per party will be accepted, cannot be used in conjunction with any other offer, photocopies will not be accepted.
4. All attractions offering a discount have confirmed their willingness to participate. All information is subject to change without notice and should any attraction close or decline to accept a voucher for any reason, Days Out UK are not liable and cannot be held responsible.
5. Days Out UK shall not accept liability for any loss, accident or injury that may occur at a participating attraction and any dispute arising must be settled direct with the attraction concerned.
6. Cash redemption value of each voucher is 0.001p.
7. You are advised to check all relevant information with your chosen attraction before commencing your journey.

Days Out UK, PO Box 427, Northampton NN1 3YN. Tel: 01604 622445

1. Each voucher entitles the holder to the discount specified by the selected attraction.
2. Valid for use until 28/02/08 (unless otherwise specified, or if attraction season finishes prior to this). Vouchers are subject to the terms, conditions and restrictions of the selected attraction.
3. One voucher per party will be accepted, cannot be used in conjunction with any other offer, photocopies will not be accepted.
4. All attractions offering a discount have confirmed their willingness to participate. All information is subject to change without notice and should any attraction close or decline to accept a voucher for any reason, Days Out UK are not liable and cannot be held responsible.
5. Days Out UK shall not accept liability for any loss, accident or injury that may occur at a participating attraction and any dispute arising must be settled direct with the attraction concerned.
6. Cash redemption value of each voucher is 0.001p.
7. You are advised to check all relevant information with your chosen attraction before commencing your journey.

Days Out UK, PO Box 427, Northampton NN1 3YN. Tel: 01604 622445

1. Each voucher entitles the holder to the discount specified by the selected attraction.
2. Valid for use until 28/02/08 (unless otherwise specified. or if attraction season finishes prior to this). Vouchers are subject to the terms, conditions and restrictions of the selected attraction.
3. One voucher per party will be accepted, cannot be used in conjunction with any other offer, photocopies will not be accepted.
4 All attractions offering a discount have confirmed their willingness to participate. All information is subject to change without notice and should any attraction close or decline to accept a voucher for any reason, Days Out UK are not liable and cannot be held responsible.
5. Days Out UK shall not accept liability for any loss, accident or injury that may occur at a participating attraction and any dispute arising must be settled direct with the attraction concerned.
6. Cash redemption value of each voucher is 0.001p.
7. You are advised to check all relevant information with your chosen attraction before commencing your journey.

Days Out UK, PO Box 427, Northampton NN1 3YN. Tel: 01604 622445

1. Each voucher entitles the holder to the discount specified by the selected attraction.
2. Valid for use until 28/02/08 (unless otherwise specified, or if attraction season finishes prior to this). Vouchers are subject to the terms, conditions and restrictions of the selected attraction.
3. One voucher per party will be accepted, cannot be used in conjunction with any other offer, photocopies will not be accepted.
4. All attractions offering a discount have confirmed their willingness to participate. All information is subject to change without notice and should any attraction close or decline to accept a voucher for any reason, Days Out UK are not liable and cannot be held responsible.
5. Days Out UK shall not accept liability for any loss, accident or injury that may occur at a participating attraction and any dispute arising must be settled direct with the attraction concerned.
6. Cash redemption value of each voucher is 0.001p.
7. You are advised to check all relevant information with your chosen attraction before commencing your journey.

Days Out UK, PO Box 427, Northampton NN1 3YN. Tel: 01604 622445

1. Each voucher entitles the holder to the discount specified by the selected attraction.
2. Valid for use until 28/02/08 (unless otherwise specified, or if attraction season finishes prior to this). Vouchers are subject to the terms, conditions and restrictions of the selected attraction.
3. One voucher per party will be accepted, cannot be used in conjunction with any other offer, photocopies will not be accepted.
4. All attractions offering a discount have confirmed their willingness to participate. All information is subject to change without notice and should any attraction close or decline to accept a voucher for any reason, Days Out UK are not liable and cannot be held responsible.
5. Days Out UK shall not accept liability for any loss, accident or injury that may occur at a participating attraction and any dispute arising must be settled direct with the attraction concerned.
6. Cash redemption value of each voucher is 0.001p.
7. You are advised to check all relevant information with your chosen attraction before commencing your journey.

Days Out UK, PO Box 427, Northampton NN1 3YN. Tel: 01604 622445

1. Each voucher entitles the holder to the discount specified by the selected attraction.
2. Valid for use until 28/02/08 (unless otherwise specified, or if attraction season finishes prior to this). Vouchers are subject to the terms, conditions and restrictions of the selected attraction.
3. One voucher per party will be accepted, cannot be used in conjunction with any other offer, photocopies will not be accepted.
4. All attractions offering a discount have confirmed their willingness to participate. All information is subject to change without notice and should any attraction close or decline to accept a voucher for any reason, Days Out UK are not liable and cannot be held responsible.
5. Days Out UK shall not accept liability for any loss, accident or injury that may occur at a participating attraction and any dispute arising must be settled direct with the attraction concerned.
6. Cash redemption value of each voucher is 0.001p.
7. You are advised to check all relevant information with your chosen attraction before commencing your journey.

Days Out UK, PO Box 427, Northampton NN1 3YN. Tel: 01604 622445

Gainsborough Old Hall

Parnell Street Gainsborough Lincolnshire DN21 2NB

One Child Free

with every full-paying adult

Cannot be used in conjunction with other offers. One voucher per party. Not valid on Bank Hols or special event days.

Expires end Feb 2008 (unless otherwise specified)

Galloway Wildlife Conservation Park

Lochfergus Plantation Kirkcudbright Dumfries and Galloway

One Child Free

with every full-paying adult

(not valid on Easter weekend or Bank holidays)

Cannot be used in conjunction with other offers. One voucher per party. Not valid on Bank Hols or special event days.

Expires end Feb 2008 (unless otherwise specified)

Garden at Hatfield House

Hatfield Hertfordshire AL9 5NQ

Two for the Price of One

with a full-paying adult

(applies to Park and Garden only; not valid for major events)

Cannot be used in conjunction with other offers. One voucher per party. Not valid on Bank Hols or special event days.

valid 7th April to end of September 2007

Gardens and Grounds of Herstmonceux Castle

Herstmonceux Hailsham East Sussex BN27 1RN

One Child Free

with every full-paying adult
(valid for Gardens & Grounds only)

Cannot be used in conjunction with other offers. One voucher per party. Not valid on Bank Hols or special event days.

Expires end Feb 2008 (unless otherwise specified)

Gilbert White's House
and the Oates Museum

The Wakes High Street Selborne Alton Hampshire

Two for the Price of One
with a full-paying adult

Cannot be used in conjunction with other offers. One voucher per party. Not valid on Bank Hols or special event days.

Expires end Feb 2008 (unless otherwise specified)

Gladstone Pottery Museum

Uttoxeter Road Longton Stoke-On-Trent Staffordshire

Two for the Price of One
with a full-paying adult

Cannot be used in conjunction with other offers. One voucher per party. Not valid on Bank Hols or special event days.

Expires end Feb 2008 (unless otherwise specified)

1. Each voucher entitles the holder to the discount specified by the selected attraction.
2. Valid for use until 28/02/08 (unless otherwise specified, or if attraction season finishes prior to this). Vouchers are subject to the terms, conditions and restrictions of the selected attraction.
3. One voucher per party will be accepted, cannot be used in conjunction with any other offer, photocopies will not be accepted.
4. All attractions offering a discount have confirmed their willingness to participate. All information is subject to change without notice and should any attraction close or decline to accept a voucher for any reason, Days Out UK are not liable and cannot be held responsible.
5. Days Out UK shall not accept liability for any loss, accident or injury that may occur at a participating attraction and any dispute arising must be settled direct with the attraction concerned.
6. Cash redemption value of each voucher is 0.001p.
7. You are advised to check all relevant information with your chosen attraction before commencing your journey.

Days Out UK, PO Box 427, Northampton NN1 3YN. Tel: 01604 622445

1. Each voucher entitles the holder to the discount specified by the selected attraction.
2. Valid for use until 28/02/08 (unless otherwise specified. or if attraction season finishes prior to this). Vouchers are subject to the terms, conditions and restrictions of the selected attraction.
3. One voucher per party will be accepted, cannot be used in conjunction with any other offer, photocopies will not be accepted.
4. All attractions offering a discount have confirmed their willingness to participate. All information is subject to change without notice and should any attraction close or decline to accept a voucher for any reason, Days Out UK are not liable and cannot be held responsible.
5. Days Out UK shall not accept liability for any loss, accident or injury that may occur at a participating attraction and any dispute arising must be settled direct with the attraction concerned.
6. Cash redemption value of each voucher is 0.001p.
7. You are advised to check all relevant information with your chosen attraction before commencing your journey.

Days Out UK, PO Box 427, Northampton NN1 3YN. Tel: 01604 622445

1. Each voucher entitles the holder to the discount specified by the selected attraction.
2. Valid for use until 28/02/08 (unless otherwise specified, or if attraction season finishes prior to this). Vouchers are subject to the terms, conditions and restrictions of the selected attraction.
3. One voucher per party will be accepted, cannot be used in conjunction with any other offer, photocopies will not be accepted.
4. All attractions offering a discount have confirmed their willingness to participate. All information is subject to change without notice and should any attraction close or decline to accept a voucher for any reason, Days Out UK are not liable and cannot be held responsible.
5. Days Out UK shall not accept liability for any loss, accident or injury that may occur at a participating attraction and any dispute arising must be settled direct with the attraction concerned.
6. Cash redemption value of each voucher is 0.001p.
7. You are advised to check all relevant information with your chosen attraction before commencing your journey.

Days Out UK, PO Box 427, Northampton NN1 3YN. Tel: 01604 622445

1. Each voucher entitles the holder to the discount specified by the selected attraction.
2. Valid for use until 28/02/08 (unless otherwise specified, or if attraction season finishes prior to this). Vouchers are subject to the terms, conditions and restrictions of the selected attraction.
3. One voucher per party will be accepted, cannot be used in conjunction with any other offer, photocopies will not be accepted.
4. All attractions offering a discount have confirmed their willingness to participate. All information is subject to change without notice and should any attraction close or decline to accept a voucher for any reason, Days Out UK are not liable and cannot be held responsible.
5. Days Out UK shall not accept liability for any loss, accident or injury that may occur at a participating attraction and any dispute arising must be settled direct with the attraction concerned.
6. Cash redemption value of each voucher is 0.001p.
7. You are advised to check all relevant information with your chosen attraction before commencing your journey.

Days Out UK, PO Box 427, Northampton NN1 3YN. Tel: 01604 622445

1. Each voucher entitles the holder to the discount specified by the selected attraction.
2. Valid for use until 28/02/08 (unless otherwise specified, or if attraction season finishes prior to this). Vouchers are subject to the terms, conditions and restrictions of the selected attraction.
3. One voucher per party will be accepted, cannot be used in conjunction with any other offer, photocopies will not be accepted.
4. All attractions offering a discount have confirmed their willingness to participate. All information is subject to change without notice and should any attraction close or decline to accept a voucher for any reason, Days Out UK are not liable and cannot be held responsible.
5. Days Out UK shall not accept liability for any loss, accident or injury that may occur at a participating attraction and any dispute arising must be settled direct with the attraction concerned.
6. Cash redemption value of each voucher is 0.001p.
7. You are advised to check all relevant information with your chosen attraction before commencing your journey.

Days Out UK, PO Box 427, Northampton NN1 3YN. Tel: 01604 622445

Go Ape! High Wire Forest Adventure
Two for the Price of One with a full-paying adult

1 free admission only when 1 of equal or greater value is purchased. Only one voucher can be used per booking. Lower value ticket goes free. Excluding school and bank holidays. Pre-Booking essential. Please call 0870 420 7876 and **quote** 'Days Out UK'. Voucher must be produced on admission

Cannot be used in conjunction with other offers. One voucher per party. Not valid on Bank Hols or special event days.

Offer valid Mon-Fri until Oct 2007

Gower Heritage Centre
Parkmill Gower Swansea West Glamorgan Wales
One Child Free
with a full-paying adult

Cannot be used in conjunction with other offers. One voucher per party. Not valid on Bank Hols or special event days.

Expires end Feb 2008 (unless otherwise specified)

Grasmere Lakeland Sports and Show
Grasmere Sportsfield Grasmere Ambleside Cumbria
Two for the Price of One
with a full-paying adult
(offer applies to adult admissions only)

Cannot be used in conjunction with other offers. One voucher per party. Not valid on Bank Hols or special event days.

Expires end Feb 2008 (unless otherwise specified)

Great Yarmouth Sea Life Centre
Marine Parade Great Yarmouth Norfolk NR30 3AH
One Child Free with a full-paying adult

1. This voucher entitles free admission to the Great Yarmouth Sea Life Centre for one child when accompanied by one full paying adult.
2. Offer expires 28 February 2008.
3. Cannot be used in conjunction with any other offer.
4. A "child" is classed as a person aged 3-14 inclusive (under 3s go free anyway).
5. No cash alternative, non-refundable; and non-exchangeable.
6. All children must be accompanied by an adult.
7. Only one voucher per party and per transaction.
8. Photocopies not accepted.
9. SEA LIFE/Sanctuaries reserve the right to alter, close or remove details/exhibits without prior notice for technical, operational or other reasons, and no refunds can be given in these circumstances.
10. SEA LIFE/Sanctuaries reserve the right to refuse entry without explanation.
Voucher Ref: DOUK.

Cannot be used in conjunction with other offers. One voucher per party. Not valid on Bank Hols or special event days.

Expires end Feb 2008 (unless otherwise specified)

Greenmeadow Community Farm
Greenforge Way Cwmbran Gwent Wales NP44 5AJ
One Child Free
with a full-paying adult
(not valid for group rates)

Cannot be used in conjunction with other offers. One voucher per party. Not valid on Bank Hols or special event days.

Expires end Feb 2008 (unless otherwise specified)

1. Each voucher entitles the holder to the discount specified by the selected attraction.
2. Valid for use until 28/02/08 (unless otherwise specified, or if attraction season finishes prior to this). Vouchers are subject to the terms, conditions and restrictions of the selected attraction.
3. One voucher per party will be accepted, cannot be used in conjunction with any other offer, photocopies will not be accepted.
4. All attractions offering a discount have confirmed their willingness to participate. All information is subject to change without notice and should any attraction close or decline to accept a voucher for any reason, Days Out UK are not liable and cannot be held responsible.
5. Days Out UK shall not accept liability for any loss, accident or injury that may occur at a participating attraction and any dispute arising must be settled direct with the attraction concerned.
6. Cash redemption value of each voucher is 0.001p.
7. You are advised to check all relevant information with your chosen attraction before commencing your journey.

Days Out UK, PO Box 427, Northampton NN1 3YN. Tel: 01604 622445

1. Each voucher entitles the holder to the discount specified by the selected attraction.
2. Valid for use until 28/02/08 (unless otherwise specified. or if attraction season finishes prior to this). Vouchers are subject to the terms, conditions and restrictions of the selected attraction.
3. One voucher per party will be accepted, cannot be used in conjunction with any other offer, photocopies will not be accepted.
4. All attractions offering a discount have confirmed their willingness to participate. All information is subject to change without notice and should any attraction close or decline to accept a voucher for any reason, Days Out UK are not liable and cannot be held responsible.
5. Days Out UK shall not accept liability for any loss, accident or injury that may occur at a participating attraction and any dispute arising must be settled direct with the attraction concerned.
6. Cash redemption value of each voucher is 0.001p.
7. You are advised to check all relevant information with your chosen attraction before commencing your journey.

Days Out UK, PO Box 427, Northampton NN1 3YN. Tel: 01604 622445

1. Each voucher entitles the holder to the discount specified by the selected attraction.

2. Valid for use until 28/02/08 (unless otherwise specified, or if attraction season finishes prior to this). Vouchers are subject to the terms, conditions and restrictions of the selected attraction.

3. One voucher per party will be accepted, cannot be used in conjunction with any other offer, photocopies will not be accepted.

4. All attractions offering a discount have confirmed their willingness to participate. All information is subject to change without notice and should any attraction close or decline to accept a voucher for any reason, Days Out UK are not liable and cannot be held responsible.

5. Days Out UK shall not accept liability for any loss, accident or injury that may occur at a participating attraction and any dispute arising must be settled direct with the attraction concerned.

6. Cash redemption value of each voucher is 0.001p.

7. You are advised to check all relevant information with your chosen attraction before commencing your journey.

Days Out UK, PO Box 427, Northampton NN1 3YN. Tel: 01604 622445

1. Each voucher entitles the holder to the discount specified by the selected attraction.
2. Valid for use until 28/02/08 (unless otherwise specified, or if attraction season finishes prior to this). Vouchers are subject to the terms, conditions and restrictions of the selected attraction.
3. One voucher per party will be accepted, cannot be used in conjunction with any other offer, photocopies will not be accepted.
4. All attractions offering a discount have confirmed their willingness to participate. All information is subject to change without notice and should any attraction close or decline to accept a voucher for any reason, Days Out UK are not liable and cannot be held responsible.
5. Days Out UK shall not accept liability for any loss, accident or injury that may occur at a participating attraction and any dispute arising must be settled direct with the attraction concerned.
6. Cash redemption value of each voucher is 0.001p.
7. You are advised to check all relevant information with your chosen attraction before commencing your journey.

Days Out UK, PO Box 427, Northampton NN1 3YN. Tel: 01604 622445

Guards Museum, The

Wellington Barracks Birdcage Walk London SW1E 6HQ

Two for the Price of One
with a full-paying adult

Cannot be used in conjunction with other offers. One voucher per party. Not valid on Bank Hols or special event days.

Expires end Feb 2008 (unless otherwise specified)

Hall's Croft

Old Town Stratford-Upon-Avon Warwickshire

Two for the Price of One
(voucher entitles one adult or one child to be admitted free of charge when accompanied by a full-paying adult)

Cannot be used in conjunction with other offers. One voucher per party. Not valid on Bank Hols or special event days.

Expires end Feb 2008 (unless otherwise specified)

Handel House Museum

25 Brook Street Mayfair London W1K 4HB

Two for the Price of One
with a full-paying adult

Cannot be used in conjunction with other offers. One voucher per party. Not valid on Bank Hols or special event days.

Expires end Feb 2008 (unless otherwise specified)

Harbour Park

Seafront Arun Parade Littlehampton West Sussex

Family Ride Books - 10 Rides for £12.00

Cannot be used in conjunction with other offers. One voucher per party. Not valid on Bank Hols or special event days.

Expires end Feb 2008 (unless otherwise specified)

Harewood House and Bird Garden

Harewood Leeds West Yorkshire LS17 9LG

Two for the Price of One
with a full-paying adult

Cannot be used in conjunction with other offers. One voucher per party. Not valid on Bank Hols or special event days.

Expires end Feb 2008 (unless otherwise specified)

Harrington Aviation Museums

Sunnyvale Farm and Nursery off Lamport Road Harrington Northamptonshire NN6 9PF

Two for the Price of One
with a full-paying adult

Cannot be used in conjunction with other offers. One voucher per party. Not valid on Bank Hols or special event days.

Expires end Feb 2008 (unless otherwise specified)

1. Each voucher entitles the holder to the discount specified by the selected attraction.
2. Valid for use until 28/02/08 (unless otherwise specified, or if attraction season finishes prior to this). Vouchers are subject to the terms, conditions and restrictions of the selected attraction.
3. One voucher per party will be accepted, cannot be used in conjunction with any other offer, photocopies will not be accepted.
4. All attractions offering a discount have confirmed their willingness to participate. All information is subject to change without notice and should any attraction close or decline to accept a voucher for any reason, Days Out UK are not liable and cannot be held responsible.
5. Days Out UK shall not accept liability for any loss, accident or injury that may occur at a participating attraction and any dispute arising must be settled direct with the attraction concerned.
6. Cash redemption value of each voucher is 0.001p.
7. You are advised to check all relevant information with your chosen attraction before commencing your journey.

Days Out UK, PO Box 427, Northampton NN1 3YN. Tel: 01604 622445

1. Each voucher entitles the holder to the discount specified by the selected attraction.
2. Valid for use until 28/02/08 (unless otherwise specified, or if attraction season finishes prior to this). Vouchers are subject to the terms, conditions and restrictions of the selected attraction.
3. One voucher per party will be accepted, cannot be used in conjunction with any other offer, photocopies will not be accepted.
4. All attractions offering a discount have confirmed their willingness to participate. All information is subject to change without notice and should any attraction close or decline to accept a voucher for any reason, Days Out UK are not liable and cannot be held responsible.
5. Days Out UK shall not accept liability for any loss, accident or injury that may occur at a participating attraction and any dispute arising must be settled direct with the attraction concerned.
6. Cash redemption value of each voucher is 0.001p.
7. You are advised to check all relevant information with your chosen attraction before commencing your journey.

Days Out UK, PO Box 427, Northampton NN1 3YN. Tel: 01604 622445

1. Each voucher entitles the holder to the discount specified by the selected attraction.
2. Valid for use until 28/02/08 (unless otherwise specified, or if attraction season finishes prior to this). Vouchers are subject to the terms, conditions and restrictions of the selected attraction.
3. One voucher per party will be accepted, cannot be used in conjunction with any other offer, photocopies will not be accepted.
4. All attractions offering a discount have confirmed their willingness to participate. All information is subject to change without notice and should any attraction close or decline to accept a voucher for any reason, Days Out UK are not liable and cannot be held responsible.
5. Days Out UK shall not accept liability for any loss, accident or injury that may occur at a participating attraction and any dispute arising must be settled direct with the attraction concerned.
6. Cash redemption value of each voucher is 0.001p.
7. You are advised to check all relevant information with your chosen attraction before commencing your journey.

Days Out UK, PO Box 427, Northampton NN1 3YN. Tel: 01604 622445

1. Each voucher entitles the holder to the discount specified by the selected attraction.
2. Valid for use until 28/02/08 (unless otherwise specified, or if attraction season finishes prior to this). Vouchers are subject to the terms, conditions and restrictions of the selected attraction.
3. One voucher per party will be accepted, cannot be used in conjunction with any other offer, photocopies will not be accepted.
4. All attractions offering a discount have confirmed their willingness to participate. All information is subject to change without notice and should any attraction close or decline to accept a voucher for any reason, Days Out UK are not liable and cannot be held responsible.
5. Days Out UK shall not accept liability for any loss, accident or injury that may occur at a participating attraction and any dispute arising must be settled direct with the attraction concerned.
6. Cash redemption value of each voucher is 0.001p.
7. You are advised to check all relevant information with your chosen attraction before commencing your journey.

Days Out UK, PO Box 427, Northampton NN1 3YN. Tel: 01604 622445

1. Each voucher entitles the holder to the discount specified by the selected attraction.
2. Valid for use until 28/02/08 (unless otherwise specified, or if attraction season finishes prior to this). Vouchers are subject to the terms, conditions and restrictions of the selected attraction.
3. One voucher per party will be accepted, cannot be used in conjunction with any other offer, photocopies will not be accepted.
4. All attractions offering a discount have confirmed their willingness to participate. All information is subject to change without notice and should any attraction close or decline to accept a voucher for any reason, Days Out UK are not liable and cannot be held responsible.
5. Days Out UK shall not accept liability for any loss, accident or injury that may occur at a participating attraction and any dispute arising must be settled direct with the attraction concerned.
6. Cash redemption value of each voucher is 0.001p.
7. You are advised to check all relevant information with your chosen attraction before commencing your journey.

Days Out UK, PO Box 427, Northampton NN1 3YN. Tel: 01604 622445

1. Each voucher entitles the holder to the discount specified by the selected attraction.
2. Valid for use until 28/02/08 (unless otherwise specified, or if attraction season finishes prior to this). Vouchers are subject to the terms, conditions and restrictions of the selected attraction.
3. One voucher per party will be accepted, cannot be used in conjunction with any other offer, photocopies will not be accepted.
4. All attractions offering a discount have confirmed their willingness to participate. All information is subject to change without notice and should any attraction close or decline to accept a voucher for any reason, Days Out UK are not liable and cannot be held responsible.
5. Days Out UK shall not accept liability for any loss, accident or injury that may occur at a participating attraction and any dispute arising must be settled direct with the attraction concerned.
6. Cash redemption value of each voucher is 0.001p.
7. You are advised to check all relevant information with your chosen attraction before commencing your journey.

Days Out UK, PO Box 427, Northampton NN1 3YN. Tel: 01604 622445

Hartlepool's Maritime Experience

Maritime Avenue Hartlepool Cleveland TS24 0XZ

One Child Free
with a full-paying adult

Cannot be used in conjunction with other offers. One voucher per party. Not valid on Bank Hols or special event days.

valid until 31 December 2007

Harvington Hall

Harvington Hall Lane Harvington Kidderminster Worcestershire

One Child Free
with 2 full-paying adults

Cannot be used in conjunction with other offers. One voucher per party. Not valid on Bank Hols or special event days.

Expires end Feb 2008 (unless otherwise specified)

Hatton Farm Village at Hatton Country World

Dark Lane Hatton Warwick Warwickshire

One Child Free
with one full-paying adult
(voucher also valid on event days code DO/07)

Cannot be used in conjunction with other offers. One voucher per party. Not valid on Bank Hols

valid until 28 October 2007

Hawk Conservancy Trust

Sarson Lane Weyhill Andover Hampshire SP11 8DY

£1.00 off Child Admission

Cannot be used in conjunction with other offers. One voucher per party. Not valid on Bank Hols or special event days.

Expires end Feb 2008 (unless otherwise specified)

Hedingham Castle

Bayley Street Castle Hedingham Halstead Essex

One Child Free
with one full-paying adult

Cannot be used in conjunction with other offers. One voucher per party. Not valid on Bank Hols or special event days.

Sun-Thur only expires 28th September 2007

Hellfire Caves

West Wycombe Caves Ltd.High Wycombe Buckinghamshire

Two for the Price of One
with a full-paying adult

Cannot be used in conjunction with other offers. One voucher per party. Not valid on Bank Hols or special event days.

Expires end Feb 2008 (unless otherwise specified)

1. Each voucher entitles the holder to the discount specified by the selected attraction.
2. Valid for use until 28/02/08 (unless otherwise specified, or if attraction season finishes prior to this). Vouchers are subject to the terms, conditions and restrictions of the selected attraction.
3. One voucher per party will be accepted, cannot be used in conjunction with any other offer, photocopies will not be accepted.
4. All attractions offering a discount have confirmed their willingness to participate. All information is subject to change without notice and should any attraction close or decline to accept a voucher for any reason, Days Out UK are not liable and cannot be held responsible.
5. Days Out UK shall not accept liability for any loss, accident or injury that may occur at a participating attraction and any dispute arising must be settled direct with the attraction concerned.
6. Cash redemption value of each voucher is 0.001p.
7. You are advised to check all relevant information with your chosen attraction before commencing your journey.

Days Out UK, PO Box 427, Northampton NN1 3YN. Tel: 01604 622445

1. Each voucher entitles the holder to the discount specified by the selected attraction.
2. Valid for use until 28/02/08 (unless otherwise specified, or if attraction season finishes prior to this). Vouchers are subject to the terms, conditions and restrictions of the selected attraction.
3. One voucher per party will be accepted, cannot be used in conjunction with any other offer, photocopies will not be accepted.
4. All attractions offering a discount have confirmed their willingness to participate. All information is subject to change without notice and should any attraction close or decline to accept a voucher for any reason, Days Out UK are not liable and cannot be held responsible.
5. Days Out UK shall not accept liability for any loss, accident or injury that may occur at a participating attraction and any dispute arising must be settled direct with the attraction concerned.
6. Cash redemption value of each voucher is 0.001p.
7. You are advised to check all relevant information with your chosen attraction before commencing your journey.

Days Out UK, PO Box 427, Northampton NN1 3YN. Tel: 01604 622445

1. Each voucher entitles the holder to the discount specified by the selected attraction.
2. Valid for use until 28/02/08 (unless otherwise specified, or if attraction season finishes prior to this). Vouchers are subject to the terms, conditions and restrictions of the selected attraction.
3. One voucher per party will be accepted, cannot be used in conjunction with any other offer, photocopies will not be accepted.
4. All attractions offering a discount have confirmed their willingness to participate. All information is subject to change without notice and should any attraction close or decline to accept a voucher for any reason, Days Out UK are not liable and cannot be held responsible.
5. Days Out UK shall not accept liability for any loss, accident or injury that may occur at a participating attraction and any dispute arising must be settled direct with the attraction concerned.
6. Cash redemption value of each voucher is 0.001p.
7. You are advised to check all relevant information with your chosen attraction before commencing your journey.

Days Out UK, PO Box 427, Northampton NN1 3YN. Tel: 01604 622445

1. Each voucher entitles the holder to the discount specified by the selected attraction.
2. Valid for use until 28/02/08 (unless otherwise specified, or if attraction season finishes prior to this). Vouchers are subject to the terms, conditions and restrictions of the selected attraction.
3. One voucher per party will be accepted, cannot be used in conjunction with any other offer, photocopies will not be accepted.
4. All attractions offering a discount have confirmed their willingness to participate. All information is subject to change without notice and should any attraction close or decline to accept a voucher for any reason, Days Out UK are not liable and cannot be held responsible.
5. Days Out UK shall not accept liability for any loss, accident or injury that may occur at a participating attraction and any dispute arising must be settled direct with the attraction concerned.
6. Cash redemption value of each voucher is 0.001p.
7. You are advised to check all relevant information with your chosen attraction before commencing your journey.

Days Out UK, PO Box 427, Northampton NN1 3YN. Tel: 01604 622445

1. Each voucher entitles the holder to the discount specified by the selected attraction.
2. Valid for use until 28/02/08 (unless otherwise specified, or if attraction season finishes prior to this). Vouchers are subject to the terms, conditions and restrictions of the selected attraction.
3. One voucher per party will be accepted, cannot be used in conjunction with any other offer, photocopies will not be accepted.
4. All attractions offering a discount have confirmed their willingness to participate. All information is subject to change without notice and should any attraction close or decline to accept a voucher for any reason, Days Out UK are not liable and cannot be held responsible.
5. Days Out UK shall not accept liability for any loss, accident or injury that may occur at a participating attraction and any dispute arising must be settled direct with the attraction concerned.
6. Cash redemption value of each voucher is 0.001p.
7. You are advised to check all relevant information with your chosen attraction before commencing your journey.

Days Out UK, PO Box 427, Northampton NN1 3YN. Tel: 01604 622445

1. Each voucher entitles the holder to the discount specified by the selected attraction.
2. Valid for use until 28/02/08 (unless otherwise specified, or if attraction season finishes prior to this). Vouchers are subject to the terms, conditions and restrictions of the selected attraction.
3. One voucher per party will be accepted, cannot be used in conjunction with any other offer, photocopies will not be accepted.
4. All attractions offering a discount have confirmed their willingness to participate. All information is subject to change without notice and should any attraction close or decline to accept a voucher for any reason, Days Out UK are not liable and cannot be held responsible.
5. Days Out UK shall not accept liability for any loss, accident or injury that may occur at a participating attraction and any dispute arising must be settled direct with the attraction concerned.
6. Cash redemption value of each voucher is 0.001p.
7. You are advised to check all relevant information with your chosen attraction before commencing your journey.

Days Out UK, PO Box 427, Northampton NN1 3YN. Tel: 01604 622445

Henry Moore Institute

74 The Headrow Leeds West Yorkshire LS1 3AH

15% discount on all publications, plus one free poster of your choice.

Cannot be used in conjunction with other offers. One voucher per party. Not valid on Bank Hols or special event days.

Expires end Feb 2008 (unless otherwise specified)

Heritage Motor Centre

Banbury Road Gaydon Warwickshire CV35 0BJ

Two for the Price of One
with a full-paying adult

Cannot be used in conjunction with other offers. One voucher per party. Not valid on Bank Hols or special event days.

Expires end Feb 2008 (unless otherwise specified)

High Beeches Gardens Conservation Trust

High Beeches Lane Handcross Haywards Heath West Sussex

Two for the Price of One
with a full-paying adult
(valid during normal opening times and event days)

Cannot be used in conjunction with other offers. One voucher per party. Not valid on Bank Hols.

Expires end Feb 2008 (unless otherwise specified)

Holly Gate Cactus Garden and Nursery

Billingshurst Road Ashington West Sussex RH20 3BB

Two for the Price of One
with a full-paying adult

Cannot be used in conjunction with other offers. One voucher per party. Not valid on Bank Hols or special event days.

Expires end Feb 2008 (unless otherwise specified)

Hollycombe Steam Collection

Midhurst Road Liphook Hampshire GU30 7LP

One Child Free
with a full-paying adult

Cannot be used in conjunction with other offers. One voucher per party. Not valid on Bank Hols or special event days.

Expires end Feb 2008 (unless otherwise specified)

Hop Farm at the Kentish Oast Village

Beltring Maidstone Road Paddock Wood Tonbridge Kent

One Child Free
with every full-paying adult

excludes 'War & Peace,' 'Monster Mania'
and music events; no cash alternative

Cannot be used in conjunction with other offers. One voucher per party. Not valid on Bank Hols or special event days.

valid until 31 December 2007

1. Each voucher entitles the holder to the discount specified by the selected attraction.
2. Valid for use until 28/02/08 (unless otherwise specified, or if attraction season finishes prior to this). Vouchers are subject to the terms, conditions and restrictions of the selected attraction.
3. One voucher per party will be accepted, cannot be used in conjunction with any other offer, photocopies will not be accepted.
4. All attractions offering a discount have confirmed their willingness to participate. All information is subject to change without notice and should any attraction close or decline to accept a voucher for any reason, Days Out UK are not liable and cannot be held responsible.
5. Days Out UK shall not accept liability for any loss, accident or injury that may occur at a participating attraction and any dispute arising must be settled direct with the attraction concerned.
6. Cash redemption value of each voucher is 0.001p.
7. You are advised to check all relevant information with your chosen attraction before commencing your journey.

Days Out UK, PO Box 427, Northampton NN1 3YN. Tel: 01604 622445

1. Each voucher entitles the holder to the discount specified by the selected attraction.
2. Valid for use until 28/02/08 (unless otherwise specified, or if attraction season finishes prior to this). Vouchers are subject to the terms, conditions and restrictions of the selected attraction.
3. One voucher per party will be accepted, cannot be used in conjunction with any other offer, photocopies will not be accepted.
4. All attractions offering a discount have confirmed their willingness to participate. All information is subject to change without notice and should any attraction close or decline to accept a voucher for any reason, Days Out UK are not liable and cannot be held responsible.
5. Days Out UK shall not accept liability for any loss, accident or injury that may occur at a participating attraction and any dispute arising must be settled direct with the attraction concerned.
6. Cash redemption value of each voucher is 0.001p.
7. You are advised to check all relevant information with your chosen attraction before commencing your journey.

Days Out UK, PO Box 427, Northampton NN1 3YN. Tel: 01604 622445

1. Each voucher entitles the holder to the discount specified by the selected attraction.
2. Valid for use until 28/02/08 (unless otherwise specified, or if attraction season finishes prior to this). Vouchers are subject to the terms, conditions and restrictions of the selected attraction.
3. One voucher per party will be accepted, cannot be used in conjunction with any other offer, photocopies will not be accepted.
4. All attractions offering a discount have confirmed their willingness to participate. All information is subject to change without notice and should any attraction close or decline to accept a voucher for any reason, Days Out UK are not liable and cannot be held responsible.
5. Days Out UK shall not accept liability for any loss, accident or injury that may occur at a participating attraction and any dispute arising must be settled direct with the attraction concerned.
6. Cash redemption value of each voucher is 0.001p.
7. You are advised to check all relevant information with your chosen attraction before commencing your journey.

Days Out UK, PO Box 427, Northampton NN1 3YN. Tel: 01604 622445

1. Each voucher entitles the holder to the discount specified by the selected attraction.
2. Valid for use until 28/02/08 (unless otherwise specified, or if attraction season finishes prior to this). Vouchers are subject to the terms, conditions and restrictions of the selected attraction.
3. One voucher per party will be accepted, cannot be used in conjunction with any other offer, photocopies will not be accepted.
4. All attractions offering a discount have confirmed their willingness to participate. All information is subject to change without notice and should any attraction close or decline to accept a voucher for any reason, Days Out UK are not liable and cannot be held responsible.
5. Days Out UK shall not accept liability for any loss, accident or injury that may occur at a participating attraction and any dispute arising must be settled direct with the attraction concerned.
6. Cash redemption value of each voucher is 0.001p.
7. You are advised to check all relevant information with your chosen attraction before commencing your journey.

Days Out UK, PO Box 427, Northampton NN1 3YN. Tel: 01604 622445

1. Each voucher entitles the holder to the discount specified by the selected attraction.
2. Valid for use until 28/02/08 (unless otherwise specified, or if attraction season finishes prior to this). Vouchers are subject to the terms, conditions and restrictions of the selected attraction.
3. One voucher per party will be accepted, cannot be used in conjunction with any other offer, photocopies will not be accepted.
4. All attractions offering a discount have confirmed their willingness to participate. All information is subject to change without notice and should any attraction close or decline to accept a voucher for any reason, Days Out UK are not liable and cannot be held responsible.
5. Days Out UK shall not accept liability for any loss, accident or injury that may occur at a participating attraction and any dispute arising must be settled direct with the attraction concerned.
6. Cash redemption value of each voucher is 0.001p.
7. You are advised to check all relevant information with your chosen attraction before commencing your journey.

Days Out UK, PO Box 427, Northampton NN1 3YN. Tel: 01604 622445

51

1. Each voucher entitles the holder to the discount specified by the selected attraction.
2. Valid for use until 28/02/08 (unless otherwise specified, or if attraction season finishes prior to this). Vouchers are subject to the terms, conditions and restrictions of the selected attraction.
3. One voucher per party will be accepted, cannot be used in conjunction with any other offer, photocopies will not be accepted.
4. All attractions offering a discount have confirmed their willingness to participate. All information is subject to change without notice and should any attraction close or decline to accept a voucher for any reason, Days Out UK are not liable and cannot be held responsible.
5. Days Out UK shall not accept liability for any loss, accident or injury that may occur at a participating attraction and any dispute arising must be settled direct with the attraction concerned.
6. Cash redemption value of each voucher is 0.001p.
7. You are advised to check all relevant information with your chosen attraction before commencing your journey

Days Out UK, PO Box 427, Northampton NN1 3YN. Tel: 01604 622445

1. Each voucher entitles the holder to the discount specified by the selected attraction.

2. Valid for use until 28/02/08 (unless otherwise specified. or if attraction season finishes prior to this). Vouchers are subject to the terms, conditions and restrictions of the selected attraction.

3. One voucher per party will be accepted, cannot be used in conjunction with any other offer, photocopies will not be accepted.

4. All attractions offering a discount have confirmed their willingness to participate. All information is subject to change without notice and should any attraction close or decline to accept a voucher for any reason, Days Out UK are not liable and cannot be held responsible.

5. Days Out UK shall not accept liability for any loss, accident or injury that may occur at a participating attraction and any dispute arising must be settled direct with the attraction concerned.

6. Cash redemption value of each voucher is 0.001p.

7. You are advised to check all relevant information with your chosen attraction before commencing your journey.

Days Out UK, PO Box 427, Northampton NN1 3YN. Tel: 01604 622445

1. Each voucher entitles the holder to the discount specified by the selected attraction.
2. Valid for use until 28/02/08 (unless otherwise specified, or if attraction season finishes prior to this). Vouchers are subject to the terms, conditions and restrictions of the selected attraction.
3. One voucher per party will be accepted, cannot be used in conjunction with any other offer, photocopies will not be accepted.
4. All attractions offering a discount have confirmed their willingness to participate. All information is subject to change without notice and should any attraction close or decline to accept a voucher for any reason, Days Out UK are not liable and cannot be held responsible.
5. Days Out UK shall not accept liability for any loss, accident or injury that may occur at a participating attraction and any dispute arising must be settled direct with the attraction concerned.
6. Cash redemption value of each voucher is 0.001p.
7. You are advised to check all relevant information with your chosen attraction before commencing your journey.

Days Out UK, PO Box 427, Northampton NN1 3YN. Tel: 01604 622445

1. Each voucher entitles the holder to the discount specified by the selected attraction.
2. Valid for use until 28/02/08 (unless otherwise specified, or if attraction season finishes prior to this). Vouchers are subject to the terms, conditions and restrictions of the selected attraction.
3. One voucher per party will be accepted, cannot be used in conjunction with any other offer, photocopies will not be accepted.
4. All attractions offering a discount have confirmed their willingness to participate. All information is subject to change without notice and should any attraction close or decline to accept a voucher for any reason, Days Out UK are not liable and cannot be held responsible.
5. Days Out UK shall not accept liability for any loss, accident or injury that may occur at a participating attraction and any dispute arising must be settled direct with the attraction concerned.
6. Cash redemption value of each voucher is 0.001p.
7. You are advised to check all relevant information with your chosen attraction before commencing your journey.

Days Out UK, PO Box 427, Northampton NN1 3YN. Tel: 01604 622445

Ickworth House Park and Gardens
The Rotunda Ickworth Bury St Edmunds Suffolk IP29 5QE
One Child Free
with a full-paying adult
Cannot be used in conjunction with other offers. One voucher per party. Not valid on Bank Hols or special event days.
Expires end Feb 2008 (unless otherwise specified)

Inigo Jones and Co Ltd
Tudor Slate Works Y Groeslon Caernarfon Gwynedd Wales
Two for the Price of One
with a full-paying adult
Cannot be used in conjunction with other offers. One voucher per party. Not valid on Bank Hols or special event days.
Expires end Feb 2008 (unless otherwise specified)

International Women's Open
Devonshire Park Eastbourne East Sussex
Save up to £8.00 off Ticket Prices!
Simply call our booking line: 01323 412000 and quote "Days Out UK"
to claim your discount when ordering.
Conditions: no cash alternative; one discount per transaction
Cannot be used in conjunction with other offers. One voucher per party. Not valid on Bank Hols or special event days.
Expires end Feb 2008 (unless otherwise specified)

Inveraray Jail
Church Square Inveraray Argyll PA32 8TX
One Child Free
with every full-paying adult
Cannot be used in conjunction with other offers. One voucher per party. Not valid on Bank Hols or special event days.
Expires end Feb 2008 (unless otherwise specified)

Jewish Museum - Camden Town
Raymond Burton House 129-131 Albert Street
London NW1 7NB
Two for the Price of One
with a full-paying adult
Cannot be used in conjunction with other offers. One voucher per party. Not valid on Bank Hols or special event days.
Expires end Feb 2008 (unless otherwise specified)

Jewish Museum - Finchley
80 East End Road London N3 2SY
Two for the Price of One
with a full-paying adult
Cannot be used in conjunction with other offers. One voucher per party. Not valid on Bank Hols or special event days.
Expires end Feb 2008 (unless otherwise specified)

1. Each voucher entitles the holder to the discount specified by the selected attraction.
2. Valid for use until 28/02/08 (unless otherwise specified, or if attraction season finishes prior to this). Vouchers are subject to the terms, conditions and restrictions of the selected attraction.
3. One voucher per party will be accepted, cannot be used in conjunction with any other offer, photocopies will not be accepted.
4. All attractions offering a discount have confirmed their willingness to participate. All information is subject to change without notice and should any attraction close or decline to accept a voucher for any reason, Days Out UK are not liable and cannot be held responsible.
5. Days Out UK shall not accept liability for any loss, accident or injury that may occur at a participating attraction and any dispute arising must be settled direct with the attraction concerned.
6. Cash redemption value of each voucher is 0.001p.
7. You are advised to check all relevant information with your chosen attraction before commencing your journey.

Days Out UK, PO Box 427, Northampton NN1 3YN. Tel: 01604 622445

1. Each voucher entitles the holder to the discount specified by the selected attraction.
2. Valid for use until 28/02/08 (unless otherwise specified, or if attraction season finishes prior to this). Vouchers are subject to the terms, conditions and restrictions of the selected attraction.
3. One voucher per party will be accepted, cannot be used in conjunction with any other offer, photocopies will not be accepted.
4. All attractions offering a discount have confirmed their willingness to participate. All information is subject to change without notice and should any attraction close or decline to accept a voucher for any reason, Days Out UK are not liable and cannot be held responsible.
5. Days Out UK shall not accept liability for any loss, accident or injury that may occur at a participating attraction and any dispute arising must be settled direct with the attraction concerned.
6. Cash redemption value of each voucher is 0.001p.
7. You are advised to check all relevant information with your chosen attraction before commencing your journey.

Days Out UK, PO Box 427, Northampton NN1 3YN. Tel: 01604 622445

1. Each voucher entitles the holder to the discount specified by the selected attraction.
2. Valid for use until 28/02/08 (unless otherwise specified, or if attraction season finishes prior to this). Vouchers are subject to the terms, conditions and restrictions of the selected attraction.
3. One voucher per party will be accepted, cannot be used in conjunction with any other offer, photocopies will not be accepted.
4. All attractions offering a discount have confirmed their willingness to participate. All information is subject to change without notice and should any attraction close or decline to accept a voucher for any reason, Days Out UK are not liable and cannot be held responsible.
5. Days Out UK shall not accept liability for any loss, accident or injury that may occur at a participating attraction and any dispute arising must be settled direct with the attraction concerned.
6. Cash redemption value of each voucher is 0.001p.
7. You are advised to check all relevant information with your chosen attraction before commencing your journey.

Days Out UK, PO Box 427, Northampton NN1 3YN. Tel: 01604 622445

1. Each voucher entitles the holder to the discount specified by the selected attraction.
2. Valid for use until 28/02/08 (unless otherwise specified, or if attraction season finishes prior to this). Vouchers are subject to the terms, conditions and restrictions of the selected attraction.
3. One voucher per party will be accepted, cannot be used in conjunction with any other offer, photocopies will not be accepted.
4. All attractions offering a discount have confirmed their willingness to participate. All information is subject to change without notice and should any attraction close or decline to accept a voucher for any reason, Days Out UK are not liable and cannot be held responsible.
5. Days Out UK shall not accept liability for any loss, accident or injury that may occur at a participating attraction and any dispute arising must be settled direct with the attraction concerned.
6. Cash redemption value of each voucher is 0.001p.
7. You are advised to check all relevant information with your chosen attraction before commencing your journey.

Days Out UK, PO Box 427, Northampton NN1 3YN. Tel: 01604 622445

1. Each voucher entitles the holder to the discount specified by the selected attraction.
2. Valid for use until 28/02/08 (unless otherwise specified, or if attraction season finishes prior to this). Vouchers are subject to the terms, conditions and restrictions of the selected attraction.
3. One voucher per party will be accepted, cannot be used in conjunction with any other offer, photocopies will not be accepted.
4. All attractions offering a discount have confirmed their willingness to participate. All information is subject to change without notice and should any attraction close or decline to accept a voucher for any reason, Days Out UK are not liable and cannot be held responsible.
5. Days Out UK shall not accept liability for any loss, accident or injury that may occur at a participating attraction and any dispute arising must be settled direct with the attraction concerned.
6. Cash redemption value of each voucher is 0.001p.
7. You are advised to check all relevant information with your chosen attraction before commencing your journey.

Days Out UK, PO Box 427, Northampton NN1 3YN. Tel: 01604 622445

Jodrell Bank Visitor Centre

Jodrell Bank Lower Withington Macclesfield Cheshire

Two for the Price of One

with a full-paying adult

Cannot be used in conjunction with other offers. One voucher per party. Not valid on Bank Hols or special event days.

Expires end Feb 2008 (unless otherwise specified)

JORVIK Viking Centre

Coppergate York North Yorkshire YO1 9WT

One Child Free

with a full-paying adult

Cannot be used in conjunction with other offers. One voucher per party. Not valid on Bank Hols or special event days.

Expires end Feb 2008 (unless otherwise specified)

Kelburn Castle and Country Centre

South Offices Fairlie Largs Ayrshire KA29 0BE

Two for the Price of One

with a full-paying adult

Cannot be used in conjunction with other offers. One voucher per party. Not valid on Bank Hols or special event days.

Expires end Feb 2008 (unless otherwise specified)

Kentwell Hall and Gardens

Long Melford Sudbury Suffolk CO10 9BA

One Child Free

with two full-paying adults
(voucher must be presented at time of purchase)

Cannot be used in conjunction with other offers. One voucher per party. Not valid on Bank Hols or special event days.

Expires end Feb 2008 (unless otherwise specified)

Killhope

The North of England Lead Mining Museum
Cowshill Weardale County Durham DL13 1AR

Two for the Price of One

with a full-paying adult
(lowest priced admission goes free)

Cannot be used in conjunction with other offers. One voucher per party. Not valid on Bank Hols or special event days

Expires end Feb 2008 (unless otherwise specified)

King Arthur's Labyrinth

Corris Craft Centre Corris Machynlleth Powys

20% off Adult Admissions to the Labyrinth

offer applies to full-priced admissions only
(cannot be used during the month of August)

Cannot be used in conjunction with other offers. One voucher per party. Not valid on Bank Hols or special event days.

Expires end Feb 2008 (NOT VALID IN AUGUST)

1. Each voucher entitles the holder to the discount specified by the selected attraction.
2. Valid for use until 28/02/08 (unless otherwise specified, or if attraction season finishes prior to this). Vouchers are subject to the terms, conditions and restrictions of the selected attraction.
3. One voucher per party will be accepted, cannot be used in conjunction with any other offer, photocopies will not be accepted.
4. All attractions offering a discount have confirmed their willingness to participate. All information is subject to change without notice and should any attraction close or decline to accept a voucher for any reason, Days Out UK are not liable and cannot be held responsible.
5. Days Out UK shall not accept liability for any loss, accident or injury that may occur at a participating attraction and any dispute arising must be settled direct with the attraction concerned.
6. Cash redemption value of each voucher is 0.001p.
7. You are advised to check all relevant information with your chosen attraction before commencing your journey.

Days Out UK, PO Box 427, Northampton NN1 3YN. Tel: 01604 622445

1. Each voucher entitles the holder to the discount specified by the selected attraction.
2. Valid for use until 28/02/08 (unless otherwise specified, or if attraction season finishes prior to this). Vouchers are subject to the terms, conditions and restrictions of the selected attraction.
3. One voucher per party will be accepted, cannot be used in conjunction with any other offer, photocopies will not be accepted.
4. All attractions offering a discount have confirmed their willingness to participate. All information is subject to change without notice and should any attraction close or decline to accept a voucher for any reason, Days Out UK are not liable and cannot be held responsible.
5. Days Out UK shall not accept liability for any loss, accident or injury that may occur at a participating attraction and any dispute arising must be settled direct with the attraction concerned.
6. Cash redemption value of each voucher is 0.001p.
7. You are advised to check all relevant information with your chosen attraction before commencing your journey.

Days Out UK, PO Box 427, Northampton NN1 3YN. Tel: 01604 622445

1. Each voucher entitles the holder to the discount specified by the selected attraction.
2. Valid for use until 28/02/08 (unless otherwise specified, or if attraction season finishes prior to this). Vouchers are subject to the terms, conditions and restrictions of the selected attraction.
3. One voucher per party will be accepted, cannot be used in conjunction with any other offer, photocopies will not be accepted.
4. All attractions offering a discount have confirmed their willingness to participate. All information is subject to change without notice and should any attraction close or decline to accept a voucher for any reason, Days Out UK are not liable and cannot be held responsible.
5. Days Out UK shall not accept liability for any loss, accident or injury that may occur at a participating attraction and any dispute arising must be settled direct with the attraction concerned.
6. Cash redemption value of each voucher is 0.001p.
7. You are advised to check all relevant information with your chosen attraction before commencing your journey.

Days Out UK, PO Box 427, Northampton NN1 3YN. Tel: 01604 622445

1. Each voucher entitles the holder to the discount specified by the selected attraction.
2. Valid for use until 28/02/08 (unless otherwise specified, or if attraction season finishes prior to this). Vouchers are subject to the terms, conditions and restrictions of the selected attraction.
3. One voucher per party will be accepted, cannot be used in conjunction with any other offer, photocopies will not be accepted.
4. All attractions offering a discount have confirmed their willingness to participate. All information is subject to change without notice and should any attraction close or decline to accept a voucher for any reason, Days Out UK are not liable and cannot be held responsible.
5. Days Out UK shall not accept liability for any loss, accident or injury that may occur at a participating attraction and any dispute arising must be settled direct with the attraction concerned.
6. Cash redemption value of each voucher is 0.001p.
7. You are advised to check all relevant information with your chosen attraction before commencing your journey.

Days Out UK, PO Box 427, Northampton NN1 3YN. Tel: 01604 622445

1. Each voucher entitles the holder to the discount specified by the selected attraction.
2. Valid for use until 28/02/08 (unless otherwise specified, or if attraction season finishes prior to this). Vouchers are subject to the terms, conditions and restrictions of the selected attraction.
3. One voucher per party will be accepted, cannot be used in conjunction with any other offer, photocopies will not be accepted.
4. All attractions offering a discount have confirmed their willingness to participate. All information is subject to change without notice and should any attraction close or decline to accept a voucher for any reason, Days Out UK are not liable and cannot be held responsible.
5. Days Out UK shall not accept liability for any loss, accident or injury that may occur at a participating attraction and any dispute arising must be settled direct with the attraction concerned.
6. Cash redemption value of each voucher is 0.001p.
7. You are advised to check all relevant information with your chosen attraction before commencing your journey.

Days Out UK, PO Box 427, Northampton NN1 3YN. Tel: 01604 622445

DAYSOUtUK
The place to look for places to go

Kirklees Light Railway
Park Mill Way Clayton West Huddersfield West Yorkshire
One Child Free
with a full-paying adult

Cannot be used in conjunction with other offers. One voucher per party. Not valid on Bank Hols or special event days.

Expires end Feb 2008 (unless otherwise specified)

DISCOUNT VOUCHER

DAYSOUtUK
The place to look for places to go

Knebworth House, Gardens, Adventure
Playground and Park
Knebworth Hertfordshire SG3 6PY
Two for the Price of One
with a full-paying adult
(valid for Park and Gardens only)

Cannot be used in conjunction with other offers. One voucher per party. Not valid on Bank Hols or special event days.

Expires end Feb 2008 (Valid Mon-Fri only)

DISCOUNT VOUCHER

DAYSOUtUK
The place to look for places to go

Knockhatch Adventure Park
Hempstead Lane Hailsham East Sussex BN27 3PR
One Child Free
with every full-paying adult
(applies to Park entry only)

Cannot be used in conjunction with other offers. One voucher per party. Not valid on Bank Hols or special event days.

Expires end Feb 2008 (unless otherwise specified)

DISCOUNT VOUCHER

DAYSOUtUK
The place to look for places to go

Lee Valley Regional Park
Stubbins Hall Lane Crooked Mile Waltham Abbey Essex
Save £3-00! One Child Free at the Lee Valley
Park Farms with one full-paying adult
(no cash alternative)

Cannot be used in conjunction with other offers. One voucher per party. Not valid on Bank Hols or special event days.

valid 1 March - 31 October 2007

DISCOUNT VOUCHER

DAYSOUtUK
The place to look for places to go

LEGOLAND Windsor
Winkfield Road Windsor Berkshire SL4 4AY
Save up to £25.00!
(Voucher entitles a maximum of 5 people to £5.00 off full admission price per
person at LEGOLAND Windsor excludes August)

Terms & Conditions: 1. Voucher to be surrendered at ticket booth. 2. Not to be
used in conjunction with any other offer, reward/loyalty programme, 2 day pass,
annual pass, group booking, online tickets, rail inclusive offers or an exclusive
event or concert. 3. Not all attractions and shows may be operational on day of
visit. 4. Height, age and weight restrictions may apply. 5. Guests under the age of
14 or those that do not meet the height restrictions must be accompanied by a
person aged 16 or over. 6. Not for re-sale, non-refundable, and non-transferable.
7. Voucher valid for admissions from 17 March-28 October 2007, excluding the
month of August and selected dates. 8. Offer limited to one per household. 9.
Offer applies irrespective of entrance price at time of use. 10. LEGOLAND
Windsor will be closed on selected weekdays in April, May, September and
October 11. voucher cannot be used in conjunction with any booking made with
LEGOLAND Holidays

17 March-28 October 2007(Excludes August)

DISCOUNT VOUCHER

300709

1. Each voucher entitles the holder to the discount specified by the selected attraction.
2. Valid for use until 28/02/08 (unless otherwise specified, or if attraction season finishes prior to this). Vouchers are subject to the terms, conditions and restrictions of the selected attraction.
3. One voucher per party will be accepted, cannot be used in conjunction with any other offer, photocopies will not be accepted.
4. All attractions offering a discount have confirmed their willingness to participate. All information is subject to change without notice and should any attraction close or decline to accept a voucher for any reason, Days Out UK are not liable and cannot be held responsible.
5. Days Out UK shall not accept liability for any loss, accident or injury that may occur at a participating attraction and any dispute arising must be settled direct with the attraction concerned.
6. Cash redemption value of each voucher is 0.001p.
7. You are advised to check all relevant information with your chosen attraction before commencing your journey.

Days Out UK, PO Box 427, Northampton NN1 3YN. Tel: 01604 622445

1. Each voucher entitles the holder to the discount specified by the selected attraction.
2. Valid for use until 28/02/08 (unless otherwise specified, or if attraction season finishes prior to this). Vouchers are subject to the terms, conditions and restrictions of the selected attraction.
3. One voucher per party will be accepted, cannot be used in conjunction with any other offer, photocopies will not be accepted.
4. All attractions offering a discount have confirmed their willingness to participate. All information is subject to change without notice and should any attraction close or decline to accept a voucher for any reason, Days Out UK are not liable and cannot be held responsible.
5. Days Out UK shall not accept liability for any loss, accident or injury that may occur at a participating attraction and any dispute arising must be settled direct with the attraction concerned.
6. Cash redemption value of each voucher is 0.001p.
7. You are advised to check all relevant information with your chosen attraction before commencing your journey.

Days Out UK, PO Box 427, Northampton NN1 3YN. Tel: 01604 622445

1. Each voucher entitles the holder to the discount specified by the selected attraction.
2. Valid for use until 28/02/08 (unless otherwise specified, or if attraction season finishes prior to this). Vouchers are subject to the terms, conditions and restrictions of the selected attraction.
3. One voucher per party will be accepted, cannot be used in conjunction with any other offer, photocopies will not be accepted.
4. All attractions offering a discount have confirmed their willingness to participate. All information is subject to change without notice and should any attraction close or decline to accept a voucher for any reason, Days Out UK are not liable and cannot be held responsible.
5. Days Out UK shall not accept liability for any loss, accident or injury that may occur at a participating attraction and any dispute arising must be settled direct with the attraction concerned.
6. Cash redemption value of each voucher is 0.001p.
7. You are advised to check all relevant information with your chosen attraction before commencing your journey.

Days Out UK, PO Box 427, Northampton NN1 3YN. Tel: 01604 622445

1. Each voucher entitles the holder to the discount specified by the selected attraction.

2. Valid for use until 28/02/08 (unless otherwise specified, or if attraction season finishes prior to this). Vouchers are subject to the terms, conditions and restrictions of the selected attraction.

3. One voucher per party will be accepted, cannot be used in conjunction with any other offer, photocopies will not be accepted.

4. All attractions offering a discount have confirmed their willingness to participate. All information is subject to change without notice and should any attraction close or decline to accept a voucher for any reason, Days Out UK are not liable and cannot be held responsible.

5. Days Out UK shall not accept liability for any loss, accident or injury that may occur at a participating attraction and any dispute arising must be settled direct with the attraction concerned.

6. Cash redemption value of each voucher is 0.001p.

7. You are advised to check all relevant information with your chosen attraction before commencing your journey.

Days Out UK, PO Box 427, Northampton NN1 3YN. Tel: 01604 622445

Leighton Buzzard Railway

Page's Park Station Billington Road Leighton Buzzard Bedfordshire

One Child Free

with a full fare paying adult

(Not valid on Christmas services in December)

Cannot be used in conjunction with other offers. One voucher per party. Not valid on Bank Hols or special event days.

Expires end Feb 2008 (unless otherwise specified)

Leighton Hall

Carnforth Lancashire LA5 9ST

Two for the Price of One

with a full-paying adult

Cannot be used in conjunction with other offers. One voucher per party. Not valid on Bank Hols or special event days.

Expires end Feb 2008 (unless otherwise specified)

LetsSubscribe.com

Save up to 85% off the cover price on a selection of top magazine titles and browse our other categories to find your special offers on a range of new products. To see the complete list and to place an order visit www.letssubscribe.com and enter partner code: 'Days'

Terms and conditions

It normally takes 6-8 weeks before you will receive your first magazine. These offers are subject to delivery in the UK. A full title list is only available from the website. Delivery charges for other products apply.

Expires end Feb 2008 (unless otherwise specified)

Lewes Castle
and Barbican House Museum

169 High Street Lewes East Sussex BN7 1YE

Two for the Price of One

with a full-paying adult

Cannot be used in conjunction with other offers. One voucher per party. Not valid on Bank Hols or special event days.

Expires end Feb 2008 (unless otherwise specified)

Lightwater Valley Theme Park

North Stainley Ripon North Yorkshire HG4 3HT

One Child Free

with one full-paying adult

(not valid on Bank holiday weekends or during August; free child must be under 1.3m in height; no photocopies)

Cannot be used in conjunction with other offers. One voucher per party. Not valid on Bank Hols or special event days.

Valid until 28 October 2007 (excludes Aug)

Days Out UK, PO Box 427, Northampton NN1 3YN. Tel: 01604 622445

Days Out UK, PO Box 427, Northampton NN1 3YN. Tel: 01604 622445

Days Out UK, PO Box 427, Northampton NN1 3YN. Tel: 01604 622445

Days Out UK, PO Box 427, Northampton NN1 3YN. Tel: 01604 622445

Days Out UK, PO Box 427, Northampton NN1 3YN. Tel: 01604 622445

Lincoln Cathedral

Minster Yard Lincoln Lincolnshire LN2 1PX

10% discount on all gift shop purchases

(when you spend £10.00 or more)

Cannot be used in conjunction with other offers. One voucher per party. Not valid on Bank Hols or special event days.

Expires end Feb 2008 (unless otherwise specified)

Liverpool Football Club Museum and Tour Centre

Anfield Road Liverpool Merseyside L4 0TH

One Child Free

with a full-paying adult

Cannot be used in conjunction with other offers. One voucher per party. Not valid on Bank Hols or special event days.

Expires end Feb 2008 (unless otherwise specified)

Llancaiach Fawr Manor

Nelson Treharris Mid Glamorgan Wales CF46 6ER

One Child Free

with every full-paying adult

(Not valid for evening tours or Bank Holidays)

Cannot be used in conjunction with other offers. One voucher per party. Not valid on Bank Hols or special event days.

Expires end Feb 2008 (unless otherwise specified)

London Aquarium

County Hall Westminster Bridge Road London SE1 7PB

One Child Free

with one full-paying adult

Cannot be used in conjunction with other offers. One voucher per party. Not valid on Bank Hols or special event days.

Expires end Feb 2008 (unless otherwise specified)

London Dungeon

28-34 Tooley Street London SE1 2SZ

One Child Free

with every full-paying adult

Cannot be used in conjunction with other offers. One voucher per party. Not valid on Bank Hols or special event days.

Expires end Feb 2008 (unless otherwise specified)

London Waterbus Company

London NW1 8AF

80p off Adult Fares

on one-way or return tickets to Camden Lock or Little Venice
(present voucher on board; not valid for fares to or from London Zoo;
one voucher per person; not for use with any other offer; seats subject to
availability)

Cannot be used in conjunction with other offers. One voucher per party. Not valid on Bank Hols or special event days.

Valid until 31 October 2007

Long Shop Museum
Main Street Leiston Suffolk IP16 4ES
Two for the Price of One
with a full-paying adult

Cannot be used in conjunction with other offers. One voucher per party. Not valid on Bank Hols or special event days.

Expires end Feb 2008 (unless otherwise specified)

Longdown Activity Farm
Longdown Ashurst Southampton Hampshire SO40 7EH
One Child Free
with one full-paying adult
(Not valid Bank Holidays or Easter Half-Term or special event days)

Cannot be used in conjunction with other offers. One voucher per party. Not valid on Bank Hols or special event days.

Expires end Feb 2008 (unless otherwise specified)

Look Out Discovery Centre
Nine Mile Ride Bracknell Berkshire RG12 7QW
One Child Free
with a full-paying adult

Cannot be used in conjunction with other offers. One voucher per party. Not valid on Bank Hols or special event days.

Expires end Feb 2008 (unless otherwise specified)

Lord's Tour and MCC Museum
Lord's Ground St John's Wood London NW8 8QN
One Child Free
with one full-paying adult.
(valid on all public tours; not valid on match tickets)

Cannot be used in conjunction with other offers. One voucher per party. Not valid on Bank Hols or special event days.

Expires end Feb 2008 (unless otherwise specified)

Lulworth Castle and Park
East Lulworth Wareham Dorset BH20 5QS
One Child Free
with every full-paying adult
(Not valid for special events)

Cannot be used in conjunction with other offers. One voucher per party. Not valid on Bank Hols or special event days.

Expires end Feb 2008 (unless otherwise specified)

M and D's Scotland's Theme Park
Strathclyde Country Park Motherwell Lanarkshire Scotland
£5.00 off
One Unlimited Ride Wristband (for a family of 4)

Cannot be used in conjunction with other offers. One voucher per party. Not valid on Bank Hols or special event days.

Valid for 2007 season only

1. Each voucher entitles the holder to the discount specified by the selected attraction.
2. Valid for use until 28/02/08 (unless otherwise specified, or if attraction season finishes prior to this). Vouchers are subject to the terms, conditions and restrictions of the selected attraction.
3. One voucher per party will be accepted, cannot be used in conjunction with any other offer, photocopies will not be accepted.
4. All attractions offering a discount have confirmed their willingness to participate. All information is subject to change without notice and should any attraction close or decline to accept a voucher for any reason, Days Out UK are not liable and cannot be held responsible.
5. Days Out UK shall not accept liability for any loss, accident or injury that may occur at a participating attraction and any dispute arising must be settled direct with the attraction concerned.
6. Cash redemption value of each voucher is 0.001p.
7. You are advised to check all relevant information with your chosen attraction before commencing your journey.

Days Out UK, PO Box 427, Northampton NN1 3YN. Tel: 01604 622445

1. Each voucher entitles the holder to the discount specified by the selected attraction.
2. Valid for use until 28/02/08 (unless otherwise specified. or if attraction season finishes prior to this). Vouchers are subject to the terms, conditions and restrictions of the selected attraction.
3. One voucher per party will be accepted, cannot be used in conjunction with any other offer, photocopies will not be accepted.
4. All attractions offering a discount have confirmed their willingness to participate. All information is subject to change without notice and should any attraction close or decline to accept a voucher for any reason, Days Out UK are not liable and cannot be held responsible.
5. Days Out UK shall not accept liability for any loss, accident or injury that may occur at a participating attraction and any dispute arising must be settled direct with the attraction concerned.
6. Cash redemption value of each voucher is 0.001p.
7. You are advised to check all relevant information with your chosen attraction before commencing your journey.

Days Out UK, PO Box 427, Northampton NN1 3YN. Tel: 01604 622445

1. Each voucher entitles the holder to the discount specified by the selected attraction.
2. Valid for use until 28/02/08 (unless otherwise specified, or if attraction season finishes prior to this). Vouchers are subject to the terms, conditions and restrictions of the selected attraction.
3. One voucher per party will be accepted, cannot be used in conjunction with any other offer, photocopies will not be accepted.
4. All attractions offering a discount have confirmed their willingness to participate. All information is subject to change without notice and should any attraction close or decline to accept a voucher for any reason, Days Out UK are not liable and cannot be held responsible.
5. Days Out UK shall not accept liability for any loss, accident or injury that may occur at a participating attraction and any dispute arising must be settled direct with the attraction concerned.
6. Cash redemption value of each voucher is 0.001p.
7. You are advised to check all relevant information with your chosen attraction before commencing your journey.

Days Out UK, PO Box 427, Northampton NN1 3YN. Tel: 01604 622445

1. Each voucher entitles the holder to the discount specified by the selected attraction.
2. Valid for use until 28/02/08 (unless otherwise specified, or if attraction season finishes prior to this). Vouchers are subject to the terms, conditions and restrictions of the selected attraction.
3. One voucher per party will be accepted, cannot be used in conjunction with any other offer, photocopies will not be accepted.
4. All attractions offering a discount have confirmed their willingness to participate. All information is subject to change without notice and should any attraction close or decline to accept a voucher for any reason, Days Out UK are not liable and cannot be held responsible.
5. Days Out UK shall not accept liability for any loss, accident or injury that may occur at a participating attraction and any dispute arising must be settled direct with the attraction concerned.
6. Cash redemption value of each voucher is 0.001p.
7. You are advised to check all relevant information with your chosen attraction before commencing your journey.

Days Out UK, PO Box 427, Northampton NN1 3YN. Tel: 01604 622445

1. Each voucher entitles the holder to the discount specified by the selected attraction.
2. Valid for use until 28/02/08 (unless otherwise specified, or if attraction season finishes prior to this). Vouchers are subject to the terms, conditions and restrictions of the selected attraction.
3. One voucher per party will be accepted, cannot be used in conjunction with any other offer, photocopies will not be accepted.
4. All attractions offering a discount have confirmed their willingness to participate. All information is subject to change without notice and should any attraction close or decline to accept a voucher for any reason, Days Out UK are not liable and cannot be held responsible.
5. Days Out UK shall not accept liability for any loss, accident or injury that may occur at a participating attraction and any dispute arising must be settled direct with the attraction concerned.
6. Cash redemption value of each voucher is 0.001p.
7. You are advised to check all relevant information with your chosen attraction before commencing your journey.

Days Out UK, PO Box 427, Northampton NN1 3YN. Tel: 01604 622445

1. Each voucher entitles the holder to the discount specified by the selected attraction.
2. Valid for use until 28/02/08 (unless otherwise specified, or if attraction season finishes prior to this). Vouchers are subject to the terms, conditions and restrictions of the selected attraction.
3. One voucher per party will be accepted, cannot be used in conjunction with any other offer, photocopies will not be accepted.
4. All attractions offering a discount have confirmed their willingness to participate. All information is subject to change without notice and should any attraction close or decline to accept a voucher for any reason, Days Out UK are not liable and cannot be held responsible.
5. Days Out UK shall not accept liability for any loss, accident or injury that may occur at a participating attraction and any dispute arising must be settled direct with the attraction concerned.
6. Cash redemption value of each voucher is 0.001p.
7. You are advised to check all relevant information with your chosen attraction before commencing your journey.

Days Out UK, PO Box 427, Northampton NN1 3YN. Tel: 01604 622445

1. Each voucher entitles the holder to the discount specified by the selected attraction.
2. Valid for use until 28/02/08 (unless otherwise specified. or if attraction season finishes prior to this). Vouchers are subject to the terms, conditions and restrictions of the selected attraction.
3. One voucher per party will be accepted, cannot be used in conjunction with any other offer, photocopies will not be accepted.
4. All attractions offering a discount have confirmed their willingness to participate. All information is subject to change without notice and should any attraction close or decline to accept a voucher for any reason, Days Out UK are not liable and cannot be held responsible.
5. Days Out UK shall not accept liability for any loss, accident or injury that may occur at a participating attraction and any dispute arising must be settled direct with the attraction concerned.
6. Cash redemption value of each voucher is 0.001p.
7. You are advised to check all relevant information with your chosen attraction before commencing your journey.

Days Out UK, PO Box 427, Northampton NN1 3YN. Tel: 01604 622445

1. Each voucher entitles the holder to the discount specified by the selected attraction.
2. Valid for use until 28/02/08 (unless otherwise specified, or if attraction season finishes prior to this). Vouchers are subject to the terms, conditions and restrictions of the selected attraction.
3. One voucher per party will be accepted, cannot be used in conjunction with any other offer, photocopies will not be accepted.
4. All attractions offering a discount have confirmed their willingness to participate. All information is subject to change without notice and should any attraction close or decline to accept a voucher for any reason, Days Out UK are not liable and cannot be held responsible.
5. Days Out UK shall not accept liability for any loss, accident or injury that may occur at a participating attraction and any dispute arising must be settled direct with the attraction concerned.
6. Cash redemption value of each voucher is 0.001p.
7. You are advised to check all relevant information with your chosen attraction before commencing your journey.

Days Out UK, PO Box 427, Northampton NN1 3YN. Tel: 01604 622445

1. Each voucher entitles the holder to the discount specified by the selected attraction.
2. Valid for use until 28/02/08 (unless otherwise specified, or if attraction season finishes prior to this). Vouchers are subject to the terms, conditions and restrictions of the selected attraction.
3. One voucher per party will be accepted, cannot be used in conjunction with any other offer, photocopies will not be accepted.
4. All attractions offering a discount have confirmed their willingness to participate. All information is subject to change without notice and should any attraction close or decline to accept a voucher for any reason, Days Out UK are not liable and cannot be held responsible.
5. Days Out UK shall not accept liability for any loss, accident or injury that may occur at a participating attraction and any dispute arising must be settled direct with the attraction concerned.
6. Cash redemption value of each voucher is 0.001p.
7. You are advised to check all relevant information with your chosen attraction before commencing your journey.

Days Out UK, PO Box 427, Northampton NN1 3YN. Tel: 01604 622445

1. Each voucher entitles the holder to the discount specified by the selected attraction.
2. Valid for use until 28/02/08 (unless otherwise specified, or if attraction season finishes prior to this). Vouchers are subject to the terms, conditions and restrictions of the selected attraction.
3. One voucher per party will be accepted, cannot be used in conjunction with any other offer, photocopies will not be accepted.
4. All attractions offering a discount have confirmed their willingness to participate. All information is subject to change without notice and should any attraction close or decline to accept a voucher for any reason, Days Out UK are not liable and cannot be held responsible.
5. Days Out UK shall not accept liability for any loss, accident or injury that may occur at a participating attraction and any dispute arising must be settled direct with the attraction concerned.
6. Cash redemption value of each voucher is 0.001p.
7. You are advised to check all relevant information with your chosen attraction before commencing your journey.

Days Out UK, PO Box 427, Northampton NN1 3YN. Tel: 01604 622445

Mersey Ferries Ltd
Victoria Place Wallasey Merseyside CH44 6QY
Save up to £1.00!
£1.00 off a return ferry adult ticket or 50p off a return ferry child ticket

Cannot be used in conjunction with other offers. One voucher per party. Not valid on Bank Hols or special event days.
Expires end Feb 2008 (unless otherwise specified)

Michelham Priory
Upper Dicker Nr Hailsham East Sussex BN27 3QS
Two for the Price of One
with a full-paying adult

Cannot be used in conjunction with other offers. One voucher per party. Not valid on Bank Hols or special event days.
Expires end Feb 2008 (unless otherwise specified)

Milestones, Hampshire's
Living History Museum
Leisure Park Churchill Way West Basingstoke Hampshire
Two for the Price of One
with a full-paying adult
(not valid for groups, joint ticket events or Christmas Gala evenings)

Cannot be used in conjunction with other offers. One voucher per party. Not valid on Bank Hols or special event days.
Expires end Feb 2008 (unless otherwise specified)

Mill Green Museum and Mill
Mill Green Hatfield Hertfordshire AL9 5PD
0.50p off a Bag of Mill Green Flour
(any size)

Cannot be used in conjunction with other offers. One voucher per party. Not valid on Bank Hols or special event days.
Expires end Feb 2008 (unless otherwise specified)

Moggerhanger Park
Park Road Moggerhanger Bedford Bedfordshire MK44 3RW
Two for the Price of One
with a full-paying adult
(can be used for guided tours of Moggerhanger House)

Cannot be used in conjunction with other offers. One voucher per party. Not valid on Bank Hols or special event days.
valid 16 June-7 September 2007

Mount Edgcumbe House
and Country Park
Cremyll Torpoint Cornwall PL10 1HZ
Two for the Price of One
(two adult tickets for the price of one full priced adult ticket)

Cannot be used in conjunction with other offers. One voucher per party. Not valid on Bank Hols or special event days.
Expires end Feb 2008 (unless otherwise specified)

1. Each voucher entitles the holder to the discount specified by the selected attraction.
2. Valid for use until 28/02/08 (unless otherwise specified, or if attraction season finishes prior to this). Vouchers are subject to the terms, conditions and restrictions of the selected attraction.
3. One voucher per party will be accepted, cannot be used in conjunction with any other offer, photocopies will not be accepted.
4. All attractions offering a discount have confirmed their willingness to participate. All information is subject to change without notice and should any attraction close or decline to accept a voucher for any reason, Days Out UK are not liable and cannot be held responsible.
5. Days Out UK shall not accept liability for any loss, accident or injury that may occur at a participating attraction and any dispute arising must be settled direct with the attraction concerned.
6. Cash redemption value of each voucher is 0.001p.
7. You are advised to check all relevant information with your chosen attraction before commencing your journey.

Days Out UK, PO Box 427, Northampton NN1 3YN. Tel: 01604 622445

1. Each voucher entitles the holder to the discount specified by the selected attraction.
2. Valid for use until 28/02/08 (unless otherwise specified, or if attraction season finishes prior to this). Vouchers are subject to the terms, conditions and restrictions of the selected attraction.
3. One voucher per party will be accepted, cannot be used in conjunction with any other offer, photocopies will not be accepted.
4. All attractions offering a discount have confirmed their willingness to participate. All information is subject to change without notice and should any attraction close or decline to accept a voucher for any reason, Days Out UK are not liable and cannot be held responsible.
5. Days Out UK shall not accept liability for any loss, accident or injury that may occur at a participating attraction and any dispute arising must be settled direct with the attraction concerned.
6. Cash redemption value of each voucher is 0.001p.
7. You are advised to check all relevant information with your chosen attraction before commencing your journey.

Days Out UK, PO Box 427, Northampton NN1 3YN. Tel: 01604 622445

1. Each voucher entitles the holder to the discount specified by the selected attraction.
2. Valid for use until 28/02/08 (unless otherwise specified. or if attraction season finishes prior to this). Vouchers are subject to the terms, conditions and restrictions of the selected attraction.
3. One voucher per party will be accepted, cannot be used in conjunction with any other offer, photocopies will not be accepted.
4. All attractions offering a discount have confirmed their willingness to participate. All information is subject to change without notice and should any attraction close or decline to accept a voucher for any reason, Days Out UK are not liable and cannot be held responsible.
5. Days Out UK shall not accept liability for any loss, accident or injury that may occur at a participating attraction and any dispute arising must be settled direct with the attraction concerned.
6. Cash redemption value of each voucher is 0.001p.
7. You are advised to check all relevant information with your chosen attraction before commencing your journey.

Days Out UK, PO Box 427, Northampton NN1 3YN. Tel: 01604 622445

1. Each voucher entitles the holder to the discount specified by the selected attraction.
2. Valid for use until 28/02/08 (unless otherwise specified, or if attraction season finishes prior to this). Vouchers are subject to the terms, conditions and restrictions of the selected attraction.
3. One voucher per party will be accepted, cannot be used in conjunction with any other offer, photocopies will not be accepted.
4. All attractions offering a discount have confirmed their willingness to participate. All information is subject to change without notice and should any attraction close or decline to accept a voucher for any reason, Days Out UK are not liable and cannot be held responsible.
5. Days Out UK shall not accept liability for any loss, accident or injury that may occur at a participating attraction and any dispute arising must be settled direct with the attraction concerned.
6. Cash redemption value of each voucher is 0.001p.
7. You are advised to check all relevant information with your chosen attraction before commencing your journey.

Days Out UK, PO Box 427, Northampton NN1 3YN. Tel: 01604 622445

1. Each voucher entitles the holder to the discount specified by the selected attraction.
2. Valid for use until 28/02/08 (unless otherwise specified, or if attraction season finishes prior to this). Vouchers are subject to the terms, conditions and restrictions of the selected attraction.
3. One voucher per party will be accepted, cannot be used in conjunction with any other offer, photocopies will not be accepted.
4. All attractions offering a discount have confirmed their willingness to participate. All information is subject to change without notice and should any attraction close or decline to accept a voucher for any reason, Days Out UK are not liable and cannot be held responsible.
5. Days Out UK shall not accept liability for any loss, accident or injury that may occur at a participating attraction and any dispute arising must be settled direct with the attraction concerned.
6. Cash redemption value of each voucher is 0.001p.
7. You are advised to check all relevant information with your chosen attraction before commencing your journey.

Days Out UK, PO Box 427, Northampton NN1 3YN. Tel: 01604 622445

1. Each voucher entitles the holder to the discount specified by the selected attraction.
2. Valid for use until 28/02/08 (unless otherwise specified, or if attraction season finishes prior to this). Vouchers are subject to the terms, conditions and restrictions of the selected attraction.
3. One voucher per party will be accepted, cannot be used in conjunction with any other offer, photocopies will not be accepted.
4. All attractions offering a discount have confirmed their willingness to participate. All information is subject to change without notice and should any attraction close or decline to accept a voucher for any reason, Days Out UK are not liable and cannot be held responsible.
5. Days Out UK shall not accept liability for any loss, accident or injury that may occur at a participating attraction and any dispute arising must be settled direct with the attraction concerned.
6. Cash redemption value of each voucher is 0.001p.
7. You are advised to check all relevant information with your chosen attraction before commencing your journey.

Days Out UK, PO Box 427, Northampton NN1 3YN. Tel: 01604 622445

DAYSOUTUK
The place to look for places to go

Moyse's Hall Museum
Cornhill Bury St Edmunds Suffolk IP33 1DX
Two for the Price of One
with a full-paying adult

Cannot be used in conjunction with other offers. One voucher per visit. Not valid on Bank Hols or special event days.

Expires end Feb 2008 (unless otherwise specified)

DAYSOUTUK
The place to look for places to go

Mr Hardman's Photographic Studio
59 Rodney Street Liverpool L1 9EX
One Child Free
with a full-paying adult

Cannot be used in conjunction with other offers. One voucher per party. Not valid on Bank Hols or special event days.

Expires end Feb 2008 (unless otherwise specified)

DAYSOUTUK
The place to look for places to go

Mr Karting
The Hangers Harbury Lane Bishops Tachbrook Leamington Spa Warwickshire CV33 9SA
Two for the Price of One
with a full-paying adult
(please telephone in advance to check availability)

Cannot be used in conjunction with other offers. One voucher per party. Not valid on Bank Hols or special event days.

Expires end Feb 2008 (unless otherwise specified)

DAYSOUTUK
The place to look for places to go

Museum in Docklands
No 1 Warehouse West India Quay Hertsmere Road London E14 4AL
Two for the Price of One
full-paying adult

Cannot be used in conjunction with other offers. One voucher per party. Not valid on Bank Hols or special event days.

Expires end Feb 2008 (unless otherwise specified)

DAYSOUTUK
The place to look for places to go

Museum of Rugby
and Twickenham Stadium Tours
Rugby Football Union Rugby Road Twickenham Middlesex London
Two for the Price of One
with a full-paying adult

Cannot be used in conjunction with other offers. One voucher per party. Not valid on Bank Hols or special event days.

Expires end Feb 2008 (unless otherwise specified)

DAYSOUTUK
The place to look for places to go

Nash's House and New Place
Chapel Street Stratford-Upon-Avon Warwickshire CV37 6EP
Two for the Price of One
(voucher entitles one adult or one child to be admitted free of charge when accompanied by a full-paying adult)

Cannot be used in conjunction with other offers. One voucher per party. Not valid on Bank Hols or special event days.

Expires end Feb 2008 (unless otherwise specified)

1. Each voucher entitles the holder to the discount specified by the selected attraction.
2. Valid for use until 28/02/08 (unless otherwise specified, or if attraction season finishes prior to this). Vouchers are subject to the terms, conditions and restrictions of the selected attraction.
3. One voucher per party will be accepted, cannot be used in conjunction with any other offer, photocopies will not be accepted.
4. All attractions offering a discount have confirmed their willingness to participate. All information is subject to change without notice and should any attraction close or decline to accept a voucher for any reason, Days Out UK are not liable and cannot be held responsible.
5. Days Out UK shall not accept liability for any loss, accident or injury that may occur at a participating attraction and any dispute arising must be settled direct with the attraction concerned.
6. Cash redemption value of each voucher is 0.001p.
7. You are advised to check all relevant information with your chosen attraction before commencing your journey.

Days Out UK, PO Box 427, Northampton NN1 3YN. Tel: 01604 622445

1. Each voucher entitles the holder to the discount specified by the selected attraction.
2. Valid for use until 28/02/08 (unless otherwise specified, or if attraction season finishes prior to this). Vouchers are subject to the terms, conditions and restrictions of the selected attraction.
3. One voucher per party will be accepted, cannot be used in conjunction with any other offer, photocopies will not be accepted.
4. All attractions offering a discount have confirmed their willingness to participate. All information is subject to change without notice and should any attraction close or decline to accept a voucher for any reason, Days Out UK are not liable and cannot be held responsible.
5. Days Out UK shall not accept liability for any loss, accident or injury that may occur at a participating attraction and any dispute arising must be settled direct with the attraction concerned.
6. Cash redemption value of each voucher is 0.001p.
7. You are advised to check all relevant information with your chosen attraction before commencing your journey.

Days Out UK, PO Box 427, Northampton NN1 3YN. Tel: 01604 622445

1. Each voucher entitles the holder to the discount specified by the selected attraction.
2. Valid for use until 28/02/08 (unless otherwise specified. or if attraction season finishes prior to this). Vouchers are subject to the terms, conditions and restrictions of the selected attraction.
3. One voucher per party will be accepted, cannot be used in conjunction with any other offer, photocopies will not be accepted.
4. All attractions offering a discount have confirmed their willingness to participate. All information is subject to change without notice and should any attraction close or decline to accept a voucher for any reason, Days Out UK are not liable and cannot be held responsible.
5. Days Out UK shall not accept liability for any loss, accident or injury that may occur at a participating attraction and any dispute arising must be settled direct with the attraction concerned.
6. Cash redemption value of each voucher is 0.001p.
7. You are advised to check all relevant information with your chosen attraction before commencing your journey.

Days Out UK, PO Box 427, Northampton NN1 3YN. Tel: 01604 622445

1. Each voucher entitles the holder to the discount specified by the selected attraction.
2. Valid for use until 28/02/08 (unless otherwise specified, or if attraction season finishes prior to this). Vouchers are subject to the terms, conditions and restrictions of the selected attraction.
3. One voucher per party will be accepted, cannot be used in conjunction with any other offer, photocopies will not be accepted.
4. All attractions offering a discount have confirmed their willingness to participate. All information is subject to change without notice and should any attraction close or decline to accept a voucher for any reason, Days Out UK are not liable and cannot be held responsible.
5. Days Out UK shall not accept liability for any loss, accident or injury that may occur at a participating attraction and any dispute arising must be settled direct with the attraction concerned.
6. Cash redemption value of each voucher is 0.001p.
7. You are advised to check all relevant information with your chosen attraction before commencing your journey.

Days Out UK, PO Box 427, Northampton NN1 3YN. Tel: 01604 622445

1. Each voucher entitles the holder to the discount specified by the selected attraction.
2. Valid for use until 28/02/08 (unless otherwise specified, or if attraction season finishes prior to this). Vouchers are subject to the terms, conditions and restrictions of the selected attraction.
3. One voucher per party will be accepted, cannot be used in conjunction with any other offer, photocopies will not be accepted.
4. All attractions offering a discount have confirmed their willingness to participate. All information is subject to change without notice and should any attraction close or decline to accept a voucher for any reason, Days Out UK are not liable and cannot be held responsible.
5. Days Out UK shall not accept liability for any loss, accident or injury that may occur at a participating attraction and any dispute arising must be settled direct with the attraction concerned.
6. Cash redemption value of each voucher is 0.001p.
7. You are advised to check all relevant information with your chosen attraction before commencing your journey.

Days Out UK, PO Box 427, Northampton NN1 3YN. Tel: 01604 622445

1. Each voucher entitles the holder to the discount specified by the selected attraction.
2. Valid for use until 28/02/08 (unless otherwise specified, or if attraction season finishes prior to this). Vouchers are subject to the terms, conditions and restrictions of the selected attraction.
3. One voucher per party will be accepted, cannot be used in conjunction with any other offer, photocopies will not be accepted.
4. All attractions offering a discount have confirmed their willingness to participate. All information is subject to change without notice and should any attraction close or decline to accept a voucher for any reason, Days Out UK are not liable and cannot be held responsible.
5. Days Out UK shall not accept liability for any loss, accident or injury that may occur at a participating attraction and any dispute arising must be settled direct with the attraction concerned.
6. Cash redemption value of each voucher is 0.001p.
7. You are advised to check all relevant information with your chosen attraction before commencing your journey.

Days Out UK, PO Box 427, Northampton NN1 3YN. Tel: 01604 622445

National Herb Centre

Banbury Road Warmington Banbury Oxfordshire OX17 1DF

10% discount on all gift shop purchases
(when you spend £10-00 or more)

Cannot be used in conjunction with other offers. One voucher per party. Not valid on Bank Hols or special event days.

Expires end Feb 2008 (unless otherwise specified)

National Horseracing Museum and Tours

99 High Street Newmarket Suffolk CB8 8JH

Two for the Price of One

with a full-paying adult

Cannot be used in conjunction with other offers. One voucher per party. Not valid on Bank Hols or special event days.

Expires end Feb 2008 (unless otherwise specified)

National Maritime Museum

Greenwich London SE10 9NF

20% off Adult Admissions to the 'Sailor Chic' Exhibition
(no cash alternative; photocopies not accepted; non-transferable)

Cannot be used in conjunction with other offers. One voucher per party. Not valid on Bank Hols or special event days.

Valid 25 July-30 Oct 2007

National Maritime Museum Cornwall

Discovery Quay Falmouth Cornwall TR11 3QY

Two for the Price of One

with a full-paying adult

Cannot be used in conjunction with other offers. One voucher per party. Not valid on Bank Hols or special event days.

Expires end Feb 2008 (unless otherwise specified)

National Museum of Costume Scotland

Shambellie House New Abbey Dumfries DG2 8HQ

Two for the Price of One

with a full-paying adult
(offer does not include entry to special events)

Cannot be used in conjunction with other offers. One voucher per party. Not valid on Bank Hols or special event days

Expires end Feb 2008 (unless otherwise specified)

National Museum of Flight Scotland

East Fortune Airfield North Berwick East Lothian

Two for the Price of One
(offer applies to adult and concession tickets; offer includes the
Concorde Experience; offer excludes Concorde boarding passes)

Cannot be used in conjunction with other offers. One voucher per party. Not valid on Bank Hols or special event days.

Expires end Feb 2008 (unless otherwise specified)

1. Each voucher entitles the holder to the discount specified by the selected attraction.
2. Valid for use until 28/02/08 (unless otherwise specified, or if attraction season finishes prior to this). Vouchers are subject to the terms, conditions and restrictions of the selected attraction.
3. One voucher per party will be accepted, cannot be used in conjunction with any other offer, photocopies will not be accepted.
4. All attractions offering a discount have confirmed their willingness to participate. All information is subject to change without notice and should any attraction close or decline to accept a voucher for any reason, Days Out UK are not liable and cannot be held responsible.
5. Days Out UK shall not accept liability for any loss, accident or injury that may occur at a participating attraction and any dispute arising must be settled direct with the attraction concerned.
6. Cash redemption value of each voucher is 0.001p.
7. You are advised to check all relevant information with your chosen attraction before commencing your journey.

Days Out UK, PO Box 427, Northampton NN1 3YN. Tel: 01604 622445

1. Each voucher entitles the holder to the discount specified by the selected attraction.
2. Valid for use until 28/02/08 (unless otherwise specified, or if attraction season finishes prior to this). Vouchers are subject to the terms, conditions and restrictions of the selected attraction.
3. One voucher per party will be accepted, cannot be used in conjunction with any other offer, photocopies will not be accepted.
4. All attractions offering a discount have confirmed their willingness to participate. All information is subject to change without notice and should any attraction close or decline to accept a voucher for any reason, Days Out UK are not liable and cannot be held responsible.
5. Days Out UK shall not accept liability for any loss, accident or injury that may occur at a participating attraction and any dispute arising must be settled direct with the attraction concerned.
6. Cash redemption value of each voucher is 0.001p.
7. You are advised to check all relevant information with your chosen attraction before commencing your journey.

Days Out UK, PO Box 427, Northampton NN1 3YN. Tel: 01604 622445

1. Each voucher entitles the holder to the discount specified by the selected attraction.
2. Valid for use until 28/02/08 (unless otherwise specified, or if attraction season finishes prior to this). Vouchers are subject to the terms, conditions and restrictions of the selected attraction.
3. One voucher per party will be accepted, cannot be used in conjunction with any other offer, photocopies will not be accepted.
4. All attractions offering a discount have confirmed their willingness to participate. All information is subject to change without notice and should any attraction close or decline to accept a voucher for any reason, Days Out UK are not liable and cannot be held responsible.
5. Days Out UK shall not accept liability for any loss, accident or injury that may occur at a participating attraction and any dispute arising must be settled direct with the attraction concerned.
6. Cash redemption value of each voucher is 0.001p.
7. You are advised to check all relevant information with your chosen attraction before commencing your journey.

Days Out UK, PO Box 427, Northampton NN1 3YN. Tel: 01604 622445

1. Each voucher entitles the holder to the discount specified by the selected attraction.
2. Valid for use until 28/02/08 (unless otherwise specified, or if attraction season finishes prior to this). Vouchers are subject to the terms, conditions and restrictions of the selected attraction.
3. One voucher per party will be accepted, cannot be used in conjunction with any other offer, photocopies will not be accepted.
4. All attractions offering a discount have confirmed their willingness to participate. All information is subject to change without notice and should any attraction close or decline to accept a voucher for any reason, Days Out UK are not liable and cannot be held responsible.
5. Days Out UK shall not accept liability for any loss, accident or injury that may occur at a participating attraction and any dispute arising must be settled direct with the attraction concerned.
6. Cash redemption value of each voucher is 0.001p.
7. You are advised to check all relevant information with your chosen attraction before commencing your journey.

Days Out UK, PO Box 427, Northampton NN1 3YN. Tel: 01604 622445

1. Each voucher entitles the holder to the discount specified by the selected attraction.
2. Valid for use until 28/02/08 (unless otherwise specified, or if attraction season finishes prior to this). Vouchers are subject to the terms, conditions and restrictions of the selected attraction.
3. One voucher per party will be accepted, cannot be used in conjunction with any other offer, photocopies will not be accepted.
4. All attractions offering a discount have confirmed their willingness to participate. All information is subject to change without notice and should any attraction close or decline to accept a voucher for any reason, Days Out UK are not liable and cannot be held responsible.
5. Days Out UK shall not accept liability for any loss, accident or injury that may occur at a participating attraction and any dispute arising must be settled direct with the attraction concerned.
6. Cash redemption value of each voucher is 0.001p.
7. You are advised to check all relevant information with your chosen attraction before commencing your journey.

Days Out UK, PO Box 427, Northampton NN1 3YN. Tel: 01604 622445

Days Out UK, PO Box 427, Northampton NN1 3YN. Tel: 01604 622445

Days Out UK, PO Box 427, Northampton NN1 3YN. Tel: 01604 622445

Days Out UK, PO Box 427, Northampton NN1 3YN. Tel: 01604 622445

Days Out UK, PO Box 427, Northampton NN1 3YN. Tel: 01604 622445

DAYS OUT UK
The place to look for places to go

National Seal Sanctuary

Gweek Helston Cornwall TR12 6UG

One Child Free with a full-paying adult

1. This voucher entitles free admission to the National Seal Sanctuary for one child when accompanied by one full paying adult.
2. Offer expires 28 February 2008.
3. Cannot be used in conjunction with any other offer.
4. A "child" is classed as a person aged 3-14 inclusive (under 3s go free anyway).
5. No cash alternative, non-refundable; and non-exchangeable.
6. All children must be accompanied by an adult.
7. Only one voucher per party and per transaction.
8. Photocopies not accepted.
9. SEA LIFE/Sanctuaries reserve the right to alter, close or remove details/exhibits without prior notice for technical, operational or other reasons, and no refunds can be given in these circumstances.
10. SEA LIFE/Sanctuaries reserve the right to refuse entry without explanation.
Voucher Ref: DOUK.

Cannot be used in conjunction with other offers. One voucher per party. Not valid on Bank Hols or special event days.

Expires end Feb 2008 (unless otherwise specified)

DAYS OUT UK
The place to look for places to go

DISCOUNT VOUCHER

National Wildflower Centre

Court Hey Park Roby Road Liverpool L16 3NA

Two for the Price of One

with a full-paying adult

Cannot be used in conjunction with other offers. One voucher per party. Not valid on Bank Hols or special event days.

Valid March-September 2007 only

DAYS OUT UK
The place to look for places to go

DISCOUNT VOUCHER

Nature in Art

Wallsworth Hall Twigworth Gloucester Gloucestershire

Two for the Price of One

with a full-paying adult

Cannot be used in conjunction with other offers. One voucher per party. Not valid on Bank Hols or special event days.

Expires end Feb 2008 (unless otherwise specified)

DAYS OUT UK
The place to look for places to go

DISCOUNT VOUCHER

Nature's World

Ladgate Lane Acklam Middlesbrough Cleveland

£1.00 off per head

For groups (pre-booked) of 20 or more

Cannot be used in conjunction with other offers. One voucher per party. Not valid on Bank Hols or special event days.

Expires end Feb 2008 (unless otherwise specified)

DAYS OUT UK
The place to look for places to go

DISCOUNT VOUCHER

Navan Centre and Fort

81 Killylea Road Armagh County Armagh Northern Ireland

Two for the Price of One

with a full-paying adult

Cannot be used in conjunction with other offers. One voucher per party. Not valid on Bank Hols or special event days.

Expires end Feb 2008 (unless otherwise specified)

1. Each voucher entitles the holder to the discount specified by the selected attraction.

2. Valid for use until 28/02/08 (unless otherwise specified, or if attraction season finishes prior to this). Vouchers are subject to the terms, conditions and restrictions of the selected attraction.

3. One voucher per party will be accepted, cannot be used in conjunction with any other offer, photocopies will not be accepted.

4. All attractions offering a discount have confirmed their willingness to participate. All information is subject to change without notice and should any attraction close or decline to accept a voucher for any reason, Days Out UK are not liable and cannot be held responsible.

5. Days Out UK shall not accept liability for any loss, accident or injury that may occur at a participating attraction and any dispute arising must be settled direct with the attraction concerned.

6. Cash redemption value of each voucher is 0.001p.

7. You are advised to check all relevant information with your chosen attraction before commencing your journey.

Days Out UK, PO Box 427, Northampton NN1 3YN. Tel: 01604 622445

1. Each voucher entitles the holder to the discount specified by the selected attraction.
2. Valid for use until 28/02/08 (unless otherwise specified. or if attraction season finishes prior to this). Vouchers are subject to the terms, conditions and restrictions of the selected attraction.
3. One voucher per party will be accepted, cannot be used in conjunction with any other offer, photocopies will not be accepted.
4. All attractions offering a discount have confirmed their willingness to participate. All information is subject to change without notice and should any attraction close or decline to accept a voucher for any reason, Days Out UK are not liable and cannot be held responsible.
5. Days Out UK shall not accept liability for any loss, accident or injury that may occur at a participating attraction and any dispute arising must be settled direct with the attraction concerned.
6. Cash redemption value of each voucher is 0.001p.
7. You are advised to check all relevant information with your chosen attraction before commencing your journey.

Days Out UK, PO Box 427, Northampton NN1 3YN. Tel: 01604 622445

1. Each voucher entitles the holder to the discount specified by the selected attraction.
2. Valid for use until 28/02/08 (unless otherwise specified, or if attraction season finishes prior to this). Vouchers are subject to the terms, conditions and restrictions of the selected attraction.
3. One voucher per party will be accepted, cannot be used in conjunction with any other offer, photocopies will not be accepted.
4. All attractions offering a discount have confirmed their willingness to participate. All information is subject to change without notice and should any attraction close or decline to accept a voucher for any reason, Days Out UK are not liable and cannot be held responsible.
5. Days Out UK shall not accept liability for any loss, accident or injury that may occur at a participating attraction and any dispute arising must be settled direct with the attraction concerned.
6. Cash redemption value of each voucher is 0.001p.
7. You are advised to check all relevant information with your chosen attraction before commencing your journey.

Days Out UK, PO Box 427, Northampton NN1 3YN. Tel: 01604 622445

1. Each voucher entitles the holder to the discount specified by the selected attraction.
2. Valid for use until 28/02/08 (unless otherwise specified, or if attraction season finishes prior to this). Vouchers are subject to the terms, conditions and restrictions of the selected attraction.
3. One voucher per party will be accepted, cannot be used in conjunction with any other offer, photocopies will not be accepted.
4. All attractions offering a discount have confirmed their willingness to participate. All information is subject to change without notice and should any attraction close or decline to accept a voucher for any reason, Days Out UK are not liable and cannot be held responsible.
5. Days Out UK shall not accept liability for any loss, accident or injury that may occur at a participating attraction and any dispute arising must be settled direct with the attraction concerned.
6. Cash redemption value of each voucher is 0.001p.
7. You are advised to check all relevant information with your chosen attraction before commencing your journey.

Days Out UK, PO Box 427, Northampton NN1 3YN. Tel: 01604 622445

1. Each voucher entitles the holder to the discount specified by the selected attraction.
2. Valid for use until 28/02/08 (unless otherwise specified, or if attraction season finishes prior to this). Vouchers are subject to the terms, conditions and restrictions of the selected attraction.
3. One voucher per party will be accepted, cannot be used in conjunction with any other offer, photocopies will not be accepted.
4. All attractions offering a discount have confirmed their willingness to participate. All information is subject to change without notice and should any attraction close or decline to accept a voucher for any reason, Days Out UK are not liable and cannot be held responsible.
5. Days Out UK shall not accept liability for any loss, accident or injury that may occur at a participating attraction and any dispute arising must be settled direct with the attraction concerned.
6. Cash redemption value of each voucher is 0.001p.
7. You are advised to check all relevant information with your chosen attraction before commencing your journey.

Days Out UK, PO Box 427, Northampton NN1 3YN. Tel: 01604 622445

DAYSOUTUK
The place to look for places to go

NCCL Galleries of Justice

Shire Hall High Pavement Lace Market Nottingham

Two for the Price of One

with a full-paying adult

Cannot be used in conjunction with other offers. One voucher per party. Not valid on Bank Hols or special event days.

Expires end Feb 2008 (unless otherwise specified)

DAYSOUTUK
The place to look for places to go

Needles Park

Alum Bay Isle of Wight PO39 0JD

Three for the Price of Two

Super-Saver ticket books

Cannot be used in conjunction with other offers. One voucher per party. Not valid on Bank Hols or special event days.

Expires end Feb 2008 (unless otherwise specified)

DAYSOUTUK
The place to look for places to go

New Forest Otter, Owl and Wildlife
Conservation Park

Deerleap Lane Longdown Marchwood Southampton
Hampshire SO40 4UH

One Child Free

with a full-paying adult

Cannot be used in conjunction with other offers. One voucher per party. Not valid on Bank Hols or special event days.

Expires end Feb 2008 (unless otherwise specified)

DAYSOUTUK
The place to look for places to go

New Metroland

39 Garden Walk Metrocentre Gateshead Tyne & Wear

Two for the Price of One

with a full-paying adult

(height restrictions in force; offer applies to Standard All-Day Passes only)

Cannot be used in conjunction with other offers. One voucher per party. Not valid on Bank Hols or special event days.

Expires end Feb 2008 (unless otherwise specified)

DAYSOUTUK
The place to look for places to go

Newby Hall and Gardens

Newby Hall Ripon North Yorkshire HG4 5AE

One Child Free

with a full-paying adult

(not valid on special event days)

Cannot be used in conjunction with other offers. One voucher per party. Not valid on Bank Hols or special event days.

Expires end Feb 2008 (unless otherwise specified)

DAYSOUTUK
The place to look for places to go

Newquay Zoo

Trenance Gardens Newquay Cornwall TR7 2LZ

£1.00 off Per-Person

for up to 6 people

Cannot be used in conjunction with other offers. One voucher per party. Not valid on Bank Hols or special event days.

Valid until 31 Dec 2007

Days Out UK, PO Box 427, Northampton NN1 3YN. Tel: 01604 622445

1. Each voucher entitles the holder to the discount specified by the selected attraction.
2. Valid for use until 28/02/08 (unless otherwise specified, or if attraction season finishes prior to this). Vouchers are subject to the terms, conditions and restrictions of the selected attraction.
3. One voucher per party will be accepted, cannot be used in conjunction with any other offer, photocopies will not be accepted.
4. All attractions offering a discount have confirmed their willingness to participate. All information is subject to change without notice and should any attraction close or decline to accept a voucher for any reason, Days Out UK are not liable and cannot be held responsible.
5. Days Out UK shall not accept liability for any loss, accident or injury that may occur at a participating attraction and any dispute arising must be settled direct with the attraction concerned.
6. Cash redemption value of each voucher is 0.001p.
7. You are advised to check all relevant information with your chosen attraction before commencing your journey.

Days Out UK, PO Box 427, Northampton NN1 3YN. Tel: 01604 622445

1. Each voucher entitles the holder to the discount specified by the selected attraction.
2. Valid for use until 28/02/08 (unless otherwise specified. or if attraction season finishes prior to this). Vouchers are subject to the terms, conditions and restrictions of the selected attraction.
3. One voucher per party will be accepted, cannot be used in conjunction with any other offer, photocopies will not be accepted.
4. All attractions offering a discount have confirmed their willingness to participate. All information is subject to change without notice and should any attraction close or decline to accept a voucher for any reason, Days Out UK are not liable and cannot be held responsible.
5. Days Out UK shall not accept liability for any loss, accident or injury that may occur at a participating attraction and any dispute arising must be settled direct with the attraction concerned.
6. Cash redemption value of each voucher is 0.001p.
7. You are advised to check all relevant information with your chosen attraction before commencing your journey.

Days Out UK, PO Box 427, Northampton NN1 3YN. Tel: 01604 622445

1. Each voucher entitles the holder to the discount specified by the selected attraction.
2. Valid for use until 28/02/08 (unless otherwise specified, or if attraction season finishes prior to this). Vouchers are subject to the terms, conditions and restrictions of the selected attraction.
3. One voucher per party will be accepted, cannot be used in conjunction with any other offer, photocopies will not be accepted.
4. All attractions offering a discount have confirmed their willingness to participate. All information is subject to change without notice and should any attraction close or decline to accept a voucher for any reason, Days Out UK are not liable and cannot be held responsible.
5. Days Out UK shall not accept liability for any loss, accident or injury that may occur at a participating attraction and any dispute arising must be settled direct with the attraction concerned.
6. Cash redemption value of each voucher is 0.001p.
7. You are advised to check all relevant information with your chosen attraction before commencing your journey.

Days Out UK, PO Box 427, Northampton NN1 3YN. Tel: 01604 622445

1. Each voucher entitles the holder to the discount specified by the selected attraction.
2. Valid for use until 28/02/08 (unless otherwise specified, or if attraction season finishes prior to this). Vouchers are subject to the terms, conditions and restrictions of the selected attraction.
3. One voucher per party will be accepted, cannot be used in conjunction with any other offer, photocopies will not be accepted.
4. All attractions offering a discount have confirmed their willingness to participate. All information is subject to change without notice and should any attraction close or decline to accept a voucher for any reason, Days Out UK are not liable and cannot be held responsible.
5. Days Out UK shall not accept liability for any loss, accident or injury that may occur at a participating attraction and any dispute arising must be settled direct with the attraction concerned.
6. Cash redemption value of each voucher is 0.001p.
7. You are advised to check all relevant information with your chosen attraction before commencing your journey.

Days Out UK, PO Box 427, Northampton NN1 3YN. Tel: 01604 622445

1. Each voucher entitles the holder to the discount specified by the selected attraction.
2. Valid for use until 28/02/08 (unless otherwise specified, or if attraction season finishes prior to this). Vouchers are subject to the terms, conditions and restrictions of the selected attraction.
3. One voucher per party will be accepted, cannot be used in conjunction with any other offer, photocopies will not be accepted.
4. All attractions offering a discount have confirmed their willingness to participate. All information is subject to change without notice and should any attraction close or decline to accept a voucher for any reason, Days Out UK are not liable and cannot be held responsible.
5. Days Out UK shall not accept liability for any loss, accident or injury that may occur at a participating attraction and any dispute arising must be settled direct with the attraction concerned.
6. Cash redemption value of each voucher is 0.001p.
7. You are advised to check all relevant information with your chosen attraction before commencing your journey.

Days Out UK, PO Box 427, Northampton NN1 3YN. Tel: 01604 622445

Norton Priory Museum and Gardens

Tudor Road Manor Park Runcorn Cheshire

Two for the Price of One
with a full-paying adult

Cannot be used in conjunction with other offers. One voucher per party. Not valid on Bank Hols or special event days.

Expires end Feb 2008 (unless otherwise specified)

Ocean Beach Pleasure Park

23 The Foreshore Sea Road South Shield Tyne & Wear

Save £10.00!
Get £25.00 worth of tokens for just £15.00
(single tokens cost 50p)

Cannot be used in conjunction with other offers. One voucher per party. Not valid on Bank Hols or special event days.

Expires end Feb 2008 (unless otherwise specified)

Old House Museum

Cunningham Place off North Church Street Bakewell
Derbyshire DE45 1DD

One Child Free
with a full-paying adult

Cannot be used in conjunction with other offers. One voucher per party. Not valid on Bank Hols or special event days.

Expires end Feb 2008 (unless otherwise specified)

Oliver Cromwell's House

29 St. Mary's Street Ely Cambridgeshire CB7 4HF

One Child Free
with a full-paying adult

Cannot be used in conjunction with other offers. One voucher per party. Not valid on Bank Hols or special event days.

Expires end Feb 2008 (unless otherwise specified)

Original Great Maze

Blake House Craft Centre Blake End Rayne Nr.
Braintree Essex CM77 6RA

One Child Free
with two full-paying adults

Cannot be used in conjunction with other offers. One voucher per party. Not valid on Bank Hols or special event days.

Expires end Feb 2008 (unless otherwise specified)

Oswaldtwistle Mills

Moscow Mill Collier Street Oswaldtwistle Accrington
Lancashire

10% Discount on Food & Drink
Purchases in Café Nova

Cannot be used in conjunction with other offers. One voucher per party. Not valid on Bank Hols or special event days.

Expires end Feb 2008 (unless otherwise specified)

DAYS OUT UK
The place to look for places to go

Palace Stables Heritage Centre
The Palace Demense Armagh County Armagh BT60 4EL
Two for the Price of One
with a full-paying adult
Cannot be used in conjunction with other offers. One voucher per party. Not valid on Bank Hols or special event days.
Expires end Feb 2008 (unless otherwise specified)

DAYS OUT UK
The place to look for places to go

Paradise Park
Avis Road Newhaven East Sussex BN9 0DH
One Child Free
with a full paying adult
Cannot be used in conjunction with other offers. One voucher per party. Not valid on Bank Hols or special event days.
Expires end Feb 2008 (unless otherwise specified)

DAYS OUT UK
The place to look for places to go

Paradise Park and Jungle Barn
16 Trelissick Road Hayle Cornwall TR27 4HB
£1.00 off standard admission prices
(for up to 5 people)
Cannot be used in conjunction with other offers. One voucher per party. Not valid on Bank Hols or special event days.
Expires end Feb 2008 (unless otherwise specified)

DAYS OUT UK
The place to look for places to go

Paradise Wildlife Park
White Stubbs Lane Broxbourne Hertfordshire EN10 7QA
One Child Free
with two full-paying adults
Cannot be used in conjunction with other offers. One voucher per party. Not valid on Bank Hols or special event days.
valid until 31st December 2007

DAYS OUT UK
The place to look for places to go

Paxton House and Country Park
Paxton Berwick Upon Tweed Northumberland TD15 1SZ
One Child Free
with a full-paying adult
Cannot be used in conjunction with other offers. One voucher per party. Not valid on Bank Hols or special event days.
Expires end Feb 2008 (unless otherwise specified)

DAYS OUT UK
The place to look for places to go

Peak Cavern
Peak Cavern Rd Castleton Hope Valley Derbyshire S33 8WS
£1.50 off a Joint Adult Ticket OR 50p off a Joint Child Ticket OR £2.50 off a Joint Family Ticket
Cannot be used in conjunction with other offers. One voucher per party. Not valid on Bank Hols or special event days.
Expires end Feb 2008 (unless otherwise specified)

1. Each voucher entitles the holder to the discount specified by the selected attraction.
2. Valid for use until 28/02/08 (unless otherwise specified, or if attraction season finishes prior to this). Vouchers are subject to the terms, conditions and restrictions of the selected attraction.
3. One voucher per party will be accepted, cannot be used in conjunction with any other offer, photocopies will not be accepted.
4. All attractions offering a discount have confirmed their willingness to participate. All information is subject to change without notice and should any attraction close or decline to accept a voucher for any reason, Days Out UK are not liable and cannot be held responsible.
5. Days Out UK shall not accept liability for any loss, accident or injury that may occur at a participating attraction and any dispute arising must be settled direct with the attraction concerned.
6. Cash redemption value of each voucher is 0.001p.
7. You are advised to check all relevant information with your chosen attraction before commencing your journey.

Days Out UK, PO Box 427, Northampton NN1 3YN. Tel: 01604 622445

1. Each voucher entitles the holder to the discount specified by the selected attraction.
2. Valid for use until 28/02/08 (unless otherwise specified, or if attraction season finishes prior to this). Vouchers are subject to the terms, conditions and restrictions of the selected attraction.
3. One voucher per party will be accepted, cannot be used in conjunction with any other offer, photocopies will not be accepted.
4. All attractions offering a discount have confirmed their willingness to participate. All information is subject to change without notice and should any attraction close or decline to accept a voucher for any reason, Days Out UK are not liable and cannot be held responsible.
5. Days Out UK shall not accept liability for any loss, accident or injury that may occur at a participating attraction and any dispute arising must be settled direct with the attraction concerned.
6. Cash redemption value of each voucher is 0.001p.
7. You are advised to check all relevant information with your chosen attraction before commencing your journey.

Days Out UK, PO Box 427, Northampton NN1 3YN. Tel: 01604 622445

1. Each voucher entitles the holder to the discount specified by the selected attraction.
2. Valid for use until 28/02/08 (unless otherwise specified, or if attraction season finishes prior to this). Vouchers are subject to the terms, conditions and restrictions of the selected attraction.
3. One voucher per party will be accepted, cannot be used in conjunction with any other offer, photocopies will not be accepted.
4. All attractions offering a discount have confirmed their willingness to participate. All information is subject to change without notice and should any attraction close or decline to accept a voucher for any reason, Days Out UK are not liable and cannot be held responsible.
5. Days Out UK shall not accept liability for any loss, accident or injury that may occur at a participating attraction and any dispute arising must be settled direct with the attraction concerned.
6. Cash redemption value of each voucher is 0.001p.
7. You are advised to check all relevant information with your chosen attraction before commencing your journey.

Days Out UK, PO Box 427, Northampton NN1 3YN. Tel: 01604 622445

1. Each voucher entitles the holder to the discount specified by the selected attraction.
2. Valid for use until 28/02/08 (unless otherwise specified, or if attraction season finishes prior to this). Vouchers are subject to the terms, conditions and restrictions of the selected attraction.
3. One voucher per party will be accepted, cannot be used in conjunction with any other offer, photocopies will not be accepted.
4. All attractions offering a discount have confirmed their willingness to participate. All information is subject to change without notice and should any attraction close or decline to accept a voucher for any reason, Days Out UK are not liable and cannot be held responsible.
5. Days Out UK shall not accept liability for any loss, accident or injury that may occur at a participating attraction and any dispute arising must be settled direct with the attraction concerned.
6. Cash redemption value of each voucher is 0.001p.
7. You are advised to check all relevant information with your chosen attraction before commencing your journey.

Days Out UK, PO Box 427, Northampton NN1 3YN. Tel: 01604 622445

1. Each voucher entitles the holder to the discount specified by the selected attraction.
2. Valid for use until 28/02/08 (unless otherwise specified, or if attraction season finishes prior to this). Vouchers are subject to the terms, conditions and restrictions of the selected attraction.
3. One voucher per party will be accepted, cannot be used in conjunction with any other offer, photocopies will not be accepted.
4. All attractions offering a discount have confirmed their willingness to participate. All information is subject to change without notice and should any attraction close or decline to accept a voucher for any reason, Days Out UK are not liable and cannot be held responsible.
5. Days Out UK shall not accept liability for any loss, accident or injury that may occur at a participating attraction and any dispute arising must be settled direct with the attraction concerned.
6. Cash redemption value of each voucher is 0.001p.
7. You are advised to check all relevant information with your chosen attraction before commencing your journey.

Days Out UK, PO Box 427, Northampton NN1 3YN. Tel: 01604 622445

Pensthorpe Nature Reserve
and Gardens
Pensthorpe Fakenham Norfolk NR21 0LN

£1.00 off Standard Admission Prices
for up to 6 people

Cannot be used in conjunction with other offers. One voucher per party. Not valid on Bank Hols or special event days.

Valid until 29 February 2008

Pettitts Animal Adventure Park
Camphill Reedham Norfolk NR13 3UA

Two for the Price of One

full-paying adult

Cannot be used in conjunction with other offers. One voucher per party. Not valid on Bank Hols or special event days.

Expires end Feb 2008 (unless otherwise specified)

Pleasure Beach, Blackpool
Blackpool Lancashire FY4 1EZ

Three Wristbands for the Price of Two
not valid on any UK Public Holidays or Sat-Mon during Bank Hol weekends; offer only applies to full priced Wristbands; lowest priced wristband goes free.
Code: 7008

Cannot be used in conjunction with other offers. One voucher per party. Not valid on Bank Hols or special event days.

Expires end Feb 2008 (unless otherwise specified)

Pleasure Island Theme Park
Kings Road Cleethorpes Lincolnshire DN35 0PL

Two for the Price of One

with a full-paying adult

Cannot be used in conjunction with other offers. One voucher per party. Not valid on Bank Hols or special event days.

Expires end Feb 2008 (unless otherwise specified)

Pleasurewood Hills Theme Park
Leisure Way Corton Lowestoft Suffolk NR32 5DZ

Three for the Price of Two
full-paying adults
(cannot be used with discount or family tickets)

Cannot be used in conjunction with other offers. One voucher per party. Not valid on Bank Hols or special event days.

Expires 30th September 2007

Poole's Cavern and Buxton Country Park
Green Lane Buxton Derbyshire SK17 9DH

20% off Adult Admissions
(A£5.40)

Cannot be used in conjunction with other offers. One voucher per party. Not valid on Bank Hols or special event days.

Expires end Feb 2008 (unless otherwise specified)

1. Each voucher entitles the holder to the discount specified by the selected attraction.
2. Valid for use until 28/02/08 (unless otherwise specified, or if attraction season finishes prior to this). Vouchers are subject to the terms, conditions and restrictions of the selected attraction.
3. One voucher per party will be accepted, cannot be used in conjunction with any other offer, photocopies will not be accepted.
4. All attractions offering a discount have confirmed their willingness to participate. All information is subject to change without notice and should any attraction close or decline to accept a voucher for any reason, Days Out UK are not liable and cannot be held responsible.
5. Days Out UK shall not accept liability for any loss, accident or injury that may occur at a participating attraction and any dispute arising must be settled direct with the attraction concerned.
6. Cash redemption value of each voucher is 0.001p.
7. You are advised to check all relevant information with your chosen attraction before commencing your journey.

Days Out UK, PO Box 427, Northampton NN1 3YN. Tel: 01604 622445

1. Each voucher entitles the holder to the discount specified by the selected attraction.
2. Valid for use until 28/02/08 (unless otherwise specified. or if attraction season finishes prior to this). Vouchers are subject to the terms, conditions and restrictions of the selected attraction.
3. One voucher per party will be accepted, cannot be used in conjunction with any other offer, photocopies will not be accepted.
4. All attractions offering a discount have confirmed their willingness to participate. All information is subject to change without notice and should any attraction close or decline to accept a voucher for any reason, Days Out UK are not liable and cannot be held responsible.
5. Days Out UK shall not accept liability for any loss, accident or injury that may occur at a participating attraction and any dispute arising must be settled direct with the attraction concerned.
6. Cash redemption value of each voucher is 0.001p.
7. You are advised to check all relevant information with your chosen attraction before commencing your journey.

Days Out UK, PO Box 427, Northampton NN1 3YN. Tel: 01604 622445

1. Each voucher entitles the holder to the discount specified by the selected attraction.
2. Valid for use until 28/02/08 (unless otherwise specified, or if attraction season finishes prior to this). Vouchers are subject to the terms, conditions and restrictions of the selected attraction.
3. One voucher per party will be accepted, cannot be used in conjunction with any other offer, photocopies will not be accepted.
4. All attractions offering a discount have confirmed their willingness to participate. All information is subject to change without notice and should any attraction close or decline to accept a voucher for any reason, Days Out UK are not liable and cannot be held responsible.
5. Days Out UK shall not accept liability for any loss, accident or injury that may occur at a participating attraction and any dispute arising must be settled direct with the attraction concerned.
6. Cash redemption value of each voucher is 0.001p.
7. You are advised to check all relevant information with your chosen attraction before commencing your journey.

Days Out UK, PO Box 427, Northampton NN1 3YN. Tel: 01604 622445

1. Each voucher entitles the holder to the discount specified by the selected attraction.
2. Valid for use until 28/02/08 (unless otherwise specified, or if attraction season finishes prior to this). Vouchers are subject to the terms, conditions and restrictions of the selected attraction.
3. One voucher per party will be accepted, cannot be used in conjunction with any other offer, photocopies will not be accepted.
4. All attractions offering a discount have confirmed their willingness to participate. All information is subject to change without notice and should any attraction close or decline to accept a voucher for any reason, Days Out UK are not liable and cannot be held responsible.
5. Days Out UK shall not accept liability for any loss, accident or injury that may occur at a participating attraction and any dispute arising must be settled direct with the attraction concerned.
6. Cash redemption value of each voucher is 0.001p.
7. You are advised to check all relevant information with your chosen attraction before commencing your journey.

Days Out UK, PO Box 427, Northampton NN1 3YN. Tel: 01604 622445

1. Each voucher entitles the holder to the discount specified by the selected attraction.
2. Valid for use until 28/02/08 (unless otherwise specified, or if attraction season finishes prior to this). Vouchers are subject to the terms, conditions and restrictions of the selected attraction.
3. One voucher per party will be accepted, cannot be used in conjunction with any other offer, photocopies will not be accepted.
4. All attractions offering a discount have confirmed their willingness to participate. All information is subject to change without notice and should any attraction close or decline to accept a voucher for any reason, Days Out UK are not liable and cannot be held responsible.
5. Days Out UK shall not accept liability for any loss, accident or injury that may occur at a participating attraction and any dispute arising must be settled direct with the attraction concerned.
6. Cash redemption value of each voucher is 0.001p.
7. You are advised to check all relevant information with your chosen attraction before commencing your journey.

Days Out UK, PO Box 427, Northampton NN1 3YN. Tel: 01604 622445

Port Lymphne Wild Animal Park

Aldington Road Lymphne Hythe, nr Ashford Kent CT21 4PD

Kid for a Quid

each child must be accompanied by a full-paying adult

Cannot be used in conjunction with other offers. One voucher per party. Not valid on Bank Hols or special event days.

Valid 1 April - 31 December 2007

Porthcurno Telegraph Museum

Porthcurno Penzance Cornwall TR19 6JX

10% off Admission Prices

(A£4.46 C£2.48)

Cannot be used in conjunction with other offers. One voucher per party. Not valid on Bank Hols or special event days.

Expires end Feb 2008 (unless otherwise specified)

Portsmouth Historic Dockyard

Visitor Centre Victory Gate Portsmouth Hampshire PO1 3LJ

20% off One All-Inclusive Ticket
(A£12.80 Concessions£10.40)

This ticket gives one entry to each of the ships, museums and other attractions at Portsmouth Historic Dockyard including HMS Victory, HMS Warrior 1860, Mary Rose Ship Hall and Museum, Action Stations and a Harbour Tour (subject to availability). The ticket is valid for one year from redemption so you can return within 12 months to see any attractions you may have missed. Cannot be used with any special rates or ticketed event. Voucher must be redeemed and no photocopies will be accepted. One voucher per person.

Cannot be used in conjunction with other offers. One voucher per party. Not valid on Bank Hols or special event days.

Valid until 31 Dec 2007

Priest House

North Lane West Hoathly nr East Grinstead W. Sussex

Two for the Price of One

with a full-paying adult

Cannot be used in conjunction with other offers. One voucher per party. Not valid on Bank Hols or special event days.

Expires end Feb 2008 (unless otherwise specified)

Pulborough Brooks RSPB Nature Reserve

Wiggonholt Pulborough West Sussex RH20 2EL

50% off One Family Ticket

(A2+C4)

Cannot be used in conjunction with other offers. One voucher per party. Not valid on Bank Hols or special event days.

Expires end Feb 2008 (unless otherwise specified)

Ramsey Rural Museum
Wood Lane Ramsey Cambridgeshire PE26 2XE

Two for the Price of One
with a full-paying adult
(applies to normal entrance fee only)

Cannot be used in conjunction with other offers. One voucher per party. Not valid on Bank Hols or special event days.

Expires end Feb 2008 (unless otherwise specified)

DISCOUNT VOUCHER

Ramsgate Maritime Museum
Clock House Pier Yard Royal Harbour Ramsgate Kent

Two for the Price of One
with a full-paying adult

Cannot be used in conjunction with other offers. One voucher per party. Not valid on Bank Hols or special event days.

Expires end Feb 2008 (unless otherwise specified)

DISCOUNT VOUCHER

Raptor Foundation
The Heath St Ives Road Woodhurst Cambridgeshire

Two for the Price of One
with a full-paying adult

Cannot be used in conjunction with other offers. One voucher per party. Not valid on Bank Hols or special event days.

Expires end Feb 2008 (unless otherwise specified)

DISCOUNT VOUCHER

Redwings Ada Cole Rescue Stables
Broadlands Epping Road Broadley Common
Waltham Abbey Essex EN9 2DH

Free Poster

Cannot be used in conjunction with other offers. One voucher per party. Not valid on Bank Hols or special event days.

Expires end Feb 2008 (unless otherwise specified)

DISCOUNT VOUCHER

Redwings Oxhill Rescue Centre
Banbury Road Oxhill Warwickshire CV35 0RP

Free Poster

Cannot be used in conjunction with other offers. One voucher per party. Not valid on Bank Hols or special event days.

Expires end Feb 2008 (unless otherwise specified)

DISCOUNT VOUCHER

Redwings Caldecott Visitor Centre
Caldecott Hall Beccles Road Fritton Great Yarmouth Norfolk

Free Poster

Cannot be used in conjunction with other offers. One voucher per party. Not valid on Bank Hols or special event days.

Expires end Feb 2008 (unless otherwise specified)

DISCOUNT VOUCHER

1. Each voucher entitles the holder to the discount specified by the selected attraction.
2. Valid for use until 28/02/08 (unless otherwise specified, or if attraction season finishes prior to this). Vouchers are subject to the terms, conditions and restrictions of the selected attraction.
3. One voucher per party will be accepted, cannot be used in conjunction with any other offer, photocopies will not be accepted.
4. All attractions offering a discount have confirmed their willingness to participate. All information is subject to change without notice and should any attraction close or decline to accept a voucher for any reason, Days Out UK are not liable and cannot be held responsible.
5. Days Out UK shall not accept liability for any loss, accident or injury that may occur at a participating attraction and any dispute arising must be settled direct with the attraction concerned.
6. Cash redemption value of each voucher is 0.001p.
7. You are advised to check all relevant information with your chosen attraction before commencing your journey.

Days Out UK, PO Box 427, Northampton NN1 3YN. Tel: 01604 622445

1. Each voucher entitles the holder to the discount specified by the selected attraction.
2. Valid for use until 28/02/08 (unless otherwise specified, or if attraction season finishes prior to this). Vouchers are subject to the terms, conditions and restrictions of the selected attraction.
3. One voucher per party will be accepted, cannot be used in conjunction with any other offer, photocopies will not be accepted.
4. All attractions offering a discount have confirmed their willingness to participate. All information is subject to change without notice and should any attraction close or decline to accept a voucher for any reason, Days Out UK are not liable and cannot be held responsible.
5. Days Out UK shall not accept liability for any loss, accident or injury that may occur at a participating attraction and any dispute arising must be settled direct with the attraction concerned.
6. Cash redemption value of each voucher is 0.001p.
7. You are advised to check all relevant information with your chosen attraction before commencing your journey.

Days Out UK, PO Box 427, Northampton NN1 3YN. Tel: 01604 622445

1. Each voucher entitles the holder to the discount specified by the selected attraction.
2. Valid for use until 28/02/08 (unless otherwise specified. or if attraction season finishes prior to this). Vouchers are subject to the terms, conditions and restrictions of the selected attraction.
3. One voucher per party will be accepted, cannot be used in conjunction with any other offer, photocopies will not be accepted.
4. All attractions offering a discount have confirmed their willingness to participate. All information is subject to change without notice and should any attraction close or decline to accept a voucher for any reason, Days Out UK are not liable and cannot be held responsible.
5. Days Out UK shall not accept liability for any loss, accident or injury that may occur at a participating attraction and any dispute arising must be settled direct with the attraction concerned.
6. Cash redemption value of each voucher is 0.001p.
7. You are advised to check all relevant information with your chosen attraction before commencing your journey.

Days Out UK, PO Box 427, Northampton NN1 3YN. Tel: 01604 622445

1. Each voucher entitles the holder to the discount specified by the selected attraction.
2. Valid for use until 28/02/08 (unless otherwise specified, or if attraction season finishes prior to this). Vouchers are subject to the terms, conditions and restrictions of the selected attraction.
3. One voucher per party will be accepted, cannot be used in conjunction with any other offer, photocopies will not be accepted.
4. All attractions offering a discount have confirmed their willingness to participate. All information is subject to change without notice and should any attraction close or decline to accept a voucher for any reason, Days Out UK are not liable and cannot be held responsible.
5. Days Out UK shall not accept liability for any loss, accident or injury that may occur at a participating attraction and any dispute arising must be settled direct with the attraction concerned.
6. Cash redemption value of each voucher is 0.001p.
7. You are advised to check all relevant information with your chosen attraction before commencing your journey.

Days Out UK, PO Box 427, Northampton NN1 3YN. Tel: 01604 622445

1. Each voucher entitles the holder to the discount specified by the selected attraction.
2. Valid for use until 28/02/08 (unless otherwise specified, or if attraction season finishes prior to this). Vouchers are subject to the terms, conditions and restrictions of the selected attraction.
3. One voucher per party will be accepted, cannot be used in conjunction with any other offer, photocopies will not be accepted.
4. All attractions offering a discount have confirmed their willingness to participate. All information is subject to change without notice and should any attraction close or decline to accept a voucher for any reason, Days Out UK are not liable and cannot be held responsible.
5. Days Out UK shall not accept liability for any loss, accident or injury that may occur at a participating attraction and any dispute arising must be settled direct with the attraction concerned.
6. Cash redemption value of each voucher is 0.001p.
7. You are advised to check all relevant information with your chosen attraction before commencing your journey.

Days Out UK, PO Box 427, Northampton NN1 3YN. Tel: 01604 622445

1. Each voucher entitles the holder to the discount specified by the selected attraction.
2. Valid for use until 28/02/08 (unless otherwise specified, or if attraction season finishes prior to this). Vouchers are subject to the terms, conditions and restrictions of the selected attraction.
3. One voucher per party will be accepted, cannot be used in conjunction with any other offer, photocopies will not be accepted.
4. All attractions offering a discount have confirmed their willingness to participate. All information is subject to change without notice and should any attraction close or decline to accept a voucher for any reason, Days Out UK are not liable and cannot be held responsible.
5. Days Out UK shall not accept liability for any loss, accident or injury that may occur at a participating attraction and any dispute arising must be settled direct with the attraction concerned.
6. Cash redemption value of each voucher is 0.001p.
7. You are advised to check all relevant information with your chosen attraction before commencing your journey.

Days Out UK, PO Box 427, Northampton NN1 3YN. Tel: 01604 622445

Redwings Stonham Rescue Centre

Stonham Barns Pettaugh Road Stonham Aspal
Stowmarket Suffolk IP14 6AT

Free Poster

Cannot be used in conjunction with other offers. One voucher per party. Not valid on Bank Hols or special event days.

Expires end Feb 2008 (unless otherwise specified)

RHS Garden Hyde Hall

Buckhatch Lane Rettendon Chelmsford Essex

Two for the Price of One

with a full-paying adult

Cannot be used in conjunction with other offers. One voucher per party. Not valid on Bank Hols or special event days.

Valid until 31 December 2007

RHS Garden Wisley

RHS Garden Wisley Woking Surrey GU23 6QB

Two for the Price of One

with a full-paying adult

(Mon-Sat only; not valid Bank Holiday weekends)

Cannot be used in conjunction with other offers. One voucher per party. Not valid on Bank Hols or special event days.

Expires end Feb 2008 (unless otherwise specified)

Ripley Castle

Ripley Harrogate North Yorkshire HG3 3AY

One Child Free

with one full-paying adult

Cannot be used in conjunction with other offers. One voucher per party. Not valid on Bank Hols or special event days.

Expires end Feb 2008 (unless otherwise specified)

Royal Marines Museum

Eastney Esplanade Southsea Hampshire PO4 9PX

Two for the Price of One

with a full-paying adult

Cannot be used in conjunction with other offers. One voucher per party. Not valid on Bank Hols or special event days.

Expires end Feb 2008 (unless otherwise specified)

Royal Navy Submarine Museum

Haslar Jetty Road Gosport Hampshire PO12 2AS

25% off Full-Priced Admissions

Cannot be used in conjunction with other offers. One voucher per party. Not valid on Bank Hols or special event days.

Valid until 31 March 2008

1. Each voucher entitles the holder to the discount specified by the selected attraction.
2. Valid for use until 28/02/08 (unless otherwise specified, or if attraction season finishes prior to this). Vouchers are subject to the terms, conditions and restrictions of the selected attraction.
3. One voucher per party will be accepted, cannot be used in conjunction with any other offer, photocopies will not be accepted.
4. All attractions offering a discount have confirmed their willingness to participate. All information is subject to change without notice and should any attraction close or decline to accept a voucher for any reason, Days Out UK are not liable and cannot be held responsible.
5. Days Out UK shall not accept liability for any loss, accident or injury that may occur at a participating attraction and any dispute arising must be settled direct with the attraction concerned.
6. Cash redemption value of each voucher is 0.001p.
7. You are advised to check all relevant information with your chosen attraction before commencing your journey.

Days Out UK, PO Box 427, Northampton NN1 3YN. Tel: 01604 622445

1. Each voucher entitles the holder to the discount specified by the selected attraction.
2. Valid for use until 28/02/08 (unless otherwise specified, or if attraction season finishes prior to this). Vouchers are subject to the terms, conditions and restrictions of the selected attraction.
3. One voucher per party will be accepted, cannot be used in conjunction with any other offer, photocopies will not be accepted.
4. All attractions offering a discount have confirmed their willingness to participate. All information is subject to change without notice and should any attraction close or decline to accept a voucher for any reason, Days Out UK are not liable and cannot be held responsible.
5. Days Out UK shall not accept liability for any loss, accident or injury that may occur at a participating attraction and any dispute arising must be settled direct with the attraction concerned.
6. Cash redemption value of each voucher is 0.001p.
7. You are advised to check all relevant information with your chosen attraction before commencing your journey.

Days Out UK, PO Box 427, Northampton NN1 3YN. Tel: 01604 622445

1. Each voucher entitles the holder to the discount specified by the selected attraction.
2. Valid for use until 28/02/08 (unless otherwise specified, or if attraction season finishes prior to this). Vouchers are subject to the terms, conditions and restrictions of the selected attraction.
3. One voucher per party will be accepted, cannot be used in conjunction with any other offer, photocopies will not be accepted.
4. All attractions offering a discount have confirmed their willingness to participate. All information is subject to change without notice and should any attraction close or decline to accept a voucher for any reason, Days Out UK are not liable and cannot be held responsible.
5. Days Out UK shall not accept liability for any loss, accident or injury that may occur at a participating attraction and any dispute arising must be settled direct with the attraction concerned.
6. Cash redemption value of each voucher is 0.001p.
7. You are advised to check all relevant information with your chosen attraction before commencing your journey.

Days Out UK, PO Box 427, Northampton NN1 3YN. Tel: 01604 622445

1. Each voucher entitles the holder to the discount specified by the selected attraction.
2. Valid for use until 28/02/08 (unless otherwise specified, or if attraction season finishes prior to this). Vouchers are subject to the terms, conditions and restrictions of the selected attraction.
3. One voucher per party will be accepted, cannot be used in conjunction with any other offer, photocopies will not be accepted.
4. All attractions offering a discount have confirmed their willingness to participate. All information is subject to change without notice and should any attraction close or decline to accept a voucher for any reason, Days Out UK are not liable and cannot be held responsible.
5. Days Out UK shall not accept liability for any loss, accident or injury that may occur at a participating attraction and any dispute arising must be settled direct with the attraction concerned.
6. Cash redemption value of each voucher is 0.001p.
7. You are advised to check all relevant information with your chosen attraction before commencing your journey.

Days Out UK, PO Box 427, Northampton NN1 3YN. Tel: 01604 622445

1. Each voucher entitles the holder to the discount specified by the selected attraction.
2. Valid for use until 28/02/08 (unless otherwise specified, or if attraction season finishes prior to this). Vouchers are subject to the terms, conditions and restrictions of the selected attraction.
3. One voucher per party will be accepted, cannot be used in conjunction with any other offer, photocopies will not be accepted.
4. All attractions offering a discount have confirmed their willingness to participate. All information is subject to change without notice and should any attraction close or decline to accept a voucher for any reason, Days Out UK are not liable and cannot be held responsible.
5. Days Out UK shall not accept liability for any loss, accident or injury that may occur at a participating attraction and any dispute arising must be settled direct with the attraction concerned.
6. Cash redemption value of each voucher is 0.001p.
7. You are advised to check all relevant information with your chosen attraction before commencing your journey.

Days Out UK, PO Box 427, Northampton NN1 3YN. Tel: 01604 622445

Scarborough Sea Life
and Marine Sanctuary

Scalby Mills Road Scarborough N Yorkshire YO12 6RP

One Child Free with a full-paying adult

1. This voucher entitles free admission to the Scarborough Sea Life and Marine Sanctuary for one child when accompanied by one full paying adult.
2. Offer expires 28 February 2008.
3. Cannot be used in conjunction with any other offer.
4. A "child" is classed as a person aged 3-14 inclusive (under 3s go free anyway).
5. No cash alternative, non-refundable; and non-exchangeable.
6. All children must be accompanied by an adult.
7. Only one voucher per party and per transaction.
8. Photocopies not accepted.
9. SEA LIFE/Sanctuaries reserve the right to alter, close or remove details/exhibits without prior notice for technical, operational or other reasons, and no refunds can be given in these circumstances.
10. SEA LIFE/Sanctuaries reserve the right to refuse entry without explanation.
Voucher Ref: DOUK.

Cannot be used in conjunction with other offers. One voucher per party. Not valid on Bank Hols or special event days.

Expires end Feb 2008 (unless otherwise specified)

DISCOUNT VOUCHER

Scone Palace

Scone Perth Perthshire Scotland PH2 6BD

Two for the Price of One

with a full-paying adult

Cannot be used in conjunction with other offers. One voucher per party. Not valid on Bank Hols or special event days.

Expires end Feb 2008 (unless otherwise specified)

DISCOUNT VOUCHER

Scotland's Secret Bunker

Crown Buildings Troywood St. Andrews Fife Scotland

One Child Free

with one full paying adult

Cannot be used in conjunction with other offers. One voucher per party. Not valid on Bank Hols or special event days.

Expires end Feb 2008 (unless otherwise specified)

DISCOUNT VOUCHER

Scottish Fisheries Museum

St Ayles East Shore Harbour Head Anstruther Fife Scotland

Accompanied Children Free

(maximum of five children per party and per transaction)

Cannot be used in conjunction with other offers. One voucher per party. Not valid on Bank Hols or special event days.

Expires end Feb 2008 (unless otherwise specified)

DISCOUNT VOUCHER

Scottish Mining Museum

Lady Victoria Colliery Newtongrange Edinburgh Scotland

One Child Free

with every full-paying adult

Cannot be used in conjunction with other offers. One voucher per party. Not valid on Bank Hols or special event days.

Expires end Feb 2008 (unless otherwise specified)

DISCOUNT VOUCHER

1. Each voucher entitles the holder to the discount specified by the selected attraction.

2. Valid for use until 28/02/08 (unless otherwise specified, or if attraction season finishes prior to this). Vouchers are subject to the terms, conditions and restrictions of the selected attraction.

3. One voucher per party will be accepted, cannot be used in conjunction with any other offer, photocopies will not be accepted.

4. All attractions offering a discount have confirmed their willingness to participate. All information is subject to change without notice and should any attraction close or decline to accept a voucher for any reason, Days Out UK are not liable and cannot be held responsible.

5. Days Out UK shall not accept liability for any loss, accident or injury that may occur at a participating attraction and any dispute arising must be settled direct with the attraction concerned.

6. Cash redemption value of each voucher is 0.001p.

7. You are advised to check all relevant information with your chosen attraction before commencing your journey.

Days Out UK, PO Box 427, Northampton NN1 3YN. Tel: 01604 622445

1. Each voucher entitles the holder to the discount specified by the selected attraction.
2. Valid for use until 28/02/08 (unless otherwise specified, or if attraction season finishes prior to this). Vouchers are subject to the terms, conditions and restrictions of the selected attraction.
3. One voucher per party will be accepted, cannot be used in conjunction with any other offer, photocopies will not be accepted.
4. All attractions offering a discount have confirmed their willingness to participate. All information is subject to change without notice and should any attraction close or decline to accept a voucher for any reason, Days Out UK are not liable and cannot be held responsible.
5. Days Out UK shall not accept liability for any loss, accident or injury that may occur at a participating attraction and any dispute arising must be settled direct with the attraction concerned.
6. Cash redemption value of each voucher is 0.001p.
7. You are advised to check all relevant information with your chosen attraction before commencing your journey.

Days Out UK, PO Box 427, Northampton NN1 3YN. Tel: 01604 622445

1. Each voucher entitles the holder to the discount specified by the selected attraction.
2. Valid for use until 28/02/08 (unless otherwise specified, or if attraction season finishes prior to this). Vouchers are subject to the terms, conditions and restrictions of the selected attraction.
3. One voucher per party will be accepted, cannot be used in conjunction with any other offer, photocopies will not be accepted.
4. All attractions offering a discount have confirmed their willingness to participate. All information is subject to change without notice and should any attraction close or decline to accept a voucher for any reason, Days Out UK are not liable and cannot be held responsible.
5. Days Out UK shall not accept liability for any loss, accident or injury that may occur at a participating attraction and any dispute arising must be settled direct with the attraction concerned.
6. Cash redemption value of each voucher is 0.001p.
7. You are advised to check all relevant information with your chosen attraction before commencing your journey.

Days Out UK, PO Box 427, Northampton NN1 3YN. Tel: 01604 622445

1. Each voucher entitles the holder to the discount specified by the selected attraction.
2. Valid for use until 28/02/08 (unless otherwise specified, or if attraction season finishes prior to this). Vouchers are subject to the terms, conditions and restrictions of the selected attraction.
3. One voucher per party will be accepted, cannot be used in conjunction with any other offer, photocopies will not be accepted.
4. All attractions offering a discount have confirmed their willingness to participate. All information is subject to change without notice and should any attraction close or decline to accept a voucher for any reason, Days Out UK are not liable and cannot be held responsible.
5. Days Out UK shall not accept liability for any loss, accident or injury that may occur at a participating attraction and any dispute arising must be settled direct with the attraction concerned.
6. Cash redemption value of each voucher is 0.001p.
7. You are advised to check all relevant information with your chosen attraction before commencing your journey.

Days Out UK, PO Box 427, Northampton NN1 3YN. Tel: 01604 622445

1. Each voucher entitles the holder to the discount specified by the selected attraction.
2. Valid for use until 28/02/08 (unless otherwise specified, or if attraction season finishes prior to this). Vouchers are subject to the terms, conditions and restrictions of the selected attraction.
3. One voucher per party will be accepted, cannot be used in conjunction with any other offer, photocopies will not be accepted.
4. All attractions offering a discount have confirmed their willingness to participate. All information is subject to change without notice and should any attraction close or decline to accept a voucher for any reason, Days Out UK are not liable and cannot be held responsible.
5. Days Out UK shall not accept liability for any loss, accident or injury that may occur at a participating attraction and any dispute arising must be settled direct with the attraction concerned.
6. Cash redemption value of each voucher is 0.001p.
7. You are advised to check all relevant information with your chosen attraction before commencing your journey.

Days Out UK, PO Box 427, Northampton NN1 3YN. Tel: 01604 622445

Scottish Sea Life Sanctuary

Barcaldine Oban Argyll PA37 1SE

One Child Free with a full-paying adult

1. This voucher entitles free admission to the Scottish Sea Life Sanctuary for one child when accompanied by one full paying adult.
2. Offer expires 28 February 2008.
3. Cannot be used in conjunction with any other offer.
4. A "child" is classed as a person aged 3-14 inclusive (under 3s go free anyway).
5. No cash alternative, non-refundable; and non-exchangeable.
6. All children must be accompanied by an adult.
7. Only one voucher per party and per transaction.
8. Photocopies not accepted.
9. SEA LIFE/Sanctuaries reserve the right to alter, close or remove details/exhibits without prior notice for technical, operational or other reasons, and no refunds can be given in these circumstances.
10. SEA LIFE/Sanctuaries reserve the right to refuse entry without explanation.
Voucher Ref: DOUK.

Cannot be used in conjunction with other offers. One voucher per party. Not valid on Bank Hols or special event days.

Expires end Feb 2008 (unless otherwise specified)

Scottish Seabird Centre

The Harbour North Berwick East Lothian Scotland

One Child Free

with a full-paying adult

Cannot be used in conjunction with other offers. One voucher per party. Not valid on Bank Hols or special event days.

Expires end Feb 2008 (unless otherwise specified)

Sealife Adventure

Eastern Esplanade Southend-On-Sea Essex SS1 2ER

Two for the Price of One

with a full-paying adult

(free ticket to be of equal or lesser value)

Cannot be used in conjunction with other offers. One voucher per party. Not valid on Bank Hols or special event days.

Valid until 31 December 2007

Seaquarium Ltd

Marine Parade Weston-Super-Mare Somerset BS23 1BE

One Child Free

with every two full-paying adults

Cannot be used in conjunction with other offers. One voucher per party. Not valid on Bank Hols or special event days.

Valid until 31 March 2008

Seaton Tramway

Harbour Road Seaton Devon EX12 2NQ

One Child Free

with every two full-paying adults

(excludes the month of August, Bank Holidays, special events, birdwatching trips and santa specials)

Cannot be used in conjunction with other offers. One voucher per party. Not valid on Bank Hols or special event days.

Expires end Feb 2008 (unless otherwise specified)

1. Each voucher entitles the holder to the discount specified by the selected attraction.

2. Valid for use until 28/02/08 (unless otherwise specified, or if attraction season finishes prior to this). Vouchers are subject to the terms, conditions and restrictions of the selected attraction.

3. One voucher per party will be accepted, cannot be used in conjunction with any other offer, photocopies will not be accepted.

4. All attractions offering a discount have confirmed their willingness to participate. All information is subject to change without notice and should any attraction close or decline to accept a voucher for any reason, Days Out UK are not liable and cannot be held responsible.

5. Days Out UK shall not accept liability for any loss, accident or injury that may occur at a participating attraction and any dispute arising must be settled direct with the attraction concerned.

6. Cash redemption value of each voucher is 0.001p.

7. You are advised to check all relevant information with your chosen attraction before commencing your journey.

Days Out UK, PO Box 427, Northampton NN1 3YN. Tel: 01604 622445

1. Each voucher entitles the holder to the discount specified by the selected attraction.
2. Valid for use until 28/02/08 (unless otherwise specified. or if attraction season finishes prior to this). Vouchers are subject to the terms, conditions and restrictions of the selected attraction.
3. One voucher per party will be accepted, cannot be used in conjunction with any other offer, photocopies will not be accepted.
4. All attractions offering a discount have confirmed their willingness to participate. All information is subject to change without notice and should any attraction close or decline to accept a voucher for any reason, Days Out UK are not liable and cannot be held responsible.
5. Days Out UK shall not accept liability for any loss, accident or injury that may occur at a participating attraction and any dispute arising must be settled direct with the attraction concerned.
6. Cash redemption value of each voucher is 0.001p.
7. You are advised to check all relevant information with your chosen attraction before commencing your journey.

Days Out UK, PO Box 427, Northampton NN1 3YN. Tel: 01604 622445

1. Each voucher entitles the holder to the discount specified by the selected attraction.
2. Valid for use until 28/02/08 (unless otherwise specified, or if attraction season finishes prior to this). Vouchers are subject to the terms, conditions and restrictions of the selected attraction.
3. One voucher per party will be accepted, cannot be used in conjunction with any other offer, photocopies will not be accepted.
4. All attractions offering a discount have confirmed their willingness to participate. All information is subject to change without notice and should any attraction close or decline to accept a voucher for any reason, Days Out UK are not liable and cannot be held responsible.
5. Days Out UK shall not accept liability for any loss, accident or injury that may occur at a participating attraction and any dispute arising must be settled direct with the attraction concerned.
6. Cash redemption value of each voucher is 0.001p.
7. You are advised to check all relevant information with your chosen attraction before commencing your journey.

Days Out UK, PO Box 427, Northampton NN1 3YN. Tel: 01604 622445

1. Each voucher entitles the holder to the discount specified by the selected attraction.
2. Valid for use until 28/02/08 (unless otherwise specified, or if attraction season finishes prior to this). Vouchers are subject to the terms, conditions and restrictions of the selected attraction.
3. One voucher per party will be accepted, cannot be used in conjunction with any other offer, photocopies will not be accepted.
4. All attractions offering a discount have confirmed their willingness to participate. All information is subject to change without notice and should any attraction close or decline to accept a voucher for any reason, Days Out UK are not liable and cannot be held responsible.
5. Days Out UK shall not accept liability for any loss, accident or injury that may occur at a participating attraction and any dispute arising must be settled direct with the attraction concerned.
6. Cash redemption value of each voucher is 0.001p.
7. You are advised to check all relevant information with your chosen attraction before commencing your journey.

Days Out UK, PO Box 427, Northampton NN1 3YN. Tel: 01604 622445

1. Each voucher entitles the holder to the discount specified by the selected attraction.
2. Valid for use until 28/02/08 (unless otherwise specified, or if attraction season finishes prior to this). Vouchers are subject to the terms, conditions and restrictions of the selected attraction.
3. One voucher per party will be accepted, cannot be used in conjunction with any other offer, photocopies will not be accepted.
4. All attractions offering a discount have confirmed their willingness to participate. All information is subject to change without notice and should any attraction close or decline to accept a voucher for any reason, Days Out UK are not liable and cannot be held responsible.
5. Days Out UK shall not accept liability for any loss, accident or injury that may occur at a participating attraction and any dispute arising must be settled direct with the attraction concerned.
6. Cash redemption value of each voucher is 0.001p.
7. You are advised to check all relevant information with your chosen attraction before commencing your journey.

Days Out UK, PO Box 427, Northampton NN1 3YN. Tel: 01604 622445

Secret Hills -
The Shropshire Hills Discovery Centre
School Lane Craven Arms Shropshire SY7 9RS

Two for the Price of One
with a full-paying adult

Cannot be used in conjunction with other offers. One voucher per party. Not valid on Bank Hols or special event days.

Expires end Feb 2008 (unless otherwise specified)

Shakespeare's Birthplace
The Shakespeare Centre Henley St. Stratford-Upon-Avon
Warwickshire CV37 6QW

Two for the Price of One
(voucher entitles one adult or one child to be admitted free of charge when accompanied by a full-paying adult)

Cannot be used in conjunction with other offers. One voucher per party. Not valid on Bank Hols or special event days.

Expires end Feb 2008 (unless otherwise specified)

Shakespeare's Globe Theatre Tour
and Exhibition
21 New Globe Walk Bankside London SE1 9DT

One Child Free
with a full-paying adult

Cannot be used in conjunction with other offers. One voucher per party. Not valid on Bank Hols or special event days.

Expires end Feb 2008 (unless otherwise specified)

Shepreth Wildlife Park
Willersmill Station Road Shepreth Nr Royston Hertfordshire

One Child Free
with two full-paying adults
(one voucher per family)

Cannot be used in conjunction with other offers. One voucher per party. Not valid on Bank Hols or special event days.

Valid until 31 December 2007

Shugborough Estate
Shugborough Milford Stafford Staffordshire ST17 0XB

Two Children Free
with two full-paying adults

Cannot he used in conjunction with other offers. One voucher per party. Not valid on Bank Hols or special event days.

Valid until 26 October 2007

Sir Richard Arkwright's Masson Mills
Working Textile Museum Derby Road Matlock Bath
Derbyshire DE4 3PY

Iwo for the Price of One
with a full-paying adult

Cannot be used in conjunction with other offers. One voucher per party. Not valid on Bank Hols or special event days.

Expires end Feb 2008 (unless otherwise specified)

1. Each voucher entitles the holder to the discount specified by the selected attraction.
2. Valid for use until 28/02/08 (unless otherwise specified, or if attraction season finishes prior to this). Vouchers are subject to the terms, conditions and restrictions of the selected attraction.
3. One voucher per party will be accepted, cannot be used in conjunction with any other offer, photocopies will not be accepted.
4. All attractions offering a discount have confirmed their willingness to participate. All information is subject to change without notice and should any attraction close or decline to accept a voucher for any reason, Days Out UK are not liable and cannot be held responsible.
5. Days Out UK shall not accept liability for any loss, accident or injury that may occur at a participating attraction and any dispute arising must be settled direct with the attraction concerned.
6. Cash redemption value of each voucher is 0.001p.
7. You are advised to check all relevant information with your chosen attraction before commencing your journey.

Days Out UK, PO Box 427, Northampton NN1 3YN. Tel: 01604 622445

1. Each voucher entitles the holder to the discount specified by the selected attraction.
2. Valid for use until 28/02/08 (unless otherwise specified. or if attraction season finishes prior to this). Vouchers are subject to the terms, conditions and restrictions of the selected attraction.
3. One voucher per party will be accepted, cannot be used in conjunction with any other offer, photocopies will not be accepted.
4. All attractions offering a discount have confirmed their willingness to participate. All information is subject to change without notice and should any attraction close or decline to accept a voucher for any reason, Days Out UK are not liable and cannot be held responsible.
5. Days Out UK shall not accept liability for any loss, accident or injury that may occur at a participating attraction and any dispute arising must be settled direct with the attraction concerned.
6. Cash redemption value of each voucher is 0.001p.
7. You are advised to check all relevant information with your chosen attraction before commencing your journey.

Days Out UK, PO Box 427, Northampton NN1 3YN. Tel: 01604 622445

1. Each voucher entitles the holder to the discount specified by the selected attraction.
2. Valid for use until 28/02/08 (unless otherwise specified, or if attraction season finishes prior to this). Vouchers are subject to the terms, conditions and restrictions of the selected attraction.
3. One voucher per party will be accepted, cannot be used in conjunction with any other offer, photocopies will not be accepted.
4. All attractions offering a discount have confirmed their willingness to participate. All information is subject to change without notice and should any attraction close or decline to accept a voucher for any reason, Days Out UK are not liable and cannot be held responsible.
5. Days Out UK shall not accept liability for any loss, accident or injury that may occur at a participating attraction and any dispute arising must be settled direct with the attraction concerned.
6. Cash redemption value of each voucher is 0.001p.
7. You are advised to check all relevant information with your chosen attraction before commencing your journey.

Days Out UK, PO Box 427, Northampton NN1 3YN. Tel: 01604 622445

1. Each voucher entitles the holder to the discount specified by the selected attraction.
2. Valid for use until 28/02/08 (unless otherwise specified, or if attraction season finishes prior to this). Vouchers are subject to the terms, conditions and restrictions of the selected attraction.
3. One voucher per party will be accepted, cannot be used in conjunction with any other offer, photocopies will not be accepted.
4. All attractions offering a discount have confirmed their willingness to participate. All information is subject to change without notice and should any attraction close or decline to accept a voucher for any reason, Days Out UK are not liable and cannot be held responsible.
5. Days Out UK shall not accept liability for any loss, accident or injury that may occur at a participating attraction and any dispute arising must be settled direct with the attraction concerned.
6. Cash redemption value of each voucher is 0.001p.
7. You are advised to check all relevant information with your chosen attraction before commencing your journey.

Days Out UK, PO Box 427, Northampton NN1 3YN. Tel: 01604 622445

1. Each voucher entitles the holder to the discount specified by the selected attraction.
2. Valid for use until 28/02/08 (unless otherwise specified, or if attraction season finishes prior to this). Vouchers are subject to the terms, conditions and restrictions of the selected attraction.
3. One voucher per party will be accepted, cannot be used in conjunction with any other offer, photocopies will not be accepted.
4. All attractions offering a discount have confirmed their willingness to participate. All information is subject to change without notice and should any attraction close or decline to accept a voucher for any reason, Days Out UK are not liable and cannot be held responsible.
5. Days Out UK shall not accept liability for any loss, accident or injury that may occur at a participating attraction and any dispute arising must be settled direct with the attraction concerned.
6. Cash redemption value of each voucher is 0.001p.
7. You are advised to check all relevant information with your chosen attraction before commencing your journey.

Days Out UK, PO Box 427, Northampton NN1 3YN. Tel: 01604 622445

Skipton Castle

Skipton North Yorkshire BD23 1AW

Two for the Price of One

with a full-paying adult

(offer applies to full-priced adult tickets only)

Cannot be used in conjunction with other offers. One voucher per party. Not valid on Bank Hols or special event days.

Expires end Feb 2008 (unless otherwise specified)

Smallest House in Great Britain

Quay Conwy Wales LL32 8DE

One Child Free

with a full-paying adult

Cannot be used in conjunction with other offers. One voucher per party. Not valid on Bank Hols or special event days.

Expires end Feb 2008 (unless otherwise specified)

SnowDome

Leisure Island River Drive Tamworth

Staffordshire B79 7ND

Two for the Price of One

Conditions: Purchase either a single tobogganing, tubing, ice skating, snowplay or snowmobile session, a group ski or snowboard lesson or a one-hour recreational pass for one person and another person goes free. Age and height restrictions may apply; valid for one person only; valid from 1st April 2007 until 30 September 2007; not to be used with any other offer/promotion; voucher has no cash value and cannot be resold; all sessions should be pre-booked; Ice Track, 'mini rink' and Snowmobiles available at varying times of the season, please phone for details.

Cannot be used in conjunction with other offers. One voucher per party. Not valid on Bank Hols or special event days.

valid 1st April 2007 until 30 September 2007

Solihull Ice Rink

Hobs Moat Road Solihull West Midlands B92 8JN

Save up to £5.00!

Family Ticket (two parents and two children or one parent and three children) for just £16.50

(Not valid Saturdays (all day or evening) or Friday evenings)

Cannot be used in conjunction with other offers. One voucher per party. Not valid on Bank Hols or special event days.

Valid until 1 November 2007

Southsea Castle

Clarence Esplanade Southsea Hampshire PO5 3PA

20% off Adult Admissions (A£2.80)

(maximum 2 discounted adults per transaction)

Cannot be used in conjunction with other offers. One voucher per party. Not valid on Bank Hols or special event days.

Expires end Feb 2008 (unless otherwise specified)

1. Each voucher entitles the holder to the discount specified by the selected attraction.
2. Valid for use until 28/02/08 (unless otherwise specified, or if attraction season finishes prior to this). Vouchers are subject to the terms, conditions and restrictions of the selected attraction.
3. One voucher per party will be accepted, cannot be used in conjunction with any other offer, photocopies will not be accepted.
4. All attractions offering a discount have confirmed their willingness to participate. All information is subject to change without notice and should any attraction close or decline to accept a voucher for any reason, Days Out UK are not liable and cannot be held responsible.
5. Days Out UK shall not accept liability for any loss, accident or injury that may occur at a participating attraction and any dispute arising must be settled direct with the attraction concerned.
6. Cash redemption value of each voucher is 0.001p.
7. You are advised to check all relevant information with your chosen attraction before commencing your journey.

Days Out UK, PO Box 427, Northampton NN1 3YN. Tel: 01604 622445

1. Each voucher entitles the holder to the discount specified by the selected attraction.

2. Valid for use until 28/02/08 (unless otherwise specified. or if attraction season finishes prior to this). Vouchers are subject to the terms, conditions and restrictions of the selected attraction.

3. One voucher per party will be accepted, cannot be used in conjunction with any other offer, photocopies will not be accepted.

4. All attractions offering a discount have confirmed their willingness to participate. All information is subject to change without notice and should any attraction close or decline to accept a voucher for any reason, Days Out UK are not liable and cannot be held responsible.

5. Days Out UK shall not accept liability for any loss, accident or injury that may occur at a participating attraction and any dispute arising must be settled direct with the attraction concerned.

6. Cash redemption value of each voucher is 0.001p.

7. You are advised to check all relevant information with your chosen attraction before commencing your journey.

Days Out UK, PO Box 427, Northampton NN1 3YN. Tel: 01604 622445

1. Each voucher entitles the holder to the discount specified by the selected attraction.
2. Valid for use until 28/02/08 (unless otherwise specified, or if attraction season finishes prior to this). Vouchers are subject to the terms, conditions and restrictions of the selected attraction.
3. One voucher per party will be accepted, cannot be used in conjunction with any other offer, photocopies will not be accepted.
4. All attractions offering a discount have confirmed their willingness to participate. All information is subject to change without notice and should any attraction close or decline to accept a voucher for any reason, Days Out UK are not liable and cannot be held responsible.
5. Days Out UK shall not accept liability for any loss, accident or injury that may occur at a participating attraction and any dispute arising must be settled direct with the attraction concerned.
6. Cash redemption value of each voucher is 0.001p.
7. You are advised to check all relevant information with your chosen attraction before commencing your journey.

Days Out UK, PO Box 427, Northampton NN1 3YN. Tel: 01604 622445

1. Each voucher entitles the holder to the discount specified by the selected attraction.
2. Valid for use until 28/02/08 (unless otherwise specified, or if attraction season finishes prior to this). Vouchers are subject to the terms, conditions and restrictions of the selected attraction.
3. One voucher per party will be accepted, cannot be used in conjunction with any other offer, photocopies will not be accepted.
4. All attractions offering a discount have confirmed their willingness to participate. All information is subject to change without notice and should any attraction close or decline to accept a voucher for any reason, Days Out UK are not liable and cannot be held responsible.
5. Days Out UK shall not accept liability for any loss, accident or injury that may occur at a participating attraction and any dispute arising must be settled direct with the attraction concerned.
6. Cash redemption value of each voucher is 0.001p.
7. You are advised to check all relevant information with your chosen attraction before commencing your journey.

Days Out UK, PO Box 427, Northampton NN1 3YN. Tel: 01604 622445

1. Each voucher entitles the holder to the discount specified by the selected attraction.
2. Valid for use until 28/02/08 (unless otherwise specified, or if attraction season finishes prior to this). Vouchers are subject to the terms, conditions and restrictions of the selected attraction.
3. One voucher per party will be accepted, cannot be used in conjunction with any other offer, photocopies will not be accepted.
4. All attractions offering a discount have confirmed their willingness to participate. All information is subject to change without notice and should any attraction close or decline to accept a voucher for any reason, Days Out UK are not liable and cannot be held responsible.
5. Days Out UK shall not accept liability for any loss, accident or injury that may occur at a participating attraction and any dispute arising must be settled direct with the attraction concerned.
6. Cash redemption value of each voucher is 0.001p.
7. You are advised to check all relevant information with your chosen attraction before commencing your journey.

Days Out UK, PO Box 427, Northampton NN1 3YN. Tel: 01604 622445

1. Each voucher entitles the holder to the discount specified by the selected attraction.
2. Valid for use until 28/02/08 (unless otherwise specified. or if attraction season finishes prior to this). Vouchers are subject to the terms, conditions and restrictions of the selected attraction.
3. One voucher per party will be accepted, cannot be used in conjunction with any other offer, photocopies will not be accepted.
4. All attractions offering a discount have confirmed their willingness to participate. All information is subject to change without notice and should any attraction close or decline to accept a voucher for any reason, Days Out UK are not liable and cannot be held responsible.
5. Days Out UK shall not accept liability for any loss, accident or injury that may occur at a participating attraction and any dispute arising must be settled direct with the attraction concerned.
6. Cash redemption value of each voucher is 0.001p.
7. You are advised to check all relevant information with your chosen attraction before commencing your journey.

Days Out UK, PO Box 427, Northampton NN1 3YN. Tel: 01604 622445

1. Each voucher entitles the holder to the discount specified by the selected attraction.
2. Valid for use until 28/02/08 (unless otherwise specified, or if attraction season finishes prior to this). Vouchers are subject to the terms, conditions and restrictions of the selected attraction.
3. One voucher per party will be accepted, cannot be used in conjunction with any other offer, photocopies will not be accepted.
4. All attractions offering a discount have confirmed their willingness to participate. All information is subject to change without notice and should any attraction close or decline to accept a voucher for any reason, Days Out UK are not liable and cannot be held responsible.
5. Days Out UK shall not accept liability for any loss, accident or injury that may occur at a participating attraction and any dispute arising must be settled direct with the attraction concerned.
6. Cash redemption value of each voucher is 0.001p.
7. You are advised to check all relevant information with your chosen attraction before commencing your journey.

Days Out UK, PO Box 427, Northampton NN1 3YN. Tel: 01604 622445

1. Each voucher entitles the holder to the discount specified by the selected attraction.
2. Valid for use until 28/02/08 (unless otherwise specified, or if attraction season finishes prior to this). Vouchers are subject to the terms, conditions and restrictions of the selected attraction.
3. One voucher per party will be accepted, cannot be used in conjunction with any other offer, photocopies will not be accepted.
4. All attractions offering a discount have confirmed their willingness to participate. All information is subject to change without notice and should any attraction close or decline to accept a voucher for any reason, Days Out UK are not liable and cannot be held responsible.
5. Days Out UK shall not accept liability for any loss, accident or injury that may occur at a participating attraction and any dispute arising must be settled direct with the attraction concerned.
6. Cash redemption value of each voucher is 0.001p.
7. You are advised to check all relevant information with your chosen attraction before commencing your journey.

Days Out UK, PO Box 427, Northampton NN1 3YN. Tel: 01604 622445

Days Out UK, PO Box 427, Northampton NN1 3YN. Tel: 01604 622445

Stratford-upon-Avon Butterfly Farm

Swan's Nest Lane Stratford-upon-Avon Warwickshire

Two for the Price of One

with a full-paying adult

Cannot be used in conjunction with other offers. One voucher per party. Not valid on Bank Hols or special event days.

Expires end Feb 2008 (unless otherwise specified)

Stromness Museum

52 Alfred Street Stromness Orkney Scotland KW16 3DF

10% discount on all gift shop

purchases when you spend £10.00 or more

Cannot be used in conjunction with other offers. One voucher per party. Not valid on Bank Hols or special event days.

Expires end Feb 2008 (unless otherwise specified)

Strutt's North Mill

Derwent Valley Visitor Centre North Mill Bridgefoot Belper Derbyshire

One Child Free

with every full-paying adult

Cannot be used in conjunction with other offers. One voucher per party. Not valid on Bank Hols or special event days.

Expires end Feb 2008 (unless otherwise specified)

Sudeley Castle, Gardens

and Exhibitions
Winchcombe Cheltenham Gloucestershire GL54 5JD

One Child Free

with every full-paying adult

Cannot be used in conjunction with other offers. One voucher per party. Not valid on Bank Hols or special event days.

Expires end Feb 2008 (unless otherwise specified)

Syon House and Gardens

Syon Park Brentford Middlesex London TW8 8JF

Two for the Price of One

with a full-paying adult

(applies to combined House & Garden tickets only)

Cannot be used in conjunction with other offers. One voucher per party. Not valid on Bank Hols or special event days.

Expires end Feb 2008 (unless otherwise specified)

Tamworth Castle

The Holloway Ladybank Tamworth Staffordshire B79 7NA

Two for the Price of One

with a full-paying adult

Cannot be used in conjunction with other offers. One voucher per party. Not valid on Bank Hols or special event days.

Expires end Feb 2008 (unless otherwise specified)

1. Each voucher entitles the holder to the discount specified by the selected attraction.
2. Valid for use until 28/02/08 (unless otherwise specified, or if attraction season finishes prior to this). Vouchers are subject to the terms, conditions and restrictions of the selected attraction.
3. One voucher per party will be accepted, cannot be used in conjunction with any other offer, photocopies will not be accepted.
4. All attractions offering a discount have confirmed their willingness to participate. All information is subject to change without notice and should any attraction close or decline to accept a voucher for any reason, Days Out UK are not liable and cannot be held responsible.
5. Days Out UK shall not accept liability for any loss, accident or injury that may occur at a participating attraction and any dispute arising must be settled direct with the attraction concerned.
6. Cash redemption value of each voucher is 0.001p.
7. You are advised to check all relevant information with your chosen attraction before commencing your journey.

Days Out UK, PO Box 427, Northampton NN1 3YN. Tel: 01604 622445

1. Each voucher entitles the holder to the discount specified by the selected attraction.
2. Valid for use until 28/02/08 (unless otherwise specified. or if attraction season finishes prior to this). Vouchers are subject to the terms, conditions and restrictions of the selected attraction.
3. One voucher per party will be accepted, cannot be used in conjunction with any other offer, photocopies will not be accepted.
4. All attractions offering a discount have confirmed their willingness to participate. All information is subject to change without notice and should any attraction close or decline to accept a voucher for any reason, Days Out UK are not liable and cannot be held responsible.
5. Days Out UK shall not accept liability for any loss, accident or injury that may occur at a participating attraction and any dispute arising must be settled direct with the attraction concerned.
6. Cash redemption value of each voucher is 0.001p.
7. You are advised to check all relevant information with your chosen attraction before commencing your journey.

Days Out UK, PO Box 427, Northampton NN1 3YN. Tel: 01604 622445

1. Each voucher entitles the holder to the discount specified by the selected attraction.
2. Valid for use until 28/02/08 (unless otherwise specified, or if attraction season finishes prior to this). Vouchers are subject to the terms, conditions and restrictions of the selected attraction.
3. One voucher per party will be accepted, cannot be used in conjunction with any other offer, photocopies will not be accepted.
4. All attractions offering a discount have confirmed their willingness to participate. All information is subject to change without notice and should any attraction close or decline to accept a voucher for any reason, Days Out UK are not liable and cannot be held responsible.
5. Days Out UK shall not accept liability for any loss, accident or injury that may occur at a participating attraction and any dispute arising must be settled direct with the attraction concerned.
6. Cash redemption value of each voucher is 0.001p.
7. You are advised to check all relevant information with your chosen attraction before commencing your journey.

Days Out UK, PO Box 427, Northampton NN1 3YN. Tel: 01604 622445

1. Each voucher entitles the holder to the discount specified by the selected attraction.
2. Valid for use until 28/02/08 (unless otherwise specified, or if attraction season finishes prior to this). Vouchers are subject to the terms, conditions and restrictions of the selected attraction.
3. One voucher per party will be accepted, cannot be used in conjunction with any other offer, photocopies will not be accepted.
4. All attractions offering a discount have confirmed their willingness to participate. All information is subject to change without notice and should any attraction close or decline to accept a voucher for any reason, Days Out UK are not liable and cannot be held responsible.
5. Days Out UK shall not accept liability for any loss, accident or injury that may occur at a participating attraction and any dispute arising must be settled direct with the attraction concerned.
6. Cash redemption value of each voucher is 0.001p.
7. You are advised to check all relevant information with your chosen attraction before commencing your journey.

Days Out UK, PO Box 427, Northampton NN1 3YN. Tel: 01604 622445

1. Each voucher entitles the holder to the discount specified by the selected attraction.
2. Valid for use until 28/02/08 (unless otherwise specified, or if attraction season finishes prior to this). Vouchers are subject to the terms, conditions and restrictions of the selected attraction.
3. One voucher per party will be accepted, cannot be used in conjunction with any other offer, photocopies will not be accepted.
4. All attractions offering a discount have confirmed their willingness to participate. All information is subject to change without notice and should any attraction close or decline to accept a voucher for any reason, Days Out UK are not liable and cannot be held responsible.
5. Days Out UK shall not accept liability for any loss, accident or injury that may occur at a participating attraction and any dispute arising must be settled direct with the attraction concerned.
6. Cash redemption value of each voucher is 0.001p.
7. You are advised to check all relevant information with your chosen attraction before commencing your journey.

Days Out UK, PO Box 427, Northampton NN1 3YN. Tel: 01604 622445

Tanfield Railway

Old Marley Hill Nr Stanley Newcastle Upon Tyne Tyne & Wear

One Child Free
with one full-paying adult

Cannot be used in conjunction with other offers. One voucher per party. Not valid on Bank Hols or special event days.

Expires end Feb 2008 (unless otherwise specified)

Tangmere Military Aviation
Museum Trust

Tangmere Chichester West Sussex PO20 2ES

One Child Free
with a full-paying adult

Cannot be used in conjunction with other offers. One voucher per party. Not valid on Bank Hols or special event days.

Expires end Feb 2008 (unless otherwise specified)

Techniquest

Stuart Street Cardiff Wales CF10 5BW

Two for the Price of One
with a full-paying adult

(cheapest ticket goes free; valid on event weekends; Code: DOUK)

Cannot be used in conjunction with other offers. One voucher per party. Not valid on Bank Hols or special event days.

Expires end Feb 2008 (unless otherwise specified)

Tenterden and District Museum

Station Road Tenterden Kent TN30 6HN

Two for the Price of One

with a full-paying adult

Cannot be used in conjunction with other offers. One voucher per party. Not valid on Bank Hols or special event days.

Expires end Feb 2008 (unless otherwise specified)

Thackray Museum

Beckett Street Leeds West Yorkshire LS9 7LN

Two for the Price of One

with a full-paying adult

Cannot be used in conjunction with other offers. One voucher per party. Not valid on Bank Hols or special event days.

Expires end Feb 2008 (unless otherwise specified)

The Animalarium

Borth Ceredigion Wales SY24 5NA

One Child Free

with a full-paying adult

Cannot be used in conjunction with other offers. One voucher per party. Not valid on Bank Hols or special event days.

Expires end Feb 2008 (unless otherwise specified)

The Deep - The World's Only Submarium

Hull East Riding of Yorkshire HU1 4DP

One Child Free
with every two full-paying adults

(code DAYS50208)

Cannot be used in conjunction with other offers. One voucher per party. Not valid on Bank Hols or special event days.

Expires end Feb 2008 (unless otherwise specified)

The Original Tour - London Sightseeing

Jews Row Wandsworth London SW18 1TB

Save Money - Book in advance
through www.theoriginaltour.com entering promotional code daysoutuk07
Alternatively, call and quote on telephone number 020 8877 2120

Cannot be used in conjunction with other offers. One voucher per party. Not valid on Bank Hols or special event days.

Expires end Feb 2008 (unless otherwise specified)

Thousand Islands Expeditions

Cross Square St. Davids Pembrokeshire Wales

10% off all Full-Priced Fares

Cannot be used in conjunction with other offers. One voucher per party. Not valid on Bank Hols or special event days.

Expires end Feb 2008 (unless otherwise specified)

Thursford Collection

Thursford Fakenham Norfolk NR21 OAS

Two for the Price of One
with a full-paying adult

Cannot be used in conjunction with other offers. One voucher per party. Not valid on Bank Hols or special event days.

Expires end Feb 2008 (unless otherwise specified)

Torquay Museum

529 Babbacombe Road Torquay Devon TQ1 1HG

One Free "Explorers" Knapsack
for Every Full-Paying Child

Cannot be used in conjunction with other offers. One voucher per party. Not valid on Bank Hols or special event days.

Expires end Feb 2008 (unless otherwise specified)

Trafalgar Celebrations at
Hartlepool's Maritime Experience
Maritime Avenue Hartlepool Cleveland TS24 0XZ

One Child Free
with every full-paying adult

Cannot be used in conjunction with other offers. One voucher per party. Not valid on Bank Hols or special event days.

Expires end Feb 2008 (unless otherwise specified)

1. Each voucher entitles the holder to the discount specified by the selected attraction.
2. Valid for use until 28/02/08 (unless otherwise specified, or if attraction season finishes prior to this). Vouchers are subject to the terms, conditions and restrictions of the selected attraction.
3. One voucher per party will be accepted, cannot be used in conjunction with any other offer, photocopies will not be accepted.
4. All attractions offering a discount have confirmed their willingness to participate. All information is subject to change without notice and should any attraction close or decline to accept a voucher for any reason, Days Out UK are not liable and cannot be held responsible.
5. Days Out UK shall not accept liability for any loss, accident or injury that may occur at a participating attraction and any dispute arising must be settled direct with the attraction concerned.
6. Cash redemption value of each voucher is 0.001p.
7. You are advised to check all relevant information with your chosen attraction before commencing your journey.

Days Out UK, PO Box 427, Northampton NN1 3YN. Tel: 01604 622445

1. Each voucher entitles the holder to the discount specified by the selected attraction.
2. Valid for use until 28/02/08 (unless otherwise specified, or if attraction season finishes prior to this). Vouchers are subject to the terms, conditions and restrictions of the selected attraction.
3. One voucher per party will be accepted, cannot be used in conjunction with any other offer, photocopies will not be accepted.
4. All attractions offering a discount have confirmed their willingness to participate. All information is subject to change without notice and should any attraction close or decline to accept a voucher for any reason, Days Out UK are not liable and cannot be held responsible.
5. Days Out UK shall not accept liability for any loss, accident or injury that may occur at a participating attraction and any dispute arising must be settled direct with the attraction concerned.
6. Cash redemption value of each voucher is 0.001p.
7. You are advised to check all relevant information with your chosen attraction before commencing your journey.

Days Out UK, PO Box 427, Northampton NN1 3YN. Tel: 01604 622445

1. Each voucher entitles the holder to the discount specified by the selected attraction.
2. Valid for use until 28/02/08 (unless otherwise specified. or if attraction season finishes prior to this). Vouchers are subject to the terms, conditions and restrictions of the selected attraction.
3. One voucher per party will be accepted, cannot be used in conjunction with any other offer, photocopies will not be accepted.
4. All attractions offering a discount have confirmed their willingness to participate. All information is subject to change without notice and should any attraction close or decline to accept a voucher for any reason, Days Out UK are not liable and cannot be held responsible.
5. Days Out UK shall not accept liability for any loss, accident or injury that may occur at a participating attraction and any dispute arising must be settled direct with the attraction concerned.
6. Cash redemption value of each voucher is 0.001p.
7. You are advised to check all relevant information with your chosen attraction before commencing your journey.

Days Out UK, PO Box 427, Northampton NN1 3YN. Tel: 01604 622445

1. Each voucher entitles the holder to the discount specified by the selected attraction.
2. Valid for use until 28/02/08 (unless otherwise specified, or if attraction season finishes prior to this). Vouchers are subject to the terms, conditions and restrictions of the selected attraction.
3. One voucher per party will be accepted, cannot be used in conjunction with any other offer, photocopies will not be accepted.
4. All attractions offering a discount have confirmed their willingness to participate. All information is subject to change without notice and should any attraction close or decline to accept a voucher for any reason, Days Out UK are not liable and cannot be held responsible.
5. Days Out UK shall not accept liability for any loss, accident or injury that may occur at a participating attraction and any dispute arising must be settled direct with the attraction concerned.
6. Cash redemption value of each voucher is 0.001p.
7. You are advised to check all relevant information with your chosen attraction before commencing your journey.

Days Out UK, PO Box 427, Northampton NN1 3YN. Tel: 01604 622445

1. Each voucher entitles the holder to the discount specified by the selected attraction.
2. Valid for use until 28/02/08 (unless otherwise specified, or if attraction season finishes prior to this). Vouchers are subject to the terms, conditions and restrictions of the selected attraction.
3. One voucher per party will be accepted, cannot be used in conjunction with any other offer, photocopies will not be accepted.
4. All attractions offering a discount have confirmed their willingness to participate. All information is subject to change without notice and should any attraction close or decline to accept a voucher for any reason, Days Out UK are not liable and cannot be held responsible.
5. Days Out UK shall not accept liability for any loss, accident or injury that may occur at a participating attraction and any dispute arising must be settled direct with the attraction concerned.
6. Cash redemption value of each voucher is 0.001p.
7. You are advised to check all relevant information with your chosen attraction before commencing your journey.

Days Out UK, PO Box 427, Northampton NN1 3YN. Tel: 01604 622445

1. Each voucher entitles the holder to the discount specified by the selected attraction.
2. Valid for use until 28/02/08 (unless otherwise specified, or if attraction season finishes prior to this). Vouchers are subject to the terms, conditions and restrictions of the selected attraction.
3. One voucher per party will be accepted, cannot be used in conjunction with any other offer, photocopies will not be accepted.
4. All attractions offering a discount have confirmed their willingness to participate. All information is subject to change without notice and should any attraction close or decline to accept a voucher for any reason, Days Out UK are not liable and cannot be held responsible.
5. Days Out UK shall not accept liability for any loss, accident or injury that may occur at a participating attraction and any dispute arising must be settled direct with the attraction concerned.
6. Cash redemption value of each voucher is 0.001p.
7. You are advised to check all relevant information with your chosen attraction before commencing your journey.

Days Out UK, PO Box 427, Northampton NN1 3YN. Tel: 01604 622445

Traquair House
Innerleithen Peeblesshire Scotland EH44 6PW
One Child Free
with a full-paying adult

Treak Cliff Cavern
Buxton Road Castleton Hope Valley Derbyshire
10% off Adult Admissions
(A£6.12)

Trolleybus Museum at Sandtoft
Belton Road Sandtoft Doncaster North Lincolnshire
1 Adult admitted
at the Concession Rate

Tropical Butterfly House, Wildlife and Falconry Centre
Woodsetts Road North Anston Nr Sheffield South Yorkshire
One Child Free
with a full-paying adult

Trotters World of Animals
Coalbeck Farm Bassenthwaite Keswick Cumbria
One Child Free
with a full-paying adult

Twinlakes Park
Melton Spinney Road Melton Mowbray Leicestershire
15% Off Admission Prices
(Valid for up to 6 people)

1. Each voucher entitles the holder to the discount specified by the selected attraction.
2. Valid for use until 28/02/08 (unless otherwise specified, or if attraction season finishes prior to this). Vouchers are subject to the terms, conditions and restrictions of the selected attraction.
3. One voucher per party will be accepted, cannot be used in conjunction with any other offer, photocopies will not be accepted.
4. All attractions offering a discount have confirmed their willingness to participate. All information is subject to change without notice and should any attraction close or decline to accept a voucher for any reason, Days Out UK are not liable and cannot be held responsible.
5. Days Out UK shall not accept liability for any loss, accident or injury that may occur at a participating attraction and any dispute arising must be settled direct with the attraction concerned.
6. Cash redemption value of each voucher is 0.001p.
7. You are advised to check all relevant information with your chosen attraction before commencing your journey.

Days Out UK, PO Box 427, Northampton NN1 3YN. Tel: 01604 622445

1. Each voucher entitles the holder to the discount specified by the selected attraction.
2. Valid for use until 28/02/08 (unless otherwise specified. or if attraction season finishes prior to this). Vouchers are subject to the terms, conditions and restrictions of the selected attraction.
3. One voucher per party will be accepted, cannot be used in conjunction with any other offer, photocopies will not be accepted.
4. All attractions offering a discount have confirmed their willingness to participate. All information is subject to change without notice and should any attraction close or decline to accept a voucher for any reason, Days Out UK are not liable and cannot be held responsible.
5. Days Out UK shall not accept liability for any loss, accident or injury that may occur at a participating attraction and any dispute arising must be settled direct with the attraction concerned.
6. Cash redemption value of each voucher is 0.001p.
7. You are advised to check all relevant information with your chosen attraction before commencing your journey.

Days Out UK, PO Box 427, Northampton NN1 3YN. Tel: 01604 622445

1. Each voucher entitles the holder to the discount specified by the selected attraction.
2. Valid for use until 28/02/08 (unless otherwise specified, or if attraction season finishes prior to this). Vouchers are subject to the terms, conditions and restrictions of the selected attraction.
3. One voucher per party will be accepted, cannot be used in conjunction with any other offer, photocopies will not be accepted.
4. All attractions offering a discount have confirmed their willingness to participate. All information is subject to change without notice and should any attraction close or decline to accept a voucher for any reason, Days Out UK are not liable and cannot be held responsible.
5. Days Out UK shall not accept liability for any loss, accident or injury that may occur at a participating attraction and any dispute arising must be settled direct with the attraction concerned.
6. Cash redemption value of each voucher is 0.001p.
7. You are advised to check all relevant information with your chosen attraction before commencing your journey.

Days Out UK, PO Box 427, Northampton NN1 3YN. Tel: 01604 622445

1. Each voucher entitles the holder to the discount specified by the selected attraction.
2. Valid for use until 28/02/08 (unless otherwise specified, or if attraction season finishes prior to this). Vouchers are subject to the terms, conditions and restrictions of the selected attraction.
3. One voucher per party will be accepted, cannot be used in conjunction with any other offer, photocopies will not be accepted.
4. All attractions offering a discount have confirmed their willingness to participate. All information is subject to change without notice and should any attraction close or decline to accept a voucher for any reason, Days Out UK are not liable and cannot be held responsible.
5. Days Out UK shall not accept liability for any loss, accident or injury that may occur at a participating attraction and any dispute arising must be settled direct with the attraction concerned.
6. Cash redemption value of each voucher is 0.001p.
7. You are advised to check all relevant information with your chosen attraction before commencing your journey.

Days Out UK, PO Box 427, Northampton NN1 3YN. Tel: 01604 622445

1. Each voucher entitles the holder to the discount specified by the selected attraction.
2. Valid for use until 28/02/08 (unless otherwise specified, or if attraction season finishes prior to this). Vouchers are subject to the terms, conditions and restrictions of the selected attraction.
3. One voucher per party will be accepted, cannot be used in conjunction with any other offer, photocopies will not be accepted.
4. All attractions offering a discount have confirmed their willingness to participate. All information is subject to change without notice and should any attraction close or decline to accept a voucher for any reason, Days Out UK are not liable and cannot be held responsible.
5. Days Out UK shall not accept liability for any loss, accident or injury that may occur at a participating attraction and any dispute arising must be settled direct with the attraction concerned.
6. Cash redemption value of each voucher is 0.001p.
7. You are advised to check all relevant information with your chosen attraction before commencing your journey.

Days Out UK, PO Box 427, Northampton NN1 3YN. Tel: 01604 622445

Twycross Zoo
Burton Road Atherstone Warwickshire CV9 3PX
One Child Free
with two full-paying adults
(not valid on Bank Holiday weekends)

Cannot be used in conjunction with other offers. One voucher per party. Not valid on Bank Hols or special event days.

Expires end Feb 2008 (unless otherwise specified)

Ulster American Folk Park
2 Mellon Road Castletown Omagh County Tyrone
Northern Ireland BT78 5QY
Two for the Price of One
with a full-paying adult
(not valid on Bank Holidays, for special events or school groups)

Cannot be used in conjunction with other offers. One voucher per party. Not valid on Bank Hols or special event days.

Expires end Feb 2008 (unless otherwise specified)

Ulster Folk and Transport Museum
Bangor Road Cultra Holywood County Down
Northern Ireland BT18 0EU
Two for the Price of One
with a full-paying adult

Cannot be used in conjunction with other offers. One voucher per party. Not valid on Bank Hols or special event days.

Expires end Feb 2008 (unless otherwise specified)

Upton House and Gardens
Upton Banbury Oxfordshire OX15 6HT
Two for the Price of One
with a full-paying adult
(cannot be used for group visits; not to be used for events outside of
normal opening hours)

Cannot be used in conjunction with other offers. One voucher per party. Not valid on Bank Hols or special event days.

Expires end Feb 2008 (unless otherwise specified)

Walsingham Abbey Grounds
and Shirehall Museum
Estate Office Common Place Walsingham Norfolk
Two for the Price of One
with a full-paying adult
(cannot be used during February)

Cannot be used in conjunction with other offers. One voucher per party. Not valid on Bank Hols or special event days.

Expires end Jan 2008 (Not valid during February)

Watercress Line
The Railway Station Alresford Hampshire SO24 9JG
Two for the Price of One
with a full-paying adult
(not valid for special events, luxury dining, real ale trains,
driving experiences or footplate rides)

Cannot be used in conjunction with other offers. One voucher per party. Not valid on Bank Hols or special event days.

Expires end Feb 2008 (unless otherwise specified)

1. Each voucher entitles the holder to the discount specified by the selected attraction.
2. Valid for use until 28/02/08 (unless otherwise specified, or if attraction season finishes prior to this). Vouchers are subject to the terms, conditions and restrictions of the selected attraction.
3. One voucher per party will be accepted, cannot be used in conjunction with any other offer, photocopies will not be accepted.
4. All attractions offering a discount have confirmed their willingness to participate. All information is subject to change without notice and should any attraction close or decline to accept a voucher for any reason, Days Out UK are not liable and cannot be held responsible.
5. Days Out UK shall not accept liability for any loss, accident or injury that may occur at a participating attraction and any dispute arising must be settled direct with the attraction concerned.
6. Cash redemption value of each voucher is 0.001p.
7. You are advised to check all relevant information with your chosen attraction before commencing your journoy.

Days Out UK, PO Box 427, Northampton NN1 3YN. Tel: 01604 622445

1. Each voucher entitles the holder to the discount specified by the selected attraction.
2. Valid for use until 28/02/08 (unless otherwise specified. or if attraction season finishes prior to this). Vouchers are subject to the terms, conditions and restrictions of the selected attraction.
3. One voucher per party will be accepted, cannot be used in conjunction with any other offer, photocopies will not be accepted.
4. All attractions offering a discount have confirmed their willingness to participate. All information is subject to change without notice and should any attraction close or decline to accept a voucher for any reason, Days Out UK are not liable and cannot be held responsible.
5. Days Out UK shall not accept liability for any loss, accident or injury that may occur at a participating attraction and any dispute arising must be settled direct with the attraction concerned.
6. Cash redemption value of each voucher is 0.001p.
7. You are advised to check all relevant information with your chosen attraction before commencing your journey.

Days Out UK, PO Box 427, Northampton NN1 3YN. Tel: 01604 622445

1. Each voucher entitles the holder to the discount specified by the selected attraction.
2. Valid for use until 28/02/08 (unless otherwise specified, or if attraction season finishes prior to this). Vouchers are subject to the terms, conditions and restrictions of the selected attraction.
3. One voucher per party will be accepted, cannot be used in conjunction with any other offer, photocopies will not be accepted.
4. All attractions offering a discount have confirmed their willingness to participate. All information is subject to change without notice and should any attraction close or decline to accept a voucher for any reason, Days Out UK are not liable and cannot be held responsible.
5. Days Out UK shall not accept liability for any loss, accident or injury that may occur at a participating attraction and any dispute arising must be settled direct with the attraction concerned.
6. Cash redemption value of each voucher is 0.001p.
7. You are advised to check all relevant information with your chosen attraction before commencing your journey.

Days Out UK, PO Box 427, Northampton NN1 3YN. Tel: 01604 622445

1. Each voucher entitles the holder to the discount specified by the selected attraction.
2. Valid for use until 28/02/08 (unless otherwise specified, or if attraction season finishes prior to this). Vouchers are subject to the terms, conditions and restrictions of the selected attraction.
3. One voucher per party will be accepted, cannot be used in conjunction with any other offer, photocopies will not be accepted.
4. All attractions offering a discount have confirmed their willingness to participate. All information is subject to change without notice and should any attraction close or decline to accept a voucher for any reason, Days Out UK are not liable and cannot be held responsible.
5. Days Out UK shall not accept liability for any loss, accident or injury that may occur at a participating attraction and any dispute arising must be settled direct with the attraction concerned.
6. Cash redemption value of each voucher is 0.001p.
7. You are advised to check all relevant information with your chosen attraction before commencing your journey.

Days Out UK, PO Box 427, Northampton NN1 3YN. Tel: 01604 622445

1. Each voucher entitles the holder to the discount specified by the selected attraction.
2. Valid for use until 28/02/08 (unless otherwise specified, or if attraction season finishes prior to this). Vouchers are subject to the terms, conditions and restrictions of the selected attraction.
3. One voucher per party will be accepted, cannot be used in conjunction with any other offer, photocopies will not be accepted.
4. All attractions offering a discount have confirmed their willingness to participate. All information is subject to change without notice and should any attraction close or decline to accept a voucher for any reason, Days Out UK are not liable and cannot be held responsible.
5. Days Out UK shall not accept liability for any loss, accident or injury that may occur at a participating attraction and any dispute arising must be settled direct with the attraction concerned.
6. Cash redemption value of each voucher is 0.001p.
7. You are advised to check all relevant information with your chosen attraction before commencing your journey.

Days Out UK, PO Box 427, Northampton NN1 3YN. Tel: 01604 622445

Waterworld
Festival Park Stoke-on-Trent Staffordshire ST1 5PU
Two for the Price of One
with a full-paying adult

Cannot be used in conjunction with other offers. One voucher per party. Not valid on Bank Hols or special event days.

Expires end Feb 2008 (unless otherwise specified)

Weald and Downland Open Air Museum
Singleton Chichester West Sussex PO18 0EU
One Child Free
with every full-paying adult
(not valid with group bookings; photocopies cannot be accepted; no cash alternative)

Cannot be used in conjunction with other offers. One voucher per party. Not valid on Bank Hols or special event days.

Expires end Feb 2008 (unless otherwise specified)

Wedgwood Visitor Centre
Barlaston Stoke-On-Trent Staffordshire ST12 9ES
Two for the Price of One
(One person admitted free when accompanied by one full-paying adult; voucher must be presented at time of purchase; not to be used in conjunction with any other offer/promotion/discount; Wedgwood Visitor Centre reserved the right to alter details without notice; subject to availablity)

Cannot be used in conjunction with other offers. One voucher per party. Not valid on Bank Hols or special event days.

Expires end Feb 2008 (unless otherwise specified)

Wellington Country Park
Odiham Road Riseley Reading Berkshire RG7 1SP
One Child Free
with every full-paying adult

Cannot be used in conjunction with other offers. One voucher per party. Not valid on Bank Hols or special event days.

Valid 16 April - 20 July 2007

Welsh Highland Railway (Caernarfon)
St Helen's Road Caernarfon Gwynedd Wales
One Free Child
with each full-paying adult

Cannot be used in conjunction with other offers. One voucher per party. Not valid on Bank Hols or special event days.

Expires end Feb 2008 (unless otherwise specified)

Westons Cider Visitors Centre
The Bounds Much Marcle Ledbury Herefordshire
One Child Free
with a full-paying adult

Cannot be used in conjunction with other offers. One voucher per party. Not valid on Bank Hols or special event days.

Expires 30 September 2007

Weymouth Sea Life Park
and Marine Sanctuary

Lodmoor Country Park Weymouth Dorset DT4 7SX

One Child Free with a full-paying adult

1. This voucher entitles free admission to the Weymouth Sea Life Park and Marine Sanctuary for one child when accompanied by one full paying adult.
2. Offer expires 28 February 2008.
3. Cannot be used in conjunction with any other offer.
4. A "child" is classed as a person aged 3-14 inclusive (under 3s go free anyway).
5. No cash alternative, non-refundable; and non-exchangeable.
6. All children must be accompanied by an adult.
7. Only one voucher per party and per transaction.
8. Photocopies not accepted.
9. SEA LIFE/Sanctuaries reserve the right to alter, close or remove details/exhibits without prior notice for technical, operational or other reasons, and no refunds can be given in these circumstances.
10. SEA LIFE/Sanctuaries reserve the right to refuse entry without explanation.
Voucher Ref: DOUK.

Cannot be used in conjunction with other offers. One voucher per party. Not valid on Bank Hols or special event days.

Expires end Feb 2008 (unless otherwise specified)

Whit Lenge Gardens and Nurseries

Whit Lenge Lane Hartlebury Worcestershire

Two for the Price of One

with a full-paying adult

Cannot be used in conjunction with other offers. One voucher per party. Not valid on Bank Hols or special event days.

Expires end Feb 2008 (unless otherwise specified)

White Post Modern Farm Centre

Mansfield Road Farnsfield Newark Nottinghamshire

Two Free Bags of Animal Feed

(one voucher per transaction)

Cannot be used in conjunction with other offers. One voucher per party. Not valid on Bank Hols or special event days.

Expires end Feb 2008 (unless otherwise specified)

Wicksteed Park

Barton Road Kettering Northamptonshire NN15 6NJ

Three Wristbands for the Price of Two

(che. pest wristband free)

(maxi... ...valid on Bank Holiday weekends;
... ...y this offer at any time)

Can... ...Bank Hols or special event days.

...pecified)

1. Each voucher entitles the holder to the discount specified by the selected attraction.

2. Valid for use until 28/02/08 (unless otherwise specified, or if attraction season finishes prior to this). Vouchers are subject to the terms, conditions and restrictions of the selected attraction.

3. One voucher per party will be accepted, cannot be used in conjunction with any other offer, photocopies will not be accepted.

4. All attractions offering a discount have confirmed their willingness to participate. All information is subject to change without notice and should any attraction close or decline to accept a voucher for any reason, Days Out UK are not liable and cannot be held responsible.

5. Days Out UK shall not accept liability for any loss, accident or injury that may occur at a participating attraction and any dispute arising must be settled direct with the attraction concerned.

6. Cash redemption value of each voucher is 0.001p.

7. You are advised to check all relevant information with your chosen attraction before commencing your journey.

Days Out UK, PO Box 427, Northampton NN1 3YN. Tel: 01604 622445

1. Each voucher entitles the holder to the discount specified by the selected attraction.
2. Valid for use until 28/02/08 (unless otherwise specified, or if attraction season finishes prior to this). Vouchers are subject to the terms, conditions and restrictions of the selected attraction.
3. One voucher per party will be accepted, cannot be used in conjunction with any other offer, photocopies will not be accepted.
4. All attractions offering a discount have confirmed their willingness to participate. All information is subject to change without notice and should any attraction close or decline to accept a voucher for any reason, Days Out UK are not liable and cannot be held responsible.
5. Days Out UK shall not accept liability for any loss, accident or injury that may occur at a participating attraction and any dispute arising must be settled direct with the attraction concerned.
6. Cash redemption value of each voucher is 0.001p.
7. You are advised to check all relevant information with your chosen attraction before commencing your journey.

Days Out UK, PO Box 427, Northampton NN1 3YN. Tel: 01604 622445

1. Each voucher entitles the holder to the discount specified by the selected attraction.
2. Valid for use until 28/02/08 (unless otherwise specified, or if attraction season finishes prior to this). Vouchers are subject to the terms, conditions and restrictions of the selected attraction.
3. One voucher per party will be accepted, cannot be used in conjunction with any other offer, photocopies will not be accepted.
4. All attractions offering a discount have confirmed their willingness to participate. All information is subject to change without notice and should any attraction close or decline to accept a voucher for any reason, Days Out UK are not liable and cannot be held responsible.
5. Days Out UK shall not accept liability for any loss, accident or injury that may occur at a participating attraction and any dispute arising must be settled direct with the attraction concerned.
6. Cash redemption value of each voucher is 0.001p.
7. You are advised to check all relevant information with your chosen attraction before commencing your journey.

Days Out UK, PO Box 427, Northampton NN1 3YN. Tel: 01604 622445

1. Each voucher entitles the holder to the discount specified by the selected attraction.
2. Valid for use until 28/02/08 (unless otherwise specified, or if attraction season finishes prior to this). Vouchers are subject to the terms, conditions and restrictions of the selected attraction.
3. One voucher per party will be accepted, cannot be used in conjunction with any other offer, photocopies will not be accepted.
4. All attractions offering a discount have confirmed their willingness to participate. All information is subject to change without notice and should any attraction close or decline to accept a voucher for any reason, Days Out UK are not liable and cannot be held responsible.
5. Days Out UK shall not accept liability for any loss, accident or injury that may occur at a participating attraction and any dispute arising must be settled direct with the attraction concerned.
6. Cash redemption value of each voucher is 0.001p.
7. You are advised to check all relevant information with your chosen attraction before commencing your journey.

Days Out UK, PO Box 427, Northampton NN1 3YN. Tel: 01604 622445

Wimbledon Lawn Tennis Museum and Tour
Museum Building All England Lawn Tennis & Croquet Club
Church Road Wimbledon London SW19 5AE
One Child Free
with a full-paying adult
(offer applies to the museum only)

Winkworth Arboretum
Hascombe Road Nr Godalming Surrey GU8 4AD
Save £5.00!
2 Adults and 3 Children admitted for £12.50

Winston Churchill's Britain at War Experience
64-66 Tooley Street London SE1 2TF
Two for the Price of One
with a full-paying adult

Wolterton Park
Erpingham Aylsham Norfolk NR11 7LY
Two for the Price of One
with a full-paying adult
(offer applies to Hall admission)

Wolverhampton Racecourse
Dunstall Park Centre Dunstall Park Wolverhampton West Midlands
Three for the Price of Two
with two full-paying adults
(offer applies to admission to the Grandstand Enclosure;
excludes Boxing Day)

Woodlands Leisure Park
Blackawton Totnes Devon TQ9 7DQ
Save up to £4.44!
12% off Individual Admissions (A&C£8.15)
(maximum of four people per voucher; no cash alternative)

1. Each voucher entitles the holder to the discount specified by the selected attraction.
2. Valid for use until 28/02/08 (unless otherwise specified, or if attraction season finishes prior to this). Vouchers are subject to the terms, conditions and restrictions of the selected attraction.
3. One voucher per party will be accepted, cannot be used in conjunction with any other offer, photocopies will not be accepted.
4. All attractions offering a discount have confirmed their willingness to participate. All information is subject to change without notice and should any attraction close or decline to accept a voucher for any reason, Days Out UK are not liable and cannot be held responsible.
5. Days Out UK shall not accept liability for any loss, accident or injury that may occur at a participating attraction and any dispute arising must be settled direct with the attraction concerned.
6. Cash redemption value of each voucher is 0.001p.
7. You are advised to check all relevant information with your chosen attraction before commencing your journey.

Days Out UK, PO Box 427, Northampton NN1 3YN. Tel: 01604 622445

1. Each voucher entitles the holder to the discount specified by the selected attraction.
2. Valid for use until 28/02/08 (unless otherwise specified. or if attraction season finishes prior to this). Vouchers are subject to the terms, conditions and restrictions of the selected attraction.
3. One voucher per party will be accepted, cannot be used in conjunction with any other offer, photocopies will not be accepted.
4. All attractions offering a discount have confirmed their willingness to participate. All information is subject to change without notice and should any attraction close or decline to accept a voucher for any reason, Days Out UK are not liable and cannot be held responsible.
5. Days Out UK shall not accept liability for any loss, accident or injury that may occur at a participating attraction and any dispute arising must be settled direct with the attraction concerned.
6. Cash redemption value of each voucher is 0.001p.
7. You are advised to check all relevant information with your chosen attraction before commencing your journey.

Days Out UK, PO Box 427, Northampton NN1 3YN. Tel: 01604 622445

1. Each voucher entitles the holder to the discount specified by the selected attraction.
2. Valid for use until 28/02/08 (unless otherwise specified, or if attraction season finishes prior to this). Vouchers are subject to the terms, conditions and restrictions of the selected attraction.
3. One voucher per party will be accepted, cannot be used in conjunction with any other offer, photocopies will not be accepted.
4. All attractions offering a discount have confirmed their willingness to participate. All information is subject to change without notice and should any attraction close or decline to accept a voucher for any reason, Days Out UK are not liable and cannot be held responsible.
5. Days Out UK shall not accept liability for any loss, accident or injury that may occur at a participating attraction and any dispute arising must be settled direct with the attraction concerned.
6. Cash redemption value of each voucher is 0.001p.
7. You are advised to check all relevant information with your chosen attraction before commencing your journey.

Days Out UK, PO Box 427, Northampton NN1 3YN. Tel: 01604 622445

1. Each voucher entitles the holder to the discount specified by the selected attraction.
2. Valid for use until 28/02/08 (unless otherwise specified, or if attraction season finishes prior to this). Vouchers are subject to the terms, conditions and restrictions of the selected attraction.
3. One voucher per party will be accepted, cannot be used in conjunction with any other offer, photocopies will not be accepted.
4. All attractions offering a discount have confirmed their willingness to participate. All information is subject to change without notice and should any attraction close or decline to accept a voucher for any reason, Days Out UK are not liable and cannot be held responsible.
5. Days Out UK shall not accept liability for any loss, accident or injury that may occur at a participating attraction and any dispute arising must be settled direct with the attraction concerned.
6. Cash redemption value of each voucher is 0.001p.
7. You are advised to check all relevant information with your chosen attraction before commencing your journey.

Days Out UK, PO Box 427, Northampton NN1 3YN. Tel: 01604 622445

1. Each voucher entitles the holder to the discount specified by the selected attraction.
2. Valid for use until 28/02/08 (unless otherwise specified, or if attraction season finishes prior to this). Vouchers are subject to the terms, conditions and restrictions of the selected attraction.
3. One voucher per party will be accepted, cannot be used in conjunction with any other offer, photocopies will not be accepted.
4. All attractions offering a discount have confirmed their willingness to participate. All information is subject to change without notice and should any attraction close or decline to accept a voucher for any reason, Days Out UK are not liable and cannot be held responsible.
5. Days Out UK shall not accept liability for any loss, accident or injury that may occur at a participating attraction and any dispute arising must be settled direct with the attraction concerned.
6. Cash redemption value of each voucher is 0.001p.
7. You are advised to check all relevant information with your chosen attraction before commencing your journey.

Days Out UK, PO Box 427, Northampton NN1 3YN. Tel: 01604 622445

Wookey Hole Caves
Wookey Hole Wells Somerset BA5 1BB

Two for the Price of One
with a full-paying adult

Cannot be used in conjunction with other offers. One voucher per party. Not valid on Bank Hols or special event days.

Expires end Feb 2008 (unless otherwise specified)

Worcestershire County Museum
Hartlebury Castle Stourport Road Hartlebury
Nr Kidderminster Worcestershire DY11 7XZ

Two for the Price of One
with a full-paying adult
(cheapest ticket goes free)

Cannot be used in conjunction with other offers. One voucher per party. Not valid on Bank Hols or special event days.

Expires end Feb 2008 (unless otherwise specified)

WWT Arundel, The Wildfowl
and Wetlands Trust
Mill Road Arundel West Sussex BN18 9PB

Two for the Price of One
with a full-paying adult
(lowest entry fee goes free)

Cannot be used in conjunction with other offers. One voucher per party. Not valid on Bank Hols or special event days.

Expires end Feb 2008 (unless otherwise specified)

WWT National Wetland Centre Wales
Llwynhendy Llanelli Carmarthenshire Wales SA14 9SH

Two for the Price of One
with a full-paying adult

Cannot be used in conjunction with other offers. One voucher per party. Not valid on Bank Hols or special event days.

Expires end Feb 2008 (unless otherwise specified)

WWT Washington Wetland Centre
Pattinson Washington Tyne & Wear NE38 8LE

Two for the Price of One
with a full-paying adult

Cannot be used in conjunction with other offers. One voucher per party. Not valid on Bank Hols or special event days.

Expires end Feb 2008 (unless otherwise specified)

Yellow Duckmarine
Unit 32 Anchor Courtyard Atlantic Pavilion Albert Dock
Liverpool Merseyside L3 4AS

Two for the Price of One
with a full-paying adult
(special mid-week offer on individual tickets - excluding school and Bank
Holidays - please quote 'Days Out UK' when booking)

Cannot be used in conjunction with other offers. One voucher per party. Not valid on Bank Hols or special event days.

Valid Sept 2007-May 2008 inclusive

York Dungeon

12 Clifford Street York North Yorkshire YO1 9RD

One Child Free

with every full-paying adult

Cannot be used in conjunction with other offers. One voucher per party. Not valid on Bank Hols or special event days.

Expires end Feb 2008 (unless otherwise specified)

DISCOUNT VOUCHER

Yorkshire Dales Falconry and Conservation Centre

Crows Nest Austwick via Lancaster North Yorkshire

One Child Free

with two full-paying adults

Cannot be used in conjunction with other offers. One voucher per party. Not valid on Bank Hols or special event days.

Expires end Feb 2008 (unless otherwise specified)

DISCOUNT VOUCHER

£20 OFF any PRAGUE booking with Superbreak

To make a booking call 0870 043 7633

Please quote "Days Out UK Prague reward"
from 8am to 11pm , 7 days a week.
To request a brochure please call 08705 499 499 or simply visit
www.superbreak.com

Expires end Feb 2008

DISCOUNT VOUCHER

£20 OFF any booking to BARCELONA with Superbreak

To make a booking call 0870 043 7633

Please quote "Days Out UK Barcelona reward"
from 8am to 11pm , 7 days a week.
To request a brochure please call 08705 499 499 or simply visit
www.superbreak.com

Expires end Feb 2008

DISCOUNT VOUCHER

£20 OFF any booking to ROME with Superbreak

To make a booking call 0870 043 7633

Please quote "Days Out UK Rome reward"
from 8am to 11pm , 7 days a week.
To request a brochure please call 08705 499 499 or simply visit
www.superbreak.com

Expires end Feb 2008

DISCOUNT VOUCHER

£20 OFF any booking to AMSTERDAM with Superbreak

To make a booking call 0870 043 7633

Please quote "Days Out UK Amsterdam reward"
from 8am to 11pm , 7 days a week.
To request a brochure please call 08705 499 499 or simply visit
www.superbreak.com

Expires end Feb 2008

DISCOUNT VOUCHER

1. Each voucher entitles the holder to the discount specified by the selected attraction.
2. Valid for use until 28/02/08 (unless otherwise specified, or if attraction season finishes prior to this). Vouchers are subject to the terms, conditions and restrictions of the selected attraction.
3. One voucher per party will be accepted, cannot be used in conjunction with any other offer, photocopies will not be accepted.
4. All attractions offering a discount have confirmed their willingness to participate. All information is subject to change without notice and should any attraction close or decline to accept a voucher for any reason, Days Out UK are not liable and cannot be held responsible.
5. Days Out UK shall not accept liability for any loss, accident or injury that may occur at a participating attraction and any dispute arising must be settled direct with the attraction concerned.
6. Cash redemption value of each voucher is 0.001p.
7. You are advised to check all relevant information with your chosen attraction before commencing your journey.

Days Out UK, PO Box 427, Northampton NN1 3YN. Tel: 01604 622445

1. Each voucher entitles the holder to the discount specified by the selected attraction.
2. Valid for use until 28/02/08 (unless otherwise specified, or if attraction season finishes prior to this). Vouchers are subject to the terms, conditions and restrictions of the selected attraction.
3. One voucher per party will be accepted, cannot be used in conjunction with any other offer, photocopies will not be accepted.
4. All attractions offering a discount have confirmed their willingness to participate. All information is subject to change without notice and should any attraction close or decline to accept a voucher for any reason, Days Out UK are not liable and cannot be held responsible.
5. Days Out UK shall not accept liability for any loss, accident or injury that may occur at a participating attraction and any dispute arising must be settled direct with the attraction concerned.
6. Cash redemption value of each voucher is 0.001p.
7. You are advised to check all relevant information with your chosen attraction before commencing your journey.

Days Out UK, PO Box 427, Northampton NN1 3YN. Tel: 01604 622445

1. Valid for use until 28/02/08 (unless chosen break becomes unavailable prior to this). Offer is subject to the terms, conditions and restrictions of Superbreak Mini-Holidays
2. Offer cannot be used in conjunction with any other offer.
3. All information is subject to change without notice and should offer become unavailable for any reason, Days Out UK are not liable and cannot be held responsible.
4. Days Out UK shall not accept liability for any loss, accident or injury that may occur, and any dispute arising must be settled direct with Superbreak Mini Holidays.
5. Offer valid for bookings for 2 persons for 2 nights or more.
6. Minimum spend before offer becomes valid: £100.00.
7. Only one voucher/discount per booking.

Superbreak Mini-Holidays 60 Piccadilly, York YO1 9WX www.superbreak.com

1. Valid for use until 28/02/08 (unless chosen break becomes unavailable prior to this). Offer is subject to the terms, conditions and restrictions of Superbreak Mini-Holidays
2. Offer cannot be used in conjunction with any other offer.
3. All information is subject to change without notice and should offer become unavailable for any reason, Days Out UK are not liable and cannot be held responsible.
4. Days Out UK shall not accept liability for any loss, accident or injury that may occur, and any dispute arising must be settled direct with Superbreak Mini Holidays.
5. Offer valid for bookings for 2 persons for 2 nights or more.
6. Minimum spend before offer becomes valid: £100.00.
7. Only one voucher/discount per booking.

Superbreak Mini-Holidays 60 Piccadilly, York YO1 9WX www.superbreak.com

1. Valid for use until 28/02/08 (unless chosen break becomes unavailable prior to this). Offer is subject to the terms, conditions and restrictions of Superbreak Mini-Holidays
2. Offer cannot be used in conjunction with any other offer.
3. All information is subject to change without notice and should offer become unavailable for any reason, Days Out UK are not liable and cannot be held responsible.
4. Days Out UK shall not accept liability for any loss, accident or injury that may occur, and any dispute arising must be settled direct with Superbreak Mini Holidays.
5. Offer valid for bookings for 2 persons for 2 nights or more.
6. Minimum spend before offer becomes valid: £100.00.
7. Only one voucher/discount per booking.

Superbreak Mini-Holidays 60 Piccadilly, York YO1 9WX www.superbreak.com

1. Valid for use until 28/02/08 (unless chosen break becomes unavailable prior to this). Offer is subject to the terms, conditions and restrictions of Superbreak Mini-Holidays
2. Offer cannot be used in conjunction with any other offer.
3. All information is subject to change without notice and should offer become unavailable for any reason, Days Out UK are not liable and cannot be held responsible.
4. Days Out UK shall not accept liability for any loss, accident or injury that may occur, and any dispute arising must be settled direct with Superbreak Mini Holidays.
5. Offer valid for bookings for 2 persons for 2 nights or more.
6. Minimum spend before offer becomes valid: £100.00.
7. Only one voucher/discount per booking.

Superbreak Mini-Holidays 60 Piccadilly, York YO1 9WX www.superbreak.com

£20 OFF any booking to PARIS with Superbreak

To make a booking call 0870 043 7633

Please quote "Days Out UK Paris reward"
from 8am to 11pm , 7 days a week.
To request a brochure please call 08705 499 499 or simply visit
www.superbreak.com

Expires end Feb 2008

DISCOUNT VOUCHER

£20 OFF any booking to DUBLIN with Superbreak

To make a booking call 0870 043 7633

Please quote "Days Out UK Dublin reward"
from 8am to 11pm , 7 days a week.
To request a brochure please call 08705 499 499 or simply visit
www.superbreak.com

Expires end Feb 2008

DISCOUNT VOUCHER

£30 OFF Your Next London Theatre Break

To make a booking call 0870 043 7633

Please quote "Days Out UK Theatre Break Reward"
from 8am to 11pm , 7 days a week.
To request a Superbreak brochure please call 08705 499 499 or simply
visit www.superbreak.com

Expires end Feb 2008

DISCOUNT VOUCHER

£20 OFF Your Next Mini Break to London

To make a booking call 0870 043 7633

Please quote "Days Out UK London Reward"
from 8am to 11pm , 7 days a week.
To request a Superbreak brochure please call 08705 499 499 or simply
visit www.superbreak.com

Expires end Feb 2008

DISCOUNT VOUCHER

£20 OFF Your Next Mini Break to Manchester

To make a booking call 0870 043 7633

Please quote "Days Out UK Manchester Reward" from
8am to 11pm, 7 days a week.
To request a Superbreak brochure please call 08705 499 499 or simply
visit www.superbreak.com

Expires end Feb 2008

DISCOUNT VOUCHER

£20 OFF Your Next Mini Break to Edinburgh

To make a booking call 0870 043 7633

Please quote "Days Out UK Edinburgh Reward" from
8am to 11pm, 7 days a week.
To request a Superbreak brochure please call 08705 499 499 or simply
visit www.superbreak.com

Expires end Feb 2008

DISCOUNT VOUCHER

1. Valid for use until 28/02/08 (unless chosen break becomes unavailable prior to this). Offer is subject to the terms, conditions and restrictions of Superbreak Mini-Holidays
2. Offer cannot be used in conjunction with any other offer.
3. All information is subject to change without notice and should offer become unavailable for any reason, Days Out UK are not liable and cannot be held responsible.
4. Days Out UK shall not accept liability for any loss, accident or injury that may occur, and any dispute arising must be settled direct with Superbreak Mini Holidays.
5. Offer valid for bookings for 2 persons for 2 nights or more.
6. Minimum spend before offer becomes valid: £100.00.
7. Only one voucher/discount per booking.

Superbreak Mini-Holidays 60 Piccadilly, York YO1 9WX www.superbreak.com

1. Valid for use until 28/02/08 (unless chosen break becomes unavailable prior to this). Offer is subject to the terms, conditions and restrictions of Superbreak Mini-Holidays
2. Offer cannot be used in conjunction with any other offer.
3. All information is subject to change without notice and should offer become unavailable for any reason, Days Out UK are not liable and cannot be held responsible.
4. Days Out UK shall not accept liability for any loss, accident or injury that may occur, and any dispute arising must be settled direct with Superbreak Mini Holidays.
5. Offer valid for bookings for 2 persons for 2 nights or more.
6. Minimum spend before offer becomes valid: £100.00.
7. Only one voucher/discount per booking.

Superbreak Mini-Holidays 60 Piccadilly, York YO1 9WX www.superbreak.com

1. Valid for use until 28/02/08 (unless chosen break becomes unavailable prior to this). Offer is subject to the terms, conditions and restrictions of Superbreak Mini-Holidays
2. Offer cannot be used in conjunction with any other offer.
3. All information is subject to change without notice and should offer become unavailable for any reason, Days Out UK are not liable and cannot be held responsible.
4. Days Out UK shall not accept liability for any loss, accident or injury that may occur, and any dispute arising must be settled direct with Superbreak Mini Holidays.
5. Offer valid for bookings for 2 persons for 2 nights or more.
6. Minimum spend before offer becomes valid: £100.00.
7. Only one voucher/discount per booking.

Superbreak Mini-Holidays 60 Piccadilly, York YO1 9WX www.superbreak.com

1. Valid for use until 28/02/08 (unless chosen break becomes unavailable prior to this). Offer is subject to the terms, conditions and restrictions of Superbreak Mini-Holidays
2. Offer cannot be used in conjunction with any other offer.
3. All information is subject to change without notice and should offer become unavailable for any reason, Days Out UK are not liable and cannot be held responsible.
4. Days Out UK shall not accept liability for any loss, accident or injury that may occur, and any dispute arising must be settled direct with Superbreak Mini Holidays.
5. Offer valid for bookings for 2 persons for 2 nights or more.
6. Minimum spend before offer becomes valid: £100.00.
7. Only one voucher/discount per booking.

Superbreak Mini-Holidays 60 Piccadilly, York YO1 9WX www.superbreak.com

1. Valid for use until 28/02/08 (unless chosen break becomes unavailable prior to this). Offer is subject to the terms, conditions and restrictions of Superbreak Mini-Holidays
2. Offer cannot be used in conjunction with any other offer.
3. All information is subject to change without notice and should offer become unavailable for any reason, Days Out UK are not liable and cannot be held responsible.
4. Days Out UK shall not accept liability for any loss, accident or injury that may occur, and any dispute arising must be settled direct with Superbreak Mini Holidays.
5. Offer valid for bookings for 2 persons for 2 nights or more.
6. Minimum spend before offer becomes valid: £100.00.
7. Only one voucher/discount per booking.

Superbreak Mini-Holidays 60 Piccadilly, York YO1 9WX www.superbreak.com

1. Valid for use until 28/02/08 (unless chosen break becomes unavailable prior to this). Offer is subject to the terms, conditions and restrictions of Superbreak Mini-Holidays
2. Offer cannot be used in conjunction with any other offer.
3. All information is subject to change without notice and should offer become unavailable for any reason, Days Out UK are not liable and cannot be held responsible.
4. Days Out UK shall not accept liability for any loss, accident or injury that may occur, and any dispute arising must be settled direct with Superbreak Mini Holidays.
5. Offer valid for bookings for 2 persons for 2 nights or more.
6. Minimum spend before offer becomes valid: £100.00.
7. Only one voucher/discount per booking.

Superbreak Mini-Holidays 60 Piccadilly, York YO1 9WX www.superbreak.com

£20 OFF Your Next Mini Break to York
To make a booking call 0870 043 7633

Please quote "Days Out UK York Reward" from
8am to 11pm, 7 days a week.
To request a Superbreak brochure please call 08705 499 499 or simply
visit www.superbreak.com

Expires end Feb 2008

DISCOUNT VOUCHER

£20 OFF Your Next Mini Break to Glasgow
To make a booking call 0870 043 7633

Please quote "Days Out UK Glasgow Reward"
from 8am to 11pm, 7 days a week.
To request a Superbreak brochure please call 08705 499 499 or simply
visit www.superbreak.com

Expires end Feb 2008

DISCOUNT VOUCHER

£30 OFF Your Next Golf Break
To make a booking call 0870 043 7633

Please quote "Days Out UK Golf Break Reward"
from 8am to 11pm, 7 days a week.
To request a Superbreak brochure please call 08705 499 499 or simply
visit www.superbreak.com

Expires end Feb 2008

DISCOUNT VOUCHER

£20 OFF Your Next Mini Break to Blackpool
To make a booking call 0870 043 7633

Please quote "Days Out UK Blackpool Reward"
from 8am to 11pm, 7 days a week.
To request a Superbreak brochure please call 08705 499 499 or simply
visit www.superbreak.com

Expires end Feb 2008

DISCOUNT VOUCHER

£20 OFF Your Next Mini Break to Stratford Upon Avon
To make a booking call 0870 043 7633

Please quote "Days Out UK Stratford Reward"
from 8am to 11pm, 7 days a week.
To request a Superbreak brochure please call 08705 499 499 or simply
visit www.superbreak.com

Expires end Feb 2008

DISCOUNT VOUCHER

£20 OFF Your Next Mini Break to Brighton
To make a booking call 0870 043 7633

Please quote "Days Out UK Brighton Reward"
from 8am to 11pm, 7 days a week.
To request a Superbreak brochure please call 08705 499 499 or simply
visit www.superbreak.com

Expires end Feb 2008

DISCOUNT VOUCHER

1. Valid for use until 28/02/08 (unless chosen break becomes unavailable prior to this). Offer is subject to the terms, conditions and restrictions of Superbreak Mini-Holidays
2. Offer cannot be used in conjunction with any other offer.
3. All information is subject to change without notice and should offer become unavailable for any reason, Days Out UK are not liable and cannot be held responsible.
4. Days Out UK shall not accept liability for any loss, accident or injury that may occur, and any dispute arising must be settled direct with Superbreak Mini Holidays.
5. Offer valid for bookings for 2 persons for 2 nights or more.
6. Minimum spend before offer becomes valid: £100.00.
7. Only one voucher/discount per booking.

Superbreak Mini-Holidays 60 Piccadilly, York YO1 9WX www.superbreak.com

1. Valid for use until 28/02/08 (unless chosen break becomes unavailable prior to this). Offer is subject to the terms, conditions and restrictions of Superbreak Mini-Holidays
2. Offer cannot be used in conjunction with any other offer.
3. All information is subject to change without notice and should offer become unavailable for any reason, Days Out UK are not liable and cannot be held responsible.
4. Days Out UK shall not accept liability for any loss, accident or injury that may occur, and any dispute arising must be settled direct with Superbreak Mini Holidays.
5. Offer valid for bookings for 2 persons for 2 nights or more.
6. Minimum spend before offer becomes valid: £100.00.
7. Only one voucher/discount per booking.

Superbreak Mini-Holidays 60 Piccadilly, York YO1 9WX www.superbreak.com

1. Valid for use until 28/02/08 (unless chosen break becomes unavailable prior to this). Offer is subject to the terms, conditions and restrictions of Superbreak Mini-Holidays
2. Offer cannot be used in conjunction with any other offer.
3. All information is subject to change without notice and should offer become unavailable for any reason, Days Out UK are not liable and cannot be held responsible.
4. Days Out UK shall not accept liability for any loss, accident or injury that may occur, and any dispute arising must be settled direct with Superbreak Mini Holidays.
5. Offer valid for bookings for 2 persons for 2 nights or more.
6. Minimum spend before offer becomes valid: £100.00.
7. Only one voucher/discount per booking.

Superbreak Mini-Holidays 60 Piccadilly, York YO1 9WX www.superbreak.com

1. Valid for use until 28/02/08 (unless chosen break becomes unavailable prior to this). Offer is subject to the terms, conditions and restrictions of Superbreak Mini-Holidays
2. Offer cannot be used in conjunction with any other offer.
3. All information is subject to change without notice and should offer become unavailable for any reason, Days Out UK are not liable and cannot be held responsible.
4. Days Out UK shall not accept liability for any loss, accident or injury that may occur, and any dispute arising must be settled direct with Superbreak Mini Holidays.
5. Offer valid for bookings for 2 persons for 2 nights or more.
6. Minimum spend before offer becomes valid: £100.00.
7. Only one voucher/discount per booking.

Superbreak Mini-Holidays 60 Piccadilly, York YO1 9WX www.superbreak.com

1. Valid for use until 28/02/08 (unless chosen break becomes unavailable prior to this). Offer is subject to the terms, conditions and restrictions of Superbreak Mini-Holidays
2. Offer cannot be used in conjunction with any other offer.
3. All information is subject to change without notice and should offer become unavailable for any reason, Days Out UK are not liable and cannot be held responsible.
4. Days Out UK shall not accept liability for any loss, accident or injury that may occur, and any dispute arising must be settled direct with Superbreak Mini Holidays.
5. Offer valid for bookings for 2 persons for 2 nights or more.
6. Minimum spend before offer becomes valid: £100.00.
7. Only one voucher/discount per booking.

Superbreak Mini-Holidays 60 Piccadilly, York YO1 9WX www.superbreak.com

£20 OFF Your Next Mini Break to The West Country
To make a booking call 0870 043 7633

Please quote "Days Out UK West Country Reward"
from 8am to 11pm, 7 days a week.
To request a Superbreak brochure please call 08705 499 499 or simply
visit www.superbreak.com

Expires end Feb 2008

£20 OFF Your Next Mini Break to Wales
To make a booking call 0870 043 7633

Please quote "Days Out UK Wales Reward"
from 8am to 11pm, 7 days a week.
To request a Superbreak brochure please call 08705 499 499 or simply
visit www.superbreak.com

Expires end Feb 2008

1. Valid for use until 28/02/08 (unless chosen break becomes unavailable prior to this). Offer is subject to the terms, conditions and restrictions of Superbreak Mini-Holidays

2. Offer cannot be used in conjunction with any other offer.

3. All information is subject to change without notice and should offer become unavailable for any reason, Days Out UK are not liable and cannot be held responsible.

4. Days Out UK shall not accept liability for any loss, accident or injury that may occur, and any dispute arising must be settled direct with Superbreak Mini Holidays.

5. Offer valid for bookings for 2 persons for 2 nights or more.

6. Minimum spend before offer becomes valid: £100.00.

7. Only one voucher/discount per booking.

Superbreak Mini-Holidays 60 Piccadilly, York YO1 9WX www.superbreak.com

X

Y

Z

Notes

Notes

Notes

Notes

Notes